THE NATIONAL PARTY CHAIRMEN AND COMMITTEES

THE NATIONAL PARTY CHAIRMEN AND COMMITTEES

Factionalism at the Top

Ralph M. Goldman

M. E. Sharpe, Inc.
Armonk, New York, and London

Library of Congress Cataloging-in-Publication Data

Goldman, Ralph Morris, 1920-
    The national party chairmen and committees : factionalism at the
top / by Ralph M. Goldman.
      p. cm.
    Includes bibliographical references.
    ISBN 0-87332-636-9
    1. Political parties—United States—History. 2. Party
committees—United States—History. I. Title.
JK2263 1990
324.273′09—dc20   90-70272
                                                CIP

JK 2263 1990 — Mar. 92

Printed in the United States of America

∞

MV 10 9 8 7 6 5 4 3 2 1

Contents

Part IV. Destruction by Faction

Part V. Formalizing the National Chairmanship

Part VI. Bureaucratizing the National Committee

Part VII. The Long View: Processes and Problems

Preface

This book traces the history of the national committee chairmanships of the two major parties of the United States. The story of the Democratic party begins in the mid-nineteenth century. The Democrats were the first to establish a national committee in 1848. In 1854, the Republican party made a national committee an integral part of its initial organization. Taken together, the institutional history of the two national committees and their chairmanships reveals much that distinguishes the party system of the United States. In addition, by following the trends in certain aspects of their institutional evolution, we are able to test, albeit in a limited manner, an analytic theory of conflict processes and organizational development.

The government-party-faction hierarchy

The relevant organizations that are in part observed in this book are the government of the United States (particularly the presidency and the Congress as the elective branches), the major political parties (Democratic and Republican), and the factions within each party.

A government is a complex organization that is established by leaders of a society according to custom or according to specifications in a written constitution. The extent to which ordinary citizens participate in the selection and accountability of governmental officers and in the decisions that make public policies is a major measure of how democratic the political system is.

This organizational framework is part of a hierarchy of organizations that facilitates political conflict, competition, and the search for consensus. Party factions compete for control of party offices and policies. Parties compete for control of governmental offices and policies. Governments often compete with other institutions, for example, the media, organized interest groups, churches, corporations, military establishments ("the military-industrial complex," for example), and others for control of the society.

In constitutional democracies, practices and rules evolve that constrain leaders to be tolerant, to negotiate, and to compromise in the process of resolving their conflicts. From this perspective, a democracy is essentially a system of conflict management that provides institutional alternatives to internal violence, for example, the judicial processes that replaced trial by combat between adversary individuals. Similarly, party leaders in constitutional systems have become the principal advocates and negotiators of the nation's political and social values, enabling them to provide opportunities for and constraints upon elite conflict.

When the above hierarchy of organizations is inverted, a faction may gain control of a party, a party may exclusively control the government, and the government may exercise extensive as well as intensive control over all facets of the society's and the citizen's life. Such a system is totalitarian and essentially a system of conflict prevention rather than conflict management.

Parties are organizations that seek to place their leaders or recognized representatives into the offices of government. Party organization is usually formal, that is, with officers, headquarters, and rules of operation. Parties will also formally present their nominees to an electorate, campaign for their election, and appeal for support through statements, platforms, manifestos, and propaganda dealing with public policy issues.

In their early stages of organizational development, parties tend to be relatively accidental and transitional bodies, operating extraconstitutionally within the context of the governmental organization. When parties endure for long periods and interact with each other in a more or less regularized manner, they become a party system.

A faction is a temporary system of cooperation among a number of recognized leaders of a political party for the purpose of influencing the decisions and conduct of the party organization as a whole.[1] A faction is usually informally organized. Its decisions usually pertain to the selection of the party's officers, nominees, or policy postures or to the distribution of party resources such as campaign funds and job patronage. Factional leaders usually have a constituency among party rank-and-file workers and regular party voters. Factions are sometimes referred to as cliques, wings, by an ideological name ("the Eastern liberals"), or the name of their principal leader ("the McKinley men"). A faction may exist as briefly as a ballot during a national nominating convention or as long as a decade or two in support of a policy such as "free silver."

An entire faction may bolt a party and set itself up as a new, independent party organization; this happened frequently during the first century of the American system. More commonly, faction leaders within a party will negotiate their differences and arrive at various trade-offs, for example, one faction's support for a nomination in exchange for another's endorsement of a platform plank.

The chairmen of party national committees hold key offices at the point where faction and party make one of their most important institutional connections. The interactions between faction and party can tell us much about how the chairmanship develops as an office, how its incumbents are selected or removed, and how chairmen behave while in office as well as about the historical development of the party as an organization.

How factional leaders conduct themselves may predict how they will behave as party and governmental leaders. The "deals" that factional leaders are willing to make may predict how well they will serve as political brokers or negotiators among the many competing interests of a heterogeneous society. As key players, factional leaders also become the rule makers for the institutionalized "political game" within which they carry on their conflicts.

In this book, the national party chairman will be viewed from several perspectives: as the manager of the national committee's affairs; as a political careerist; as a representative of a faction in his or her party. Relationships between chairmen and other major party leaders, particularly the titular leaders, will be given special attention. The functional development and political significance of the office of national chairman will be examined. The historical account will follow the flow of events chronologically. All this will describe significant conflicts that have institutionalized parties as vital agencies in the management of political conflict in the United States.

Conflict processes and organizational development

In his presidential address to the American Political Science Association, E.E. Schattschneider viewed conflict as the essential element of politics and conflict management as the central practice of politics:

> If politics is the management of conflict, it is necessary first to get rid of some simplistic concepts of conflict. Political conflict is not primarily or usually a matter of head-on collisions or tests of strength, for a good reason: intelligent people prefer to avoid tests of strength, about matters more serious than sports, unless they are sure to win.
>
> Nor is political conflict like an intercollegiate debate in which the opponents agree in advance on the definition of the issues. The definition of alternatives is the supreme instrument of power; the antagonists can rarely agree on what the issues are because power is involved in the definition. He who determines what politics is about runs the country because the definition of the alternatives is the choice of conflicts, and the choice of conflicts allocates power.
>
> Political strategy deals therefore with the exploitation, use, and suppression of conflict. Conflict is so powerful an instrument of government that all regimes are of necessity concerned with its management. . . . The grand strategy of politics deals with public policy concerning conflict. This is the policy of policies, the sovereign policy—what to do about conflict.[2]

Theoretically, some of the developmental patterns of an organization may be inferred from a history of the conflicts surrounding its principal executive office. The outcomes of these conflicts may, in fact, predict whether or not the organization is viable. At minimum, this kind of data and analysis may provide valuable information to those leaders who must manage the present affairs and further development of the organization.

Conflicts may determine how incumbents in the principal executive office are likely to behave, what functions and tasks they are expected to perform, and what kinds of persons are likely to hold the office or be removed from it. As will be explained in the concluding chapters of this inquiry, issues in conflict may arise from and have consequences on basic structural features of the office and the organization that it heads.[3]

To illustrate, assume that a national committee chairman issues a policy statement of his own formulation on some public issue such as welfare. Assume too that his policy is contrary to the party's platform or the position taken by the dominant faction in the national committee. A factional conflict ensues. The conflict may be resolved in one or more of at least three ways. The chairman may retract his statement, apologize for having made it, and promise never again to presume to make policy statements of his own formulation. His changed behavior is the structural change; he has "learned a lesson" and the conflict has "socialized" him somewhat. When this type of change occurs, we may call it a socialization process.

A second kind of conflict resolution may involve the creation of new rules about what chairmen in general may or may not do with respect to party policy statements. This new specification of a chairman's duties and prerogatives changes the organizational structure by further formalizing the office; it is a formalization outcome.

A third outcome of the conflict may be to remove the incumbent chairman from office by firing or forced resignation. This may be described as an investiture (in this case, divestiture) process.

Combinations of two or more of these conflict causes or outcomes are possible, for example, firing the incumbent (investiture process) and writing new rules for the job (formalization process).

The three processes are referred to here as socialization, formalization, and investiture. This analytical typology of conflict processes helps narrow the focus of an otherwise unmanageably large institutional history. The three perspectives suggest questions to be asked and events to be chosen in tracing the factional conflicts associated with the development of the national chairmanship and the national committee. Some of the conflicts are about personal behavior (socialization process), some are about task expectations pertinent to the office (formalization process), and some about how an incumbency is achieved (investiture process). In all cases, there are structural consequences for the office and the organization. These structural consequences *in seriatim* comprise the developmental history of the office and, less directly, of the organization.

In the developmental histories of the national committees and the national chairmanships, an economical way of tracking the relevant factional data is to follow the major party and factional events as they manifest themselves at party national conventions and during presidential campaigns, as is often done in this book. National factions reveal themselves most often in these circumstances.

The semiautonomous national agencies

Organizationally, neither major party in the United States is an integrated whole at its national level. Rather, each national-level party organization is a relatively loose network of semi-autonomous organizations. These include: the party-in-the-Senate, the party-in-the-House, the national convention, the presidential campaign organization, the party-in-the-electorate, the national committee, and the national chairman as chief executive of the national party headquarters. The national-level agencies of the two major parties reflect the separation of powers principle. Nothing distinguishes the U.S. parties from parliamentary or authoritarian parties more than this plurality of semiautonomous national-level units. The U.S. national parties are structurally ill suited to march in solid phalanx or hierarchical order as is almost always the case in political parties elsewhere in the world.

Each of these semiautonomous agencies has a membership and executives of its own. One national party agency may exert temporary influence over the others, usually through the overlapping membership of particular persons. Each of these national-level organizations recruits its own officers with substantial independence from the others. Each member of each semiautonomous agency relates to the different party units at the national level in a different way.

Party-in-the-Senate

Once in the Senate, a senator's party affiliation takes on particular significance primarily when that body is being organized, that is, the majority party is entitled to control the senior offices of the Senate and all its committee chairmanships. A senator automatically becomes a member of his party's conference in the Senate. The conference chooses the president *pro tempore* of the Senate (when it is the majority party), its own chairman and secretary, the party's floor leader and whips, the membership of its committee on committees or steering committee, its committee on Senate patronage, and its senatorial campaign committee. The conference also chooses the party's policy committee.

Party-in-the-House

Congressional district constituents tend to vote the party ticket, largely because most candidates for representative are less well known than senators. This party-ticket constituency tends to obligate the representative to deal carefully with party matters in the House. Arrival to the House of Representatives carries automatic membership in the party's House caucus. The majority party wins the powerful speakership. The caucus selects its own officers, the party's floor leader, the whip, the members of (in the Democratic case) a steering and policy committee, standing committee chairpersons, the members of the congressional campaign committee, and the party's House patronage committee.

In general, coordination in so large a body as the House of Representatives has promoted party organization in many forms. House Democrats have developed an elaborate system of party management. In practice, for example, the whip is not a single person, but really an organization of nearly thirty assistant whips and others. The powerful steering and policy committee, chaired by the Speaker, consists of about twenty-nine members representing specific interests in the party. Even the unwieldy party caucus has arrogated to itself larger powers and greater participation in House operations. In recent years, the House has also seen the growth in a number of special caucuses: the Black caucus, the Hispanic caucus, the women's caucus, and liberal and conservative caucuses. These special caucuses endeavor to transcend party lines, but more often than not they have more members from one party than the other.

National convention

Every four years the party recreates its most comprehensive representative body, the national convention. Every state and territorial party organization in the Union sends a delegation to the great national quadrennial meeting to write a platform of public policies upon which the party will stand, prepare rules for the governance of the party as a national organization, nominate its slate for president and vice-president, and designate the membership of the national committee as the party's governing body between conventions.

The presidential nomination rather than national party self-governance has dominated the concerns of national conventions since their founding in 1832. Candidate and ideological factionalism, as the evidence of this volume demonstrates, rather than principles of rational organization, have been the principal engine of convention action. Platforms are more often encyclopedias of public issues than specific programs for legislative and executive action. Delegate selection through primary elections has placed voter popularity above peer assessment as the party's principal standard for selecting nominees and other leaders. By the end of one week, the national convention disbands, leaving the future of national party affairs in the hands of the nominee's campaign organization, the national committee, and the party national chairman.

Campaign organization

The nominee's campaign organization is a special short-term organization that takes shape and leads the party during the period from the end of the national convention until election day. The sources of personnel for this operation have been numerous and varied. The campaign organization's chief executive may be a personal and trusted friend, the manager of his preconvention campaign, a representative of an adversary faction, the national committee chairman, or even an executive from a public relations firm. Subordinate campaign staff may also come from as many sources.

The presidential campaign organization is a distinct corporate body. As such, it may receive federal election funds, incur debts, hire and fire personnel, and cooperate with or ignore party agencies. Some nominees may try to operate it as though it were an assembly representative of the entire spectrum of interests in the party; others will prefer a tight ship consisting of only loyal co-workers. How the campaign organization is composed and directed may furnish clues to the manner in which the nominee is likely to manage his administration if elected. The way the campaign organization handles the party platform and the debates over public policy also helps forecast the programmatic approach of the nominee's prospective administration.

Party-in-the-electorate

The electorate is rarely viewed as an organization. Yet on election day the mobilized electorate systematically registers, with constitutional finality, its decisions regarding the personnel to fill the principal offices of government. How each voter casts his or her ballot has consequences for the composition of the electoral college, the party-in-the-Senate, the party-in-the-House, the partisan character of state and local governments and party organizations, the makeup of the national committee, and even the delegations to the next national convention.

In recent years, roughly 40 percent of the voters have referred to themselves as Democrats, 25 to 30 percent as Republicans, and about 33 percent as Independents. Intensity of identification varies within each group. The party-in-the-electorate is therefore a subdivision of the total electorate: party "regulars," who vote with the party through thick and thin, plus all the others—from leaners to switchers—whose votes make a difference in the party's fortunes.

National committee

From all appearances, the national committee is an organization subordinate to the national convention. Representatives to the national committee are designated by each state's delegation to the national convention. The national committee serves as the convention's interim organization. In both parties, each state and territory is entitled to at least three people—one man, one woman, and the state party chairperson—as its core representatives. The Democrats apportion more than this minimum according to the size of the delegation to the national convention. The Democrats also provide several seats to representatives of Democratic governors, mayors, congressional leaders, young Democrats, women, and others.

The national committee tends to be more of a political environment than an operating agency. With some distortion, it perpetuates the intraparty power relationships manifest at the national convention. The committee is a place to test factional and candidate influence. It is often a sounding board for the national chairman or, if in office, the president. It is a place to discuss and possibly ameliorate grievances and competing interests. Above all, it is the specific party agency to which the national party chairman is beholden.

National chairmanship

"Floating" among all these semiautonomous national-level agencies is the national chairman and his headquarters staff. By now, it should be evident that the national chairman is not the chief executive of a neatly structured hierarchy. He and his headquarters are only one of several semiautonomous agencies. How he performs may depend on political skill, luck, political circumstances, personal ambition, factional connection, and so on. The national chairman may try to serve as a party broker among the several semiautonomous agencies or factions, particularly when different agencies are controlled by different factions. He may be a political recluse, filling the office either to prevent someone else from controlling it or to hold it until a preferred successor is available to fill it. In brief, the national chairman is only one of several leaders of a multiheaded organization called "the national party."

What may be said with confidence is that the national chairmanship has been at the center of national factional developments throughout the history of each major party. Factional conflict has had much to do with the manner in which individuals have been chosen for or removed from the office, the kinds of persons who have been its incumbents, and the kinds of job descriptions and expectations held for the office. These developments may be observed by investigating the national committee's investiture, socialization, and formalization processes.

A word about methodology

There are several ways of investigating and reporting history. A chronicle recites events in chronological order, describing which actors did what and in what sequence. A colligation endeavors to apply selected major concepts, for example, socialization, investiture, and formalization processes, to the information of a chronicle in order to interpret the facts and thereby convert the chronicle into a significant narrative. Finally, there is the genetic explanation, which is the historian's closest approach to testing hypotheses and producing predictive knowledge. Genetic explanation seeks to find the reasons for, and the causes of, behavior and events. This volume is a colligation about the institutional history of a particular political office—the party national chairmanship—and of the agency—the national committee—of which it is a part.

Historiography is necessarily a less than scientific enterprise. It must deal with all of the pitfalls of *ex post facto* inquiry, wherein independent variables have already occurred and the researcher must start with observation of the dependent variables. This is the reverse of the more rigorously scientific experimental procedure wherein the researcher can manipulate and measure the independent variable and at the same time observe if there is concomitant variation in the dependent variable. Pitfalls notwithstanding, historiography can be systematic, guided by—albeit not a test of—a hypothesis, particular concepts, or specific questions. By applying the questions raised by conflict process theory, this book aims to meet the standards of systematic historiography. This report also seeks to encourage the recent revival of historical methods in the study of political institutions.

National Party Chairmen

Democratic National Chairmen

	Date of election
Benjamin F. Hallett	May 22, 1848
Robert M. McLane	June 5, 1852
David A. Smalley	June 6, 1856
August Belmont	June 23, 1860
Augustus Schell	July 10, 1872
Abram S. Hewitt	June 29, 1876
William H. Barnum	March 3, 1877
Calvin S. Brice	June 12, 1889
William F. Harrity	July 21, 1892
James K. Jones	July 11, 1896
Thomas D. Taggart	July 26, 1904
Norman E. Mack	July 25, 1908
William F. McCombs	July 15, 1912
Vance C. McCormick	June 15, 1916
Homer S. Cummings	February 26, 1919
George White	July 20, 1920
Cordell Hull	November 1, 1921
Clement L. Shaver	August 11, 1924
John J. Raskob	July 11, 1928
James A. Farley	July 2, 1932
Edward J. Flynn	August 17, 1940
Frank C. Walker	January 18, 1943
Robert E. Hannegan	January 22, 1944
J. Howard McGrath	October 29, 1947
William M. Boyle, Jr.	August 24, 1949

Frank E. McKinney	November 1, 1951
Stephen A. Mitchell	August 29, 1952
Paul M. Butler	December 5, 1954
Henry M. Jackson	July 17, 1960

The following chairmen are not covered in this book:

John M. Bailey	January 22, 1961
Lawrence O'Brien	August 31, 1968
Fred R. Harris	January 14, 1969
Jean Westwood	July 14, 1972
Robert Strauss	December 9, 1972
Kenneth Curtis	January 7, 1977
John C. White	December 29, 1977
Charles A. Manatt	February 28, 1981
Paul G. Kirk, Jr.	February 2, 1985
Ronald H. Brown	February 10, 1989

Republican National Chairmen

	Date of election
Edwin D. Morgan	February 23, 1856
Henry J. Raymond	June 8, 1864
Marcus L. Ward	September 3, 1866
William Claflin	June 3, 1868
Edwin D. Morgan	June 6, 1872
Zachariah Chandler	July 8, 1876
James D. Cameron	December 17, 1879
Marshall Jewell	July 2, 1880
Dwight M. Sabin	December 12, 1883
Benjamin F. Jones	June 26, 1884
Matthew S. Quay	July 11, 1888
James S. Clarkson	July 29, 1891
Thomas H. Carter	May 10, 1893
Marcus A. Hanna	June 19, 1896
Henry C. Payne	June 20, 1904
George B. Cortelyou	June 23, 1904
Harry S. New	December 6, 1907
Frank H. Hitchcock	July 8, 1908
John F. Hill	December 12, 1911
Victor Rosewater	June 6, 1912
Charles D. Hilles	July 9, 1912

William R. Willcox	June 28, 1916
William H. Hays	February 13, 1918
John T. Adams	June 6, 1921
William M. Butler	June 13, 1924
Hubert Work	June 21, 1928
Claudius H. Huston	September 9, 1929
Simeon D. Fess	August 7, 1930
Everett Sanders	June 16, 1932
Henry P. Fletcher	June 6, 1934
John D.M. Hamilton	June 12, 1936
Joseph W. Martin, Jr.	July 9, 1940
Harrison E. Spangler	December 7, 1942
Herbert Brownell, Jr.	June 29, 1944
B. Carroll Reece	April 1, 1946
Hugh D. Scott, Jr.	June 26, 1948
Guy G. Gabrielson	August 9, 1949
Arthur E. Summerfield	July 11, 1952
C. Wesley Roberts	January 17, 1953
Leonard Hall	April 11, 1953
H. Meade Alcorn, Jr.	January 22, 1957
Thruston B. Morton	April 12, 1959

The following chairmen are not covered in this book:

William E. Miller	June 3, 1961
Dean Burch	July 18, 1964
Ray C. Bliss	January 23, 1965
Rogers C.B. Morton	April 15, 1969
Robert J. Dole	January 15, 1971
George Bush	December 11, 1972
Mary Louise Smith	September 17, 1974
Bill Brock	January 15, 1977
Richard Richards	January 18, 1981
Paul Laxalt (general chairman)	January 29, 1983
Frank J. Fahrenkopf	January 29, 1983
Lee Atwater	January 18, 1989

Acknowledgments

This book has been long in gestation and made possible only with the help and encouragement of many. The study began as a doctoral project at the University of Chicago, under the guidance of Professors Avery Leiserson and Charles Hardin. Initial financial assistance came from a Social Science Research Council fellowship. Subsequently, Dr. Paul T. David, then director of Governmental Studies at The Brookings Institution in Washington, DC, recommended its inclusion in the institution's research program and provided precious counsel as chairman of my advisory committee. Funds were forthcoming from a Ford Foundation grant to The Brookings Institution. At Brookings, my colleague Richard C. Bain gave generously of his time and advice, and Alice E. Robinson provided dedicated research assistance.

Research proceeded during my tenure as a member of the Michigan State University political science faculty, where I received an All-University Research Grant and time away from teaching duties, thanks to then Dean Alfred L. Seelye of the College of Business and Public Service and Professor Joseph La-Palombara, chair of the Department of Political Science.

Advice regarding conceptualization and sources of data came in abundance from Professor Arthur N. Holcombe of Harvard University, Emil Hurja, Irving Brant, Dr. E. Francis Brown of the *New York Times*, John D.M. Hamilton, Dr. Floyd E. McCaffree of the Republican National Committee, and Grey Leslie and Marion Watts of the Democratic National Committee. Long overdue are thanks to Dr. Sheilah Mann of the American Political Science Association for invaluable editorial suggestions made some time ago.

The staffs of several historical societies and libraries were particularly helpful. They included: Dr. Paul Buck, Dr. C. Percy Powell, and the staff of the Manuscripts Division of the Library of Congress; Charlotte D. Conover of the New Hampshire Historical Society; M. Halsey Thomas of Columbia University's Low Memorial Library; Stephen T. Riley of the Massachusetts

Historical Society; Clifford K. Shipton of the American Antiquarian Society; Margaret Larson of the Clements Library at the University of Michigan; Polly Quinn of the University of Vermont Library; Clara E. Follette of the Vermont Historical Society; Mattie Russell of the Duke University Library; Wayne Andrews of the New York Historical Society; and the staffs of the New Jersey Historical Society and the Historical Society of Pennsylvania. Mrs. G. Macculloch Miller gave much appreciated permission to examine and quote from the William C. Whitney Papers.

Theda Cullen, Adaline Gall, Margaret Blough, Beatrice Katamoto, Edith Starr, and Mariko Spitz were among the loyal troops that helped put information on cards and manuscript on paper.

For advice that led to substantial modifications of an earlier draft of the manuscript, my gratitude goes out to Professor L. Sandy Maisel of Colby College. Cynthia Maude-Gembler of Syracuse University Press gave encouragement when the project hit unexpected publishing shoals at another university press. The enthusiasm and technical support of editor Barbara Leffel and the staff of M.E. Sharpe Publishers were particularly gratifying.

I must, of course, acknowledge sole and full responsibility for the more or less adequate distillation that follows. I hope the final product offers some solace to all who have helped and waited, including those patient members of the author's family. Thank you, one and all.

Ralph M. Goldman
Reston, Virginia

Part I
In the Beginning

1 | Early National Parties as Personal Networks

By the mid-eighteenth century, the Tory and Whig parties were the established political parties of Great Britain and were principally active in Parliament. In several British colonies there were partisan counterparts of the British parties, namely, the Crown and Country parties, respectively. As in the mother country, the colonial parties engaged each other regularly in the colonial legislatures. American politicians differed from their counterparts in the mother country because, from the outset, they were primarily concerned with their constituencies, that is, the electorate. Thus, colonial parties were more electoral than parliamentary.

Local caucusing, campaigning (or electioneering, as it was known), and grass-roots organizing received serious attention. Grass-roots politics and decentralization remain characteristic of U.S. party development. A half-century passed after the founding of the Republic before a major party established its first formal *national* chief executive office, that is, the Democratic national chairmanship. Even today, organization continues to be a prime concern of American party leaders. Decentralization and loose structure are still major characteristics, although there is a firm trend toward centralization.

1

Most of the Founders were uncomfortable with the concept of popular sovereignty and particularly with political parties as organizers of the popular will. They drew this attitude from the contentious history of the British party system and from the writings of such critical British observers as Lord Bolingbroke. The Founders were also quite familiar with the partisan squabbling in the colonial legislatures, which was either joined or derided by the colonial press. Popular sovereignty was suspect, even though the tiny American electorate consisted mainly of property-owning Caucasian males, that is, less than 5 percent of the total population, including children. In his Farewell Address, President George Washington reinforced the emerging antiparty tradition by warning against parties. Even Thomas Jefferson, builder of the first loyal opposition party, was ambivalent from time to time on the subject of parties.

The exceptions to this antiparty tradition were James Madison and Alexander Hamilton. Madison wrote of the importance of "factions," the commonly used synonym for political parties, in his much-quoted *Federalist Paper* #10. He also created and led the Democratic-Republican caucus in the first sessions of the House of Representatives. Hamilton, as secretary of the treasury, was the behind-the-scenes leader of the "Hamiltonian," or Federalist, bloc in Congress.

Party lines were well drawn by the Third Congress, with Madisonians (now also known as Democratic-Republicans) dominating the House of Representatives. In the country and the electorate, party organizations appeared in state legislatures as caucuses and in the cities and counties, as patriotic clubs and democratic societies. What national party organization existed depended entirely upon the pens of Jefferson and Hamilton, whose prolific correspondence was all that bound state and local political leaders of like mind together in the coordination of their election strategies and efforts. Jefferson and Hamilton were, for all practical purposes, the national chairmen of their respective parties.

When Hamilton urged his fellow Federalists to better organize themselves as a party at the local level, his counsel was ignored; the Federalist leaders refused to acknowledge that they were a political party. Not long after, the Federalists disappeared from the state and local ballots, whereupon almost every politician referred to himself as a Democratic-Republican or Jeffersonian Republican. This was the "Era of Good Feelings," a euphemism for a one-party system that lasted for the decade from 1814 to 1824.

The young nation sprawled and spread during the 1820s and 1830s. As its borders and population changed, so did its politics. In the national arena, new constituencies mixed with the old, for example, labor in the cities joined with farmers at the frontiers. Suffrage was extended to unpropertied white males. New political interests came to life. Presidential politicians worked diligently to mobilize the political fragments. Henry Clay produced an oppositionist patchwork— the War Hawks—in the West to confront the Virginia Dynasty (Jefferson, Madison, and Monroe) in the East. The remnants of Federalism in New England fell in line behind the Adamses and Daniel Webster. Of them all, only Andrew Jackson's colleagues organized a party that endured.

Even as presidential parties organized themselves around their heroes, different factions within each party made themselves visible. Factionalism soon acquired regional dimensions, for example, North versus South, Northeast versus West. These factions became powerful enough to destroy the National Republican party, the Whig party, and others prior to 1856 and to come within a breath of destroying the Democrats—and the nation—in 1860. One major arena of factional struggle was the contest between leaders of the parties in Congress and leaders of the presidential wings. It took little time for the principle of separation of powers that was applied to the national government to find its way into the factionalism of the political parties.

2

The politicians around Andrew Jackson intended to collect the Jacksonian following into a potent and durable political organization. In time, a number of otherwise independent state party organizations united to form a "holding company" to capitalize the fame of Old Hickory.[1] Once accomplished, they converted the holding company into a more formal national party organization.

After his inauguration, Jackson gave careful attention to the political composition of his administration. He wanted his cabinet to be his administrative arm; the six states represented in it constituted one-third of the votes in the electoral college and were also the principal sources of Jackson's popular support. For advice in matters of party and political management, Jackson turned to a more intimate group: the Kitchen Cabinet.*

For counsel regarding broad strategies of political organization, Jackson relied mostly on Martin Van Buren, leader of New York's Albany Regency. Van Buren was, in effect, the leader of the Kitchen Cabinet. He later became Jackson's secretary of state, vice-president, and heir apparent. Secretary of War John Henry Eaton was another favored adviser, long an intimate friend and Jackson's personal biographer. Senator Thomas Hart Benton of Missouri, John Forsyth of Georgia, and Robert Hayne of South Carolina were Jacksonian activists in matters of congressional relations.

The membership of the Kitchen Cabinet changed over the years. Jackson's long-time aide Major William B. Lewis, brother-in-law to Eaton and principal promoter of the Jackson-for-president movement in the early 1820s, participated while serving as a federal auditor; Lewis later broke with Jackson on the national bank issue. Duff Green edited the *Telegraph*, the administration's chief newspaper, but soon fell out with the Jacksonian cause. Isaac Hill was known as "the Marat of the Kitchen Cabinet" because heads fell under the system of patronage he devised. Editor of the leading Democratic newspaper in New Hampshire, Hill headed the Jacksonian party in that state, keeping it Democratic over the decades from 1832 to 1852. Hill's organization issued the official calls for the first Democratic national conventions. Another consultant to the Kitchen Cabinet was Roger B. Taney, Maryland lawyer and attorney general in the reorganized cabinet after 1831.

The publicists were the key activists in the Kitchen Cabinet. They maintained

---

*An unofficial and informal group of personal advisers who presumably worked out political strategies in the White House kitchen.

the lines of communication between President Jackson and the new mass electorate. Isaac Hill's newspaper, for example, was a formidable voice for Jackson. Other key journalists included Amos Kendall and Francis P. Blair. Educated at Dartmouth and later a teacher at Groton, Kendall moved to Kentucky in 1814, where he became a tutor for the Henry Clay family. A journalist, he eventually became editor of the leading newspaper in the state, the *Angus*. Kendall's support of Jackson was an influential factor in the West. Blair was also a Kentuckian, long associated with Kendall and the latter's successor as editor of the *Angus*. When Duff Green's handling of the *Telegraph* became unsatisfactory, Kendall arranged for Blair to launch a new Jackson newspaper, the *Globe*, which began publication on December 7, 1830. Both Kendall and Blair worked well with Van Buren and became masters of the press battles that helped transform the Jacksonian following into the Democratic party.

The Kitchen Cabinet was never more than advisory. Jackson made up his own mind. "I should loath myself," he wrote, "did any act of mine afford the slightest color for the insinuation that I followed blindly the judgment of any friend in the discharge of my proper duties as a public or private individual."[2] Furthermore, the members of the group were too transient ever to have the opportunity to control Jackson. Nonetheless, the Kitchen Cabinet was an informal national party staff with substantial influence upon the political strategies Jackson chose and the tactics he used to win his battles.

Gradually, Jackson's vice-president, John C. Calhoun of South Carolina, became a political opponent and a problem for his administration. Calhoun, along with Henry Clay, was a nationalist prior to his vice-presidential campaign in 1824. Calhoun had endorsed most of Clay's American System platform, which promised protective tariffs to New England and internal improvements to the West, but gave very little to the South. However, Calhoun was in favor of reducing tariffs, a policy that had strong support in the South. In the 1824 presidential race, Calhoun ran for the vice-presidency on both John Quincy Adams' and Andrew Jackson's tickets in different states. He was elected as Adams' vice-president. After 1824, however, Calhoun began an ideological shift that eventually placed him at the head of the states' rights cause. The price for Calhoun's support of Jackson's candidacy in 1828 was tariff reform—and the vice-presidency.

William H. Crawford of the Richmond Junto and Martin Van Buren of the Albany Regency shared the objective of blocking Calhoun's presidential ambitions. The bitterness between Calhoun and Van Buren supporters became extreme even before Jackson's inauguration in March 1829.[3] This rivalry lent unusual heat to what should have been a minor social crisis: the social ostracizing of Peggy Eaton.

Jackson's old friend, Secretary of War John Henry Eaton, had married Peggy O'Neale, a Washington tavern-keeper's daughter, two months before Jackson's inauguration. At the inaugural and thereafter, Peggy Eaton was subjected to an ostentatious snub from the other cabinet wives led by Floride Calhoun. Sympathetic to the Eatons and recalling the distresses that politics had heaped upon his own deceased wife, Jackson asked the men of the cabinet to intercede with their wives. Widower Van Buren took a position alongside Jackson and Eaton in this affair. Calhoun, on the other hand, supported the cabinet majority in its refusal to intercede. Thereafter, few cabinet meetings were called. After 1830, Calhoun began to feel the full force of Jackson's hostility.

Jackson had pledged himself to a single term in the presidency. As Clay proceeded to mobilize the National Republican opposition and as Calhoun became an overt contender for the leadership of the Jackson party, Van Buren and the Kitchen Cabinet reached the conclusion that only the renomination of the president himself could lay low both the Clay threat from without and the Calhoun faction within. Early in 1830, two New York newspapers, the *Courier* and the *Enquirer*, opened the campaign for Jackson's renomination.

Meanwhile, in Congress during January 1830, the historic Webster-Hayne debate on the nature of the Union took place. The Jacksonian leaders viewed the crusade in favor of the states' rights doctrine as a major threat to the sectional combination upon which their support rested. Jackson's second annual message of the following December declared that it was within the power of Congress to protect industry by using tariffs and that it was not within the power of any state to nullify an act of the national legislature. Robert Hayne, as a South Carolinian, fervently set forth the nullification doctrine formulated by Calhoun in 1828. Daniel Webster replied with a classic appeal for union and patriotism. The issue between Jackson and Calhoun was thus sharply drawn. On January 22, 1831, the *Globe* reported that the president would not decline a second term; Calhoun's presidential aspirations were now in jeopardy.

In March and April, Jackson followed Van Buren's strategy and began to remove the Calhoun supporters from his cabinet. In order to give the president a free hand to reorganize his cabinet, Van Buren and Eaton volunteered to resign. Ingham, Branch, and Berrien followed suit, but not without public references to the pressure that had been put on them. One member of the new cabinet came from Louisiana and another from Maryland, but on the whole the pro-Calhoun South was no longer represented. The Jacksonians were ready to proceed into the campaign of 1832, but not before revamping the Kitchen Cabinet.

The Anti-Masonic party issued its call for a national nominating convention, the first such convention. In February 1831, the New York City National Republicans adopted the same procedure, a national convention to nominate Clay. Since Van Buren had proposed the concept of national nominating conventions four years earlier, the Kitchen Cabinet was also predisposed to this new nominating method.

A month after the cabinet reshuffle, Amos Kendall visited Isaac Hill in New

Hampshire to discuss means for uniting the Jacksonian party. While there, he received the following message from Major Lewis, still a member of the Kitchen Cabinet:

> Many of our friends (and the most judicious of them) think it would be best for the Republican members of the respective Legislatures to propose to the people to elect delegates to a national convention . . . about the middle of next May. That period is preferred to prevent an improper interference by members of Congress who, about that time, will leave this city for their respective homes. If the friends of the administration, when brought together from every part of the Union, in convention, cannot harmonize I know of no other plan by which it can be done.[4]

Lewis closed his letter with the suggestion that the New Hampshire legislature lead off with the proposal. Hill arranged to have this done on June 25, 1831, issuing the convention call, a function later performed by the party's national committee. Duff Green's pro-Calhoun *Telegraph* promptly denounced the convention as a scheme to nominate Van Buren.

The president had other plans for his former secretary of state. Jackson appointed Van Buren to be ambassador to Great Britain in the belief that, after two or three years out of the country, Van Buren could return to the cabinet in time to regain his position as Jackson's successor in 1836.[5] This intention was evident from Major Lewis' failure to mention Van Buren as a vice-presidential candidate, instead suggesting Philip P. Barbour of Virginia, former Speaker of the House of Representatives, and two others. Van Buren departed for Great Britain during the summer as an interim appointee to be confirmed when Congress reconvened.

The vote on confirmation came January 25, 1832. The National Republicans and four Calhoun men voted against confirmation, creating a 23 to 23 tie. As presiding officer, Calhoun broke the tie by voting against confirmation. The Jacksonians rose to the challenge. Senator Benton, looking directly at Calhoun, shouted, "You have broken a minister and elected a vice-president." Jackson wrote Van Buren, "The insult to the executive would be avenged by putting you into the very chair which is now occupied by him who cast the deciding vote against you."[6]

The Democratic-Republican national convention had a larger attendance from more states than either the Anti-Masonic or the National Republican conventions. The Jacksonians followed the Anti-Mason example by adopting a unit rule for delegation voting and a special majority, the two-thirds rule, to nominate. The purpose was to avoid letting divided votes in the convention give the public the impression of party disunity. After approving a motion to concur in the many state legislative nominations of Jackson, the convention proceeded directly to a vice-presidential vote. The Calhoun supporters concen-

trated their votes on Barbour, but to no avail. Van Buren received 208 of the 283 votes cast.

This first Democratic-Republican national convention next turned to matters of permanent organization. Simon Cameron of Pennsylvania, who three decades later would be a member of President Abraham Lincoln's cabinet, offered a resolution that a national nominating convention be held every four years. However, the motion was tabled.

A presidential campaign organization was authorized and was composed of state corresponding committees appointed by the respective state delegations to the convention. A national central committee, with an unspecified number of members, was to be designated by the chairman of the convention. An "address to the nation," that is, a platform, was not to be prepared by national party officials, but left to state organizations to be handled as best suited to local conditions.[7]

These simple organizing arrangements were prodigious for the times and were made with an eye to permanency. The Anti-Mason and National Republican meetings, however, never convened again after their first gatherings; the Democratic-Republican meeting did, and continued to do so. A major step in the incorporation of Jacksonian democracy had been successfully consummated.

3

President Jackson began his second term with a new vice-president, Martin Van Buren. The outgoing vice-president, John C. Calhoun, became the spearhead of the states' rights movement. In 1832 and 1836, Calhoun's South Carolina threw away its electoral vote in the factional stalemate between Calhoun's Nullifiers and the pro-Jackson Unionists, a stalemate that began to be felt throughout the South. In the Southern frontier states, prior to 1836, including Jackson's own Tennessee, there was mounting resistance to the probability that Van Buren would be Jackson's successor. In the Northeast and the West, on the other hand, the exertions of Van Buren and his allies began to produce impressive state party organizations.

Federal patronage was used with skill to ensure party discipline. The *Globe*, as the official party newspaper, was able to coordinate policy positions on major issues and to give a semblance of unity to party affairs generally. Van Buren was indefatigable in his personal contacts and correspondence.[8] For Van Buren, the business of creating a national political party was essential and honorable work in a democracy:

> But knowing, as all men of sense know, that political parties are inseparable from free governments, and that in many and material respects they are highly useful to the country, I never could bring myself for my part to deprecate their existence. . . . The disposition to abuse power, so deeply planted in the human

heart, can by no other means be more effectively checked; and it has always struck me as more honorable and manly and more in harmony with the character of our People and of our Institutions to deal with the subject of Political Parties in a sincere and wiser spirit.[9]

In 1835, the Jacksonians again turned to the national convention as a means for tightening party lines behind a single national ticket. To capture the initiative in a divided field, the national nominating convention was held early, on May 20, 1835, in Baltimore, Maryland. The purpose of the convention was stated clearly enough by its chairman, Andrew Stevenson of Virginia, former Speaker of the House of Representatives from 1827 to 1834:

> Efforts will no doubt be made to . . . put in jeopardy, and possible defeat the election of a president by the people, in their primary colleges. . . . The democracy of the union have [sic] been forced to look to a national convention, as the best means of concentrating the popular will, and giving it effect in the approaching election. It is, in fact, the only defense against a minority president.[10]

The roll call showed 612 delegates present, representing twenty-two states. Most of this large number, however, were from Maryland, giving the convention more the appearance of a mass rally than a representative assembly. Vice-President Van Buren received the 1836 presidential nomination without opposition.

The Jackson-Van Buren managers then proposed Richard M. Johnson of Kentucky, hero of the Indian wars of the West, as vice-president. The South, particularly Virginia, expressed strong objections. To overcome the two-thirds nominating requirement, the Jackson-Van Buren managers attempted to change the rule from two-thirds to a simple majority. This was the first of a century-long series of attempts to repeal the two-thirds rule. The motion was defeated. Johnson was nevertheless nominated by a bare two-thirds vote, 178 to 87, but at the cost of Virginia's support in the campaign and election. Virginia not only refused to pledge its energies to the campaign, but, after the convention, nominated its own vice-presidential candidate, John Tyler.

The convention failed to name a national or central campaign committee or committee of correspondence. It did, however, select a committee to prepare an address to the nation at some time after the convention. Represented on the committee were the Jackson leaders from New York, Virginia, New Hampshire, Maryland, North Carolina, and Mississippi. The work of this postconvention platform committee was published in the *Globe* on July 31, 1835, and filled ten columns.[11]

The convention vote on the vice-presidency revealed the first serious fissure in the Jacksonian party and was further reflected in the failure of any nominee to win the requisite majority of electoral college votes for vice-president. This was

the first and only election in which the choice of vice-president was made in the Senate.*

The Whig opposition had adopted the strategy of running several strong regional candidates for president. The strategy may not have won the election, but it did result in significant inroads into Democratic strength in many states. The decline in the Democratic vote in the South—Alabama, Georgia, Louisiana, Mississippi, North Carolina, and Virginia—averaged 34 percentage points. An average decline of 33 percent was registered for the Democrats in the West and Southwest: Illinois, Indiana, Missouri, and Tennessee. On the other hand, the average Democratic vote rose 11 percent in the New England states, reflecting in part the rise of New England's abolitionist movement. Van Buren's losses in the South indicated the sharpening of the North-South split in the Democratic party-in-the-electorate, that is, the rank-and-file party workers and the loyal party voters in the electorate. The election marked a decline in the extent to which one-party states dominated the national elections and began a period in which politics became competitive throughout the nation, with Democrats and Whigs evenly matched in most states. In close elections, the cost of factionalism was bound to come high.

The presidential campaign of 1836 also marked the advent of slavery as an explicit and emotional national issue. The abolitionists petitioned Congress to forbid slavery in the District of Columbia. The petition roused the ire of Southerners whose economic interests depended on the institution of slavery. Southern leaders repeatedly asked President Van Buren his views on slavery. Van Buren took the position that the states had jurisdiction over slavery strictly within their own boundaries and that the Constitution did not give Congress the power to interfere either in the states or in the District of Columbia.[12]

The years 1837–1841 were particularly consequential for the development of the Democratic party. The premises for Van Buren's policies regarding the independent treasury, public lands, and the slave issues turned the Democratic party toward new principles of political philosophy. For example, Van Buren could see no reason why private state or national banks should be employed as depositories for government money. In May 1837, he ordered the suspension of specie payments by the banks. The economic Panic of 1837 ensued, for which he was blamed. This set the tone of factional and partisan controversy.

---

*Richard Johnson of Kentucky, the Jacksonian convention's nominee for vice-president, was the bachelor father of illegitimate daughters whom he had by a mulatto slave. He lived openly with the slave, educated the daughters, and left them his fortune in his will. This earned him the hostility of the slave state leaders, who withheld their votes from him in the electoral college. Thus, he failed to get the requisite absolute majority in the electoral college, and the selection went to the Senate in accordance with the Twelfth Amendment to Article II, Section 1, of the Constitution. He was unopposed, and the Senate Democrats elected him.

In September 1837, Van Buren called Congress into special session to consider the "Divorce Bill" that would create an independent sub-treasury for the deposit of public funds. The proposal completely obliterated party lines. The Senate vote on the sub-treasury bill in particular revealed the split between the conservative forces in the Democratic party in Congress and the Van Buren administration. After much debate, the administration, led by Wright and Benton, rallied enough votes to pass the bill, 26 to 20. In the House, however, the conservatives were successful in tabling the bill, 119 to 107. An opposition group among the Democrats had cooperated with the Whigs to reject the bill. In the event, the two state organizations—New York and Virginia—that had been the pillars of the Democratic national coalition also had split apart.

On December 12, 1837, former president and now Representative John Quincy Adams presented a petition in the House asking for the abolition of slavery in the District of Columbia. According to Thomas Hart Benton,[13] this petition was followed on December 20 by "the most disturbing movement the subject of slavery ever made in our Congress," namely, the departure of the Southern members from the hall to deliberate among themselves what lines of conduct they should follow.[14]

In the Senate, Calhoun introduced a series of resolutions defining the character of our government and the rights of the slave states under it. The debates on these resolutions were bitter and protracted. According to Benton:

> These resolutions, and the debate to which they gave rise, and the modification which they underwent, and the final vote upon them, constitute the most important proceeding on the subject of slavery which has ever taken place in Congress. They were framed to declare the whole power of Congress upon the subject, and were presented for a "test" vote, and as the future "platform" and "permanent settlement" of the law on the slavery question. The first four related to the states, and the rights of slavery in them under the guarantee of the constitution. The fifth related to the District of Columbia, and to the Territory of Florida [that being the only slave territory then in the Union], placed the abolition of slavery therein in the hands of Congress, but forbid [it] by high expedient reasons.[15]

The vote on the slavery question did not repeat the division revealed by the sub-treasury bill. Almost all Democrats supported Calhoun's efforts to prevent the question of slavery from becoming an issue. The final vote on the adoption of the first five of Calhoun's resolutions was typical. Democrats, including Southern leaders, maintained a unified front, with thirty-five in favor of passage and nine opposed. These nine were mainly senators from the Northeast.

Another test came in 1839. It required two months to organize the new House of Representatives. The party balance was 119 Democrats and 118 opposition members, with 5 members from New Jersey unable to be seated because of seating contests. Selection of the Speaker resulted in another setback for Van

Buren's administration. The chief candidates were John Bell of Tennessee, a Whig, and George W. Jones of Virginia for the Van Buren side. Neither Bell nor Jones could win the whole vote of their respective parties. A Calhoun man— Dixon H. Lewis of Alabama—also failed. Finally, the Whigs and conservative Democrats united on Robert M.T. Hunter and elected him. The vote breakdown was 119 for Hunter, 55 for Jones, 24 for George M. Keim of Pennsylvania, and 34 spread among 10 other candidates. Van Buren's influence was in decline as the time for the third Democratic-Republican national convention on May 5, 1840, approached.

Van Buren had been preparing for 1840 for some time. On February 8, 1840, Silas Wright received from the president a draft of "hints" that contained 103 handwritten pages. This document included principles upon which the party should run, organization strategies for the various states, and so forth. Van Buren evidently felt that his greatest opponent was fraud. He strongly urged organizations within the Democratic-Republican party to guard against frauds by opposition.[16]

Administration managers worked diligently to keep the factional ferment to a minimum. Preferring not to risk divisions on the floor of the convention, the Van Buren supporters moved that a committee of one representative from each state consider the subject of nominations. This committee issued a report stating that no opposition had been found to Van Buren's renomination and that no vice-presidential candidate had been chosen. The committee's report was adopted by simple majority and constituted the entire nominating procedure. Three vice-presidential candidates subsequently entered the field: Vice-President Richard Johnson, Littleton W. Tazewell of Virginia, and James K. Polk of Tennessee.

The Whigs, meanwhile, were nominating states' rights Democrat John Tyler to second place on their "Tippecanoe and Tyler, too" ticket.

The 1840 Democratic-Republican national convention was also the one in which the party name was simplified. Henceforth, it was called the Democratic party.

2 | Establishing the National Committee and Its Chairmanship

Jackson and his party managers left the modern Democratic party with a predilection for strong presidential leadership and for nurturing party strength in the presidential electorate, at times more so than in the legislative arena. In contrast to the party versus Congress factionalism exhibited in the Weed-Clay rivalry among the Whigs, the Democrats enjoyed an abundance of presidential leadership on the electoral side. Jackson and Van Buren lent energy and direction to the party-in-the-electorate, even after they left presidential office.

With keen organizational sense, Van Buren moved swiftly into the role of out-party leader after his defeat in 1840. Jackson continued to be a source of elder-statesmanly advice and influence to any Democratic leader who solicited his views. John Tyler's succession to the presidency upon William Henry Harrison's death created some confusion by giving the Democrats a third titular leader whose party identity was somewhat ambiguous. All three men turned to the national conventions as the chosen arenas of battle. James K. Polk, another Democrat skilled in electioneering and party management, was the convention's choice as Tyler's successor.

The attitude of these men toward the party reinforced the Democratic predilection for strong national party agencies capable of mobilizing the presidential electorate. National factional battles were therefore carried forward mainly in the national conventions, during the conduct of presidential campaigns, and in connection with the national party chairmanship. In contrast, sectional differences between Northern and Southern Democrats in Congress on the issues of slavery, annexation of new territories, and the admission of new states to the Union kept the development of Democratic party leadership off balance for more than two decades. Congressional Democrats found it necessary to learn the ways of the national conventions and other national party agencies.

1

Loss of the election to Harrison left Van Buren titular leader of an out-party, the first president nominated by a national convention to hold this unofficial status. The prestige of having twice received the presidential nomination of his party and having previously served in the vice-presidency and presidency assured Van Buren a leadership role even in defeat. Van Buren did not take his unspecified responsibilities lightly. He wrote in his *Autobiography* that party organization is the greatest need of a party in defeat, suggesting his conception of the problems of an opposition party.

> Always under similar circumstances, the rank and file of a political party, taught by adversity the folly of their divisions, looked to a discontinuance of them to soothe its mortification, and long delays in accomplishing a cordial reconciliation are invariably attributed to the policy inhibition of leaders.[1]

Anticipating the 1840 defeat, Francis P. Blair, editor of the *Globe*, had written to Jackson at the Hermitage arguing that the party ought to plan to restore itself "by the re-election of Mr. Van Buren." He suggested that Jackson correspond with party leaders to determine "the best means of recovery."[2]

Vice-President Tyler's succession to the presidency in April 1841 raised a serious threat to Van Buren's future. As a Virginia states' rights Democrat on the Whig ticket in 1840, Tyler had contributed substantially to Van Buren's defeat. As president, Tyler again dedicated himself to the defeat of nationalism and centralization as represented by Clay on the Whig side and by Van Buren among Democrats. Tyler's key associate in this objective was Senator Robert J. Walker, the "Wizard of Mississippi." "As an adroit political fixer, Walker knew no equal, unless it was Van Buren—the Van Buren of earlier days."[3]

Walker has been one of the forgotten political giants of mid-nineteenth-century American history.[4] He was just forty years of age when Tyler became president, in his fourth year as senator from Mississippi, and he was the spokesman for the Southeast. As the 1844 Democratic national convention approached, Walker assumed leadership of one of the three annexationist groups opposed to Van Buren's renomination.

Democratic victories in the local and congressional elections of 1841 and 1842 brought a flood of congratulations to Van Buren's home in Lindenwald, New York. "Lindenwald was becoming another Monticello."[5] Van Buren had supported and gained the support of leading figures in Democratic state organizations and media. Among the latter were Thomas Ritchie, editor of the Richmond *Enquirer;* Samuel Medary, editor of the *Ohio Statesman;* Amos Kendall, postmaster general under Van Buren; Gideon Welles, editor of the *Hartford Times;* and others.

Robert J. Walker was born to politics, educated for politics, and married into a political family. His father was a justice of the Pennsylvania supreme court, and Walker was trained to be a lawyer. His wife belonged to the Bache-Dallas political dynasty of Pennsylvania. An ardent Jacksonian even before he moved from Pennsylvania to Mississippi in 1826, by 1832 he was leader of the Jackson party in Mississippi. At the 1840 Democratic convention, Walker served on the committee that made the report on nominations. Re-elected to a second term in the Senate in 1842, he became a confidant of President Tyler.

In the summer of 1843, Medary visited Van Buren at Lindenwald and found him seemingly unaware of movements in the party to replace him as the nominee in 1844.[6] During his travels, Medary found the opposition to be more formidable than he had supposed. Kendall, for his part, carried on a large private correspondence in an often vain search of allies who could be counted on to help in the 1844 Van Buren campaign. Late in 1841, Van Buren received word from Joel Poinsett of South Carolina that John C. Calhoun would also campaign for the nomination. Among those working for Calhoun were such former Jackson and Van Buren loyalists as Senator Levi Woodbury of New Hampshire, David Henshaw of Boston, and Isaac Hill of New Hampshire.

Another threat to Van Buren was the manner in which President Tyler was dispensing patronage, strongly suggesting that Tyler was interested in succeeding himself as the regular Democratic candidate rather than as a Whig. Furthermore, the president was apparently moving into an anti-Van Buren alliance with Calhoun. As Blair's *Globe* carried on its anti-Tyler and anti-Calhoun tirades, the Calhoun newspaper, *The Spectator*, argued against Van Buren's "re-eligibility" on grounds that he had been soundly defeated in 1840 and his renomination would be an "imposition" upon the party faithful.

Duff Green, Tyler's emissary to Great Britain, wrote Calhoun that the Van Burenites would control the 1844 convention. Green hoped that Tyler might receive the nomination, but now, in November 1842, looked to the president's friends to hold only the balance of power.[7]

The Van Buren forces, in control of many state organizations, assumed that the nomination could be theirs if the national convention were held as early as possible and if they left delegation voting procedure (unit rule, per capita voting, etc.) to the judgment of each state delegation. The Calhoun people and others thought that they could further their causes by putting off the convention to the latest possible date and by voting under a per capita rule. The latter issue was fought over in several state conventions. Eventually, Van Buren agreed that a later convention would be necessary in order to conciliate the Calhoun people. The apparently innocuous issues of the convention's date and the delegation voting method had become the subjects of critical factional tests and transactions.

A further test of Van Buren's influence came in the fight for the speakership and the printer's contract of the Twenty-eighth Congress in 1843. The printing contract went to Francis Preston Blair, Van Buren's man, by an 80 to 30 vote margin. The speakership went to the Van Buren candidate, 128 to 59. The pro-Van Buren surge was felt in Democratic state organizations throughout the country. In the Senate during January 1844, the Van Buren forces joined the Whigs in rejecting four of Tyler's nominations to federal offices.

In January 1844, Calhoun announced that he would not allow his name to go before the convention. Duff Green proposed a movement to call a separate convention that would leave only the Van Buren delegates at the official Baltimore convention. Lewis Cass of Michigan, whose support was necessary for Green's scheme, sought to dissuade Green, indicating that he did not "believe much" in third parties and that "experience" proved that such organizations "could not exist in our country."[8] By 1844, Lewis Cass, James Buchanan, and Robert Johnson had removed themselves from the field of candidates.

Meanwhile, President Tyler was eagerly pursuing negotiations to annex Texas. Although the admission of Texas as another slave state would be a threat to the North, most of the Democratic party press, Andrew Jackson, and Robert Walker were unqualifiedly in favor of immediate annexation. The leading political issue during the spring of 1844 was annexation, which focused around the annexation treaty signed by Calhoun as secretary of state on April 12, 1844.

Van Buren could not escape having to take a stand. Early in April, a letter from W.H. Hammet, Democratic congressman from Mississippi, invited Van Buren to speak out on the constitutionality and expediency of immediate annexation of Texas. On April 27, Senator Henry Clay declared himself opposed to immediate annexation and was roundly criticized by leaders in both parties. On the very same day, Van Buren's reply to Hammet was published in the *Globe*. Van Buren thought that the annexation of Texas was clearly constitutional, but denied its expediency. He saw war with Mexico as the probable outcome. He further considered annexation a source of sectional bitterness. The Hammet letter immediately raised serious doubts about Van Buren's availability, particularly as a unifier of the party. The Hammet letter also united the opposition to Van Buren's renomination.

Van Buren's letter was generally interpreted as putting him in the antiannexation camp. Among the annexationists were Calhoun's followers, rabidly opposed to Van Buren; Calhoun himself had entered Tyler's cabinet just prior to the Democratic national convention. A second group of annexationists was the Southern leadership led by Robert Walker. A third group consisted of middle-states delegations led by Cave Johnson, manager of the unusual Polk-for-vice-president movement. Fourteen state party conventions, four congressional district conventions, and one party caucus in a state legislature nevertheless instructed their delegations to support Van Buren for a third presidential nomination. The votes committed in this fashion numbered 159, that is, 18 votes short of two-thirds, assuming that two-thirds would be needed to nominate.

At the convention, Senator Walker immediately moved readoption of the two-thirds rule for nomination. Debate raged for two days. There was talk of running three candidates, similar to the Whig strategy in 1836. Wrote James K. Polk from his residence in Tennessee, "Surely, there is patriotism enough among leaders yet to save the party. This can only be done by uniting on *one* candidate. . . . The idea which has been suggested of running three candidates . . . ought not to be entertained for a moment."[9]

The two-thirds rule was readopted by a 148 to 118 vote. The critical votes were Virginia's 17. George C. Dromgoole, head of the Virginia delegation, Speaker of the House of Representatives, and a Van Buren supporter of long standing, was a principal decision maker in the important vote. Virginia withdrew from the floor of the convention and cast its decisive ballot at the end of the roll call. The possibility of a renomination for the Democratic party's first titular leader ended there. Twenty-nine of the 159 voters who had been pledged to Van Buren failed to vote for him; 16 uninstructed delegates supported him, for a net loss of 13. Van Buren received 146 votes on the first ballot, 31 votes short of the necessary two-thirds.

The Walker-Dromgoole maneuver created a stalemate for seven nominating ballots. The supporters of Johnson, Cass, and Buchanan were unable to unite among themselves; nor was any one of them able to draw votes from the Van Buren side. Polk's name was added to the presidential candidate roster on the eighth ballot. Most of his forty-four votes came from the Van Buren wing of the Massachusetts delegation, a concession of defeat. The bandwagon moved quickly on the ninth ballot, and Polk was nominated amid an uproarious ovation, the first dark-horse nominee in the brief history of national conventions. The convention system thus demonstrated itself to be an institution capable of producing an unexpected solution to factional stalemates.

2

Having retired Van Buren, Senator Walker promptly moved to conciliate the supporters of the deposed leader, personally proposing Silas Wright, Van Buren's close associate in New York politics, for vice-president. Wright declined and second place went instead to Walker's brother-in-law, George M. Dallas of Pennsylvania.

Looking to the future, Cave Johnson reminded the national convention that practical means for winning the election would have to be created. Benjamin Butler of New York, as chairman of the Committee on Resolutions, recommended appointment of a Committee on Political Tracts for the ensuing campaign. A five-member committee, little used in the campaign, was appointed.

Congressman Dromgoole moved and the convention approved formation of a central committee of fifteen members to undertake immediate organization of the party throughout the Union.[10] However, over one-third of the states were not represented on the fifteen-member committee. The appointment of members to the central committee, to reside in Washington, seems to have been left to a caucus of the Democratic members of Congress. As it later turned out, none of the factional leaders dared convene the caucus for fear of alienating all the others. When it was eventually organized, the 1844 central committee was the immediate predecesssor of the all-states membership of the first national committee in 1848.[11]

After returning to Washington, Senator Walker again assumed leadership as the unofficial national chairman of the party. Throughout June, July, and August, he labored prodigiously. He initiated the organization of the central committee, wrote the address to the people, served as the go-between in the negotiations to have President Tyler withdraw from the presidential race, and induced the Tyler and Calhoun newspapers to support the Polk-Dallas ticket. Walker was chosen chairman of the central committee, probably during June, expecting to serve in that capacity only temporarily:

> I was chosen chairman, and consented to remain here [in Washington] and discharge the duties of that office, until relieved by a substitute who was expected to take my place during the present month [August], and enable me before the close of August to return to Mississippi. In this expectation I have been disappointed.[12]

Walker successfully used the central committee to draw together the disparate elements of the Democratic campaign. He asked Polk for a letter "to use discreetly" to win the support of the conservative Democrats whose votes would influence election results in Maine, Connecticut, New York, and New Jersey.[13] President Tyler expressed the hope that his "friends"—some 150,000 of them—would be treated as equals (referring, of course, to the extensive federal patronage) in the event that Polk should be elected. In response, Walker, performing the patronage duties of future national chairmen, asked Jackson and Polk for letters "of a character to put Tyler's friends at perfect ease."[14]

Favorable actions fell into place in good order. Polk made appropriate pledges regarding Tyler's friends. Blair's *Globe* ended its verbal assaults on President Tyler. Tyler terminated his candidacy. The Calhoun press mounted the Polk-Dallas bandwagon. Walker's work bore rich fruit.

The address to the people was the final delicate task. A misstep on the annexation issue could be fatal. To please both the North and the South, Walker prepared two versions of the same address. One version, entitled "The South in Danger," *seemed* to put the Democratic party on record favoring the extension of slavery into Texas. This version was widely distributed in the South. The second version, substantially the same as the first, but with a few key phrases altered, was distributed in the Northern constituencies. This was done early in October. Communication was too slow for comparisons to reach the attention of most voters until after the November elections. The pamphlets' effect was positive in both sections of the country. The postelection uproar over the pamphlet tactic was drowned out by the celebration over Polk's victory.[15]

3

The presidential prize was becoming well worth the effort. The federal job patronage during the 1840s and early 1850s had an estimated monetary value of $50 million.[16] Polk's postmaster general Cave Johnson oversaw the removals and resignations of 11,000 of the 14,000 postmasters; 11 out of every 14 postmasters as compared with the 1 out of every 8 in the simpler patronage days of Andrew Jackson.[17] The economic resources of the federal government were expanding in size and influence, particularly with respect to letting contracts for supplies for frontier policing and, later, for the Mexican War. The lands acquired as the result of that war and the discovery of gold in California heightened the eagerness of party leaders to win control of the presidency.

The Polk cabinet was largely composed of men experienced in party affairs: James Buchanan to head the State Department, Robert Walker in Treasury, William L. Marcy in War, George Bancroft in Navy, John J. Mason as attorney general; and Cave Johnson as postmaster general. Walker and Johnson were, of course, the national convention managers who produced this dark horse president. Mason's Virginia sent the delegation that had put an end to the Van Buren candidacy. Bancroft's wing of the Massachusetts delegation was responsible for starting the convention bandwagon to Polk. Marcy of New York and Buchanan of Pennsylvania represented the two most powerful states in the electoral college.

With such political talent in his cabinet, Polk naively declared his intention to serve a one-term presidency and, further, expected to be able to avoid destabilizing maneuvers pertaining to the succession. Regarding all this, Andrew Jackson suggested:

> No aspirant to the succession will be in [Polk's] Cabinet unless, over his own signature, he disavows all such intentions and this is made known to the people. He [Polk] will not permit himself, as Mr. Monroe did, to be surrounded with strife by having candidates for the Presidency in the Cabinet.[18]

In addition to the several members of the cabinet, particularly Secretary of State Buchanan, the field of presidential aspirants included Senator John C. Calhoun of South Carolina, Senator William Allen of Ohio, Senator Lewis Cass of Michigan, Senator Thomas Hart Benton of Missouri, and Governor Silas Wright of New York.[19] Polk categorically rejected suggestions that he himself stand for re-election in order to unite the party.[20]

The president eventually comprehended the lack of logic of the political vacuum created by his one-term pledge, but seemed unable or unwilling to do anything about this:

> I have a nominal majority of Democrats in both Houses of Congress, but am in truth a minority in each House. The disappointments about office among the members [referring to the distribution of patronage], and the premature contest which they are waging in favor of their favorites for the Presidency in 1848, are the leading causes of this lamentable state of things.[21]

Polk deplored the fact that "the Federalists (*sic*) are always united and vote with the minority of the Democratic party upon every administration measure."[22] Polk looked with particular disapproval upon Secretary of State Buchanan's excessive concern with the matter of the presidential nomination.

On December 23, 1847, Buchanan had an interview with the president on this subject. It was generally understood among the members of Congress, Buchanan reported, that the president favored Cass for the nomination. Polk denied this emphatically, declaring that the Democratic party would have to make its own choice without his interference. When the secretary of state departed, Polk made the following entry in his diary, "Mr. B. seems to have been so much absorbed with the idea of being President that I cannot rely, as formerly, upon his advice given in Cabinet upon public subjects."[23]

More than one member of the cabinet, however, was interested in the Buchanan candidacy. Postmaster General Cave Johnson was a Buchanan man almost from the moment the Polk administration came into office. After 1848, Johnson worked diligently to line up former Cass supporters for Buchanan in 1852.[24] If Polk hoped to keep politics out of a cabinet made up of master politicians, he was foredoomed to disappointment. If Polk had a distinct preference for his successor, he never stated it explicitly, even in his diary, although there are numerous indications that he probably preferred Cass.[25]

4

As the Democratic national convention of 1848 approached, editor Gideon Welles of Connecticut set down an estimate of the candidate situation in a memorandum to himself. Welles thought Cass of Michigan was in the lead, Levi

Benjamin F. Hallett's career reflected the party ferment and changes occurring in New England during the decades from 1820 to 1848. Upon graduation from Brown University in 1816, he embarked upon journalistic pursuits in Providence, Rhode Island. Returning to his native state of Massachusetts in 1827, he became an editor of the Boston *Advertiser*. However, his writings on behalf of the growing prohibition, abolition, and antimasonic movements were so extreme, he was compelled to resign four years later. At this juncture, he gave full time to the Anti-Mason party, editing several of its publications in Massachusetts and becoming acquainted with Thurlow Weed, then leader of the New York Anti-Masons. (By 1848, however, Weed was principal manager of the Whig presidential campaign.)

In 1831, the Massachusetts Anti-Masons were second only to the National Republicans in popular support. But when antimasonry waned following Jackson's re-election in 1832, Hallett was instrumental in leading his party into the Democratic-Republican organization, particularly after the Jacksonians stepped up their fight against the National Bank. Thereafter, Hallett became a radical Democrat, vociferous in his defense of the abolition cause. This radicalism mellowed, however, and by 1844 Hallett was one of the principal leaders of the Tyler-Calhoun faction in the Massachusetts Democratic party, bent upon conciliating the North-South split in the national party. In 1847, this faction defeated the Van Burenites and nominated Caleb Cushing for governor. This put Hallett into the chairmanship of the party's state central committee. In 1848, New England Democratic leaders, chief among them Hallett, supported the cause of Judge Levi Woodbury of New Hampshire as a regional "favorite son."

Woodbury of New Hampshire next, and Buchanan trailing. Welles did not mention Silas Wright; New York was divided to the point of sending two delegations—the antislavery Barnburners and the pro-South Hunkers—"[t]he decision in the New York case and that of the two-thirds rule will be likely to affect the result."[26] Then, alluding to the organization-conscious Polk leadership, Welles continued:

> Unfortunately, we have no great and master minds which draw to them general confidence, and give to things a right direction. Nor have we any absorbing questions generating a wholesome distinction or correct party principles. The administration has endeavored to acquire for itself a strong party character, but has failed to create a party attachment. It has trusted too much to organization, and not sufficiently mindful of principles.[27]

The national convention had special guidance from congressional sources. On January 24, 1848, rather than the national committee, a conference of Democratic senators and representatives, with Senator Sam Houston of Texas as chairman, issued the call setting the time and place of the national convention.[28] At the convention, Senator Jesse D. Bright of Indiana, the leading parliamentarian in the Senate and a trusted ally of President Polk, exercised floor leadership, particularly on matters of agenda, parliamentary procedure, and organization.[29] Assisting Bright was Benjamin F. Hallett, a former leader of the Anti-Masonic party, but now chairman of the Massachusetts Democratic state committee and spokesman for most of the New England delegations.

The convention again adopted the two-thirds rule, whose application seemed likely to stop the candidacy of Lewis Cass. The first nominating ballot gave Cass 125 votes, Woodbury 58, Buchanan 55, and Dallas 3. Hallett led the New England swing from Woodbury to Cass. Buchanan supporters, willing to wait for another opportunity, joined the Cass parade. The nomination went to Cass on the fourth ballot. The platform, in large part the work of Hallett, was conciliatory to the South.

Later in the proceedings, Senator Bright moved "that a committee be appointed for the purpose of calling the next Democratic National Convention; that said committee be composed of one member from each State, to be appointed by the delegations from each State; and that said committee be authorized to fix the time and place of holding said Convention."[30] This motion was tabled along with another motion specifically designating Pittsburgh and the second Monday of June 1852 as place and time of the next convention.

Benjamin Hallett then proposed "that a committee of fifteen, to be named by the President of this convention, be appointed to promote the Democratic cause, and to be designated as the Democratic Central Committee of the United States."[31] Hallett had in mind the reestablishment of the same kind of central committee that was headed by Robert J. Walker in 1844. After some consultation, and undoubtedly taking into account that in 1846 Congress had passed legislation requiring that all presidential electors be chosen on the same first Tuesday in November, Senator Bright offered the following amendment, "Ordered, that a committee of one from each State, to be named by the respective delegations, be appointed to promote the Democratic cause, with power to fill vacancies, and to be designated 'The Democratic National Committee.' "[32]

What Bright had originally proposed as a committee to issue the next convention call and Hallett had intended as a committee to direct the national campaign were now incorporated into a proposal for a permanent interim committee representative of all state parties with power to fill vacancies in its membership. The Bright amendment was approved and the first national committee established.

The state delegations named their respective representatives on the national committee, and the convention adjourned. Benjamin F. Hallett was chosen the first Democratic national committee chairman. It is not clear how or when Hallett was chosen. The wording of his resolution for a central committee of fifteen to be appointed by the president of the national convention suggests that he may have been designated by Andrew Stevenson, permanent chairman of the convention, probably in consultation with Senator Bright and the Cass managers.

There are several apparent reasons for Hallett's selection. He led the decisive New England shift from Woodbury to Cass, thereby starting the Cass bandwagon. He was chairman of the platform committee whose Northern majority wrote a plank on the slavery-abolition issue that was conciliatory to the South. The party's national chairman, as had Robert Walker before him, was expected to produce campaign propaganda. Hallett's achievements with the platform made him the logical man for the propaganda job. Hallett also contributed to the regional balance in the party's national leadership; the nominees came from the Northwest and the Southwest, Hallett from New England, the national committee secretaries from the Middle Atlantic area and the South. Perhaps most influential were Hallett's long years of experience in party and campaign management.

Despite the national convention's success in creating the party's first permanent national body outside of Congress and, with it, the party's highest formal permanent office—the national chairmanship—victory eluded the party in the ensuing election. Chairman Hallett conducted most of his campaign activities from Boston. He made frequent public appearances at rallies. At his state's Democratic convention in the fall, he prepared the platform, which was later entitled "One Hundred Reasons for Voting for Cass," a major campaign document.[33]

The keynote of the Democratic campaign was "organization," and, in the opinion of Gideon Welles, the election was "more a conflict of organizations than of any exciting controverted question."[34] Organization, however, was not enough to surmount the crippling effects of a bolt by a faction that refused to recognize the legitimacy of a nomination made by the party's national convention. The New York Barnburners bolted to form the Free Soil party, with former President Van Buren heading the ticket. Van Buren's 300,000 votes were more than enough to deny the electoral votes of New York, Massachusetts, and Pennsylvania to Cass. A similar fate awaited the Whigs in 1852, that is, electoral defeat was concurrent with formalization of the party's national committee structure. The Van Buren bolt and the Democratic defeat launched a new phase in the development of the national party system in which factional bolts assumed tactical importance.

3 | Federalist, National Republican, and Whig Antecedents

The modern national Republican party was not established until 1856, at which time its organizers created the party's national committee and national chairmanship. However, there were partisan forebears dating from the founding of the Republic. Alexander Hamilton was the one-man national committee for the Federalists just as Thomas Jefferson was for the Democratic-Republicans. The Federalists were replaced for the most part by the National Republicans. Since neither the Federalists nor the National Republicans were interested in organizing the electorate on any enduring basis, their followers were readily brought into the Whig party of the 1830s to 1850s.

For a time, the Whigs verged on becoming a well-organized party, only to fall victim in the mid-1850s to the divisive slavery issue. Local factions in the Whig and Free Soil parties joined to form the present Republican party: in Ripon, Wisconsin, on February 28, 1854, or, as others claim, in Jackson, Michigan, on July 6, 1854. Born of defecting factions from other parties, the Republicans have since had their own lively factional history.

1

Organizing a national-level party structure was a major problem for these predecessors of the Republican party. Staunch promoters of a strong national government under the new constitution, often referred to as "the party of the Constitution," the Federalists nevertheless were conceptually antiparty and refused to engage seriously in the grass-roots work of party organization. Recalling with disdain the partisan strife of British politics, they viewed "factions," that is, parties, as machines of conflict, and conflict meant disunity at a time when national unity was needed. In commenting on the activities of the controversial patriotic societies during the years under the Articles of Confederation, General George Washington conceded that these groups might serve a useful purpose at the local level, but were objectionable in national matters.[1] This became a typical Federalist view.

Nearly the entire membership of the First Congress was Federalist: all twenty-six members of the Senate and fifty-three of the sixty-five members of the House of Representatives. Although "above party" and often perturbed by the partisan tensions between Hamilton and Jefferson in his cabinet, President Washington nevertheless tended to favor Federalist policies. By the time the Third Congress met, most members were either Hamiltonians or, because of James Madison's leadership of the overt opposition, Madisonians, that is, Federalists or Democratic-Republicans. In his message to this Congress in November 1794, Washington made a point of condemning the activities of "certain self-created societies." The reference was to some twenty-four local Democratic-Republican societies. His message was followed by a Federalist attempt to pass an even more condemnatory congressional resolution, a move that made Washington appear to be more of a partisan than he wanted.

Hamilton was a Federalist who understood party politics. Events gave him a rare opportunity to demonstrate that partisanship could be compatible with patriotism. Jefferson was elected president in 1800 only because his arch-rival, Hamilton, trusted him with the future of the young republic. When a stalemate in the electoral college and the House of Representatives occurred between the two Democratic-Republican candidates, Jefferson and Aaron Burr, Hamilton, uneasy about Burr's reputation and ambitions, asked his Federalist colleagues in the House to break the stalemate in Jefferson's favor.

Hamilton also recognized that the Jeffersonian electoral success rested upon energetic grass-roots organization, that is, mobilization of voters by those very local societies that Washington had condemned. In 1802, Hamilton suggested a plan for a national Federalist association to be called "The Christian Constitutional Society." This society would be organized under a president and a twelve-member national council. There would be "sub-directing Councils" of thirteen members for each state and as many local branches as possible. Financed by a five dollar annual fee, this association would diffuse information about, and promote the election of, "fit" men through its use of newspapers, pamphlets, "a lively correspondence," and public meetings. The association would also pursue "charitable and useful" activities, particularly in the growing cities, through relief societies for immigrants and vocational schools for workers.[2] Hamilton's Federalist colleagues would have none of it.

2

The first congressional caucus to nominate a candidate for president in 1796 was a Democratic-Republican affair, imitated by congressional Federalists in later years. As the number of Federalists elected to Congress and other public offices grew fewer and fewer, the Federalist congressional caucus became increasingly unrepresentative and unpopular, its nominations carrying little weight with the electorate. A better way had to be found to bring Federalists in and out of public office together for consultation. In 1808, a committee of correspondence appointed by the Federalist-controlled Massachusetts legislature proposed that a secret convention be held in New York with delegates from as many states as possible.[3]

Delegates from eight of the seventeen states met in New York during the third week of August 1808 and put together a Pinckney-King ticket. A second secret convention in 1812 was attended by delegates from eleven states, passed a resolution supporting George Clinton for president, and created a committee of correspondence apparently to send literature forth from Philadelphia. This was the last secret Federalist convention and the last of the party's activities in any national sense. This left only the Democratic-Republicans, who now called themselves simply Republicans. A one-party Republican era ensued until the arrival of "the age of Jackson." Technically still Democratic-Republicans, by 1840 the Jacksonians were calling themselves Democrats.

3

In the election of 1824, General Andrew Jackson, then serving as senator from Tennessee, received 352,062 votes from the eighteen states that chose their presidential electors by popular vote (elsewhere state legislatures chose presidential electors). This was a popular plurality that produced something less than the absolute majority required in the electoral college. The presidential election went into the House of Representatives where Speaker Henry Clay, also a candidate, eventually withdrew in favor of John Quincy Adams. Thereafter, "Jackson men" claimed to be the true successors of the Jeffersonian Republicans while the "Adams men" (in large part Federalists) called themselves National Republicans to reflect their centralizing policies.

The Jackson managers, soon joined by Senator Martin Van Buren of New York, arranged to have the Tennessee legislature nominate the general again in 1825. This time they organized voters until a victory was achieved in 1828. The Adams men, for their part, were handicapped by a leader, who, in the Federalist tradition of his father's day, derided all things connected with political parties. The National Republicans were never as well organized as the Jacksonians, except in some cities and states in New England. By 1828, a generation prior to the creation of the first permanent national party committee, each major party had a central corresponding committee in Washington.[4] In press and pamphlet, the central committees hurled charges and countercharges at each other's candidates. "Federalist" and "Jacksonian" were used as terms of denigration. The central committees also served as communications centers for consultations among party leaders in Congress.

Between 1827 and 1830, significant precedents for party organization at the national level were established by the new Anti-Mason party of New York. The leading promoter of these developments was the young editor of the *Anti-Masonic Enquirer*, Thurlow Weed. The Anti-Masons adopted the delegate convention as their principal mode of organization. The New York state Anti-Mason convention of February 1829 issued a call for a national convention to be held on September 11, 1830, in Philadelphia. Each state's delegation was entitled to a number of seats and votes equal in size to its combined representation in the two houses of Congress. This voting structure mirrored the apportionment of votes in the electoral college. Each state party could elect delegates in any manner it wished.

Dominated by Weed's New York delegation, the Philadelphia convention devoted itself to matters of permanent organization. The convention decided to meet again in Baltimore, on September 26, 1831, to nominate candidates for president and vice-president of the United States. Before disbanding, the convention also appointed a three-member national committee of correspondence to take care of interim details.

At the Baltimore convention, there were 116 Anti-Masons representing thirteen states. This was the nation's first national nominating convention. Leading their respective delegations and the convention as a whole were Weed, destined to be a future founder of the Whig and Republican parties, and Benjamin F. Hallett of Massachusetts, who in 1848 became the first national committee chairman of the Democratic party. The previously appointed three-member National Anti-Masonic Committee continued in office.[5]

4

When the House of Representatives pondered its presidential choice in 1824, Speaker Clay expressed his exasperation in private correspondence, "I am compelled to be an actor in the public concern here. And an actor in such a scene! An alternative made up of Andrew Jackson and John Quincy Adams. . . . My duty was that of passive submission [to these alternatives]."[6]

From 1825 to 1828, the pressure of the Jackson juggernaut was countered by an uneasy collaboration among the nation's four leading nationalists. John Quincy Adams and Henry Clay, although personally incompatible, nevertheless cooperated for several years in the promotion of the American System concept, that is, protective tariffs and internal transportation improvements that would help the development of U.S. industry. Daniel Webster, as the chief devotee of the centralizing theories of Alexander Hamilton, was helpful in Congress, carrying with him about twenty-five representatives and four senators who clung to the old Federalist label and policies. The vice-president, John C. Calhoun, although a Southern nationalist in many respects, during his

1824–1828 term, became increasingly outspoken in defense of states' rights.

The ambitions and ages of these four made unity among them difficult. Each was presidential material. Each was in the prime of his political life: Adams 57, Clay 47, Webster and Calhoun 42. President Adams' attitude toward political parties and toward those who opposed him was unquestionably the most serious obstacle to successful collaboration. Adams entertained the old Federalist distrust of party organization per se but, unlike his father, John Adams, would not concede the inevitability of parties in democratic communities. He abhorred the manner in which democracy deified competition.[7] In his inaugural address he warned against being "palsied by the will of our constituents." Adams' shortcomings as a party leader were succinctly summarized by Thurlow Weed:

> Mr. Adams, during his administration, failed to cherish, strengthen, or even recognize the party to which he owed his election; nor as far as I am informed, with the great power he possessed did he make a single influential friend.[8]

Adams' refusal to use patronage as the cement of party organization was a constant irritation to Clay and Webster, who favored appointments for partisan supporters.[9] Adams opposed every form of activity that involved party. He opposed nominating activities, the *sine qua non* of party. He railed against the sins of party in no uncertain terms: the impropriety of private interviews between members of Congress and the president with regard to nominations to appointive public office; the tendency to misinterpret all statements "infected with the venom of party"; the extreme difficulty, even for men in the highest offices, to act properly in delicate situations; and the malignant aspect that a want of candor and explicitness gives to incidents trivial or insignificant in themselves. He opposed the use of money in election campaigning on grounds that once the principle was established, there could logically be no limit on the amount of expenditure.[10]

Adams minced no words about his attitude toward those who opposed him. They were endowed, he believed, with every trait of evil. He spoke of John Randolph of Virginia, a Jeffersonian, Samuel D. Ingham, a staunch Calhoun supporter, and others in Congress as "skunks of party slander."[11] It was therefore particularly ironic that the most vehement Jacksonian charge against Adams was that he had entered a partisan and corrupt bargain with Clay in order to win the presidency. Corrupt bargain or not, the fact was that Clay did become Adams' secretary of state. Adams, in the tradition of the day, must have understood that this cabinet post was widely considered a stepping stone to the presidency.

Clay and, particularly, Webster were aware of the need for party organization, friendly newspapers, campaign funds, and patronage. Clay kept his eye on local party developments in the Southwest and the West. Webster looked to party matters in New England and the mid-Atlantic states. Clay suggested free distribution of certain newspapers during election campaigns. Webster acted as an unofficial party treasurer for the Adams men, since most of the funds for the National Republican cause came from New England. When the successes of the Jackson men in the New York elections of 1827 foreshadowed Adams' defeat for re-election in 1828, the best Clay and Webster could do was to look forward to building a new party from whatever would remain of the National Republican organization.

After Jackson's victory in 1828, Adams returned to Washington as a congressman from Massachusetts, never again to cope with party matters, much to his satisfaction. Webster, having been elected to the Senate in 1827, prepared to assume a greater role as a member of the anti-Jackson forces. The chief mantle of opposition leadership, however, fell to Clay, who returned to Congress as a senator in 1831. Webster was pleased to follow Clay's lead, believing that only Clay could carry the party of protection and internal improvements to victory.[12] By 1829, the designation "National Republican" was firmly fixed in the press when referring to the Adams-Clay-Webster school of nationalists.[13]

Clay had favored Adams over Jackson in 1824 because he considered Jackson's popularity a threat to his own aspirations. Despite a resolution from the Kentucky legislature urging him to support Jackson, Clay thought his own chances for the presidency would be enhanced if he took the traditional route through the office of secretary of state. In supporting Adams, however, Clay forfeited much of his popular support in the frontier states. Four years later, Jackson swept to victory in Kentucky, Ohio, and Missouri, all formerly Clay states. Upon his departure from the cabinet in 1829, Clay was generally recognized as the leader of the anti-Jackson forces, yet he won his bid for re-election to the Senate in 1831 by only the slimmest majority in the Kentucky legislature.

Clay's performance as an electoral strategist never equalled his remarkable talents as a legislative strategist—"Henry Clay understood politicians perfectly, simple voters not so well."[14] Clay never learned the secret of successfully mobilizing popular votes. His nicknames reflect this distinction: the "Great Commoner" for his defense of the common people during the Alien and Sedition debates of 1798–1799, the "Chief" for his leadership of the War Hawks in Congress, the "Great Pacificator" for engineering the Compromise of 1820.[15] Clay was most at home among his legislative colleagues and at his best defending the constitutional prerogatives and institutional integrity of Congress. He never gathered around himself a group of advisers capable of managing his electoral affairs. This in part may also explain why the National Republicans never built an enduring national organization.[16]

5

After taking his seat in the Senate in 1831, Clay attempted to build common ground for the multifaction anti-Jacksonians. His best prospects were within the

Senate, where the Democratic majority of only four votes in 1831 was reduced to a 20–20 tie in 1833. The House, on the other hand, maintained overwhelming Democratic majorities until 1837. The state electorates were bound to be the most difficult of all to mobilize. States with about 40 percent of the electoral college votes were firmly under Jacksonian control; states with only 13 percent of the votes were held by steadfast National Republican organizations. Another 27 percent of the electoral votes were reasonably within National Republican reach: Indiana, Kentucky, Louisiana, Ohio, and New York. If carried, these states could bring the two major parties abreast of each other. South Carolina, despite growing hostility to Jackson, remained committed to Calhoun.

The rupture that had been developing between President Jackson and Vice-President Calhoun burst apart in 1831, when the cabinet was reshuffled to eliminate the pro-Calhoun members. Calhoun had become increasingly dedicated not only to blocking Secretary of State Van Buren's rise to the presidency, but also to promoting the cause of states' rights. In seeking an entente with Calhoun, Clay modified his own high tariff position almost to the point of alienating Webster and the New England manufacturers. At the same time, Clay endeavored to strengthen his hand in the West by proposing that revenue from the sale of public lands be used for internal improvements. When Jackson vetoed the Maysville Road Bill, Clay used the veto as a symbol of "Executive Usurpation," a political evil against which all good anti-Jacksonians could march. The battle cry was reinforced by the fact that Jackson had vetoed more bills than all his predecessors combined.

Another campaign issue was the recharter of the National Bank. Most anti-Jacksonians—Clay, Webster, even Calhoun—were supporters of the bank. Jackson's original position was one of mild opposition. He expected that the bank's rechartering would be handled by Congress quietly and in due course. Rechartering would ordinarily have come up after the 1832 election. Instead, Clay urged Nicholas Biddle, the bank's president, to apply for recharter early enough to throw the issue into the presidential campaign. Webster endorsed this tactic. Significantly, the bank, with its large network of officers and debtors, was in contact with a considerable portion of the population in every state.[17] In the absence of extensive National Republican organization, the bank could indirectly serve as the party's grass-roots army. After careful consideration, Biddle decided to hurl down the gauntlet by asking Congress for an early renewal.

Another organizational question concerned finding the most effective way to place Clay's name in nomination. The *National Intelligencer* at Washington, whose large circulation made it an important link among the anti-Jacksonian elements, in 1830 proposed Clay for the presidency. The National Republicans also revived the congressional caucus, which met weekly during the winter of 1830 and 1831 to discuss, among other things, overall opposition strategy. One member was appointed from each state to confer with political associates back home. These state representatives reconvened in January 1832 to set the "opposition's course of policy." Policy differences among its members were numerous, the stigma of "King Caucus" was still fresh in the public mind, and, in the end, the caucus fell apart as a mechanism of consultation.[18]

A solution to the question of nominating method was eventually suggested by the procedures of the Anti-Masonic party. The Anti-Masons not only opposed Jackson, a Mason, but also supported the Adams-Clay American System. The leading Anti-Masonic editor and organizer, Thurlow Weed, had virtually been President Adams' political manager for western New York in the 1828 presidential campaign. But there were hurdles to overcome.

In the months between the Anti-Masonic organizing convention in Philadelphia in 1830 and its 1831 nominating convention in Baltimore, the Anti-Masonic leadership sought a nationally acceptable presidential candidate. They came up with three names: Henry Clay; Supreme Court Justice John McLean of Ohio, former postmaster general under Monroe and Adams; and former Attorney General William Wirt of Virginia. Clay was more interested in the Anti-Masonic endorsement than in nomination; the Anti-Masons were committed to make a nomination, not an endorsement. McLean would accept the nomination only if assured that all anti-Jacksonians would unite behind him; such assurances could hardly be forthcoming. Wirt, who demanded no conditions, became the Anti-Masonic nominee.

During the winter and spring of 1830 and 1831, state and local National Republicans also were turning to the delegate convention as their nominating procedure. While working out plans for a state organization, a National Republican committee of seventy in New York City recommended on February 9, 1831, that a state convention be held at Albany in June for the purpose of endorsing Clay, to be followed by a "National Convention" to be held at Philadelphia.[19]

The National Republicans instead met in Baltimore on December 12, 1831. Over 150 delegates attended, representing seventeen states. There was no doubt who would be the nominee. Unlike later national conventions, voting was by individual delegate rather than state delegation. As the vote for Clay neared a majority, it was moved and voted to complete the nominating procedure by acclamation. Then, George William Fairfax of Virginia made the only reference to national party organization, moving "that a central state corresponding committee be provisionally appointed in each where none are now appointed, and that it be recommended to the several states, to organize subordinate corresponding committees in each county and town."[20]

The National Republican campaign began promptly. Clay and Biddle mobilized the full resources of the National Bank throughout the country, spending the unprecedented sum of $80,000 for propaganda of all kinds. The bill to recharter the bank was sent to Jackson early in July. If Clay expected simply another veto against which he could cry "Executive Usurpation," he seriously misjudged Jackson. The president's shattering veto message placed the supporters of the bank squarely on the side of "the rich and powerful" against the interests of "the humble members of society." The bitter debate continued long beyond the 1832 election.

Clay had again erred in his estimate of the electorate. Compared to 1828, the Jacksonians increased the margin of their pluralities in nearly every state, including Clay strongholds in New England. In Pennsylvania, the Anti-Masons displaced the National Republicans as the principal minority party. In Vermont, the Anti-Masons temporarily took the state entirely out of National Republican hands. Only in Clay's own Kentucky did the voters buck the national tide by turning in a National Republican majority.

Thus Henry Clay earned the dubious distinction (shared with the Anti-Masons' William Wirt) of becoming the first presidential nominee of a national party convention to suffer defeat in the general election. Clay would have been the first out-party titular leader if his party had survived to the next election.

6

Jackson's second term was a period of rapidly shifting leadership alliances and highly inflammatory policy debates. When the South Carolina legislature called a special state convention to issue an Ordinance of Nullification, the very concept of a federal union was put to test. The ordinance declared the federal tariffs of 1828 and 1832 null and void insofar as enforcement within South Carolina was concerned. On the same day, President Jackson issued a proclamation declaring the national government sovereign and indivisible. No state could refuse to obey the law, and no state could leave the Union. To support the presidential proclamation, the administration submitted a Force Bill to Congress authorizing military measures if necessary to preserve federal interests in South Carolina, in this case, the collection of tariffs. Over the next three decades this issue destroyed the Whigs, gave rise to the Republican party, divided the Democratic party, and sent the nation into civil war.

The Jacksonians favored tariffs for revenue only, but were not willing to abandon the principle that tariffs could also protect domestic products. Calhoun, now senator from South Carolina, wanted to abandon the protection principle completely. Webster sided with Jackson in seeking to preserve the superiority of the central government. Clay, so recently defeated for the presidency, assumed the role of mediator in an effort to regain his diminished prestige. The compromise he negotiated provided for gradual reduction of all duties to the revenue level, abandonment of the protection principle, repeal of South Carolina's Ordinance of Nullification, and passage of Jackson's Force Bill.

Hardly had the dust settled when President Andrew Jackson set off another storm by removing public funds from the National Bank during September

Thurlow Weed was born on November 15, 1797, the son of a "migratory person" in a Catskill Mountain community just west of the Hudson River in New York. At nine he was shifting for himself as a cabin boy on a river sloop. His adolescent years were spent alternately on his father's backwoods farm, as an army private during the War of 1812, and as an employee in printing shops. In his early twenties, Weed moved west to Chenango County to establish a weekly journal, subsequently founding the Onondaga County *Republican* and the Rochester *Telegraph*. In 1828, he founded the *Anti-Masonic Enquirer,* which supported the Adams administration nationally and the Anti-Masonic cause locally.

Elected to the state assembly in 1829, Weed left the *Enquirer* to set up the *Albany Evening Journal,* backed by leading Anti-Masons. This paper was to become one of the most powerful political organs in the country. The Anti-Mason defeats in the New York elections of 1832 turned Weed toward new party affiliations. As a first step, Weed and his associates nominated a list of presidential electors in 1832 evenly divided between National Republicans and Anti-Masons, intending to swing to either Clay or Wirt depending on which seemed best able to beat Jackson. In the following years, Weed lost hope for the Anti-Masons and the National Republicans and devoted himself to organizing the Whig party.

1833. When the public funds were withdrawn, Nicholas Biddle, president of the bank, redoubled his efforts to forge a solid political alliance among Clay, Calhoun, and Webster. He succeeded in forestalling a Webster-Jackson rapprochement that seemed in the making during the nullification crisis. Biddle did succeed in reuniting the old-line Federalists, the National Republicans, and the Calhoun states' righters in their opposition to "King Andrew." But the insurmountable obstacle to complete unity continued to be the presidential aspirations of Clay, Calhoun, and Webster.

Meanwhile, Jackson's Kitchen Cabinet was determined to build a cohesive party in Congress and a well-organized party-in-the-electorate. These Jacksonian managers took vigorous steps in friendly state party organizations and at the national conventions to bring the party-in-the-electorate into harmony with the party's congressional organization. In contrast, the anti-Jackson forces, which would eventually be united under the Whig label, were not as happily focused and united in pursuing their organizational requirements.

For the two decades from the mid-1830s to the mid-1850s, the direction of the Whig forces swung back and forth between Henry Clay operating from Congress and Thurlow Weed working among the electorate. Clay was convinced that presidents rose and fell as a consequence of events in Congress. Weed was equally convinced that winning the presidency first required an understanding of the new presidential electorate. Weed was a master builder of electoral organizations designed to facilitate control of the officeholders elected by the party.[21]

While the anti-Jacksonians in Congress maneuvered and intrigued, new developments were taking place in the electoral opposition to the president. During the midterm congressional and local elections of 1834, many anti-Jackson candidates referred to themselves as Whigs, thereby emphasizing an analogy between their own battle against "King Andrew" and that of the British Whigs against King George III and King William IV.

7

As Jackson withdrew federal deposits from the National Bank, Nicholas Biddle countered by withholding or calling loans that had been made by the bank, hoping thereby to precipitate an economic crisis. In New York, Democratic Governor William L. Marcy established a system of state credit for those put under duress by Biddle's move. At a Fourth Ward political meeting in Albany, attended by Anti-Masons and National Republicans, Thurlow Weed denounced "Marcy's Mortgage" and Jackson's fiscal policies. This issue and this meeting were among many called to inaugurate the Whig party of New York. While Weed favored the name "Republican" for the new party, his preference would have to wait the next two decades for fulfillment.[22]

Weed exercised his influence as a Whig leader through the New York state central committee and the *Albany Evening Journal*. His power rested on several pillars: the collection and distribution of party funds through his connections with New York business people; the planning of party strategies; the activities of the state legislature and through the promotion of the destinies of leading Whig politicians, among them, William H. Seward and Horace Greeley.

Nationally, Weed opposed Clay's concept of party and Clay's type of presidential candidacy based in the Congress. Weed favored instead the military hero—William Henry Harrison, Zachary Taylor, John C. Fremont, and Ulysses S. Grant—as electorally more attractive in the Jackson tradition. Weed also took the long view regarding his party-building work, for example, his words in 1834 regarding Whig prospects in its first campaign were, "Our party as at present organized, is doomed to fight merely to be beaten."[23] He later made the same appraisal when he backed General Fremont as the first presidential nominee of the new Republican party in 1856. Fremont, Weed thought, would lose, but would leave a relatively well-established party for a Seward candidacy, Weed's preference for 1860.

The New York City election of April 1834 was the first major local test for the new party. It ended in a drawn battle. The Democrats elected the mayor; the

Whigs carried both branches of the city council and control of most of the city patronage.[24]

However energetic the Whigs may have been in their local and state organizations, they admittedly had "no common understanding in relation to the affairs of the general [national] government."[25] The absence of a nationwide organization moved William Henry Harrison to complain of the lack of a "committee of vigilance" that might bring unity out of a house divided against itself.[26]

Unable to bring the anti-Jacksonians together behind a single national ticket, Biddle and the *Intelligencer* advocated the strategy of running several regional leaders—Daniel Webster in New England, Hugh L. White in the South, William Henry Harrison in the West—popular enough to prevent a Democratic majority in the electoral college, placing the final choice again in the House of Representatives. Clay pondered the question of his own candidacy for some time before concluding that the popular tide was not with him. He then fell in with the Biddle strategy.[27] With his career steeped in the doctrine of legislative opposition and influenced by the caucus maneuvers of 1824, Clay probably also felt that a stalemated House of Representatives might yet turn to him, its former Speaker, as its dark-horse choice.

A Whig national nominating convention was not held in 1836. None of the Whig leaders were confident that a national convention would produce an acceptable compromise. No national convention had yet been put to the test of doing so; the first occurred at the Democratic convention of 1844. Not all the Whig leaders, however, failed to appreciate the popularity of the national convention as a nominating instrument. Hoping to pull support from the ranks of the frontier Jacksonians, a self-styled "Democratic-Republican committee" called a "national convention" at Harrisburg, Pennsylvania, for December 1835 to provide an aura of special legitimacy to the nomination of General Harrison.[28]

The Whig strategy was to no avail. The Jacksonians swept Van Buren into office. Among the Whig candidates, General Harrison made by far the best showing. Weed, whose New York organization gave Harrison strong support, sponsored a rally in New York City two months after the 1836 election to put Harrison's name in the running for 1840. Nicholas Biddle also appreciated the availability of the hero of Tippecanoe and advised that the general remain silent on all matters of political creed and public policy lest his chances be jeopardized. Henry Clay, encouraged by the economic depression that befell the Van Buren administration in 1837 and by Whig congressional victories in the midterm elections, activated his own alliances and candidacy.

8

In New York, Thurlow Weed strengthened his forces by electing one protégé, William H. Seward, to the governorship and putting another, Horace Greeley, in charge of a political journal, *The Jeffersonian*. Weed respectfully urged Clay to withdraw from the national race in favor of a national ticket that could have greater popular appeal. Clay, of course, did not agree. Clay supporters, contrary to their legislative predilections, began to press for a Whig national convention. Weed agreed, worked out a convention strategy, and enlisted the help of the Webster managers to carry it out.[29]

A Whig congressional caucus called for the national nominating convention on December 4, 1839. There, Harrison and Webster associates led the floor fight on behalf of the keystone of the Weed strategy, namely, a unit rule whereby a majority within a delegation could commit the votes of the entire delegation. As a result, the first ballot put Clay short of a majority: Henry Clay 103, William Henry Harrison 91, and Winfield Scott 57. Weed, controlling most of the Scott delegates, shifted them to Harrison. The Clay supporters were furious and refused to name one of their own leaders for second place on the ticket. Consequently, as bait to dissident Democrats, John Tyler, a Virginia Democrat, was nominated for vice-president.

Popular unrest in 1840 produced a Whig victory. Harrison's name was unencumbered by association with former leaders and former issues. The Whig "hard cider and log cabin" campaign, with its campaign songs, mass rallies, parades, and demagoguery, was unprecedented in presidential politics. Webster, Clay, and Tyler stumped the country in a great show of party unity. The agency that probably gave the greatest direction to the national campaign was the Whig's *Log Cabin*, edited by Horace Greeley. According to Greeley, the paper's inspiration and sponsorship came from "the councils of our friends at Albany," that is, Weed.[30] "Old Tippecanoe" was elected, and Tyler, too.

Weed's triumph, that is, the nomination and election of Harrison in 1840, had its darker side. Profound factional differences were appearing in the New York Whig party, focused around two men whom Weed had started on their careers: William H. Seward and Millard Fillmore. Within a dozen years the Seward-Fillmore rivalry would destroy the Whig party nationally. More immediately, an exasperating misfortune for Weed was the death of President Harrison five months after his election. This put Tyler, a former Democrat, into the White House and lost for the Whigs their first major opportunity to use the presidency to consolidate a national party. Tyler's efforts to create a nonpartisan administration also gave Henry Clay an unexpected opportunity to reassert his leadership of the Whig party.

During his first days in office, Harrison appointed a cabinet in consultation with Clay and Webster. Clay had apparently turned down the offer of a post in order to remain leader of the party in Congress; the Whigs had just won their first majorities in both houses (the Twenty-seventh Congress). Instead, a staunch Clay supporter was appointed attorney general. The Webster faction was represented in the Harrison cabinet by Webster himself as secretary of state.[31] Clay and Webster were influential in the composition of Harrison's inaugural address, which condemned the "excessive" use of the executive veto. This was in keeping with the Whig theory of legislative supremacy.[32]

From the moment of Harrison's death, Tyler encountered constitutional and other difficulties. As the first vice-president to succeed upon the death of a president, was Tyler an acting president or a president in his own right? Tyler took the oath of office as president, but a constitutional debate ensued that clouded the title during his entire administration. By asserting in his inaugural address the independence of the executive branch, Tyler stirred Whig doubts about his ideological purity. After inheriting Harrison's cabinet, Tyler kept it intact for six months, but turned for political advice to his own kitchen cabinet, a Jacksonian practice that further disturbed Whig leaders.

9

Clay at once became active in mobilizing his congressional forces and repairing his road to the White House. In the special session of Congress in 1841, Clay's supporters were placed in key positions on the standing committees. The party caucus was given an active role in the promotion of the Whig legislative program, particularly Clay's cherished American System of high protective tariff, internal improvements, and rechartering of a national bank. Clay outlined this legislative program in a resolution presented to the Senate on June 7, 1841.

Congress soon sent Tyler a bill reestablishing a national bank. The president vetoed it; his states' rights philosophy could permit no concession to such an instrument of nationalism. This was the first open battle between Tyler and the Clay Whigs. Clay suggested that since Congress as the immediate representatives of the people had passed the legislation, Tyler should have been guided by this legislative judgment. Otherwise, Clay declared, the president ought to have resigned his office upon finding himself unable conscientiously to receive the instructions of Congress.[33] This was an extreme statement of legislative ascendancy over the executive. Not since the elder Adams had entertained the thought during his altercation with an unfriendly faction of the Federalist party had the idea of resignation from the presidency been so seriously formulated. Whig constitutional theory and Clay's drive for undisputed party leadership were harmonizing.

Tyler vetoed a second bank bill on September 9, 1841. His cabinet solidly opposed his action. On September 11, all members of the cabinet, except Webster, resigned. Once again Clay seemed within striking distance of the presidency. Whig theory required that resignation of a cabinet should compel the resignation of the "prime minister," that is, the president, as well. If Tyler resigned, the president pro tempore of the Senate, the elderly and ill Samuel L. Southard, a loyal Whig, would succeed to the presidency, perhaps followed by the election of Clay to that office. This parliamentary strategy was intended for a presidential system and would again be attempted during the administrations of Abraham Lincoln and Andrew Johnson. President Tyler, however, held a different concept of the separation of powers. On September 13, he submitted the names of a new cabinet, with the exception of Webster, for Senate confirmation.

Clay convened a Whig congressional caucus that same day. The caucus issued a manifesto regretting that the president "by withdrawal of confidence from his real friends in Congress and from the members of his Cabinet . . . has voluntarily separated himself from those by whose exertions and suffrages he was elevated to that office." [34] In short, Clay and the caucus read President Tyler out of the Whig party.

Caleb Cushing of Massachusetts issued his own manifesto urging the Whigs of the country to ignore the "caucus dictatorship." Tyler's position was probably best stated by his new secretary of the navy and long-time friend, Abel Upshur:

> [Tyler] is now determined to take a middle course, avoiding ultraism on both sides, and aiming at the approbation of the temperate and sober minded of both parties. . . . I verily believe that he is determined on this course. He speaks of his re-election without any sort of reserve, as a thing that may or may not be, and as a thing which he may or may not seek.[35]

With Clay as leader of the organized opposition to Tyler's administration, it seemed inevitable that Tyler should move slowly back to the Democratic party. His various cabinet reshufflings between 1842 and 1844 were evidence of such a course. In 1844, Tyler went so far as to appoint Calhoun as his secretary of state. Finally, despite relinquishing all hope of his own re-election, Tyler maintained his candidacy with two objectives in mind: to prevent the nomination of Van Buren by the Democrats and to prevent Clay's victory in the election. Hence, a "Tyler convention" met in Baltimore on May 27, 1844, the same day as the regular Democratic convention, and gave its nomination to the president. The Democrats denied their nomination to Van Buren and gave it to James K. Polk, a dark horse, instead.

Meanwhile, the "Old Chief" was in the Whig saddle, Clay's chances for renomination in 1844 only modestly challenged by such perennials as Winfield Scott, John McLean, Daniel Webster, and the faction-ridden Weed-Seward forces. The Whig congressional caucus set the nominating convention date for May 3, 1844. At the Whig convention, Thurlow Weed was conspicuous for his absence. Clay received the nomination by acclamation.[36] After much discussion about the method of choosing a vice-presidential candidate, Theodore Frelinghuysen was nominated. Disappointed Fillmore managers blamed the absent Weed for preventing their man from getting second place; the New York factional struggle boiled on.

With the Democrats split over the question of annexing Texas and with Tyler running on his own ticket, Whig leaders were astonished to see a united Democratic party come out of that party's national convention. They were just as stunned three months later when, after receiving assurances from Polk's managers that Tyler's followers would be welcomed back into the Democratic party to share the patronage, Tyler withdrew from the presidential race. Clay lost by only 38,000 votes in the more than 2.6 million cast. Tyler, having failed to organize an effective party behind his own titular leadership, did achieve his other main objectives, namely, the retirements of Martin Van Buren and Henry Clay.

4 | The Republicans: Old Factions Create a New Party

Between the territorial accessions of the Mexican War and the state secessions leading to the Civil War, the disruption of party politics grew in intensity and consequence. Van Buren's Free Soil bolt from the Democratic party in 1848 added to the Whig following. Between 1853 and 1856, Whig factions bolted to join the new coalition that became the modern Republican party. The only political certainty seemed to be the difference in the ways Henry Clay and Thurlow Weed approached the nation's electorate.

1

In December 1845, Congress voted to bring Texas into the Union. Most Whigs in Congress opposed annexation, but enough Southern Whigs broke party lines to carry the measure. Sectionalism was taking a firm hold as the basis of Whig factionalism. This tendency was reinforced by the declaration of war on Mexico in May 1846. Factions in both major parties were deeply divided over the political implications of acquiring new territories. The Wilmot Proviso passed by the House of Representatives—but not by the Senate—in 1847 required that slavery should be excluded from new territories. Southern Whigs joined Southern Democrats in opposing the Wilmot Proviso; Northern Whigs supported the measure.

The war with Mexico produced its military heroes and at least three Whig presidential candidates. General Zachary Taylor seized the disputed lands that prompted the U.S. declaration of war; his victories at Buena Vista put him at the forefront of potential Whig candidates for 1848. General Winfield Scott, a hero since the War of 1812 and a perennial candidate, received a boost from his military achievements at Vera Cruz. Captain John C. Fremont, "Pathfinder of the West," declared California a free republic and cemented a reputation that in 1856 won him the first presidential nomination of the Republican party.

Congressional Whigs generally considered Clay out of the running; the Old

Chief was approaching seventy years old and carried the scars of too many defeats. Age also disqualified Webster. The most prominent younger Whigs included Senators John J. Crittenden of Kentucky, Clay's ally and heir apparent, and John M. Clayton of Delaware, whose oratorical gifts gave him national prominence. Crittenden and Clayton were possible compromise candidates in the event of a North-South stalemate.

As the Mexican War progressed, Taylor's candidacy took on momentum. Crittenden became one of his key proponents. Thurlow Weed, troubled locally by rivalry between the Seward and Fillmore factions, also believed Taylor would be another vote-getting military hero. As early as 1846, Weed advised the general to refrain from committing himself on public issues. Members of Congress formed a Taylor club and called themselves the Young Indians. As a result of Taylor's southern origin, even Southern Whigs began to unite behind him.

Although Weed's *Albany Evening Journal* continued to speak of Taylor as a sure winner for the presidency, Weed himself had reservations that reflected the divided state of Whig opinion in the North. Most New York Whigs, particularly Millard Fillmore, favored Clay. Weed considered Clay a retired hero and Taylor a hero likely to be elected. Yet, Weed distrusted Taylor's express opposition to national conventions as presidential nominating institutions. Recalling President Tyler's unfortunate efforts at nonpartisanship, Weed also worried about the general's ambiguous political affiliation, observing that "Taylor cannot get a Whig nomination unless [he] promises to be a Whig President."[1] Weed often spoke of John Clayton as the best compromise candidate, although he also thought that the convention could well give the nomination to Winfield Scott. Probably the best explanation of Weed's ambivalent views was his uncertainty about the prospects for New York's William H. Seward in a deadlocked convention. Would it be possible to have Seward named as a compromise candidate or to have him win second place on the ticket? How could the 1848 national convention best be exploited in a buildup for a future Seward candidacy?

On April 10, 1848, Clay adopted an unprecedented strategem. Contrary to the customs of the day, he declared himself a candidate for the presidency. This announcement was intended to block Crittenden's efforts on Taylor's behalf. The announcement probably alienated more supporters than it won. About two weeks later, Taylor confirmed his Whig affiliation in a widely publicized letter to his brother-in-law. Contrary to their position in 1844, the Clay supporters now favored holding a national convention. Taylor made it clear to his supporters that he would not withdraw his candidacy even if he failed to secure the Whig convention's nomination.[2] Some pro-Taylor extremists threatened to boycott the convention. In the absence of a national committee, the call for the convention again came from the Whig congressional caucus.

The convention outcome was unpredictable. Clay was the choice among party regulars, but Taylor was seen as a possible winner. Clay's support was centered

in the North and West, Taylor's in the South. Despite the inroads of Taylor's Young Indians, Clay still held the loyalty of most of his party in Congress. A poll of congressional Whigs in December 1847 showed 90 members for Henry Clay, 60 for Zachary Taylor, and 19 for Winfield Scott.[3]

The Clay men controlled the organization of the convention, but the authority of the convention as a nominating institution remained in doubt. A proposal to require all candidates to pledge their support to the nominee of the convention was rejected. The Taylor men indicated that they were authorized to withdraw his name from the Whig campaign if he were not nominated.[4] Weed tried to negotiate with the Taylor managers, but was burdened by failing to be the master in his own house, that is, New York. The Fillmore men in the New York delegation were for Clay, and one of their number was temporary chairman of the convention. In view of the near-equal strength of the Clay and Taylor movements, Weed continued to entertain hopes for Seward.[5]

The first ballot gave Taylor 111 votes, Clay 97, Scott 43, Webster 22, Clayton 4, and McLean 2. On the fourth ballot, with 140 votes needed to nominate, Taylor had 171 and the nomination. New York was slow to join the Taylor bandwagon, and this proved costly to Weed in the vice-presidential contest. Fourteen names were put in nomination for second place, chief among them Abbott Lawrence of Massachusetts, Thomas Ewing of Ohio, and Millard Fillmore and William Seward of New York. In such a numerous field, Seward's name was withdrawn. On the second ballot, the nomination went to Fillmore. The decision further exacerbated the factionalism among New York Whigs.[6]

The convention provided no executive organization to run the national campaign. This function was for the most part left to the Whig congressional executive committee headed by Truman Smith of Connecticut. Smith had served on this committee in the "log cabin" campaign of 1840. He brought to the Taylor canvass much of the same approach. It was a successful campaign consisting of mass rallies, parades, and song. Former President Van Buren's bolt from the Democratic to the Free Soil party was worth 54 electoral votes for Taylor.

2

Weed and Seward acted swiftly to assure themselves a solid role in the new Taylor administration. They succeeded, although they trod heavily on Vice-President Fillmore's toes in the process. Seward and Weed were particularly successful in obtaining presidential patronage.[7] As a consequence, most Southern Whigs came to believe that Seward dominated the Taylor administration.[8]

Taylor faced a hostile majority in both houses of Congress. Yet, although the Democrats were in the majority, the contest for the speakership of the House of Representatives in December 1849 required sixty-three ballots. Factional chaos reigned within both major parties, aggravated by the rise of the Free Soilers. The

North-South struggle in each party focused particularly on the disposition of the slave issue in new territories acquired in the Mexican War: California, New Mexico, and Utah.

In his message to Congress, Taylor enunciated "the President's Plan," recommending the admission of California and New Mexico under conditions that would allow each to determine whether or not to allow slavery. Since the legislatures of the two territories were predominantly antislavery, the President's Plan would have tipped the balance of power in Congress in favor of the free states. The President's Plan had the support of Seward and most Northern Whigs. It provoked hot words from Southern Democrats and Whigs. Both sides of the issue awaited a statement from Henry Clay.

Clay did not disappoint them. He offered a grand compromise. In response to Northern demands, he proposed keeping California free of slavery and abolishing the slave trade in the District of Columbia. To the South he promised territorial governments in New Mexico and Utah without the requirements of a Wilmot Proviso, thereby leaving the slavery question to the future. He also promised tighter federal enforcement of the fugitive slave laws and a generous cash settlement in the Texas-New Mexico boundary dispute. The Whigs responded divisively. Fillmore, Webster, and the Southern Whigs, joined by Democratic Senator Stephen A. Douglas of Illinois, supported the Clay compromise. Congress began to lean toward Clay's solution. Then, on July 9, 1850, in the midst of the great debate, President Taylor died. Fillmore succeeded to the presidency. Taylor's plan would undoubtedly give way to Clay's Compromise of 1850. Additionally, for a second time, Thurlow Weed's political fortunes were crushed by a presidential death.

The consequences of Fillmore's elevation were felt quickly. The Compromise of 1850 was enacted. At the Whig state convention in New York in September 1850, Fillmore's "Silver Gray" faction bolted, leaving that body to the Seward-Weed "Woolly Heads." During the spring of 1851 Fillmore conducted a wholesale removal of Seward-Weed adherents from federal posts in New York.

His health failing, Henry Clay renounced his own ambitions for renomination and instead endorsed Millard Fillmore.[9] He fervently denounced those who would make the Whig party into an abolition party and warned that he would favor a new party—a Union party—if they persisted. In particular, Clay opposed Seward's presidential aspirations.

As Northern Democrats sought a Northern candidate with Southern principles, Northern Whigs veered toward the abolitionist Free Soilers. Southern Democrats were either threatening secession or acquiescing to the principles of the compromise. Southern Whigs, although discussing formation of a Union party, were slowly moving into the Democratic party or retiring from active politics. Party politics were indeed fluid.

Samuel F. Vinton had been an Ohio congressman for twenty-two years, from 1823 to 1837 and again from 1843 to 1851. A moderate on the slave issue, Vinton declined nomination for Speaker of the House while the Polk administration was in office, becoming instead chairman of the powerful Ways and Means Committee. During the Taylor administration, Vinton was not only a leading Taylor Whig in Congress, but also the senior Whig in the House of Representatives. In Congress, few Westerners equaled Vinton's influence. In 1851, he ran unsuccessfully for the governorship of Ohio.

A caucus of senators and representatives met on April 9, 1852, to decide upon a time and place for the next Whig national convention. When a Kentucky Whig took the occasion to introduce a resolution endorsing the finality of the Compromise of 1850, the meeting adjourned in an uproar. On April 24, after a considerable number of Southerners had absented themselves, the caucus met again and voted down the Kentuckian's motion, 56 to 18. The Southerners were indignant and parted with expressions of regret about the future of the Whig party.

At the national convention, Southern Whig platform strategy included trading planks endorsing the protective tariff and improvement of rivers and harbors in exchange for a plank asserting the finality of the Compromise of 1850. This quid pro quo became part of the final platform. Southern Whigs also united in support of a Fillmore-Webster ticket. Thurlow Weed was absent on a tour of Europe, but Seward was present, supporting General Winfield Scott. For a third time the Seward-Weed alliance was placing its bets on the electoral magnetism of a military hero.

The North-South split appeared on the very first ballot: 133 (all but 16 from the South) for Fillmore, 131 for Scott, and 29 for Webster. One hundred and forty-seven votes were need to nominate. The deadlock held for 53 ballots. Then a few votes from border states shifted to Scott: 8 from Virginia and 3 each from Tennessee and Missouri. The final vote was Scott 159, Fillmore 112, and Webster 21.

It was a costly victory for the Seward-Weed faction. The nomination rejected an incumbent president and denied itself the resources of that office for the forthcoming campaign. In addition, influential Whig elder statesmen were lost to the campaign: Webster died just before the November elections and Clay, who had endorsed Fillmore, died on June 29 before giving his approval of the Scott ticket. Weed remained absent in Europe. Not only was the Whig leadership destroyed, so also was its electoral foundations. The Whigs carried only Massachusetts, Vermont, and Kentucky.

3

On the last day of the long and difficult national nominating convention, Judge William Jessup of Pennsylvania, a floor leader for the Northern wing, offered the following series of resolutions on organizational matters: (1) that future Whig national conventions be composed of as many votes as the states had in the electoral college; (2) that the convention of 1856 be held in Louisville, Kentucky, at a date to be determined later; (3) that a national committee of one from each state be appointed, with Samuel F. Vinton of Ohio as chairman; and (4) that the state delegations recommend to the convention the names of their members on the national committee.

A New Jersey delegate repeated the nomination of Vinton to be chairman of the national committee. The convention approved, in effect giving Ohio two members on the national committee. The thirty-one members of the first and only Whig national committee included many who would shortly become leading figures in the founding of the Republican party: William P. Fessenden of Maine, Aaron F. Stevens of New Hampshire, George Hodges of Vermont, Simeon Draper of New York, Andrew G. Curtin of Pennsylvania, John D. Defrees of Indiana, and Abraham Lincoln of Illinois.[10]

National-level organization came to the Whigs too late; the party was in its death throes. Completion of national-level organization did not save the Whig party from limbo. The political centrifuge created by the Kansas-Nebraska Act tore the national parties into fragments after 1853. Whigs split into North and South factions. Anti-Nebraska Democrats bolted. Dissenting factions in both major parties filled the lodges of Know-Nothingism in search of a new political affiliation. The ranks of the Free Soil party swelled. Out of this confusion came the new Republican party, whose capacity for attracting and assimilating dissatisfied local party groups brought it early electoral successes.

By 1854, Know-Nothingism invaded the Whig party, particularly in the South. The nativist secret society was joined in large numbers by former Whigs in Maryland, Virginia, the District of Columbia, Georgia, and Alabama. The movement emerged as the American party, whose candidate for president in 1856 was none other than former President Fillmore. On the other hand, the new Republican party—made up largely of Northern Whigs and free-soil Democrats—later nominated General John C. Fremont and succeeded in carrying eleven states to the Whig's three.

From the West during 1853 and 1854 came a flood of letters to the *New York Tribune* telling of steps being taken to form the new Republican party. The first organizational steps were taken in Ripon, Wisconsin, on February 28, 1854, and in Jackson, Michigan, on July 6. Editor Horace Greeley responded with encouragement for any movement opposing the Kansas-Nebraska "iniquity," but at first he clung fondly to the Whig party, and deprecated the Abolition or Third Party movement in politics, as calculated fatally to weaken the only great National organization which was likely to oppose an effective resistance to the persistent exactions and aggressions of Slave Power.[11]

New York Whig leaders were reluctant to join the rush to Republicanism, but this attitude did not last for long. By May 24, 1854, Greeley's newspaper proclaimed editorially the urgent need for a new sectional party. Two days later, Thurlow Weed, in his *Albany Evening Journal*, urged lovers of freedom to join the Whigs, adding, "when we find another [party] equally right in its principles, and more able and willing to carry them out, we will urge voters to go for that one." In June and July, Greeley warmed appreciably toward the prospects for a Republican party in New York. In mid-October, Greeley mused that perhaps a new party should have been launched in time for the fall elections. Early in November, he began to criticize Weed's Albany machine for having prevented the founding of a new party.

4

During the summer of 1855, Weed, conceding to the flow of political events, took steps to promote an amalgamation of his Woolly Head Whigs with the new Republican organization. He was ready to leave the moribund Whig party to Fillmore's Silver Gray faction. To accomplish the merger, Whigs and Republicans held simultaneous state conventions in Syracuse, New York, on September 26. Horace Greeley managed the Republican side. Guiding the Whigs was Edwin D. Morgan, chairman of the Whig state central committee. When the Whig-Republican merger was consummated, Morgan was chosen as chairman of New York's first Republican state committee.[12] Accompanying Morgan into the Republican party were a master politician, Thurlow Weed, and a presidential hopeful, Senator William H. Seward.

Elsewhere, the venerable Francis P. Blair, who had had helped Martin Van Buren create the Free Soil party six years earlier, pondered the possibility of his returning to the Democratic party in the hope of swinging its policies closer to his interpretation of Jeffersonian-Jacksonian principles. As he mulled over the matter in the retirement of his Silver Spring, Maryland, plantation, there came a bid from the Republican Association of Washington, District of Columbia, which was formed June 19, 1855, that he become president of the group.

Should the former editor of the *Globe* desert his old friend Van Buren and carry his Free Soil following into the new party? After some hesitation, Blair concluded that there was little he could do nationally with the sectionally concentrated Free Soil vote and less he could do within the Democratic party. The times required a new organization. Blair allowed himself to be elected by the District of Columbia Republican Association with the understanding that he would immediately resign from the presidency with a letter for publication. His

At 44, Edwin D. Morgan, whose substantial wealth was earned as a wholesale grocer in New York City, also enjoyed an estimable reputation as a high-minded civic leader. About a half dozen years earlier, he established a close friendship with Thurlow Weed and made frequent campaign contributions to the Whig cause in the city and the state. His public service included his election to the presidency of the New York City board of aldermen and the New York state senate.

letter of December 1, 1855, concurred in the aims of the association and was given wide circulation. The voice of the old Jacksonian was still powerful enough to cause countless Democrats to come over to the Republicans.[13]

The search for a presidential nominee went forward along with the Republican organizing campaign. The perennial John McLean was too advanced in years. Salmon P. Chase was too rabidly antislavery to be acceptable to the moderates. The Seward candidacy, carefully nurtured by Thurlow Weed, was not to be risked in the very first Republican national campaign.

Shortly after publication of his letter, Blair proposed General John C. Fremont for the Republican nomination. Fremont was the Pathfinder of the West who remained enough of a novice in politics to be unburdened by past views and enemies. Weed's old faith in military heroes was touched. Early in January 1856, New York State Chairman Morgan, Speaker of the House Nathaniel P. Banks, *New York Evening Post* editor John Bigelow, Frank Blair, and others conferred and expressed approval of the Fremont candidacy. Physically absent but politically represented at this meeting were Weed, Greeley, and Blair's Free Soil colleagues.[14]

Acting independently of the New York group, David Wilmot and Lawrence Brainerd, Republican state chairmen for Pennsylvania and Vermont, respectively, consulted late in December 1855 with the editors of the Pittsburgh *Gazette*. They planned a strategy for welding together a Republican organization at the national level. On January 17, 1856, there appeared in the press two announcements from Republican sources. One was a statement by the District of Columbia Association urging that similar associations be formed throughout the states, all to act in concert as a national committee to disseminate political information among the people.

The other was a call, addressed to "the Republicans of the United States," for an "informal convention" at Pittsburgh, on February 22, 1856. The convention was called by A.P. Stone of Ohio, J.Z. Goodrich of Massachusetts, David Wilmot of Pennsylvania, Lawrence Brainerd of Vermont, and William A. White of Wisconsin—all Republican state chairmen. Other names were added later.[15] It is possible that the Pittsburgh rally was originally intended to promote Salmon P.

Chase's candidacy. The *New York Tribune*, however, was in a position to alter the direction of the meeting by emphasizing that the purpose was to perfect Republican national organization.[16]

Delegates, mostly self-appointed, came from sixteen Northern and eight Southern states. On the eve of the convention, several leading delegates, among them Edwin D. Morgan, held an informal meeting to plan the organization of the convention.[17] They invited Francis P. Blair to serve as convention chairman.

At the convention, a Committee on National Organization, made up of one delegate from each state, recommended the formation of a "National Executive Committee" of nineteen members, patterned after the 1852 Whig national committee. Morgan's appointment to the chairmanship of this committee was recommended and approved. A platform statement, whose preparation was generally credited to the editor of the *New York Times*, Henry J. Raymond, a close associate of the Seward-Weed interest—was adopted. A national nominating convention was scheduled for June 17, 1856. When Horace Greeley declared himself in favor of Fremont, the Pathfinder's nomination was assured.

Executive Committee Chairman Morgan opened the convention, setting a precedent by making an introductory address. He reported on his correspondence with the leaders of the Northern wing of the American (Know-Nothing) party, which had just split with their Southern colleagues over the slavery issue. A special committee was appointed to prepare an invitation to them and all other parties to join the Republicans.

The convention next appointed the first Republican national committee, doing so before the nomination and platform were considered. The convention's resolution directed that

> a committee of one from each State and Territory represented in this convention be appointed by the several delegations respectively to report the name of one person from each State and Territory to constitute the Republican National Committee for the ensuing four years—such committee, when appointed, to elect their [*sic*] own chairman.

The convention next confirmed the nominating consensus by choosing Fremont on a single ballot.

5

The national committee met immediately after the convention. Edwin D. Morgan was elected national chairman. As secretary, the committee chose the committeeman from Illinois, Norman B. Judd, a political friend of Abraham Lincoln. A treasurer was not designated, but in August 1856 John T. Howard of New York was placed in charge of collected funds, a major portion of which came from Chairman Morgan.

There was a natural and informal division of labor in the management of the Fremont campaign and the Republican national committee. The campaign was conducted by a small group. Chairman Morgan looked after finances, contributing $8,000 himself and raising about $15,000 from others. More money came in during the closing days of the campaign. Blair handled relations with Free Soilers and the Northern wing of the American party, helping them get onto the new Republican bandwagon. Weed specialized in party organization and personnel. Greeley's *Tribune* office became the propaganda center. A *Semi-Weekly Tribune* was the out-and-out campaign sheet. Greeley also prepared a campaign handbook for speakers and rank-and-file party workers. Mrs. Elizabeth Benton Fremont, John Bigelow, and Charles James handled the mail.[18]

Even though many local Republican organizations were incomplete or in the hands of novices, Morgan and Weed exerted every effort to have the new national party make an impressive showing on its trial run. Their organizing skills were fully manifest. The national committee was effective as a clearinghouse for problems arising in the states, especially the pivotal ones. Morgan was successful as a national fund raiser, despite contributors' loyalties to state organizations. Even when Republican contributors were reluctant to give to the national committee, they often followed Morgan's recommendations concerning key states deserving help.[19] The results were impressive. In their first national campaign, the Republicans carried eleven of the thirty-one states and displaced the Whigs as the principal minority party in four other states.

Organizing work did not end on election day. The Republican national committee performed impressively in the territories and the midterm congressional campaign of 1858. When migration of settlers to Kansas and Nebraska was expected to determine whether these territories would come into the Union as free or slave states, the Republican national committee played a secret but vital role in helping supporters of freedom move west. Morgan, for example, wrote to Gideon Welles regarding affairs in the Kansas Territory:

> We do not mention what we have done, even to our friends, as the usefulness in Kansas of the persons sent, might be abridged thereby. Possibly even this (which of course is attended with some expense) may have been unnecessary, but we do not . . . take much for granted in anything connected with the present Administration.[20]

The national committee and the Republican Executive Congressional Committee coordinated their activities for the 1858 midterm contest. Members of Congress and representatives of Republican state committees across the country met in Washington on March 24 to map out strategy. The conference asked the national committee to assume several duties: raise funds for campaign literature;

invite state and local party committees to clear campaign documents with the Republican Executive Congressional Committee before publishing them; keep state chairmen informed of the progress of the midterm campaign. Much of the initiative rested with the congressional leaders, but important functions were nonetheless performed by the national committee. When the returns came in, the Republicans had won control of the House of Representatives. In addition, National Chairman Morgan was elected governor of New York.

Presidential candidates now loomed at every corner of the Republican horizon: William Seward, promoted by Weed; Salmon Chase, vigorously free soil; William Dayton, Fremont's partner on the national slate in 1856; Simon Cameron, the undisputed Republican leader in pivotal Pennsylvania; Edward Bates of Missouri, an antislavery Whig in a slave state and Horace Greeley's first choice; and Abraham Lincoln, now known for his debates with Stephen A. Douglas, his Ohio speeches, and his great address at Cooper Union in New York City.

Factional lines were being drawn at every turn. At the national committee meetings of May 25 and December 22, 1859, debate arose on the extent to which local party conditions in Pennsylvania and New Jersey—which were extremely factionalized—should be taken into account in the 1860 convention call. The conservatives wanted to be sure to invite *all* Pennsylvania and New Jersey factions; the radicals wanted to exclude all except those who gave full support to the free-soil spirit of the 1856 platform. The conservatives prevailed.[21]

The important choice of a convention city was made at the December meeting. The Seward men wanted New York City. The Chase men favored Cleveland or Columbus. The Bates people insisted upon St. Louis. An impasse was developing when National Committee Secretary Judd suggested Chicago as a compromise. Poker-faced, he pointed out that since Illinois had no prominent candidate of its own (Lincoln's name was never among those mentioned), Chicago would be neutral ground. Most of the committee swallowed this rationale, and in the final ballot Chicago was chosen.[22] Taking Lincoln's candidacy more seriously than did "Old Abe" himself, Judd did not overlook any opportunity that might offer advantage. Judd even wanted to be convention chairman, but decided to steer clear of a contest when David Wilmot's name was presented. Instead, Judd had himself put in charge of seating the delegates.[23]

As the Republicans gathered in the famous Wigwam convention hall, journalist Murat Halstead observed that "the principal lions in this house are Horace Greeley and Frank P. Blair, Senior."[24] These two were as one in their opposition to Seward's candidacy. Greeley was so outspokenly in the Bates camp that he could not get himself chosen as a delegate in the Weed-controlled New York delegation. Thurlow Weed was confident that Seward would prevail, Weed having "imported" two or three thousand Seward followers from New York for the occasion.

The Lincoln managers worked less conspicuously. David Davis, a presiding judge of the Illinois circuit courts before which Lincoln had practiced, placed himself in charge of the Lincoln forces. Judd, on the arrangements committee and in his capacity as secretary of the national committee, was busy elsewhere. The Lincoln managers' initial objective was to stop Seward. Others, particularly Horace Greeley, shared this same purpose, and, insofar as they did, served the Illinois cause.

The Seward-Weed-Morgan group seemed in the ascendancy until the nominations began. As the thousands of New York "spectators" made their way to the Wigwam galleries to hear Seward named, they found to their exasperation that the seats had been taken by thousands of local Chicagoans. Judd had been busy at his seating duties. When Evarts nominated Seward, there was modest applause in the galleries. When Norman Judd rose to nominate Lincoln, the galleries burst into a deafening din. The sheer impact of the noise moved Lincoln from dark horse into scoring position. The results of the first ballot were Seward, 173½; Lincoln, 102; Cameron, 50½; Chase, 49; Bates, 48; and scattered votes for others. Weed saw the threat and began to explore the possibility of Lincoln's accepting the vice-presidency on a Seward ticket. Davis' reply was "No."[25] On the second ballot, Weed and the rest of the convention were startled by the unexpected shift of Cameron's Pennsylvania votes to Lincoln.[26] The third ballot gave the nomination to Lincoln.

Weed was crushed with disappointment. Asked to nominate a candidate for second place, the Seward men refused. Anxious to conciliate the vanquished faction, the Lincoln managers invited Governor Morgan to be on the ticket, but he categorically refused. The place then went to Hannibal Hamlin of Maine. David Davis and Leonard Swett appreciated the implications of Seward-Weed intransigency and hurried to visit Weed the moment the convention adjourned. They found Weed sad but not angry, and, before a week had passed, they brought Weed and Lincoln together in Springfield, Illinois.

Meanwhile, the Republican national committee met in Chicago on May 18 and elected Governor Morgan for another term as chairman. Conciliation of the Seward-Weed people was essential for unity and victory. A seven-member executive committee was created to allow for a balanced representation of factions. Other internal crises in the party were successfully put off until after election day.

6

Although four political parties were in the field, the election of 1860 was basically a two-party competition in individual states. In twenty-seven of the thirty-three states the combined vote of two of the candidates was 85 percent or more. Only six states (California, Connecticut, Delaware, Massachusetts, Missouri, and Oregon), with a total of thirty-eight electoral votes, experienced any substantial multiparty spread in the voting, most involving a three-way split.

Together, John C. Breckinridge and John Bell carried that one-third of the electoral college that normally went Democratic. The remaining two-thirds went to Abraham Lincoln, with the exception of twelve votes for Stephen A. Douglas. With over a hundred electoral votes lost from the South, the Democratic party's future rested in large measure upon its capacity to rebuild its strength in Ohio. Certain Republicans considered their control of the presidency safe so long as the South could be kept out of the presidential election process. This subsequently became the principal strategic objective of the Radical Republican faction.

The seven competitive states clustered into three regional groupings: Ohio, Illinois, and Indiana (with 47 electoral votes) in the Midwest; New York and New Jersey (42 electoral votes) in the East; and California and Oregon (7 electoral votes) in the West. Of these, the two heavyweights were New York (35 votes) and Ohio (23 votes), and around these two an East versus West factionalism among Democrats developed quickly. The "War Democrats" gathered around Democratic National Chairman August Belmont and other New York leaders; the "Peace Democrats" collected behind Congressman Clement L. Vallandigham of Ohio.

It was Belmont who led the War faction in support of Lincoln's effort to preserve the Union by military means. Congressman Vallandigham, opposed to military measures, put his energies into developing a compromise for the North-South struggle. As his proposals and personal leadership failed to take hold, Vallandigham veered more and more into obstructionism.

The constituency basis for Democratic factionalism had important consequences in later years on President Lincoln's conduct of the Civil War, his re-election strategy, and his plans for postwar reconstruction. Lincoln's own electoral stronghold in the Midwest was little challenged by the Peace Democrats. The Southern Democrats were out of the national political picture, at least for the duration of the war. Lincoln's relations with the War Democrats in the East were excellent. The idea was to bring together Midwest Republicans and Eastern War Democrats. Wishing to minimize his Republicanism and maximize his support among Democrats, by 1864 President Lincoln was willing to head a "Union" party ticket with a War Democrat, Andrew Johnson, as his running mate.

Meanwhile, at the close of 1860, as Republicans faced their first experience as the governing party of the nation, the heterogeneous elements comprising the party began to revert to their factional origins: old-line Whigs versus former Free Soilers, conservatives versus radicals, administration versus congressional wings. The issues were several and fundamental. Who would control the distribution of public offices, and hence the Republican party? How should the party respond to the threat of Southern secession? How moderate or extreme should the party's position on slavery be?

In the postelection maneuvering, all initiative for coping with the momentous challenge of secession was lost. President Buchanan awaited a statement of preference from president-elect Lincoln. The president-elect, by no means the undisputed leader of his party and not yet the responsible head of government, maintained silence. If the Republicans had a leader at all, it was Senator Seward, who had been one of the party's principal spokesman during its first six years. But Seward's new role under a Republican president had yet to be determined.

Part II
Disintegration and Reintegration

5 | The Era of War and Peace Democrats

Sectionalism was the basis of organized factionalism in the Democratic party during the years leading up to, during, and following the Civil War. The North-South division made prewar national party leadership a Janus-like affair, with the ultimate test and failure occurring in the nominating conventions of 1860. East-West factionalism became exacerbated during the war, stirred by differences in attitude toward the South and the war. This sectional division persisted around the issue of monetary policy—hard or soft money—during Reconstruction. Democratic titular leaders exercised relatively little influence, and national chairmen, notably Benjamin Hallett and August Belmont, found themselves almost single-handedly keeping the party organizationally alive.

1

Lewis Cass, never actively assuming the titular leadership, was returned to the U.S. Senate after his defeat in the presidential race of 1848. The years 1849 to 1851, however, found National Chairman Hallett deeply involved in his new role as factional broker. More than most Democratic politicians, Hallett sat directly on the horns of his party's slavery dilemma. In his early days, within the confines of Massachusetts party politics, he had been a vocal abolitionist. By the end of his term as national party chairman in 1852, Hallett was at the head of the pro-South Doughface minority in his state party. Holding together a state party splintered by the great North-South debate over slavery called upon every lesson of brokerage and compromise he had learned.

Throughout the nation the party was in similar distress. Local Democratic organizations were disintegrating. A movement for a new party, a Union party, based on the Compromise of 1850, was attracting many Democrats.[1] Democratic leaders around the country looked to the fledgling national committee to produce unity and a workable national organization. Democrats were also seeking a "national" candidate for 1852, one who could run on the principle: "The Compromise—a final settlement."

The bitterness of the factional differences made the search a difficult one. The Hunker element wanted to conciliate the South, where Democrats were strongest. The Barnburners and Free Soilers wanted an immediate end to the institution of slavery. The states-righters were adamant in their defense of that institution. Within the sectional and ideological factions were many personal followings. Lewis Cass, although inactive as titular leader, had enough support to win a simple majority in the 1852 convention, but not the nominating two-thirds majority. His claim to the nomination rested primarily upon seniority; few believed he could win the election. Chairman Hallett and most of the New England leadership were Cass' greatest source of support, second only to Judge Levi Woodbury.

James Buchanan, Polk's secretary of state, was as anxious for the nomination as Cass was indifferent. Influential and capable political strategists supported Buchanan's claims: William R. King of Alabama, who presided over the Senate when Vice-President Fillmore succeeded to the presidency; John Slidell, former minister to Mexico, who later became one of the South's leading secessionists; August Belmont, New York head of the banking House of Rothschild; Cave Johnson of Tennessee; and Isaac Toucey of Connecticut—in all, a formidable group. Other possible candidates were: William L. Marcy, Polk's secretary of war and the candidate of New York Barnburners, William O. Butler, Sam Houston, and Stephen A. Douglas, the rising voice of Western Democracy and the youngest among the candidates. Sectionalism and slavery were well embedded in the candidacies.

New England was not the usual source of presidential talent for the Democratic party. However, Van Buren's Barnburner bolt of 1848 was strongest in the Northeast and required strong healing potions. Woodbury seemed to be the one man who could bring New England Democrats back into line. When his death on September 4, 1851, deprived New England of an outstanding candidate, Democratic leaders turned to William O. Butler. When Congressman John C. Breckinridge, a Southern leader, referred to Butler as a states-righter, this immediately made Butler unavailable as a representative of abolitionist New England. Some New Englanders then thought of Senator Benton; others of Sam Houston. Finally, the "Concord Cabal" (a group of influential New Hampshire railroad lawyers) and Levi Woodbury's brother-in-law, Isaac O. Barnes of Massachusetts, settled upon Mexican War General Franklin Pierce as their candidate.

By April 1852, General Gideon Pillow, who claimed credit for being Polk's nominator in 1844, also became interested in Pierce. Pillow was influential with the Douglas forces. By May, Caleb Cushing and his associates in Massachusetts were behind Pierce. Hallett and Greene agreed that Pierce would be their second choice after Lewis Cass. If Cass and Buchanan reached a stalemate, Pierce was assured the votes of New England and the West.[2]

Robert Milligan McLane was of distinguished forebears and destined for a career among the elite of U.S. politics. His grandfather, Colonel Allen McLane, served under LaFayette and Lee in the Revolution and as a collector of the port under every president from Washington to Jackson. His father, Louis McLane, was Jackson's minister to Great Britain in 1829, secretary of the treasury in 1831, and secretary of state in 1833.

Admitted to the bar in Washington, DC, in 1840, Robert McLane was more interested in politics than in clients. He took an immediate and commanding position as a public speaker in Maryland and made extraordinary efforts to carry the state for the Democrats in the Polk campaign of 1844. A year later he was elected to the state legislature and in 1847 went to Congress. McLane retired at the end of the Thirty-first Congress, having lent full support to the Compromise of 1850. Robert Walker, who established a lucrative legal practice after his retirement from the Polk administration, and his thirty-six-year-old colleague, Robert McLane, were retained to defend the rights of certain claimants to quicksilver mines in California. They made the long trip to the West Coast together, and it is likely that they performed some party duties to ensure California's admission to the Union as a Democratic state. In 1852, McLane hurried back to Maryland to attend the national convention as a delegate and to serve as Maryland's national committeeman.

The 1852 convention balloting followed the dark-horse precedent of 1844. Cass, Buchanan, and Douglas were deadlocked for thirty-four tedious counts. On the thirty-fifth ballot, Franklin Pierce was added to the list of candidates. Pierce received only twenty-nine votes for the next ten ballots, with his major support coming from Virginia. On the forty-ninth ballot, he won the nomination. Buchanan and Douglas backers were pleased with Cass' demise. The Cass men were happy that Buchanan and Douglas had been eliminated. To the "Buchaneers," however, went the privilege of naming the vice-presidential candidate: William R. King, a Southern champion of the compromise and Buchanan's personal friend.

Chairman Hallett called a meeting of the national committee for June 7. The campaign was discussed. The advice of the party's elder statesmen was that Pierce should limit his campaign activities to noncommittal letters, occasional journeys to one or two important centers, and dignified retirement in Concord, New Hampshire. The burden of the campaign was to fall to those stationed in

Washington, that is, to the national committee, to a Washington resident committee appointed by it, and to the Democratic members of Congress. Pierce would be hailed as Andrew Jackson's successor, "Young Hickory of the Granite Hills." The Jackson Democratic Association of Washington would raise the first hickory pole of a "Granite Club" campaign.

To be "the chief manager at Washington," the national committee chose as its chairman a nearby resident, the committeeman from Maryland, Robert McLane, son of a cabinet member under Andrew Jackson, an old friend of vice-presidential candidate King, and a representative of the mid-Atlantic states supporting a balanced North-South ticket. Benjamin B. French, former clerk of the House of Representatives and currently president of the Jackson Democratic Association in Washington, was elected national committee treasurer. Three secretaries were selected to facilitate regional communication; these were the committeemen from New Hampshire, Ohio, and Mississippi. A five-member resident committee, including Pierce's personal manager, was created to serve at the hub of the campaign.

McLane's election "as the Chairman of the Executive Committee that conducted the Presidential Canvass"[3] was not universally greeted with joy. Edmund J. Burke, a former New Hampshire congressman who had labored diligently and effectively to win preconvention support for Pierce, was in a position to express himself quite candidly to the nominee:

> I do not think our Central Executive Committee is made up of the right sort of men. Robert McLane of Baltimore is chairman. He is a man of talents, but I think he has not the industry, nor the practical experience necessary for getting up good political tracts.[4]

To Burke, G.C. Hebbe complained that the national committee "ails with deplorable imbecility," unable to collect money and, upon bad advice, giving printing contracts to the "wrong" newspapers.[5] Aware of the delicate factional situation, Burke nonetheless wrote to the nominee that he anticipated that Pierce would be elected mainly "because all cliques of the Democracy are united on you."[6] Chairman McLane, whether deliberately or not, was apparently pursuing the nominee's strategy—the less partisan campaign exposure, the better. McLane limited himself to campaigning in his own state.

Before it departed from Washington in June, the national committee authorized what came to be known as "the levy." Wrote Benjamin Hallett to a political colleague:

> The Democratic National Committee, for the purpose of publishing and distributing documents from Washington all over the Union, have [sic] "Resolved that—each member of this Committee will procure from his state for defraying the expenses of the National Executive Committee in Washington not less than $100 from each Congressional District, to be forwarded to the

Treasurer, B.B. French, Esq., at Washington.''. . . I would suggest that you make out a list, or employ someone to do it, assessing a sufficient number of Democrats such sums as they will cheerfully contribute to make up the $100, for which purpose I appoint you Finance Committee for your District. . . . Let not Massachusetts be behind other States in furnishing their quota, so necessary to disseminate truth.[7]

With 233 congressional districts from which to collect, a fund of about $20,000 was expected. The collection fell far short of this target.

The members of the national committee hoped to receive another $60,000 from Democrats in the country's financial centers: $25,000 from Wall Street in New York, $15,000 from Chestnut Street in Philadelphia, $10,000 from State Street in Chicago, and $10,000 from Baltimore. C.H. Peaslee, Pierce's manager on the resident committee in Washington, was chiefly concerned with this aspect of fund-raising.

Raising funds in New York was particularly difficult, given the strident Barnburner-Hunker factional conflict there. Peaslee tried to arrange for representatives of all factions to meet with Chairman McLane. Of the twenty invited, only three or four Barnburners showed up. Additionally, the New York national committeeman began to complain of Peaslee's intrusive fund-raising activities. Two wealthy New Yorkers, Samuel J. Tilden and J.S. Thomas, were barely successful in raising $1,500 by mid-August. Only a large contribution from August Belmont in the closing days of the campaign prevented a financial catastrophe for the national committee. When the election was over, Chairman McLane reported proudly:

> To those who have witnessed the manner in which Presidential Canvasses have been conducted in recent years, it will appear almost incredible that the expenses of the National Committee in this Canvass of 1852 scarcely exceeded ten thousand dollars for printing and other necessary election expenses.[8]

In Washington, Democrats in Congress during a long session produced a large number of floor speeches intended for use as campaign material. On July 6, a caucus of Democratic members placed the management of the Washington *Union*, which had been a somewhat neglected party organ, into the experienced hands of John Forney, clerk of the House of Representatives. The resident committee concentrated on the preparation and distribution of ''valuable documents,'' employing some thirty clerks in the process. During September, the resident committee sent out a letter to Democratic newspapers and all delegates to the national convention listing the documents that should have reached them and warning that there may be possible interference with their delivery. The committee also requested reports on local conditions.

The campaign continued listlessly. Both parties avoided debate on the Compromise of 1850. James Buchanan wrote to Marcy: ''On both sides unexampled apathy prevails; but this is favorable to the Democratic party."[9] By subordinating the conflict between Northern and Southern Democrats, the ill-managed campaign organization was adequate enough to beat a Whig party so split that it went out of business soon after the election.

2

After hardly a year in office, the Pierce administration was rent with dissatisfaction and revolt on the part of Southern Unionists, Northern Hunkers, Free Soilers, and Westerners. Some thought this was the result of the president's poor choice of his senior officials. Others argued that "the continued policy of dodging issues and the continual fear of displeasing someone was destroying the moral calibre of the leaders of the Democracy."[10] Disappointed office seekers and neglected local factions were nursing grudges. Pierce's position regarding his own renomination caused additional confusion. He refused to use the patronage on his own behalf, although his subordinates did not seem restrained in this connection. His personal traits made him appear a weak candidate. His lack of leadership was further damaged by the consequences of Stephen A. Douglas' Kansas-Nebraska Bill.

Senator Douglas' original bill simply organized the Nebraska Territory, with no reference to the issue of slavery. The enactment in final form, however, repealed the Missouri Compromise, organized two territories instead of one, and adopted the principle of "squatter sovereignty" for determining whether a territory would be free or slave. The Free Soil party, the Northern Whigs, and the Northern Know-Nothings rushed to settle Kansas and save it from slavery. The South countered, and civil war raged in the territory. Pierce's administration adopted a policy of neutrality and sent federal troops to maintain "law and order."

The repeal of the Missouri Compromise and the Kansas disorders were attributed to Douglas, an accusation that made him unavailable for the 1856 nomination. Similarly, the resentment that the president's neutrality generated among Northern Democrats ended Pierce's chances.[11] The only other major contender was James Buchanan who, in the course of seeking the presidential nomination in 1844, 1848, and 1852, had gathered an extensive personal organization and powerful support. Two of his major backers were Senator John Slidell of Louisiana and banker August Belmont of New York.

During Buchanan's tenure as Polk's secretary of state, Slidell unobtrusively assumed leadership of the Buchanan-for-president movement. Slidell, leader of a major faction in Louisiana Democratic politics, brought another important recruit into the Buchanan camp in 1849 when August Belmont, twenty-three years his junior, married his niece, the daughter of Jan Slidell Perry.

Slidell-Belmont preconvention organizing work was exacting, extensive, and unostentatious. The Buchaneers feared only one contingency: a Pierce-Douglas

August Belmont, son of a wealthy Prussian landowner, was head of the Rothschild banking firm's New York branch. A naturalized citizen, Belmont's first vote was cast for Polk in 1844. Through Robert J. Walker, Polk's secretary of the treasury, Belmont came to know Buchanan and Slidell. After joining Slidell in the Buchanan cause, Belmont set about to finance a pro-Buchanan newspaper in New York, becoming a leader of the New York "Softs," the faction that generally supported President Pierce's position on the North-South issue.

alliance at the convention. To meet this possibility, Slidell went to Cincinnati to direct the strategy in person.[12]

In the summer of 1856, the national party was weak in organization and leadership. The president had hardly been a source of strength. The national committee had neither the inclination nor the procedure for devising plans to bolster party unity. National Chairman McLane provided no inspiration. The delegates arriving for the national convention were confused by the circumstances surrounding them. The Buchanan men did not seem to be active. Douglas' and Pierce's plans were unclear. How does a political party depose its own president without losing face with the electorate? How does a new generation of politicians retire an old leadership?

The Buchanan faction won the permanent chairmanship of the convention and control of the standing committees. Once again former National Chairman Hallett assumed the delicate task of writing the platform. To keep inflammatory talk off the floor, Hallett moved the adoption of a "gag rule" requiring that all platform resolutions be referred without debate to the Committee on Resolutions. Contrary to the procedure at the 1852 convention, the platform was adopted prior to the nomination. Significantly, the platform made no reference to the Pierce administration, although many of its principles were adopted, including a version of Douglas' "squatter sovereignty" doctrine. Hallett worked out language that pledged the party to popular sovereignty, but not until a territory had reached the statehood stage. This permitted favorable regional interpretations during the campaign.

Once again the factional struggle in New York—this time between the pro-Pierce Softs and the pro-Buchanan Hards—furnished a critical test of the temper of the Democracy. Once again the convention sidestepped. In a close vote, 137 to 123, it ordered both factions to be represented on an equal basis. This was entirely to Slidell's liking. The Pierce managers, on the other hand, now realized that they could never obtain the necessary two-thirds vote. The first ballot results—Buchanan 135$\frac{1}{2}$ Pierce 122$\frac{1}{2}$, Douglas 33, and Cass 5—in effect denied

The son of a Vermont surgeon, David Allen Smalley received legal training in his uncle's law firm. Douglas, who did not depart from his native state until 1833, and Smalley were close personal and professional friends in their early years. The latter practiced law and politics in Jerico, Vermont, serving as its postmaster from 1832 to 1836. In 1836, when he moved to Burlington, Smalley was still an ardent Jacksonian. In 1842, he won election as a Democratic state senator in a normally Whig county. Later he divided his time between his lucrative practice and the chairmanship of the Democratic state committee. At the national convention of 1852, Smalley was a convention vice-president and a co-worker of Benjamin Hallett on the resolutions committee; Vermont voted for Douglas for forty-eight ballots. Smalley served on the national committee and supported the 1852 Pierce campaign. In 1853, the president appointed him collector of customs.

an incumbent president renomination, the first of such retirements.

The Pierce managers slowly shifted votes to Douglas. On the sixteenth ballot, the vote stood: Buchanan 168, Douglas 122, Cass 6, and 0 for the president. A deadlock was in the making when Douglas' manager announced the withdrawal of his candidate's name. The forty-three-year-old Illinoisian was willing to step aside for Buchanan, who was twenty-two years his senior. Douglas anticipated another chance in 1860 or 1864. Meanwhile, a show of unity was necessary to bring party victory in 1856.

Following Buchanan's nomination, Hallett, speaking for the platform committee, introduced a resolution unequivocally approving Pierce's administration. The convention secretary scribbled, "Adopted, with long and rapturous applause, and unanimously."[13] A weak president had been deposed, and his administration had been endorsed. The last of the old leaders, a Northerner, had been nominated. The way seemed clear for younger men.

A young Southerner was needed on the ticket in 1856. Thirty-five-year-old John C. Breckinridge graciously declined the honor. The Douglas forces, however, insisted that a Southerner participate in the canvass. David Allen Smalley rose during the balloting to say: "The delegation of Vermont, believing that no Democrat has a right to refuse his services when his country calls, have instructed me to cast the five votes of Vermont for the talented, accomplished, and eloquent son of Kentucky, John C. Breckinridge."[14] With that, Breckinridge was nominated on the second ballot. Smalley was the Douglas spokesman, the leader of the Vermont delegation, and a boyhood schoolmate and lifelong friend of Senator Douglas.[15]

The thirty-one members of the national committee met at the close of the convention on June 6 and again on June 12. Only three of its members were carryovers from the previous committee: David Allen Smalley of Vermont, William Clark of Virginia, and James Pratt of Connecticut. The most experienced campaigner of the three, Smalley had other qualifications that made him a logical choice for chairman. He was a neighbor and appointee of President Pierce, an unwavering Douglas man, a New Englander, a supporter of the squatter sovereignty doctrine, and instrumental in recruiting an eminent Southerner for the ticket. Smalley also had a reputation for "remarkable powers of organization" and was expected to act vigorously in the conduct of the campaign.[16]

By 1856, the national committee had grown to such a size as to require an executive committee to provide continuous supervision of the campaign. Previously, supervision was the work of a resident committee or an informal executive committee. The executive committee was now formalized, and it was expected that John Slidell would become its chairman.[17] Slidell, however, preferred to work informally from his position in the Senate and to give his main attention to the guidance of the Washington *Union*, the leading party newspaper. Instead, C.L. Ward of Pennsylvania was elected executive committee chairman. The executive committee then chose a resident committee to coordinate matters in Washington.

As before, three secretaries were chosen by the national committee to represent different sections of the country. A committee was created to procure publication of the convention proceedings. The national convention had selected Charleston, South Carolina, as the meeting place for the 1860 convention, leaving the time of the convention to be determined later by the national committee.

The campaign was carefully organized. Buchanan remained at his home in Lancaster, Pennsylvania, receiving visitors and conducting correspondence. He did both actively, to the point of writing to party leaders at the township level. The executive committee carried on fund-raising, which included "the levy" of $100 per congressional district. The resident committee distributed campaign pamphlets and served as a speakers bureau.[18] Senator Slidell and Howard Cobb took over direction of the *Union* for the period of the campaign.

As late as mid-July the executive committee was still "poorly organized" and "awfully lethargic." An informal caucus of fifty national committeemen and congressional leaders was convened and it was decided to combine the executive and the resident committees, having the latter serve as a subcommittee on documents. A second subcommittee on finance was added.[19] Meanwhile, the resident committee labored prodigiously preparing and distributing reading matter, requesting statistics and voting lists from county chairmen, and encouraging the organization of Keystone Clubs for Buchanan. By August 1, it was sending out 40,000 pieces of mail a day.

Shortly after this reorganization, C.L. Ward, on behalf of the finance subcommittee, sent Buchanan a financial report. A $20,000 debt had accumulated in the first month of the campaign, but only $3,900 was on hand, collected from Washington banker W.W. Corcoran, Senator Douglas, and John Forney. "Slidell and Douglass [*sic*] have agreed to go together to New York about the 4th of August, and see commercial men," he added hopefully. The trip was not made until September, and then only by Slidell. On one occasion in August, Ward enlisted the help of Augustus Schell, the New York committeeman, for a fund-raising trip to Boston.[20]

In September 1856, when the newly organized Republican party in its first national campaign won a landslide majority in the Maine elections, the matter-of-fact Democratic organization was jarred into a sense of urgency. Maine had voted Democratic in the three previous presidential elections. The situation now required Democratic victories in Pennsylvania and Indiana to offset the Maine loss.

Senator Slidell stepped in to save the day. He declared "the Wall Street War" by announcing that he wanted to raise $50,000 in that financial center. With Schell's help, certain influential merchants were invited to a private conference in Room 1 of the New York Hotel, organized the New York Hotel Committee, and pledged themselves to raise $50,000. This was followed by a flood of speakers, campaign literature, organizers, and money going into Pennsylvania and Indiana. Both voted Democratic on election day. There were estimates that $500,000 was used in Pennsylvania alone, of which $150,000 came from the South, $50,000 from August Belmont, and $100,000 from other Wall Street figures. The expenditures set a record.

Despite the great effort, Buchanan became a minority president, receiving only 45 percent of the popular vote. Five of the sixteen free states and fourteen of the fifteen slave states supported him. Buchanan's political debt to the South and Vice-President Breckinridge's availability to succeed him foreshadowed difficult times for the Douglas candidacy in 1860.

3

In the formation of the cabinet, Slidell exercised the greatest influence by far. As a consequence, when Senator Douglas vigorously recommended Robert J. Walker for secretary of state, Buchanan ignored the advice. Even in Douglas territory in the Northwest, Senators Slidell and Jesse D. Bright of Indiana controlled the bulk of the administration's patronage.

The Buchanan years witnessed intensifying conflict over the slavery issue. The Supreme Court's Dred Scott decision challenged the Douglas principle of popular sovereignty and strengthened the states' rights wing of the Democratic party. This was a small disturbance when compared to the row stirred up by the Lecompton affair.

If Buchanan and Douglas did not agree on what the Kansas constitution ought to say regarding slavery, both men did agree that the state constitution as a whole should be submitted to popular vote. After the Kansas constitution was drafted at Lecompton, however, the only section left to popular decision was the one governing slavery. The people were able to vote for "constitution with slavery clause" or "constitution with no slavery." In another part of the document, not subject to separate popular vote at all, was a clause fully protecting slave property regardless of the results of the referendum. The "no slavery" clause won in the popular vote. Ignoring the inclusion of a clause protecting slave property, President Buchanan recommended congressional approval of the Lecompton constitution. Douglas objected strenuously and broke openly with the administration.

Slidell now proceeded to conduct a bold campaign in the Senate to read Douglas out of the party and to accelerate the withdrawal of patronage from Douglas supporters in the hope that this might affect the results of Douglas' campaign for re-election to the Senate in 1858. The repercussions were national. Democrats throughout the country now chose sides as Buchanan Lecomptonites or Douglas Anti-Lecomptonites. Among the latter was August Belmont.[21]

Douglas affronted the South further when he enunciated his Freeport Doctrine during debates with Abraham Lincoln. Congress, he contended, could not force slavery upon a territory against the will of its people. Lecomptonites (favoring slavery) and Republicans (opposing slavery) worked hard to defeat Douglas' re-election, which they failed to do.

During 1859, two events were of substantial propaganda value to the extremists and secessionists in the South. First, Hinton Helper's *Impending Crisis*, a book aiming to show the submerged *white* classes in the South how great was the burden that slavery imposed on them, was officially endorsed by the Republican party. Southern Ultras cited the endorsement as proof that the "Black Republicans" were interested in promoting revolt in the South.[22] Second, John Brown's futile attempt to arm the slaves in the vicinity of Harpers Ferry, although entirely a project of Brown's fanatical mind, was seized upon and magnified by the partisan press into a major armed conspiracy against the South. The nation became conditioned to a sense of crisis.

As far as the Southern Ultras were concerned, defeat of the Republicans was an imperative for maintaining the Union. Since, in their view, Douglas was no better than a Republican, his defeat in the national convention was another condition on which there could be no compromise. The Buchanan faction warmly subscribed to this latter view. However, these were found to be mutually exclusive conditions: a Breckinridge nomination by the Democrats would assure a Republican victory.[23]

Meanwhile, Douglas men were organizing for the nomination fight. By late summer of 1859, an unofficial Douglas headquarters was established in New York. Its steering committee included August Belmont, Dean Richmond, John Jacob Astor, and others capable of putting together a sizable preconvention campaign fund. Belmont had broken with Buchanan and Slidell over the Lecompton issue and Slidell's treatment of the Douglas wing of the party.

An anti-Douglas majority on the national committee, at its meeting of December 7, 1859, took steps to limit any advantage that Douglas might gain from having his friend Smalley in the chairmanship. It reconstituted the 1856 resident committee—the group that coordinated the Buchanan campaign—and placed it in charge of arrangements for the national convention at Charleston. Six or seven of the resident committee members represented the Buchanan and the Southern wings of the party. Only three members—Representative C.L. Vallandigham of Ohio, John A. Logan of Illinois, and Miles Taylor of Louisiana—were Douglas supporters. It was a Buchanan committee arranging a convention in an anti-Douglas city.

Douglas continued to be the principal contender up to the day of the convention. The anti-Douglas men were finding it difficult to unite upon a candidate of their own, although the Buchanan following did favor Vice-President Breckinridge. The Ultras had several favorites, but spent most of their energy whipping up popular passions and keeping the political spotlight on themselves and away from Southern conservatives and moderates.

Failure to organize the House of Representatives during the seven-week period from December 5 to February 1 was symptomatic of the uncompromising spirit of the times. William Pennington, a New Jersey Whig, was finally elected Speaker by a majority of one vote.

4

According to one careful analysis, the South had no unified, well-considered political strategy during 1859 and 1860. A determined group of "positive actionists," centering in South Carolina, sought sufficient unity among leaders in the fifteen slave states to enable them to make certain demands of the expanding North regarding the protection of slave property. The Helper book and the John Brown raid failed to galvanize this unity. Several sensational plans were contemplated and held in reserve by these extremists during the speakership struggle, but went unused. Lincoln's nomination placed the Buchanan-Southern alliance closer to the Ultra position than anticipated. The voices of the Southern moderates were never organized or loud enough.[24] The polarizing maneuvers were reminiscent of the activities of the radical colonists during the days of the Boston Tea Party.

The bitterness, harnessed by John Slidell, carried over into the national convention. Slidell was determined to prevent Douglas' nomination. Surrounded as he was by the enemy faction, Chairman Smalley nevertheless did achieve a small coup of his own. He saw to it that the largest block of admission tickets were sent to pro-Douglas delegates, particularly those from New York and Illinois.

For this he was vigorously denounced at the national committee meeting, but his action was not rescinded or repudiated.

The pendulum of victory swung back and forth between the two factional alignments. By a margin of one vote, the national committee gave the temporary chairmanship of the convention to a Douglas man, Thompson B. Flournoy of Arkansas. Caleb Cushing, a moderate anti-Douglas man and a highly respected parliamentarian, received the permanent chairmanship. The Douglas men then won, in a 198 to 101 vote, a modification of the unit rule, limiting its application to those delegations required to vote as a unit by their state conventions. After this demonstration of strength, the Douglas men agreed to Slidell's plan for adopting the platform before the nominations. In the now-customary New York delegation seating contest, the Douglas men succeeded in excluding the Fernando Wood group and seating the Regency delegation led by Dean Richmond and August Belmont.

This was about as far as the give-and-take went. The fifteen Southerners on the platform committee, with the members from California and Oregon in tow, held a slender majority. Their majority report called for a platform that promised congressional protection of slave property. The principal minority report—there was another submitted by Benjamin Butler—was written by Douglas men. It reiterated the 1856 squatter sovereignty plank and added the observation that the entire slavery issue was now a matter for judicial—Supreme Court—determination. After some delay and filibustering, the Buchanan-Ultra alliance succeeded in sending the reports back to the platform committee. The vote for recommittal was 152 to 151.

In committee, the Douglas men expressed their willingness to acknowledge publicly that a difference of opinion within the Democratic party did exist with respect to slavery, to omit reference to the 1856 platform, and to stand by the decisions of the Supreme Court. When a floor vote was reached, the Douglas men were able to muster 165 to 138 in favor of their minority report. Richardson, the Douglas manager, rose to make a peace offer, but was put off as a 238 to 21 vote passed the preamble and first clause of the all-Douglas platform. A Southern walkout began, Alabama in the lead, and Mississippi, Louisiana, South Carolina, Florida, and Texas following. The seceders immediately organized their own Constitutional Democratic national convention.

All efforts at reconciliation failed. When the balloting for the nomination began, Convention Chairman Cushing ruled that the two-thirds necessary to nominate would have to be based on the whole number of convention votes, 303, rather than the 252 delegates present. After 57 ballots, the Douglas men were still far short of the 202 votes needed. The convention adjourned, to meet again in Baltimore on June 18, 1860. The seceders, waiting to be recalled to the regular convention by the announcement of a compromise candidate, were confronted instead with the necessity of returning to their constituencies for a new mandate. Their Constitutional Democratic convention adjourned to meet again at Richmond on June 11.

Chairman Smalley had opened the Charleston convention, but did little more. His status as chairman ended when he turned the gavel over to Flournoy, the temporary chairman of that body. From the temporary chairman, organizational continuity passed to the permanent chairman, Caleb Cushing, who reopened the convention in Baltimore. His departure from the Douglas convention to the Breckinridge convention lent a certain parliamentary authenticity to the actions of the latter gathering.

The six weeks between Charleston and Baltimore witnessed a great battle for moral and numerical advantage. In Congress, Jefferson Davis of Mississippi repeated the demand of the Southern Ultras for a Congressional Slave Code. Douglas replied that only a majority at the national convention, and not a minority in the Senate, could properly prescribe what would be the test of party fidelity.[25] The bolters decided to attempt a return to the Baltimore convention. Their test would be the composition of the roll. Would the Douglas or the Buchanan-Ultra delegations be admitted?

The Constitutional Democrats—the Charleston seceders—met as planned in Richmond on June 11, but postponed action until after the meeting of the regular convention in Baltimore. A week later in Baltimore, Caleb Cushing brought down his gavel. Attention immediately focused upon the work of the credentials committee. The Douglas men were ready to admit the bolters from Mississippi, Texas, Arkansas, Georgia, Florida, and South Carolina, but emphatically rejected those from Alabama and Louisiana, that is, the Yancy and Slidell states. One majority and two minority credentials reports were offered, the latter two insisting upon the readmission of the Alabama and Louisiana bolters.

The Douglas majority report carried, 199^1/$_2$ to 150. This time Virginia led the march out, followed by North Carolina, Tennessee, California, Oregon, half of Maryland, most of Kentucky, Missouri, and Arkansas. Douglas men in the other Southern states kept their seats. Caleb Cushing was among the last to depart. The vice-presidents of the convention elected a new permanent chairman, and the nominations were made: Senator Stephen A. Douglas for president, and Senator Benjamin Fitzpatrick of Alabama for vice-president.

At the seceders' convention, Temporary Chairman Charles W. Russell of Virginia turned over the chair to Cushing as soon as the latter arrived. The platform defeated at Charleston was now adopted. Breckinridge and Lane were nominated. The seceders claimed that their convention included 231 regularly elected delegates from nineteen states and that the true chairman of the Democratic national convention, Caleb Cushing, was their presiding officer. Actually, only about 115 authentic votes from the old convention were represented, full delegations coming from only three states. The 58 Northern delegates were primarily Buchanan officeholders.

Cushing was authorized to appoint a National Democratic Executive Committee. He chose sixteen men, one from each of eleven Southern states and five residents of the District of Columbia. This was by no means a nationally representative group in the usual sense. On the nine-man finance subcommittee were John Slidell and former national committeeman Augustus Schell, Belmont's factional rival in New York.

The Douglas national committee followed the traditional procedures of organization. However, before it was able to select its officers, it was confronted with an unprecedented situation: Senator Fitzpatrick declined the vice-presidential nomination. With H.H. Sibley acting as chairman, the national committee met on June 25 in Washington and, assuming the prerogative, voted to tender the nomination to Herschel V. Johnson of Georgia, who accepted. The following day, August Belmont was elected national chairman.

On May 9, a National Constitutional Union convention, made up of former Southern Whigs and Americans acting to ''uphold the Constitution,'' nominated John Bell of Tennessee and Edward Everett of Massachusetts. The Bell and Douglas organizations later cooperated in many places out of common fear of the temper of the Breckinridge following. This informal cooperation bore fruit in Kentucky, North Carolina, and Missouri, where Breckinridge electors were subsequently beaten.

Four major political parties entered the campaign of 1860. All four candidates vowed loyalty to the Union. An otherwise dull canvass was enlivened by Douglas' sensational and unprecedented tour of the country in behalf of his own candidacy and by the enthusiasm generated through the Republican ''Wide Awake'' marching clubs. President Buchanan told a rally in front the White House that neither nomination was regular and that every Democrat was free to make his own choice. Ex-President Pierce wrote to ex-National Chairman Hallett that he saw nothing in the convention proceedings to bind the delegates to ''party fealty'' and would himself support the Breckinridge-Lane ticket:

> It is of less consequence to discuss who were right and who were wrong upon the question of membership in the Convention, than it is to determine how the Democratic party, which united, is invincible, can avert the calamity of an irreconcilable breach.[26]

Hallett passed the letter on to the Breckinridge managers, who made campaign capital of it.

The Northern Democrats and their newspapers continued to view the Breckinridge Democrats as ''a factious minority.''[27] In the Senate, negotiators tried to achieve fusion of the Douglas-Breckinridge-Bell tickets or withdrawal of each in favor of the strongest candidate of the three on each state's ballot. Collections and factional negotiations, particularly in New York, consumed time and produced little reward. The usual congressional district levy brought almost nothing.

Although Belmont primed the personal contribution pump with $1,000 of his own, July passed without a penny more in the national committee till. Contributors were facing a choice among several tickets, each likely to lose if the others did not retire.

That September, fusionists in New York could not agree upon anything better than a proportioned distribution of New York's 35 electoral votes: 18 to Douglas, 10 to Bell, and 7 to Breckinridge, *if* the combined list should carry the state. Belmont now sent frantic pleas to Blanton Duncan and other rich Southern conservatives to supply the funds he had been unable to obtain in the Northern financial centers. This brought some money, but hardly enough. Douglas finally put up his own money for running campaign headquarters. By this time the "Little Giant," as Douglas was called, despaired of winning and began his final tour of the South (where he was least likely to gain electoral votes) in a bold attempt to dissuade his countrymen from taking the dangerous road to secession.

5

The election of a Republican president, Abraham Lincoln, and the death of Stephen A. Douglas in 1861 left the Democrats in defeat and without a titular leader. The responsibilities for formal leadership rested with National Chairman Belmont. Secession took the normally Democratic South out of the party, opening the way to a new factionalism that responded to the 1860 returns.

Although four political parties were in the field, the election of 1860 was basically a two-party competition in individual states, as noted in the previous chapter. In twenty-seven of the thirty-three states in the Union, the combined vote of the two leading candidates was 85 percent or more. Thirteen of these twenty-seven gave 150 of 303 electoral college votes to Lincoln. Three others (Kentucky, Tennessee, and Virginia) put 39 electoral votes in the Bell column. Ten two-candidate states supported Breckinridge with 69 votes. One other state (New Jersey), with a basically two-party division, split its electoral vote, 4 for Lincoln, and 3 for Douglas. Only six states (California, Connecticut, Delaware, Massachusetts, Missouri, and Oregon), with a total of 38 electoral votes, experienced any substantial multiparty divisions, most involving a three-way split. Together, Breckinridge and Bell carried the one-third of the electoral college that normally went Democratic. The remaining two-thirds went to Lincoln, with the exception of Douglas' 12 votes.

The Republicans considered their control of the presidency safe so long as the South could be kept out of the presidential election process. With over 100 electoral votes from the South lost to it, the Democratic party's future rested upon its ability to rebuild its strength in Ohio and seven other competitive states, together adding up to 96 electoral votes. The seven competitive states clustered into three regional groupings: Ohio, Illinois, and Indiana (with 47 electoral votes) in the Midwest; New York and New Jersey (42 electoral votes) in the East; and California and Oregon (7 electoral votes) in the West. Of these, the two heavyweights were New York (35 votes) and Ohio (23 votes).

An East versus West factionalism was quick to develop: the "War Democrats" gathering around National Chairman Belmont and other New York leaders; the "Peace Democrats" backing Clement L. Vallandigham of Ohio and New York City's Mayor Fernando Wood. Mayor Wood was a leader of Tammany Hall, which regularly took bargaining advantage in the closeness of New York's elections. Tammany established a tradition of opposing the rest of the state party, particularly in the closely contested presidential elections, thereby putting itself in the position of controlling the decisive swing vote. This threat enabled Tammany leaders to bargain for favorable patronage and other deals from the national party.

Belmont and the War faction supported President Lincoln's effort to preserve the Union by military means. Congressman Vallandigham, eager to assume the fallen mantle of Stephen A. Douglas, put his energies into developing a compromise for the North-South struggle. Vallandigham's plan purported to (1) preserve the Union, (2) satisfy the secessionists, and (3) give the Old Northwest a greater role in the affairs of the nation.

The rationale for Vallandigham's plan was a somewhat distorted theory of economic sectionalism that emphasized the interdependence of the Northwest and the South to the exclusion of the East. Vallandigham's plan also called for a new kind of constitutional sectionalism. The country was to be divided into four sections, and a majority of the presidential electors within each of the four sections would be necessary to choose a president. Certain laws were to be passed only with the assent of the senators of each section. Secession would be a legal right, but only when approved by all the legislatures of a section. The plan was an amalgam of states' rights theory and Calhoun's concept of concurrent majority. It proposed nothing less than a new system of separation of power under which the South could feel safe. The plan responded to the South's deepest political concern: access to and influence in the federal government.

As his proposal and leadership failed to take hold, Vallandigham veered more and more into radical rhetoric and obstructionism: criticism of every Lincoln war measure as "another cruel weapon" of coercion; opposition to the conscription law; endless proposals for a negotiated peace that would give victory to neither Union nor Confederacy and in which the Northwest would play a major mediatory role.[28]

By 1863, many Peace Democrats of the Northwest began to organize secretly to supplement or replace the regular party machinery. The Knights of the Golden Circle and similar societies evolved into the Order of American Knights, and, subsequently, into the Sons of Liberty. These clandestine political societies had military subsidiaries. The judge advocate general of the United States reported that some 340,000 of the half-million members were persons trained for military service. The Southern press and some of the South's military leaders sympathetically took up the cause of a separate "Northwest Confederacy." War Democrats and Unionists living in the Northwest countered by establishing clubs called "Loyal Leagues."

A crisis developed from a combination of circumstances including the transfer of General A.E. Burnside from the Army of the Potomac to the Department of the Ohio and the defeat of Vallandigham for re-election to Congress. Burnside arrived at his new post eager to erase the humiliating circumstances of his transfer. Vallandigham returned to Ohio eager to erase his recent election defeat by running for governor in 1863. Burnside ordered the arrest of all persons declaring sympathy with the southern Confederacy.

Vallandigham interpreted Burnside's order as a direct challenge and, on May 1, 1863, to overflow audiences, delivered two "disloyal" addresses. He was arrested on May 5, denied a writ of habeas corpus, tried, and convicted of treason by a military court. President Lincoln commuted the sentence and instructed the military authorities to send Vallandigham into exile in the Confederate states, subject to the original sentence of imprisonment if he returned.

At its June state convention, the Ohio Democratic party defiantly nominated the exile as its candidate for governor. Before another month had passed, Vallandigham set up headquarters on the Canadian side of Niagara Falls, whence he conducted a campaign notable for its brazenness. His defeat by a vote of 247,000 to 185,000 did not end his career, but it was the beginning of a decline in the influence of the Peace Democrats.[29]

Lincoln's election discredited most of the old leadership of the Democratic party. August Belmont, for example, interpreted the 1860 election results as a repudiation of Buchanan more than an endorsement of Lincoln.[30] From 1860 to 1872, Belmont's home in New York City served as something of a permanent national party headquarters.[31]

As the secession movement gathered force in 1860, Belmont shared with many Northern conservatives the impression that a peaceable separation of the "cotton states" would bring on a popular reaction against those Southern leaders who preferred to leave the Union permanently and that such a reaction would compel an "early reconstruction." This illusion was shattered by the attack on Fort Sumter, South Carolina, in April 1861. Belmont promptly joined Senator Douglas in unqualifiedly supporting Lincoln's actions to suppress the rebellion and preserve the Union.[32]

Belmont's influence proved to be important for the Civil War effort. He wrote to Baron Rothschild in the House of Commons and to Lord Dunfermline in the House of Lords emphatically predicting victory for the Northern states and deploring the British government's contemplated recognition of the Confederacy as a full belligerent. Belmont saw the seceding states as a rebellious minority, pure and simple, and he averred that the British had no business interfering in the domestic affairs of the United States. Belmont's influence in the court of Louis Napoleon was a decisive factor in frustrating the efforts of his wife's uncle, John Slidell, to bring the French empire to the side of the Confederacy.

Belmont never lost sight of his party responsibilities. In the fall of 1862, New York's Democratic Governor Horatio Seymour won a spectacular victory over James S. Wadsworth for a second term as governor. Seymour had long been one of the principal figures in the New York Democratic party: governor in 1853; a dark horse during the Charleston impasse of 1860; a promoter of the state fusion electoral ticket in that campaign. In 1862, Seymour was thought to be the best man to return the state to the Democratic column nationally. He was the choice of old-time Whigs in the Constitutional Union party, former Hunker Democrats, and Van Buren-Tilden Barnburners. His campaign speeches even won the applause of Thurlow Weed, now the Republican leader in the state. Seymour's election gave the state party a candidate for the presidency in 1864. In fact, two-thirds of Seymour's inaugural address was devoted to national affairs, hitting the Lincoln administration in its constitutional weak spots.

By the spring of 1864, however, both Seymour in the East and Vallandigham in the Northwest had run into so many political mishaps that both were considered out of the presidential race. Vallandigham had been exiled by the federal government and repudiated by the voters of Ohio. Seymour's opposition to the conscription law enabled the Republican press, without basis in fact, to blame him for the New York draft riots of July 1863. He favored volunteer recruiting as a more desirable method for filling all the needs of the military. This position pleased neither War nor Peace Democrats.

A more available presidential prospect was General George B. McClellan, whose in-and-out adventures at the head of the Union armies and whose political persecution at the hands of the Radical Republicans made him a popular martyr as well as a sharp critic of Lincoln's war management. As early as June 1863, Thurlow Weed asked McClellan to participate in a New York war rally with the object of pushing "Little Mac" to the fore as a Union party candidate. Democratic Chairman Belmont was also trying to draw McClellan onto the path to the presidency.[33]

The Democratic situation was further unsettled by the activities of Republican leaders William H. Seward, Thurlow Weed, Edwin Morgan, and the Blairs, who were arranging to drop the Republican party name in favor of the "Union" designation. A Union party would bring together all men, Democratic and Republican alike, eager to keep Lincoln in office, save the country from the excesses of the Radicals and the "treachery" of the Copperheads, or Peace Democrats, and prevent Northern defeat at the hands of the Confederacy. This move presented a serious temptation for many War Democrats. Patriotic feelings were strong; party and factional politics were very much in flux in 1864. When the Union Lincoln Association of New York was organized by Simeon Draper, Chairman Belmont, addressing an audience at Cooper Union, found it necessary to warn Democratic leaders not to be beguiled by the new organization.[34]

Assuming that McClellan was hardly a sure winner and observing that the Republicans were in factional turmoil, Belmont and his associates thought 1864 a good year for dilatory tactics. They decided to call a late national convention on July 4. Postponement would enable the Democrats to join in the Radical Republican attacks upon Lincoln. Postponement would also give the Democrats more time to think over the implications of Andrew Johnson's nomination as vice-president on Lincoln's Union ticket and perhaps to effect some pacification among their own uneasy factions.

Samuel J. Tilden, the party's state chairman in New York, refused to agree to Vallandigham's nomination nor would he commit himself to McClellan. The elder Frank Blair tried to dissuade McClellan from running against the president. Vallandigham strutted about. By the time Belmont called the 1864 convention to order, however, it was fairly certain that McClellan would be the nominee.

The convention convened with New York Governor Seymour as permanent chairman. Tilden went onto the resolutions committee, where, by the close vote of 13 to 11, he managed to defeat Vallandigham's bid for its chairmanship. Despite his defeat, Vallandigham was able to get the committee to approve, again by a narrow margin, a plank condemning the "experiment of war" and demanding immediate cessation of hostilities. Tilden and Belmont, with memories of 1860 fresh in mind, backed away from a divisive floor fight on this plank, and the convention gave its approval. Then, with cool inconsistency, the convention went on to nominate for president a general, who, by his prosecution of the war that it had just "disapproved," had become its hero.

At the national committee meeting immediately following adjournment, Belmont was the only person nominated for national chairman.

Democratic electoral hopes died with the reports of Union victories in the South. At about the same time, the Radical Republicans withdrew their objections to the Lincoln-Johnson ticket. As a final blow, in the last days of the campaign, an extremist group calling itself the War Democratic party, not to be confused with the faction of the same name, held a makeshift convention in New York to announce its support of the Lincoln administration.[35]

Lincoln's re-election caused widespread demoralization among Democrats. McClellan's departure for a stay of several years abroad left the party once again without a titular leader. The only Democrat holding a major national office was Vice-President Andrew Johnson, the Unionist Democrat whom Lincoln had recruited for his ticket. But who could be sure how much of a Democrat the "Union" vice-president would continue to be?

Elsewhere, the machinery of the national party once again devolved upon its national chairman, August Belmont. In the sixteen years since its creation, the national committee had been substantially formalized, particularly in connection with its convention arrangement and presidential campaign functions. Every state in the Union was represented on the national committee, but the selection of its officers had already begun to reflect principles of sectional and factional representation. The chairmanship increasingly tended to go to men not only who were recognized party leaders, but also who were of wealth capable of making substantial financial contributions to the national campaigns. August Belmont's repeated elections to the national chairmanship also indicated that the principal national leadership of the Democratic party was in New York during the Civil War and Reconstruction eras.

6 | Repairing the Broken Party and Nation

A bloody civil war is not easily forgotten nor its scars easily concealed. Nor is a divided political party easily reunited, particularly one that, having failed to hold the country together, seemed to become several parties: a Northeastern war party, a Midwestern peace party, and a Southern secessionist party. New political issues—for example, monetary policy, civil service reform, and tariff reduction—held the potential for aiding the forgetting process and even, possibly, bringing forward new party leaders.

The Democratic party, under the caretakership of National Chairman August Belmont, was not without fresh sources of leadership. As the nation passed through an era of Reconstruction, so did the national Democratic party. New York, with its varied population and large electoral vote, also proved to be the largest reservoir of new Democratic talent, among whom were Samuel J. Tilden and Grover Cleveland.

1

As a radical-conservative factionalism intensified among the Republicans, National Chairman Belmont and other Democrats considered how to make the most of it, particularly after a series of impressive Democratic victories in the 1867 local elections. In addition, the bidding for the 1868 Democratic presidential nomination was wide open. General McClellan, still abroad, was not interested. President Andrew Johnson's party loyalty had been blemished and his defeats at the hands of the Radical Republicans were costly. The vice-presidential nominee on the 1864 ticket, George Pendleton of Ohio, was very interested, despite a nasty feud with Vallandigham for control of the Ohio Democratic organization. The Blairs, consistent and persistent, felt that a popular Union general would attract voter support, and spoke of the availability of Winfield Scott Hancock and Frank Blair, Jr. Robert J. Walker, heavy with years and political sagacity, wrote Tilden a meticulous analysis containing six reasons why Hancock was "the only one who can certainly be elected."[1]

Although Pendleton and Hancock were popular in the West, their candidacies did not sit well with the "Hard Money" men in the East. Hard Money meant high interest and a restricted volume of currency. Pendleton wanted easy credit and cheap money for his agricultural constituencies. New York leaders, without whose support a nomination would be meaningless, were at a loss to find their own candidate. Horatio Seymour had taken himself out of the running, although Tilden, as Democratic state chairman, continued to speak of him as a prospect. Many, including Seymour, favored Senator Hendricks of Indiana, a "Sound Money" midwesterner able to win the support of the Southern delegations. The excitement of the impeachment trial of President Johnson, at which Chief Justice Salmon P. Chase presided with exemplary fairness and dignity, revived Chase's perennial candidacy.

At the 1868 national convention, Horatio Seymour again was elected permanent chairman. The platform emphatically approved various greenback proposals and favored a tariff for revenue only, both having become compelling issues in national affairs. The acclaim that accompanied approval of these planks ended Hard Money hopes, including Belmont's, of slipping quietly past the currency issue.[2]

Pendleton's strength was again demonstrated on the first ballot. He led with 105 to Johnson's 65 and Hancock's $33^1/_2$ votes; $113^1/_2$ votes were scattered among others. By the fifteenth ballot, the votes had concentrated around Pendleton, Hendricks, and Hancock. On the nineteenth ballot, Pendleton withdrew, and the vote was Hancock $135^1/_2$, Hendricks $107^1/_2$, and 73 for several others, including 4 votes for Seymour. At the twenty-second ballot, the spokesman for Ohio, where Pendleton and Vallandigham had reached a truce, cast that state's vote for Seymour. Amid the uproar, the convention's presiding officer shouted, "Your candidate I cannot be."[3] Next, New York transferred its 33 votes from Hendricks to Seymour. In moments it was unanimous. To add the military touch, the convention unanimously nominated General Frank Blair, Jr., for second place.

At the national committee meeting, August Belmont was again elected national chairman. An unusual motion was made to dispense with an executive committee, but it was not carried. Its proponents felt that management of the campaign should be concentrated in the hands of a small number of Seymour's intimates, and this is how it was eventually done. From a managerial point of view, Horatio Seymour and Samuel J. Tilden did not believe a representative body such as the executive committee, with its own internal interests to reconcile, was the appropriate mechanism for conducting a hard-hitting and efficient campaign.

The anomalies of the campaign were soon evident. The presidential candidate had been named over his protest. Seymour and Belmont were Hard Money men

Augustus Schell was the most famous of four brothers prominent in New York City financial circles. His older brother, Richard, was known as one of the most daring operators on Wall Street. The younger brothers, Robert and Edward, became presidents of leading banks. Augustus Schell, specializing in corporation law, was granted admission to the bar of the New York Supreme Court in 1833. He became a Democratic ward leader and then a district leader during the 1840s. When Schell joined, Tammany had already become almost entirely the city's Democratic party organization.

A spokesman for the Hard Shell faction (economic conservatives willing to tolerate the institution of slavery), Schell was elected chairman of the Tammany General Committee in 1852. As the Tammany candidate for governor, Schell lost the nomination to Horatio Seymour in the factional negotiations that took place. From 1853 to 1856, Schell served as Democratic state chairman. He worked energetically during the Buchanan campaign and was rewarded with the collectorship of the port of New York. He resigned from this post during the 1860 national convention, where he supported Breckinridge. He devoted the next few years to amassing a large fortune in the expanding railroad systems of the country.

Cessation of Civil War hostilities once more brought Schell to the fore politically. He joined Horace Greeley and other prominent citizens in an effort to have the imprisoned Jefferson Davis released on bail. Schell and Republican editor Horace Greeley cooperated in advocating early reincorporation of the South into the Union.

---

called upon to implement a Soft Money platform. Belmont entered the campaign discouraged and in poor health, and several hostile New York leaders accused him of being lukewarm to the cause. The Republican nominee was a war hero, Ulysses S. Grant.

Avoiding involvement with the national committee, Seymour remained virtually out of sight until the last days of the canvass. However, he actively participated in the campaign's operations. Tilden performed as his principal manager. On July 20, unhappy with the lethargic party machinery, Seymour authorized Tilden to establish the Order of the Union Democracy to supplement the party's efforts. Tilden became chief of these campaign clubs and Augustus Schell vice chief.

The Democratic campaign of 1868 plodded along in a half-hearted way. Many Democratic newspapers criticized Seymour's views. After discussing the progress of the campaign with Chicago industrialist Cyrus H. McCormick,

Seymour wrote to Tilden on September 26 proposing "a fresh presentation of our purposes" to be expounded after consultation with a "privy council" of some ten or twelve persons. "Up to this time," Seymour complained, "with the exception of my consultations with you and two or three others, I have been almost isolated in my position." The "two or three others" undoubtedly included Schell and McCormick.

As for the national committee chairmanship, it appeared that Belmont was unable or unwilling to contribute much. He and others had particular difficulty accommodating to the returning Southern wing of the party. In comparison, Schell appeared to be regaining his former stature in the national organization, facilitated by his good relations with many of the Southerners.

2

After Grant's election, New York's ascendancy in the national party was threatened by Seymour's retirement and by the growing influence of the Tweed Ring. "Boss" William Marcy Tweed gained control of both the city and the state governments in 1870. Public reaction, informed by the exposés carried in the *New York Times*, was angry, as were the more responsible Democratic leaders.

During 1871, Tilden initiated a campaign of public investigations and legal suits intended to break the hold of the Tweed Ring over the Democratic state convention. His allies included Seymour, Schell, Belmont, Francis Kernan, Abram S. Hewitt, and a host of other distinguished Democrats. The movement was extremely effective. The ring lost its grip in the elections of 1871, and its leaders were dispersed or faced trial. Tilden was on his way to becoming a reform candidate for governor and, not long after, a reform candidate for the presidency.

During 1872, the uncertain status of several New York leaders left the national party leadership in a quandary. The 1868 nominee had retired; Belmont was in his last year as national chairman. The confusion was magnified by the exodus of reform Republicans from their party to form a new party. The inevitable question was asked: Could a Democratic alliance with the newly organized Liberal Republicans produce a victorious coalition?

Among those available for the Liberal Republican nomination were Justice David Davis, Lincoln's close associate and member of the Supreme Court. Nominally a Republican, Davis was generally regarded as the choice of a majority of the conservative Democrats. National Chairman Belmont let Republican Senator Carl Schurz know that Charles Francis Adams, an independent Republican, could undoubtedly win the support of the Democratic party. Leaders of various nonpartisan reform movements as well as certain conservative Eastern Democrats were ready to back Adams if his ticket included any one of several prominent midwesterners: Trumbull, Cox, or Palmer. Party regulars among the Liberal Republicans and the Democrats were well disposed toward a David Davis-Horace Greeley ticket.

When the Liberal Republican national convention began its work on May 1, 1872, a Davis-Fenton-McClure alliance supported Davis for president and Greeley or Curtin for second place. This group, called "The Politicians," represented experienced leadership and the substantial votes of Liberal Republicans and reform Democrats in Illinois, New York, and Pennsylvania. The Politicians were opposed by "The Great Quadrilateral," Bowles, Halstead, White, and Watterson, four leading reform editors who publicly disapproved of Davis. Sharing their views was Senator Schurz, convention chairman.

As balloting proceeded, the Politicians abruptly shifted their support to Horace Greeley. The Schurz-Trumbull-reformist vote kept Charles Francis Adams ahead, though short of a majority. Gratz Brown's followers in the Missouri delegation, opposed to Adams and to Schurz' domination of the convention, swung their influence behind Greeley. This was supported by a dramatic, well-planned, and noisy "stampede." Thus, the Politicians succeeded in nominating Greeley and Gratz Brown, but, for each nomination, the usual motion to make the nomination unanimous was bitterly voted down.

The wholly unexpected nomination of such an old foe as Horace Greeley left the Democratic leadership with a frustrating dilemma. They had no outstanding candidate of their own and entertained small hope of defeating the incumbent, President Grant. They had already carefully paved the way for a Democratic endorsement of a Liberal Republican nominee. Opposition to endorsement of Greeley was pronounced in New York, New Jersey, Pennsylvania, and Delaware; important elements in the South were quite willing to make the endorsement. Southern Democrats saw Greeley as a friendly candidate, and the Democratic press of that section rallied behind him. Greeley also had an important Democratic ally in New York: Augustus Schell.

In the end, an almost unanimous Democratic convention endorsed the Liberal Republican platform and the Greeley-Brown ticket. The only public surprise at this convention was the presentation of Schell's name to represent New York on the national committee. It had been expected that John Kelly, a new power in Tammany Hall, would succeed Belmont. Once seated as committeeman, Schell's name was put forward for the national chairmanship.

"There is a bitter fight between Augustus Schell and Cyrus H. McCormick, the Chicago reaper man, for the Chairmanship," read the New York Times report of the national committee meeting. "It is a battle of millions."[4] This was the first time that a divided vote in a chairmanship election was publicly recorded. The vote was: Schell 23, McCormick 7, Prince 1, and 1 blank.

With Greeley as the nominee and Schell as national chairman, it now seemed feasible to find ways to reincorporate Southern Democrats into the national party. Transcending party, both men had a public record of reconciliation with the South.

In most states, electoral college slates were apportioned between Liberal Republicans and Democrats without serious friction. Most of the Democratic leaders and party regulars carried out their pledge to support Greeley, but hardly did so cheerfully. Greeley had too long a record of Democrat bashing. Tilden was typical, remaining a spectator in the national campaign, but laboring hard for the New York state ticket.

Schell's biographer devotes exactly one sentence to describe the Democratic chairman's part in the campaign.[5] Elsewhere it was observed that he contributed enough money to make several men rich. In the *New York Times* list of pro-Greeley contributions, however, Schell does not appear as a major source of funds.[6] The campaign's direction and heaviest field work fell to Greeley himself. He coordinated the work of two national committees and proved tireless in consultation and attention to campaign details.

Greeley's defeat was described as "disastrous" for the Democratic party. Indeed, the margin of defeat in the popular votes—763,000 behind Grant—and electoral votes was without precedent. The *New York Times* could say, with evidence if not impartiality, that "the final death of the Democratic party is to be ascribed to Horace Greeley."[7] Greeley's own death occurred before the electoral college met, which added a note of deep personal tragedy to the election outcome.

3

The Democrats never permitted their party organization to be absorbed by the coalition of 1872. The bolting Liberals were the ones who suffered losses in patronage and congressional prerogatives at the hands of vengeful Radical Republicans. The Democrats, instead, were now identified in the popular mind as the party of reform and change. Although many Liberal leaders returned to the Republican fold, the bulk of the rank-and-file Liberals, particularly in the West, found their way into local Democratic organizations.

The two Grant administrations and the issue of corruption among Grant's officials and friends made the case for reform in the public service an unbeatable symbol in national politics. This carried over into party reform. In New York, the small band of Democratic reformers who fought the Tweed Ring organized themselves into the Apollo Hall Democracy.

Among the Apollo Hall leaders was a twenty-nine-year-old corporation lawyer named William C. Whitney, one day to become Grover Cleveland's Warwick.* Nine generations of Puritan stock and Williston Seminary, Yale, and Harvard were behind young Whitney when he came to New York in 1864 to set

---

*A reference by William C. Whitney's biographer to Earl Richard Warwick, the fifteenth century "kingmaker" who was reputedly responsible for the elevation of Edward IV and Henry VI to the throne.

Abram S. Hewitt's career was of the log-cabin-to-riches stamp. Born in 1822 at Haverstraw, New York, Hewitt was reared in a house almost bare of furnishings. When his family moved to New York City, Hewitt entered the Grammar School of Columbia College as a free student, later winning a scholarship. He earned his way, in part, by tutoring. Among his pupils was Edward Cooper, the son of the genius of the new age of iron and railroads, Peter Cooper. Abram and Edward had been classmates at Columbia, but illness caused the latter to fall behind. With the help of Hewitt's tutoring, young Cooper graduated in 1843. Twenty-two years old, Hewitt, suffering from eyestrain, gave up the legal studies upon which he had already entered. After some hesitation, Peter Cooper permitted his son to take Hewitt as a partner in the management of an iron mill in Trenton, New Jersey. In 1847, "Cooper & Hewitt" became the firm's name. Eight years later, Hewitt married Edward's sister.

Hewitt cast his first vote for Zachary Taylor and the Whig ticket in 1848. For a brief period he worked with the Whigs, a reaction against the Democratic tariff of 1846, a heavy burden on the iron industry. However, inclination and personal friendships soon brought him into the Democratic organization. Among his intimates were Lorenzo Shepard, Robert J. Walker, and Samuel J. Tilden. He had known Tilden since the days when he read law in various New York City law offices. Hewitt spent much of his year at his New York residence, just across Gramercy Park from the Tildens. In 1871, Hewitt joined Tilden and Edward Cooper in their efforts to reorganize Tammany. Hewitt and civic reform were loosely identified with each other in New York City during the second half of the century.

up his practice. He joined Apollo Hall in 1870 and earned prominence for his anti-Tweed utterances. Another reorganizer of Tammany Hall by early 1872 was John Kelly. Kelly was instrumental in gaining the position of grand sachem for Augustus Schell.

Meanwhile, Samuel J. Tilden and Abram S. Hewitt assumed leading roles in the reorganization of Tammany. In time, Tammany itself began to look like a reform movement. Although Apollo Democrats found it difficult to believe that the Tilden-Hewitt influence would change the Tammany Tiger's stripes, in a short time, Apollo Hall closed down. William C. Whitney was among those elected to the Tammany General Committee.

When Tilden ran for governor of New York in 1874, Hewitt put time, money, and oratory into the campaign, although, as always, Tilden was his own manager. In this election, Tilden strongly urged Hewitt to stand for Congress from the Tenth District. The "Sage of Gramercy Park" saw the wisdom of having a close friend in Washington while he made his own way as a reform governor in Albany. Both men were elected. [8]

In Washington, Representative Hewitt spoke often in favor of two policies: a tariff for revenue only and hard money. Most of the time Hewitt listened and served as Tilden's advance scout in national politics. In Albany, Governor Tilden prepared heavy guns. John Kelly, still Tilden's political friend, helped out in anti-Tweed clean-up. William C. Whitney was appointed corporation counsel for the city of New York. Tilden renewed his friendship with Illinois leader Cyrus McCormick. National Chairman Augustus Schell, the grand sachem of Tammany, was, for the moment, sympathetic to the Tilden cause. Tilden's masterful breakup of the New York Canal Ring, whose members had accumulated fortunes through fraudulent repairs of the state's canals, made 1875 and 1876 favorable years for pro-Tilden presidential talk around the country.

John Kelly had ideas of his own about the part Tammany should play in the presidential choice and the Democratic party. As 1876 approached, his relationship with Tilden cooled perceptibly. National Chairman Schell, as Kelly's grand sachem, was in "Honest John's" corner for the next maneuver.

On January 28, 1876, Schell convened conferences in Washington with members of the House Democratic caucus—Hewitt among them—and with the executive committee of the national committee. The meetings concerned the rehabilitation of the party organs at Washington, particularly the reactivation of the national committee's executive committee. Senator Theodore Randolph of New Jersey was made vice-chairman of the executive committee, William H. Barnum of Connecticut, treasurer, and A.D. Banks of Mississippi, resident secretary. Randolph was a "party man," cautious in his factional allegiances, but always for the regularly nominated ticket. Randolph did not doubt that Tilden could give the country an excellent administration, but he frequently questioned whether Tilden could be nominated in view of his poor following in the South.[9]

Tilden's defeat of the Canal Ring made him "the Democrat best qualified" to drive out the corruption that flourished during Grant's administration. Tilden's hard money views, however, were quite controversial. Since Pendleton first proposed the Ohio Idea, the currency question had become the focus of agrarian discontent. The panic of 1873 made the currency shortage a critical problem, but one that Congress refused to face. In 1874, Grant vetoed a bill setting January 1876 as the date for redemption of greenbacks. In 1875, payments were officially deferred until 1879. In frustration, the Greenback party was organized in 1876 to mobilize popular opinion in the wake of the failures of the Granger movement, the Liberal Republicans, and the independent farmers' parties to do so. Although the main strength of the new party was in the Old Northwest and in most of the South, influential easterners like Peter Cooper were thoroughly in accord with its objectives.[10]

William H. Barnum made his fortune expanding his father's iron
foundry business, investing in land companies, and manufacturing car
wheels. In 1866, when he first ran for Congress from his home district
in Connecticut, Barnum's Republican opponent was another man of
great wealth, Phineas T. Barnum of circus renown, but no relative. William H. won after a heated campaign and served in the House until
1876. In 1868, the year of the Seymour-Grant contest, he was treasurer of the Democratic congressional campaign committee, coming
into friendly association with party managers Tilden, Schell, and Belmont in New York. Through Tilden he became acquainted with a fellow
ironmaster, Abram S. Hewitt, and the three men soon became operators of the Iron Cliffs Company, an enterprise that owned rich iron
mines in the Marquette district of Michigan. To fill the Senate vacancy
created by the death of Connecticut's Orris S. Ferry, Governor Charles
R. Ingersoll appointed James English in December of 1875. Before the
state legislature could meet to confirm this choice, however, Barnum
had consummated enough political deals to be the one chosen by a
narrow majority.

The new Democratic treasurer, Senator-elect Barnum, was an avowed Tilden
man. He was in constant touch with William T. Pelton, Tilden's nephew, regarding fund-raising matters.[11] As Barnum quietly passed the hat for funds, the
public advocacy of Tilden's candidacy was left to Manton Marble, who was just
about to retire from the editorship of the *New York World*. Marble corresponded
with other Democrat editors and with local party leaders. Hewitt talked up the
Tilden candidacy among members of Congress and helped organize a "Southern
Committee" to draw reluctant Southern Democrats onto the bandwagon.

When the New York state convention proposed Tilden for the presidency on
April 26, 1876, the absence of applause was deafening. The state party organiza-
tion agreed grudgingly to support Tilden. Facing such organizational hostility,
Tilden realized that he would have to create his own organization and publicity
channels, as he had for Horatio Seymour in 1868. A Newspaper Publicity Bureau was established to serve this end. This was soon succeeded by a Literary
Bureau. Tilden sank some unnamed amount of his own funds into the latter.
Edward Cooper, his father's Greenback politics notwithstanding, gave
$20,000. A private advertising agency was hired to do some of the preconven-
tion work.

Resisting all this were anti-Tilden Democrats who were heartened when John
Kelly openly joined them. Prior to the national convention, one-hundred-twenty

prominent Democrats signed a circular declaring themselves opposed to Tilden. At the convention itself, John Kelly hoisted over Tammany headquarters a banner stating: "New York, the largest Democratic city in the Union, is uncompromisingly opposed to the nomination of Samuel J. Tilden because he cannot carry the State of New York."[12]

The Republican nomination of Hayes a few days earlier no longer left the Democrats with a monopoly on the "Reform" symbol. Nonetheless, Manton Marble's draft platform, constructed around the phrase "Reform is necessary," was approved, 651 to 83. Tilden was nominated on the second ballot; Hendricks, his runner-up for first place, was given the vice-presidential nomination. Hard and soft money factions were thus able to unite on a reform platform.

Congressman Hewitt succeeded Schell as national committeeman from New York, "doubtless by the wish of Mr. Tilden," according to Hewitt's later record of it. "On this committee, I was at once made the chairman. It was understood that in taking this place I became the personal representative of Governor Tilden, as I was his intimate personal friend."[13]

Secretary-Treasurer Prince, now in his sixteenth year in this position, was elected as secretary only; the two positions were now separated. Chairman Hewitt appointed nine members to the executive committee. Senator Barnum's name moved to fifth on the executive committee roster from the ninth place it had been in 1872. The customary Washington resident committee functions were turned over entirely to Chairman Hewitt. A New York headquarters at Everett House on Union Square was placed in the charge of Tilden's nephew, Colonel Pelton.[14] After Congress adjourned, Hewitt joined the New York headquarters.

Edward Cooper, though not a member of the committee, was made national committee treasurer. In this position, Cooper received and disbursed $150,000. However, it was reliably estimated that a total of $500,000 in contributions was raised for the entire campaign. Tilden contributed a minimum of $100,000, with Hewitt and Cooper giving the next largest amounts. As "penance" for earlier opposition to Tilden, August Belmont gave $10,000 for the Indiana and Ohio campaigns. Barnum gave money, too, and was one of the principal Democratic orators. As a national committee agent, the Connecticut senator took $60,000 for speakers and literature in the intense Indiana campaign, assisted in the management of last-minute operations there, and helped save the state by 5,084 votes.[15]

Tilden carried his preconvention distrust of the regular party organization into the campaign, even though the national party's chief executive was one of his closest friends. Consultation between the two was made difficult by Tilden's duties in Albany as governor. Hewitt later described the beginning of the breach between the two men as follows. Tilden had been attacked throughout the summer for favoring federal assumption of the Southern war debts, but he refused to utter a word on the subject. On October 24, Hewitt went to Tilden with a prepared letter repudiating the charges. Tilden refused to sign. Hewitt threatened to withdraw from the campaign; the issue seemed that important. Finally, after making certain changes, Tilden approved. Knowing well the governor's chronic cautiousness, Hewitt hastened away from the Tilden residence, only to be overtaken shortly by a servant who had been sent to retrieve the document for further consideration. Hewitt refused to return it, and it went out to the newspapers. Hewitt later believed that Tilden never forgave him.[16]

4

Both Republican and Democratic versions of the November count gave Tilden 250,000 more popular votes than Hayes. The unofficial electoral college vote favored Tilden, 203 to 166. However, returns from Louisiana (8 electoral votes), South Carolina (7 votes), Florida (4 votes), and Oregon (1 elector) were tardy and uncertain. The Democrats could be sure of only 184 electoral votes; they needed 185 to elect their man. The Republicans were certain of only 166, including all 3 from Oregon. The crisis was an unfortunate climax to what had been a particularly rough presidential campaign during which the Republicans had waved "the bloody shirt," blaming the Southern Democrats for the Civil War.

The Civil War had ended eleven years earlier. Since then, the South had been more torn by Reconstruction than it had been by cannon and shell. The Black as postwar voter and militiaman was the constituency upon which Republican state governments in the South had been constructed. Carpetbaggers amd scalawags were everywhere. The terror of the Ku Klux Klan and the anti-Republican rifle clubs were part of the white man's subterranean resistance to Black-based authority. The chaos brought strikes, riots, massacres, and the rise of demagogues of the style of "Pitchfork" Ben Tillman. The Southern ballot box was regularly drenched in blood and fraud, compelling President Grant to send federal troops to preserve order.

The editors of the influential *New York Times* refused to concede Hayes' defeat, claiming that South Carolina and Louisiana were Republican and that the four votes of Florida would be decisive in giving the election to Hayes by a majority of one vote in the electoral college. Frequent requests from Democratic headquarters for *New York Times* reports of the results betrayed the uncertainty of the Democratic officials. The *Times* managing editor, John C. Reid, raced to Republican national headquarters to report the doubts in the Democratic camp. Republican Chairman Zachariah Chandler boldly announced, "Hayes has 185 votes and is elected!"[17] Each party's national committee at once dispatched party officers, legal counsel, and money to South Carolina, Louisiana, and Florida.

The two parties, through their press and local organizations, seemed to be hostile armies jockeying for position during the four months before inauguration, elements in each ready and eager to engage in armed conflict once again if necessary. President Grant appreciated the imminence of another civil conflict and declared that he would accept any nonmilitary solution worked out in Congress. Fortunately, Hayes and Tilden were patriots and men of moderation, even in this exceptional conflict. Each had personally conducted himself with great dignity and reserve during an otherwise bitter campaign. Pressures for another civil war came from other sources.

Hewitt, as congressman and national chairman, was in the midst of Democratic maneuvers. He helped the Democratic caucus organize a permanent advisory committee, consisting of eleven representatives and six senators. This committee met frequently during the crisis, either at Hewitt's house or at Speaker Samuel J. Randall's. According to Hewitt's later testimony, Tilden was constantly consulted.

Later efforts by Tilden followers to make Hewitt the scapegoat for Democratic defeat left the matter of Hewitt's reliability a moot question. Tilden, for his part, used many agents—Chairman Hewitt, Speaker Randall, Colonel Pelton— and designated no particular one as his sole spokesman. Tilden sent most of his messages via Pelton, but his final views were announced through Randall.

Hewitt, with his usual independence, leaned heavily upon his Democratic associates in Congress for advice. To Tilden, Hewitt may have become more a spokesman for the Democratic legislators than his own agent. During December, Hewitt's zeal got the better of him. He wrote an address intended to launch mass rallies throughout the nation on January 8. Tilden, appreciating the incendiary nature of such meetings, refused to approve the address.

Pressures for solution of the impasse came from outside the party and Congress. As Congressman James A. Garfield of Ohio put it, the nation's Democratic businessmen were more anxious for peace than for Tilden.[18] Certain businessmen in particular were instrumental in the outcome. Thomas Scott of the Texas and Pacific Railroad and Collis Huntington of the Southern Pacific and Central Pacific lines were bitter protagonists for a congressional subsidy to build a Southern railroad route to the Pacific. The *quid pro quo* for congressional votes in support of the subsidy were congressional votes helpful in seating Hayes— classic legislative logrolling. The debate over the proposed subsidy exacerbated North-South divisions among the Democrats and facilitated the election of Hayes.[19]

On March 2, 1877, the findings of the special electoral commission were announced, giving the disputed returns to the Republican nominee. In the corridors of the Capitol, Hewitt collapsed of shock and exhaustion. Somewhat recovered the following day, Hewitt decided to resign immediately as national chairman. Although he resumed his "old relations of friendly intercourse with Mr. Tilden,"[20] Hewitt and Tilden no longer shared political confidences.

Hewitt's resignation, however, did not signal his retirement from politics. He had, after all, salvaged what he could for the Democratic party: an indirect Republican commitment that federal troops would be withdrawn from the disputed southern states, thereby allowing the states to return to the Democratic party. He remained national committeeman from New York, reappointed to that position in 1880, and he continued to serve his congressional district for another four terms. Hewitt was elected mayor of New York in 1887 and was repeatedly mentioned as a candidate for the presidency.

Among the senior members of the executive committee at this time, in terms of years of service, was Senator Barnum of Connecticut, who was also the closest to Tilden. "After some discussion," the executive committee assumed the responsibility for electing him to succeed Hewitt in the chairmanship.[21]

The reception to Barnum's election was far from enthusiastic. The press editorialized that only wealth set him on a par with such predecessors as Belmont and Hewitt. Barnum had none of their intellectual training, sense of high purpose, or capacity for personal leadership, according to the *New York Times*. It was generally believed that Barnum considered politics a game—to be played to win—and that his money was his sole entree into a field worthy of better men.[22] In later years, the Republicans conferred upon Barnum the unflattering nickname "mule-buyer." This was based on the story that while in command of the last-minute campaign effort in Indiana in 1876, Barnum received from Chairman Hewitt a dispatch authorizing him to "buy seven more mules," that is, draw campaign funds amounting to $7,000. When Indiana gave its electoral vote to the Democrats, the Republicans credited their loss to Barnum's skill as a "mule-buyer."[23]

Tilden, over sixty years of age and afflicted with arthritis and other ailments, went into semiretirement. Nevertheless, his allies maintained his availability, arguing that Tilden had been a victim of fraud at the hands of his enemies and stupidity among his friends. In April 1878, Henry Watterson, editor of the influential *Louisville Courier-Journal* and a member of the Democratic House advisory Committee of Eleven during the disputed election, set out to find a scapegoat for Tilden's failure.

Watterson condemned "that bobolink," former National Chairman Hewitt, for misrepresenting Tilden's views regarding the Electoral Commission Bill and for suppressing a last-minute telegram of disapproval from Tilden.[24] Manton Marble supported Watterson in the quarrel, reporting that Tilden had explicitly advised Hewitt of his disapproval of the bill. Hewitt called the lie on both accusations and referred his accusers to Tilden himself for the real facts. Tilden's vindication of Hewitt was made tardily and with much indirection.

The righteous indignation of Tilden's followers was fueled further by the disclosures of the Potter Committee's congressional investigation of the conduct of the 1876 election in Louisiana and Florida. The committee, appointed by

House Democratic leaders, uncovered a host of illegal acts perpetrated by the Republican managers. The floor debate on the committee's report was concluded with a speech by Hewitt. Public opinion saw only good in the Democrats and evil in the Republicans, that is, until the *New York Tribune* published a series of disclosures about Democratic conduct in the contested states.

What the *Tribune* published was a long series of "cipher telegrams" that had passed between Colonel Pelton, Tilden's nephew, and Manton Marble in connection with bribery negotiations for the purchase of Tilden votes. The Republicans charged Tilden with responsibility for the activities of Pelton and Marble. The Potter Committee resumed its investigation. Its findings exonerated Tilden and Hewitt of personel knowledge of the negotiations, leaving Pelton and Marble utterly without defense. The scandal all but ended Tilden's chances for renomination in 1880.

5

Tilden's misfortunes and his silence about his own plans for 1880 set off new factional contention as leaders moved into position for the 1880 national convention. When John Kelly's anti-Tilden maneuvers were defeated in the New York State convention of 1878, Kelly bolted the party, had himself nominated for governor on a separate ticket, and thereby contributed to the defeat of the state Democratic slate that fall. Loss of the governorship was a telling blow to the Tilden forces and encouraged Senator Thomas F. Bayard, a high-tariff protectionist, to seek delegate support in New York for his 1880 presidential candidacy. Bayard's candidacy also became an issue among Democratic factions in Pennsylvania.

The Tilden men in Pennsylvania were led by Speaker Randall. Their adversaries were led by Senator William A. "Coffee-pot" Wallace, a manager of General Winfield Scott Hancock's campaign for the 1880 nomination. A former state chairman and head of Pennsylvania's national convention delegations in 1872 and 1876, Wallace was considered a master of the dubious practice of applying coffee to new citizens' voting papers to give them the appearance of age. Wallace was an aggressive operator who seems also to have been the source of rumors that he might replace Barnum as national chairman.[25] As factional tensions increased in New York, Pennsylvania, and Ohio, National Chairman Barnum began to receive urgent requests that he mediate the disputes. Barnum settled very little.[26]

Democratic leaders were of three views regarding the 1880 nomination. First, there were those—Manning, Blair, Bigelow, Watterson, Faulkner, and others— who believed that Tilden wanted the nomination, but would do nothing overt to get it. Second, there was the group who thought that Tilden would not himself run, but expected to name the nominee. The likeliest successor in this case would be either Henry B. Payne, William C. Whitney's father-in-law and for many years one of Ohio's outstanding Democrats, or Speaker Randall of Pennsylvania. Kind words were also being circulated in favor of National Chairman Barnum. Barnum's term in the Senate had ended in 1879, and he seemed eager for greater prizes; much was made of his close friendship with Tilden and his executive ability. A *New York Times* editorial observed, "Not being a man of words, [Barnum] is not so well known as many others, even as his position in his party brings him out occasionally; but he is, nevertheless as hard a worker and as dangerous a man to fight as any Democrat in the country."[27]

A third group of Democrats were firmly anti-Tilden. Among these were supporters of Thomas Ewing, Allen G. Thurman, Thomas F. Bayard, Thomas A. Hendricks, and Winfield Scott Hancock, candidates considered at previous conventions. Ewing had little organized strength. Tilden was decidedly opposed to Thurman, Bayard, and Hendricks, all cheap currency advocates. This left General Hancock of Pennsylvania, famous for repulsing the Confederate armies at Gettysburg. Hancock had been one of the two principal candidates in the deadlocked convention of 1868.

Tilden's titular leadership was taken seriously. In the absence of cues from him, most delegates were in doubt about their votes when they arrived in Cincinnati for the convention.[28] As Daniel Manning departed from New York for the convention, Tilden told him that he would not accept the nomination unless it were unanimous and, since unanimity seemed most unlikely, his first choice was Payne and second Randall. Almost simultaneously Tilden sent a telegram to Payne asking him to accept second place on a Tilden ticket. Payne agreed.[29] Tilden also gave Manning a letter that hinted that his health might not permit him to accept the nomination even if it should be offered. Dated June 18, 1880, and addressed to the New York delegation, the letter was to be read to the convention at an appropriate time. The letter was long and ambiguous. In it Tilden asked for "an honorable discharge." He said that he wished to "lay down the honors and toils of even *quasi* party leadership, and to seek the repose of private life."[30] When read to them, the New York delegation decided to interpret the letter as a withdrawal.

The first ballot put Hancock in the lead with 171 votes, Bayard second with 153^1/$_2$, Payne third with 81, Thurman fourth with 68^1/$_2$, and the rest scattered over a large field. During an overnight adjournment, Bayard and Hendricks delegates started a Hancock boom. On the first roll call of the morning, Hancock had 320 votes. In the middle of the roll call, in a stiking move, Pennsylvania threw all its votes to Hancock. Evidentally, "Coffee-pot" Wallace had been at work uniting the divided Pennsylvania delegation. Before the second ballot ended, Hancock had 705 votes and the nomination. Even though the convention had refused to seat his delegation, John Kelly hastened to the platform to pledge his support to the nominee.

The Bayard and Hendricks contingents were mainly southern and midwestern soft-money men. The Tilden and Payne followers were for a hard-money policy. Hancock straddled the issue and won Bayard-Hendricks votes for taking the neutral ground. William C. Whitney, still a Tilden lieutenant, observed to a friend after the convention: "Yes, it has gone as I foresaw, but not as I hoped. If Mr. Tilden had been frankly out two weeks before the Convention, we could have nominated Payne."[31]

With Hancock as nominee and Tilden still a major power in the Democratic party, the selection of a national chairman became a test of influence. Control of the chairmanship now carried with it a large role in the campaign and in preparations for the next national convention. Despite his wretched health, Tilden was determined to remain in the political picture. As a consequence, Smith M. Weed, Tilden's aide, and Barnum had several conversations with Hancock's representatives, who were more than happy to enlist Tilden's support.[32] One condition for this support was the re-election of Barnum for purposes of temporary organization when the national committee met on June 24. The committee then adjourned until July 13 to allow time for further Tilden-Hancock negotiations.

Wallace was Hancock's choice for national chairman. Hancock-Wallace supporters argued that there was no precedent for disregarding the wishes of the nominee. The converse of that argument was that precedent did not dictate that the nominee's wishes must always prevail, which was the retort of the Tilden followers. The Tildenites further argued that they remained a powerful sector of the party and deserved recognition. In addition, they said, Barnum was a far better fund raiser than Wallace.

Speculation continued until Wallace announced his ineligibility because of nonmembership on the national committee. The chairmanship then went to Barnum "unanimously."[33] Wallace was elected chairman of the congressional campaign committee. Thus, the Tilden men would still control the national committee and national convention machinery in 1884. Some went so far as to predict that Barnum's re-election meant Tilden would control a Hancock administration.[34] It is, of course, problematic how much deference Hancock would have paid Tilden, although the general did in fact pay a visit during the campaign to Tilden's residence at Greystone to receive advice and support.

Tilden made some speeches on behalf of Hancock, but the skilled hand of the old master was absent from the direction of the campaign. Nor did Hewitt, who was on the executive committee, have his heart in the cause. In midsummer, Hewitt went to Europe and, falling ill, was detained in London for some time.

Hewitt also committed a major political faux pas when he declared the forged Morey letter to be authentic. The letter suggested that Garfield favored unlimited Chinese immigration, a policy that was viewed as an affront to westerners and U.S. labor. The letter, presumably addressed by Garfield to an officer—later found to be nonexistent—of a Massachusetts employers' society, was published two weeks before the election. The letter, however, was a fraud, a fact fully confirmed before election day, compelling Hewitt to apologize to Garfield. Hewitt's biographer, Allan Nevins, blames Chairman Barnum for the hasty action.[35] The Morey "sensation" backfired in Garfield's favor.

As the campaign drew to a close, Barnum and Scott were having extreme difficulty raising funds, General Hancock was still uncommitted on any public issue, Hewitt and Speaker Randall were apologizing to Garfield, and, to Tilden's dismay, Tammany's John Kelly was giving the national slate strong support. Declared the *New York Times* gleefully, "Ex-Senator Barnum, who will probably soon be ex-Chairman Barnum, will retire into private life covered with infamy."[36] Although Garfield carried the electoral college, his plurality of 7,400 popular votes in approximately 9 million cast made this one of the closest returns on record.

Hancock, like Tilden, went to his grave with the firm conviction "that he had been really elected and then defrauded."[37] There was a movement, headed by Barnum and Kelly, to contest the returns; both claimed that there were at least 20,000 illegal Republican votes cast in New York. No legal challenge materialized and the gloom of twenty years of defeat settled heavily upon the Democratic leaders.

6

No sooner had election day passed when old reform alliances in New York were revived with the objective of driving out John Kelly. In New York City, Abram S. Hewitt, William C. Whitney, and Hubert O. Thompson organized the County Democracy to compete with Tammany. Tilden's upstate organization, under State Chairman Daniel Manning, helped whenever it could.

The anti-Tammany alliance weakened as the 1882 gubernatorial race approached. The Republicans were divided between Stalwart and Half-Breed factions. It seemed to be a year for a Democratic victory. The County Democracy favored Hewitt for the nomination, but Tilden, whose supporters were likely to control the convention, failed to respond favorably. Hewitt refused to allow his name to be put in nomination unless he had Tilden's explicit support. The County Democracy put forward Edward Cooper instead.

As second choice to Cooper, Whitney proposed Grover Cleveland, the reform mayor of Buffalo. The strategy was to have the County Democracy vote shift to Cleveland "at the proper time." The proper time came on the second ballot when the two front-runners in a field of seven candidates were deadlocked with 123 votes each. Cleveland was third with 71 votes. The County Democracy vote, plus some others controlled by Manning, started the stampede to Cleveland. David B. Hill, mayor of Elmira and in later years a thorn in Cleveland's side, was nominated for lieutenant governor.[38] Cleveland won the election, and the Tilden organization had an heir.

With Hancock retired from politics, Tilden was the principal elder in the Democratic clan. National Chairman Barnum, always a loyal Tildenite, continued to talk of Tilden's "inevitable" election to the presidency.[39] However, Tilden was becoming more and more of a recluse at his Greystone estate, and most of his influence was felt through his younger associates: State Chairman Manning and Colonel Daniel Lamont. As governor and an admirer of Tilden, Cleveland also sought his advice. To Tilden's delight, Cleveland left Tammany completely out of the patronage of 1883 and embarked upon an explosive public quarrel with John Kelly.

Nationally, the tariff issue was rapidly becoming the principal issue between the parties and among factions within each party. Customs receipts were creating a bulging Treasury surplus. Access to the surplus was a matter of growing congressional interest. The Republicans, finding the "bloody shirt" a somewhat worn garment during the campaign of 1880, had turned to an attack upon the Democratic platform phrase—"a tariff for revenue only"—in the hope of winning support from both capital and labor. Hancock's foolish remark in the campaign that the tariff was a "local issue" helped the Republican strategem.

In the House of Representatives, two former Tilden men were becoming spokesmen on opposing sides of the tariff queston: Abram Hewitt for reduction and Samuel J. Randall supporting protection. Pennsylvania became the home of protectionism, with Randall Democrats and Cameron Republicans the principal protectionists.

From Maryland came another frequently heard voice on the tariff issue: Democratic Senator Arthur Pue Gorman, who styled himself an "incidental protectionist." Gorman, like many of his Senate colleagues, was not a protectionist on every commodity. For example, he favored the reduction of tin ore duties; Maryland—incidentally—was one of the major centers of the canning industry in the country at that time.[40] Another bastion of protectionist influence was Connecticut, whence came Chairman Barnum, a leader in the protectionist iron industry.

The national committee met on February 22, 1884. Factional strength was tested in the selection of the convention city. Chicago was chosen over St. Louis by a vote of 21 to 17 on the third ballot, a vote that the press interpreted as a victory for the protectionists.

Recalling Wallace's ineligibility for the national chairmanship in 1880 because of nonmembership on the national committee, the committeeman from South Carolina recommended the adoption of a rule that would enable the national committee to choose its chairman from outside the committee if it were deemed advantageous to do so. Consideration of the motion was postponed by a 17 to 15 vote. The motion was reintroduced and adopted during the national convention.

The 1884 presidential favorites were Thomas F. Bayard, Allen G. Thurman, and Grover Cleveland. Manning, Hewitt, and Whitney were operating Cleveland headquarters, doing their utmost to counteract Tammany threats to bolt should Cleveland be the nominee and denying rumors that Randall was Tilden's real favorite. Tammany's John Kelly tried to eliminate the unit rule in order to break Manning's control of New York's 72 votes, but lost in a 463 to 322 vote. Cleveland's strength appeared on the very first ballot, his 392 votes well ahead of Bayard's 170, Thurman's 88, and Randall's 78. When Pennsylvania's protectionists, Randall and Wallace, climbed onto the bandwagon, Cleveland had the nomination. To balance the ticket, Hendricks was named for the vice-presidency, thereby assuring that the pivotal states of Indiana and New York would remain Democratic.

Cleveland wanted Daniel Manning to be national chairman, but Barnum, Gorman, and Wallace were also important possibilities. Barnum, now sixty-six and a protectionist, had declared his wishes to retire; he later became the largest contributor to the Cleveland campaign. Wallace, a protectionist, had been Hancock's preference for chairman in 1880 and was now second choice of many members of the national committee. Next was Gorman, the most skillful political manager of the three, who had acquired experience on the congressional campaign committee. William L. Scott, a staunch Tilden man, although not on the national committee, was eligible under the new rules and was a possible successor to Barnum.[41]

When the national committee met again in New York City, Barnum was absent. Gorman was selected temporary chairman. The New York committeeman at once nominated Barnum to be national chairman. He was perceived to be Cleveland's choice and was elected "by acclamation." Barnum, Gorman, Dawson, Bradley B. Smalley, Vilas, Miller of Nebraska, and Patrick Kelly of Minnesota were appointed a subcommittee on the organization of the campaign to consult with the nominee in Albany as well as with those members of the congressional campaign committee then in New York. Five days later, the national committee reconvened to receive the report of the subcommittee. A twenty-member executive committee was appointed by Barnum, with himself as chairman. A subcommittee of seven was given the active management of the campaign; its chairman was A.P. Gorman.

There was again much dissatisfaction among party officials and political commentators over Barnum's re-election. Barnum's only assignment, however, was to make supervisory trips through the western states. The real management of the campaign fell to Gorman, Manning, and Whitney.

Although these three managed the campaign, Cleveland himself did several things of consequence. He demonstrated his regard for Tilden by asking him to examine and comment upon the letter of acceptance. When, on July 21, 1884, a Buffalo paper told the story of bachelor Cleveland's affair with a woman named Maria Halpin and the illegitimate son presumably born of this union, Cleveland handled the scandal himself. Through his Buffalo friends, he requested that they "tell the truth." Doubting that the child was his, but willing to assume the responsibility for its support, Cleveland was able to ride out this storm.[42]

Republican nominee James G. Blaine made the tariff his principal campaign issue, hoping thereby to exacerbate Democratic factionalism. Rather than respond, Gorman directed a continuing attack upon Blaine's personal integrity. Gorman was particularly concerned with a threatened Tammany revolt and the effect this would have upon the Catholic vote; John Kelly had been toying with the notion of supporting Ben Butler's third-party Greenback candidacy. Gorman eventually won over grudging support from the Tammany organization.

Gorman sent a stenographer to trail Blaine about New York City during the last days of the campaign and, during his reading of the stenographer's notes, caught the implications of Reverend Burchard's reference to the Democrats as the party of "Rum, Romanism, and Rebellion." Gorman also appreciated the affront to the common man that could be read into the semisecret prosperity dinner tendered to Blaine at Delmonico's by the better-heeled members of the business community. Both events were reported far and wide, in Rum-Romanism-Rebellion handbills and in "Royal Feast of Belshazzer: Blaine and the Money Kings" cartoons.

Senator Gorman, in effect, was the party's national chairman. Barnum's role was secondary, except in terms of monetary contributions. Commenting on his own role, Whitney later wrote to the president-elect:

> Pay no attention to newspapers or other advocacy of me [for a Cabinet post]. You owe me nothing. . . . Senator Gorman is in my opinion a pretty safe adviser. He has grown upon me day by day. I hope you will ask his opinion of people you are thinking of. . . .[43]

The election returns were so close, particularly in New York, that both parties formally claimed victory. It seemed to be 1876 and 1880 over again. Mobs swirled around the streets of New York and Boston. The threat of riots hovered everywhere. The final official returns showed that Cleveland had carried New York's 36 electoral votes by the bare margin of 1,200 popular votes and therefore had won the electoral college by 219 to 182.

Gorman worried that the new president might neglect the party organization in the distribution of the vast federal patronage. He took it upon himself to place before Cleveland a list of party leaders who should be called to Albany for consultation in this regard.[44] Cleveland, however, followed his own judgment on patronage matters. As a consequence, before a year had passed, he found himself dealing with various revolts within the party, particularly from the David B. Hill and Gorman organizations in New York and Maryland, respectively.[45] The president agreed to modify his approach to appointments thereafter.

Twenty years of effort by New York's Democratic leaders had at last brought one of their number to the presidency. In that time, national committee chairmen—Belmont, Hewitt, and Barnum—played significant factional roles. Belmont kept the War Democrats behind Lincoln's conduct of the Civil War and did so without losing Democrats to the Republican party. Hewitt facilitated the return of the southern wing to the national party, albeit as part of the hopeless campaign of a Liberal Republican nominee. Barnum held onto the chairmanship on behalf of Tilden, who dominated party affairs for most of this period.

With Cleveland's arrival to the presidency, the issues of war or peace, soft or hard money policy, Reconstruction, and civil service reform faded into the past. Some of the old issues took new forms. New issues emerged. And with them, yet another Democratic factionalism took shape. One consequence of factionalism was the diminution of the role of the Democratic national chairman in party affairs.

7 | Radical Republican Capture of Committee and Chairmanship

The electoral circumstances of the Republican victory in 1860 invited a virulent factionalism. Lincoln was a minority president, having received only 40 percent of the popular vote. In contrast, the Congress elected with Lincoln was overwhelmingly Republican. In the Senate there were 31 Republicans to 10 Democrats and 8 from other parties. In the House, the line-up was 105 Republicans, 43 Democrats, and 30 others. These were the quantitative grounds for subsequent claims that Congress held a more authoritative mandate than the president. In later elections, as indicated in Table 1, the Republican majorities in Congress became more lopsided, hence presidential-congressional relations more aggravated. The election statistics lent special authority to the old Federalist-Whig argument for legislative supremacy over the executive, a philosophy that would be successfully implemented by the Radical Republicans.

1

The second session of the Thirty-sixth Congress convened in December 1860. There was a general inclination to view the secessionist crisis as a political flurry that would soon dissipate itself. Both houses of Congress began to seek the compromise that would once and for all time settle the trouble between the nation's sections. The House appointed a Committee of Thirty-Three for this enterprise, the Senate a Committee of Thirteen.

As president-elect, Lincoln began indirectly to make known his opposition to compromise. Lincoln believed that the secession movement could and would be suppressed within the South itself, without blandishments from the federal government. Lincoln's attitude was made public in Greeley's *Tribune* on December 22, 1860. Through Thurlow Weed, Lincoln requested Senator Seward to introduce certain anticompromise resolutions to the Committee of Thirteen. Seward complied reluctantly after making his own modifications in the resolutions. In

Table 1

Congressional Parties, 1961–69

Year	House of Representatives		Senate	
	Republicans	Democrats	Republicans	Democrats
1861–63	105	43	31	10
1863–65	102	75	36	9
1865–67	149 (Union)	42	42 (Union)	10
1867–69	143	49	42	11

Source: Bureau of the Census, *Historical Statistics of the United States, 1789–1945* (Washington, DC: Government Printing Office, 1949).

this episode, personal relations between Lincoln and Seward were as much at issue as those between the sections of the Union.

Control of the Republican party and the selection of the new cabinet were inextricably connected. With the secession crisis as a backdrop, the first scene of an intraparty drama took place between its senior members: Lincoln and Seward. Seward had been a leader in national politics long before Lincoln, and the New Yorker intended to maintain his status. Immediately after the election, Weed suggested that Lincoln pay a visit to Seward at Auburn, New York, to discuss the policy of the new administration and the selection of the cabinet. Lincoln brushed aside this raw display of condescension toward a president-elect. Thurlow Weed then suggested a neutral place and was again rebuffed. On December 10, Weed received an invitation, sent indirectly through Swett, to come to Springfield. Nine days later, Weed presented himself to the president-elect and carried away Lincoln's resolutions to be introduced by Senator Seward.

Lincoln eventually chose Seward as his secretary of state. As soon after inauguration as the appointment became official, Seward gave every indication that he intended to be prime minister of the new administration. On April 1, 1861, he sent "some thoughts for the President's consideration," an unsolicited and presumptuous communication that listed what Seward believed should be the administration's foreign and domestic policy and urging that, whatever policy would be determined, it should be energetically prosecuted either by the president or "some member of the Cabinet."[1] In fact, given the similarity of their political constituencies in Illinois and New York, their ideological and policy orientations were also quite similar.

Lincoln's patient reply, written the same day, completely rejected Seward's attempt to apply parliamentary theory to the U.S. presidency and firmly asserted

A brief experience in the mercantile business and a $1,000 stake provided by his father sent twenty-year-old Zachariah Chandler westward from New Hampshire in 1833. He settled in Detroit and established a retail dry goods store with his brother-in-law. The partnership was dissolved three years later, but Chandler retained the business establishment, the first in Detroit history to reach a sales volume of $50,000 in a single year, an accomplishment hailed by the community as a mercantile triumph. Between 1840 and 1850, the business was converted into a wholesaling enterprise. Chandler, having acquired large wealth, delegated its management to others so that he might devote time to politics.

In February 1851, Chandler was the Whig candidate for mayor of Detroit. Both the city and the state were Democratic strongholds, but Chandler was able to roll up a 349-vote majority in a total vote of about 3,500. A year later he was the Whig nominee for governor. He received 11,000 more votes than any previous Whig gubernatorial candidate, but fell 8,000 votes short of his Democratic opponent.

Chandler was one of the founders of the Republican party in Michigan in 1854 and, two years later, its successful candidate for the U.S. Senate, where he became known as a "fire-eater." The two most rabid Radicals during the critical winter of 1860–61 were "Zack" Chandler and "Bluff Ben" Wade of Ohio. In February 1861, Chandler created a sensation by asserting in a letter to Michigan's Governor Austin Blair: "Without a little blood-letting, this Union will not, in my estimation, be worth a rush."[2]

that the president alone would decide and prosecute administration policy. The reply made future official relations between the two men clearer; the personal relationship also tended to improve. Throughout the Civil War and during Lincoln's campaign for re-election, Secretary of State Seward remained the ranking member of the cabinet and, eventually, a loyal Lincoln supporter. But the parliamentary theory of government had advocates on a far more challenging scale in another quarter.

2

Grounds for factional division within the Republican party could be attributed to the characteristics of the party's electorate. All one-party Republican states and some other safe ones were in New England, where Republican support had been recruited from Free Soil and former Whig elements. New England Republicanism was directly heir to Federalist-Whig preference for the legislature as the seat of party leadership as well as for the abolition of slavery. Radical Republicanism in Congress drew some of its more dignified leaders from New England: Charles Sumner of Massachusetts, William Pitt Fessenden of Maine (the principal philosopher of plans to substitute a parliamentary for the presidential system), and John P. Hale of New Hampshire, who had been a presidential nominee of the Free Soil party.

Republicanism in the Midwest was of two types. The older states—Illinois, Indiana, and Ohio—had been competitive states since 1824; these states pursued an ideological moderation taught by competitive politics. The newer states—Iowa, Michigan, Minnesota, and Wisconsin—had on the average participated in only three presidential elections and were for the most part frontier democracies with electorates created by inclusive suffrage laws. These states had less competitive, more populist politics than the older states. Out of the moderation of the older states came the Lincolnian reluctance to deal severely with the South. From the newer states came the demagoguery that was a mark of Radical Republicanism, as exemplified by Zachariah Chandler.

During his many later years in national politics, Chandler was nearly always in the midst of Radical Republican operations, a vigorous and skillful organizer and campaigner. Chandler and Wade's readiness for civil war, however, was not shared by northeastern mercantile leaders. The Republicanism of New York and New Jersey was conservative and moderate, somewhat like the Republicanism of the older states of the Midwest. The Seward-Weed leaders were accustomed to competitive party politics and confident that electoral fortunes could take a favorable turn for their party in some future regular election.

The goal of New York businessmen and financiers, Republican National Chairman Morgan among them, was to prevent civil war, protect their investments in the South, and maintain peaceful trade throughout the nation and with the rest of the world. This attitude transcended party lines in New York. Democrat National Chairman Belmont supported Thurlow Weed's prewar advocacy of a compromise. Chicago merchants also placed pressure for conciliation upon Lincoln's friend, Senator Lyman Trumbull. Chandler's response to compromise sentiment was to upbraid the business world and to express the hope that Republican jitters would not spread to the president-elect.[3]

Congressional leaders and most members of the cabinet soon realized that Lincoln would consult little with them. Although relationships between Lincoln and Seward improved, the rest of the cabinet was not taken into the president's confidence. After a brief but futile attempt to make them meaningful, regular meetings of the cabinet were dropped entirely.

As for members of Congress, Lincoln's military actions, taken while Congress was away from Washington, posed the question: Is not Congress the only constitutional agency authorized to declare war? The answer depended on whether Lincoln was dealing with a "war" or an "insurrection." He called it the latter. Congressmen and senators were convened in special session nearly three months after Fort Sumter's fall and did not relish being confronted with the *fait accompli* of military engagement. A long series of executive acts had placed severe limits on congressional options. In fact, there was no alternative but to approve Lincoln's proclamations.

Meanwhile, the Union forces met their first catastrophe at Bull Run. The only good news came from General George B. McClellan's command, which had saved West Virginia for the Union. McClellan displayed consummate skill in organizing and directing his forces. On July 25, Lincoln gave him full command of the defense of Washington. By fall, General Winfield Scott—now a Republican—was retired, and McClellan—a Democrat—was made the chief of military operations.

There were an estimated eighty Democrats among the one hundred ten generals of the army of 1861, and the principal among them—McClellan—was a former "Buchaneer" who supported James Buchanan for president and held avowed proslavery sentiments. Why was not the great Republican, General John C. Fremont, put in charge? In a nation accustomed to elevating its successful generals to the presidency, any military criteria applied by Lincoln in selecting McClellan were lost among charges of treason to his party.

When Congress reconvened in December, Zachariah Chandler immediately proposed a committee of three to investigate the "disasters" of Bull Run and Edward's Ferry. From this proposal came the Committee on the Conduct of the War, originial members of which were Benjamin F. Wade, Zachariah Chandler, and Andrew Johnson, two Republicans and one Democrat representing the Senate, and Daniel W. Gooch, John Covode, George W. Julian, and Moses F. Odell, three Republicans and a Democrat representing the House. It was basically a Radical committee, with Wade and Chandler exercising active leadership. They were assisted by George Julian, son-in-law of abolitionist Joshua Giddings, as principal spokesman for the Radicals in the House. Andrew Johnson's fateful presence as the Democratic minority member undoubtedly had much to do with his subsequent difficulties with the Radicals when he became president.

After the second Union defeat at Bull Run, Secretary of War Edwin M. Stanton proposed McClellan's dismissal. Stanton had the support of three cabinet members, particularly Secretary of the Treasury Chase. The support of Secretary of the Navy Gideon Welles would have established a cabinet majority favoring the proposal. Only Seward and Blair were for retention of McClellan. Welles refused to sign the Stanton-Chase manifesto and the proposal never came to a test. Had the proposal accomplished its purpose, Lincoln would have appeared to be merely the "prime minister" of his cabinet, as in parliamentary systems. Unable to accomplish their purposes through the cabinet, the Radicals retreated to their stronghold in the Senate.

3

In his Emancipation Proclamation of 1862, Lincoln again acted in his role as commander-in-chief during the absence of Congress on a highly political matter. The proclamation took the wind out of Radical sails. Chase, an abolitionist who should have been the most pleased, presented the gloomiest countenance.[4]

The November elections proved unfavorable to the administration and afforded an opportunity for new demonstrations of Radical strength. Their next blow was aimed at Seward, whose removal had by now become an important Radical objective. After a secret caucus on December 16, 1862, nine Republican senators were chosen to present the anti-Seward case to the president. Known as the Collamer Committee, its prepared statement to the chief executive in effect instructed him to remove Seward and all the Democratic generals, blaming them for causing most of the Union's military disgraces and for the recent Republican defeats at the polls. The committee also cautioned the president that his official political theories and policy would have to be based upon the "combined wisdom and deliberation" of himself and his "cabinet council."[5]

This was a clear challenge to Lincoln's presidential powers and a statement of the Radical interpretation of the constitutional functions of the cabinet. Anticipating the crisis, Seward handed an undated resignation to the president. Lincoln's dilemma was a serious one. How was he to keep one faction from destroying his coalition cabinet and yet himself remain master of the situation? The only answer was to create a counterdilemma for Chase, who was undoubtedly the principal anti-Seward conspirator.

Lincoln invited the Collamer Committee to return on the following evening and asked all members of the cabinet, with the exception of Seward, to attend. In the course of the conversations, Chase was put in the position of either agreeing with the complaints of his Senate cohorts or remaining loyal to his chief. He did neither too well and the next day submitted his resignation. Triumphantly, the president, with two key resignations in his hands and a show of great impartiality, asked both Seward and Chase to remain "in the public interest."[6] Lincoln had again frustrated a scheme to revise the presidential system. But he still had to contend with an aggressive Radical faction.

The Radicals were deterred, but not defeated. They continued their march on the presidency, which eventually led to a vindictive reconstruction policy for the South and the near-impeachment of a president.

4

The state and congressional returns of fall 1862 made it evident to Lincoln that he would have to look for support for the war through some combination of War Democrats and conservative Republicans. The president henceforth systematically avoided reference to the Republican party in his political statements. In local organizations, the name "Union" began to replace "Republican."[7] When the Sewardites, for example, found themselves no longer in control of the Republican party in New York, they began to build a new Union organization. The Union party name first came into prominence in the 1850s when men in both the Democratic and Whig parties thought of uniting behind the Compromise of 1850. Early in 1864, Weed wrote to Senator Morgan that he had been in consultation with prominent New York War Democrats and that all were convinced that an immediate reconstruction of parties, excluding Radicals and Copperheads, was feasible.[8]

The major national parties were objects of fragile loyalty up to the time of the Hayes-Tilden election in 1876. Such men as Edwin M. Stanton, Benjamin R. Butler, John A. Logan, Ulysses S. Grant, and Andrew Johnson, for example, were Democrats in 1860, but Republicans or Unionists by 1868. On the other side, Seward, Chase, Welles, Blair, and Bates—all members of Lincoln's Republican cabinet—were wholly out of sympathy with the political party that nominated Grant; Chase came close to getting the Democratic nomination to oppose Grant. The Blairs were the most notorious of the "party-hoppers," moving through the Democratic, Free Soil, and Republican parties, and back to the Democratic party within a period of twenty years.

By 1864, Seward, Morgan, and Weed were dedicated to Lincoln's re-election. The Cookes, Jay and Henry, on the other hand, were using the new federal banking organization and a small army of government war bond salesmen to promote the cause of Secretary of the Treasury Salmon P. Chase. Weed called Chase to task for converting the Treasury Department into a political machine.[9] National Chairman (now Senator) Morgan said sorrowfully that candidate Chase would probably not "subside" until after the nomination had been made.[10]

Despite his defeat in 1856, General John C. Fremont's name appeared regularly in the lists of presidential possibilities. He was a favorite of the Radicals. A Fremont-for-president movement started in Missouri in 1861, even though Lincoln had just removed the inept general from the command of the western military districts. Fremont clubs, particularly the ones in Illinois and New York, sent delegates to a Fremont nominating convention in Cleveland on May 31, 1864. About four hundred delegations attended; none were leading Radicals. The nominations were John C. Fremont of New York for president and former Tammany leader and Congressman John Cochrane of New York for vice-president. The ticket was a dubious one, judging from the fact that both candidates were from the same state, hence, under the Constitution, not able to serve together if elected.

As the Chase and Fremont causes fluctuated, the fortune of the Lincoln candidacy were similarly unsteady. Since the establishment of the national convention as a nominating system, no incumbent president had yet won a renomination

Henry J. Raymond arrived in New York shortly after graduation from the University of Vermont at the age of twenty. He applied for a job with Horace Greeley's *New Yorker*. Instead of hiring Raymond for the *New Yorker*, Greeley took him onto the *Tribune*. Raymond did not stay long with Greeley's paper, moving on to the New York *Courier and Enquirer* where he made a reputation as a newspaper editor. Raymond became acquainted with Thurlow Weed in 1848 when the latter was looking for a prospective purchaser of the *Albany Evening Journal*. The two became close friends after Raymond won election as a state assemblyman in 1849 and became speaker of the lower house shortly thereafter. In 1851, Raymond founded the *New York Times*. When Greeley departed from the old political alliance of Seward, Weed, and Greeley, Raymond took his place and won election as lieutenant governor of New York as a consequence. At the Republican convention in Pittsburgh, Pennsylvania, in 1856, Raymond wrote the party's first national platform. A dedicated Lincoln supporter, Rayond wrote a five-hundred-page *History of President Lincoln's Administration*, advance notices for which appeared on the eve of the 1864 national convention. Raymond attended the convention at the head of the New York delegation.[11]

followed by electoral success. The anti-Seward elements in New York were cool to Lincoln. During the early part of 1864, even though "Union Lincoln Associations" were growing in number, the entire New York press, with the notable exception of Henry J. Raymond's *Times*, was skeptical of the president's renomination.

Possibly to allow local pro-Lincoln Republican organizations time to put on their Union party caps, National Chairman Morgan delayed by two months convening the national committee to issue the national convention call. When the committee met on Washington's birthday in February 1864, it took upon itself the unusual prerogative of changing the party's name. The convention call did not use the word "Republican." The call was issued by "the Executive Committee created by the National Convention held at Chicago" in 1860. It was addressed to "all qualified voters who desire the unconditional maintenance of the Union," inviting them to a "Union National Convention."[12]

In its February 23 report of the meeting, Greeley's *New York Tribune* referred to the "National Republican Committee." On the same day, Raymond's *New York Times* designation was "National Union Committee," particularly noting that the call was broad enough to include any who wished to see "the rebellion" [Lincoln's term] suppressed. New York anti-Sewardites appealed to the executive committee of the national committee to postpone the 1864 national convention until September 1. Raymond's *New York Times* interpreted this as a scheme to defeat Lincoln. Postponement, it editorialized, would merely give the Fremont movement an opportunity to gather momentum.

Although most of the convention delegates were friendly to Lincoln, to demonstrate some degree of independence, they voted 440 to 4 to seat the Radical delegation from Missouri.[13] As chairman of the resolutions committee, Raymond read a brief platform, which was accepted unanimously. Simon Cameron of Pennsylvania moved Lincoln's nomination by acclamation. Raymond pointed out that a vote by delegation would give the nomination greater moral effect. Raymond's recommendation carried; the first ballot gave 484 votes for Lincoln and 22 from Missouri for General Grant.

A scramble for second place ensued, with the New York factional fight in dead center. Vice-President Hannibal Hamlin, Andrew Johnson, and Don M. Dickinson were the principal candidates. The Weed group opposed their fellow New Yorker, Dickinson, arguing that Andrew Johnson, a War Democrat, was the man to balance a Republican president on a Union party ticket. Exhortations from Weed, Preston King, and Raymond, pointed to Johnson's humble origins, war record, pure character, and ability to unite the New York factions. Their arguments proved effective. Johnson was named on one ballot. Johnson's antislavery letter of acceptance helped deflate the troublesome Fremont candidacy.[14]

Senator Morgan moved from the chairmanship of the national committee to chairmanship of the Union Executive Congressional Committee for the period of the campaign. Morgan's colleague, Henry J. Raymond, was chosen as the new chairman. Conspicuous for his absence from the Union national committee roster was Zachariah Chandler. The Radicals were boycotting this campaign. Marcus L. Ward of New Jersey and William Claflin of Massachusetts were two new names on the committee.

Probably after consultation with President Lincoln, Chairman Raymond was authorized to appoint a five-member executive committee with headquarters in New York. The executive committee, to become the center of significant factional controversy in 1866, consisted of William Claflin, Marcus L. Ward, George R. Senter of Ohio, Samuel A. Purviance of Pennsylvania, and John B. Clark of New Hampshire.[15]

5

The Radicals remained hostile, tacitly supporting the Fremont third-party nomination and stubbornly opposing the president's legislative program. On December 8, 1863, Lincoln had presented to Congress his plan for posthostilities reconstruction in the South. It offered full pardon, with a few exceptions in the higher ranks, to all who fought in the armies of the Confederacy on condition that they take an oath of allegiance to the United States government and agree to accept the presidential proclamations and congressional enactments relative to slavery. Whenever 10 percent of the citizens of a Southern state formed a government and applied for readmission, it would again become a part of the United States.

Lincoln's assumption was that the states of the Confederacy had never departed from the Union, but were conducting an insurrection. The Radicals considered the breach between the sections complete; readmission of Southern states was to be allowed only under the most stringent conditions. Bound up with these differences was the equally fundamental issue of the proper constitutional relationship between the executive branch and Congress in arriving at these decisions.

The Radicals put forward their own Congressional Plan, which declared that Confederate readmission was a matter for Congress, not the president, to decide. Henry Winter Davis and "Bluff Ben" Wade were the major spokesmen for the Congressional Plan. The Wade-Davis Bill was passed on July 2, 1864. Lincoln killed it with a pocket veto and, by presidential proclamation, put his own reconstruction plan into effect six days later. The Radicals were incensed. On August 5, a Wade-Davis manifesto declared Lincoln's proclamation a "stupid outrage on the legislative authority of the people," a gross encroachment of executive power, and an attempt to win rebel electoral votes for Lincoln.

The manifesto burst forth in the midst of the presidential campaign. On August 14, the anti-Seward contingent in New York started a movement to have Lincoln abdicate the nomination and have the party convene another convention in September. Greeley's *Tribune* supported the abdication proposal. National Chairman Raymond, in communication with state leaders everywhere, was beginning to believe that "we don't stand the ghost of a chance in November."[16] Even Thurlow Weed was telling the president that his re-election seemed impossible. Republican despondency was reaching its lowest when the news came on September 2 that Sherman had marched into Atlanta. The emotional lift was enough to sweep aside talk of a negotiated peace and carried the administration back into office.[17]

According to James G. Blaine's analysis of the political complexion of the Thirty-ninth Congress, the Senate elected with Lincoln in 1864 had 34 Republicans, 11 Democrats, and 5 "Administration Republicans." Blaine lists Edwin D. Morgan as a Republican and Henry J. Raymond as an Administration Republican.[18] The House had 135 Republicans, 41 Democrats, and 8 Administration Republicans. These categories were uncertain. During this period party labels were lightly held. Not even the editor of the *Congressional Directory*, Ben Perley Poore, presumed to record who was a Radical Republican, Conservative Republican, Administration Republican, Unionist, War Democrat, or Peace Democrat.

According to Blaine's assessment, in a Senate of 50 members, the 34 non-Administration Republicans were susceptible to pressure from the Radical faction; only 26 were needed for an absolute majority. Similarly, in the 184-member House of Representatives, 93 constituted a majority, but there were 135 non-Administration Republicans available to produce a majority. So long as the South's absent 22 Democratic senators and 58 Democratic representatives could be kept out of the count, the Radicals would be able to run Congress and the country on their own terms.

With political and military victories behind him, Lincoln proceeded to put into effect the Presidential Plan for Southern reconstruction. In this he had, for the moment, ample Congressional support. In February 1865, his supporters were able to bring about the defeat, 80 to 65, of a Radical bill declaring that no representative should be admitted from the rebel states until Congress gives its approval.

On the evening of April 14, Lincoln was assassinated. The following day Andrew Johnson became the third vice-president to succeed to the presidency. On May 26, 1865, the last Confederate army surrendered. Between May and December, Johnson appointed provisional governors for all the returning states. Conventions were held, state legislatures elected, senators and representatives chosen, and civil governments restored.

Partisan anomaly was now heaped upon factional paradox. With the cessation of hostilities, would Johnson be a Democrat, a Unionist, or a Republican? If the latter, which kind of Republican: conservative or Radical? His adoption of Lincoln's reconstruction policy, the glorification he received from the Democratic and Southern press, and the support given him by the conservative *New York Times* was sufficient to convince the Radicals—particularly Ben Wade and Zachariah Chandler, who had been on the Committee on the Conduct of the War with Johnson—that the president would never be one of them.

6

As early as August 1865, the Radicals began planning how to control the party machinery in Congress. The wiser men among the conservatives had no illusions about the quality of the foe. Morgan and Raymond wrote to their mentor, Thurlow Weed, warning that the Radicals would not have peace except on their own terms.[19] Throughout 1866, the *New York Times* did all it could to dissociate the president from the Democratic party, but the Democratic press clung to him resolutely. In addition to his activities as editor of the principal administration newspaper and as chairman of the Union national committee, Raymond was now a freshman congressman with the added duty of leading the meager administration forces in the House of Representatives. Raymond's Achilles' heel was his inexperience as a legislative tactician.

Just prior to the opening of Congress, a caucus of Republican and Union party legislators was held. A committee of seven was appointed to report appropriate resolutions to the caucus. Most of the members of this committee were Radicals. Thaddeus Stevens was selected as its chairman, Raymond was one of an unsuspecting minority. Stevens then presented a resolution calling for the appointment of a joint congressional committee of fifteen to inquire into the condition of the seceded states and to report whether all or any of them were entitled to representation in either house. The joint committee was to be permitted to report at any time. The entire Republican-Union caucus unanimously approved the resolution, and a joint committee was established on the first day of the new Congress. Eight of the fifteen members of the joint committee, soon called "The Directory," were Radicals.

Raymond and the conservatives had been taken in and were not long in realizing it. The Lincoln view had been that the Southern states never left the Union, hence there could be no doubt that they were entitled to representation in Congress. The caucus resolution reopened the entire question and the Radicals kept it open. Raymond and his colleagues tried to recover their fumble by attempting to have all matters pertaining to representation referred to the Committee on Elections, but the Radicals were not about to compromise. On December 18, Stevens, in a speech before the House, served notice that Southerners would not be readmitted to Congress until the supremacy of the Republican party was assured. Raymond made an eloquent but futile defense of the Lincoln-Johnson policy.

It was no longer Republican vs. Democrat, Unionist vs. Copperhead, but president vs. the Directory. Realizing this, those inveterate party builders, the Blairs, once again assumed the task of party reorganization, this time aimed at an alignment that would be moderate on Southern reconstruction and general economic policy and favorable to Andrew Johnson. According to the Blairs' biographer, "Driven from the Republican party by the Radicals, the Blairs were left adrift to cast about in the political waters of a troublous era. They were forced to reorganize a party or retire from public life. They had no intention of retiring."[20] Wisconsin Senator James R. Doolittle, long an ally of the Blairs, became the midwife of the new movement.

Legislative-executive relations began to take on the pace of political tennis: the Radicals passing legislation and the president returning vetoes. In March, after several vetoes, a Civil Rights Bill, making Blacks citizens and conferring large powers upon United States marshals, district attorneys, and judges to enforce their equal rights before the law, was sent to the president and returned with the usual veto. This time the Radicals moved with determination and design. A pair was broken; a pro-Johnson senator was unseated; persuasion and a relentless party whip were employed. Most important, three fence-sitting Republican senators finally were shoved into the Radical tent; William M. Stewart of

Nevada, Waitman T. Willey of West Virginia, and Edwin D. Morgan of New York. The critical and most influential vote was that of Senator Morgan and was greeted with great applause. Although an associate of Seward, Raymond, and Weed, all of whom were supporting Johnson, Morgan also had been a consistent champion of racial equality. Confronted with a choice between factional and ideological loyalties, he decided in favor of the latter, even at the cost of the president's prestige.

By spring of 1866, the president and the Directory were taking extreme positions. Even Chairman Raymond was moved to write to Thurlow Weed asking the venerable politician to exert a moderating influence on Johnson.[21] On the other hand, Senator James R. Doolittle was busily at work with the Blairs building a Johnson political organization and preparing for a pro-Johnson midterm national convention. Should it be an organization within the Democratic or the Union party? Or should it be a third party? Some former War Democrats had indicated their willingness to give way to Republican leadership in a new third party. Such Johnson Republicans as Raymond and Seward would support a Johnson party only if it grew up within the Union party organization.

Sponsors of the Union party midterm convention deemed it essential that National Chairman Raymond attend. After some delay in backing the convention, Seward advised the national chairman that since the object of the meeting was primarily consultation, Union men should attend in order to prevent its falling into the hands of the Copperheads, that is, the Democrats eager to conciliate the South. Raymond told the president that he would have nothing to do with the formation of a new party. However, if the convention were simply to seek the election of members of Congress favorable to the admission of loyal Southern representatives—War Democrats in some places, Union men in others, Raymond thought much good might be accomplished. The president replied, according to Raymond's version of the interview, that this was precisely what he desired: a loyal Congress, but no new party. The Union national chairman was thus prevailed upon to participate in this untried vehicle of titular leadership.[22]

William B. Reed of Philadelphia, working with Montgomery Blair and Senator Doolittle, took special pains to urge Democratic national committee chairman August Belmont, Tammany leader Fernando Wood, and Charles O'Connor to attend the forthcoming Johnson convention. For Belmont, the convention seemed an excellent opportunity to keep the president from going over completely to the Republicans. But he recognized the opportunity as more apparent than real. After all, Seward was backing the convention and the president was unwilling to commit himself politically that year to anything more than the election of a pro-Johnson Congress. Furthermore, Union National Chairman Raymond would be attending in a leading capacity. In short, there would be much risk and little reward for the Democrats. Belmont decided to stay away from Philadelphia.

Marcus L. Ward, a New Jersey candle manufacturer, entered active politics at about the age of forty-three as the Republicans were organizing their new party in his state. By the time the Civil War broke out, Ward was head of the party's state organization. Shortly thereafter he won national prominence for his sponsorship of a veterans aid service. He was elected governor in 1865. A year later, the Democrat who opposed him in the gubernatorial race led a New Jersey delegation into the pro-Johnson midterm convention, prompting Ward to join the countermoves of the Radicals.

The Johnson convention was called for August 14, 1866, by the National Union Executive Committee of Washington, a merger of the District of Columbia National Johnson Club and the National Union Club. Neither group was directly connected with the Union national committee. Raymond decided to attend the midterm pro-Johnson convention as an individual and not as an officer of the Union national committee.

From the standpoint of the Radicals, the Johnson midterm convention was the equivalent of organizing a new political party.[23] They went on the attack. William Dennison, James Harlan, and James Speed resigned from Johnson's cabinet. A Southern Loyalist Convention was set for September 3 to be held in Philadelphia. To give the impression of independent action, a separate convention of Northern Radicals was called for the same day in the same city.

Senator Doolittle presided at the Johnson convention and Raymond participated actively. The latter's leadership prevented the seating of three famous Copperhead Democrats: C.L. Vallandigham, Fernando Wood, and Henry Clay Dean. Raymond was also chief draftsman of the convention's declaration of principles and its address to the people. As it concluded, the convention established a national Union executive committee, a nine-member resident executive committee at Washington, and a large committee on finance. Charles Knap served as chairman of the latter two committees. Throughout the midterm congressional campaign, President Johnson was in close touch with the Knap Resident Committee, but completely ignored the National Union Executive Committee, upon one occasion refusing to give it an audience when it convened in Washington.[24]

On August 20, 1866, Samuel A. Purviance of Pennsylvania wrote to New Jersey's Governor Marcus L. Ward suggesting that "our Committee" should meet simultaneously with the Southern Loyalist convention in September to determine what action ought to be taken now that National Chairman Raymond had attached himself to "the new party." Purviance was fearful that the public might think the committee "had gone over" to the enemy along with Raymond.

"Mr. Raymond may possibly deserve to meet with us for the purpose of making a formal withdrawal."[25] Purviance did not make clear whether "our Committee" referred to the entire Union national committee or to its executive committee. Ward assumed it was the executive committee, heartily agreed with Purviance's recommendations, and forwarded them to other members of the executive committee: Governor Claflin and John B. Clark.

On August 21, John D. Defrees of Indiana, an old hand at party tactics, and three other committeemen published a call for a meeting of the Union Executive Committee in Philadelphia on September 3, the date of the Radical conventions. One of these committeemen subsequently denied that he had authorized the use of his name. On August 22, Greeley's *Tribune*, with extraordinary promptness, carried the call, and Defrees mailed copies to the members of the national committee. Greeley's feud with Raymond was now entering a new phase.

Raymond comprehended what lay ahead. On August 25, he issued his own notice for a meeting of the National Union Executive Committee in New York City on the same day fixed by the Radicals. This immediately brought a cutting public rebuke from Governor Ward, who wrote:

> You have deemed it wise and proper to abandon the great Union Republican party [*sic*] of the country, and to connect your name and influence with a new organization designed to destroy and defeat the cause with which I sympathize, and of which I am, in some small degree, a representative. Your public action has been such that I cannot acknowledge your right to use the title, under which the meeting has been called. . . . All who would respond to your call would be regarded as betraying the party they have ceased to represent.[26]

Governor Ward's participation gave added authority to the Radical maneuvers. In attendance at the convention of the Northern Radicals were Ward and Governors Andrews, Morton, Curtin, and Hawley; Senators Chandler, Wade, Lane, Morgan, Sprague, Wilson, and Cole; and Generals Butler, Burnside, Garfield, Geary, Schurz, and Schenck. James Speed was chairman for the Southern Loyalists. Both conventions adjourned with declarations supporting Congress against the president. Neither gathering appointed a standing committee to implement convention objectives following adjournment.[27] Permanent national organization was being taken care of in another way.

As the Radical conventions met in Philadelphia on September 3, two separate meetings of Union national committeemen were taking place in New York and Philadelphia. In New York, the gathering was in response to National Chairman Raymond's call. The only members to show up were Raymond, Secretary Sperry, Cuthbert Bullitt of Louisiana, T.G. Turner of Rhode Island, John B. Clark, William Claflin, and one or two others. Sperry charged that the Philadelphia meeting was illegal. All agreed that no meeting could function without a quorum. Claflin, taking the position of a middle-of-the-roader, recommended adjournment and suggested that the action then taking place in Philadelphia be ignored since that meeting had been called without proper authority, that is, action by the full national committee at a regular meeting. Raymond stated that he would retain the national committee funds and financial records until such time as a proper and legal transfer could take place if necessary.[28]

Fifteen committeemen appeared at the Philadelphia meeting, less than half the full national committee. They proceeded to pass several momentous resolutions. One expelled Raymond, Sperry, and Senter for having an "affiliation with [the Union party's] enemies." Another filled Sperry's place and called upon the New York State central committee to name a new national committeeman. Governor Ward was unanimously chosen national chairman. A committee was appointed to prepare an address to the nation, the draft of which was submitted by Horace Greeley to Chairman Ward during the next fortnight. Before the Philadelphia meeting adjourned, there was discussion of the money and records held by Raymond, but no decisions were reached; some $20,000 or more was involved.[29]

On September 5, two days after the action taken in Philadelphia, a state convention met in Syracuse, New York, steered by the omnipresent Horace Greeley. Characterized as a "new party movement" by Raymond's *New York Times*, this state convention endorsed the Philadelphia expulsion of Raymond and named Greeley as the state party's new representative. The Radicals had succeeded in cutting the ground from under Chairman Raymond and in taking the chairmanship away from the Republican conservatives.

7

The Radicals filled the halls of Congress as a result of impressive victories in the midterm elections. This enabled the Thirty-ninth Congress to place on the statute books a number of notorious laws: the first Reconstruction Act, the Tenure of Office Act, the Conduct of the Army Act, the second Reconstruction Act, the third Reconstruction Act, an act admitting North Carolina, and a joint resolution setting aside the 1868 electoral vote of Louisiana and other states.

The high point in the struggle between congressional and presidential leadership came with the impeachment trial of President Johnson during March, April, and May 1868. If they could control the South and Congress, the Radicals reasoned, why not the presidency? The president of the Senate was Ben Wade, next in line for the presidential succession since no vice-president was then in office. Two-thirds of the Senate was now anti-Johnson. All that was lacking was reasonable grounds for Johnson's impeachment and removal from office.

The Tenure of Office Act, curbing the president's power of removal by requiring the advice and consent of the Senate, was intended to protect Radical officeholders. It might serve equally well as grounds for impeachment. Secretary of War Stanton was removed in December 1867, after provoking a dispute with the president. The Senate refused to accept Johnson's reasons or acknowledge his right to remove Stanton from his cabinet. Johnson appointed General Ulysses S. Grant and persisted in regarding him as Stanton's legal successor. The president was then charged with violation of the Tenure of Office Act, and this became the basis for impeachment.

The Senate trial lasted from March 13 to May 26. The critical test vote was taken on May 16, only four days prior to the Union Republican national convention. Thirty-six votes were necessary to convict. Thirty-five senators voted for conviction and nineteen for acquittal. A single vote kept the presidency out of Radical hands, but the proceedings ended Johnson's renomination prospects.

When the national committee had met in December 1867 to prepare the convention call, Chairman Ward thought it should be referred to as the National Union convention. Horace Greeley disagreed, and the matter was momentarily set aside. The name Union Republican was the compromise. The Union Republican title continued in use until shortly after the 1872 national convention, at which time the original Republican designation was restored.

The Radicals had a second shot at Johnson at the Union Republican national convention. Early in 1866, when New York Democratic leaders had quietly begun a Grant-for-president movement, Thurlow Weed hastened to launch a huge public demonstration to pin the Republican label on the general. With equal speed, the Radical leaders took the Grant movement away from Weed. By October 1866, Grant was writing letters sympathetic to the Radicals.

In control of the national chairmanship, the Radicals soon made it clear that the conservatives would be barred from influence in the 1868 convention. Chairman Ward was among the most zealous in marshalling Grant delegates. The dramatic public break between the general and his former commander-in-chief, President Johnson, came when Grant refused to assume Stanton's place as secretary of war. This did no harm to the Grant-for-president cause. Grant was nominated without opposition, and elected.

The presidency now belonged to the Radicals, the major prize in a long effort. They had begun by capturing control of Congress, then the Republican party's national chairmanship and national convention, and finally the hero of the Civil War. Commenting on the Johnson impeachment episode, Walter Bagehot wrote:

> A hostile legislature and a hostile executive were so tied together, that the legislature tried, and tried in vain, to rid itself of the executive by accusing it of illegal practices. . . . This was the most striking instance of disunion between the President and the Congress that has ever yet occurred, and which probably will occur. Probably for many years the United States will have great and painful reason to remember that at the moment of all their history, when it was most important to them to collect and concentrate all the strength and wisdom of their policy on the pacification of the South, that policy was divided by a strife in the last degree unseemly and degrading. . . .[30]

8 | Stalwarts, Liberals, and Reconstruction among Factions

With Grant's election to the presidency in 1868, Radical control of the national government seemed unchallengeable. With such power, however, came opportunities for corruption and other excesses, but not without resistance and opposition. Liberal Republicans, Democrats seeking to reunite their Northern and Southern constituencies, and reformers of all political stripes contested the policies and personnel of the Directory, or Stalwarts as they were now called. Despite the transitional turmoil of the Reconstruction era, the Republicans were nevertheless able to hold the White House until 1884.

1

The unanimous nomination of Ulysses S. Grant by the Union Republican national convention in 1868 obscured a new factionalism perceptible in the close four-way battle for the vice-presidential nomination. Three of the four principal candidates were leading members of the Radical-controlled Congress. Ben Wade was the front-runner, Radical president of the Senate representing the interests of the Directory. Speaker Schuyler Colfax of Indiana was a moderate acceptable to both Radicals and conservatives. Senator Henry Wilson of Massachusetts, spokesman for New England Republicanism, came from a free-soil tradition that was increasingly dissatisfied with the tactics of the midwestern Radicals. The only major noncongressional candidate was Governor Reuben Fenton of New York, an eastern conservative who came from the Weed bailiwick. The first ballot gave Wade 147 votes, Fenton 126, Wilson 119, Colfax 115, and 114 votes to others. With Colfax and Wade each holding down a third of the convention's votes on the fifth ballot, Wilson's New England support swung to Colfax, giving him the nomination and the Radicals a resounding defeat.

During the convention, factional policy differences began to focus on currency and tariff legislation. The Radicals passed legislation requiring rapid

William Claflin, born in Massachusetts, moved to St. Louis as a young man and became a successful shoe manufacturer as well as an ardent member of the Free Soil party. Upon his return to Boston, his business brought him wealth and his free soilism a seat in the lower house of the state legislature. Claflin later was chosen chairman of the Republican state central committee and was elected lieutenant governor.

repayment of the war debt and retirement of the cheap currency issued during the war. To farmers this meant credit scarcity and price deflation, particularly in agricultural commodities. There were also lingering philosophical disagreements about the impeachment proceedings against President Johnson. Many Republicans failed to see a legitimate party need for the action, but did see how an impeachment could undermine a constitutional system so recently preserved at the cost of civil war. These issues persisted well beyond the convention.

Following the convention, the national committee, not unexpectedly, unanimously chose William Claflin to be national chairman. Claflin was, after all, a senior member of the national committee's executive committee, enjoying great public esteem. In 1866, Claflin was an intermediary between the Radical and conservative factions. He was also one of the New England leaders who swung the critical vote to Colfax. There is some evidence that the Republican practice of consulting the nominee before choosing the national chairman was begun on this occasion.[1] William E. Chandler, not related to Zachariah Chandler, became the new secretary.

Claflin was the undisputed leader of his state organization, nominated for governor just after he became national chairman. Of this nomination he wrote to Marcus Ward, "I had no such idea when I saw you in Chicago or I should not have taken the Chairmanship." Even his most uncompromising opponents stepped aside so that Claflin's gubernatorial nomination could be made unanimous.[2]

President Grant's first cabinet, with the notable exception of Hamilton Fish, became a collection of incompetent personal friends. Chairman Claflin, after being elected governor in Massachusetts, grieved for the predicament of his colleagues in Washington. The president refused to consult party leaders and withdrew into a political cocoon. In one critical case, the Senate rejected Grant's friend, A.T. Stewart, as secretary of the treasury on a minor technicality. The alternative recommended by the Radicals was George S. Boutwell of Massachusetts. Boutwell's appointment was a reminder to the new president that the Senate's victory over Andrew Johnson would not be used lightly. A more substantial test came when Grant recommended repeal of the Tenure of Office Act, which gave the Senate excessive control over federal patronage. Political bones were broken during this fracas and led to a surrender by Grant.

It did not take long for the more calculating Radicals to develop a strategy to meet the new circumstances. Why not keep Grant confined to his cocoon and *assume* the role of his inner circle? As a result, there emerged the notorious "Senatorial Clique," "Stalwart Cabal," or "Politicians" as the group was variously known. This inner circle of Republicans in the Senate came to dominate both Grant administrations. Its leaders included Roscoe Conkling of New York, Zachariah Chandler of Michigan, Simon Cameron of Pennsylvania, and Oliver P. Morton of Indiana, each not only a leader in the Senate, but also the boss of his state party organization. Together, these four controlled about ninety votes in the electoral college. They enjoyed the advantages of Morton's intellectual and oratorical talents, Conkling's social polish and commercial connections, Chandler's senatorial seniority and organizing genius, and Cameron's long experience with the more sordid side of partisan and electoral combat. The Stalwarts were also adept heirs of Radical legislative tactics.

The distribution of the federal patronage became an avalanche of promotions for Stalwart followers to the exclusion of nearly all other Republican interests. The appointment process and the smell of corruption in several states and around the presidency led Senators Carl Schurz, Charles Sumner, and Lyman Trumbull to assume the leadership of antiadministration Republicans. As reformers, they gave priority to the cause of civil service. They also stood for tariff reduction and for a liberal Southern policy—universal amnesty and home rule—in order to bring the turbulent, Klan-ridden South out of its economic, social, and political morass.

Hoping to strike a telling blow at these reform Republicans, Conkling tried to reorganize the New York City central committee by establishing his own. The object was to get rid of its chairman, Horace Greeley. Greeley's committee members refused to recognize the new committee and continued to function. When efforts were made at the 1871 state convention to conciliate the competing city committees, Conkling intervened to prevent a solution. The Greeley faction walked out, and the following year its members were active in the Liberal bolt from the Republican party.

Meanwhile, in Congress, independent Republicans encouraged several investigations of the administration. As these investigations began to reveal abuses, Greeley's *Tribune* became increasingly critical of Grant. Elsewhere, disgruntled local Republican factions—Schurz men in Missouri, Fenton Republicans in New York, Trumbull followers in Illinois, Sumner supporters in Massachusetts, the Julian-Defrees faction in Indiana, the Austin Blair group in Michigan, the Curtin-McClure alliance in Pennsylvania, and many others, all much neglected in the

William E. Chandler graduated from Harvard Law School in 1854 and immediately entered New Hampshire politics. In 1863, he became speaker of the state's house of representatives. Chandler won national renown as a pamphleteer and political manager during the campaign for Lincoln's re-election. In 1864, he was appointed solicitor and judge advocate general of the Navy Department by Lincoln. Three months later, he was elevated to first assistant secretary of the treasury by Johnson. In this office, he became a close political and personal friend of financier Jay Cooke. Chandler supported Grant as early as April 1866 and resigned as assistant secretary in November 1867.

---

distribution of federal patronage, began to refer to themselves as Liberal Republicans. Greeley preferred to wait and see how strong the new party movement would become before personally committing himself. The story of his nomination for president by the Liberal Republicans and the Democrats is told elsewhere.[3]

In the regular Republican camp, National Chairman Claflin had mixed feelings about the prospects of another four years of Grant, particularly since Grant's friend, General Ben Butler, had wormed his way into control of most of the federal patronage in Massachusetts. While Claflin publicly seemed happy to be named a vice-president of the Grant Club of Boston, privately he wrote to William E. Chandler, "the dose swallows hard."[4]

An uneventful Republican convention renominated Grant. It replaced Colfax with Henry Wilson of Massachusetts in a bid for liberal Republican support. With the new vice-presidential candidate from his own state, the unenthusiastic Claflin took a back seat on the national committee. Edwin D. Morgan, now sixty-one and one of the party's grand old men, returned to his former job as national chairman. Defeated for re-election to the Senate in 1869 and waiting out the Stalwart-Liberal factional struggle in the New York organization, Morgan had his eye on the upcoming 1875 senatorial race. Morgan's thirty-five-year-old cousin, John Pierpont Morgan, only a year earlier had created the partnership of Drexel, Morgan & Company. Free to give time and money to the national campaign, Edwin D. Morgan was happy with the opportunity to remain politically active. Although twice again defeated for elective office, Morgan's standing in the party remained high until his death in 1883.

William Chandler was re-elected national committee secretary. Zachariah Chandler headed the Republican Congressional Campaign Committee. It was the latter Chandler who launched a biting "bloody shirt" campaign against Greeley.

2

In many respects the return of Morgan, the first Republican national chairman, to that office sixteen years after the founding of the party symbolized a second beginning as a national political organization. By 1872, the party was beginning to accommodate to a broadly competitive national two-party system. Partially in response to the new competitiveness, the next two decades would see the rise of powerful state party machines in both parties and the modification of doctrines of presidential-congressional relations to take into account the influence of these machines.

The depression of 1868 was a spur to labor union organization in the East and the new Granger movement in the West. With Grant's re-election in 1872, the defecting Liberal Republicans lost not only their claim to committee prerogatives in Congress, but also voter support around the country. In the West, the losses were to the Democrats, the Grangers, and the Greenback party; in the East and South, primarily to the Democrats.[5]

The liberals who remained loyal to the Republican party took up their cudgels once again as the scandals of Grant's second administration were brought to light and civic reform became a major issue. The Republican Stalwarts held fast to their domination of Grant's regime, but became somewhat uneasy as the presidential bug bit several of the coalition's own leaders. There also began to emerge a third faction, the "Half Breeds," made up of moderate Republicans, particularly those of the Hayes type who sought to win Southern conservatism away from the Democratic party.

The Republican leadership was deeply divided on the "Southern Question." From Reconstruction on, various strategies for dealing with this question were tried and failed. The Radicals and the Stalwarts favored strict enforcement of Black voting rights and were undisturbed by the prevalence of carpetbag Southern state governments. Grant maintained troop garrisons in several Southern states. Republican campaign managers waved the "bloody shirt," symbol of the disloyalty of Southern Democrats who led the rebellion and the "untrustworthiness" of Northern Democrats seeking reconciliation with the former rebels. By 1876, it was evident to most Republican observers that the policy of military intervention had simply hardened Southern resentment, which had begun to take organized form as secret societies such as the Ku Klux Klan.

First steps in the liquidation of the harsh Reconstruction policy of the Stalwarts were taken in anticipation of the 1876 Republican national convention. In a letter to Pennsylvania Republican leaders, President Grant kept in doubt his availability for a third term. In the House of Representatives, Democrats and liberal Republicans joined to prevent such a prospect. By a vote of 233 to 18 in December 1875, the House resolved that any departure from the two-term tradition would be considered "unwise, unpatriotic, and fraught with peril to our free institutions."

Elsewhere, Republican Stalwarts were being defeated for office. Zachariah Chandler, eighteen years in the Senate and its senior member in continuous service, failed to be returned by Michigan in 1875. Grant appointed him secretary of the interior to keep him in Washington. National Chairman Morgan was beaten in his bid for the Senate. In 1877, seventy-six-year-old Simon Cameron was getting ready to turn the Pennsylvania dynasty over to his son, Don, resigning from the Senate in his favor. Only Conkling in New York and Morton in Indiana held out against the negative electoral tide.

There was no dearth of contenders for the Republican nomination in 1876. Preeminent was James G. Blaine, long in the limelight because of his personal feud with Conkling, his leadership of the Half Breeds, and his long service as Speaker of the House. However, the exposure of correspondence known as the Mulligan letters implicated Blaine with the malodorous Union Pacific Railroad and cast a pall over his candidacy. On the Stalwart side, Morton and Conkling were active. The fourth major contender was Benjamin Bristow, whom Grant had appointed as secretary of the treasury in 1874 as a concession to the reformers. Rutherford B. Hayes, John F. Hartranft, and Marshall Jewell were favorite sons in their respective states. Hayes had been a sober, efficient, but colorless governor of Ohio for two terms. Hartranft's candidacy was Simon Cameron's way of tying up Pennsylvania's 58 votes. Postmaster General Jewell, later national chairman, came from pivotal Connecticut.

Upon opening the national convention, Chairman Morgan spoke feelingly in favor of an "honest money" plank and wished the convention well in its hard task. The initial ballot gave Blaine 285, Morton 124, Bristow 113, Conkling 99, Hayes 61, Hartranft 58, Jewell 11, and Wheeler 3. For four ballots the situation remained unchanged. Deals were hard to make. The Stalwarts could not imagine any one of their number winning on a civil service reform platform such as the convention had adopted, nor would any one of them give a single vote to Blaine. The reformers could not go over to Blaine because the Mulligan letters had stained the armor and reputation of the "Plumed Knight."

When the time seemed ripe for a compromise, Ohio's Senator John Sherman threw his weight behind Governor Hayes. He concentrated pressure mainly on Zack Chandler. The Michigan delegation had been dividing its vote among Bristow, Blaine, and Hayes. On the fifth ballot, Michigan united upon Hayes. This influenced the sixth ballot, during which Hayes moved to second place behind Blaine. The Stalwarts, with the exception of Don Cameron, now went all out for Hayes. Cameron anticipated Blaine's inevitable try for the nomination four years later and cast half of Pennsylvania's votes for him. With a reform candidate from the Midwest at the head of the ticket, the selection of Wheeler for vice-president was a bow to the East and the Stalwarts.

The Stalwarts promptly began to maneuver for control of the presidential campaign organization. There was much tension about naming the officers of the national committee. Instead of electing them in Cincinnati at the close of the convention, the committee adjourned to meet in Philadelphia on July 8. Hayes wanted the chairmanship to go to his friend, Governor Noyes.[6] Conkling was working to win the position for his colleague, A.B. Cornell, who had just replaced Edwin D. Morgan as New York's national committeeman. The national committee meeting was spirited. At the second session a vote was taken: 22 for Zachariah Chandler, 11 for Noyes, and 10 for Cornell. On the second ballot, Chandler received an absolute majority of 26, although, surprisingly, Stalwarts from nearly every closely contested two-party state—Connecticut, Ohio, Illinois, Indiana, New York—had voted against him. William E. Chandler declined reelection as secretary.

Wrote Godkin in the *Nation*, "Just think of a Civil Service Reform party making Zack Chandler chairman of the Executive Committee!"[7] The press objected that Chandler could not be secretary of the interior and national party chairman at the same time; it was declared a glaring breach of faith in light of the entire movement to separate party from federal officeholding.

Carl Schurz, hoping to lead the Liberal Republicans back into the party, was annoyed; to him, Zack Chandler was *the* spoilsman. During the campaign, nonetheless, Schurz gave Hayes a strong endorsement. In July, the Liberal Republican national committee annulled its call for a national convention and endorsed the Hayes-Wheeler nominations.

The Republican campaign was completely in Zachariah Chandler's hands. His was the experience and the talent. This was possibly the roughest campaign in Chandler's long and rough career. Hayes never objected to Chandler's waving of "the bloody shirt" against the Democrats.

Chandler had to deal with the South's restiveness over continued military occupation in several states, a military circumstance attributed to Grant and the Republicans. Furthermore, Democratic candidate Samuel J. Tilden was too much of a master politician to be easily beaten. The greatest challenge occurred when it became evident that the outcome would be in dispute and might hang on one electoral college vote. Chandler carried forward the postelection battle with the forcefulness that characterized his entire political career. His claim of victory was immediate. His coordination of Republican strategy in Congress was astute. The Republican victory was confirmed four months later by the special electoral commission established by Congress. To assure Hayes' assumption of office and to avoid any crisis arising from popular demonstrations or violence, he was sworn in as president secretly on March 3, 1877, and publicly the next day.

It was therefore a rude blow for Chandler when President Hayes appointed Carl Schurz to replace him as head of the Department of Interior and then made Schurz' friend, Evarts, secretary of state. When the attorney generalship was offered to Chandler's son-in-law, Eugene Hale, it was firmly declined. Over Simon Cameron's vigorous protest, George W. McCrary replaced Don Cameron as secretary of war. However, when Stalwart Oliver P. Morton insisted that his lieutenant, Richard W. Thompson, be named secretary of the navy, Hayes agreed. As a first major step toward reincorporating the South into the Union, David M. Key, an ex-Confederate and Democrat, was made postmaster general.

Opposed by major segments of his party, Hayes nonetheless inaugurated a policy of troop withdrawal, nonintervention, and conciliation in the South. He went so far as to appoint Southern Democrats to important federal posts in that section. Hayes hoped that enough conservative Southern Democrats could be converted to the Republican party to give the "natural" two-party divisions in the electorate there a chance to come into being. If this could be brought about, it seemed to him worth abandonment of the carpetbaggers and Black leaders. But it did not come about. Republican congressmen, governors, and other Southern state officers were roundly rejected in the elections of 1878 and 1880.

The cabinet selections thoroughly alienated the Stalwarts. The withdrawal of federal troops from South Carolina and Louisiana, surrendering these states to local Democrats, led to the estrangement of Blaine. Hayes' Southern policy was his own, and he was condemned for it by both Stalwarts and Half Breeds. The leaders in control of the Republican national organization soon found themselves fully out of sympathy with the man they had worked so strenuously to place into the presidential chair. Hayes' support of civil service reform added to their uneasiness.

3

The Democrats won control of both houses of Congress in 1878, and the executive and legislative branches were soon bogged down in partisan antagonism. The most serious dispute was over currency policy. The expanding U.S. economy continued to demand more and more currency with which to carry on its business. To those who might benefit from cheap currency and inflation, the recent discovery and mining of a plentiful silver supply seemed a worthy monetary companion to the short supply of paper and gold. In 1876, Richard P. Bland, a Democratic representative from Missouri, and William B. Allison, a Republican senator from Iowa, provided the leadership of the pro-silver forces. Their Bland-Allison bill called for a bimetallic currency system. Hayes' veto of the bill assured that the issue of bimetallism would have the saliency of the tariff debate.

On January 1, 1879, the Resumption Act was scheduled to take effect. At this time, government bonds were to be redeemed. It was expected that the rush to redeem bonds would strain the Treasury Department's capacity to pay in specie. Nevertheless, Secretary of the Treasury John Sherman and President Hayes were determined to test the standing of federal credit by strictly complying with the provisions of the act. The great rush to turn worn-out paper into solid gold never materialized; the government's credit rating remained at a peak in all the money markets in the world. These positive developments embellished Sherman's reputation, and he moved into the front ranks of Republican aspirants for the presidency. By 1880, he had President Hayes' cordial but tacit support.[8]

After spending most of his retirement at home in Michigan, National Chairman Chandler was able to take the oath of office as senator once more in February 1879. Within a month he resumed his former stature as a leading national figure, but, in the midst of a fall stumping tour for his party, "Old Zack" died.

Chandler was the first national party chairman to die on the job. With the 1880 national convention only months away, his succession was of immediate concern to those who appreciated how factionally significant the chairmanship had become. In that strategic post, Chandler had in fact been working actively for the nomination of Blaine.[9]

The standing of another Stalwart was being tested at the same time. In a major patronage confrontation with President Hayes, Senator Conkling went down to defeat. As a consequence, Conkling's lieutenants, Chester A. Arthur and A.B. Cornell, were removed from federal posts in New York. Determined to reestablish his political prestige, Conkling put his organization in high gear and elected Cornell governor of New York. He then proceeded to mobilize for the national convention by advocating a third term for former President Grant. Joining the Grant movement were the Camerons of Pennsylvania and John A. Logan of Illinois, the latter replacing the recently deceased Oliver P. Morton in the Stalwart leadership. With this in mind, Grant's return to the United States from a world tour in September 1879 was followed by a well-orchestrated tour of the United States.

Secretary of the Treasury Sherman was in third place in the sweepstakes. Lacking in personal warmth, he could not compete with the glamor of either Blaine or Grant, but he had the makings of a compromise candidate. On good terms with both sides, he was related to Don Cameron through the latter's recent marriage to his niece, Elizabeth Bancroft Sherman.[10] Substantial sections of the business community favored Sherman as a sound-money man. As secretary of the treasury, Sherman also controlled a large patronage, whose beneficiaries were pleased to support his candidacy. On the negative side, Sherman was identified with a Republican administration that was unpopular among Republican leaders.

4

The choice of a national chairman to succeed Chandler was looked upon as one test of Grant's strength in the national committee, and the selection of a conven-

Andrew Jackson was beginning his second term when Don Cameron was born on May 14, 1833. His father, Simon, had been at various times a newspaper editor, a construction contractor, and a local banker. Simon Cameron was also a Jacksonian Democrat, credited with uniting the Pennsylvania delegation behind Van Buren for the vice-presidency at the first Democratic national convention in 1832. Don persuaded his father to allow him to learn the banking business and, starting out as a clerk at the Middletown Bank, eventually succeeded his father as its president. Shortly after his tour as Lincoln's minister to Russia, the elder Cameron returned to the Senate where, as a leader of the Radical and Stalwart inner circle, he continued in office until his resignation in favor of Don in 1877. The Republican caucus of the Pennsylvania legislature voted 133 to 1 to name Don Cameron as the successor to his father; he was re-elected for a full term in January 1879.

tion city was another. Conkling proposed New York's national committeeman, A.B. Cornell, who was then campaigning for governor, but who resigned as committeeman upon becoming governor. William Kemble, representing Pennsylvania, also stepped down. The New York and Pennsylvania seats were then taken by Thomas C. Platt and Donald Cameron. The latter became the new candidate of the Grant men for the chairmanship.[11] William P. Frye, Maine national committeeman, was Blaine's choice. It was argued in Cameron's favor that his tenure would be brief and that his duties would involve little more than opening the national convention.

When the chairmanship vote was taken on December 17, 1879, a Sherman-Grant combination mustered 22 votes out of 42 for the bare majority electing Cameron. John T. Averill of Minnesota received the 19 Blaine votes, and Thomas C. Platt was given 1 vote.[12]

The strategic role of the national chairman in the handling of national convention preparations was again demonstrated in 1880. The Republicans had dropped the unit rule at the 1876 convention. Anxious to reestablish the unit rule, Cameron, Conkling, and Logan pushed through resolutions at their respective state conventions in Pennsylvania, New York, and Illinois recommending this rule change. At the same time, they collectively put together 109 Grant delegates. As convention time neared, the 109 votes were augmented by the selection of 197 Stalwart delegates in other states, bringing the total to 306. If the unit rule were reinstated, 63 anti-Grant votes in New York, Pennsylvania, and Illinois would automatically be counted in the Grant column, bringing the new total to 369, 9 short of the 378 votes necessary to renominate the former president.

The Stalwart strategy was to have the national committee select a pro-Grant temporary convention chairman. This temporary chairman would be able to make a decision favoring the unit rule, which could probably be sustained by a floor vote. If the national committee did not choose a pro-Grant temporary chairman, one would be nominated from the floor. In the ensuing contest, National Chairman Cameron would be in a position to declare the unit rule in effect for the purpose of electing the temporary chairman.

The plan was discovered before the national committee met on May 31. An anti-Grant majority of twenty-seven members—mostly Blaine and Sherman men led by William E. Chandler and James A. Garfield, respectively—agreed that Cameron should be forced to show his hand. They asked him to entertain a motion against the unit rule. When the anti-unit-rule motion was made, Cameron refused to entertain it on grounds that the committee had no authority to act on the rules of the convention. Cameron held his ground defiantly, overruling all appeals from his decision. As the debate raged through the night, Cameron's removal was proposed. The attitude of the sergeant-at-arms, a Logan man from Illinois named Strong, was important to know, since it would be up to him to recognize either Cameron or Cameron's successor as the proper person to call the convention to order. Strong consulted legal counsel and, when he was advised that the national committee had the right to depose its chairman at any time, he announced that he would recognize whomever the national committee appointed.

Cameron's position was now untenable. The opposition to the Grant faction, however, was unwilling to invoke its removal power, believing that a public breach between the factions would be irreparable. A tentative compromise was reached in the selection of Senator George F. Hoar as temporary chairman of the convention. Hoar was not associated with any of the major candidates and was well known for his impartiality. The unit rule question now shifted to the convention's rules committee, where the Grant men submitted a minority report. When the convention voted down the minority report, 449 to 306, Grant's chances for renomination ended. Nevertheless, the stubborn 306 Grant votes remained united on every ballot throughout seven tumultuous days.[13]

With Grant as the candidate of the Stalwarts, Blaine of the Half Breeds, and Sherman of the administration, the situation was ripe for another dark horse. On January 6, 1880, James A. Garfield had been overwhelmingly elected senator from Ohio, with the support of John Sherman. Shortly after, Garfield began to receive letters, signed anonymously, suggesting that he was the man to be president. Governor Charles Foster of Ohio, a lukewarm Sherman supporter who was ready to move the Ohio delegation to another man at the right time, and Governor T.L. Pound of Wisconsin made it clear to Garfield as early as February that he was their favored candidate. In saying this, they had the support of Wharton

Barker, a Philadelphia banker and editor of the *Pennsylvania Monthly*, and Henry C. Lea, both leaders of the Union League headquartered in Philadelphia. Blaine's manager, William E. Chandler, was fully aware of the possibility of a Garfield nomination. On April 14, Chandler wrote to a colleague that "if (Garfield) is nominated I shall heartily support him."[14]

In the convention, Roscoe Conkling and James A. Garfield became rival leaders in the floor debates on numerous parliamentary questions. As chairman of the committee on rules, Garfield defended the abolition of the unit rule and supported the resolution that instructed the national committee to prepare a new plan of apportionment for discussion at the 1884 convention. Garfield opposed Conkling's resolution to eject from the convention any delegate who would not unqualifiedly pledge his support to the candidates nominated. It was also Garfield who placed John Sherman in nomination.

The first ballot for the presidential nomination gave Grant 304, Blaine 284, Sherman 93, Edmunds 34, Washburne 30, and Windom 10. Twenty-eight ballots were taken the first day, but the basic situation remained unchanged. Pennsylvania cast 2 votes for Garfield on the twenty-third ballot. On the thirty-fourth ballot, Governor Pound threw Wisconsin's 16 votes to Garfield. On the thirty-fifth ballot, Indiana gave him 27 more. On the thirty-sixth ballot practically the entire Blaine and Sherman support moved over to Garfield. New Yorker Chester A. Arthur was nominated for second place on the ticket, but even this did not conciliate the Conkling-Cameron-Logan coalition.

On June 8, the day on which the Republican convention adjourned, National Chairman Cameron called a "snap" meeting of the national committee; only the Stalwarts had been informed of the call. The intention was to choose the officers of the national committee without regard to Garfield's wishes. On hearing of this maneuver, William E. Chandler arrived in time to prevent further action. Cameron's rash behavior before and after the convention caused much concern about his future in the chairmanship and in the campaign.

William E. Chandler was the best qualified to comment on these concerns. "I trust that you will give a little personal thought to the organization of the National Committee," he wrote to the nominee, "and that by the first of July Mr. [W.C.] Cooper [Ohio's national committeeman and a friend of Garfield] will have ready a wise and acceptable programme." Chandler categorically opposed the re-election of Cameron and referred to the snap meeting as a "direct violation of the understanding." "After the concession of Arthur's nomination further subserviency to the bosses would be unwise and would gain no votes," he wrote, adding:

> It is difficult to say what is the best organization of the Committee. The chairmanship has come to assume exaggerated proportions since Secretary [Zachariah] Chandler held the place. . . . Declining to be Chairman of the Committee myself, I only want to prevent a bad organization.[15]

Marshall Jewell entered Connecticut politics shortly after his family's tannery interests prospered between 1861 and 1865 because of the wartime demand for leather. He won election as governor in 1869 after several unsuccessful attempts. Jewell helped carry his closely contested state for Grant in 1868 and again in 1872, in the latter years serving on the executive committee of the national committee. He was rewarded in 1873 with appointment as minister to Russia. Shortly thereafter he became postmaster general, a position whose patronage gave him substantial connections with party leaders throughout the nation and familiarity with the party's problems in the South. When he failed to receive a position in the Hayes cabinet, Jewell went into semiretirement. He absented himself from the national convention of 1880 because of his former service in Grant's cabinet and his declared opposition to a third term. Nevertheless, Jewell received a substantial number of votes in the vice-presidential balloting.

Chandler thought the committee's field of action would be relatively limited in this campaign since Ohio, as the candidate's home state, would take care of itself, and Arthur would undoubtedly be helpful in New York, New Jersey, and Connecticut.[16]

To a letter Chandler wrote Marshall Jewell of Connecticut, Jewell replied:

> I quite agree with you on Committee matters. We must keep Cameron and Logan to work in harmony but hardly want them as Chairman. Governor Dennison suggested [Charles] Foster. Not a bad idea either. You are really the only fit person for it. I don't want it and hope not to have to take it though perhaps if you and the others of my friends say so I will do it. But we must have an A 1 Secretary. There is no Congressional Committee now or corps of clerks to get out documents in Washington.[17]

J.M. Forbes, the committeeman from Massachusetts, also gave his opinion to Garfield.

> After our late experience with the Conkling Bosses in the Committee, it is not safe in my judgment nor quite consistent with self respect to leave Senator Cameron in the Chair—but we need not make war on them. The Chairman should represent those who beat them at Chicago.[18]

Garfield agreed that it would be necessary to make a peace offering to the Conkling-Cameron-Logan group. He met with Cameron in Harrisburg to discuss the matter. Word got out to other members of the national committee, and many became "pretty stark mad about the prospect of serving under C." Fortunately, Cameron declined on June 28 for reasons of health.[19] This left Garfield free to think of persons from more friendly sources.

Eugene Hale, Marshall Jewell, and J.M. Forbes suggested William Chandler, but the latter categorically refused.[20] Forbes also brought up Foster's name, querying, "What think you of him with a good executive committee whose chairman might generally represent the committee in New York?"[21] Chandler in turn recommended Jewell, to which Forbes responded:

> I have a letter from Hale which looks as if he would take the chairmanship if properly offered—but you no doubt see obstacles. [Probably a reference to Hale's close affiliation with Blaine.] As to Governor Jewell—as a last resort— I should accept your judgment—but should as a figurehead prefer Halsey [George E. Halsey of New Jersey]. . . . Jewell says he will not take an active part.[22]

Blaine sent a belated warning: "Hope you will not elect C [Cameron] for Chairman."[23]

Garfield finally wrote to the Ohio national committeeman, Charles Foster, offering "some suggestions":

> I understood that it has been the custom of the Committee to consult the candidates on the National ticket in reference to the selection of Chairman and Secretary because of the somewhat close and confidential relation which must exist between these officers and the candidates in the conduct of the campaign.[24]

Calling attention to the fact that all the national committeemen were chosen at the convention *before* the nomination was made, Garfield pointed to the lack of organic relation between himself and the national committee and the limitations upon his recommending a chairman. He hastened to add, however, that he felt sure "all are anxious to make the ticket successful." Since the two most rigorously contested centers were the New York-Connecticut-New Jersey region and Indiana, Garfield felt that the campaign chairman should be selected "with a view to his familiarity with the political elements in that quarter [New York], and his general acquaintance with the leading Republicans of the whole country." Not knowing whether the committee wished him to make a positive selection, he listed four men as suitable: Eugene Hale, William E. Chandler, Richard C. McCormick, and Marshall Jewell, adding, "I shall be glad if the Committee can secure the services of Thomas C. Platt as secretary. His acquaintance with the political elements in the State of New York would make his services of great value." [25]

At the national committee meeting on July 1, Foster moved that the temporary chairman, Jewell, appoint a committee of five to make recommendations on permanent organization. Jewell appointed Charles Foster of Ohio, William E. Chandler of New Hampshire, John M. Forbes of Massachusetts, John A. Logan of Illinois, and Stephen W. Dorsey of Arkansas. These men met in an adjoining room for over an hour and finally postponed their report until the following morning.

After Cameron withdrew, the Conkling forces made a stand for Platt to be chairman. Of the four men suggested by Garfield, only Jewell had expressed any inclination to accept; Foster, Chandler, and Forbes insisted that Jewell receive the position. As a concession to the minority faction, Logan was permitted to name the national committee secretary. He named Stephen W. Dorsey.

Dorsey was known to be "a politician of the cheapest type." He would be among the principals accused of the Star Route frauds the following year. William Chandler, sophisticated in the ways of his adversaries and in the importance of the secretary during the campaign, demanded that Dorsey pledge not to "annoy" (i.e., blackmail) the candidate if chosen for this important campaign position. Dorsey gave his word, which eventually proved worthless. At the meeting next day, the selections were confirmed. [26]

Almost immediately, Dorsey, with Conkling's connivance, embarked upon a high-handed and successful attempt to undermine Jewell's management of the campaign. Jewell found himself competing with Dorsey for control of the details and losing. Stalwarts circumvented him and dealt directly with Dorsey. Wrote Richard C. McCormick to William Chandler, "Jewell has been badly used and is a model of patience to submit without making a row."[27]

In the midst of the campaign, Conkling insisted upon assurances from Garfield that the New York organization would be treated well in the distribution of Federal patronage. Dorsey, Chandler, and others recommended that Garfield make the trip from Ohio to New York, ostensibly to consult with the national committee at its August 5 meeting. Jewell was extremely uncertain about the wisdom of the trip, and Garfield was inclined to agree with him. The nominee eventually did go to New York for the national committee meeting. Conkling absented himself lest he be blamed for any arrangements made. Garfield met with Morton, Arthur, Platt, and Crowley. This resulted in Morton's assumption of the chairmanship of the finance subcommittee of the national committee. Subsequently, Conkling made himself available for extensive speaking engagements.

The Maine election took place in September and those in Ohio and Indiana in October. Jewell told Garfield that Blaine would undoubtedly take care of Maine and that "the great fight is in Indiana" where it is "mainly a question of finances." He indicated that he had secret information that the Democrats had already sent "roughs" and "repeaters" from Baltimore.[28] Maine showed a Democratic trend, and Blaine charged that the Democrats had sent $70,000 to $100,000 to that state only four days before the election and were generally using money as never before. Jewell, ever hopeful, felt that a defeat in Maine would stir businessmen to open their purses at last. He reported that Wharton Barker was active among Union Leaguers in Philadelphia: "They will raise enough money to carry that state."[29]

Garfield was elected to the presidency in November 1880 despite the prolonged dragging of Stalwart feet during the campaign. Significantly, he did not carry a single Southern state.

5

Obligated to the Sherman and Blaine delegates for his nomination, Garfield's plan was to distribute the federal patronage so as to draw the Blaine forces closer to his administration and, by so doing, outweigh the Stalwart leadership. Patronage distribution rapidly became a free-for-all. The lush patronage post of collector of the Port of New York went to a Blaine man, whereupon Conkling and Platt resigned from the United States Senate in protest. Garfield's postmaster general investigated persons extracting exorbitant fees for carrying the mails, and found National Committee Secretary Dorsey, a Stalwart, among them. Completely ignored in the patronage and the rest of the excitement was National Chairman Jewell, who returned to retirement with the complaint: "I see no object in my going on and paying money for politics. All I get is criticisms. So I have called a halt."[30]

As tension between Garfield and the Stalwarts reached a shrill pitch, Garfield was shot by Charles Guiteau, a Stalwart office seeker, and two months later died.

Chester A. Arthur assumed the presidency on September 19, 1881, under the most difficult circumstances. An experienced politician, he moved rapidly toward recombination of factional alliances. In so doing, he surprised many, removed much of the cloud of suspicion that hung over his rise to the presidency, and improved his chances for nomination in his own right in 1884. Arthur made peace with the Republican reform element by his endorsement of civil service legislation. He called a Blaine man, William E. Chandler, into his cabinet as secretary of the navy, and together they struggled with the declining fortunes of the Republican party in the South.

Both Garfield and Arthur took steps to set aside Hayes' conciliatory attitude toward the conservative Democrats in the South. Instead, they placed their hope on the long-term development of Southern business interests and the education of Southern youth. Garfield and Arthur also began to abandon the Southern Black leadership and the defense of Black suffrage. At about this time, radical populists among the Democrats, dissatisfied with the leadership of Democratic conservatives, began to defect in nearly every state in the South and to organize independent parties. To the astonishment of regular Republicans in the North, President Arthur and William E. Chandler, who had castigated Hayes for his conciliatory policy, adopted a strategy of alliance with these independent movements.

During Arthur's administration, another problem of major importance to the Republican national party arose. What should be the voting strength apportioned to the Southern delegations at the Republican national conventions? Arthur, seeking renomination in 1884, resisted all proposals to reduce Southern voting strength. By 1888, Southern rotten borough* representation was an established feature of Republican conventions, even as Republican hopes of fostering the vote for their party in the South were all but abandoned.[31]

While new electoral alliances were explored with the Southern independents bolting from the Democratic party, federal patronage was used to strengthen established Republican forces in order to keep Southern delegations in President Arthur's corner in the national committee and at the next national convention. Alternatively, the insatiable patronage appetite of the Stalwarts continued to be fed with crumbs. Relations between Arthur and Conkling became extremely strained, the latter's usual aggressiveness inhibited only by the Stalwart affiliation of Garfield's assassin and the reflection it cast on the Stalwarts generally.

National Chairman Jewell died on February 10, 1883. Recalling the consequences of hasty decision on the Zachariah Chandler succession, the national committee moved slowly this time, not meeting to choose a new chairman until ten months after the vacancy occurred. Secretary of the Navy Chandler again seemed the man most suited for the job, but his official position ruled him out. At first the Arthur leaders put up John M. Forbes of Massachusetts, but the pro-Arthur committeemen from the South raised objections to anyone from the home of abolitionism. The Logan following united on ex-Senator J.B. Chaffee. The Blaine leaders had no candidate.

When the national committee met, its first business was the selection of Chicago as the convention city. In the voting it became evident that President Arthur's supporters were facing a Blaine-Logan alliance. Having dropped Forbes as their candidate for chairman, the Arthur men recommended Senator Dwight M. Sabin of Minnesota, who had not yet become identified in the public mind with any faction.

The Southern committee members had a great deal of difficulty accepting Sabin. Additionally, the Southerners were being helped by Logan in defeating efforts to decrease Southern representation at the national convention; they felt constrained to await Logan's word on the chairmanship. In the midst of the maneuvering, the Logan representative withdrew Chaffee's name and agreed to vote for Sabin "in the interest of harmony."[32] The uncommitted Blaine men and the Southern members fell into line, making the election by acclamation.

---

*A term from English history and usage, rotten boroughs were grossly overrepresented districts, often with almost no inhabitants.

A manufacturer of railroad cars and agricultural machinery in his home state, Dwight M. Sabin's efforts in politics won for him in 1876 the chairmanship of the Minnesota Republican state committee, an important post in the politics of the Northwest. On the executive committee of the national committee during the Garfield campaign, Sabin spent much time in New York City where Arthur, Conkling, and other Stalwarts came to know him well.

Sabin commented: "I am doubtless as much surprised as the country at large will be." Logan's supporters later commented that the choice of Chicago for the convention would offset any administration advantages gained by Sabin's election.[33]

At the next national committee meeting in June 1884, a combination of Blaine-Logan votes prevailed in giving the convention's temporary chairmanship to Powell Clayton.[34]

Conspicuous in his absence from the 1884 national convention was William E. Chandler. It had been expected that he would be President Arthur's principal manager, but Chandler's divided loyalties kept him away. He had been on the Blaine-for-president trail long before Arthur became his chief.

The Arthur convention management apparently was "a botch from beginning to end."[35] Even National Chairman Sabin was unable to deliver any of his delegation's votes except his own to Arthur. Arthur's managers found temporary allies in the reform wing. The independent Republicans were dead set against Blaine. When Chairman Sabin nominated Powell Clayton for temporary presiding officer, the reformers joined the Arthur men in choosing John Lynch of Mississippi from the floor. The vote, 424 to 384, revealed Sherman and Logan support for Lynch, but this was the extent to which the anti-Blaine forces could cooperate. The delegates from the Southern states gave Arthur a hard core of 195 votes, barely one-fourth the membership in the convention; 411 votes were necessary to nominate.

When the third ballot had been completed, the vote was Blaine 375, Arthur 274, Edmunds 69, Logan 53, Sherman 25, and a scattering for others. Tom Platt rocked the convention when he suddenly declared that "it was Blaine's turn now," casting 28 New York votes for Conkling's old rival. Platt, assuming the position in New York politics left vacant by Conkling's retirement, was not willing to sacrifice new opportunities for old feuds. On the fourth ballot, the Logan men from Illinois trumped with 34 votes to give Blaine the prize. Logan received the vice-presidential nomination.

During the postconvention speculation regarding the chairmanship, Stephen B. Elkins, Blaine's convention manager, was thought to be the most prominent

Benjamin Franklin Jones was born sixty years earlier in Washington County, Pennsylvania, Blaine's birthplace and boyhood home. Jones' main political experience prior to 1884 was his work with the American Iron and Steel Association, of which he later became president, and in the cause of the protective tariff. Although not a delegate, Jones attended the 1884 national convention, actively promoted the Blaine cause, and became Pennsylvania's national committeeman during the proceedings.

possibility. To the independent Republicans, however, Elkins represented the quintessence of corrupt politics.[36] Instead, Blaine pulled another candidate out of the hat: Benjamin Franklin Jones, senior partner in Jones, Laughlin & Company (later Jones & Laughlin Steel Company of Pittsburgh). When he was announced as Blaine's choice for chairman, Jones declared, by way of explanation, that the nominee and he had been personal friends for over thirty years, reaching back to Blaine's boyhood in Pennsylvania.

The Republican press received his selection with favor, characterizing him as "a business man of the highest character and of the soundest judgment . . . free from the objections which would have been urged to a mere politician."[37] The Republican party was interested in business prosperity. Its new chairman was presumed to represent the best in the business community.

The campaign witnessed an important Republican factional development. Independent and reform Republicans simply refused to go along with the Blaine candidacy. An organizational meeting at New York was called for July 22 by the Independent Republican Committees of New York, Boston, New Haven, and Buffalo. George William Curtis presided; the conference rejected third-party strategies. The "Mugwumps," as they were called, decided to attack their party's nominee from within the party. Therefore, as Democratic orators and press hacked away at Blaine's personal record, the Mugwumps joined in. The Mugwumps uncovered new Mulligan letters, reviving the charges that had foreclosed Blaine's nomination in 1876.

The close margin of Blaine's defeat set loose a torrent of recrimination among Republican politicians. Most vituperative was Chairman Jones. During a trip to New York in December, the national chairman "intervened" openly in local politics by declaring himself opposed to former President Arthur's candidacy for New York's Senate seat; Arthur's free trade views were what made him "unacceptable." Jones went on to accuse President Arthur and his cabinet members of failure to support the Blaine ticket, thrice avoiding political conferences with Jones himself, making no contributions to the national committee, and allowing only one member of the administration to make a pro-Blaine speech.[38]

The charges created a sensation and were greeted with denials and attacks upon Jones for making "unjust" complaints and for "indecent" participation in New York affairs. Secretary of the Navy William E. Chandler reminded Jones that as a political "unknown" who had led his party to defeat, he might do well to remain silent. Whereupon Jones repeated his charges and added that he did not think much of Chandler either, nor of Chandler's assistance during the campaign.[39]

In a *Chicago Tribune* interview a month earlier, Chairman Jones more calmly had observed that the national committee would wind up its campaign business with all bills paid, contrary to popular report. In subsequently discussing the election results, he confessed his surprise at the size of the independent vote and attributed the loss of New York to the Burchard incident. What of Blaine's chances in 1888? "I doubt that Blaine will ever run again," responded Jones.[40] Blaine himself told friends that he considered the campaign a disaster "personally, politically, pecuniarily."[41]

For Republicans in general, the defeat meant the loss of the presidency for the first time in a quarter of a century and the total loss of the Solid South. The "Plumed Knight" turned to travel in Europe and the preparation of the second volume of his *Twenty Years of Congress*.

Part III
Stabilizing the Pinnacle

9 | Party Elders as National Chairmen

As president, Grover Cleveland gave little attention to party organization, least of all to the national chairmanship. The chairmanship now seemed to be an honorific offering to older leaders and, at times, an immobilized hostage to a faction. The active management of presidential campaigns became the work of the nominee and his intimate friends, as in the cases of Grover Cleveland and William Jennings Bryan. Relatively minor aspects of the national committee's functions, such as the selection of convention dates and locations, became the testing grounds of factional strength.

1

After the elections of November 1881, President-elect Cleveland gave places in his cabinet to his personal managers, Daniel Manning and William C. Whitney. Manning had served as Cleveland's principal link to the Tilden men. He accepted the treasury post, but ill health forced him to relinquish it after two years. Whitney was appointed secretary of the navy over the opposition of anticorporation western leaders, who argued that Cleveland was showing excessive favor to the moneyed interests of the East. For a brief time, National Chairman Barnum's friends boomed his name for the cabinet, but Cleveland never gave this possibility much thought. Arthur Pue Gorman continued as senator from Maryland; his growing influence in the distribution of federal patronage and his participation in the determination of tariff and currency policy assured him a large future in Democratic politics.

In his annual message of December 1885, the president asked that the Bland-Allison law, requiring the coinage of a fixed amount of silver, be terminated. The treasury was paying out millions in gold, the long-standing basis of the nation's currency, in exchange for equivalent millons of the more slowly circulating silver coin. This policy presented a constant threat to the treasury's stock of gold, to business confidence, and to the savings of the thrifty Americans, Cleveland argued. The issue remained a live one, with Congress declining to act upon the president's recommendations.

Cleveland's policy toward the tariff, expressed in his annual message of December 1887, raised factional troubles to a high pitch within the party. The surplus of federal revenues over expenditures had been ignored for too long. Cleveland decided to devote his entire annual message to the one issue of tariff revision. As he prepared the message, he heard important voices pro and con, cautioning or encouraging: the Randalls, the Gormans, and the Barnums of the party arrayed against the Carlisles, the Hewitts, and the Scotts. William C. Whitney, with an eye to the 1888 presidential contest, advised the president to "take it easy" or to postpone the issue, but the president did not heed.[1]

Cleveland's tariff message of December 6, 1887, set the topic and the tone of national politics for the following presidential year. It was substantive in dealing with a real problem that affected many constituencies. It was Jacksonian in its broad emotional appeal to "the masses" to unite against "the interests." In some ways, it was a campaign address that confirmed Cleveland's availability for renomination in 1888 without his appearing to seek it. The message gave him the political initiative, and debate proceeded on his terms and around his name. Whitney admitted that "it was a winning issue." "Your position," he told the president, "has been greatly raised."[2]

As soon as the message reached Congress and the public, James G. Blaine, traveling in Paris, declared his disapproval. Vacationing in Europe, the Republican titular leader reaffirmed the principle of protection as Republican doctrine. Since Blaine was considered the logical choice for renomination by the next Republican convention, his statements made the issue seem to be a personal one between Cleveland and himself. Meanwhile, in Congress, the Mills Tariff Reduction Bill was introduced and bandied about until mid-July.

The protectionists in the Democratic party were not idle or reluctant to take up the challenge of Cleveland's tariff message. Senator Gorman had a great deal to say during the next meeting of the national committee on February 22, 1888, and, with Barnum in the chair, the opportunity to say it. Nothing was said directly about the tariff message, but the debate over the choice of convention date and place was unusually protracted. Gorman moved that the convention be held late, on July 3. Several other dates were proposed. William L. Scott, as the committeeman closest to the Cleveland administration, tried to prevent a clear demonstration of Gorman's strength in the committee. When the final ballot was cast, however, Gorman's July 3 was preferred over June 5 by a vote of 28 to 19.

The choice of a convention city required fourteen ballots. The committee was evenly divided among three cities: San Francisco, Chicago, and St. Louis. Gorman led the fight for San Francisco, Scott was for Chicago. An overnight recess was taken after the eleventh ballot. When the count remained unchanged next morning on the twelfth ballot, Scott moved to reconsider the convention date, but lost 24 to 23. On the thirteenth ballot it was still San Francisco 17, Chicago 16, and St. Louis 13. However, on the fourteenth, 3 Chicago votes shifted to St. Louis and nearly all the San Francisco votes followed. Scott then moved to reconsider the date, and June 5 was chosen, 29 to 17.[3]

Thus, the Cleveland group had its way on the convention date, but not without the size of the protectionist opposition being revealed. While Gorman acknowledged that Cleveland's renomination was a foregone conclusion, he was well aware that there were the issues of the platform, campaign management, and postelection patronage over which to bargain further.

Meanwhile, in January 1888, the Cleveland forces in Pennsylvania demonstrated their strength by unseating the protectionist state chairman, Representative Samuel J. Randall, and replacing him with William L. Scott, leader of the tariff reform faction. The Cleveland-reductionist forces were gathering themselves successfully.

The protectionist-reductionist dispute went forward in the national convention's resolutions committee. Editor Henry Watterson, leading the low-tariff wing, was elected committee chairman, beating Gorman by the close vote of 22 to 20.[4]

Gorman now set aside his protectionist cloak and cast himself in the role of mediator between the factions. Cleveland had given Gorman a draft tariff plank that avoided reference to the Mills Bill, then still pending congressional decision. The draft was written in such moderate language as to avoid putting the president out on a limb as a free trader. Gorman, without revealing its authorship, showed it to Randall, the leader of the extreme protectionists, who remarked that it suited him but that "the Cleveland crowd would kick." Gorman said he thought he could manage them.[5]

The convention took the unusual step of renominating Cleveland first and then receiving the report of the platform committee. The moderation displayed by Cleveland and Gorman notwithstanding, the reductionists put a strong tariff plank into the platform, and, by a separate resolution, the convention endorsed the Mills Bill.

"The first important questions to be settled are the selection of the leader of the National Committee and [the New York] State Executive Committee," Cleveland observed. "If anyone has any very clear ideas on these subjects, I am not aware of it."[6] When the national committee meeting of June 26 commenced, Gorman proposed the immediate election of a national chairman. The Cleveland spokesman, Scott, requested postponement. In a long speech, he pointed out that it was not of overshadowing importance who was chairman of the full committee, for that body did not have very much to do in the campaign. The really important thing, he declared, was the makeup of the executive committee. The chairman of this committee should be someone who could take active personal

The son of a Presbyterian minister, Calvin Brice earned an outstanding reputation as a corporation lawyer in the Cincinnati bar before he had reached his mid-twenties. At that age he turned his talents to railroad financing and management, supplementing this with stockholding interests in banks, mining, and public utilities. Brice participated only intermittently in Ohio party politics before 1888, acting as a Tilden elector in 1876 and a Cleveland elector in 1884. Actually, after 1884 he spent most of the year at his New York City home, a fact that the Republican press played up when he ran for the Senate from Ohio in 1890. Between 1884 and 1888, Brice became keenly interested in public office. His long association with vice-presidential nominee Thurman in railroad development and his social relations with such national political figures as Whitney, Gorman, and others while living in New York apparently whetted his political appetite. The incumbent senator from Ohio, Henry B. Payne, father-in-law of William C. Whitney, was about to retire from politics because of advanced age. Payne and Thurman agreed that Brice should inherit the senatorial toga.

charge of the canvass and devote his whole time to it. There was a brief adjournment during which Scott learned that most of the committeemen favored the retention of Barnum as chairman. With no other candidate coming from Cleveland, Scott acquiesced, and Barnum was re-elected by acclamation.[7]

In 1884, the executive committee managed the campaign, but this time a separate campaign committee was created by the national committee. National Chairman Barnum served on it *ex officio* and was authorized to select the other eight members. The campaign committee was also authorized to select its chairman either from its own members, the membership of the national committee, or "any other person" not a member of either of these.[8] The precedent was now formally set for a nominee to choose his campaign manager. Among those on the campaign committee were Gorman, Scott, and the committeeman from Ohio, Calvin Brice.

South Carolina's Dawson sounded out Barnum about focusing the campaign on the tariff issue. Barnum "neither assented or [*sic*] dissented." Dawson's concern was to find a campaign manager who could handle the issue "well." He also assured President Cleveland that "Mr. Gorman had refused point blank to be chairman of the committee and assured me that he would not occupy any official position in this campaign." Barnum was not interested and was planning to concentrate his energies in Connecticut and New Jersey, hoping to carry them "by the free use of money, in a legitimate way of course." Brice was not the kind of man, Dawson added, who could bother with the menial details of a literary bureau. Others were also limited in different ways, according to the South Carolinian.[9]

The choice finally narrowed to Calvin Brice. Vice-presidential candidate Thurman and Senator Gorman warmly recommended the lawyer-railroad promoter. While Brice shared the general protectionist attitudes of the majority of the business leaders of his day, he apparently had issued no controversial public statements on the subject. A White House conference was called for Sunday morning, July 15. Lamont asked Barnum to have Brice attend. At the appointed time, Barnum, Brice, Whitney, and Scott were greeted by Colonel Lamont and ushered into the president's study. There the six men conferred most of the day.

Whitney later wrote to his wife: "It was arranged that Bryce [sic] should be chairman of the Executive Committee [sic] and that lets one responsible man in to shoulder the campaign."[10] After the conference, Whitney invited Barnum and Brice to dinner, and the minutiae of campaign organization were discussed far into the evening. Arrangements were made for a meeting of the campaign committee the following Wednesday, over which Senator Gorman presided. Congressman Scott nominated Brice, and the Ohioan formally accepted the chairmanship of the campaign committee.[11]

Probably the most significant fact about the selection of Calvin Brice was the search for a "neutral" man that preceded it. The Democratic factions were constrained to present a united front to the public and to the Republican opposition in order to minimize the agitation caused by Cleveland's tariff message. Factional accommodation should have ended with the appointment of Barnum and Brice, but problems continued into the campaign, for which vigorous leadership was entirely lacking.

Brice set up New York headquarters practically alone. It soon became evident that he was not familiar with state factional matters, particularly in the eastern states, and that he himself was waiting for signals to be called. Most persons connected with the campaign organization looked to Cleveland's secretary, Colonel Lamont, as the team's quarterback. Barnum did some field work, but according to certain Democrats, he grossly neglected the campaign in his own state. Gorman and his state organization sat on their hands. "Gorman's obvious, apparent apathy even leads us to hope we may carry Maryland," reported one Republican state leader to his party's nominee, Benjamin Harrison.[12]

As F.W. Dawson had predicted in July, Brice became annoyed with the operation of a literary bureau. On August 18, Brice abruptly turned the entire bureau over to a subordinate. Three weeks later, Brice wrote Lamont that while the campaign was proceeding well, most of the contributions were going to the state committees directly rather than to the national committee. Brice then asked for further relief from headquarters duties so that he might "look around for money."[13]

On July 21, 1888, the Mills Tariff Reform Bill, implementing the reductionist position taken by the president, was passed in the House by 162 to 149 votes. Only four Democrats voted against the bill; three Republicans and three Independents crossed lines to vote in support. The vote was strictly partisan. The president's prestige was greatly enhanced. In the Senate, the Republicans followed a strategy of delay and substitution. Congress adjourned on October 20, after the campaign was well under way, without having sent the bill or the substitute Allison Bill to the president.

The poor management of the Democratic campaign organization may be judged from the handling of the Sackville-West and the "blocks-of-five" incidents. The British minister's letter, undiplomatically favoring Cleveland's reelection, was dated September 13, but was "exposed" by the Republican managers on October 24, leaving little time for a Democratic rebuttal. The Republican press played it up conspicuously. The Democrats barely had time to demand Sackville-West's recall. On October 30, President Cleveland made this request of the British government, a move that confirmed the existence of the letter and that seemed a confession of guilt.

The blocks-of-five incident was even more poorly handled. On October 31, 1888, the *Indianapolis Sentinel* exposed a letter from the Republican national treasurer instructing his Indiana party workers to organize the "floaters" in that state into "blocks-of-five" and let "none get away." The apathetic Democratic managers did nothing with this powerful evidence and Republican managers were able to bluff out of the situation. Cleveland's popular plurality of more than ninety-thousand votes did him little good in the electoral college, where Harrison received a majority. Cleveland retired to a law practice in New York.

William H. Barnum died on April 30, 1889, in his seventy-first year. The selection of a successor received little attention among Democratic politicians. Few were interested in taking on the chairmanship in a time of defeat. Some of the potential candidates elicited hostility. As one correspondent expressed it to Cleveland when asking him to use his influence to prevent Gorman from being chosen, "Mr. Gorman has done you enough injury."[14] Gorman, for his part, expressly did not want the position.

Gorman, Scott, and others on the national committee joined in asking Brice to accept; Cleveland apparently did not intervene. Brice's factional affiliations were still ambiguous. The *New York Times* referred to him as "a strong tariff reform man" at the time.[15] On June 12, Brice was chosen unanimously. Six months later, he was deep into a campaign for election to the United States Senate from Ohio. Once elected, Brice was repeatedly characterized in the press as "New York's third Senator," for his frequent residence and many political associates in New York City.[16] Contrary to the impression that he was a reductionist, Brice soon joined Gorman as the most outspoken Democratic protectionists in the Senate.[17]

At the meeting in which Brice was chosen national chairman, the national

William Francis Harrity managed his first political campaign on behalf of his law partner, who ran for the state senate in 1880. Within two years Harrity became chairman of the Democratic city committee of Philadelphia and a member of the executive committee of the state central committee. His work in the Cleveland campaign of 1884 won him the postmastership of Philadelphia. When one of Pennsylvania's few Democratic governors, Robert E. Pattison, was re-elected in 1890, Harrity became Pattison's secretary of the Commonwealth. Harrity promptly began building Cleveland support in the state, with the governor as second choice should the former president withdraw.

committee also voted to continue the campaign committee. Brice was authorized to fill all vacancies on it. Thus, the tendency toward subcommittee specialization continued.

2

As the time for the 1892 Democratic nomination approached, Cleveland, still practicing law, remained silent about his availability. The only president to seek a third nomination after losing his second election was Martin Van Buren. The two-thirds rule stopped Van Buren and was still at hand as a potential obstacle to a third Cleveland nomination.

Cleveland's silence ended when it came to the issue of currency policy. On February 10, 1891, he wrote a brief public letter in which he declared unqualifiedly that free coinage of silver was a "dangerous and reckless experiment."[18] The newspapers of the agricultural South and West loosed an avalanche of abuse upon the ex-president. New York's Democratic governor and senator-elect, David B. Hill, sounded off in favor of an "honest, bimetallic coinage," warning the party in New York against "those who would have run us into collision with our fellow-Democrats in other States."[19] This was Hill's bid for the support of the free-silver Democrats at the next national convention.

Elsewhere, other anti-Cleveland forces were gathering momentum. Senators Arthur P. Gorman of Maryland, John M. Palmer of Illinois, and Daniel W. Voorhees of Indiana conferred with Governor Hill. In Ohio, factional bitterness remained as the aftermath of Chairman Brice's election to the Senate in 1890; Governor Campbell took leadership of the anti-Cleveland men. Brice maintained a semblance of neutrality through 1890 and 1891, but by early 1892, it was clear that he was also opposed to Cleveland and even considered himself a presidential candidate.[20]

The sudden death of William L. Scott of Pennsylvania created a serious void in the Cleveland leadership on the national committee. Cleveland's supporters in Pennsylvania proposed William Francis Harrity, secretary of the Commonwealth, to replace Scott. His opponent was the anti-Cleveland state party chairman, James Kerr.

During his fatal illness, Scott had arranged for Harrity to hold his proxy on the national committee. Harrity was spoken of not only as Scott's successor but also as the choice of the Cleveland men to replace Brice as national chairman. In January 1892, however, Brice appointed State Chairman Kerr to fill the Scott vacancy. The Harrity group immediately decribed this as a "usurpation of power," challenged Brice's right to make the appointment, and announced their intention to override it in the state committee.[21] When the state committee met several days later on January 20, 1892, Kerr was defeated for state chairman, 43 to 32, Brice's appointment was rescinded, 59 to 10, and Harrity was elected as national committeeman, *viva voce* and unanimously.[22]

At the national committee meeting on January 21, nine cities presented their claims when the business moved to the choice of a place for the convention. The voting lasted for fifteen ballots, at which time Chicago was chosen, 27 to 18. After the meeting, many Democrats denounced the choice as a Brice-Gorman-Hill "trick." Trick or not, the selection of Chicago was perceived as a Cleveland setback. The opponents of Cleveland's renomination were encouraged to make their next move.

As soon as the national convention call was issued, New York State Chairman Charles F. Murphy called a Democratic state convention for February 22. No state convention had ever been held earlier than April 20. The Hill faction's object was to catch the Cleveland people either napping or snowbound in the northern areas of the state. The audacity of the Hill-inspired move brought a sharp reaction in the press and among Democrats throughout the nation.

The "snap convention" awakened the Cleveland men—Whitney, Vilas, Dickinson, Harrity, and others. In March, Cleveland wrote a long letter to Whitney in which he analyzed the party situation. The ex-president harked back to the speakership fight in the Democratic congressional caucus the preceding December. There had been a three-way contest to determine who would be nominated to succeed Speaker Thomas B. "Czar" Reed in 1891. Charles F. Crisp of Georgia was chosen over Roger Q. Mills and William M. Springer. In Cleveland's opinion, Gorman and Brice were the power brokers who turned the scales in favor of Crisp. "This was the beginning of our woes," Cleveland declared. Those in the congressional party who chose the Speaker will also destroy the hopes of the Democratic party, he continued,

> and Gorman and Brice with them. Do they not see that the Chairman of our National Committee and the man who occupies Gorman's leading position, cannot escape political damnation, if without an effort on their part, they allow their crew to navigate the ship on the rocks of Free Coinage?

. . . Cannot you in some way spur Gorman and Brice to some activity in behalf of the Democratic party?[23]

In April, Brice began to tell others that Cleveland would probably never get the necessary two-thirds vote for the nomination. Denying that he was pro-Hill, Brice explained that he expected Cleveland and Hill to neutralize each other. As time passed, Brice set aside the "can't get two-thirds" argument and joined the "Cleveland cannot carry New York" chorus.[24]

The lackadaisical pace of the Cleveland preconvention campaign disturbed Harrity. He finally wrote to Whitney, "I hope we may have an opportunity of having a talk with you prior to the Chicago Convention. . . . It seems to me that the time has come when a little closer organization of our political friends is necessary."[25]

On June 3, Whitney sent out invitations for a strategy conference to Cleveland leaders in New Hampshire, Massachusetts, Pennsylvania, Vermont, Wisconsin, New York, Connecticut, Minnesota, West Virginia, Indiana, and elsewhere. The time was June 9, and the place was Whitney's home in New York City.[26]

The conferees delved into the entire gamut of questions pertaining to the convention: the organization of the convention; the seating of contesting delegations; nominating speeches; the platform. The group constituted itself as a steering committee and made a careful estimate of Cleveland strength. The convention would have 900 delegates; 600 votes would be required to nominate. Their estimate, as of June 9 was 563 for Cleveland, 111 doubtful, and 224 opposed.[27] The estimate was conservative. At the convention, there were well over 600 votes for the Cleveland group's choice for permanent chairman. Cleveland was easily nominated on the first ballot.

During the convention's closing moments, it was moved "that the National Committee is authorized and empowered in its discretion to select as its Chairman and also as the Chairman of its Executive Committee persons who are not members of the said National Committee." This motion reiterated the principle established at the 1888 convention, namely, that an "outsider" to the national committee could be chosen as its chairman. As the resolution was adopted unanimously, a murmur filled the convention hall: "That means Whitney!"[28] Whitney's quiet leadership had overcome formidable obstacles and had done so without closing the door to future party harmony.

Cleveland at once gave his attention to campaign organization. He wrote that Whitney should be, at least nominally, at the head of the campaign. Knowing that Whitney had other preferences, Cleveland asked William S. Bissell to get as many friends, far and wide, to bombard the financier with letters asking him to accept the national committee chairmanship.[29] Democratic leaders everywhere did not need this encouragement. Nearly a full volume of correspondence in the Whitney Papers attests to his popularity.[30]

Gorman and Brice were ready to agree to whatever Whitney suggested. The latter's momentary hesitation encouraged them to hope for control. "The short of it," observed William F. Vilas, "is that the attempt is being quietly made to retain the control of the Committee by Hill and Brice by keeping Brice as Chairman. You will see at once what that means for the future, if not for the present."[31]

However, Whitney made up his mind quickly. "[Whitney] is convinced that he can accomplish more by being a free lance, unburdened with the details that fall upon the Chairman, than by accepting the Chairmanship," C.H. Jones sadly communicated to Dickinson. "His declination will have a dampening effect upon our party. . . . For twelve years the Chairman of the National Committee has been a burden for the Democratic party to carry instead of a help," Jones added, without mentioning the names of either the deceased Barnum or the incumbent Brice.[32]

Meanwhile, Whitney was urging the chairmanship on Harrity, to which Harrity courteously demurred. This predicament saddened the presidential nominee. "The refusal of both yourself and Harrity to serve . . . is a dreadful set-back," Cleveland declared. Whitney again conferred with Harrity, this time with greater success. Harrity suggested that Whitney write to Governor Pattison at Harrisburg, while he himself consulted with friends. Pattison replied that although he had planned to have Harrity run the Pennsylvania campaign, it was agreeable that he be named national chairman. Three days later, Harrity consented.[33]

Harrity worked like a drone, but always in Whitney's shadow. Cleveland somewhat unfairly referred to the young Pennsylvanian as "Whitney's clerk."[34] Quincy called him the "nominal head" of the national committee.[35]

A major threat to Cleveland's election chances was Populist enmity, rooted in widespread agricultural discontent. In the South and Midwest, the Populist appeal was mainly agrarian. However, the farther west one traveled, the greater the Populist emphasis on the free and unlimited coinage of silver. President Harrison, the Republican nominee, admitted that some coinage ratio between gold and silver might be desirable, but felt that the United States could best act on this at the forthcoming International Monetary Conference rather than independently of other nations. For advice on Democratic silver policy, Whitney turned to Benton McMillin of Tennessee and William Jennings Bryan of Nebraska.[36]

McMillin was in his seventh term in Congress and knew the politics of the border states thoroughly. Bryan, just turned thirty-two, had a better than average knowledge of midwestern affairs. The latter was to be the more interesting consultant, for Bryan would influence every Democratic national convention from 1896 to 1924, inclusive. Bryan would also be unique in that he would be the only national party titular leader to lose two elections and yet receive a third nomination. He was eventually called everything from "madman" to "the greatest enigma in American political history, enough like Henry Clay to be his blood brother."[37]

Whatever advice McMillin and Bryan gave Whitney, Cleveland heeded none of it. Cleveland stood firm against "doubtful experiments" (free coinage of silver) with the nation's currency.[38] The election gave Cleveland 5,556,000 popular votes, Harrison 5,175,000, and Weaver 1,041,000. The Populist leaders argued that Cleveland owed his election to Weaver's candidacy. Many of the Democratic managers agreed and, as a consequence, became susceptible to Populist demands in 1896.[39]

3

As the president-elect awaited his second inauguration, the horizons filled with signs of impending economic collapse. Congressional leaders and financiers called with unprecedented urgency for the repeal of the Sherman Silver Purchase Act, which they blamed for the precarious condition of the gold supply, credit, and prices. Cleveland agreed to call a special session of Congress in February to repeal the act.

By May, the Panic of 1893 was in progress. In August, the special session convened and wrangled until November before passing the repeal. The West and the agrarian South blasted the president as "the tool of Wall Street." In Congress, a powerful group of silverite leaders opposed repeal, including Senators James K. Jones, George Vest, Edward C. Wolcott, Fred T. Dubois, William M. Stewart, William A. Peffer, and Henry M. Teller, and Representatives Richard P. Bland, William Jennings Bryan, and Joseph M. Bailey.

At the beginning of the House debate, there were about 173 antisilver men, 114 silverites, and 69 doubtful representatives. During the debate, in which William L. Wilson, Bourke Cockran, and Tom Reed gave eloquent voice to the administration's position, the most impressive prosilver speeches came from Congressman Bryan.

His second administration was not a happy one for Cleveland. There was no way he could escape blame for the depression. His veto of the silver seigniorage bill intensified the hostility of the silver forces in the South and the West. General labor unrest culminated in the Pullman strike in Chicago in July 1894. Over the protest of Illinois Governor John P. Altgeld, Cleveland sent federal troops into the troubled area to break the strike, earning labor's and Altgeld's lasting enmity.

In Congress, Representative William L. Wilson sponsored the administration's reductionist tariff measure. In the Senate, its management was entrusted to James K. Jones. The House bill met stubborn opposition in the Senate, where it was padded with over 600 amendments. Senator Gorman was the leader of "the amenders." What should have been called the Wilson-Jones Bill came to be known as the Wilson-Gorman Tariff.

The Senate bill so altered the original measure that the president, in a public letter

James K. Jones, senator from Arkansas, was considered an expert in financial legislation and one of the silverite leaders on most friendly terms with the Cleveland administration. Educated by private tutors on his father's plantation and admitted to the bar after privately reading law, Jones rose rapidly in state politics during the Reconstruction era and won his first term in the lower house of Congress in 1880. In 1884, Jones managed the speakership fight for a tariff-reductionist candidate against the protectionists. His candidate, John G. Carlisle, won and appointed Jones to the Ways and Means Committee where he became spokesman for the reductionists. In 1885, Jones was elected to the Senate by the Arkansas legislature. In the Senate he led the Cleveland administration forces for tariff reduction during his first term. During his second term, beginning in 1891, Jones became increasingly involved in the leadership of the silver cause.

to Congressman Wilson on July 2, denounced the failure of "certain Democrats" to keep the party's pledges. On July 23, Gorman addressed a stinging reply from the Senate floor. Senator Jones made no response. The Senate version was passed in August and became law without Cleveland's signature. Ben Tillman promised to stick a pitchfork in Cleveland's "old ribs."[40] Missouri's Champ Clark compared Cleveland, Benedict Arnold, and Aaron Burr.[41] The less extreme of the old Southern leaders—Jones, Vest, Harris, Bland—saw silver as the issue upon which to challenge the president's party leadership.

In the fall elections of 1894, the Republicans returned to the House 284 strong; the Democrats limped in with 104 seats. The Populists polled 1,471,600 votes and were more certain than ever of greatly influencing the coming presidential race. It was a staggering personal defeat for President Cleveland. The casualties included Congressman Bryan, who found new employment as editor-in-chief of the *Omaha World-Herald* and as a much in demand lecturer on the silver problem, the one issue that transcended all others in symbolizing popular discontent.

National free-silver groups proliferated. From among Ohio silver Democrats came the initiative for creating an American Bimetallic League. In 1895, silver Republicans founded the National Bimetallic Union that merged with the American Bimetallic League in January 1896 to form the American Bimetallic Union, more popularly known as the National Silver party. Silver Republicans began to close ranks behind Senators Henry M. Teller of Colorado and Fred T. Dubois of Idaho. In April 1895, silver Democrats in Illinois led by the Altgeld faction sponsored prosilver resolutions that came out of state conventions in Texas, Mississippi, and Missouri.

In July, Senators James K. Jones of Arkansas, Isham G. Harris of Tennessee, and David Turpie of Indiana issued a call for a conference of "bimetallic" Democrats in Washington. At the August 15 conference, more than nineteen states were represented by nearly 100 persons. The conference's Provisional Executive Committee, consisting of Jones, Harris, and Turpie, was enlarged. A committee of one from each state was authorized, to be known as the Bimetallic Democratic National Committee. The chairman of this committee was Senator Harris, James K. Jones was treasurer, and Thomas O. Towles was secretary. "The thing we are to fight for is the control of the next National Convention," wrote Governor William J. Stone to editor William Jennings Bryan.[42]

At the meeting of the Democratic national committee in January 1896, the sound-money forces won a victory fraught with peril. The silverites backed St. Louis as the convention city. The sound-money contingent favored New York. Senator Jones warned that the silver men would hold a separate convention if New York were chosen. After twenty-nine ballots, the selection was made: Chicago, 26, St. Louis, 24. Senator Jones' warning was the first authoritative word uttered by the silverites regarding the possibility of bolting the party.

Probably the greatest deterrent to a thorough mobilization of sound-money delegations was Cleveland himself. His failure to renounce interest in a third term came too late to help such men as Brice, whose state convention endorsed a silver plank despite his personal fight against it. Even National Chairman Harrity's Pennsylvania sent a silver delegation. Whitney disregarded all entreaties to head the sound-money group at Chicago and did not change his mind until three weeks before the convention.

Whitney hardly expected an eastern sound-money man to get the nomination. If he could hold 312 of the 930 delegates, however, he would be able to prevent a silverite nomination and perhaps work out a compromise on bimetallism. President Cleveland was uncompromising in his stand against free silver, "We can survive as a party without immediate success at the polls, but I do not think we can survive if we have fastened upon us, as an authoritative declaration of party policy, the free coinage of silver."[43]

The candidates included Cleveland, a factor rather than a candidate, and silver Republican Henry M. Teller, a favorite of the Populists and the Silver party. Governor John P. Altgeld was ineligible because of foreign birth. The two strongest silverite contenders were Richard P. Bland and Horace Boies. Bland had very influential backing—James K. Jones, Altgeld, and most of the Bimetallic Democratic National Committee. Neither he nor Boies had great support in the Silver party or among Populists.

4

William Jennings Bryan's candidacy was hardly noticed, not even in Bryan's own *Omaha World-Herald*. It was not until spring of 1896 that it became generally understood among Democratic politicians that the thirty-six-year-old Bryan considered himself a presidential candidate. Until then he had been concentrating his efforts on addresses to special groups, on his *Omaha World-Herald* editorials, on his extensive personal correspondence, and on his long lecture tours through the South and the West where his unique oratorical gifts won a fervent following.

Bryan took pains to clarify his own position on the possibility of a silverite bolt from the Democratic party. Just as the gold Democrats would probably not support a free-silver Democrat, so ought the free-silver Democrats refuse to support a gold Democrat, he wrote. No compromise was possible between monometallism and bimetallism, hence a bolt by either the silverites or the gold Democrats was to be expected.[44] Bryan advocated an alliance among silver Democrats, silver Republicans, and Populists in opposition to the gold tickets that might be put forward.

Many Populist party leaders favored endorsing Bryan if he could win the Democratic nomination. Silver Republicans rated Bryan second only to Henry M. Teller as their presidential choice.[45] When Bryan asked Governor Altgeld if his support would be forthcoming if Bryan were placed in nomination, Altgeld responded that he found "everywhere great admiration for you but an almost unanimous sentiment that you are not available for president this time." Altgeld further observed that the "situation looks dangerous because of possible division among silver men."[46]

The Democratic national committee met just prior to the convention to settle seating contests and to choose a temporary chairman for the convention. The Nebraska seating contest, with Bryan at the head of the silver delegation, was considered the most important one. The national committee voted against seating the Bryan delegation. The chairmanship vote was taken after Senator Jones warned that the convention's majority ought not be ignored in making the decision. Jones was spokesman for what had come to be known as "the Senatorial Clique." The clique included James K. Jones, Isham G. Harris, George Vest, Edward Bates, Joseph C.S. Blackburn, Benjamin Tillman, William T. Stone, Francis M. Cockrell, and Governor John P. Altgeld, all favoring Bland.

Senator Jones continued as spokesman for the silver cause on the floor of the convention. The national committee's recommendation for temporary chairman was set aside in favor of Silverite John W. Daniel, 556 to 349. The committee on credentials, where there was a 27 to 16 silver majority, seated the Bryan delegation, and the convention approved, 558 to 368.

The platform came next. An Altgeld composition, it featured support for the 16 to 1 ratio of silver to gold and full repudiation of "government by injunction," that is, Cleveland's breaking of the Pullman strike two years earlier. When the resolutions committee completed its work, its chairman, Senator Jones, called on Bryan to arrange the debate on the platform. Bryan's version of this incident makes much of the "unexpected stroke of luck" and reveals the somewhat impersonal relationship between Jones and Bryan:

> My ambition had been to be chairman of the Committee on Resolutions, but I found that Senator Jones aspired to that place, and as he was a much older man, and the president [sic] of the bimetallic organization formed at Memphis, I did not care to be a candidate against him, and gave up the thought of that place. . . . The request [to organize the debate] came as a surprise. . . . After the Convention was over and Senator Jones had been made Chairman of the National Committee at my request, I asked him how he happened to turn the defense of the platform over to me. I know that it was not with any thought of favoring me as a candidate, because he was a supporter of Mr. Bland and too loyal to him. . . . Senator Jones answered my question by saying that I was the only one of the prominent speakers who had not had an opportunity to address the Convention. . . . He knew of the part I had taken in the organizing of the fight and how I had traveled over the country for a year helping in many states and said that his invitation to me was due entirely to a sense of fairness.[47]

Bryan arranged that Senator Jones read the platform. Benjamin Tillman would open the debate for the silver side. David B. Hill, William F. Vilas, and William E. Russell would follow with the sound-money argument. Bryan would close the argument for silver.

That evening at his hotel room, as Bryan wrote his dispatch for the *Omaha World-Herald*, a delegation of Silver Republicans interrupted to present the claims of Senator Teller for the Democratic nomination. Could Mr. Bryan be enlisted in favor of Henry M. Teller? Bryan replied:

> I am perfectly willing to vote for Senator Teller myself because I regard the money question as the paramount issue, but the silver Democrats have won their fight, while the silver Republicans lost in their convention, and it will be easier to bring the minority silver Republicans to us than to take the majority silver Democrats over to a Republican nominee.[48]

With disconcerting candor, Bryan concluded that he felt he could make a stronger fight than any lifelong Republican. "I expect to be the nominee of the convention," he told the astonished delegation.[49]

When the "Boy Orator" rose to make his speech the next day, he was aware that: (1) within the silver faction, the Bland and Boies candidacies were about to stalemate each other, (2) because of the narrow two-thirds majority, the silver leaders could not afford a drawn-out nomination contest, (3) many southern delegations were either uncommitted to any candidate or had Bryan as their second choice, (4) no silver Democrat could as readily win the endorsement of the Populists, the Silver Republicans, and the National Silver party as Bryan himself, (5) among the major silver leaders, Tillman was friendly, Daniel uncommitted, and Altgeld influenced by a strong pro-Bryan group in the Illinois delegation, and, above all, (6) the one question upon which at least 626 of the delegates could be fully united was free silver.

When Bryan closed his speech with the ringing words—"We shall answer their demands for a gold standard by saying to them, you shall not press down upon the brow of labor this crown of thorns. You shall not crucify mankind upon a cross of gold."—the silverites had a man around whom they could unite.

Throughout the balloting, there were 162 sound-money men who refused to vote for any candidate. The first ballot gave Richard P. Bland 235, William Jennings Bryan 137, Robert E. Pattison 97, Joseph Blackburn 82, John R. Mc-Lean 54, Horace Boies 67, Claude Matthews 37, Benjamin R. Tillman 17, and a scattering for others. Two attempts were made to abolish the two-thirds rule, but Senator Jones blocked them. On the fourth ballot, Bryan had 280, Bland 241. Altgeld withdrew to consult and sadly returned to give Bryan Illinois' 48 votes. The nomination was made on the fifth ballot.

The convention fell apart in the naming of a vice-presidential nominee. Sixteen names were put in nomination. Two hundred sixty delegates were absent or declined to vote; the gold faction had gone home the day before. The leaders on the first ballot were Joseph E. Sibley with 163, John R. McLean 111, Arthur Sewall 100, George F. Williams 76, and Richard P. Bland 62. On the second ballot, it was Bland 294, McLean 158, Sibley 113, Sewall 37. Although Bryan withheld Nebraska's vote so as not to reveal a preference, privately he voted for McLean as a gesture to the moneyed interests. James K. Jones' Arkansas delegation voted for Sewall, who eventually was nominated. The platform and the candidates were silverite through and through.

The Democratic national committee met July 11 and elected Senator Jones as its chairman. According to Bryan:

> The main reason for this was that the Senator had been the head of the organization through whose efforts we had won the Convention, and was therefore the logical man to lead the fight during the campaign. I had a personal reason in addition, namely, that it gratified my own desire to show my appreciation of the favor he did me in giving me an opportunity to defend the platform before the Convention.[50]

Jones was not a member of the national committee, but his election was made possible by the convention rule of 1892 that allowed the appointment of an outsider. Jones was the first Democratic outsider chosen, although from the point of view of his congressional status, he was in most respects more of an "insider" than the nominee himself.

5

The campaign was complex. The Democratic campaign organization could not be completed until the Silver Republicans, the National Silver party, and the

Populists had acted to endorse Bryan's candidacy. It was certain that the sound-money Democrats would create problems, probably by bolting. Nor was it going to be easy for the older silver leaders to become enthused over the Boy Orator as their new leader. Governor Stone was frank enough to tell Bryan:

> I follow you because the party has made you its leader. I am glad the leader is a man I can respect and honor for his sincerity, his ability and his manhood; but I want it understood that I am not going to sneeze because you take snuff.[51]

Senator Teller sent word that he was about to confer with Dubois and others about winning a Silver Republican endorsement of Bryan. "I have written to all the Populist leaders . . . urging them to nominate you and I made it impossible for my name to be used."[52] The Silver Republican endorsement was promptly given.

The Populist national convention presented a different picture. Most of the 1,400 delegates were fearful of being "sold out" to the Democratic party. This was particularly true of southern Populists, who had spent six years in an all-out battle against southern Democrats. These antifusionists were a poorly organized majority at the convention. The fusionist minority, led by James B. Weaver, was well organized, working for an endorsement of Bryan and Sewall. For three days prior to the convention, Democratic Chairman Jones consulted with the fusionists.

Senator Marion Butler came up with a compromise plan. Would the anti-fusionists go along if a radical southern Populist—Tom Watson—were substituted for Sewall on the ticket? Rumors circulated among convention delegates that the Democratic managers would withdraw Sewall in favor of a Populist if Bryan were endorsed. The compromisers made the unusual suggestion that the vice-presidential candidate be nominated first. This change was approved 738 to 637, and Watson received the Populist nomination for vice-president, $539^1/_2$ to 257.

The following morning the delegates read in the newspapers a telegram from Bryan to Jones asking that his name be withdrawn if Sewall were not also endorsed. Charges were made that the convention's chairman, Senator William V. Allen of Nebraska, had withheld this information from the convention. The newspapers also carried a statement by Senator Jones denying that he had ever agreed to the withdrawal of Sewall.

Senator Allen refused to recognize the message from Bryan and hurried the balloting along. The antifusionists caucused on a proposal to bolt, but reached no decision. They departed from St. Louis in no mood to cooperate with the campaign.[53]

The campaign activities of four political parties—Democrats, Populists, National Silverites, and Silver Republicans—now needed to be coordinated. This was partly accomplished by creating a multiparty advisory committee to the Democratic national committee, consisting of six Democrats and six representatives from the other three parties. One individual served as treasurer of both Democratic and National Silver national committees.

Chairman Jones frequently lost patience with the southern Populists who, he said, "are out for nothing but spoils."[54] It was September before membership of the advisory and other committees was completed. It took weeks to accomplish fusion slates of presidential electors in twenty-eight states. The Republican press rejoiced over the troubles of the "Popocrats."

Meanwhile, conservative Democrats in the East decided to concentrate on congressional and local races and possibly to come out for a third-party ticket in support of the gold standard. On July 23 and 24, a conference of sound-money leaders took place in Chicago. At an August 7 meeting, a national committee of thirty-five was organized and a nominating convention called. On September 2, the National Democratic party, that is, the Gold Democrats, was formally established; John M. Palmer and Simon B. Buckner were nominated after President Cleveland had declined to be its nominee.

The new party's finance committee was a formidable roster: Charles J. Canda (former treasurer of the regular Democratic national committee) as chairman, William C. Whitney, former Democratic Chairman Abram S. Hewitt, August Belmont the Younger, George Foster Peabody, William R. Grace, John D. Crimmins, Roswell Flower, Don M. Dickinson, and others. This group was wealthy and politically experienced. President Cleveland and his cabinet enthusiastically supported the new ticket. Only the necessity of conducting further legislative business with Congress kept Cleveland from participating in the Gold Democrats' campaign.[55]

The campaign of the Gold Democrats was concentrated in five midwestern states: Indiana, Kentucky, Michigan, Minnesota, and Kansas. They intended to draw off enough Democratic votes from Bryan to assure state pluralities for McKinley.[56] The Republican national committee contributed an unspecified amount of money to the Gold Democratic campaigns in these states.

As Chairman Jones struggled with campaign organization and the fusion of electoral college slates, Bryan conducted a one-man stumping campaign that broke all records. He traveled 18,000 miles across twenty-nine states and directly addressed over five million people.[57] It was a contest of communication techniques: railroad and rostrum vs. Republican National Chairman Mark Hanna's 120 million campaign documents, 1,400 campaign speakers, and overwhelming newspaper support for the Republican nominee, William McKinley. It was also a contest of money; most estimates set Democratic resources at about $300,000 and Republican funds at $2,500,000. The ideological content of the rhetoric was unprecedented: rich against poor, proletariat against capitalists, farmers against Wall Street. Republican speakers rarely mentioned Bryan, but attacked Governor John P. Altgeld of Illinois as the embodiment of revolution.

Bryan lost the election 6,511,073 to McKinley's 7,107,822 popular votes and by 176 to 271 in the electoral college. Contrary to expectations, the Populists made little difference either way. The defeat opened an era of recurring Democratic defeats and continued inability to organize a national headquarters that could compete effectively. The weaknesses of the national committee and its chairmanship also reflected the prominence and tenacity of William Jennings Bryan, who proved to be a titular leader who would not go away.

10 | Bryan: Titular Leader with Tenure

William Jennings Bryan understood national conventions and titular leadership. His acute strategic sense dominated the next four Democratic national conventions. His aggressive assumption of the titular leadership gave him tenure in a phantom office in a minority party. His adversaries in the Democratic party found it difficult to ignore or get rid of him. Essentially a political loner and always suspect of party regulars, Bryan did nothing to develop a stronger national party organization. If anything, he used the office of national chairman as a bargaining chip with which to keep important factions loyal. His successor as titular leader, Woodrow Wilson, was equally inattentive. Not until the 1920s, under the chairmanships of Cordell Hull and John J. Raskob, was serious consideration given to building an organization at the national level.

1

The national leadership of the Democratic party retired en masse after election day 1896. President Cleveland retreated to Princeton. Financier Whitney returned to his business interests. Gorman suffered temporary loss of his Senate seat in 1899, but returned in 1903. Benjamin Tillman, John W. Daniel, and George Vest continued in the Senate, substantially diminished in influence because of the fading Populist and silverite movements. Thomas Watson became virtually a political recluse for eight years. Failing re-election in the Illinois gubernatorial race, John P. Altgeld ended active participation in politics, with a brief return during the mayoralty race of 1899 in which he unsuccessfully challenged Carter H. Harrison's control of the Chicago Democratic organization. David B. Hill left the Senate to resume his law practice; his personal following in New York declining in influence. William J. Stone returned to the practice of law at the end of his term as governor of Missouri, and succeeded George Vest as United States senator in 1903. The departures made way for a new generation and a new factionalism.

The leaders who did not retire were titular leader Bryan and his national chairman, Senator Jones. Bryan just kept right on running for the presidency. His postelection mail ran into several hundred thousand pieces, including messages and advice from major party figures. Arthur Sewall wrote, "This battle beyond a question must be fought over again in 1900, and my present judgment is that it ought to be fought on the single issue of free coinage of silver." Ben Tillman urged the "Silver Knight" to "gird on your armor for a continuation of the fight."[1]

National Chairman Jones was returned to the Senate by the Arkansas legislature in the fall of 1897, despite a determined Populist opposition. In the Senate, Jones remained a low-tariff and free-silver leader. The thirty-six-year-old titular leader and his fifty-seven-year-old national chairman were inescapably of different vintages. It was bound to be difficult for the older man to take orders from the younger, yet it was inevitable that the younger man would be holding the initiatives as he endeavored to consolidate his resources for a second try at the presidency.

The 1896 Democratic campaign had been one of unprecedented complexity, particularly from the perspective of Chairman Jones. Bryan had almost single-handedly conducted his own unprecedented stumping tour, proclaiming the greed of Wall Street and the need for free silver. The nominee left the extra-heavy organizational chores on the shoulders of Chairman Jones, not least of which was the coordination of four political parties.

Jones came out of the campaign irritated by his young leader and by the impossible duties that had been imposed upon him. He publicly criticized Bryan's conduct of the campaign. Against Jones' advice, Bryan insisted upon making a second tour of the East. In Jones' opinion, this section of the country was lost, and the candidate should have spent his precious time elsewhere, particularly in the Midwest. "I haven't a particle of doubt," Jones told the press, "that had he not gone skylarking through the East, but had devoted his time to Michigan, Indiana, Illinois, Ohio, Minnesota, and other of the states where we knew there was a strong and growing silver sentiment, he would have won the election."[2]

The Republican McKinley administration came to office at the beginning of an era of prosperity and national self-confidence. The Union now filled the land space between the Atlantic and Pacific. The country's enterprising but impolitic sons were prospecting in Alaska, unsettling a monarchy in Hawaii, selling supplies to Cuban revolutionaries, filibustering up and down Central America, investing in South American enterprises, projecting an interoceanic canal across Nicaragua, and, at home, pressing ahead with industrial expansion and advanced stages of monopolistic concentration. The shortage of currency—the major economic justification for the free-silver movement—was "solved" by the discovery of new gold deposits in the Klondike region and the improved exploitation of old deposits in the western mining states. The Spanish-American War gave the youthful nation colonial possessions that may well have been the envy of its European elders.

Bryan, meanwhile, went into lecture tour work on a large scale. He was a surefire drawing card for clubs, institutional fund raisers, and speaking bureaus. During 1897, 1898, and 1899, he traveled a total of 92,720 miles and earned the nickname "the Chautauqua King." His usual topics were money, trusts, and imperialism. What amounted to a four-year presidential campaign tour earned him a great deal of money. He turned to his profession as a lawyer only once, to argue and win a famous Nebraska railroad rate case before the United States Supreme Court. He published a lengthy exposition of the 1896 campaign, *The First Battle*, which also brought a good income.

Bryan's public activities were essentially a one-man business, with his wife serving as business manager. His writing and lecture tours absorbed nearly all of his time. The officers of the national committee demurred. National Chairman Jones cautioned him to speak only to college students free of charge. Treasurer William P. St. John added that a paid lecture tour would tend to cheapen Bryan's status as party leader. Both men joshed Bryan about his forthcoming book, *The First Battle*, remarking that it ought to be quite thorough since Bryan "had three years in which to write it."[3]

What Jones and St. John failed to appreciate was the semireligious fervor of thousands upon thousands of Bryan's followers in both the party rank and file and the leadership. An example was a strategically placed Bryan contact man in northern Texas, Dr. Charles M. Rosser, director of a mental institution, whose lecturing work carried him to all parts of the lower South and Southwest. On the eve of the 1896 election, Rosser wrote Bryan: "No matter what be the result tomorrow, you will be greater than any other man since Christ." George F. Washburn, manager of the Populist headquarters in Chicago, added: "I still believe you are the divinely appointed one to lead us." The Bryan Papers in the Library of Congress contain countless such letters.[4]

Bryan's efforts at strengthening grass-roots organization and raising funds soon ran up against the skepticism, inertia, and factional cross-currents of the Democratic leadership. In Missouri, Bryan followers started an organization called "The Democratic Volunteers." The object was to establish local clubs that eventually could be chartered by a National Association of Democratic Clubs. Some $100,000 and over eight hundred workers went into the movement. But, to the disappointment of its leaders, Governor Stone of Missouri, National Chairman Jones, and the officers of the Democratic congressional campaign committee refused to get involved until it had proven itself further. Another three years passed before Chairman Jones turned his attention to the National Association of Democratic Clubs. In April 1900, Jones offered and

William Randolph Hearst accepted the presidency of the association.[5]

Party fund-raising also bogged down. When Bryan consulted with Jones about matters of organization and funds, the national chairman responded, "I think we will have no difficulty in effecting a thorough and complete organization of the Democratic party if we can raise the money necessary to defray the expenses of the movement."[6] However, it took Chairman Jones until the fall of 1898 to get around to setting up a Committee on Ways and Means to raise funds for furthering "the cause of bimetallism."[7] He appointed Governor Stone of Missouri, former Governor Altgeld of Illinois, Populist Senator Allen of Nebraska, and Silver Republican Senator Teller of Colorado to this committee. Jones served as chairman. William H. ("Coin") Harvey, the ardent free-silver editor, was appointed general manager of the committee.

Within six months Harvey resigned in disgust. In his letter of resignation, he described his success in collecting $40,000 at an expense of only about 10 percent. Harvey then leveled a long indictment against Chairman Jones.

1. Jones refused to call a meeting of the Ways and Means Committee.

2. Jones opposed Harvey's plan to have agents solicit funds. Jones argued that people would contribute voluntarily, despite the fact that Harvey had demonstrated that less than 5 percent of the funds had been given voluntarily.

3. Jones turned down William Randolph Hearst's offer to provide editorial support to an authorized fund-raising campaign.

4. Jones refused to call a meeting of friendly state chairmen and never did get around to calling a meeting of friendly congressmen, as he had promised.

Harvey then turned his verbal assault upon former Governor Altgeld, who had by then become a candidate for mayor of Chicago. Not only was Altgeld running on an independent ticket, but he had failed to reiterate his loyalty to Bryan and the 16 to 1 coinage ratio. Harvey objected to Altgeld's failure to try to win a nomination through the party's regular nominating agencies. If the Ways and Means Committee condoned this kind of behavior in one of its members, Harvey argued, how could the party's state and local committees cooperate wholeheartedly in its efforts?

Harvey resigned in March 1899. Several weeks after, Stone, Teller, and Allen resigned from the Ways and Means Committee, leaving only Jones (in Switzerland at this time) and Altgeld. Altgeld stubbornly refused to resign until August. Meanwhile, at the July 20, 1899, meeting of the national committee, the Ways and Means Committee was confirmed as an integral part of the national committee machinery, its membership set at seven, and specific financial duties assigned to it.[8]

2

Democratic factional struggles continued in state organizations across the nation, complicated by shifts and changes within the Populist and Silver Republican

---

Norman E. Mack (originally McEachren) was the Ontario-born publisher and editor of the Buffalo *Daily Times*. In the presidential campaigns of 1884, 1888, and 1892, Mack supported his fellow Buffalonian, Grover Cleveland, serving in 1892 as chairman of the national convention's committee to notify Cleveland of his nomination. In 1896, the Buffalo *Times* was ardently pro-silver and pro-Bryan. A man of great tact and party regularity, Mack's newspaper became the authentic voice of the Democratic leadership in western New York.

---

parties. Although there was rarely voiced any doubt that Bryan would receive a second nomination, anti-Bryan feeling manifested itself in a variety of ways: delays in public endorsements of Bryan's leadership, debates over the proper emphasis to be given the money issue in the 1900 platform, and decisions about party procedures. While there was no real challenger for the presidential nomination, there were great differences in enthusiasm for Bryan.

The Bryanites won early factional victories in Massachusetts. In Ohio, on the other hand, John R. McLean, who had been ruled out by Bryan for the 1896 vice-presidential nomination, maintained his ascendency in the state organization and withheld its support from Bryan until the very last minute. In Maryland, Arthur P. Gorman did nothing to discourage Gorman-for-president booms. In New York, commitments were postponed because of the changes accompanying the return of many Gold Democrats into the regular organization.

After the election, the Gold Democrats decided to establish a permanent headquarters in New York City and asked their national chairman, William D. Bynum, a former Indiana congressman, to take charge at a salary. Bynum took on the job in spring of 1897, producing sound-money literature and maintaining contact with many midterm candidates for Congress. However, by September 1898, Bynum was ready to conduct a dissolution meeting of the Gold Democratic national committee, having ordered the treasurer to refund money on hand proportionally to all contributors. The national committee however, chose to continue as a formal group and appointed a new chairman. Meeting again in July 1900, the committee decided that it had lost not only its principal leaders and main sources of financial support, but also its issue. The committee voted not to name a third-party ticket, but declared that it was the duty of all sound-money Democrats to join in defeating Bryan's second candidacy.[9]

The return of the Gold Democrats to the parent party gave the money issue a significance it might not otherwise have had in 1900. Perry Belmont, himself "loyal," but whose brother August was a leading Gold Democrat, spoke out on behalf of the sound-money "regulars," in a widely publicized address in which he rejected the infallibility of the 16 to 1 coinage ratio. Norman E. Mack, Democratic leader in Buffalo, New York, observed sadly that the Gold Democrats were not coming back into the party as graciously as one might hope.[10]

The Gold Democrats forced the money issue into the ongoing factional battle between New York's ex-Governor David B. Hill and Tammany's Richard Croker. As chairman of the Erie County Democratic committee, Mack assumed the role of mediator. Croker favored full reiteration of the 16 to 1 plank and succeeded in getting one of his Tammany men on the platform committee of the 1900 convention. Hill, on the other hand, wanted milder demands in a "brief" reiteration of the 1896 platform, but urged top priority to two new issues: imperialism and monopoly. "Give us the best quality of crow you can," he asked Bryan.[11]

Chairman Jones, in his blunt and undiplomatic way, stood four square for the 1896 money plank. His position did not help matters, particularly in 1898, when several factional elements sought to negotiate greater intraparty unity. Writing to Bryan, Jones reported:

> Many men approach me on this question of "getting together." My answer invariably to them is, that we would be very glad to have all Democrats squarely back in the fold; that the party will not deviate one hair's breadth from the line already marked out for us, and that it will be necessary either to come in without conditions or, in my opinion, join the Republicans. I always do this in as courteous a way as I can, and try not to be offensive.[12]

Bryan was willing to move to other issues. This was especially true after the Spanish-American War made imperialism an all-consuming question. In the summer of 1898, the governor of Nebraska appointed Bryan a colonel in a volunteer regiment for duty in Cuba. But Republicans, most notably Theodore Roosevelt, monopolized the glory. Bryan's regiment remained bottled up in Florida. Bryan resigned his commission in December and joined the chorus of anti-imperialist opinion in the country.

Opposing imperialism, but in favor of ratification of a peace treaty with Spain, Bryan refrained from trying to use his influence as the Senate struggled over the treaty's ratification. The upper house approved the treaty by a single vote more than the necessary two-thirds. Andrew Carnegie and the Anti-Imperialist League complained that one word from Bryan would have beaten the treaty. Senator Jones regretted exceedingly that Bryan had taken "so prominent and pronounced a stand in favor of ratification."[13]

In preparing for the national convention of 1900, Senator Jones once again called upon the editor of the *St. Louis Republic*, Charles H. Jones, to prepare a draft of the platform. This platform, counseled the national chairman, ought to be more carefully weighed than the last one. In a conciliatory mood, he further advised that "we should avoid the *appearance* of receding from any position we held in '96," yet leave the way open for those who wish to come back to the party.[14]

Not all who wished to return were interested in doing so peaceably. As Congressman William Sulzer of New York, one of the more prominent vice-presidential candidates, reported to Bryan:

> There seems to be some effort among a few of the oldtime leaders who were opposed to you or lukewarm in 1896 to get control of one-third of the delegates to the Kansas City convention in order to force a compromise on the platform and make terms with the candidate.[15]

Sulzer's information was accurate. The convention's platform committee accepted the old 16 to 1 silver plank by the narrow margin of 26 to 24, but only after it was agreed that anti-imperialism and antitrust planks would share the limelight.

The first organizational decision to test Bryan's titular leadership involved the Harrity case. A supporter of Grover Cleveland and the gold standard, former national chairman Harrity had retired from politics in the midst of the 1896 campaign, retaining only his position as Pennsylvania's national committeeman. Controlled by silverites, the Pennsylvania Democratic state convention in the fall of 1897 ousted Harrity as national committeeman and designated James M. Guffey in his place. Harrity challenged the action in an appeal to the national committee.

Chairman Jones anticipated a 40 to 5 vote by the committee confirming Harrity's removal. When about half the committee members had returned their ballots on the issue, Jones, in astonishment, saw the vote going 2 to 1 in favor of retaining Harrity. Jones sent an appeal to Bryan, suggesting that most committeemen were uncertain about the issues at stake and about their right to remove Harrity. An extensive correspondence ensued. Bryan was reminded that "the defeat of Mr. Guffey, as you know, means a serious wound to the silver forces in Pennsylvania." Guffey asked Bryan to intercede with the national committee, saying that the committeemen would change their votes only if Bryan asked them to do so. Bryan did ask, and the vote was brought to an end in June, with Guffey becoming the new committeeman from Pennsylvania.[16]

3

During the spring of 1899, Chairman Jones prepared to depart for a European rest tour on the advice of his physician. His departure was the occasion for several organizational developments that occurred under the clear assumption that Bryan would make the race in 1900.

Jones appointed former Missouri Governor William J. Stone as acting chairman in his absence, with authority to submit Jones' resignation if this were advisable at any time. To assist Stone, Jones appointed an advisory committee to the campaign committee, which included: George F. Williams, the Bryan leader in Massachusetts; Norman E. Mack of New York; Stephen M. White of California; former Governor John P. Altgeld of Illinois; and Daniel J. Campau of Michigan, chairman of the campaign committee.

Stone had been one of the doubtfuls in the Harrity case, and some Bryan men were inclined to eye him with suspicion. However, shortly after his appointment as acting chairman, Stone reaffirmed his loyalty to Bryan and free silver, charging that the Gold Democrats were obviously planning to try to control the national convention. "I stand ready to fight the old battle over again if necessary," he declared.[17]

Stone called available members of the national committee to an informal meeting on May 25 in St. Louis. The conference was a preliminary discussion on the choice of issues for 1900. Bryan attended. Campaign issues were discussed in a general way. Particular attention was given to the Altgeld-Harrison contest in Chicago and its implications for the national committee's ways and means committee. A subcommittee was appointed to draft rules of organization and procedure for the national committee. Plans were made for a formal meeting on July 20.[18]

With Bryan still present, the national committee considered the rules prepared for it by the special subcommittee. Of approximately fourteen rules submitted, only three were adopted. These specified that officers of the national committee were to serve until the close of the national convention. The position of vice-chairman was formally established, and Acting Chairman Stone was elected as its first incumbent. The executive committee was reduced in size to eleven and its authority over all other subcommittees of the national committee clarified.

Among the subcommittees authorized were the ways and means committee and a press committee. On the assumption that Bryan was to be the nominee, executive, ways and means, and press subcommittee appointments were made to continue in effect through the campaign (with only minor changes). Bryan recommended a successor to the deceased treasurer, William P. St. John, and the appointee also served through the campaign of 1900.[19]

Unity on Bryan's renomination could not conceal factional disunity in the national party. When National Chairman Jones returned to the United States in October, choices of convention date and city were yet to be made. Another national committee meeting was called for February 22, 1900, at which the silver and anti-silver factions regrouped.

The silver people, with Altgeld and Williams as their spokesmen, favored an early convention to give ample time for organizing the campaign. They were particularly concerned about coordination with Populists, Silver Republicans, and other remnants from 1896. Arthur P. Gorman spoke for a later date, possibly after the Republican convention. Of the fifty committee votes, twenty-eight were cast for July 4, twenty-one for June 14. Gorman's preference carried. On the

Born at Waterford, Ireland, in 1856, Thomas Taggart arrived in the United States as a young child, his parents first settling in Ohio and later moving to Garrett, Indiana. Taggart's irregular rural school education came to an end when he decided at the age of twelve that he should contribute to the family's income. His father was railroad baggage master at Xenia, Ohio, and the young son became a handyman at the depot, amd later a waiter at its restaurant. Taggart continued these occupations at Garrett and Indianapolis. He arrived in Indianapolis at the age of seventeen and soon became known for his energy and Irish wit. He was just over twenty-one when he became manager of the Indianapolis railroad depot restaurant. Shortly after, with the support of friends, he purchased the Depot Hotel, which he operated for about seven years. During this time, he became deeply involved in Democratic ward politics. The auditorship of Marion County, in which Indianapolis is located, was worth some $50,000 in fees and had been in Republican hands for several decades. Taggart captured the position for the Democrats in 1866 and held it for eight years. At the beginning of his incumbency, he liquidated his holdings in the Depot Hotel. At the end of the term, Taggart became proprietor of the Grand Hotel, and later the Denison Hotels, in Indianapolis. Meanwhile, he was elected Marion county Democratic chairman in 1888 and Indiana state chairman in 1892.

After the campaign of 1894, State Chairman Taggart turned to the race for mayor of Indianapolis. He was elected and served three terms. While mayor, he was chosen Indiana's national committeeman, a position in which he served from 1900 to 1912. When he declined to run again for the mayorality in 1901, he purchased property at French Lick Springs and, because of the famous sulphur spring at that location, developed it into one of the world's best-known health resorts. For nearly four decades, from 1892 until his death in 1929, Taggart headed the Democratic organization in Indiana.

question of city, Vice-Chairman Stone had been promoting Kansas City since early November, and Kansas City was chosen without difficulty.[20]

By 1900, there was widespread confusion among the multiparty forces that had favored free silver. The southern middle-of-the-road Populists, having left their party in 1897, conducted a separate nominating convention in Cincinnati on May 11, 1900. The fusionist Populists held their nominating convention at Sioux Falls, South Dakota, on the same date. Large numbers of Silver Republicans attended the latter, which rededicated itself to Bryan and free silver.

On the selection of a vice-presidential nominee at Sioux Falls, Bryan and Chairman Jones suggested the name of a little-known Populist. The strategy was to have the fusionists nominate someone inoffensive to the Democratic convention, thereby making it simpler to arrange a Populist withdrawal in favor of the eventual Democratic vice-presidential nominee. The Populist convention ignored the advice and nominated the popular national chairman of the Silver Republican party, Charles A. Towne. This action added fuel to the flames of the Democratic vice-presidential race, for which New York alone had five men available, Congressman Sulzer the front-runner among them.[21]

Factionalism and interparty problems produced a strong undercurrent at the otherwise colorless Democratic convention in Kansas City. The Democratic national committee selected the convention's temporary chairmen on a 24 to 22 vote. Platform issues were resolved by narrow margins. Agreement on the vice-presidential nominee stalled as Democrats, Silver Republicans, and Populists consulted. The compromise was former Vice-President Adlai E. Stevenson. Wild demonstrations for Bryan were the only evidence of any enthusiasm.

A crisis in relations between Bryan and National Chairman Jones was evident even prior to the convention. Rumor of Jones' resignation had circulated all during the period of his illness and absence in 1899. Jones issued several emphatic denials. Despite his readiness to criticize his chief in public, Jones' loyalty to the party and to Bryan had never been in question. Some advisers to Bryan thought that Jones had "neither the breadth nor capacity intellectually nor the health physically" to carry on the contest in 1900. Others proposed that "someone experienced in conducting campaigns in close northern states where the art of organization has been developed" ought to be named national chairman. One individual with these competencies was Thomas Taggart of Indiana.[22]

Jones became quite uncertain just where he stood with Bryan. After consulting his physician, Jones assured Bryan that he could cope with the physical strain of a campaign, provided the work was shared with others:

> Somehow the impression got out that I was not to be Chairman in the coming campaign and this resulted in my getting many letters urging me not to decline to act. I wrote evasive answers but many things were said which I confess made an impression on me. . . . If you think it politic to have someone else or that it will increase our chances in any degrees to make a change, don't hesitate to say so.[23]

A week before the national convention, it was announced that Jones would succeed himself as national chairman. Bryan was not inclined to change horses in midstream, nor could he easily disregard Jones' apparent desire to continue. Bryan once again intended to conduct a personal campaign, and, in a sense, was simply abdicating responsibility for national organizational matters.[24]

The management of the 1900 Democratic campaign was a repetition of 1896, perhaps with fewer intricacies. The national organization lacked firm direction and enthusiasm. The decision to have or not have a headquarters in New York City remained unresolved until mid-September. Senator Gorman and others waited until October to announce their support of Bryan. Such dubious techniques as the "endless chain" method of raising funds (each Democrat to solicit contributions from a half-dozen or so other Democrats) left much to be desired. Bryan, as usual, carried on his own personal operation. He had a poor press and explored the possibility of launching a large daily newspaper in New York and Chicago. This need was fulfilled when William Randolph Hearst endorsed his candidacy and founded the Chicago *American* as the Bryan paper in the mid-western metropolis.[25]

Chairman Jones went through most of the campaign with an easy optimism that often upset his colleagues. Visiting New York in August, he casually reported to the nominee that "things look well." He wrote, without apparent concern, that the party might lose some votes for its anti-imperialism stand and "in the West some Silver Republicans have abandoned us and gone back to the old party." He was nonetheless confident that victory was in the wings.[26]

Jones may have based his optimism on the fact that about ten of the forty-five states seemed in doubt, and several of them—Idaho, Indiana, Kentucky, Nebraska, and Utah, for example—seemed good Bryan territory. The Democrats were sure of at least fifteen one-party states and the Republicans just as sure of an equal number. When the McKinley landslide rolled in, Jones was "completely stunned" and ready to blame the loss on coercion and corruption.[27]

Just days after the election, discussions were under way regarding the next presidential nominee. Would the Democrats have to look to another? The younger leaders expressed the hope that Bryan would continue "as the aggressive and forceful leader of the Party." Chairman Jones went so far as to suggest a third nomination for Bryan.[28]

An important element in the party took exception to Jones' suggestion. Speaking as a leader of the former Gold Democratic party, Don M. Dickinson of New York expressed the hope that both elements of the Democratic party—the silver and the gold men—could reunite soon. "It was only through Bryan's defeat that the desired reorganization could be brought about. Hence, it was that this year the gold men gave their strength to McKinley instead of setting up a candidate as in 1896."[29]

At the same time, the regular New York organization was eager to return to its old ascendancy in national Democratic politics, as in the days of the first Belmont, Tilden, and Cleveland. In fact, Tammany boss Charles F. Murphy was so nostalgic that he recommended renominating the sixty-four-year-old Cleveland. On the other side of the Democratic fence in New York, former Governor and Senator David B. Hill began to suggest the availability of a fellow New Yorker, Judge Alton B. Parker. Prior to his appointment to the bench, Parker had been Democratic state chairman in New York, winning a notable political reputation for his leadership of the campaign of 1885 which swept Hill into the governorship and carried the state ticket with him.

At forty, William Jennings Bryan was the first presidential nominee to suffer defeat twice consecutively. For Bryan, however, defeat in an election for the presidency was hardly synonymous with defeat in leadership of the Democratic party. Part of the armory of the active leader who has suffered electoral defeat is his capacity to threaten to again become a candidate. "I am not a candidate for any office," he said in 1901; "however, I would not enter into a bond never to become a candidate."[30] Bryan was not about to relinquish his titular leadership and turn his party over to its conservative wing. Consequently, he inaugurated a weekly newspaper called the *Commoner*, began work on a book entitled *The Second Battle*, continued his speaking engagements, but on a more limited scale and with more religious subject matter.

Meanwhile, the national party headquarters disappeared, the only evidence of its existence being several files of records and campaign documents in the custody of various national committee officers. Chairman Jones, although declining in health, continued as an elder statesman in the United States Senate.

4

McKinley's assassination and Theodore Roosevelt's succession to the presidency in 1901 turned national political discourse sharply in a progressive direction. The shift gave fresh impetus to Bryan's brand of reformism and democratic philosophizing, as articulated in the *Commoner*. In his articles and editorials, Bryan favored a federal income tax, direct election of United States senators, independence for the Philippines, prohibition, women's suffrage, a department of labor with cabinet status, publicity of election campaign expenditures, and other radical reform proposals of his day. Having laid the groundwork for a political alliance between the agrarian and labor elements in U.S. politics during the campaigns of 1896 and 1900, he continued to present himself as a spokesman for the farmer and the worker.

Some of Bryan's philosophy of politics was revealed during his advocacy of popular election of senators. Following a Madisonian line, Bryan was firm in his dedication to the dogma, as he called it, of majority rule:

> There is no reason to believe that a majority will always be right. There is, however, a reason to believe that the rule of a majority is more apt to be right than the rule of the minority. Truth has such a persuasive power that a minority in possession of the truth generally grows into a majority, but until it becomes a majority, it cannot insist upon recognition. . . . If we deny to the majority the right to rule, there is no basis on which to build. If a minority rules, it must rule by force, for the moment it secures the consent of the majority, it is no longer a minority.[31]

In proposing direct popular election of senators, Bryan was confident that "the people can be trusted with the direct choice of their public servants."[32] He was also confident that one of the indispensable instruments of that direct choice was the political party. Despite his general disinterest in matters of party organization, Bryan fully supported Theodore Roosevelt's suggestion that the government appropriate money for the legitimate expenses of parties, arguing that this could be justified on the same ground that the printing of ballots by the government had been in earlier years.[33]

In 1902, Bryan's prestige was still sufficient to bring him an invitation to address the inaugural crowds witnessing the installation of the first president of the Republic of Cuba. In 1903, however, he became the object of much unfavorable publicity in connection with his services as executor of the will of a New Haven wholesale grocer, P.S. Bennett. After the Bennett case was favorably disposed, Bryan turned to an extended foreign tour under the auspices of the Hearst newspapers. With editor Henry L. Stoddard as his companion, he traveled for nine weeks to Cuba, Mexico, Europe, and Russia, writing dispatches about his trip for the Hearst syndicate. Upon his return to New York, Bryan received an enthusiastic political welcome that only thinly veiled the growing factional tensions.

William Randolph Hearst had been preparing to make himself heir to the Bryan following. One of Bryan's aides, Millard Fillmore Dunlap, became Hearst's political manager in Illinois. However, Illinois Democratic boss, Roger Sullivan, quickly put an end to the Hearst movement by handpicking a Parker delegation to the national convention. Hearst supporters chose their own delegation. Dunlap called upon his former chief, Bryan, for help, and Bryan consented to lead the fight on behalf of the Hearst delegates at the national convention. Meanwhile, Hearst won election to Congress in 1903.

Bryan-Hearst setbacks started early. At the January 1904 meeting of the national committee, St. Louis was chosen over Chicago as the convention city, 28 to 21. Bryan's old adversary, Arthur P. Gorman, led the anti-Chicago forces.

Several procedural matters concerning the prerogatives of the national chairman were raised. The national committeeman from the District of Columbia had died. In his place Chairman Jones had appointed Edwin Sefton, a practicing lawyer in the district who had long been Jones' secretary. When his appointing authority was challenged at the meeting, Jones pointed out that it had always been the custom that during recesses of the committee the national chairman fill any vacancies that occur. Jones then inquired what the pleasure of the committee would be. Sefton resigned. Some confusion concerning the technicalities ensued during which a parliamentary motion was defeated, 26 to 22, in what appeared to be a division between Bryan and anti-Bryan elements. The matter was referred to a special committee.

In another discussion at the meeting, committeeman John T. McGraw of West

Virginia observed that a great deal of preparatory information gathering and clerical work could be done between January and the time of the convention. This preparation would presumably be of great value to the succeeding national committee and to the nominees. He particularly referred to data that could be compiled for the campaign texbook so that it could be issued in time to be useful and to other information on national organizational matters. The committeeman from Kansas moved that the national chairman undertake the work, and the motion passed, to which Chairman Jones commented, "If there had been embodied in the motion something about where we are going to get the money to do all this, it would have been a little more complete and effective." Jones' complaint notwithstanding, the pressures for preconvention preparation for the presidential campaign increased with the passage of the years.[34]

The party's two living titular leaders symbolized the ongoing factional polarization. A few days after the committee's action, former President Cleveland made an appearance before an anti-Bryan audience. In reply to a public statement by Bryan calling for a reaffirmation of bimetallism, Cleveland recommended to his fellow Democrats that they abandon "obsolete issues."[35]

In New York, David B. Hill worked diligently and effectively to line up Parker votes. During one of Bryan's trips to New York, Hill made every effort, through Norman E. Mack, to arrange a conference. Mack failed, for Bryan would do nothing to lend encouragement to the Parker movement. By paying his respects to Mayor George B. McClellan, Jr., of New York City before leaving town, Bryan indicated that he would support any anti-Hill, anti-Parker tactics that Murphy and Tammany might undertake. This gesture produced no results. After much talk about drafting Cleveland again for the presidency, Murphy finally joined Hill in endorsing Parker at the New York State convention. Hill then won over Sullivan of Illinois. Gorman of Maryland and Guffey of Pennsylvania were cool about Parker, but with no candidate of their own they eventually joined the movement.

For a time there was some speculation that Guffey of Pennsylvania might support Parker if the national chairmanship were forthcoming. This rumor was denied and never became more than newspaper speculation. There was, however, one politician who never denied an intense interest in the national chairmanship: Tom Taggart of Indiana. All through the early months of 1904, Taggart carried on a full-fledged campaign for the chairmanship, with Senator Joe Bailey of Texas acting as his manager.[36]

In Chicago, on April 23, 1904, Bryan declared somewhat gratuitously that he was not a candidate for renomination. Elsewhere, the Hearst boom was collapsing even before getting off the ground. At the national convention in July, Bryan led and lost the fight to seat the Hearst delegation from Illinois by a vote of 647 to 299. Bryan led a more successful fight in the platform committee, where an anti-bimetallism plank was dropped in favor of silence on the currency issue.

The nominating and seconding speeches were of particular interest. Among those placed in nomination were: Judge Alton B. Parker of New York; William Randolph Hearst of Illinois, one of whose seconding speeches was delivered by Clarence Darrow; Francis M. Cockrell, Senate minority leader; Edward C. Wall of Wisconsin, whose nominator pointedly charged that many of Parker's supporters had failed to campaign and vote for Bryan in 1896 and 1900; and several others. After all the states had nominated, seconded, or passed, Bryan went to the rostrum and asked that the rule limiting speeches be suspended. This was a tactic that Bryan would employ in future conventions. Suspension was granted in 1904, without opposition.

In his opening words, the Peerless Leader revealed how much he considered the titular leadership an active responsibility:

> Eight years ago a Democratic national convention placed in my hand the standard of the party and commissioned me as its candidate. Four years later that commission was renewed. I come tonight to this Democratic Convention to return the commission.

With his most spellbinding rhythms, Bryan continued:

> You may dispute whether I have fought a good fight, you may dispute whether I have finished my course, but you cannot deny that I have kept the faith.[37]

He implored his listeners to nominate a man whom the West could accept. He seconded the nomination of Cockrell, but mentioned several others including Hearst, who would be acceptable. His list did not include Parker. The convention listened respectfully, but did not accept his advice. Parker received 679 of the convention's 1,000 votes.

As the vice-presidential nominations were proceeding, a telegram arrived from Parker that threw the convention into an uproar. "I regard the gold standard as firmly and irrevocably established. . . . As the platform is silent on the subject, my view should be made known to the Convention, and if it is proved to be unsatisfactory to the majority, I request you to decline the nomination for me at once."[38]

Bryan took the podium again and shouted to the infuriated delegates, "From the tactics they pursued, you should have known it was not compromise they demanded, but surrender."[39]

In composing a reply to Parker, the embarrassed convention leadership resorted to some sleight of hand, "The platform . . . is silent upon the question of the monetary standard, because it is not regarded by us as a possible issue in this campaign, and only campaign issues are mentioned in the platform." A vote of 794 to 191 authorized the sending of the telegram.[40]

5

Even before the convention, Taggart's campaign for the national chairmanship approached success. Gorman and Guffey removed themselves as candidates. August Belmont, one of Parker's close associates, was considered until his defection to the Gold Democrats in 1896 and 1900 was recalled. As the convention delegations arrived in St. Louis, it was generally conceded that the chairmanship would go to Taggart. The Indiana delegation to the last man devoted itself to his election.

After the convention had nominated Parker, William F. Sheehan of New York successfully moved that National Chairman Jones convene the fifty-three newly designated national committeemen in New York City. Another resolution authorized the national committee to fill any vacancies occurring on the national ticket before election day.

Chairman Jones called a meeting of the national committee in St. Louis after the convention, at which time the Taggart supporters insisted that their man be elected national chairman at once. Chairman Jones said that it was "unheard of" to organize the committee without first consulting the nominee.[41] Norman E. Mack of New York, presumed to be Parker's spokesman, also pointed out how discourteous this would be to the party's new leader. Mack agreed that the committee might simply adopt a resolution endorsing Taggart, which it did. Jones added that the St. Louis meeting was in fact out of order since it was not consistent with the resolution adopted by the convention, which required that the new committee meet in New York City.

The chairmanship discussion moved to New York City. Taggart's closest political associate, John W. Kern of Indiana, pressed an aggressive fight on behalf of his fellow Hoosier. The opposition to Taggart began to unite upon Gorman as an alternative. Kern charged that this would constitute "dumping" Taggart, and added, "We don't want an old fogey at the head of the Committee."[42] Kern visited Parker, wired Taggart to come to New York City, speculated publicly about the prospects of losing Indiana for the Democrats, and darkly anticipated other difficulties. Meanwhile, Mack suggested to the press that either Gorman or Sheehan would be national chairman. As the national committee gathered, Gorman, Sheehan, and Belmont formally took themselves out of the chairmanship race. Chairman Jones arrived, promising Parker that the silverites would support him. At the July 26 meeting, Tom Taggart was unanimously elected chairman. The presidential nominee had acceded to the pressure.[43]

The Parker leaders decided to surround Taggart with organizational arrangements. New Yorker Sheehan made a motion, which was adopted,

that the Chair be authorized to appoint not to exceed two vice-chairmen, as his judgment may determine; that the Chair be authorized to appoint an Executive Committee of not less than five nor more than seven members; that the Chair be authorized to appoint a Finance Committee of not less than three nor more than five members, and if in the judgment of the Chair these two committees should be amalgamated into an Executive Committee, then the Executive Committee shall be composed of seven members; that if at any time the exigencies of the campaign should, in the judgment of the Chairman of the National Committee, require it, or if it becomes advisable at any time for the proper conduct of the campaign, that the Chairman of the National Committee be authorized to appoint a committee or committees for any State or States as the occasion may demand.[44]

McGraw of West Virginia further moved that the executive committee, when selected, be authorized to elect a treasurer of the national committee and report its choice immediately to the national chairman.

When organized, the executive committee was clearly conservative, dedicated to Parker, and anti-Bryan in composition. Most of the members had been Gold Democrats in 1896. William F. Sheehan of New York was chairman. The members included New York banker August Belmont; petroleum magnate James M. Guffey of Pennsylvania; Ohio multimillionaire John R. McLean, an old foe of Bryan; ex-Senator James Smith of New Jersey; Senator Thomas S. Martin of Virginia; and Timothy E. Ryan of Wisconsin. Although not appointed to the executive committee, Senator Gorman was virtually a member. George Foster Peabody was named treasurer by the executive committee. Peabody was an outspoken sound-money man. Delancey Nicoll, a noted New York corporation lawyer who had voted for McKinley in 1896, was appointed vice-chairman and *ex officio* member of the executive committee. This was a group that could represent Parker well and constrain Chairman Taggart if necessary.

The Parker telegram on the gold standard and the composition of the executive committee left no doubt that the gold faction of the East wished nothing more than to remove silver and Bryan as influences within the party.[45]

Chairman Taggart's approach to the campaign indicated that he was a willing prisoner of the eastern wing. One political journalist described Taggart as a "home ruler" in party politics, that is, one who believes that each state organization should do most of its own planning and managing of the campaign. "The new chairman is not a man who will worry about issues except as they may be of service in securing votes."[46] It was expected that Taggart would devote most of his attention to strengthening party organization in the doubtful states, wards, and even precincts. At one point in the course of the campaign, Taggart sadly observed that the contest was "apathetic" and attributed this to the fact that campaign documents had replaced torchlight parades and brass bands.[47]

William Jennings Bryan came into the Parker campaign with a bombshell of his own. In the *Commoner* on July 15, 1904, he indicated that he would support Parker for four reasons: the anti-imperialist stand of the party; the platform declaration favoring reduction of the standing army; Roosevelt's agitation of the race issue; and Roosevelt's warlike postures. However, wrote Bryan, Parker was wrong on the money question, the antitrust issue, and the problems of the laborer, "[T]he fight on economic questions . . . is not abandoned. As soon as the election is over, I shall . . . undertake to organize for the campaign of 1908."

A few days later on July 22, Bryan announced a program for radical Democracy, reiterating that "immediately after the close of the campaign I shall start out to reorganize the Democratic Party along radical lines." In so many words, Bryan was publicly forecasting Parker's defeat and readying himself to reassert his titular leadership.

11 | Management by State and National Party Bosses

As the out-party for the first time in a quarter of a century, Republican leaders in 1885 looked to their organizational shortcomings with renewed determination. Their attention was focused primarily on the structure of the competitive environment in the presidential electorate: a group of safe Republican states matched by a South that was solidly Democratic; several large pivotal states that were closely contested; systems of local election administration that were less than pure. The era was reminiscent of the party competition of the 1840s and 1850s. The era would test the leadership's organizational and tactical skills.

1

For many Republicans, James G. Blaine's narrow defeat in 1884 did not retire their titular leader from politics. The Republican national committee still remained under the control of Blaine leaders at its meeting of December 1887. When President Cleveland devoted an entire annual message to Congress calling for tariff reduction, Blaine promptly issued a response. The two 1884 adversaries, poised at opposite sides of the tariff question, seemed so ready for a repeat contest in 1888 that the Republican national committee pursued the unusual course of outlining the party platform in advance of the national convention. Everything seemed set for Blaine's renomination.

Early in February 1888, National Chairman Benjamin F. Jones received an unexpected letter from Blaine, then in Florence, Italy, serving notice that his name would not go before the national convention again. The shocking news evoked expressions of exasperation, secret conferences, and the usual query, ''Does he mean it?'' Party officials spoke of forcing the nomination upon Blaine, but more realistically began looking over the field for new possibilities.[1]

Much of the uncertainty concerning Blaine's availability originated in the vigor of his reply to Cleveland's tariff message. Even the remote prospect

Matthew Quay had been in Pennsylvania politics since prior to the Civil War, weaving in and out of that state's complex factionalism, receiving appointments from various Republican governors as secretary of the Commonwealth. He became chairman of the state central committee in 1878 and joined Don Cameron in the United States Senate in 1887.

of his renomination encouraged Republican politicians to support their former nominee. It was also possible that Blaine intended to wait out the likely re-election of an incumbent Democratic president and return to the arena in 1892, when the Republican nomination would be much more valuable.

Others were available for 1888. Senator John Sherman of Ohio, a presidential candidate in 1880 and 1884, was still running. Indiana's Benjamin Harrison, grandson of President William Henry Harrison, had been mentioned as presidential material for several years, particularly since he was governor of one of the most closely contested states. Senator William B. Allison of Iowa, the cheap currency advocate, was another major contender.

Sherman was in a particularly strong position. He had been President Hayes' first choice for the nomination in 1880 and had since been developing contacts among the new southern Republican leadership. Although President Arthur thoroughly controlled the southern delegations in 1884, Sherman had also personally and assiduously solicited their support. After Arthur, he was the second choice of many. Arthur's failure to receive the nomination and Blaine's defeat in the election left Sherman heir to this constituency. Their loyalty was strengthened by Sherman's election as president pro-tem of the Senate upon the death of Vice-President Hendricks in 1885, placing him a heartbeat away from the presidency.

Sherman's hold on southern delegate support did not go unchallenged. One consequence of the chase for 1888 convention votes was increased skepticism on the part of southern conservatives that the Republican leadership was sincere about helping to rebuild their state parties. In effect, what was occurring in the Republican parties of the South was the rise of party officials without party voters. The main stock-in-trade of these officials was their national convention votes. They were unburdened by the necessity of also delivering electoral college votes on election day, a responsibility that was carried by state party leaders elsewhere.[2]

It was in the conduct of Sherman's preconvention campaign that Marcus A. Hanna, one of Sherman's managers, began to acquire the experience and contacts that served him so well in his later successes as a party leader.

Marcus A. Hanna was the son of an Ohio physician who had run for Congress as a Whig in 1844. Hanna entered the family's food-merchandising business, becoming its head during his mid-twenties. In 1864, he married the daughter of one of the city of Cleveland's most successful coal and iron merchants. A few years later he became a partner in his father-in-law's firm, and, in 1877, the firm became M.A. Hanna and Company. In an era of big business consolidation and un-paralleled economic expansion, Hanna won a reputation unique among employers for his views on labor-management relations. "Organized labor and organized capital are but forward steps in the great industrial evolution that is taking place," he argued; successful arbitration requires "thorough and effective" organization on both sides.[3] Around 1880, Hanna's attention turned to politics. He bought the *Cleveland Herald* and acquired a reputation as an effective fund raiser. By 1883, Hanna had become a leading manager of the Sherman-for-president movement.

As early as November 1886, Benjamin Harrison wrote that he expected Blaine to get the 1888 nomination

> if he wants it, and he will want it and ask for it unless he concludes that the opposition in his own party is so strong as to make a second defeat probable. In that event, he and his friends will (within limits) be able to name the candidate. He will want a man who can probably win and who will be friendly. But I shall have an opportunity to talk with you this winter, and that is better than to confide in the pen.[4]

Harrison's manager in 1888 was the attorney general of Indiana, Louis T. Michener. Soon after Blaine's withdrawal, Stephen B. Elkins, who had been Harrison's manager in the 1884 convention, wrote to Michener, "I am doing, in a quiet way, all the work I possibly can in Harrison's behalf. If the New York delegation should agree upon him, I think that would secure his nomination. . . . [Gresham] is out of the question [as a good candidate]."[5]

Barring the nomination of Blaine by acclamation, Elkins felt Harrison's appeal seemed the strongest, and he advised Michener to cultivate the Gresham following so as to make Harrison their second choice. The general strategy included an effort to have the Blaine delegates come to the convention uninstructed and unpledged.[6]

Tom Platt kept the New York delegation uncommitted. Pennsylvania boss Matthew Quay made public statements about Sherman's strong prospects, but privately

James S. Clarkson was the national committeeman from Iowa, publisher of the *Des Moines Register*, and holder of interests in banks, railroads, and other properties. Clarkson had been particularly active in the Blaine campaign of 1884, spending most of his time in New York in constant consultation with Elkins and for a time in charge of the speakers bureau.

left himself available for a *quid pro quo* from Harrison. Quay made sure to report to Michener and John B. Elam, Harrison's law partner, all the trials and tribulations of his efforts to unite Pennsylvania behind Harrison. Michener's own estimates indicated that one-third of the Pennsylvania delegates were for Harrison.

"Senator Quay is trying hard to unite them," Michener reported to Harrison. "His idea is that his state can nominate if he can solidify it. He wants recognition for Pennsylvania in the Cabinet."[7] While Quay named no one man to be recognized, he did state a preference for the War Department, the portfolio held by his predecessor, Simon Cameron, and one for which his own experience seemed to qualify him. Since Quay wanted assurances in writing, Michener and Elam went so far as to draft a letter for Harrison's signature approving this arrangement, to which Harrison replied, "No!"—unobtrusively written on the envelope of the letter.[8]

Iowa's was another critical delegation, led by James S. Clarkson and pledged to Senator Allison. Clarkson played his cards cagily. He met in New York with Elkins and agreed to an alliance between Harrison and Allison.[9] Shortly after, Clarkson dined with Joseph Medill, editor of the *Chicago Tribune* and a Gresham advocate, leaving the impression that Gresham was considered favorably in the Allison camp.[10]

Hanna and Quay arrived at the convention as leaders of the Sherman forces, with authority from Sherman "as broadly as language can confer it" to negotiate with members of other delegations.[11] Up to the convention itself, Sherman was convinced that his main opponent was Blaine. He strongly urged Quay and Hanna to stand firmly together to prevent Blaine's nomination.[12]

At the convention, in a field of fourteen candidates, Sherman held the lead up to the sixth ballot. The shift putting Harrison ahead began on the seventh. On the eighth ballot Clarkson announced the withdrawal of Allison's candidacy, completing the swing to Harrison. Quay, who had been voting most of Pennsylvania's strength for Sherman, jumped on the bandwagon belatedly.

2

There was no dearth of advice given Harrison regarding the national chairmanship. William J. Sewell of New Jersey wrote:

> If the Chairman is to be in active charge of the campaign, he should be very carefully selected, and should come from New York City, if possible; he should have the confidence of the business community so as to enable him to raise the sinews of war.[13]

The committeeman from Harrison's state, John C. New, might be helpful in the West, thought Sewell, but not as national chairman.

After conferring with Elkins and Reed of Maine, Harry H. Smith proposed Quay for the chairmanship, giving five reasons:

1. Indiana could be managed quite adequately by Harrison himself, Dudley, and New.

2. This left New York, New Jersey, and Connecticut as the most doubtful areas, in which the tariff would be the main issue, requiring a known tariff man (Quay).

3. The chairman "should not be a man who would use the power and influence of the office of Chairman with a view of political preferment." (Quay?)

4. "He should not be a member of any faction in his state or section where hostility would be aroused or engendered by his selection which would in the least endanger the ticket in that state." (Quay)

5. He should possess "recognized political ability." (Quay)[14]

Other advisers expressed apprehension that Harrison might let the selection of executive and national committee chairmanships go by default to the New York group and urged him to name men from the West.[15] According to Clarkson, Harrison asked him to accept the chairmanship. Clarkson, however, advised that the "Old Grant Crowd" should be placated by the selection of Senator Quay. When Harrison acquiesced, Clarkson asked the leaders of the independent faction of Pennsylvania if they had any objections to Quay. None was made, and Quay was chosen.[16]

Another version was offered by Louis T. Michener:

> Harrison asked me to represent him at the meeting of the [National] Committee in New York early in July. I went reluctantly because I knew that the contest for the chairmanship would be most disagreeable for me for General James S. Clarkson of Iowa, who had been prominently connected with the Committee in the past, and who had helped in nominating Harrison in Chicago would be a candidate, and would be supported by my dear friend General W.W. Dudley and other powerful men. I said all that to Harrison, but he insisted that I must go and gave me full authority, saying also that he would approve whatever I did. I spent forty-eight hours in New York most uncomfortably in this battle. I had made up my mind on the way to support Senator M.S. Quay of Pennsylvania if Mr. Morton and his friends were agreeable to him. In consultation I learned that they favored Senator Quay. I had found that a decided majority of the committeemen favored General Clarkson, but I believed that this could be changed by a motion in the Committee to elect Senator Quay if made in the name of the ticket. That motion was made by John

C. New, the Indiana committeeman, and supported by the member from New York; whereupon a large majority voted for Senator Quay. Then General Clarkson was elected Vice-Chairman; J. Sloat Fassett of New York, Secretary; and General W.W. Dudley, Treasurer. The officers were all skilled and industrious party managers and organizers, and they led a more efficient and a successful campaign.[17]

The campaign moved rapidly into high gear. Clarkson reported to Harrison that "our committee is perfectly harmonious in its personnel."[18] However, the political era was highly competitive and the campaign soon ran into trouble. On October 31, the Indianapolis *Sentinel* published the contents of the "blocks-of-five" circular, a letter allegedly issued by Treasurer W.W. Dudley on national committee stationery to local leaders in Indiana, saying, "Divide the floaters into blocks of five and put a trusted man with necessary funds in charge of these five and make him responsible that none get away and that all vote our ticket."

Quay denounced the *Sentinel* revelation as a lie and promised to prosecute for theft from the federal mails. Dudley instituted legal suits, although these subsequently were dropped. The Quay-Dudley bluff kept enough voters in doubt to enable the Republicans to carry Indiana by 2,300 votes.[19]

The situation in the New York campaign is best told in the words of historian Allan Nevins:

> On the Saturday before election the [Republican] National Committee paid through a state leader $150,000 for bribery. It was all used for the purpose of three "movements"—the James O'Brien movement, estimated at 10,000 votes; the Coogan movement, estimated at 30,000; and the John J. O'Brien or Eighth District movement, an unknown quantity. The *Mail and Express* declared that the Coogan movement promised Harrison and Miller 20,000 more votes than it really polled; the James O'Brien movement 10,000 more than it polled; and that the John J. O'Brien movement kept its word pretty well for Harrison but miserably for Miller. In other words, the *Mail and Express* was angry because a costly attempt to buy votes in New York City had broken down—only half of them had stayed bought![20]

3

The Republican plurality in New York was only 13,000, but the state's electoral college votes elected Harrison. Nationally, the Democrats had a plurality—some 96,000 votes. The narrow margin of victory gave special point to Chairman Quay's postelection comment that Harrison "would never know how close a number of men were compelled to approach the gates of the penitentiary to make him President."[21] As a consequence, Quay expected to have a large influence upon patronage in the Harrison administration.

President Harrison, however, proceeded to make appointments according to his own judgments. James G. Blaine was called out of retirement to head the

State Department. Tom Platt did not receive the Treasury Department, although he insisted that it had been promised to him.[22] Quay thought Clarkson should receive the position of postmaster general and its vast patronage; instead it went to John Wanamaker, Quay's rival in Pennsylvania Republican politics. Clarkson, who credited Harrison's election to Quay and Platt, was appointed first assistant postmaster general. Clarkson observed that "things are not turning out as expected"; his loyalty to Harrison began to cool as his sympathies for Quay warmed.[23] Harrison-Quay differences became public in the contest for the speakership of the House of Representatives in December 1889. Harrison favored William McKinley; Quay favored Thomas B. Reed. Reed won in a close vote. Harrison had to confront Quay's hostility in the Senate and Reed's in the House throughout his administration.

National Chairman Quay was not without his own problems. On February 10 and March 3, 1890, the *New York World* devoted sixteen columns to an exposé of Senator Quay's conduct while secretary of the Commonwealth and state treasurer of Pennsylvania. The charges against Quay included (1) while secretary of the Commonwealth, between 1879 and 1882, Quay took money from the state treasury (not a difficult achievement in prebudget days), lost $260,000 of it in speculations, and was saved from exposure by the timely assistance of Don Cameron; and (2) even though this offense was widely known, Quay was elected state treasurer in 1885, and in this office he used some $400,000 in state funds for new private speculation. There were immediate demands from reform Republicans that Quay resign from the national chairmanship. He twice called and as many times postponed meetings of the national committee. Finally, he declared that he would not resign under fire and would do so only after the midterm elections in the fall.

On the congressional front the main issues of public debate continued to be the tariff, currency, and civil service reform, the latter called "the trifling thing of hobby riders" by Republican Vice-Chairman Clarkson.[24] Two other issues reached a new level of importance: the growth of monopolistic business enterprises and, with the Republicans again controlling the presidency, the question of a strategy for halting the rise of a South that was solidly Democratic. There was significant legislative activity on most of these matters during 1890: the Sherman Silver Purchase Act, designed to ease the currency shortage; the McKinley tariff, raising duties to new highs; and the Sherman Antitrust Act. Civil service reform went into reverse, particularly in the Post Office Department under John Wanamaker and his first assistant, James S. Clarkson. Half of the 2,700 postmasters subject to presidential appointment were removed or resigned to be replaced by Republicans. Of the 56,000 postmasterships that were not presidential appointments, 49,000 were similarly displaced.[25]

Possibly the most difficult problem confronting national Republican leaders was the continued loss of party strength in the South. White supremacy legislation and practices had begun to disenfranchise Blacks entirely. Where Blacks did still have the vote, they felt completely abandoned by the Hayes-Garfield-Arthur policies. Some northern Republicans agreed with Senator Philetus Sawyer of Wisconsin: "What's the use of bothering about the South!"[26] After long and careful study, President Harrison reached the conclusion that a federally protected ballot box in southern states would reap Republican votes there; this meant a willingness to return to the use of troops as in Reconstruction days.

Henry Cabot Lodge introduced the principal bill in the House in March 1890, where it eventually passed on July 2 by a vote of 155 to 149. In the Senate, the bill ran into agenda difficulties, competing against the pending tariff and silver legislation. Under Senator Gorman's leadership, the Democrats began to filibuster the elections bill, now called the Force Bill, and in so doing, impeded consideration of the McKinley tariff. At this point, Quay and Cameron of Pennsylvania moved to postpone action on the election bill, and protectionists in both parties carried the motion. Despite Harrison's efforts to revive the election measure in his message to Congress in December 1890, the Quay maneuver put an end to further efforts to build a Republican party in the South.[27]

The Republicans lost seventy-eight seats in the House in the fall elections. Agrarian unrest in the South and the West motivated voters to elect nine representatives and two senators running on independent and Populist tickets. Twice this number of Democrats went to Congress pledged to the Populist programs of the farmers' organizations. The following year, the Populist party was established nationally. In Pennsylvania, Quay's gubernatorial candidate was defeated and the overthrow of "Quayism" was hailed.

The cry for National Chairman Quay's resignation was renewed. The announcement finally came on July 19, 1891. Quay let it be known that Vice-Chairman Clarkson was the man best fitted to succeed him; Clarkson had resigned from his position as first assistant postmaster general in August 1890. There was some speculation about just how the change would be formalized. Clarkson issued a statement concerning the powers of the executive committee:

> The Executive Committee has unquestionably the power to act upon a resignation, as the National Committee had empowered it to transact its business, but not to elect to fill vacancies in the committee. Should Mr. Quay resign, the Vice-Chairman would take his place until the full committee selected a new Chairman.[28]

This statement would later take on special importance in connection with the selection of Clarkson's successor in 1892.

The Quay resignation put a new face on the question of the Republican nominations in 1892. Quay declared that Secretary of State Blaine could be nominated if he consented to be a candidate. Clarkson, on the other hand, dodged questions regarding his preference between Harrison and Blaine. He did observe that Harrison had been a faithful executive, "lacking only in personal popularity."[29]

Returning from Europe just as the news of Quay's resignation was released, Clarkson wrote to President Harrison expressing his readiness to acquiesce to any plan of reorganization that met with the president's approval. He went into some detail about his personal plans to buy a newspaper either in Chicago or New York and perhaps to purchase *Cosmopolitan Magazine*. Clarkson continued:

> I can readily recognize that from this time on, with the high duty resting upon the administration to strengthen the party in every possible way for its next great contest, all the men in controlling places ought to be those who possess your confidence and can be fully trusted by you. . . . You and Blaine—with the friendship that exists, or ought to exist, between you—and with the supreme power that you together have in the land—can save the party from *any* contest and give it the necessary power of union and harmony as the first requisite for success in '92.[30]

The executive committee met on July 29. Indiana's national committeeman, John C. New, perhaps the most prominent of the friends of the administration, was not present and no friendly proxy was there to take his place. Louis T. Michener lamented this absence, for it left the impression that the administration had no friends on the executive committee or that Harrison was not interested in party affairs. Either notion was likely to influence unfavorably the bandwagon riders among the federal officeholders. Michener himself kept away from the gathering only because he did not have New's proxy.

At the meeting, Quay resigned from both the executive and the national committees; "Blocks-of-Five" Dudley followed suit. Despite his earlier statement regarding the limited powers of the executive committee, no objection was raised when Clarkson was elected by the executive committee to several capacities: national chairman, chairman of the executive committee, and treasurer, the latter position until someone else could be found.

4

Those at the executive committee meeting apparently agreed that Blaine would never be a candidate unless the convention tendered the nomination in some extraordinarily flattering manner. Nor could he accept it while in Harrison's cabinet. Michener later wrote to the president's secretary that the leading politicians seemed determined to maneuver matters so as to make themselves sought after by presidential candidates. He judged that Platt, Alger, Clarkson, and Dudley held the key to the situation and that their subordinates would henceforth handle the Blaine boom while "the politicians" remained silent.[31]

George B. Cortelyou's Huguenot ancestors played a leading role in the settlement of New York in the mid-seventeenth century. Son of a successful businessman, Cortelyou's college education was largely in literature and music at private schools. As he turned twenty, he felt the need for a practical skill and attended a stenographic school, a decision of great importance to his later rise in politics. Of Republican anteced-ents, he had an active interest in party affairs, founding the Young Men's Republican Club of Hempstead, New York, while still a youth. In 1884, at twenty-two, he became a leading member of the Plumed Knights, a Blaine campaign organization. At that time he was appointed stenographer and private secretary to the Republican appraiser of the port of New York. With Blaine's defeat, Cortelyou became a stenogra-pher in the New York superior court, where he achieved a reputation as a medical as well as a legal stenographer. For a brief number of years he was principal of a college preparatory school in New York and from 1889 to 1891 private secretary to the Post Office Department inspector in charge of the New York area. In the spring of 1891, he became pri-vate secretary to Harrison's fourth assistant postmaster general. Cortelyou performed his official duties with such skill that, although known to have been an active assistant to the Harrison managers, he was requested to stay on to manage the fourth assistant's office after Cleveland's re-election. Hearing of Cortelyou's reputation for efficiency, President Cleveland in 1895 appointed him presidential stenographer and later executive clerk. Cortelyou continued in this position under Mc-Kinley, meanwhile earning an LL.B, LL.M., and an LL.D. at various Dis-trict of Columbia law schools.

Although not publicly committed to any candidate, Clarkson held frequent conferences with the anti-Harrison leaders. As Blaine's health deteriorated, there were rumors that the Blaine men would unite upon McKinley or Allison. In selecting Minneapolis as the convention city, seven national committee ballots were required. The choice was viewed as a defeat for the Harrison group, which had supported Cincinnati.

Benjamin Harrison, James G. Blaine, and William McKinley were the three principal names before the national convention in 1892. Louis T. Michener was once more Harrison's personal manager; National Committeeman New was Harrison's official floor manager. Michener had the invaluable secretarial assis-tance of George B. Cortelyou. His most frequent adviser was Thomas H. Carter of Montana. Other assistance came from Wisconsin's National Committeeman Henry C. Payne.

Born and educated in Illinois, and a practicing lawyer for a brief spell in Iowa, Thomas H. Carter made his permanent residence in Montana, where he specialized in mining law. Although the Montana Territory was Democratic, as a Republican Carter won election as its representative to Congress in 1888. In Congress, Carter developed a strong friendship with Speaker Reed and was soon assigned to the secretaryship of the Republican congressional campaign committee. When Carter failed to win re-election in 1890, Harrison, as a gesture to the silver Republicans of the Northwest, appointed Carter as head of the Land Office of the Department of Interior. Carter resigned from this position just prior to the 1892 convention, which he attended as a Harrison manager without delegate status.

Massachusetts-born Henry Clay Payne was the son of a local public official of modest means and obvious Whig affiliation. Payne completed a secondary school education, worked for a short period as a clerk in a dry goods and clothing establishment, and, at age twenty, moved to Milwaukee, Wisconsin, where he achieved considerable success in the insurance business. His first activities in politics took place in 1872 when he helped organize the city's Young Men's Republican Club. As a consequence, he was offered the postmastership of Milwaukee in 1873, but did not accept the position until 1876. Payne held the postmastership for ten years and used it most effectively as a political base. He gave special attention to improvement of the money order branch from which many of the foreign-born in the city remitted money to families in the homeland. By 1881, as head of the Milwaukee "Post Office Clique," Payne displaced the incumbent party boss, Elisha Keyes, as head of the state organization. He served successively as secretary and chairman of the state central committee and, after 1888, as Wisconsin Republican national committeeman. Payne managed the Harrison campaigns in several midwestern states in 1888 and 1892. After leaving the Milwaukee postmastership in 1885, Payne involved himself in a variety of public utility operations, in 1889 becoming president of the Wisconsin Telephone Company and in 1895 president of the Milwaukee Street Railway Company.

The Blaine forces were directed by Matthew Quay and National Chairman Clarkson, the latter's partisanship now out in the open. McKinley's manager was Mark Hanna, who had transferred his allegiance to McKinley in Ohio politics largely as a consequence of Sherman's advancing age and ineptitude in the 1888 nominating fight. Among these managers were one former (Quay), one incumbent (Clarkson), and four future (Carter, Hanna, Payne, and Cortelyou) national chairmen.

The relative strength of the major candidates was not at all clear as the 1892 convention opened.[32] Harrison had put off his decision to run again until shortly before the convention, giving Michener very little time to organize his support. Blaine's intentions were unknown until three days before the convention, when he abruptly resigned as secretary of state, a move that Michener attributed to Mrs. Blaine's pique over President Harrison's refusal to promote her son-in-law to brigadier general. "The National Committee is engineering the opposition," Michener told Charles Foster, "and doing it in the Committee headquarters. The feeling against the Committe is very bitter."[33]

Michener believed that the Blaine people were really trying to nominate McKinley. McKinley was publicly pledged to President Harrison, but during a private conference Michener found Hanna noncommittal. Michener's scouts at the convention brought reports that McKinley was attending several anti-Harrison conferences and that Hanna had on hand several crates of McKinley badges, pennants, and portraits.

Management of the 1892 convention seemed to be in the hands of the Blaine supporters: Clarkson, who opened the proceedings as national chairman; J. Sloat Fassett, a Platt man, who received the temporary chairmanship. At this point, Michener pulled his first coup by nominating McKinley for permanent chairman. Quay complimented Michener for the cleverness of this strategy, stating, "We will have to support McKinley for the place, although we had planned that he should be on the floor. This makes it impossible for McKinley to Garfield* the convention."[34]

The next test came with the resolution of the disputed delegation seats. The fight for Alabama's 22 votes was the most critical. The national committee had turned the matter over to a special subcommittee of three just prior to the convention; Quay was its chairman. When its report came to a vote on the convention floor, the Harrison delegates were seated by the uncomfortable winning margin of 463 to 423$\frac{1}{2}$. This vote dampened the Blaine boom. Had Ohio voted with Blaine men on the Alabama case, Chairman Clarkson later observed, Harrison could have been defeated.[35]

---

*To "Garfield" a convention refers to the Republican national convention of 1880, which gave its presidential nomination to Congressman James A. Garfield for his reasoned and moderate floor speeches that calmed the intense factionalism of that gathering.

Many delegates continued to entertain doubts about Harrison's strength, and one suggested holding a rally of all the Harrison men. Michener recommended that an element of secrecy and mystery be employed, lest the more fickle Harrison adherents shy away in fear of being caught on a losing team. Word of the rally was passed to a "Committee of Forty" and to thirty other key men in the different delegations. Each was instructed which delegates to see and, at the proper time, to say only these words: "Come with me and you will see something that has never before been seen, and that you will love to think of all your life. Put your faith in me."[36] About 468 persons, representing 521 convention votes, took the bait and shortly found themselves in nearby Market Hall cheering for Harrison. When told the news, Quay could not understand how the meeting had been called without his getting wind of it. He added: "The fight will go on just the same."[37]

The first ballot gave Harrison $535\frac{1}{6}$, Blaine $182\frac{1}{6}$, and McKinley 182; $6\frac{2}{3}$ either voted for others or did not vote. Mark Hanna had told Sherman that he believed the use of McKinley's name in opposition to the president's would do more good than harm. In the belief that 1892 was not a Republican year, Hanna said to McKinley, "Well, William, that is what I call a damn tight squeak!"[38]

There was little enthusiasm for the president's renomination. Harrison very quickly encountered difficulties in putting together the campaign and permanent organizations. Michener would not take the national chairmanship. In Michener's words:

> The President wished me to take the chairmanship, but I declined for professional reasons. That was the only time that I ever declined to render any service that he requested; and in later years I regretted that declination. . . . Platt, Quay and other malcontents, with their insidious and harmful advice and conduct, would have had no influence with my management.[39]

With respect to the national chairmanship, Garrett A. Hobart of New Jersey proposed Clarkson as the person to give the Blaine men a direct responsibility for the success of the national ticket. P.E. Quigg of the *New York Tribune* suggested Thomas H. Carter as "the best man available to handle Platt."[40] Carter was not a member of the national committee, but a rule adopted in 1888 permitted nonmembers to serve on the executive committee.

Harrison hoped that the national chairman would come from New York. The press mentioned Horace Porter, but he declined the dubious responsibility of converting Platt into a Harrison enthusiast. A conference with Cornelius N. Bliss, wealthy New York financier and recent chairman of the state committee, found him unwilling to assume the thankless job of welding party factions into a team. Bliss was contented to help as treasurer and fund raiser.[41] Chris Magee, a rival of Quay in Pennsylvania, was prominently mentioned. The name of William J. Campbell of Illinois received some attention. As the national committee convened, Harrison confided to Chauncy Depew, "We are today attempting an organization of the National Committee, amid some distracting influences which I had hoped would not appear."[42]

Just prior to the national committee meeting, Chairman Clarkson asked the president for an interview regarding the committee's organization.[43] Clarkson later reported the results of the interview to the committee. Thanking the members of the committee for their expressions of confidence and support, Clarkson told them that the president wanted some other man, but had not designated which one. Carter, Campbell, William A. Massey of Delaware, and Person Colby Cheney of New Hampshire had been among those mentioned by Harrison. Only Campbell and Cheney were members of the national committee. Henry C. Payne, speaking for the Harrison men, nominated Campbell, who was elected by acclamation. Carter was appointed secretary.

The committee's choice of William J. Campbell as national chairman was not a happy one for President Harrison. The forty-two-year-old Chicago lawyer had three times been elected president of the Illinois Senate and was a loyal Blaine man in 1880 and 1884. Harrison was trying to win over the Blaine supporters outside of New York and Pennsylvania.

On the floor of the Senate, Campbell's appointment was the occasion for caustic comment by Senator Vest of Missouri, "He haunted my meat committee . . . from one end of the country to the other, representing Armour and his beef monopoly at Chicago. He is the man who advised Armour . . . to refuse to obey our subpoenas."[44] Campbell had accepted the chairmanship with the understanding that certain private business engagements might make it impossible for him to serve. After efforts to adjust these engagements, Campbell, in conference with Carter, Elkins, Michener, Spooner, and Rusk, concluded that it would be impossible to do so. On July 5, Carter announced Campbell's resignation. The executive committee was called to accept the resignation and elect a successor.[45]

Chairmanship speculations started again. When the name of Edward Rosewater, owner of the *Omaha Bee*, came up, Clarkson made it clear that he would not serve on the same executive committee with the national committeeman from Nebraska. Michener observed that Rosewater was "surely one of the most disagreeable men I ever knew." The favorites among Republican leaders in Washington seemed to be Clarkson and Carter. In desperation, Harrison drafted a telegram to Henry C. Payne; Philetus Sawyer agreed to sign it. "Either you or Spooner must take the Chairmanship," wired the Wisconsin senator; "The situation is urgent." At the same time, Harrison's private secretary wired Spooner, "Every effort has been made to secure the gentleman you suggested [probably Rosewater] but it has failed. Matter must be settled before National Committee meets." Would Spooner accept the chairmanship? After giving sincere assurances of friendship for Harrison, Payne and Spooner refused.[46]

The executive committee met on July 16. Campbell's resignation was accepted. Clarkson nominated, and Henry C. Payne seconded, Thomas H. Carter, the national committee secretary, for the chairmanship. The vote was unanimous. Nothing seems to have been said about the authority by which the executive committee elected the national committee's chairman or the fact that Carter was not a member of the national committee. The new vice-chairman, M.H. De Young, waited until after the election to raise these parliamentary questions.

In December, De Young inquired whether the executive committee had the authority to accept Campbell's resignation. Only the full national committee could accept a resignation, he argued. Until such acceptance, said De Young, he as vice-chairman carried the chairmanship. Carter's election was to the chairmanship of the executive committee only.

Campbell and Carter at first denied the validity of De Young's position, but when the full national committee met at Louisville in 1893, Carter quietly handed the gavel over to De Young. A resolution retroactively confirming the July 1892 action of the executive committee was ruled out of order. Campbell's resignation was accepted as of the current date, May 10, 1893, and Carter was elected national chairman in proper fashion. On none of these occasions was Carter's nonmembership on the national committee mentioned. He became the first "outsider" to be chosen for the Republican national chairmanship.[47] Six new states participated in the 1892 election—North Dakota, South Dakota, Montana, Washington, Wyoming, and Idaho. The new Northwest was presumably Chairman Carter's specialty.

5

In the campaign of 1892, the country knew the two candidates as presidents, Harrison and Cleveland. There was little that could be added to their personal portraits. Public discussion hinged upon the tariff, the defeated election law, and the arbitary rule of "Czar" Reed in the House of Representatives. In the West and the South, that large portion of the electorate not yet attached to either major party and uneasy about the deteriorating agricultural economy found its way into the camp of Populist candidate James B. Weaver.

Against the odds, Carter succeeded in uniting most of the Republican factions. An ailing James G. Blaine issued a statement in support of the ticket. Matthew Quay sent a lieutenant to campaign headquarters in August. He himself arrived late in October, whereupon Carter deferred to the advice of the veteran campaigner, particularly regarding the contests in New York and Pennsylvania.

Platt was more difficult to please. Platt's complaint was personal: the president apparently thought of him as merely a political boss, "not good enough to be a friend."[48] After much maneuvering and letter writing, Harrison wrote to Platt, "I have concluded to dispense with all intermediaries and to address you directly, with absolute frankness." The president made three points. First, there would be no promises—"Every appointment will be left open until the time for making it arrives." Second, he had the highest personal regard for the New York chieftain—"I have never intentionally done or omitted anything out of any personal disrespect." And third, Platt would have to make the next move:

> You will not expect me to apologize for getting the nomination—nor I you for having tried to prevent it. . . . It has seemed to me that it would be very desirable, as well on your account as mine, that our [contemplated] meeting should be anticipated rather than followed by any steps you may decide to take.[49]

Platt replied that he would look forward to their conference and put in his first appearance at Republican headquarters on August 29.[50] Nevertheless, that fall, Harrison failed to carry New York's thirty-six electoral votes.

Defeated by his old adversary Grover Cleveland, Harrison returned to his law practice in Indiana, to the writing of books and lectures commenting on the history of the United States, and, at age sixty, to retirement from active party leadership.[51] Neither Harrison nor his long-time manager, Michener, felt that the ex-president should seek renomination in 1896 or exercise titular leadership of any kind. On the renomination, Harrison wrote to Michener after the 1894 midterm elections: "I am not very anxious just now to make myself more popular. Indeed I am somewhat tempted to do something very unpopular for safety."[52]

In view of Harrison's difficulties with Republican state bosses and with the management of the national organs of his own party during a time of close competition between the parties, his comments on intraparty splits and bolts, although made with regard to the Democratic party, are of more than passing interest. Harrison left office at the end of an era in which the two major national parties had achieved a level of electoral organization that in many respects was similar to that at the end of the 1836–1852 period. Factional bolts, new third parties, and large-scale shifts among party leaders and voters particularly marked the years between 1852 and 1856 and again the years from 1892 to 1896. Disintegration of the national parties was a fundamental problem after 1852. It re-emerged in 1896. Harrison observed:

> I have never had so much respect for so many Democrats as I have now. That party has once more exhibited its capacity to be ruptured, and *a party that can not be split is a public menace*. When the leaders of a party assembled in convention depart from its traditional principles and advocate doctrines that threaten the integrity of the government, the social order of our communities and the security and soundness of our finances [a reference to the free silver issue], the party ought to split [a reference to the bolt of the Gold Democrats after the nomination of William Jennings Bryan] and it dignifies itself when it does split. A bolt is now and then a most reassuring incident.[53]

6

One of the consequences of the 1892 Republican defeat was the emergence of Mark Hanna as the party's leading organizational talent. Even while serving as a national convention manager for the Sherman cause in 1888, Hanna had William McKinley in mind as a future presidential candidate. Hanna was later on hand in Washington to manage McKinley's unsuccessful contest with Reed for the House speakership. In 1891, he ran the McKinley campaign for governor of Ohio. With Harrison's defeat in 1892, Hanna immediately began the campaign for McKinley's presidential nomination. This would have to be accomplished over the resistance of the Republican leadership in the Senate, the so-called "Combine." As Senator Platt put it:

> Abundantly supplied with money, and able to command any number of millions he needed, Hanna really began his campaign to make McKinley President, immediately after the defeat of Harrison in 1892. He had the South practically solid before some of us awakened. Then he picked off enough Western and Pacific Slope States.[54]

The Combine included Senators William E. Chandler of Maine, Matthew Quay of Pennsylvania, Thomas Platt of New York, W.B. Allison of Iowa, Shelby M. Cullom of Illinois, and Speaker Thomas B. Reed. Platt's favorite-son candidate was Governor Levi P. Morton; Quay declared himself a candidate; and Allison's campaign was managed by J.S. Clarkson. Probably the most serious candidate was Speaker Reed, who had the friendly but unpledged support of such men as Theodore Roosevelt and Senator Henry Cabot Lodge as well as Quay, Platt, National Chairman Carter, Chandler, and others.

With Hanna directing his campaign, McKinley was re-elected governor of Ohio in 1893. As McKinley and Reed forces on the Republican national committee began to choose up sides, Chairman Carter gave up his chairmanship of the executive committee to campaign for his own re-election to the Senate as well as to withdraw to neutral ground in the developing battle for the presidential nomination. Speaker Reed's preconvention manager became chairman of the executive committee. The chairman of the Republican congressional campaign committee was a McKinley man. The two committees competed strenuously for control of the midterm campaign.

The returns brought Republican victories in the election, whereupon Hanna turned over management of his business enterprises to his brother, rented a winter home in Georgia, and made it into a mecca for the many southern Republican leaders with whom he had become acquainted during the Sherman candidacy. On December 9, 1895, permanent McKinley headquarters were established in Washington. Party veterans looked askance at such behavior, considering it premature and undignified.

On January 7, 1896, Quay, Platt, Clarkson, Manley, and Filley conferred and adopted a favorite son strategy to stop McKinley. Thomas B. Reed would hold New England. Levi P. Morton would be New York's candidate, Matthew Quay would be Pennsylvania's. William Allison would tie down Iowa, Benjamin Harrison would run in Indiana, Shelby M. Cullom in Illinois, and Cushman K. Davis in Minnesota. Meanwhile, National Chairman Carter and other pro-silver committeemen moved into a balance of power position between the McKinley and Reed factions on the national committee, and this became critical when the roll of the national convention was to be composed. There was talk of ousting Carter for his "immoderate" free-silver views. Platt, who encouraged the ouster rumors, suspected that Carter and the silver committeemen might favor McKinley at some critical point. The McKinley men were quick to defend Carter's retention as chairman.

Former President Harrison's withdrawal as a possible candidate came in February 1896. By the end of April, after a series of state conventions had selected delegates, it was estimated that McKinley had 360 votes, about 100 short of a majority. The Reed campaign all but collapsed at the end of April when the Vermont state convention, thought to be in his camp, declared itself for McKinley. This denied Reed the solid support he had expected in New England, and the blow was magnified on the following day when the Illinois convention went for McKinley. On May 27, after serious division among New York Republicans, one of the principal state leaders, Warner Miller, announced for McKinley.

At the national convention, there were 156 seating contests, 128 of which were in the southern delegations. The critical test came in the Alabama contest, which was settled by a vote of 38 to 7 in favor of the McKinley delegates; Chairman Carter also voted with McKinley.

The tariff was McKinley's forte in the policy field; both he and Hanna wanted to give it maximum attention in the platform and the campaign. Hanna hoped to deal with silver through a mild or ambiguous currency plank. At the convention, however, he was confronted with a choice between a militant free-silver minority and the strong gold sentiment of such eastern Republicans as Platt, Quay, and Lodge.[55] The Saturday before the convention, in Hanna's hotel room, Hanna, W.R. Merriam of Minnesota, Henry C. Payne of Wisconsin, H.H. Kohlsaat of Chicago, and Nicholas Murray Butler of New York argued about how to handle the gold plank. Initially Hanna believed that a strong stand for gold might embarrass his candidate. Payne presented the best possible reasons for including the plank. Merriam and Kohlsaat agreed with Payne. Hanna telephoned McKinley at Canton and the latter consented to go along with whatever seemed best. Hanna then approved an out-and-out gold plank.[56]

The silver delegates on the platform committee attempted to push through three different resolutions favoring free silver, but all were voted down by 41 to 10. The floor test on the silver issue was voted down by a vote of $818^1/_2$ to

$105^{1}/_{2}$. About 34 silver delegates bolted the convention. National Chairman Carter was the only leading silverite to keep his seat.[57]

McKinley received $661^{1}/_{2}$ votes on the first ballot, and thus the nomination. The convention acknowledged Hanna's remarkable accomplishment by calling him to the rostrum to acknowledge the applause and to deliver a speech. Instead of waiting the customary two or three weeks, the national committee elected Hanna as chairman immediately at the close of the convention.[58]

In contrast to the deep split in the Democratic party, unity was achieved among the Republicans as a result of Hanna's decision on the gold plank and his extraordinary conduct of the election campaign. Active in the campaign was former President Harrison, who spoke frequently in New York, Virginia, and his home state of Indiana. Never before had a presidential campaign been as thoroughly organized, as much campaign literature and speeches communicated to the electorate, and as much money raised and expended. Hanna's managerial achievements were unprecedented and have been thoroughly documented elsewhere.[59]

Two full-fledged Republican headquarters, in Chicago and New York, were established. There was a division of labor under Hanna's direction among national committee, congressional campaign committee, and such nonparty groups as the Protective Tariff League.[60] Expenditures were without parallel to that date; some informed estimates put the figure as high as $7 million by the national agencies alone.[61] A complete commercial bookkeeping and auditing system was installed to keep track of the flow of funds. On October 14, the *New York Journal* revealed that Hanna had sent out a circular letter to several banks in Newark, New Jersey, assessing them 1/8 of 1 percent of their capital stock for support of the campaign. This was confirmed and was found to be the fund-raising procedure in several states. Standard Oil, for example, gave $250,000. The national committee produced an estimated 120 to 225 million pamphlets and other documents.

Mark Hanna's activities were probably the most discussed of any politician in that day. An industrial statesman, chief executive of his national party, and, with McKinley's victory, dispenser of a vast government patronage, National Chairman Hanna was declared by many to be the public figure most representative of the energy, prosperity, optimism, and other qualities of Americans generally during this era of U.S. history.[62]

12 | Expansion of Presidential and Chairmanship Resources

The growth in the resources of the presidency was dramatic after 1896. The Spanish-American War, the administration of the nation's overseas dependencies, demands for federal intervention in various aspects of national economic life such as the monopoly-dominated industries, and World War I gave the executive branch an enlarged bureaucracy, additional patronage, and purchasing power that exceeded anything known previously. Presidents found themselves with unprecedented tools of influence.

National leadership tended to fall into two styles: "quiet" and "vocal." The McKinley approach was to employ the new tools of the presidency without fanfare. According to his personal secretary, George B. Cortelyou, McKinley unobtrusively exercised even greater political skills than those so often attributed to Mark Hanna. In contrast, Theodore Roosevelt used the new political tools to fashion his own special dynamic presidential leadership and succeeded to the point of naming his successor, William Howard Taft. Woodrow Wilson gave a parliamentary interpretation to the new presidency, trying to follow the British tradition of strong prime ministerial leadership.

But even such vocal and vigorous leaders as Roosevelt and Wilson met with frustration when opposed by alliances of state party bosses serving in the United States Senate. These legislators controlled their respective state party machines and electorates. Presidents had to deal not only with voters, but also with party and congressional politicians.

The national party chairmanship also passed through substantial evolution and growth during this period. There was need for national party agencies to keep pace with the organizational developments elsewhere in the nation, particularly in the presidency, industry, communication, transportation, and finance. The concept of year-round national party operations and permanent national headquarters gained general acceptance among party leaders during the decades between 1900 and 1930. The trend was speeded along by the need to deal with increasing numbers of nationally organized interest groups.

1

After Hanna's many years as a McKinley associate and promoter bore fruit in McKinley's election, the public impression was that he nominated and elected this president and dominated his administration. The Hearst newspapers were the principal source of the notion that Hanna dominated McKinley. The testimony of many contemporaries is quite different, namely, that Hanna treated McKinley with conspicuous deference—"Together these two made one perfect politician."[1]

McKinley was himself a thoroughly experienced politician. He knew how to make his own decisions. Like Hanna, he was a behind-the-scenes political operator. For most of McKinley's first administration, the relationship between the two men was mutually supportive. McKinley tended to remain behind the scenes, despite his occupancy of the presidency. However, Hanna tended to place himself in the forefront of Republican political affairs as a spokesman and as a target for the opposition. His name became synonymous with "plutocrat" in the Democratic party's lexicon. This high profile was particularly evident after he became a candidate for a seat in the United States Senate.

President McKinley intended to reward Hanna by appointing him postmaster general. Most of the federal job patronage at this time consisted of postmasterships. Certain that most of the patronage would be cleared with him in his position as national chairman, Hanna preferred the independence and power of a seat in the Senate to a relatively subordinate position in the cabinet. In conversation with a friend as early as 1892, Hanna made it clear that the only public office he ever had dreamed of occupying was that of United States senator and that he felt there was little chance of reaching this goal. Possibly his hero worship of Senator John Sherman was involved; Sherman had been Hanna's ideal as a senator from the time Hanna was old enough to vote.[2]

Hanna suggested to President McKinley that a suitable vacancy would be created in the Senate if John Sherman were to be appointed secretary of state. McKinley hesitated, since the assumption was that Ohio's Governor Asa Bushnell would be willing to appoint Hanna to Sherman's seat. Ohio's Senator-elect Foraker openly declared his opposition to such an arrangement. McKinley finally made the request and Sherman accepted, recommending that Bushnell appoint Hanna as his successor. A six-week stalemate followed. McKinley eventually exerted his personal influence, and Bushnell made the appointment. Hanna took his seat in the Senate in 1897, but bitterness over the pressure persisted in Ohio.[3]

The Ohio legislature met in January 1898 to fill the full senatorial term. Hanna was one of several in the running. He won, with administration backing, in a vote of 71 to 70. It was no small tribute to the president's diplomacy that even under these conditions he retained the affection of Foraker and his adherents. Hanna's election was questioned in the Third Session of the Fifty-fifth Congress on grounds that it had been won by bribery, but evidence was never produced and the charges were dropped.

Thereafter, in his multiple roles as national chairman, confidant of the president, chief distributor of the federal patronage, business leader, and senator from a powerful and pivotal state, Hanna rapidly became the principal figure in the Republican party in Congress. He was at once admitted to the coterie of conservative Republicans who controlled the upper chamber. He was courted and flattered. He did not in false modesty discount his growing prestige by abjuring allusions to his influence over the president. Tom Platt of New York and Matthew Quay of Pennsylvania continued to dislike Hanna rather intensely. Another Platt (Orville), of Connecticut, was Hanna's closest friend in the Senate, and among his intimate associates were such influential senators as William P. Frye of Maine, Alfred B. Kittridge of South Dakota, Spooner of Wisconsin, Aldrich, and Allison.

Frye observed that Hanna had more calls on the Senate floor than any other six men. Frye lent him use of the vice-president's chamber because of Hanna's lameness. Hanna's famous corned beef hash breakfasts at the Cameron mansion on Lafayette Square became a forum for leadership consultations over many years. An invitation to one of these breakfasts came to be a much awaited distinction among Washington politicians.

When Hanna declined McKinley's offer of the postmaster generalship, he in turn recommended that the post go to Henry C. Payne of Wisconsin, the vice-chairman of the national committee. Despite Hanna's forceful presentation of Payne's qualifications, the president never made this appointment. Apparently the president and Payne had difficult relations in previous years when McKinley was a congressman and Payne a lobbyist for the Northern Pacific Railroad. Instead, Charles Emory Smith of Pennsylvania became postmaster general. Smith's appointment did not alter the fact that Hanna was to control patronage distribution. Even McKinley cleared many presidential appointments with Hanna.

There could be no doubt that Hanna organized patronage distribution to the best advantage of the president.[4] He distributed patronage through the national committee and the regular Republican organization in those states having Democratic senators. He had referees in each state who were usually the national committeeman, the state committee chairman, and the defeated candidates for Congress in each district. As a rule, their judgment prevailed.

There was of course a connection between Hanna's control of the patronage and his leadership of congressional Republicans; he assumed that post office appointments were the ''property'' of the representative of the district concerned.[5] Hanna was also careful to reduce hostility among potential allies. For example, he went out of his way in 1898 to offer Senator Platt of New York assistance in the campaign for the state's Republican congressional slate.

President McKinley gave Hanna a particularly free hand in the distribution of patronage in the South. McKinley was aware of the significance of the southern votes in the Republican national convention. Thus, when national committee vice-chairman Payne tried in 1899 to revive the issue of improved apportionment of state delegate strength in the national convention, both McKinley and Hanna promptly discouraged him.

In a letter to McKinley, Payne pointed out that seven southern states cast less than half as many Republican popular votes as Ohio, yet had three times as many delegates at the convention. Anticipating no contest for the nomination in 1900, Payne expressed the hope that the apportionment rules would be reformed. He specifically proposed introducing a resolution at the December 1899 national committee meeting making Republican popular votes cast in the state rather than the number of electoral college votes serve as the basis of convention representation. In raising the issue, Payne reflected the widely felt disenchantment within the party regarding the inequities of convention apportionment. McKinley and Hanna, however, resisted weakening so solid a source of pro-McKinley votes in the next convention.

2

As Senator Hanna's power on Capitol Hill grew, there were reports of personal coolness between him and the president. The first evidence of strain came in connection with certain new appointment rules recommended to the president by the Civil Service Commission in 1899. The proposals created a flurry of uncertainty among local Republican party workers. From Europe, where he was vacationing, Hanna urged the president to settle the issue in a hurry, threatening to stay on in Europe if the president failed to get directives out in time to reassure the party workers in Ohio. The new rules that came forth two weeks later involved minor changes, and party workers were indeed reassured.[6] However, rumors persisted that Hanna was no longer the unchallenged distributor of federal jobs. He had instead become the leader of the Republican party in the Senate, a place, he told a friend, that he would not exchange for the presidency itself.[7]

As the national committee meeting of December 1899 approached, sources close to Hanna disclosed that he would not seek the national chairmanship again in 1900.[8] By January, Hanna himself indicated that he would not be a delegate to the convention nor would he be available for the convention's permanent chairmanship. Hanna was at this time crippled by rheumatism and indicated that he was not well enough to manage the campaign. To his chagrin, he was not coaxed to remain nor told that he was indispensable nor asked to sacrifice himself for the president and the party. McKinley appeared to be taking him at his word.

> It is impossible to accept the theory that McKinley had been antagonized by Hanna's increasing power in the Senate and before the people. Hanna owed his prestige in the Senate to his hold on the federal patronage. He enjoyed that hold by favor of the President and was sick with fear of losing it.[9]

The president's uncharacteristic coldness to Hanna suggested some recent cause of offense. Besides, except by sinister reputation, Hanna was relatively unknown beyond Ohio and Capitol Hill. Not until the end of May did McKinley decide to ask Hanna to serve again as national chairman.[10] This arrangement was confirmed at a conference between the president and the senator on June 9.

President McKinley's renomination in 1900 was assured. The vice-presidential nomination was the convention's principal contest. The principal actors were Hanna of Ohio, Quay of Pennsylvania, and Platt of New York. The battle began after 1896 when Quay's political fortunes in Pennsylvania suffered several setbacks. His followers became locked into an intense rivalry with the Wanamaker faction. During his trial for alleged misuse of state funds, Quay was denied re-election to the Senate by the state legislature. His acquittal came after the legislature had adjourned, but the governor immediately appointed him to the vacant Senate seat. The appointment was challenged in the Senate, where Quay lost in a vote of 33 to 32. Voting against Quay were Senators Hanna and, surprisingly, Platt.

Quay vented his antagonism toward Hanna in particular by favoring the selection of New York's Governor Theodore Roosevelt for second place on the 1900 national ticket. A vociferous reformer and dramatic campaigner, Roosevelt had long been a thorn in the side of the regular Republican organization in New York. Roosevelt's exploits as leader of the Rough Riders in Cuba during the Spanish-American War typified the muscular, expansionist mood of the country and projected "Teddy's" fame across the nation. Platt was eager to "kick Roosevelt upstairs" into the relatively harmless post of vice-president. Hanna, even without a strong candidate of his own, vigorously opposed Roosevelt's nomination.[11]

On the morning the convention opened, Hanna shouted at Payne: "Don't any of you realize that there's only one life between that madman and the Presidency?" Payne, a Roosevelt supporter, blandly pointed out that Hanna controlled the convention and could change the direction of events. "I am not in control!" Hanna stormed. "McKinley won't let me use the power of the Administration to defeat Roosevelt. He is blind, or afraid, or something!"[12]

Quay's objective was to further undermine Hanna's influence. His first move was to propose, without warning, a new method of apportionment of convention votes, thereby reviving an issue that National Committee Vice-Chairman Payne had been forced to drop at the recent national committee meeting. Payne's motion had been defeated by a coalition of southern and Pennsylvanian votes. Quay's proposal revived the threat to the influence of the southerners, but he agreed to withdraw his resolution on condition that the southern leaders support Roosevelt. Hanna thus lost his usual control of the southern delegates. President McKinley kept aloof from the entire situation, but did instruct Hanna, through Charles G. Dawes, that he "not interfere with the vice-presidential nomination."[13] Hanna acquiesced, and Roosevelt's nomination followed.

On June 21, the national committee met and re-elected Hanna as its chairman. Hanna named several members of the executive committee, including Vice-Chairman Payne and representatives of several pivotal states: Wisconsin (Payne), Maine (Manley), West Virginia (Scott), and Indiana (New). By mid-July, representatives of Illinois (Stewart), Missouri (Kerens), New York (Gibbs), and New Jersey (Murphy) were added. Quay did not wish to serve, leaving Pennsylvania unrepresented. By mid-August, Chairman Hanna set up the now customary campaign advisory committee.

Hanna's organizing and campaigning efforts were comparable to those of 1896. The Republican national committee collected about five million dollars. Toward the end of the campaign, Republicans were delivering an estimated 7,000 speeches each week as compared to 2,500 by the Democrats. The national headquarters, which had previously been located in a private, brownstone home on Fifth Avenue in New York, were now in the Metropolitan Life Building at One Madison Avenue. At the height of the campaign in October, the national committee offices looked very much like the executive offices of a large factory or railroad. The Chicago branch of the national committee was also in a large office building. The Republican executive committee was synchronized into a smooth strategy-making team. It received almost daily reports from state committees, and these state committees in turn were in close touch with local committees.

Hanna turned supervision of most of the office operations of the national committee over to Vice-Chairman Payne. He himself embarked upon a campaign tour of the Midwest where he was widely thought of as a "money-bags of Wall Street" manipulating the McKinley administration. For example, at the Democratic national convention of 1900, Governor Altgeld of Illinois alluded to Hanna as follows, "The Republican Party, which was born of humanity, which came into the world with a mission, which was a mighty moral force in the time of Lincoln, has become a mere criminal instrument in the hands of Mark Hanna."[14]

The president tried to dissuade Hanna from exposing himself to hostile audiences, but Hanna insisted upon making himself better known in that region. Hanna also argued that his appearances might help Republicans carry the legislatures of South Dakota and other states.[15] Perhaps it was this tour that led Speaker

Henderson to comment on election day that a Hanna-for-president movement was about to get under way, with 1904 as the goal. By the end of November, Hanna found it necessary to issue denials of interest in the presidency and to indicate his plans to retire at the end of his senatorial term.

After his re-election, one of President McKinley's first projects was to embark upon a tour of the nation in a campaign to educate the people on two policy issues: the control of trusts and the extension of commercial reciprocity. In the freedom afforded by his second term, McKinley apparently intended to change from a "quiet" to a "vocal" type of president, using appeals to the people as a tactic for putting pressure on Congress. His choice of these subjects implied that as chief executive he was prepared to challenge the agenda of Congress, particularly in the Senate where Mark Hanna was a principal figure.[16]

3

The United States Senate at the turn of the century was a formidable collection of political potentates. McKinley had dealt indirectly with its leaders during his first term, aided by the fact that Hanna and others had conscientiously represented his interests there. When Vice-President Hobart died in 1899, McKinley remarked that his deceased running mate had been one of the friendly forces in the fierce struggles in the Senate who helped carry out his policies between 1897 and 1899.[17] However, public disenchantment with the Senate was increasing in the light of widespread bribery in the state legislatures that then elected United States senators. The movement for direct election of senators was gaining support; in the House of Representatives resolutions proposing a constitutional amendment for direct election of senators were passed in 1893, 1894, 1898, 1900, and almost unanimously in 1902. By 1911, the Senate concurred, and two years later the states adopted the amendment.

McKinley's imminent encounter with the Senate seemed mandated by the overwhelming popular vote in his re-election. In fact, he had hardly taken the oath of office when he had to issue denials of interest in a third term: "I not only am not and will not be a candidate for a third term, but would not accept a nomination for it, if it were tendered me."[18] Three short months later President McKinley was dead at the hands of an assassin.

McKinley's death only momentarily postponed the presidential-congressional struggle. That struggle was shortly personified and activated by the emergence of Theodore Roosevelt and Mark Hanna as the principal protagonists for the 1904 Republican presidential nomination.

Hanna's declining political fortunes were given a lift, ironically enough, by McKinley's death. Hanna could now become a spokesman for the Senate against the executive without fear of personal embarrassment. On the other hand, Roosevelt suffered from certain weaknesses, including the fact that no vice-president constitutionally succeeding to the presidency upon the death of the incumbent had yet won a presidential nomination in his own right.

Roosevelt was not long in assuming control of the Republican party as well as the presidency. In doing so, he once again demonstrated his skill in accommodating the requirements of practical politics and the appearances of reform. His first cabinet appointment elevated National Committee Vice-Chairman Payne to postmaster general.

Prior to the 1900 national convention, Payne had campaigned throughout Wisconsin and the Midwest to generate a popular demand for Roosevelt's nomination to the national ticket. Payne's effectiveness in the 1896 campaign had prompted Hanna to recommend him to McKinley for the postmaster generalship. Despite McKinley's refusal to make the appointment, Payne remained loyal. Next to Hanna, he was probably the main architect of the sucessful 1900 campaign. Hence, Hanna could hardly oppose Payne's appointment. At the same time, it put into a key patronage position a skilled party practitioner who demonstrably had Roosevelt's interest at heart. Nor could the civil service reformers, whose hero Roosevelt had long been, complain. Through his convention reapportionment proposals, Payne was known to advocate a reduction in southern influence at the national conventions. Hence the reformers could expect Payne, as postmaster general, to clean up the post office appointments in the South.

President Roosevelt's next major political move was in the Jacksonian tradition. He embarked upon a noisy campaign against big business. By February 1902, his attorney general initiated legal proceedings against J.P. Morgan's Northern Securities Company for violation of the Sherman Antitrust Act.

Reaction came quickly as reports of a Hanna-for-president boom began to circulate. Said the *New York Times*, "The feeling is spreading in Washington that Mr. Hanna is far more likely to be nominated for the Presidency in the next Republican convention than Mr. Roosevelt."[19] The newspaper also reported that Roosevelt was not popular among Republican senators and that the recent Ohio Republican state convention seemed thoroughly united behind Hanna.

But Mark Sullivan believed that Hanna never hoped to outdistance Roosevelt's rapidly growing strength with the people. Instead, knowing that Roosevelt could not get to the White House without his party's nomination, Hanna, as national chairman in control of the machinery, thought he could put Roosevelt under obligation by getting him nominated.[20] Thus on July 6, 1902, Hanna indicated publicly that he would run for president only if it became clear that the Republican party did not want Roosevelt. This statement came at a moment when Hanna was being credited for steering the Panama Canal legislation through Congress, which was considered a major political feat.

The Roosevelt managers were not idle. Postmaster General Payne assumed leadership of Roosevelt's preconvention work, assisted by two former national chairmen—Clarkson and Quay—and others with strong anti-Hanna sentiment.

Payne sent Clarkson South to mobilize the southern delegates. Clarkson's principal tactic was to perfect the patronage referee system in the South in order to determine which patronage appointments should be recognized by the administration. The referees were held responsible for identifying prospective appointees who combined competence and "correct" leadership loyalties.

When Clarkson's activities were reported in the press, Roosevelt denounced the reports as "particularly malicious and slanderous." In a letter to Clarkson, Roosevelt wrote:

> I do not want the nomination unless it comes freely from the people of the Republican states because they believe in me, and because they believe I can carry their States. And in the South I want to make it clear as a bell that I have acted in the way I have on the Negro question simply because I hold myself the heir of the policies of Abraham Lincoln.[21]

During 1902 and 1903, the Hanna movement suffered two serious setbacks. In May 1902, over 147,000 anthracite miners struck against the coal operators. The price of coal rose from $5 to $30 per ton. Hanna's renown as a philosopher of cordial labor-management relations brought him into the situation, but by mid-August it was clear that his efforts to end the strike had failed. On October 1, President Roosevelt took the then unprecedented step of inviting the operators and the miners' leaders to Washington to try to reach a settlement. After three weeks of maneuvering, the parties submitted to arbitration, and the miners resumed work. Roosevelt's success was a dramatic contrast to Hanna's failure.

The second setback came in spring of 1903. In May, Hanna's long-time rival, the senior senator from Ohio, Joseph B. Foraker, issued a statement recommending that the Ohio state convention, scheduled to meet in June, endorse President Roosevelt for nomination in 1904. Foraker's object was to cut the ground from under Hanna in his own state.

Hanna immediately and angrily issued a counterstatement in which he urged the Republicans of Ohio not to commit themselves on the presidential nomination a year ahead of time. He further said, "I am not, and will not be, a candidate for the presidential nomination. [But] on account of my position as chairman of the Republican National Committee, I am supposed to have a vital interest in the results in Ohio."[22] Hanna felt severely challenged in his role as a presidential politician.

At the same time, Hanna telegraphed President Roosevelt that his statement did not imply hostility to the Roosevelt cause, but merely reflected a concern for Ohio's best interests at the national convention. To which Roosevelt replied: "I have had nothing whatever to do with raising this issue. Inasmuch as it has been raised, of course, those who favor my administration and my nomination will favor endorsing both, and those who do not will oppose." Hanna succumbed immediately, "In view of the sentiment expressed, I shall not oppose the endorsement of your administration and candidacy by our state convention.''

Hanna's death ten months later seemed an anticlimax to his political demise at the hands of Foraker and Roosevelt.

Vice-Chairman Payne assumed the acting chairmanship of the national committee. Payne had indicated to friends, even before Hanna died, that he would retire from politics after the national convention because of poor health. When Payne collapsed in April 1904, it was certain that a new national chairman would be chosen after the nomination of Roosevelt.

4

New York's Governor Odell was prominently mentioned as a successor in the chairmanship. This, it was argued, would allow Elihu Root to run for governor and generally restore Republican harmony in that important state. But President Roosevelt and Odell had never been on good political terms. Roosevelt initially wanted Elihu Root, W. Murray Crane, or Cornelius N. Bliss for the chairmanship. The latter recommended George B. Cortelyou, preferring for himself the position of national committee treasurer.[23] The suggestion of Cortelyou, the new secretary of commerce and labor, was provocative.

Cortelyou was initially a Harrison supporter, as noted earlier. In 1895 President Cleveland invited him to serve as presidential executive clerk. Cortelyou had also served as presidential secretary to McKinley and was retained by Roosevelt. When the Department of Commerce and Labor was created by Congress in February 1903, Roosevelt, impressed by Cortelyou's great executive talents, nominated him for the new cabinet post.

Cortelyou was not well known by the general public, having been almost exclusively a behind-the-scenes political adviser. Ironically, a major objection to his becoming national chairman was his "political inexperience." Quipped the *New York Times*:

> Can anyone imagine this courteous and high-principled gentleman successfully grappling with sudden campaign exigencies of a kind that would have caused "Zack" Chandler to retire to the committee back room for lonely communion with his soul or have given Mark Hanna pause even in a crowded hour? . . . Think of Mr. Cortelyou "buying mules," ordering a resort to "soap," organizing "blocks of five," or even "frying fat."[24]

Another objection was that Cortelyou had at one time been a Democrat, referring to his service as Cleveland's secretary. Some Republican leaders were also reluctant to choose a national chairman so long in advance of the national convention. Aside from Cortelyou's merits, the basic issue was whether the senators, through their state party organizations, or the president would control the national chairmanship, the campaign, and the national party machinery.

From the day that Cortelyou's name was first mentioned until he was elected national chairman on June 23, President Roosevelt insisted upon his prerogative to name the national chairman. He made this clear in a letter to the Massachusetts national committeeman:

> Please wire me in full about opposition to Cortelyou. People may as well understand that if I am to run for President that Cortelyou is to be Chairman of the National Committee. I will not have it any other way. Please give me the names of people opposed to him; and you are welcome to tell each of them what I have said. . . . I regard opposition or disloyalty to Mr. Cortelyou as being simply an expression of disloyalty to the Republican party.[25]

Meanwhile, the acting national chairman, Postmaster General Payne, was running into difficulties in his governmental role. Civil service reformers were loosing a crescendo of criticism of the Post Office Department as the mainstay of the party patronage system. In 1903 and early 1904, a series of post office scandals perpetrated during the tenure of the preceding postmaster general were brought to light. With Payne, a high party official, holding the postmaster generalship, the newspapers did their best to implicate him.

Payne responded by initiating a thorough investigation and making appropriate dismissals. He displayed less discretion in his great annoyance with the press attacks, which simply invited renewed attacks. His predicament was complicated by a rule he issued in spring of 1904.

Postmasters, Payne stated, were not prohibited from joining political clubs or making voluntary financial contributions on premises outside governmental offices or buildings, nor from acting as delegates to county, state, or congressional district conventions. However, continued his ruling, they must not serve as chairmen of political organizations, nor make themselves unduly prominent in local political matters. Although this was ordinarily an appropriate administrative ruling, the embarrassment for Payne arose out of the fact that he was acting chairman of the national committee and would be the presiding officer at the opening of the Republican national convention. Despite his difficulties and the fact that his health continued to fail, Payne remained Roosevelt's main link with those state organizations that could assure him the nomination in 1904.[26]

Roosevelt had good reason to be concerned about conditions in the state parties. The disproportionate Republican majorities in many states had led to a rampant insurgency among the younger generation of politicians demanding their place in the party. Robert M. La Follette had just won the governorship in Wisconsin and was rapidly becoming a leader of insurgents beyond his state's borders. The president, anticipating the requirements of the national convention, found himself relying upon the loyalty of the Old Guard in many states. In a sense, the contention over the national chairmanship was evidence of Old Guard fears that the president, a progressive at heart, would not remain loyal to them after the nomination. As later developments

revealed, their fears were well founded. Acting Chairman Payne suffered an apoplec-
tic stroke on the eve of the June 16 national committee meeting. At the meeting, most
of the national committeemen were in revolt over the selection of Cortelyou. Since
most of the committee would continue as members after the convention, the basic
issue was control of the committee. Senators Penrose, Gallinger, Scott, Allen,
Hansbrough, and Governor Murphy were the most vocal in opposition to Cortelyou.

Among those working in Cortelyou's behalf were Cornelius N. Bliss and
Charles G. Dawes. Working with them closely were Senator Henry Cabot
Lodge, Payne, and others. The president's representatives held in abeyance a
telegram from Roosevelt insisting upon Cortelyou's election. The telegram was
not needed. On June 21, the national committee elected Payne as its chairman for
the duration of the convention. On June 23, after a new national committee had
been designated by the national convention, Cortelyou was elected as Payne's
successor. Many of the committeemen refrained from voting. No vice-chairman
was appointed. Wrote Dawes in his diary:

> Cortelyou's selection marks the final transition from the rotten condition of
> party management as it was before Hanna's day to an absolutely clean basis.
> Hanna was distinctly an improver of conditions. Cortelyou will still further
> perfect them since he will even more strenuously than Hanna insist on clean
> methods of campaigning.[27]

Payne and Cortelyou's preconvention work on behalf of President Roosevelt
paid off. The national committee decided more than sixty seating contests from
thirteen states in favor of factions friendly to Roosevelt. However, the conservative-progressive splits appearing in 1904 were destined to reach major proportions by 1912. The debate over the number of votes to be allowed Hawaii—two
or six—particularly foreshadowed the future; principles of representation were
argued long and carefully to make the record clear and to educate the delegates.
The problem of reapportioning representation in the Republican national convention was not to be set aside soon or lightly.[28]

As might be expected from his previous executive achievements, Chairman
Cortelyou proved to be an outstanding campaign organizer. For example, in his
Journal observations about the work of the Midwest branch of the national
committee, Charles G. Dawes was pleased that "at last we have a committee
whose work is untainted by fraud of any kind in its business departments."
Dawes indicated that great savings were being made because the old system of
having bureaus within the committee and permitting bureau chiefs to let contracts (often while taking commissions) was now abolished and replaced by
greater accountability on the part of the executive committee in financial matters.
Compared to 1904, the campaigns of 1896 and 1900 had been extravagant
spending orgies, according to Dawes.[29]

Harry S. New was born into a political family. His father was treasurer of the United States under Grant and consul general at London under Benjamin Harrison. His father was also publisher of the Indianapolis *Journal*, where the young Harry began his career as a reporter. New was born in Indianapolis on December 31, 1858, and was educated at Butler University. After sharing with his father the editorship of the Indianapolis *Journal* for several years, New shifted his interest to participation in elective politics. In 1896, he was elected to the state senate and served as a delegate to the national convention at St. Louis. After brief service in the Spanish-American War, he was chosen national committeeman from Indiana in 1900. Following the 1904 responsibilities in the Midwest regional office, New was elevated to the vice-chairmanship of the national committee in 1906 and to the chairmanship in 1907. He became a United States senator in 1917, postmaster general under Harding in 1923, and was reappointed to the post by Coolidge in 1925. Between 1900 and 1912, New was generally considered "one of the most powerful political figures of the Middle West," according to the *New York Times* (May 10, 1937).

Frank Harris Hitchcock, son of an Ohio Congregationalist clergyman, was a descendant of early colonial settlers in Boston. He received his primary and secondary education in that city, entering Harvard in 1887. While at college, he was active in the Young Republican movement, earning election as a precinct committeeman. After a year of law school in Cambridge, he went to work in the U.S. Department of Agriculture in 1891. While a junior civil servant in Washington, DC, he studied law at Columbian (later George Washington) University. There he made the acquaintance of another part-time student, George B. Cortelyou. Hitchcock received the LL.M. in 1895, a year before Cortelyou received his degree. Two years later, Hitchcock was promoted to chief of the Division of Foreign Markets in the Department of Agriculture. Cortelyou invited him to become chief clerk of the new Department of Commerce and Labor when it was established in 1903. In 1905, Hitchcock followed Cortelyou into the Post Office Department as first assistant postmaster general. He became Republican national chairman in 1908 and postmaster general in 1909. Some of his innovations in the latter capacity earned him the title "Father of the United States airmail."

5

As the Old Guard had feared, the new chairman began to appoint a new generation of Republican politicians to strategic positions in the national party. After so
many years in the White House, Cortelyou knew party people in every state and
in every faction. Cortelyou even declined to put Postmaster General Payne on
the executive committee. Payne's death in October, as Hanna's and Quay's
earlier in the year, marked the passing of an older generation of Republican
leaders. Cortelyou, with Roosevelt's approval, was quick to replace them with
loyal and ambitious younger men. Among these, for example, were the forty-six-
year-old national committeeman from Indiana, Harry S. New, and thirty-seven-
year-old Frank Hitchcock, Cortelyou's principal assistant in organizing the new
Department of Commerce and Labor. New handled the campaign literature of
the Midwest office; Hitchcock became assistant secretary of the national committee.

Cortelyou's intimate knowledge of party personnel was further demonstrated
by his appointments to the executive and advisory committees. He assigned five
members of the executive committee to eastern headquarters in New York City,
including several who had opposed his appointment. Six other members of the
executive committee were attached to western headquarters in Chicago.

The advisory committee was large, composed of key politicians from all
sections of the country. Although this group never met, its members communicated frequently with the national chairman concerning the progress of the campaign in their respective states. The interests of the House of Representatives
were represented by Speaker Cannon and those of the Senate by President pro
tem Frye. Possibly Cortelyou's principal adviser on this committee was former
Governor W. Murray Crane of Massachusetts.

Bitter factional fights, particularly in New York and Wisconsin, were handled
with dexterity by the new chairman. When the state supreme court of Wisconsin
upheld the La Follette ticket as the regular one instead of the Stalwart ticket
headed by Senator Spooner, a friend of Roosevelt, both the president and
Cortelyou urged the Stalwarts to withdraw. This was done, and the La Follette
ticket was subsequently thoroughly beaten.[30]

Even the rambunctious Teddy Roosevelt, who probably never conducted a
quiet political campaign in his life, was deferential to the wishes of his reserved
national chairman. Roosevelt was eager to campaign actively against his Democratic opponent, Alton B. Parker, but acquiesced to Cortelyou's insistence that he
follow the McKinley technique of taking refuge on a front porch.

Roosevelt kept in close touch with Cortelyou, in one instance writing, "I
wonder whether President McKinley bothered Hanna as I am bothering you."[31]
At one point Roosevelt cautioned Cortelyou against bargaining with businessmen in connection with the Northern Securities case, to which Cortelyou indig-

nantly responded that he thought of himself as having "a fair degree of moral fibre." Roosevelt continued to write, call, and advise on the details of the campaign.

As it turned out, Cortelyou's fund-raising activities provided the principal excitement of an otherwise lethargic presidential campaign. On October 1, Joseph Pulitzer's *World* asked how much the beef, steel, tobacco, and other trusts were contributing to Cortelyou's coffers. The *New York Times* suggested that Cortelyou was exploiting knowledge he had gained as secretary of commerce and labor to put pressure upon large corporations for campaign contributions. When the Democratic nominee, Judge Alton B. Parker, took up the issue shortly before election day, Cortelyou urged the president to enter the campaign in rebuttal.

It was common in that day for corporations to contribute large sums of money openly to political campaigns. On October 26, Roosevelt insisted that if the Standard Oil Company had given his campaign a large contribution, it would be returned directly, an offer that was never implemented. On November 6, Chairman Cortelyou publicly reported that the campaign fund was made up of contributions from about four thousand people and had totaled only half as much as the fund raised in 1896. In view of the aforementioned reforms in the accounting of Republican national committee funds, there is little question that this was a relatively penurious campaign. The campaign finance issue had little effect upon the result—an overwhelming victory for Roosevelt.[32]

When Postmaster General Payne died in October, President Roosevelt offered that cabinet position to Cortelyou. Difficulties arose because the appointment would legally have to take effect before election day, hence would become a vulnerable target for Democratic propaganda. Instead, the incumbent first assistant postmaster general was promoted to the cabinet post for the duration of the administration. In March 1905, National Chairman Cortelyou took over the Post Office Department, bringing with him Frank Hitchcock as first assistant postmaster general.

It was not yet well established that the party national chairman of a successful presidential campaign would be rewarded with the postmaster generalship. When he entered the cabinet, Cortelyou announced that he would retire as national chairman as soon as certain business matters were resolved. He did not resign, however, until January 1907 when President Roosevelt was about to appoint him as secretary of the treasury. In this way, it became accepted practice over the next four or five decades for the postmaster general to hold both the national party chairmanship and a cabinet position at the same time.

As postmaster general, a position he had aspired to for nearly a decade, Cortelyou became a political figure in his own right. On November 8, 1904, after Roosevelt had announced that he would not seek another term, Cortelyou was at once named in the press and among party leaders as a probable successor. Privately, Cortelyou told his friend Charles G. Dawes that he would "let the future take care of itself."[33] But Cortelyou was too practical a politician to let the future go entirely unguided. A major part of Cortelyou's energies during the interim between election day and his appointment as postmaster general, and during his long delayed resignation from the national chairmanship, was occupied filling patronage vacancies with politicians friendly to Roosevelt and himself. He gave no quarter to the "Hanna Old Guard."[34]

Roosevelt entered his first full presidential term under favorable political circumstances. Most Americans were enjoying continued prosperity, with the exception of some farmers and, during the brief depression of 1907, some Wall Street financiers. His overwhelming defeat of Parker inhibited trouble-making among Republican leaders. His continuing vociferations against the trusts gave the rising forces of progressivism the comfort of having a friend in the White House.

Above all, Roosevelt's dramatic activities in the field of international relations shook his countrymen into an awareness that the United States now held new status as a world power, with commensurate military obligations. The colorful colonel of Spanish-American War fame pressed insistently upon Congress for resources to build a strong army and navy, particularly the latter. Roosevelt had a comprehension of the problems of international relations that was "extraordinary," and, according to at least one eminent historian, "superior to that of most presidents and secretaries of state." He understood the rivalries between Britain and Germany and between Germany and France and the threat that these held for world peace. He appreciated the rising importance of the Far East. He predicted the Russian Revolution three decades before the event.[35] As a consequence of his views and conduct of foreign affairs, Roosevelt elevated the presidency, and, concomitantly, party leadership to the stature of world leader. He thrust domestic politics into world politics, paving the way for two other international activists, Woodrow Wilson and Franklin D. Roosevelt.

Part IV
Destruction by Faction

13 | Wilson's "Parliamentary" Presidential Parties

Parker's defeat was a shattering one for the conservative wing of the Democratic party. The unhappy electoral fact confronting Democratic politicians was that their party's popular vote for president had dropped from a high of 46 percent in 1896 to a low of 37 percent in 1904. With the exception of a temporary rise in the middle of the Wilson presidency to 49 percent in 1916, the Democratic vote would remain below 43 percent until 1932.

1

William Jennings Bryan tenaciously refused to abdicate the titular leadership. The responsibilities and performance of the national committee and the national chairmen continued to be limited. At the same time, various Democratic state party organizations grew influential, led by the machines of powerful senators or governors. However, the state "bosses," one of whom was National Chairman Taggart, were increasingly interested in the national chairmanship and attentive to the coalitions required to control it and, thereby, possibly the national conventions.

In New York, David B. Hill announced that he would retire from politics. Parker quietly did the same. Bryan, for his part, looked to the future. A headline in the *Commoner* of November 11 drove home the mission: "Prepare for 1908— Democracy versus Plutocracy—The Election's Lesson."

As promised, Bryan began preparations for a third nomination. He conducted a speech-making tour of the Mississippi Valley. He published pledge cards in the *Commoner* on which his followers could promise to take an active part in local primaries. Meanwhile, it was becoming increasingly evident that the man in the White House, Theodore Roosevelt, seemed to have adopted the political style and progressive policies for which the public had known Bryan, a fact that Bryan himself was more than once compelled to acknowledge and endorse.

From the fall of 1905 to the late summer of 1906, Bryan and his family embarked upon a comprehensive world tour. American reporters met him everywhere, and the trip was extremely valuable for the publicity it received back home.

During his absence, several New York Democratic leaders began to note— aloud—that Bryan could easily qualify as the party's leader in 1908. In some ways, these endorsements were a recognition of Bryan's increasing conservatism. They could also have been a reaction to the progressive programs that were gaining ground with Theodore Roosevelt's capture of the Republican party. Finally, the Democratic leaders may have wished to head off William Randolph Hearst's aggressive efforts to win over all of Bryan's radical following by taking strong stands for public ownership. The Indiana Democratic state convention of 1906, under the firm leadership of National Chairman Taggart and John W. Kern, applauded Bryan as "that wise and conservative statesman."[1]

Chairman Taggart had political and personal reasons for drawing closer to the "Peerless Leader." With Hill and Parker retiring, a new Democratic leadership was emerging in New York, and this development would have major consequences on Taggart's influence in the national organization. Taggart was also having problems at home, where an unfriendly governor was conducting an investigation of gambling activities at his French Lick Springs Hotel. The hotel's casino was raided, patriotically enough, on July 4, 1906, and the national chairman seemed about to be inundated by scandal.

In view of his difficulties, Taggart resigned as treasurer of the Indiana Democratic state committee and indicated that he would not seek the national chairmanship again in 1908. A move was nevertheless initiated to oust him as national chairman. The movement's chances depended largely upon Bryan's attitude. Bryan refused to join the attack on Taggart and observed that the Hoosier's status as national committeeman from Indiana was a matter to be decided by the Democrats of that state. Indiana Democrats were, of course, in Taggart's corner.[2]

Bryan was less friendly to Roger Sullivan of Chicago. Sullivan had been responsible for Bryan's defeat in the Illinois seating contest of 1904. When Sullivan was elected as Illinois' national committeeman, Bryan demanded his immediate resignation on the grounds that Sullivan was too closely allied with big corporations. The demand was not likely to result in a resignation, but it did create a furor in the newspapers and reminded Bryan's followers that he was still antiboss and anticorporation.

Looking to 1908, Bryan had yet to win the nomination and to develop a winning issue for the election. He took the occasion of an inquiry from Senator Jones during the summer of 1906 to declare:

> I shall do no more to secure another nomination, and do not want one unless conditions seem to demand it. . . . There are, however, certain reforms which I

would like very much to see accepted, and to assist in the acceptance of these reforms I am willing to become the party candidate again.[3]

With respect to a campaign issue, Bryan realized that history and Theodore Roosevelt had caught up with his own early radicalism. In a statement to reporters while in Europe, he said: "I am more radical than ever, while the platform of the Democratic party is essentially conservative." He added, "What used to be called radical is now called conservative. The doctrine has not changed, but public sentiment is making progress."[4]

Bryan's homecoming at the end of August 1906 was celebrated by a mammoth Democratic rally at Madison Square Garden in New York City. Some eighteen governors and fifteen senators as well as nearly every prominent Democrat in the country attended. As Bryan came ashore, Chairman Taggart was the first to shake his hand. Close by stood Roger Sullivan and a host of other Democratic dignitaries. That night, in an overflowing Madison Square Garden, Bryan reviewed with particular eloquence the entire gamut of Democratic symbols and issues. The surprise, and presumably the issue for 1908, came when Bryan declared that the railroads "must *ultimately* become public property."[5]

This was Hearst's issue. The publisher immediately conferred with Bryan to determine what significance the declaration might have for his own ambitions. Dissatisfied with Bryan's responses, Hearst founded a third party, the Independence League, on May 3, 1907, hoping thereby to draw the radicals away from Bryan. Meanwhile, Bryan began backing away from the position taken at Madison Square Garden. By July 26, 1907, Bryan wrote in the *Commoner*, "Government ownership is not an immediate issue."[6]

The big issue for the campaign was set forth at the national committee meeting of December 1907. Chairman Taggart called upon the caustic leader of the southern silverites, "Pitchfork Ben" Tillman, to offer a resolution of commendation for Perry Belmont, a leading New York sound-money man and brother of August, the former Gold Democrat. The resolution extended the party's thanks to Belmont for his leadership in the movement for legislation to require publicity of campaign finances. Thus, Taggart hoped to divest the party of the big-money image it had acquired during Parker's campaign, at the same time taking advantage of revelations that Standard Oil and the New York Life Insurance Company had contributed hundreds of thousands of dollars to the 1904 Roosevelt campaign. Even though Perry Belmont's brother, August, had given the Democratic national committee $250,000, the Democratic campaign fund of $620,000 in 1904 was hardly a match for the Republican's fund.[7]

The 1908 national convention at Denver conducted its business expeditiously. In one of his rare absences from these gatherings, Bryan remained at home in Fairview, Nebraska, sending his brother Charles to represent him. A Pennsylvania seating contest between Bryan and anti-Bryan delegates from Philadelphia became a floor test of Bryan's strength. His delegates were seated by a 3 to 2 majority.

After Bryan's nomination, the convention chose Tom Taggart's good friend, John W. Kern, for second place on the ticket. To settle the perennial procedural problems arising from national committee vacancies due to death or resignation, the convention passed a rule designating the state committees as the agencies with authority to fill such vacancies.

The national committee retired to Lincoln, Nebraska, to consult with Bryan concerning the organization and leadership of the campaign. Bryan addressed the group and endorsed its statements as well as the convention's statements favoring publicity of campaign contributions and expenditures. The nominee asked the committee not to accept any contributions from any corporation, to make public all contributions above $100, to set a maximum of $10,000 for contributions, and to publicize committee finances before rather than after an election. Chairman Taggart, always a practical man, qualified Bryan's statements by observing that these principles applied to national but not to local party committees.

Bryan evidently had given little thought to the selection of a national chairman. He was going to run his own personal campaign again and, on the basis of his observations in three previous presidential races, viewed the chairmanship as an instrument for keeping the organization "regulars" loyal or at least unopposed. At Lincoln, he had no nomination to make for chairman. The national committeeman from Nebraska moved, and it was unanimously carried:

> that a committee of eleven, of which the Chairman of this Committee [Taggart] shall be a member, be appointed by the Chair [Taggart] to confer with the candidates for President [Bryan] and Vice-President [Kern] and to select the permanent officers of this Committee, and the Chairman so selected be authorized to appoint such Committees as may be necessary for the management of the campaign, such Committees to have full power to act.[8]

In less abstruse language, the national committee delegated its elective authority to a subcommittee of eleven and gave any new national chairman full power to complete the campaign organization.

Eleven days later, the special committee of eleven met in Chicago to choose Norman E. Mack of New York as national chairman. Mack was probably the most "regular" Democrat of all, having successfully served in the difficult role of intermediary between the Parker and Bryan leaders in 1904. As national committeeman from New York, Mack served as Parker's spokesman on the national committee, yet was not a member of Taggart's executive committee, which was completely dominated by the sound-money faction.

Asked if he had found the ideal national chairman for the 1908 campaign, Bryan replied: "I'm afraid not. If the man existed who would make an ideal Chairman, he would be running for President instead of me."[9] In later years,

Bryan commented that the selection of Mack was, as far as he was concerned, a gesture of recognition of the "Eastern Democracy."[10]

The special committee of eleven decided other organizational matters. A Bryan associate, the national committeeman from Nebraska, was chosen vice-chairman of the national committee. As treasurer, the subcommittee chose Charles N. Haskell, governor of Oklahoma and chairman of the platform committee at Denver. Chairman Mack was directed to send a letter to members of the national committee concerning adoption of a systematic plan of raising campaign funds and another letter to the editors of Democratic newspapers urging them to help raise funds through popular subscriptions. The principal campaign headquarters was to be located in Chicago and an eastern headquarters in New York City.

The campaign was dull. Very few experienced Democratic politicians expected Bryan to beat the formidable combination of President Roosevelt and his chosen successor, William Howard Taft. Although his new third party was hardly a serious threat, Hearst did have a powerful chain of newspapers dedicated to Bryan's defeat. Bryan sent Senator Pettigrew of North Dakota to discuss with Arthur Brisbane what could be done about regaining Hearst's support, but Hearst would have none of it. Even Bryan's friend, Clarence Darrow, joined Hearst.

The publisher proceeded to use his new political party as a platform to expose the "corrupt moneyed interests" controlling both major parties. The big issue was money and corruption. As part of this campaign, the Hearst papers published a collection of letters written by the Standard Oil Company, its allied corporations, and several eastern railroad magnates to a number of public men concerning campaign contributions. Among those implicated were Republican Senator Foraker, who had just been defeated in his effort to stop Taft's nomination, and Governor Haskell, treasurer of the Democratic national committee.

However, President Roosevelt made the most of the sensational charges. From the White House on September 22, the president issued a statement charging Bryan with insincerity in his so-called "campaign against the interests":

> There is a striking difference in one respect, however, in the present posts of Governor Haskell and Senator Foraker. Governor Haskell stands high in the counsels of Mr. Bryan and is the treasurer of his national campaign committee. Senator Foraker represents only the forces, which, embittered, fought the nomination of Mr. Taft.[11]

Roosevelt pointed out how "the great and sinister moneyed interests" had opposed his administration and Mr. Taft's and "seemed now behind Governor Haskell."

Bryan responded by reiterating that Standard Oil had in the past supported Roosevelt and was now supporting Taft. He defended Haskell and demanded proof of the charges. Roosevelt issued a lengthy report showing Haskell's relationship with a subsidiary company of Standard Oil. Haskell resigned as Democratic national committee treasurer on September 25. After a few additional parries, the controversy subsided. Then, in surprise to all, John D. Rockefeller, Sr., issued a statement in support of Taft. It was the final note; it was too late for Bryan to respond, nor did he wish to spend more energy defending his national committee's officers.

2

Election day ushered in Bryan's third defeat, a distinction that matched Henry Clay's. Characteristically, Bryan intended to give the toga of titular leadership another hard wearing. He again went on a newsworthy foreign tour, this time to South America. He attended the Democratic state convention in Nebraska on July 26, 1910, as the leader of temperance forces seeking a county-option plank and was resoundingly defeated.

Shortly after the 1908 election, National Chairman Mack became concerned about the fact that the official leadership of the national party had no rostrum from which to express itself. Bryan and his paper the *Commoner*, a personal rather than a party organ, always seemed to stand in the way of other official party communications. Mack proposed that a national monthly magazine devoted to the interests of the Democratic party be founded, but nothing came of the suggestion.[12]

Democratic and progressive victories in the fall congressional and gubernatorial races across the country gave the sinking titular leader the straw he needed to maintain his influence in the presidential developments of 1911 and 1912. The growing breach between conservative and progressive wings of the Republican party, symbolized by the alienation of ex-President Roosevelt from President Taft, gave Bryan grounds for claiming that Democratic radicalism, or progressivism, whose leading representative he was, still had much to accomplish and could expect many successes ahead. As Democrats available for the presidential nomination began to come forward, Bryan anticipated an open national convention in which the prize would go to the best coalition builder. It would be reminiscent of the multicandidate convention of 1896, and Bryan was a past master in manipulating divided conventions.

Among the principal names in the Democratic ring was Champ Clark of Missouri, who had served in the House of Representatives since 1893 and became Speaker when the Democrats took control in 1911. With a large network of friends in the national party, Clark was elected permanent chairman of the convention that nominated Judge Parker. Clark was particularly well liked by organization regulars.

A second prospect was Oscar Underwood of Alabama, a southern conservative who had served many years as Democratic floor leader in the House of Representatives and in 1911 had become chairman of its Ways and Means Committee. Another available conservative was Governor Judson Harmon of Ohio, who had been attorney general during Cleveland's second term. Harmon had substantial support in the Northeast.

A fourth candidate was Woodrow Wilson, a Virginian, political science professor, and president of Princeton University since 1902. Although his origins were conservative, Wilson took on the mantle of progressivism soon after he was nominated for the governorship of New Jersey in 1910. Wilson's dramatic and hard-hitting campaign style, his personality, and his break with the Democratic "bosses" who nominated him for governor held the attention of the entire New York press for some time. This in turn helped make Wilson's progressivism known to the rest of the country.[13]

For William Jennings Bryan, the progressive choice lay between Speaker Clark and Governor Wilson. Bryan made this clear in a speech delivered August 14, 1911, at Columbus, Ohio, in which he eliminated Harmon, whom he considered suspiciously close to Wall Street. But Bryan refused to take a firm position favoring either Clark or Wilson. He relished his new role, which held all kinds of possibilities: his own renomination, the possibility of naming his successor (as Roosevelt had recently done for Taft), a high position in a Democratic administration.

Bryan sent questionnaires to the candidates to test their orthodoxy as progressives. During much of 1911 and 1912, the *Commoner* published letters from his readers urging him to run again; each time Bryan denied that he was a candidate. When specifically asked by Champ Clark if he meant to run, Bryan invariably said, "No." Bryan kept himself in the public eye by, on one occasion, devoting an entire speech in praise of Speaker Clark and, on another, lauding the new "radical" governor of New Jersey. As time for the national convention approached, it was clear that Bryan intended to have a major part in it.[14]

Clark's campaign had been going on for a long time. He viewed the presidency as a proper promotion from the speakership after lengthy service to his party and country. For years he had been nurturing his relationships with the party regulars as well as with Bryan. Clark considered himself a close personal friend of Bryan. He repeatedly asked the Nebraskan if he intended to be a candidate in 1908, indicating his reluctance to move aggressively in his own behalf until he had assurances that Bryan would not be offended.

The Wilson movement was something else again. After assuming the presidency of Princeton, Wilson spoke frequently on public affairs. His personality and the content and style of his presentations caught the attention of George Harvey, one of William C. Whitney's chief lieutenants during the Cleveland years and now publisher of *Harper's Weekly* and *North American Review*. In 1906, the world of higher education was deeply impressed by the adoption at

William F. McCombs, born in Arkansas in 1876, was the son of a rice plantation owner. Permanently lame as the result of a childhood accident, he led a somewhat protected life, receiving his elementary education from his mother and private tutors. He trained for college at a Tennessee prep school and entered Princeton for his undergraduate degree. He received a law degree from Harvard in 1901, established a practice in New York City, and, socially, concentrated his attentions upon his Princeton and Southern Society associations. Wilson and McCombs were extremely stubborn men; this and other incompatible facets of their personalities made it inevitable that their relationship would experience substantial tension.

Princeton of one of Wilson's greatest academic reforms, the preceptorial system. As a consequence, Harvey's publications began to speak of Wilson as presidential material.

The university president was mentioned for the United States Senate in 1907, and, in 1908, was considered by many easterners as an appropriate balance on a ticket headed by Bryan. Wilson would have nothing to do with the vice-presidential spot, and even declined to share a speaking platform with Bryan. Before 1908, Wilson was generally thought of as a conservative intellectual. The "progressive" Wilson began to appear during his struggles with the trustees of Princeton, in the conduct of his campaign for governor, and in gubernatorial successes in pushing substantial reform proposals through the New Jersey legislature.

Harvey, who was instrumental in persuading the New Jersey Democratic leaders to nominate Wilson for governor, took steps prior to 1910 to launch a full-blown Wilson-for-president campaign. However, Wilson's mounting progressivism began to embarrass Harvey, a conservative, and the people from whom Harvey was soliciting financial and other support. This brought the Harvey operation to an abrupt end in 1911. In its place there developed another group of Wilson enthusiasts, united around the fact that Wilson was a southerner.

Several leaders in the Southern Society of New York, some former students of Wilson, and other southern friends began to plan ways of placing Wilson conspicuously before the nation. Among these leaders were two New York lawyers, William F. McCombs of Arkansas and Walter F. McCorkle of Virginia, and one editor, North Carolinian Walter Hines Page of *World's Work* magazine. McCombs had been an honor student under Wilson at Princeton from 1894 to 1898. Page, an ardent advocate of educational and agrarian reform in the South, had been a personal friend since 1882.

In February 1911, James C. Sprigg, a Democratic progressive and reform

Vance Criswell McCormick was the publisher of two Harrisburg newspapers, the morning *Patriot* and the evening *News*. He was one of the first Wilson enthusiasts during the preconvention period, and four years later became Wilson's national committee chairman. Of Scotch-Irish ancestry, McCormick was born in Harrisburg in 1872. He attended Yale, where he became captain of the football team and received his bachelor's degree in 1893. Several years later, he returned to receive a master's degree. McCormick entered politics in Harrisburg soon after he left Yale and was elected to the city council in 1900. He was only twenty-nine when elected mayor and gave the city a vigorous reform administration. Some time after his term as mayor, he and A. Mitchell Palmer began a long struggle against the Democratic machine in Pennsylvania, in one election year bolting the gubernatorial nomination on grounds that "it had been corruptly made."[15] He subsequently served in several capacities in the Wilson administration and unsuccessfully ran for governor in 1914.

---

leader in Newark, McCorkle, and several others approached Wilson about organizing a movement for the presidential nomination. Wilson suggested that McCorkle see Page. The following month Page arranged a meeting among Wilson, McCorkle, McCombs, and himself to examine the organizational and strategic requirements of such a movement. They agreed that Wilson should make a speaking tour to the West Coast and that a publicity office be established in New York City. A fourth leader of the Southern Society of New York soon joined the Wilson group: William Gibbs McAdoo of Georgia. McAdoo became a prominent New York lawyer, and, in 1911, as president of the Hudson and Manhattan Railroad Company, gained renown for directing the building of the Hudson tunnel between New York and New Jersey.

During March, while Wilson was in Atlanta, William Jennings Bryan appeared at Princeton to give an address. Mrs. Wilson wired the governor to return for the occasion, and thus, for the first time, Bryan and Wilson met.

Upon his return from a highly successful speaking tour in the South and West, Wilson arrived in Washington on June 4 and consulted with his small inner circle: Page, McCombs, Vance C. McCormick of Pennsylvania, Frank P. Stockbridge, who had been Wilson's publicity man during the western trip, and Joseph P. Tumulty, a young New Jersey legislator whom Wilson had appointed as his private secretary. The group was eager to form a full-scale preconvention organization and embark upon a national campaign.

However, Wilson preferred to keep the organization limited and informational only. An information bureau was therefore established, and Wilson appointed

Stockbridge to run it. Wilson gave McCombs the task of raising money to support the bureau. McCombs was quite successful, concentrating his efforts mainly among Princeton alumni and his own acquaintances in New York City.

Early on, Wilson sought support from Democratic organizations in neighboring states. This was particularly true of Pennsylvania, where a progressive faction was giving the established party leadership, led by James M. Guffey, a rough time. Guffey, who had himself arrived at his present position by unseating former National Chairman Harrity, was particularly responsive to his factional problems. Leading the newly organized progressives were McCormick, A. Mitchell Palmer, and Representative William B. Wilson. After futile efforts to reshuffle the party machinery to accommodate both factions, the two wings went their separate ways, creating two Democratic state committees. Eventually, both factions responded to the overwhelmiong sentiment in the state and endorsed Woodrow Wilson's candidacy. This was Wilson's first endorsement and his largest single bloc of delegate votes throughout the nominating contest.

Another recruit to the Wilson bandwagon during the fall of 1911 was Edward M. House, a reform-minded Texan who had been involved in several party campaigns in his home state and at the time resided in New York City. A man of means who was deeply fascinated by presidential politics, House at first backed Mayor William J. Gaynor of New York for the 1912 nomination. He joined the Wilson movement at about the time that Wilson was conducting a tour of Texas at the request of the state's potent Wilson-for-president organization. The two men met through George Harvey at House's New York apartment on November 24, 1911, and developed a significant political friendship.

During October, Wilson formally designated McCombs as his campaign manager. McCombs had become de facto leader of the activities of the inner circle. With full responsibility for the Wilson organization, McCombs almost singlehandedly raised funds and created Wilson organizations in the states. McCombs also methodically went about establishing contact with newspaper editors and well-known public figures who might be sympathetic to Wilson. By December he felt that something more than the New York information bureau was needed. He established a branch office in Washington and appointed a Raleigh newspaperman to head it. The Washington office created and distributed campaign literature and press releases to 800 daily and 6,000 weekly newspapers around the country. The Washington office was also the main point of contact with congressional leaders sympathetic to the Wilson cause.

Strains that ultimately led to a break between McCombs and Wilson began to appear as the former increasingly made himself the liaison to the Democratic bosses and regulars. Wilson had successfully fought the bosses in New Jersey. Furthermore, Wilson was conducting himself as though issues rather than organization would bring him the nomination. McCombs became uneasy as Wilson seemed more and more to turn to McAdoo and House for political counsel.

There was the inevitable status problem arising out of their original professor-student relationship; neither man ever became accustomed to the fact that they were now peers. McCombs' difficulties also extended to his relations with subordinates in the organization; for example, by convention time, three publicity directors at the New York office had been hired and fired.

3

January 8, 1912, was a day of intense political maneuvering. The national committee held its first meeting of the presidential year. The Jackson Day dinner featured speeches by all major presidential aspirants. Bryan was very much in evidence at both occasions, this time attending the national committee meeting as a proxy holder. National Chairman Mack, who had withdrawn to New York politics following the defeat of 1908, opened the proceedings. Bryan immediately referred to the contest between James M. Guffey and A. Mitchell Palmer, the progressive challenger, over the Pennsylvania national committee seat.

In the Pennsylvania seating contest of 1898, the principle had been established that the national committee was the ultimate judge of the eligibility and qualifications of its members. In that instance, and with the intervention of Bryan, Guffey displaced Harrity as national committeeman. Early in 1904, authority to fill committee vacancies was again questioned when Chairman Jones appointed his former secretary to fill the District of Columbia seat. The seating procedure was presumably settled by a resolution passed at the 1908 convention that designated the state committees as the responsible agencies for choosing interim national committeemen to fill vacancies.

The Guffey-Palmer dispute again raised the issue of seating procedure. Bryan expressed his disagreement with the principles underlying the 1908 convention resolution. Drawing an analogy between the national committee and the United States Senate, Bryan argued that each of these bodies had the right to determine who may sit as its members. In seating contests and proxy disputes, Bryan continued, the national committee should not have to abide by the decisions of a state committee. The Vermont committeemen replied that only the Democratic national convention held the power to determine the membership and procedure of the national committee; in passing the 1908 rule, it had employed this power. With Chairman Mack, Tom Taggart, and Roger Sullivan supporting Guffey, the latter's right to the seat was upheld 30 to 18, with 4 abstaining. The matter did not end there.

The national committee proceeded to other business. The convention date and city were chosen. A three-member auditing committee reported that the financial report of the treasurer was correct. An arrangements subcommittee of sixteen members was chosen. Apparently for the first time, a committee on resolutions composed of five members was appointed to work on a preliminary draft of the platform. The Jackson Day dinner was far more exciting.

By the end of 1911, Wilson appeared to be the front-runner for the nomination. The other candidates and several leading conservative newspapers began a stop-Wilson effort, publishing a letter he had written in 1907 to a Princeton trustee expressing the hope that some way might be found to "knock Mr. Bryan once for all into a cocked hat!" The revelation would presumably alienate Bryan from Wilson. The Wilson men were deeply perturbed.

Bryan was at the home of Josephus Daniels, the North Carolina editor and a friend of both men, when news of the Wilson letter broke. Daniels did what he could to calm the Nebraskan, but apparently his efforts were not necessary. Bryan was too skillful a politician to be easily driven from his strategic pivotal position. As he traveled to Washington for the Jackson Day dinner, Bryan let word reach the Wilson people that no grudges would be borne. When it came his turn to speak at the dinner, Wilson offered a glowing tribute to Bryan's leadership. The entire incident turned out happily for the Wilson movement.

At about this time, the Champ Clark campaign began to develop strong momentum. Its leadership was based mainly in Congress. Senator William J. Stone of Missouri, the former national committee vice-chairman, launched the Clark boom in November 1911. Former Senator Fred T. DuBois of Idaho headed the Clark national headquarters in Washington.

As the presidential primaries got under way, Clark's many colleagues in Congress provided critical support in several local delegation contests. Clark and Wilson slates battled in California, Illinois, Maryland, Massachusetts, and Nebraska; Clark won all of the races. Wilson beat Clark in Oregon, South Dakota, and Wisconsin. Harmon carried only his home state, Ohio, and Underwood entered the Georgia primary unopposed. Clark was also favored by the entire Hearst newspaper chain.

Wilson's major difficulty, as McCombs explained to him in letter after letter, was the refusal of local organization leaders—the regulars—to join the Wilson side. The low point of the Wilson campaign came in May 1912. The McCombs organization had run out of money. Wilson was ill. Colonel House began to express doubts that Wilson could be nominated and predicted that Bryan would probably be the nominee. Ever eager to be a president-maker, House wrote to Mrs. Bryan pledging his support of her husband if he were again the Democratic nominee.[16]

The Roosevelt Bull Moose bolt from the Republican party offered the Democrats their best chance in two decades to capture the presidency. The Democratic national convention, still operating under the two-thirds rule, would be sufficiently divided to give nearly every major candidate in it a veto over the others. A convention stalemate could easily occur. No one expected an ambitious titular leader like Bryan, even one who had been defeated three times, to retire from the field. Democratic politicians knew and feared the prospect of another Bryan circus.

Homer Stille Cummings, son of an inventor, cement manufacturer, and Lincoln Republican, was born in Chicago in 1870. From the Heathcote School in Buffalo, the youth entered the Sheffield Scientific School of Yale University, receiving his bachelor's degree in 1891 and a Yale law degree two years later. Upon admission to the Connecticut bar, he entered into a partnership with Samuel Fessenden and G.A. Carter in Stamford, both eminent in the state's politics. An active Democrat, Cummings was elected mayor of Stamford in 1900 and served for three terms. When first elected mayor, he was also chosen national committeeman for Connecticut, a position he held until 1925. At the end of his second term as mayor, he made an unsuccessful race for congressman-at-large, returning in 1904 to serve his final term as mayor. He became corporation counsel in 1908 and rose rapidly to a position of leadership in the New England bar. Democratic national chairman in 1919 and 1920, Cummings subsequently became attorney general in Franklin D. Roosevelt's cabinet from 1933 to 1939.

What would Bryan's objectives be? Did he wish to deliver his progressive following to the eventual nominee and thus place the latter under obligation? Did he want to develop a stalemate that might ultimately compel the party to turn to him once again? There is evidence and testimony that make each interpretation seem likely. Bryan may have entertained both objectives, retreating from one to the other as events unfolded.

During spring of 1912, National Chairman Mack asked Bryan to serve as temporary chairman and keynote speaker of the convention. The gesture was undoubtedly rooted in mixed motives. As current titular leader, Bryan was the senior man available for the honorific duty. It was also true that allowing Bryan to have his great oratorical moment early in the proceedings might break the force of his inevitable subsequent speeches. Bryan's reasons for declining were probably equally mixed. In his *Memoirs*, Bryan offers the following explanation, "Some of the metropolitan papers were construing my neutrality between the two leading candidates as evidence of a desire to be a candidate myself. I was afraid that I would be accused of trying to stampede the convention."[17]

The arrangements committee met in Baltimore on June 20, still confronted with the problem of choosing a temporary chairman. The Clark supporters advocated Congressman Ollie M. James, a Clark man and friend of Bryan. The Wilson followers proposed Senator James A. O'Gorman, the New York progressive leader who had joined the Wilson camp in January. National Chairman Mack, with the support of Tom Taggart and Roger Sullivan, promoted the 1904 standard-bearer, Alton B. Parker. On an 8 to 8 vote, the subcommittee recommended Parker to the full national committee.

When the full national committee met on June 24, Homer Cummings of Connecticut, who had been in charge of the group handling temporary organization, rose to explain why the subcommittee had chosen Parker. Bryan had declined to be a candidate; the Clark and Wilson people were not likely to agree on anyone; Parker was considered the second senior man in the party after Bryan; his selection would be "good politics." After further wrangling, the results of the national committee vote were Parker 31, James 20, and O'Gorman 2.

In Bryan's view, the choice of Parker represented a victory for the party's mcst conservative elements. Bryan now had an issue upon which to ride into the convention. It was precisely the issue that could help him separate out the progressive sheep from the "reactionary" goats. Bryan proceeded to wire Clark, Wilson, and several progressive favorite-son candidates (ignoring Harmon and Underwood), asking them to stand by him in his opposition to Parker. Bryan invited each of them to wire him their assurances of support.

There was some disagreement among Wilson's associates over the content of a reply. McCombs redrafted a straddling statement that Wilson had previously issued to the editor of the *Baltimore Sun*. Tumulty and Mrs. Wilson urged a straightforward response. Wilson accepted their advice, his reply beginning with the words, "You are right."[18] McCombs considered the statement fatal, for it was bound to alienate the Tammany and New York delegates permanently. However, when Clark's noncommittal reply became public, it was clear that Wilson would be the principal progressive candidate, second only to Bryan. Despite McCombs' concerns, Wilson's strategy was apparently based upon the assumption that he had little to lose and everything to gain.

As the convention opened, some 436 delegates were instructed for Clark (including Bryan himself) and only 248 for Wilson; 726 votes were required to nominate. The convention was bound to be a strenuous one, but few expected it to last forty-six ballots, a record to that date.

When National Chairman Mack reported the committee's recommendation of Parker for the temporary chairmanship, Bryan rose to make a floor nomination: John W. Kern of Indiana, the vice-presidential nominee in 1908. Bryan pointed out that the friends of both progressive candidates, Clark and Wilson, had been favorably disposed to Ollie James at the national committee meetings. In choosing Parker, the committee was compelling a progressive convention and public to listen to a conservative keynote address. Intimating what was to come later in the convention, Bryan condemned the moneyed interests allegedly trying to run the Democratic party. "You cannot frighten [the Democratic party] with your Ryans nor buy it with your Belmonts," he shouted, making the issue as personal as possible.[19]

Kern took the podium to decline, appealing to Parker and the New York delegation to accept a compromise. When no response came from the New York delegation, Kern nominated Bryan for temporary speaker as "the only man to lead the people's side."[20] In the vote that followed, Parker received 579 and Bryan 508. The Underwood and Harmon people went almost entirely for Parker. Most of the Wilson vote went to Bryan. The Clark delegates were about evenly divided. Bryan had succeeded in separating out the sheep from the goats at the relatively low cost of losing the temporary chairmanship. As the convention proceeded to its next business, over 100,000 telegrams descended upon it from across the nation, most decrying the conservatives' tactics.

After listening to Parker's keynote speech, the convention moved on to the report of the rules committee. This committee brought forth another test of strength with respect to the application of the unit rule. A majority of the rules committee proposed that each delegation be allowed to make up its own mind about the unit rule. A minority report, taking cognizance of the new presidential primaries, requested that district delegates be bound by the instructions of their congressional district primaries. The disagreement originated in Ohio, where Wilson carried several districts, but Harmon won statewide. The Harmon majority in the state was trying to bind the Wilson district delegates. The long convention debate resulted in a Wilson victory, the minority recommendation receiving $565\frac{1}{2}$ to $492\frac{1}{3}$ votes. The conservative victory on the temporary chairmanship was now offset by a progressive victory on rules.

The next item of business was the selection of a permanent chairman; Congressman Ollie James' selection pleased all sides.

There was mounting concern over Bryan's intentions. Much of the convention's behavior was clearly in reaction to the thrice-defeated titular leader. Josephus Daniels, in his memoirs, reports typical opinions. National Chairman Mack told Daniels prior to the convention that "if Bryan will let matters take their course, busy himself with the platform, he will be the nominee. . . . In fact, New York, while not now for Bryan, would prefer to vote for his nomination than to see Wilson the nominee." On the other hand, Carter Glass of Virginia thought that Bryan was trying to stop Champ Clark "with the concealed hope and the expectation of prolonging the contest and receiving the nomination."[21]

It was apparent to Bryan that the Clark leaders, especially William J. Stone of Missouri, favored Parker as part of a bid for New York support for their candidate later in the convention, an arrangement subsequently confirmed by events. Bryan, in consultation with his brother Charles, decided that another attempt to ostracize the New Yorkers and unite the progressives was needed. As the nominating speeches were about to begin, Bryan asked and received special permission to introduce a resolution.

The Bryan resolution was presented in two parts. The first asked the convention to declare itself "opposed to the nomination of any candidate for president who is the representative of or under obligation to J. Pierpont Morgan, Thomas

F. Ryan, August Belmont, or any other member of the privilege-hunting and favor-seeking class.'' The second part demanded the ''withdrawal from this convention of any delegate or delegates'' representing these interests.[22]

The reaction of the delegates is vividly described in every account of the 1912 Democratic convention. Delegates ''screeched,'' ''frothed at the mouth,'' cursed and insulted Bryan. One delegate went so far as to offer a $25,000 reward to the person who would assassinate Bryan.[23] During the debate, Bryan withdrew the second clause. The first passed by a vote of 883 to 201$^1/_2$. Bryan had again succeeded in dramatizing himself and the conservative-progressive split and his own irreconcilable stand against ''the interests.''

With 726 votes needed to nominate, the first ballot showed Clark ahead with 440$^1/_2$, Wilson 324, Harmon 148, Underwood 117$^1/_2$, and the rest scattered. Any combination of 363 votes could veto the nomination under the two-thirds rule. Most of the Underwood strength lay in the South and held second-choice preferences for fellow-southerner Wilson. McCombs, at the head of the Wilson organization, obtained binding assurances that Wilson and Underwood delegates would remain steadfastly loyal to their first choices, but would be ready to move to their second choices only after consultation with each other.

On the tenth ballot, New York shifted its ninety votes from Harmon to Clark. This gave Clark a simple majority; in previous conventions this would have been followed by nomination. From Sea Girt, New Jersey, Wilson was in telephone contact with McCombs, McAdoo, Daniels, and others. Wilson sent two telegrams to McCombs, one at his own initiative, authorizing withdrawal at an appropriate time. McCombs was deeply discouraged. McAdoo and Daniels, however, indicated that they were still highly optimistic.

Later, a bitter controversy erupted over the withdrawal telegrams. According to Wilson, McCombs requested the authorization. McCombs claimed that Wilson volunteered it. By not announcing the withdrawal, McCombs believed he saved the nomination for Wilson. From Wilson's point of view, his nomination was put into jeopardy by McComb's discouragement. Two outcomes of this story are beyond controversy: Wilson lost faith in McComb's political judgment, and McComb's paranoia regarding Wilson's attitude toward him was aggravated beyond repair.[24]

In the balloting to this point, Nebraska's sixteen votes, including Bryan's, were nearly all committed to Clark. On the fourteenth ballot, when the bandwagon shift to Clark failed to materialize, Bryan rose again to ask for unanimous consent to explain his vote. He was opposed to any candidate receiving New York's support, as Clark now was. He therefore wished to change his vote from Clark to Wilson. He promised to shift his vote from Wilson at any time that the latter received New York votes. Few votes changed; the effect of Bryan's move was to prolong the stalemate. Whichever way New York went, Bryan now had a basis for throwing his influence in the opposite direction. This presumably would lead to a compromise candidate. The convention adjourned for a Sunday holiday at the end of the twenty-sixth ballot. The vote was Clark, 463$\frac{1}{2}$, Wilson, 407$\frac{1}{2}$, Underwood, 112$\frac{1}{2}$.

McCombs, not the most reliable source, offers the only direct testimony that Bryan actively sought the nomination for himself. Around midnight Saturday, McCombs was invited to Bryan's hotel room. There, according to McCombs, Bryan said, "McCombs, *you* know that Wilson cannot be nominated. *I* know that Clark cannot be nominated. You must turn your forces to a progressive Democrat like me." McCombs denied that Wilson was defeated, and hurriedly left the room.[25]

During the Sunday holiday, Bryan blandly told reporters that there was every reason why the progressives should be able to get together to make the ticket. He then suggested several relatively secondary political figures—Kern, James, O'Gorman, Culberson, and Rayner—as acceptable progressives. Noticeably omitted were Wilson's name and his own.

The balloting resumed on Monday. The titular leader's influence was significantly absent during the next twenty ballots. The convention had spent over half its time disengaging from the old leadership. It now turned to the problem of finding a consensus for a new one.

The Murphy-Sullivan-Taggart triumvirate, with 178 votes among them, made a direct bid to the largest Wilson delegation in the convention, Pennsylvania with 76 votes. The bosses proposed that A. Mitchell Palmer be a compromise candidate. Palmer and Vance McCormick declined the offer and continued to be the backbone of the Wilson movement throughout the convention. A similar offer was made to Texas, whose 40 votes remained solidly for Wilson. Meanwhile, the convention made small and slow additions to Wilson's strength. On the twenty-eighth ballot, Taggart led Indiana from its favorite son to Wilson. After the forty-second ballot, when Clark's votes had fallen below the one-third mark, Sullivan put Illinois in the Wilson column. On the forty-sixth and final ballot, Underwood released his delegates to complete the nomination of Wilson.

The convention was now able to adopt a progressive platform and select a vice-presidential candidate. McCombs indicated his support of Indiana's favorite son, Thomas R. Marshall. Apparently McCombs had, without Wilson's knowledge, agreed to a *quid pro quo*. Wilson preferred another, but reluctantly went along with the arrangement. This was yet another incident that aggravated relations between Wilson and McCombs. As a consequence, the selection of a national chairman developed into an extremely difficult matter.

The circumstances were summarized by Josephus Daniels. "The secretiveness of McCombs, his bad advice at the Baltimore Convention, and his jealousy of McAdoo had cost him Wilson's confidence and created an embarrassing situation."[26] These problems notwithstanding, McCombs' large role in the nomination campaign made him the logical choice for national committee chairman.

McAdoo, whose relations with Wilson had grown increasingly cordial during the previous weeks, would probably have been the nominee's personal choice. Bryan was reportedly in favor of retaining the incumbent, Norman E. Mack. Joseph E. Davies of Wisconsin was being promoted by many midwesterners. Many national committeemen, thinking of the negative public impression if Wilson failed to choose McCombs, strongly recommended the nominee's former student. After two weeks of hesitation, Wilson agreed to the election of McCombs.

However, Wilson hardly intended to have McCombs run his election campaign. Using National Committeeman Hudspeth of New Jersey as his channel of communication, Wilson embodied his plans for the campaign in a long memorandum. Wilson also named the other officers of the national committee: McAdoo as vice-chairman, Joseph E. Davies as secretary, and Henry Morgenthau as chairman of the finance committee.

McCombs was bitterly opposed to placing McAdoo in so prominent a position. McCombs also preferred that the executive committee be made up of leaders of different factional interests in the party, for example, Charles F. Murphy, Tom Taggart, William J. Stone, John H. Bankhead, and others. Wilson insisted upon a committee made up almost entirely of men who had loyally supported him before the nomination. McCombs, who had been ill during the preconvention campaign, collapsed in exhaustion immediately afterward. On August 12, he was stricken with neurasthenia and was literally removed from the rest of the campaign by his disability. He also suffered severe psychological disabilities. In the words of his secretary, Maurice Lyons:

> From the month of July, when he was first stricken, Mr. McCombs was a changed man. He seemed suspicious of everyone any way connected with the campaign. In his abnormal condition he concluded that Mr. McAdoo, especially, sought to undermine him, and when I endeavored to quiet him he responded in a manner that caused me to gasp.[27]

Other difficulties beset the campaign. Tensions developed between the Chicago and New York headquarters. Fund-raising posed problems. Wilson wanted all contributions over $1,000 returned, leading his associates to develop a popular appeal for small contributions through the newspapers. The small contributions, as usual, proved unsubstantial, and the large ones eventually were accepted. The McCombs-McAdoo rivalry produced strife within the campaign staff, particularly when McAdoo assumed full leadership of the campaign following McCombs' collapse.

Another major problem was the struggle within the New York organization, a battle that seemed likely to cost Wilson the electoral votes of the largest state in the Union. In 1911, a small group of progressive Democrats in the state legislature won the election of James A. O'Gorman to the United States Senate despite

Boss Murphy's support for the candidacy of William F. Sheehan. Hoping to rid the state of Tammany control entirely, these same progressives met shortly after the national convention and, under the leadership of State Senator Franklin D. Roosevelt, bolted the party, organizing the "Empire State Democratic Party." Murphy was determined to maintain control. Wilson was put in the position of having to make a choice between the two factions.

On September 23, Wilson followed a familiar pattern. He joined the fight against the bosses, particularly Murphy. At the Democratic state convention in October, Murphy capitulated and agreed to a compromise candidate for governor. The Franklin D. Roosevelt party thereupon withdrew its slate of state candidates and pledged support to the regular Democratic nominees.

There were few surprises in the election outcome. The campaign reduced itself to a battle between Wilson and Theodore Roosevelt. President Taft's candidacy had no other apparent objective than to deny victory to Roosevelt. Wilson received less than a majority of the popular vote, but carried the electoral college votes in forty-two of the forty-eight states. After sixteen years in the wilderness with Bryan, the Democratic party once again controlled the White House. A new generation of party leaders emerged around Wilson and dominated party affairs well on into the New Deal era.

4

With the possible exceptions of James Madison and Martin Van Buren, no president has written so extensively about presidential party leadership as Wilson.[28] There were important differences among these prolific presidential authors. Madison and Van Buren were consummate political practitioners long before reaching the presidency; Wilson was not. Furthermore, each man wrote during quite different periods in the institutional development of the executive and legislative branches of the federal government. Madison considered party organization essential in Congress and in campaigns for the presidency. He did not advocate strong party leadership by incumbent presidents. Van Buren, following the Jacksonian example, favored strong direction of party affairs while in the presidency as well as in the titular leadership of the opposition.

Wilson carried the institutional argument a step further. The party was vital in legislative affairs, but mainly in the manner of the British parliamentary system. The party was important during presidential campaigns, but only as it followed the nominee's, not the party boss's, lead. The party leadership was most demanding on the presidency itself, in which position a man was simultaneously the spokesman for both the party and the nation as well as the molder of the public opinion from which the party and nation draw support for their policies.

There were relevant personality difference between Wilson and his two eminent predecessors. Madison and Van Buren were negotiators, compromisers, and builders of political alliances. These were characteristics amenable to a system of divided governmental powers. Wilson, on the other hand, was "burdened with serious, at times crippling, temperamental defects" that often only fortuitously fitted the requirements of governmental leadership in the early years of his presidency:

> Though forced to operate within a governmental system of divided powers and checks and balances, Wilson's driving, essentially autocratic, leadership was for a number of years politically acceptable and successful. This achievement was due in large measure, of course, to the character of the situation at the time, which favored political reforms and strong leadership.[29]

Wilson articulated his enthusiasm for the British cabinet and parliamentary system of government during his career. A major advantage of the British system, he argued, was that both executive and legislative authority are vested in the leaders of the dominant party. The prime minister and his cabinet participate directly in the legislative process, initiate all important legislative propositions, and can be held accountable for their legislative program. The keenest criticism of that program is forthcoming from the opposition, and the ensuing debate clarifies the issues and informs public opinion. Wilson's behavior in the presidency, particularly his promotion of entire legislative programs and his tactic of taking issues "to the people" for public debate, was based upon his expectation that it was possible for the American system to follow more closely the British.

Wilson's later views of the presidency, possibly a consequence of his growing personal interest in this office, differed from his earlier acceptance of congressional ascendancy. In a new edition of *Constitutional Government in the United States*, published in 1908, Wilson took the position that the presidency was the main seat of governing power in the nation.[30] Wilson had, of course, been watching Theodore Roosevelt function as an activist president, the first since Lincoln. Wilson's revised view argued that the president automatically becomes the leader of his party through his selection by a nominating convention. Once a nominee is chosen, he stands before the country as the symbol of the party. Inevitably, the party must be led by its presidential candidate during the campaign, which is precisely the behavior Wilson followed during the 1912 contest.

Once a president is elected, "he cannot escape being the leader of his party except by incapacity and lack of personal force, because he is at once the choice of the party and of the nation. He is . . . the only party nominee for whom the whole nation votes." It then is entirely up to the president himself whether he becomes the leader of the nation. "His is the only national voice in affairs. Let him once win the admiration and confidence of the country, and no other single voice can withstand him . . . if he leads the nation, his party can hardly resist him." Through the exercise of persuasion and appeals to public opinion, according to Wilson, the president could also exercise leadership over Congress. Wilson concluded that the presidency was declining as a mere executive office and rising rapidly as a political office. When the power of initiative and direction of pubic policy lies in a single person leading a disciplined party, he believed, the people can rest assured that the power will be used responsibly.

As he prepared to assume office, the first tests of Wilson's theories of party were applied in connection with the appointment of his cabinet and the distribution of federal patronage. In view of his growing distrust of McCombs, it was to be expected that he would keep the national chairman at arm's length on appointments. However, it was less predictable that Wilson would justify his treatment of McCombs in the way that he did or that he would disregard the regular party leaders in key organizations around the country as much as he did.

When McCombs appeared in Princeton the day after the election to discuss patronage matters, he found Wilson unreceptive, even unwilling to dismiss his stenographer from the room during their conference. According to McCombs' account, Wilson said: "Before we proceed, I wish it clearly understood that I owe you nothing. . . . Remember that God ordained that I should be the next President of the United States. Neither you nor any other mortal or mortals could have prevented that!" As the tense interview proceeded, McCombs reported that he had been "commissioned by members of the national committee" to leave appointment suggestions with the president-elect, which he did and departed.[31]

Wilson's views on the selection of a cabinet are summarized in a paragraph of his book on *Constitutional Government in the United States*:

> Self-reliant men will regard their cabinets as executive councils; men less self-reliant or more prudent will regard them as also political councils, and will wish to call into them men who have earned the confidence of their party. The character of the cabinet may be made a nice index of the President's theory of party government; but the one view is, so far as I can see, as constitutional as the other.[32]

Although Wilson conducted lengthy interviews with the members of the party leadership, basically he distrusted them and collected most of his information about prospective cabinet officials through Colonel House, Walter Hines Page, and Tumulty. The press particularly seemed to enjoy speculating over the manner in which Wilson would "dispose of" Bryan. Concluding that the former titular leader would have to be recognized, Wilson offered Bryan the post of secretary of state.

The Wilson cabinet turned out to be a cross between a political council and an executive council. Bryan was the only appointee with a national following, and his appointment was a major gesture to progressivism. Wilson's preference for McAdoo over McCombs for treasury indicated to whom he would be turning for advice on party affairs. Other party advisers were Postmaster General Burleson, who had been chairman of the Democratic caucus of the House of Representatives, and Secretary of the Navy Daniels, who had been director of publicity for the national committee during the campaign. Most of the others in the cabinet, particularly McReynolds, Lane, Houston, and Garrison, were appointed on the basis of experience, merit, or some other relevant factor.[33]

Wilson's approach to titular leadership of the Democratic party was revealed in other ways. His strong predilection for the civil service merit system was severely tried in the distribution of presidential patronage. At the time, about 40 percent of the 470,000 civil employees of the federal government were subject to appointment through examination. More than 50,000 of these were postmasters, district attorneys, collectors of customs, and other officials appointed directly by the president. Wilson's initial intention was to review each candidate's file. He began to do this for postmasterships during his very first days in the White House.

Dissatisfied with the qualifications of a substantial number of the candidates, Wilson was inclined to set aside all the traditional procedures of appointment. Postmaster General Burleson presented a strong case for following the usual procedure of congressional recommendation, suggesting that those nominations with shortcomings in qualifications could be returned to the appropriate congressman for a new nomination. Inundated by the sheer volume of appointments to be made, Wilson eventually retreated to more traditional practices, relying primarily upon the recommendations of department heads, intimates on the national committee such as Thomas J. Pence, and his secretary, Tumulty. As a consequence, loyal personal followers, important progressives, and supporters of Wilson's programs were often overlooked. Many appointments went to local organizations and factions. Thus, through their handling of the federal patronage, Wilson's staff led the president into concessions that improved the chances of immediate party cooperation at the cost of long-run reorientation of the party's leadership and policies.[34]

5

Once in office, Wilson lay a strong hand on executive-congressional relations. His personal popularity carried over from the election campaign. He developed a presence by various personal activities, such as reading his messages to Congress in person. Even though Wilson made few efforts to do so prior to 1918, he always held in abeyance the threat to "go to the people." For a time Wilson contemplated an alliance with congressional Progressives, revealing greater concern for his legislative program than for party unity. However, he soon found that regular Democrats were surprisingly responsive to ordinary party pressures and to presidential patronage. Out of office for seventeen years, congressional and local Democrats were willing to bend in Wilson's direction for a while. Wilson and his associates, for their part, proved willing to crack the patronage whip. Under these circumstances, Wilson was able to hold the Sixty-third Congress in special session for the unprecedented period of a year and a half.

With Burleson's help, Wilson was also able to convert the party caucus in the House of Representatives into an effective instrument for promoting the presidential program. The president kept up a barrage of messages and personal pressures. Thus, the Underwood-Simmons tariff and the Glass-Owen currency bills became "party issues" instead of ordinary economic measures; their passage represented major political victories for Wilson. Most of Wilson's other legislative proposals were passed during the year-and-a-half-long session with less difficulty. As the session ended in October 1914, World War I was beginning in Europe and drew Wilson's attention away fom his domestic program. However, when confronted with the re-election contest in 1916, Wilson again gave priority to the passage of a progressive domestic program, which was significant in holding progressive support.[35]

Wilson did not exercise much party leadership, however, during the 1913 elections of United States senators by state legislatures where there were several excellent prospects for Democratic-Progressive alliances. Wilson's failure to get involved lost him an opportunity to strengthen the forces of his adherents in Congress.[36]

Rebuffed by Wilson for a cabinet post, McCombs took refuge in the national chairmanship. Prior to Wilson's inauguration in 1913, rumors circulated that McCombs would be offered the ambassadorship to France by Secretary of State Bryan, a prestigious but extremely expensive foreign post. The offer would have been ironic: too expensive for him to accept, and offered by the man (Bryan) he had opposed for secretary of state. At a National Press Club reception in his honor prior to the inauguration, McCombs publicly announced that he would not seek nor accept any office under the Wilson administration.[37]

The national committee met on the day after Wilson's inauguration. The main item on the agenda was the selection of a new vice-chairman to succeed McAdoo, who had moved on to the cabinet. McCombs feared that the occasion was part of a "McAdoo-Tumulty plot" to remove him from the chairmanship. After the committee passed the usual resolutions of commendation of the national chairman for his leadership in the recent campaign, McCombs made it clear that he would not relinquish the chairmanship until his term had run out at the next national convention. He then argued for broadening and regularizing the work of the committee:

> I do not believe that, after an election, whether it results in victory or defeat, a committee should be dormant until a few months before another election. We should be in thorough cooperation all the time. . . . In order to assure a continuation of what we have accomplished, we must continue [like] an organized army. . . . Two years from now, when we meet strong opposition, we can maintain ourselves in Congress and reorganize for the Presidential battle of 1916.[38]

To implement McCombs's goal, the national committee agreed to continue the headquarters in New York and open a Washington office under the supervision of Thomas J. Pence. Plans were discussed for national committee cooperation with the congressional campaign committee in the 1914 campaign. These discussions led to the establishment of a joint campaign committee two months later.[39]

To succeed McAdoo as vice-chairman, the national committee chose Homer S. Cummings, the national committeeman from Connecticut. It was assumed that Cummings, in his new capacity, would take an active part in coordinating the activities of the national committee and the congressional committee during the midterm election.

Later in 1913, President Wilson again offered McCombs the ambassadorship to France. McCombs again declined on grounds of the expenses involved and the diversion such a position would create from his immediate objectives of establishing and advancing himself in the legal profession. Although he made no public comment about it, another reason McCombs declined was to advance himself in New York politics. His position as national chairman put him in a good position for doing so. He was helped somewhat by Wilson's express willingness to clear all presidential patronage matters in New York through him.[40]

It did not take long for McCombs to became deeply involved in the labyrinth of New York Democratic factionalism. In anticipation of a bid for re-election in 1914, Governor Martin Glynn sought tighter control over the state organization and President Wilson's endorsement. Wilson suspected Glynn of having a too close association with Tammany and remained aloof. Glynn asked McCombs to intercede with the president.

On February 9, 1914, Wilson, Glynn, and McCombs conferred at the White House and projected plans to reorganize the New York party by eliminating Charles F. Murphy from the leadership of Tammany and electing William Church Osborn as state chairman. As legal adviser to State Senator Franklin D. Roosevelt in 1910, Osborn was identified with the Wilson progressives. Governor Glynn also agreed to withhold all state patronage from the Tammany organization. Subsequently, Murphy conceded to Osborn's election as state chairman, but only when the president and the governor agreed to accept his own continued leadership of Tammany. Rather than risk losing federal patronage, the Tammany men in the state senate agreed to support Governor Glynn's patronage appointments, which were presumably being made to strengthen his gubernatorial candidacy.[41]

McCombs came out of these elaborate transactions in a good position to be the party's candidate for United States senator. However, there were other hurdles. Governor Glynn offered McCombs his choice of the chairmanship of the New York Public Service Commission or of the New York Democratic party. McCombs would be able to manage Glynn's campaign for re-election from either position. According to the editor of McComb's autobiography, "McCombs' intimates asserted that the Glynn offers were all a part of the White House conspiracy to oust him from the National Chairmanship."[42]

McCombs took into account the relatively poor off-year election prospects for the Democrats in New York and decided to play a waiting game. Although frequently mentioned as an outstanding candidate for senator that year, he suggested the names of others. He declined the Glynn offers on grounds that his law practice would suffer and that his duties as national chairman precluded involvement in the state campaign on anything more than a part-time basis. As it turned out, the Democrats lost both the governorship and the senatorial race in that election. McCombs made his race for the Senate in 1916.

Whatever his state of mind, McCombs' tribulations concluded two decades during which the party's titular leaders—William Jennings Bryan and Woodrow Wilson—managed, in one way or another, to impede the institutional development of the national committee and the national chairmanship. Bryan, basically a political loner, never took either seriously. Wilson was overtly hostile. Another decade would pass before the Democratic national committee and its chairmanship would come into their own.

14 | The Chairmanship among Embittered Factions

As though President Wilson's lack of interest were not enough to retard their development, the national committee and its chairmanship were further encumbered by the distractions of World War I and the bitterness of a Democratic factionalism rooted in the last hurrahs of a stubborn Solid South, the power plays of urban machines, the distresses of Prohibition, and the dislocations of the postwar economy. As the Wilson era came to its close, the outline of the 1920s Democratic party troubles was already in view.

1

In 1914, the Democratic national committee assumed a large role in the midterm congressional elections. The manager of the Washington headquarters, Thomas J. Pence, issued a campaign pamphlet enumerating the achievements of the Wilson administration early in the campaign, specifically, the first week of February. The strategy was to link the congressional races to Wilson's great popularity. The national committee actively supported the fieldwork of the congressional campaign committee in the northern and eastern states. During the summer, the president expressed his desire to make a far-flung speaking tour on behalf of Democratic candidates. To gather information on political conditions and to prepare an itinerary for the president, Chairman McCombs began a tour of the West late in July.

In August, the first Mrs. Wilson died. The blow was a shattering one for Wilson and became the major reason for his reluctance to stump the country that fall. Another factor that undoubtedly diverted him from active campaigning was the deepening crisis in the international field, ultimately leading to the outbreak of world war. As international tensions intensified, so did Wilson's popularity at home. This popularity was the coattail to which the national committee hoped to devote its particular attention. The president, however, limited his campaign efforts to extensive letter writing on behalf of congressional candidates. This combination of personal and international circumstances compelled Wilson to remain in the traditionally passive presidential role during midterm campaigns. This was not what he intended nor did he repeat this pattern four years later.[1]

As it had since the early days of the Republic, the midterm elections resulted in losses of seats in the House of Representatives for the party controlling the presidency. The Democrats lost fifty-eight seats, but maintained a majority of nineteen votes. Republicans and anti-Wilson Democrats alike began to read the vote as a rejection of the president.

Renominating and re-electing Wilson in 1916 were by no means foregone conclusions, despite the advantages of incumbency. Wilson had, after all, been elected by a minority of the popular vote in 1912. At its meeting of February 13, 1915, the executive committee of the Democratic national committee agreed in principle that the campaign to renominate and re-elect President Wilson should begin without delay. Strongly favoring early activity were Vice-Chairman Homer S. Cummings, A. Mitchell Palmer, chairman of the executive committee, and Frederick B. Lynch of Minnesota. National Chairman McCombs, however, was unwilling to be rushed and handled changes in the national committee staff accordingly, that is, slowly. Meanwhile, supporters of William Howard Taft and Theodore Roosevelt began to make gestures of reconciliation on the Republican side.

Early in April, the secretary of the national committee, Joseph E. Davies, resigned to accept a presidential appointment as chairman of the Federal Trade Commission. McCombs promptly stated that there would be no need to fill the vacancy immediately. The president and his associates wanted Thomas J. Pence of the Washington headquarters to succeed Davies, although it was conceded that the national chairman held the authority to name a secretary. The Pence appointment was held up until the December meeting, at which time he was chosen.[2]

The Pence incident stirred up rumors that the White House was trying to get McCombs to resign. Joseph P. Tumulty, Wilson's secretary, found it necessary to issue frequent denials of the rumor. In June, Frederick B. Lynch was elected chairman of the executive committee and of the finance subcommittee to succeed Palmer. At this juncture, there was speculation that either Lynch or Vice-Chairman Cummings was being prepared to succeed McCombs.

Secretary of State Bryan's resignation at just this time in protest of the president's handling of relations with Germany added spice to the speculations. McCombs himself issued a statement on June 16 in which he said, "There is no intention whatever on my part of resigning as chairman of the Democratic national committee. My term will expire at the conclusion of the next national convention."[3] McCombs' resignation was forthcoming, however, on April 25, 1916. The White House, releasing a cordial exchange of letters between Wilson and McCombs, indicated that the resignation would take effect after the national convention in June.

The list of those who publicly denied their availability for the chairmanship was impressive: Homer Cummings, Frederick B. Lynch, Henry Morgenthau, William Gibbs McAdoo, Albert S. Burleson, and Joseph P. Tumulty. The search for a successor pointed most directly to Vice-Chairman Cummings and the executive committee chairman, Lynch. At this same time, Morgenthau resigned as ambassador to Turkey; his name was added to the speculation. Morgenthau made it clear that his resignation was intended only to free him to organize a "nonpartisan league" to promote Wilson's re-election. Tumulty suggested Senator Ollie James of Kentucky as a possibility. At one point just prior to the national convention, the leaders of Tammany announced their support of Senator Tom Taggart of Indiana for another term in the chairmanship.[4]

Much of the difficulty in choosing a national chairman originated in the doubts that Democratic politicians had about whether Wilson could be re-elected. Magnifying these doubts was Wilson's romantic interest in Mrs. Edith Bolling Galt, which was expected to alienate the support of many women voters. After several conferences with Democratic leaders, Postmaster General Burleson went so far as to suggest to Secretary of the Navy Daniels that the latter diplomatically request the president to put off his marriage until after the election, a suggestion that Daniels gingerly declined. The wedding took place before Christmas 1915.[5]

There was no question that the national convention would renominate Wilson. Wilson's influence was also felt in the preparation of the platform, many planks of which he drafted personally and others of which had his approval. One particular sentence congratulated the president for his diplomatic victories and for having "kept us out of war." The phrase made the president uneasy, even more so when the keynote speaker, Governor Martin Glynn of New York, alluded to it. The convention responded so wildly that the pacificism issue became the theme of the campaign, much to Wilson's discomfort.[6]

As the national convention convened, the selection of a successor to the national chairmanship remained unresolved. A great many national committeemen were reportedly strongly in favor of Vice-Chairman Cummings. McCombs also announced his preference for Cummings. The president was understood to favor Solicitor General John W. Davis of West Virginia. A. Mitchell Palmer arrived at the convention city leading a boom for Vance McCormick, then director of the Federal Reserve Bank at Philadelphia.

One of the earliest Wilson supporters in 1912, McCormick had the added advantage of a large following among Theodore Roosevelt's Progressives. McCormick was the 1914 gubernatorial candidate of both the Democrats and Progressives in Pennsylvania, and Theodore Roosevelt stumped the state for him. According to Josephus Daniels, Wilson esteemed McCormick "as a brother."

The president's personal adviser, Colonel House, had for over a year approached the 1916 campaign as a problem of winning the votes of former Progressives and Independents, which led House to recommend McCormick as one who could attract non-Democratic votes.[7]

Although Democratic chairmen had several times previously been selected from outside the membership of the national committee, McCormick's nonmembership became the occasion for expressions of discontent with President Wilson's management of party affairs. The debate was started by a resolution of the national committeeman from Ohio, Edmund H. Moore. The resolution was intended to throw full responsibility for the presidential campaign on Wilson personally. It explicitly gave him full power to select an entire campaign committee, thus freeing the national committee from its usual campaign functions. After lengthy discussion, Vice-Chairman Cummings announced his opposition to the Moore resolution. He was joined by Norman Mack of New York and Fred Talbott of Maryland.

Not until the Moore resolution was defeated by a recorded vote did the committee move to the selection of Vance McCormick as national chairman. The other officers chosen were Cummings, again as vice-chairman, Congressman Carter Glass to replace Thomas J. Pence (recently deceased) as secretary, Wilbur W. Marsh of Iowa as treasurer, Frederick B. Lynch as chairman of the executive committee, and Henry Morgenthau as chairman of the finance committee.

McCormick took over active management of the eastern and national headquarters in the Forty-second Street Building in New York City. Senator Thomas J. Walsh was placed in charge of the western headquarters in Chicago. The national headquarters bureaus were headed by Daniel C. Roper in the organization bureau, Robert W. Woolley in the publicity bureau, and Hugh C. Wallace in the foreign bureau. A campaign committee was chosen. At the September 1 meeting of the national committee, two women were in attendance as proxies for other committeemen, the first time women took formal part in Democratic national party councils.[8]

From the outset, the campaign was short of money. Although some 170,000 persons contributed, relatively few did so in substantial amounts. Special endorsements were obtained from Henry Ford, Thomas Edison, and John Burroughs. Ford spread word of his endorsement through a special (and expensive) series of newspaper advertisements. The president decided against stumping across the country and, in fact, made very few speeches. At national party headquarters in New York, Colonel House, McAdoo, and Morgenthau caused occasional consternation by assuming informal direction of many aspects of the campaign.[9]

New York Democratic leaders accepted the recommendation of President Wilson and Assistant Secretary of the Navy Franklin D. Roosevelt that Samuel Seabury be nominated for governor. A similar recommendation of Secretary

McAdoo for senator ran into a factional squabble. McCombs' name was injected as a possible compromise. McCombs won the Democratic primary, but, along with Seabury, lost by a small margin in the November election.

The outcome of the Wilson-Hughes contest was also close. Wilson again won with less than 50 percent of the popular vote. The final vote in California was uncertain for many days, prompting both national chairmen to send observers and legal counsel to the Far West to protect their party interests.

With Wilson's re-election assured, Chairman McCormick and Vice-Chairman Cummings initiated steps to strengthen the national organization. The New York headquarters was moved to the Woodward Building in Washington, where Assistant Treasurer W.D. Jameson and Assistant Secretary W.R. Hollister undertook fund-raising activities because a $200,000 indebtedness had been incurred. At this permanent headquarters, Chairman McCormick made plans for "Wilson banquets" and for establishing 2,000 local finance committees to solicit contributions.

2

In conjunction with the congressional campaign committee, McCormick started up preparations for the 1918 midterm campaign. The more than one hundred employees at party headquarters during the 1916 campaign had been reduced to a mere handful after the election, but the Woodward Building office continued thereafter to be a beehive of activity. This was especially true after the spring of 1917, at which time both Democratic and Republican national headquarters agreed to cooperate in the sale of Liberty bonds.[10]

The United States declared war against the Central Powers on April 6, 1917. President Wilson resisted suggestions that he create a war cabinet based upon a coalition between the major parties. Nevertheless, an impressive roster of Republicans were soon appointed to important positions in Wilson's war administration, including General John J. Pershing, General Robert E. Wood, Admiral Mark Bristol, Admiral W.S. Sims, Harry Garfield of Williams College, Julius Rosenwald, Robert S. Brookings, Robert S. Lovett, William H. Taft, Edward Stettinius, Charles Schwab, Herbert Hoover, and others.

The president assigned control over imports, exports, and blockade matters to National Chairman McCormick. By winter of 1917, McCormick was functioning as chairman of the War Trade Board and a member of the American Mission to Europe, headed by Colonel House. Under the circumstances, Vice-Chairman Cummings became acting chairman and assumed responsibility for midterm campaign operations.

In his memoir of the war period, Herbert Hoover refers to the 1918 congressional campaign as "an unhappy interlude."[11] By October 1918, the end of the war seemed imminent. On October 24, President Wilson, despite the bipartisanship of his appointments, launched a partisan attack upon the Republican party and especially its members in Congress. Said the president:

> If you [the American people] have approved of my leadership and wish me to continue to be your unembarrassed spokesman in affairs at home and abroad, I earnestly beg that you will express yourselves unmistakably to that effect by returning a Democratic majority to both the Senate and the House of Representatives... The return of a Republican majority to either house of the Congress would . . . certainly be interpreted on the other side of the water as a repudiation of my leadership.

The president thus staked his personal reputation and leadership upon an election in which he had no official part and about which he undoubtedly knew that incumbent presidential parties invariably lose seats in off-year congressional returns.

Herbert Hoover refers to this statement as a "mystery" and attributes it mainly to "politicians who pushed Mr. Wilson into an action so entirely foreign to his nature and his previous non-partisan conduct of war affairs." The statement and the campaign strategy it signified were opposed by Secretary of State Lansing, Secretary of Agriculture Houston, Secretary of the Interior Lane, and Attorney General Gregory. The major proponents were Presidential Secretary Tumulty and Postmaster General Burleson. On grounds that "the president's hand in the treaty negotiations would be greatly weakened if the election went against him," Hoover himself addressed a public letter to fellow-Republican Frederic Coudert of New York on November 2 supporting the Wilson appeal for a Democratic Congress. Republican National Chairman Willcox denounced Hoover, and this letter subsequently became the basis for charges at later Republican national conventions that Hoover was really a Democrat.

Upon closer analysis, President Wilson's midterm campaign strategy was perhaps not as "foreign" to his nature as Herbert Hoover believed. Wilson's most characteristic political response to opposition to his policies was to "go to the people." In their psychological study of Wilson, the Georges explain his use of this procedure as follows:

> What Wilson needed for peace of mind, when political deadlocks with his opponents developed, was a practical device which would enable him to "test" his contention that he better represented the will of the people than did Congress (or, in other situations, the Princeton Board of Trustees, the New Jersey Legislature, the Allied negotiators in Paris), a device which, therefore, would serve as a psychological and political safety valve against any autocratic tendencies within him. The device which he most often used for this purpose was the "appeal to the people."
> That "public opinion" could be made the immediate arbiter in his power conflicts with his opponents was indeed a comforting thesis. It served to relieve Wilson of the responsibility to compromise when deadlock was reached.[12]

As the end of the war approached, Wilson saw looming around him growing hostility not only to his demands for almost absolute wartime executive powers but also to the manner in which he requested and executed these powers. By 1918 congressional opinion was beginning to take on the scope and intensity of the antipresidential attitudes prevalent during the Jackson and Lincoln administrations. When some legislators proposed a congressional committee to oversee war expenditures, Wilson referred to it as an "espionage committee" and would have none of it. Legislative-executive relations deteriorated. By the fall of 1918, Republicans were looking forward eagerly to the possibility of winning control of Congress. They were determined to put an end to the era of strong presidents that they had had to endure under Theodore Roosevelt and Woodrow Wilson.

Possibly the most determined opposition to Wilson on personal as well as institutional grounds came from the Republican faction headed by Senator Henry Cabot Lodge of Massachusetts. In August 1918, Lodge was elected Republican Senate floor leader. Over the years that followed, the vendetta between Lodge and Wilson became a major factor in the conduct of U.S. foreign relations. Not only was Lodge his party's floor leader, but he was also the ranking Republican on the Senate Foreign Relations Committee. Thus, he was in line to become the committee's chairman if the Republicans were to win a Senate majority at the midterm elections. This prospect was undoubtedly reason enough for President Wilson to risk making an appeal "to the people."

Wilson lost his gamble. The Republicans captured control of both houses of Congress. Ex-President Roosevelt and Senator Lodge were quick to reiterate Wilson's own pre-election interpretation of a Democratic defeat: a vote by the American people of no-confidence in Wilson's leadership. Yet, the narrow forty-nine to forty-seven Republican majority in the Senate was hardly a very solid basis for Lodge's bitter opposition to presidential proposals.

3

The Germans sued for peace in October 1918. On January 12, 1919, the Paris Peace Conference held its first formal meeting. Throughout the conference, Wilson was harassed by the public statements of Henry Cabot Lodge, now chairman of the Senate Foreign Relations Committee, challenging Wilson's view of the American position. Wilson returned from Europe on July 8 and shortly thereafter presented the peace treaty, together with its Covenant for a League of Nations, to the Senate for ratification. The treaty was referred to the Foreign Relations Committee.

Senator Lodge's public position was that he favored American entry into a League of Nations only if the covenant could be so revised as to protect certain basic interests of the United States. Lodge's strategy was to assume a revisionist position in order to delay and, if possible, defeat the league proposal. His objec-

Although a newcomer to the national committee, Cordell Hull, at forty-eight, was hardly new to national politics. His father was a Tennessee farmer, merchant, lumberman, and banker who accumulated a modest fortune. While attending country schools and normal schools, Hull assisted in his father's farming and timber operations. He read law privately and subsequently graduated from the law program at Cumberland University in Tennessee. Barely twenty-one, he was elected to the Tennessee House of Representatives, where he served for four years. After active service in the Spanish-American War, he returned to Tennessee to enter law practice. In 1903, through an appointment to fill a vacancy, he became judge of Tennessee's fifth judicial circuit. Three years later he was elected to Congress. Hull specialized in economic and monetary problems and was one of the Democrats active in the revolt against Speaker Cannon in 1911. As a result, Hull won membership on the House Ways and Means Committee, which in effect became the new steering committee of the House. While on this committee, he served conspicuously in the formulation of economic policies under the Wilson administration.

---

tives were fairly evident to many observers: to humiliate Wilson personally, to protect American sovereignty, to reassert legislative ascendancy over the executive, and to create the issue for the next election contest in 1920. Lodge was not only majority leader of the Senate, but also an old hand at presidential politics. The Republican leadership in the Senate was positioning itself to become the most influential element in the 1920 Republican national nominating convention.

As Democratic National Chairman McCormick became increasingly involved in the duties of the American Peace Commission during the fall of 1918, the pressures of these activities compelled him to turn over the party chairmanship to another. This occurred during the congressional campaigns; Vice-Chairman Cummings carried the brunt of that work. McCormick finally resigned in December. At the national committee meeting of February 26, 1919, Homer S. Cummings was chosen to succeed him. The national committee also called for a complete reorganization in anticipation of a "militant" campaign in 1920.

Cummings had hardly assumed party leadership when he found himself urging nonpartisanship upon the citizenry. On March 7, 1919, Republican National Chairman Will Hays in effect launched the 1920 presidential campaign on the theme of nationalism versus the League of Nations. Five days later, Democratic Chairman Cummings responded with the assertion that the projected league was "too great a question to become partisan." Nevertheless, at its May 28 meeting, the Democratic national committee passed a resolution acknowledging that the League of Nations was the paramount issue before the country. The resolution urged prompt approval of the peace treaty and the league covenant. Cummings underscored the resolution in a formal address, saying, "While I do not consider the League of Nations Covenant a party issue at this time, I do say that it would strengthen the pressure on the President to run again if it should be defeated in the Senate."[13] This was the first public intimation by a responsible party leader that Wilson might be available for a third term.

Throughout 1919, organizational questions were under constant consideration by the new national chairman. In March, he selected a new executive committee and appointed to it such experienced hands as Norman E. Mack, W.W. Marsh, A. Mitchell Palmer, and E.H. Moore as well as such new figures as Cordell Hull of Tennessee. National party headquarters were again moved, this time from Washington to New York, a more convenient location for Cummings, whose residence was in Connecticut.

During June and July, Chairman Cummings toured the states from the Mississippi to the Pacific Coast to consult with Democratic leaders. Upon his return to party headquarters, he declared that he found the people overwhelmingly in favor of early ratification of the peace treaty.

The perennial problem of fund-raising came up at the September meeting of the executive committee. The director of finance advocated establishing a goal of $5 million, with the money raised by popular subscription. He hoped for between one and two million contributors.[14] The executive committee also created several regional campaign zones around the nation to facilitate the work of the national committee.

The question of a third term for President Wilson was raised at this meeting in connection with making statements to the press. The presence of Assistant Secretary of the Navy Franklin D. Roosevelt, not a member of the committee, was generally interpreted as having a bearing upon the third-term issue. Norman E. Mack put it this way, "You can say for me that if the League of Nations Covenant is beaten in the United States Senate, the next national convention will nominate Woodrow Wilson by acclamation, and we won't give a damn what he has to say about it."[15] Mack's remarks were a touching demonstration of loyalty to his chief, who at that very moment was experiencing a tragic conclusion of his nationwide speaking tour on behalf of the treaty.

The treaty had been dragging through the Senate, slowed down by requests for information, proposals of mild reservations, and pressures to amend. Wilson insisted that the treaty be ratified "exactly as it stood." In August, the treaty was still in the Foreign Relations Committee. Wilson once again decided to overcome his opponents by going to the people. On September 3, he embarked upon an extended and passionate tour of the country in defense of the treaty and the league. On September 28, he showed signs of suffering from sheer physical exhaustion. Four days later, he was overcome by a stroke that paralyzed the left side of his body.

Wilson would not allow Mrs. Wilson or his physician to divulge the seriousness of his condition. During the height of the debate over the league in October, the president was literally incommunicado. He continued, however, to insist that he would accept no compromises or reservations, not even the mild ones now being proposed by Lodge. The treaty failed in the Senate; the vote was an overwhelming 53 to 38 against ratification.

When Congress reassembled in December, the spirit of compromise was nowhere in evidence. On December 14, a White House statement indicated that the president was not considering a "concession of any kind." In a letter dated January 8, to be read to the Jackson Day dinner in Washington by Chairman Cummings, Wilson made a typical proposal—that the league issue be taken to the people.

> If there is any doubt as to what the people of the country think on this vital matter, the clear and single way out is to submit it for determination at the next election to the voters of the Nation, to give the next election the form of a great and solemn referendum.[16]

Speculation grew regarding the president's interest in a third term. William Jennings Bryan came into the picture again, opposing the president and urging ratification with reservations. The party seemed headed for another stalemated convention. Retention of the two-thirds rule became a subject of grave discussion among the leaders.

The third-term question was now an integral part of Wilson's fight for the League of Nations Covenant. This was even more so when, again in March 1920, the peace treaty was rejected by the Senate. There were third-term precedents. Grant in 1880 and Theodore Roosevelt in 1912 challenged, although unsuccessfully, the two-term tradition. Bryan, while never elected, established the precedent of a third nomination. Although the president's illness and confinement complicated the preconvention maneuvers, activity favoring his candidacy persisted nonetheless.[17]

Bryan was not about to be left out. His followers revived the Bryan Leagues. Bryan himself made much of the fact that he was the party's principal spokesman on the Prohibition amendment soon to go into effect. Former Secretary of the Treasury William Gibbs McAdoo, now Wilson's son-in-law, was mentioned often. McAdoo, however, was handicapped by the appearance of being a "crown prince," which made him a convenient target for the more outspoken anti-Wilson sentiment.[18] Another candidate was Attorney General A. Mitchell Palmer, whose anti-Communist investigations led to the arrest of thousands of "suspects" and kept his name in the headlines. Others candidates named in the press were John W. Davis, ambassador to England, National Chairman Cum-

George White was a successful oil-driller and financier, with interests in Ohio, West Virginia, and Oklahoma at the time of the request from Cox to assist Moore in the preconvention campaign. Born in Elmira, New York, in 1872, White was raised and schooled in Pennsylvania until he was nineteen years old. He received his bachelor's degree from Princeton in 1895, having been a student in two of Woodrow Wilson's classes during his senior year. White taught school for three years and then embarked upon a prospecting venture in the Klondike for another three years. When he returned, he settled in Marietta, Ohio, engaged in the oil production industry, and won election to the Ohio House of Representatives, in which he served from 1905 to 1908. His election from a district that was predominantly Republican gave him a statewide reputation as an effective campaigner. In the Ohio assembly, he became a leader of the Dry forces favoring the Prohibition amendment. He was elected to Congress in 1910 and 1912, where he became a close friend of Representative James M. Cox, succeeding him on the Ways and Means Committee when Cox ran for governor. Probably the two most popular members of the House of Representatives at that time were Cordell Hull of Tennessee and George White. White failed to be re-elected in 1914, was returned to Congress in 1916, but again failed to be elected in 1918. Democratic national chairman in 1920, White became a two-term governor of Ohio in 1930.

---

mings, and the three-time governor of Ohio, James M. Cox.

The Cox candidacy was one of the best organized. During the spring of 1920, the governor asked National Committeeman Edmund H. Moore to manage his preconvention campaign and George White to assist. The Wilson-Bryan differences and the McAdoo-Palmer candidacies held promise of a divided convention in which the major factions would have difficulty obtaining the necessary two-thirds vote. This was the familiar setting for choosing a compromise candidate.

Cox, Moore, and White had a combination of skills and attributes ideal for advancing a compromise candidacy. Cox was a Democratic "winner," having been elected several times in a predominantly Republican state. He was a Wet who had strictly enforced the state prohibition laws as governor. Moore was a "manager's manager," having close associations with Charles Murphy of Tammany, Roger Sullivan and George Brennan of Illinois, James Nugent of New Jersey, and Tom Taggart of Indiana. White, as a former Princeton student, was a friend of the president, a Dry, and a popular member of the House of Representatives.

Other factors favored Cox. The Republican nomination of Senator Warren G. Harding of Ohio helped. Ohio was a pivotal and hotly contested state, its electorate a weathervane indicator of trends in the nation. In New York, Governor Alfred E. Smith was that state party's favorite-son candidate, but he and the Tammany leaders were looking for a second choice, that is, a candidate who was Wet, had a good labor record, and was not too closely associated with the Wilson administration. Cox met these qualifications. Prior to and during the Republican national convention, Governor Smith, Murphy of Tammany, and other party leaders met at Tom Taggart's French Lick Springs Hotel to coordinate strategies.

During the week following the Republican convention, newspaperman Louis Seibold was invited to spend a few days at the White House. Seibold's account of the president's activities and state of health won for him a Pulitzer Prize—his reports testifying to Wilson's general good health in the course of a day's work. The timing of the invitation and the publication of Seibold's report on the eve of the Democratic national convention were interpreted as evidence of Wilson's active interest in a third nomination.

Additional evidence came from another direction. Seibold's visit to the White House took place on June 15 and 16. In a letter dated June 18, the president's son-in-law, William G. McAdoo, advised Assistant Secretary of the Treasury Jouett Shouse that Wilson would not permit his name to go before the convention. Shouse and others immediately shifted their support to the candidacy of Secretary of the Treasury Carter Glass. Glass visited the president on June 19, just before leaving for the national convention. According to Glass' report, President Wilson considered McAdoo's letter to be a final withdrawal and thought that Palmer's nomination would be "futile" and Cox's a "joke."[19]

Wilson clearly possessed the enthusiastic support of the convention delegates. When his picture was unfurled at the opening of the convention, the demonstration was prolonged and intense. Only the New York delegation kept its seats, with two or three important exceptions. Franklin D. Roosevelt engaged in some vigorous pushing and pulling to carry off the New York standard for the Wilson parade.

Wilson's influence was felt in the moving keynote address by National Chairman Cummings in support of the League of Nations Covenant. Wilson's hand was also seen in the work of the platform committee chairman, Carter Glass. Bryan led the Drys on the committee in a vigorous fight for a Prohibition plank. Bourke Cochran of Tammany pressed for a Wet plank. The fight was carried to the floor, where both Wet and Dry planks were defeated, and the platform, as reported by Glass, adopted.

Twenty-four candidates received votes on the first ballot. Of these, only four received more than 100 votes: McAdoo received 266 votes, Palmer, 256, Cox, 134, and Smith, 109. Seven hundred and twenty-nine votes were needed for the nomination. Cox reached a peak of $454\frac{1}{2}$ votes on the fifteenth ballot, leading McAdoo by more than 100. The race reduced itself to a two-man match on the thirty-ninth ballot. Cox received the nomination on the forty-fourth ballot.

At various critical junctures in the proceedings, there was renewed talk of turning to President Wilson as the candidate upon whom the party could unite. Wilson himself resisted many requests for public comment. As the convention opened, Chairman Cummings let it be known that "there will be no attempt to dictate from the White House." But former Chairman McCombs had this bitter word to say:

> When the great war broke out in 1914, naturally America was more or less dazed and was willing to accept any kind of leadership which might draw it through a possible difficulty. In this moment the chief executive again repeated that he was the leader of his party, a conception theretofore never entertained by an American. . . It was in such a manner that for the first time in the history of this country autocracy came into being. . . At San Francisco we again return to true democracy.[20]

As the deadlock continued, Secretary of State Bainbridge Colby wired the president that at the first appropriate moment he would request suspension of the convention's rules in order to place the president's name in nomination. Before sending the telegram, Colby talked with Mrs. Wilson, who told him that the president was willing to have his name presented if the move was generally approved by the administration leaders present in San Francisco. Colby called a conference for Sunday morning, July 4, which was attended by Chairman Cummings, Senator Joseph T. Robinson, and those cabinet members attending the convention, with the exception of Attorney General Palmer. Many felt that nomination of Wilson would not resolve the convention's problem, and would possibly expose the president to a humiliation. The group advised against carrying out Colby's suggestion, and the third-term movement ended.[21]

In the opinion of one student of this episode, "Colby was not working in the dark regarding the President's real desires."[22] Woodrow Wilson's third-term position has been summarized by David Lawrence as follows:

> My impression is that Wilson wanted the nomination primarily as a vindication of League of Nations policy. I am sure he realized that he was not well enough to serve another term in the Presidency. But with Wilson the nomination in itself would have been a vote of confidence by his own political party. He had . . . an ingrained feeling that confidence by a party should be shown periodically, just as it is in Britain. The fact that Bainbridge Colby was prepared to nominate Wilson fits with my theory that the whole thing had to do with vindication of his League of Nations policy. I believe he would have declined to run if he had been nominated.

Since Cox's nomination was interpreted as a defeat for the administration, the vice-presidential place was offered to an administration man. Franklin D. Roosevelt was an anti-Tammany Wilsonian who was nonetheless a good friend of Governor Smith. He was nominated by acclamation after several others withdrew.

4

The convention over, the national committee turned to its customary task of selecting new officers. On July 10, Chairman Cummings had indicated in a telegram to President Wilson that he was "pretty well tired out and sorely needed a vacation." Cummings indicated that in his opinion National Committee Secretary Kremer of Montana, Congressman Hull of Tennessee, then chairman of the congressional campaign committee, or McLean of North Carolina would do a competent job in the chairmanship, especially if supported by a good campaign committee. The president replied with a telegram stating that "the success of the party in this campaign depends upon your retaining the chairmanship of the National Committee. No one else has the same vision and enthusiasm." Cummings was the administration's choice, but any administration choice was unacceptable to the group of party leaders who had conferred prior to the convention at French Lick Springs.[23]

The day after the nomination, Cox's preconvention manager, Ohio National Committeeman Edmund H. Moore, announced that he would not become national chairman. Moore offered as his explanation his need to return to his law practice after having given so much time and effort to politics. What Moore did not say was that he shared the views of the French Lick Springs conferees: anyone connected with the administration had to be kept out of the campaign.

Those conferees—Governor Alfred E. Smith, Charles F. Murphy of Tammany, Thomas Taggart of Indiana, Roger Sullivan and George E. Brennan of Illinois—were old political friends of Moore. It was Brennan, according to the reports of William H. Crawford of the *New York Times*, who proposed that a subcommittee of the national committee be appointed to consider the problem of the chairmanship. Since Brennan was not a member of the national committee, his proposal was presented by others and adopted.[24] Thus, with Moore taking himself out of the running and Cummings too closely associated with President Wilson, the subcommittee began its search for a compromise candidate for the chairmanship.

In his memoirs, Cox recalls that "Hull was my personal choice." Known among his colleagues as "one of the silentest statesmen we have," Hull was popular among party leaders and, through his work on the congressional campaign committee, experienced in the problems of national political contests. However, Moore vetoed Hull. According to Cox's explanation:

> Moore was a man whose dislikes were as strong as his likes, and not until recently did I know, and then from Mr. Hull himself, the reasons for his opposition. During the convention, Moore had not got on pleasantly with

Chairman Cummings and Secretary J. Bruce Kremer of Montana. Moore, as Mr. Hull put it, erroneously thought that the Tennessean was too closely aligned with both Cummings and Kremer.[25]

The recommendation of George White as a compromise has been credited to two sources: Moore and vice-presidential candidate Roosevelt. It is probable that both men acted simultaneously and at the suggestion of the same combination of leaders. White was closely associated with Moore in Ohio politics and the Cox preconvention effort. Roosevelt undoubtedly served as a channel of communication between the administration people and the French Lick Springs forces.

When Cox agreed to have White as national chairman, Moore resigned so that the Ohio state central committee could elect White to succeed him as national committeeman. The national committee elected White and chose other officers, among them, three vice-chairmen. For the first time a woman was selected as a vice-chairman.

After White had been selected, Cummings expressed his dissatisfaction with the way the matter had been handled. He presented his views during a visit to the White House on July 26. He told President Wilson that Cox, Roosevelt, and White were "for me and at least 95 percent of the Committee was for me." Wilson then asked for an explanation of Cummings' failure to be selected, to which the former national chairman replied, "I am sorry to say that Governor Cox yielded to pressure. Moore and Marsh [Wilbur W. Marsh of Iowa; the national committee treasurer] threatened to resign."[26]

One other difficulty was relevant to the selection of the national chairman: the manner in which the League of Nations issue was to be handled in the campaign. Moore and the French Lick Springs leaders preferred to subordinate the league issue. The covenant having again been voted down by the Senate, politicians generally considered the handling of treaty ratification as the greatest failure of the Wilson administration. Cox and Roosevelt, however, held other views. Contrary to Moore's advice, Cox went to Washington shortly after the convention to visit with President Wilson. Roosevelt was present at the meeting. In Cox's words:

> As the nominee of our party, the leadership of the campaign passed from [Wilson] to me. . . There was some doubt at this time as to whether Mr. Wilson would live long. I would have reproached myself everlastingly if he had passed on without my going to him as an earnest of fealty to the cause which he had led.[27]

President Wilson was confined to a wheelchair during the meeting. His apparent poor health made a deep impression upon Cox, as reported by Roosevelt. Wilson indicated that he would do all he could to help the campaign.

Both Wilson and Cox subsequently issued statements of unity and optimism to the press. Cox's statement indicated that the league would be *the* issue.

Meanwhile, White was busily taking over national committee facilities. There were headquarters offices in Washington, New York, and Chicago. The offices in New York occupied the eleventh floor of the Grand Central Palace. This headquarters was to be White's main base during the campaign, other headquarters space being rented at the Murray Hill Hotel. Coincidentally, the owner of the Grand Central Palace was Coleman du Pont, an ardent supporter of Harding. This may have had something to do with the fact that Democratic headquarters were padlocked on election day on grounds that the month's rent of $2,900 had not been paid.[28]

Echoing part of an earlier statement by Governor Cox, White announced that the campaign would be fought on the issue of progressivism. When asked if progressivism would be taking the place of the league as the chief issue, White said, "I do not think that the League of Nations is the chief issue." This was a direct contradiction of former Chairman Cummings' statement, who, upon leaving the White House after his conference with the president, said that the league would undoubtedly be the leading issue, particularly since the league was popular in the West. In White's view, "progressivism [is] the real issue west of the Mississippi."[29]

The big city Democratic organizations cut themselves loose from the Cox campaign as soon as it became a League of Nations crusade. Tammany leaders were rarely, if ever, seen at national headquarters in New York. The New York City Board of Elections, under Tammany influence, ordered separate ballots to be printed for presidential electors. President Wilson's main campaign effort was his $500 contribution to the national committee for an educational fund on behalf of the League of Nations issue. The contribution was the beginning of a "Match the President" campaign fund.

The Democratic ticket faced still another difficulty, one much less visible in view of the limited scientific knowledge of that day regarding American electoral behavior. The 1920 election was the first in which women were eligible to vote on a nationwide basis. While there is very little evidence to indicate how women divided in their presidential preferences that year, it is clear that relatively few participated, and these were mainly from the higher socioeconomic groups. According to more recent studies, women in such groups tend not only to be active participants in politics, but also tend to vote Republican. This, combined with the lethargy of the Democratic city organizations, the disinterest of Bryan, and the incapacity of Wilson, resulted in an overwhelming defeat for Governor Cox. The Harding landslide gave the Republicans a 59 to 37 margin in the Senate and a 296 to 135 majority in the House. Even popular Alfred E. Smith was swept out of office, although by a small margin.

5

The closing of the Wilson era in presidential politics was perceptively reviewed in *World's Work*, one of the leading news magazines of the day:

> The one definite outcome of the San Francisco Convention is the elimination of Woodrow Wilson as the dominant force in American public life. . . Mr. Wilson's health in itself makes this inevitable; more significant still, the San Francisco Convention clearly showed that the President no longer controls his own party organization. . .
>
> Only two men have dominated the Democratic Party to the same extent as Mr. Wilson; these were Thomas Jefferson and Andrew Jackson. The influence of both extended to their periods of retirement. Ceasing to be President, Jefferson and Jackson became "sages"; the party leaders constantly consulted them on party policies and their approval was a powerful auxiliary in political campaigns. Dominant as Mr. Wilson has been for eight years, it seems inevitable that the role of "sage" will be denied him. The two Presidents who immediately succeeded Jefferson were his political disciples; Jackson's successor was his own selection; the party policies in both cases represented merely a continuation of the policies of the "master." But in San Francisco the forces in the Democratic Party which are most antagonistic to Mr. Wilson emerged triumphant.
>
> Probably the most important aspect of the Convention was the decisive influence exercised by such practical political leaders as Charles F. Murphy of New York, James R. Nugent of New Jersey, George E. Brennan of Illinois, and Thomas Taggart of Indiana.[30]

The article goes on to recall how Wilson, in September 1912, indicated his contempt of Murphy by refusing to be photographed in the same group with him, leaving a luncheon table at which Murphy was a guest. While governor of New Jersey, Wilson's difficulties with Nugent reached the point of a violent scene in the governor's office, when Wilson, in tones loud enough to reach the newspaper reporters, ordered Nugent to "get out" of the room. In the case of Sullivan, who had led the Illinois delegation to Wilson in 1912, the president refused to acknowledge any political obligation and early threw the influence of his administration against the Sullivan machine. Similar treatment was given the Taggart organization in Indiana.

Woodrow Wilson's personality was such that he could not help but act as though the presidency was what he thought it should be, that is, a prime ministerial position in a parliamentary system. This, of course, affected the way he dealt with the organizational leadership in his party. Any successes he may have had in practical party management may in part have been because he was too busy with other matters to interfere with the more pragmatic judgment of some of his colleagues. For example, had Wilson not been overwhelmed by other duties in his first months in office in 1913, his colleagues might never have been able to utilize the federal patronage as an instrument for strengthening his administration.

Wilson's final failure as a party leader was his mishandling of the 1920 national convention. Wilson was utterly untutored in the behavior of national conventions; in fact, he favored legislation eliminating them. Unlike Jefferson and Jackson, Wilson refused to select and boost a successor. It was his personal vindication that he most sought from the national convention, namely, its enthusiastic endorsement of the League of Nations Covenant. Wilson's basic amateurishness in party affairs made the development of the national committee and the chairmanship irrelevant not only for the promotion of his own programs but also for the extension of his influence beyond the period of his administration. He left behind a cranky and divided party.

15 | Self-Defeat: Roosevelt Progressives versus Taft Conservatives

Progressivism and conservatism were the salient factional rubrics in both major parties during the Roosevelt-Taft administrations, in no small way a consequence of the activities of the Democrats' William Jennings Bryan and the Republicans' Robert M. La Follette. In this setting, the Republican national chairmanship became a bone of bitter contention, at times occupied by men who wished they could be engaged elsewhere.

1

With President Roosevelt unwilling to seek another nomination, four or five Republican heirs-apparent were being discussed by 1907. Among these were Vice-President Fairbanks of Indiana, Attorney General Philander C. Knox of Pennsylvania, Senator Albert B. Cummins of Iowa, Governor Charles E. Hughes of New York, Postmaster General Cortelyou, and Secretary of War William Howard Taft. Hughes was elected governor of New York as recently as 1906 and enjoyed the qualities of a progressive reformer whose style and philosophy were conservative. National Chairman Cortelyou was a rising star slated for promotion to secretary of the treasury. An overriding consideration was the possibility (threat, some thought) that Roosevelt would change his mind and again want to be the party's standard-bearer.

In March, 1906, Roosevelt tried to discourage Secretary of War Taft from seeking a place on the Supreme Court. Said the president: "There are strong arguments against your taking this justiceship. In the first place, my belief is that of all the men who have appeared so far you are the man who is most likely to receive the Republican nomination, and who is, I think, the best man to receive it."[1]

William Howard Taft was born into one of the foremost political families of Ohio. While still a young man of twenty-nine, Taft was appointed to an unexpired term on the superior court of Cincinnati by Governor Foraker, later winning election by an overwhelming majority. In 1890, he was appointed solicitor general of the United States by President Harrison. At about this time he became acquainted with the young chairman of the Civil Service Commission, Theodore Roosevelt, and they formed a warm friendship. As chairman of President McKinley's second commission to establish civil government in the Philippines, Taft earned a reputation as a conciliator and administrator. His absence from the country in 1902 and 1903 enabled him to remain uninvolved in the political skirmishes among Hanna, Foraker, and Roosevelt. He also began to be considered as a presidential prospect.

Sensing the buildup of a potential rival for the 1904 nomination, President Roosevelt offered Taft an appointment to a Supreme Court vacancy. Others wanted him to enter the race for the governorship of Ohio, which would have drawn him into a debilitating factional conflict. The Supreme Court appointment, long cherished by Taft, would have removed him entirely from party politics. Taft cordially declined both invitations.

In a second attempt to dispose of a potential rival, Roosevelt asked Taft to be secretary of war. Taft accepted, finally willing to associate himself with the Roosevelt administration. In 1904, he helped appreciably in the Roosevelt campaign. The bonds of friendship and mutual trust between the two were so strong by 1905 that, whenever Roosevelt was away from Washington, matters were left so that Taft was in effect the pro tem president. By then, Roosevelt obviously had Taft in mind as his successor in 1908.[2]

Shortly after the 1906 midterm election, Roosevelt began to make personnel changes aimed at controlling the 1908 national convention. He promoted Postmaster General Cortelyou to secretary of the treasury. This took Cortelyou out of the patronage-rich Post Office Department and gave First Assistant Postmaster General Frank Hitchcock a freer hand to round up Roosevelt loyalists for 1908. For postmaster general, Roosevelt chose George Meyer, former ambassador to Russia, who had been recommended by two trusted friends, Senator Henry Cabot Lodge and Nicholas Murray Butler.

Other personnel changes bore more directly on control of the national party. On January 7, 1907, after his elevation to the treasury post, Cortelyou resigned from the national chairmanship. Harry New, who had been chosen for the vice-chairmanship in 1906, filled the vacancy as acting chairman. Among those eager to win the chairmanship away from New was Senator N.B. Scott of West Virginia. Scott was one of Foraker's chief lieutenants in the Senate and a warm supporter of Vice-President Fairbanks' presidential aspirations, certainly more so than Fairbanks' fellow Hoosier, Harry New. Scott had the advantage of seniority, that is, nineteeen years of service on the national committee. Rather than risk any early indications of weakness, the several candidate interests on the national committee agreed to postpone the election of a new chairman until the end of the year.[3]

Throughout 1907, Frank Hitchcock, with the knowledge and approval of Postmaster General Meyer, began to gather preconvention pro-Roosevelt commitments from prospective southern delegations. This was accompanied by much public speculation that the president was probably trying to make a choice from among Governor Hughes, Secretary Cortelyou, and Secretary Taft. Some observers guessed that Hitchcock was using these preconvention efforts to boost the chances of his former chief, Cortelyou. This interpretation was supported by the several instances in which Roosevelt and Meyer overruled Hitchcock's selections of southern patronage conferees.

At the December 6 meeting of the national committee, Acting Chairman New was confirmed as permanent national chairman. In the corridors, the national committeemen expressed themselves guardedly about the relative chances of Hughes, Knox, Fairbanks, Cortelyou, and Taft. The southern committeemen pledged themselves to act as a bloc in urging a third term upon Roosevelt. Chairman New forecast a warm contest.

In the selection of a convention city, a factional split appeared along candidate lines, with the southern coalition in the strategic middle. The southerners defeated the selection of Kansas City, ostensibly because it was a "Taft town." Chicago was chosen as a result of Hitchcock's manipulation of the southern bloc, leading to speculation in the press that this was a victory for Cortelyou. Hitchcock insisted that he was for Roosevelt and no one else. A few days later, on December 12, President Roosevelt declared emphatically that he would not run for a third term. This was interpreted as a blow to the Cortelyou cause, which had presumably been using the president's name as a stalking horse.

Hitchcock and the southerners, it turned out, were in Taft's corner all along. Late in January 1908, Hitchcock resigned from the Post Office Department upon the advice of Postmaster General Meyer in order to assume full-time management of Taft's preconvention campaign.[4] By the third week of March, Hitchcock claimed for Taft 552 of the 980 delegates.

Opposition to the Taft nomination came from both the progressive and the conservative poles of the Republican spectrum. Wisconsin, selecting a La Follette delegation under its new presidential primary law, not only supported its native son, but also won notoriety at the convention by offering, unsuccessfully, radical minority planks on railroad legislation, direct election of senators, and limitation of campaign funds.

Some 219 seats were contested by the "Allies," as Taft's opponents were known, but, of these, 216 were awarded to Taft supporters. At the convention, Senator Lodge, Roosevelt's close friend, was selected as permanent chairman. A new plan of convention apportionment, similar to the Quay plan to reduce southern strength, was defeated by 506 to 471; southern delegations were joined by a sufficient number of pro-Taft northerners to accomplish this. After this critical test, William Howard Taft was nominated with relative ease.[5]

Victor Rosewater, thirty-seven years old, was a Nebraska-born journalist following his father's footsteps in Nebraska politics. The family owned the *Omaha Bee*. The younger Rosewater received his bachelor's, master's, and doctoral degrees from Columbia University, having held the first university fellowship in political science in 1892–93. His doctoral dissertation on "Special Assessments: A Study in Municipal Finance" was published and received substantial notice.

Rosewater returned to Omaha and became managing editor of the family paper in 1895. He also assumed public positions: regent of the University of Nebraska, member of the Omaha Public Library board of directors, and activist in city and state Republican politics. The elder Rosewater had been a national committeeman from Nebraska and the younger Rosewater also found his political interests drawn to national party affairs. During 1907, Rosewater acted as Charles H. Morrill's proxy on the national committee and was subsequently elected national committeeman under the new Nebraska primary election system. In the Taft campaign of 1908, Rosewater, selected for a place on the executive committee of the national committee, served as director of publicity for the western headquarters in Chicago.

The selection of a national chairman to manage the campaign was a more difficult decision than the presidential nomination. There were many candidates. Acting Chairman New hoped that he would be retained. President Roosevelt favored Postmaster General Meyer, but the latter resisted on grounds that this would risk his being subject to charges that he had all along been using the Post Office Department to campaign for Taft. Furthermore, Meyer was sincerely interested in completing several of his favorite post office projects, including those concerned with postal savings banks and the parcel post.

Potential chairmen were available in Taft's home state: Ohio. Former Governor Myron T. Herrick, backed by vice-presidential nominee James S. Sherman, actively sought the position. Taft's manager in Ohio, Arthur I. Vorys, resenting Hitchcock's leading role in the preconvention work, thought himself eligible. Even Taft's brother, Charles, suggested himself as a possibility. The national committee appointed a subcommittee, headed by Powell Clayton, to assist in the search.

Supporters of the various candidates for chairman were unusually active even before departing the convention city. At his room in the Congress Hotel in Chicago, the new national committeeman from Nebraska, Victor Rosewater, called a meeting of some newly elected members of the national committee to compose a petition supporting Hitchcock. According to Rosewater, the petition eventually had the signatures of a large majority of the national committee and was telegraphed to Taft. Rosewater's claim is that it "added the final weight needed to turn the scale in Hitchcock's favor against the maneuvering of the wiley wire-pullers for the beaten 'Allies.' "[6]

The principal decision makers were, of course, Roosevelt and Taft. On July 8, at a conference of the executive committee and others at Hot Springs, Taft indicated his support of Hitchcock, and the executive committee, apparently acting on behalf of the entire national committee, formally confirmed this choice. Part of the arrangement was to give Vorys complete charge of the campaign in Ohio.[7]

President Roosevelt threw himself energetically into the campaign, delivering speeches in Taft's behalf, passing along political information to Hitchcock, making frequent recommendations about speakers and issues, and generally offering counsel on strategy and tactics; in short, "watching every phase of it with great care and circumspection to counteract every unfavorable tendency and to push promptly every tactical advantage."[8] Some newspapers even asserted that the real campaign manager was not Hitchcock, but the president himself.

However, those on the inside knew that Hitchcock dominated the campaign organization, made his own decisions, and kept his own counsel. Almost alone, Hitchcock determined to delay the party's maximum campaign effort until October on the assumption that William Jennings Bryan would exhaust himself and his campaign material early in the contest. Hitchcock even ignored requests from the nominee. For example, one source of embarrassment to Taft was the presence of a du Pont on the executive committee. The Powder Trust, of which the du Ponts were a part, was then being investigated by the Department of Justice. Taft suggested to Hitchcock that it was perhaps unwise to have a du Pont in so prominent a party position, but Hitchcock made no change. Only after President Roosevelt wrote the national chairman on the matter did du Pont resign. Hitchcock was also reluctant to call meetings of the national committee's executive and advisory committees, doing so only when pressured by Postmaster General Meyer.[9]

In October, in a flood of literature and speakers, the Republican campaign went into high gear. Taft conducted an extensive tour of the country, even invading the Solid South. Although the electorates of most states were heavily Republican, the election outcome nonetheless depended upon a few states, which, leaning Republican, remained relatively competitive. Hitchcock directed his maximum campaign efforts to these few states, with results that were soon fairly predictable. Taft won, coming within four electoral votes of the number forecast by Hitchcock on the basis of the data in his card index reporting system.

In keeping with recently established practice, Hitchcock was designated by President-elect Taft be the new postmaster general.[10] There were those who tried to dissuade Hitchcock from taking the cabinet position on grounds that the

John F. Hill, born in 1855 and educated as a physician, became instead a publisher of periodical journals in Augusta, Maine, in 1879. Ten years later, he was elected to the state house of representatives and in 1892 moved on to the state senate. He served as a member of the Maine Executive Council in 1898 and 1899, winning election as governor for two terms in 1901 and 1903. His work in the Taft nomination campaign of 1908 led to his appointment by the Maine delegation to the national committee.

national party needed a skilled manager. "Some of us believed that he (Hitchcock) could make the chairmanship of the national committee of greater usefulness to the party than any cabinet portfolio and it had been given out that the new President would not countenance its retention if he went into the official family."[11] Separating the chairmanship from the postmaster generalship at this particular time turned out to be one of Taft's more serious political misjudgments.

On the eve of inauguration, March 3, Hitchcock named the former governor of Maine, John F. Hill, as vice-chairman of the national committee. The appointment was made after conferring with members of the national committee. The choice was announced to the press as "substantially an action of the committee."[12] The procedural precedent thus established became a significant point of contention in 1911 and 1912.

A friend of Boston-bred Hitchcock, Hill had been an important factor in mobilizing northeastern support during Taft's nomination campaign. The selection of Hill was obviously intended to keep control of the national committee in friendly hands. When Hitchcock resigned from the chairmanship on inauguration day, Hill automatically became acting chairman, and served in this position until December 12, 1911, when the national committee formally elected him chairman.

2

During the Roosevelt administration, the progressive wing of the party received attention and opportunity that it might never have had otherwise. Roosevelt's actions regarding railroads, trusts, and conservation, as well as the 1908 platform promises of tariff revision, set a relatively firm policy mold into which a Taft administration would have to fit. As a consequence, the progressive wing, vigorously led by Robert M. La Follette, gained substantial support outside the northern Midwest. However, the conservative wing, as vigorously led by Nelson Aldrich of Rhode Island, held the majorities within both the party and the Republican electorate.

The 1908 national convention not only rejected progressive platform planks but also went out of its way to choose a rank conservative for the vice-presidency. At the time, Taft reported his uneasiness about the convention's failure to give representation to the progressives. When he became president-elect, Taft found himself titular leader of a dividing party. He remained unhappy and immobilized by this condition.[13]

Taft anticipated that his main factional troubles would manifest themselves in the Senate. He hoped that Roosevelt or Elihu Root would seek the New York Senate seat. "[Root] would be a tower of strength for me in the Senate. The personnel of the Senate is changing so rapidly that it has an important bearing on the entire administration."[14] In another letter to Roosevelt, as the latter departed for a two-year African hunting trip, Taft observed:

> I have no doubt that when you return you will find me very much under suspicion by our friends in the West. Indeed, I think I am already so, because I was not disposed to countenance an insurrection of 30 men against 180 outside the caucus. [Referring to the effort of the midwestern Republicans in the House to defeat the re-election of Cannon as Speaker.] I knew how this would be regarded, but I also knew that unless I sat steady in the vote, and did what I could to help Cannon and the great majority of the Republicans stand solid, I should make a capital error in the beginning of my administration in alienating the good will of those without whom I could do nothing to carry through the legislation to which the party and I pledged. Cannon and Aldrich have promised to stand by the party platform and to follow my lead. . . . Of course, I have not the prestige which you had or the popular support in any such measure as you had, to enable you to put through the legislation which was so remarkable in your first Congress; but I am not attempting quite as much as you did then.

Although Taft apparently was more ready to help the insurgents than Roosevelt, the new president failed a crucial test (in the eyes of the progressives) by refusing to join the revolt against Speaker Cannon.[15] The House in this Congress had 219 Republicans to 172 Democrats. About 30 progressive Republicans joined the minority Democrats, led by Champ Clark of Missouri, and, as a result, Cannon's escape was narrow.

Taft's lack of political skill manifested itself elsewhere. In composing his cabinet, Taft sought Roosevelt's advice, then failed to take most of it. He reappointed Knox, Meyer, and Wilson to positions other than those they had held under Roosevelt. Although Wright had been appointed by Roosevelt, with Taft's knowledge, to succeed Taft as secretary of war, Taft failed to reappoint Wright. Straus and Garfield, regular Republicans, were excluded from the Taft cabinet; two Democrats were included. The cabinet changes and the uncertainties they engendered caused a tempest of factional recriminations.

Abiding by the 1908 Republican platform, President Taft called a special session of Congress to revise the tariff. The Senate of 1909 had a Republican majority of 60 to 32. Its deliberations led to the Payne-Aldrich tariff, which was passed by a vote of 45 to 34. The bill went to a conference committee, to which Speaker Cannon unexpectedly appointed at least four high-tariff men. Taft recognized that a certain amount of duplicity had been committed, but reconciled himself to the final bill.

When the bill came to a vote in the Senate, it passed 47 to 31, with seven Republicans voting against it. In the House the vote was 195 to 183, with twenty Republicans voting "no." The new tariff only slightly reduced the rates on certain items and discriminated against midwestern products. Taft approved the bill, called it the best that could have been produced under the circumstances and shortly after toured the Midwest to defend his position. The entire episode succeeded only in further alienating the progressives.

The alienation was aggravated further by Taft's dismissal of Gifford Pinchot, chief forester of the Department of Agriculture and a hero of the conservation movement, for insubordination in a controversy with Secretary of Interior Ballinger. The incident, projected out of all proportion by the difficult personalities involved, left the impression that the progressives no longer had access to the White House.

Speaker Cannon's domination of the House of Representatives became an issue again in 1910. On March 17, Representative George W. Norris of Nebraska, a progressive Republican, offered a resolution authorizing the House, rather than the Speaker, to appoint the powerful Committee on Rules, excluding the Speaker from membership on the committee. Two days later, the resolution was adopted, 191 to 155, with every Democrat and some thirty Republicans voting for it. The progressive victory was spectacular and deepened the split within the Republican party.

When Roosevelt returned from his African trip on June 18, 1910, he was given a ticker-tape welcome as his carriage proceeded up Broadway in New York. He soon began his new job as associate editor of the weekly, *The Outlook*. In his first formal public statement, Roosevelt announced, "I am ready and eager to do my part so far as I am able in helping solve problems which must be solved." This was not the statement of a political retiree.[16]

Shortly after, Roosevelt was invited to the White House for a personal visit. Roosevelt offered various reasons for delay. President Taft became displeased and reluctant to repeat the invitation, but finally a reunion was arranged to take place at the summer White House. En route, Roosevelt asked Senator Lodge to remain with him during the visit so that the stay would be primarily social.[17]

Thereafter, Roosevelt remained at his home in Oyster Bay and received a stream of political visitors. Many observers noted that there seemed to be a greater number of insurgents than regulars calling upon the ex-president. In August, the New York Republican state committee rejected, by a 20 to 15 vote, a motion to recommend Roosevelt to be temporary chairman of its state convention. Instead, the committee chose Vice-President James S. Sherman, a dedicated foe of the progressive wing. In a published letter, President Taft expressed his unhappiness over the incident and hoped that steps would be taken to avert a division in the New York party.

The split soon encompassed much more than the New York party. Roosevelt, dissatisfied with Taft's apparent abandonment of his progressive programs and convinced that Taft was incorrigibly inept in party affairs, was ready to return to the partisan fray. In late August, Roosevelt embarked upon a tour of the West ostensibly to support Republican congressional campaigns there. The trip took on the reality of a former president seeking to reestablish his claim to the party's titular leadership. On August 31, before an audience of Kansas progressives, Roosevelt announced his program for a "New Nationalism," an eighteen-point program made up almost entirely of progressive planks. In the same speech, Roosevelt made oblique remarks about men "whose eyes are a little too wild to make it safe to trust them" (La Follette) and men "who make promises before election that they do not intend to keep" (Taft).[18]

President Taft also undertook a ten-day campaign tour of the Midwest in October. Leading members of the Taft administration were heavily engaged in similar stumping tours. The congressional campaign committee chose most of its campaign speakers from among the conservatives. In this way, the midterm election polarized the progressive-conservative leaderships. There was talk of creating a third party. However, Senator Jonathan Dolliver of Iowa, one of the progressive leaders, in a Senate speech on June 13, announced that the insurgent strategy would be to work within the Republican party.

Among both Republicans and Democrats, the progressive message seemed to be well received by the voters in the primaries and the general elections of 1910. Progressive Republicans enjoyed victories in the primaries in Idaho, New Hampshire, Wisconsin, Michigan, California, and Washington. At the New York Republican state convention, despite the rejection he suffered from the state committee, Roosevelt captured the temporary chairmanship by a vote of 568 to 443; the victory was counted in favor of the progressives. On the Democratic side, Woodrow Wilson, campaigning on a straight progressive platform, succeeded in the gubernatorial race in New Jersey. Progressive Democrats also won in the gubernatorial elections in New York, Ohio, Massachusetts, Connecticut, and Oregon. One of the major Republican victories was Hiram Johnson's in California, a progressive stronghold.

The year 1911 seemed entirely devoted to factional jockeying and preliminary organizational work among the supporters of Taft, Roosevelt, and La Follette. On January 23, 1911, the formation of the National Progressive Republican League was announced. It was intended to be a vehicle for the La Follette candidacy. The charter members included most of those men who had participated in the progressive congressional campaigns of 1909–10: Senator Bourne as

Ohio-born Charles D. Hilles, after completing his formal education at Oxford Academy in Maryland, devoted over twenty years to youth welfare work. Fifteen of these years were spent as an officer and eventually president of the Boys' Industrial School at Lancaster, Ohio. The promotion to president came with the help of a political friend, Arthur I. Vorys, who later became one of William Howard Taft's campaign managers in Ohio. In 1902, Hilles was hired as superintendent of the New York Juvenile Asylum at Dobbs Ferry. He maintained his Republican connections in Ohio, helped Vorys on a confidential basis during the Taft campaign in 1908, and became well known among Republican leaders in New York. His work in the Taft campaign led to his appointment as assistant secretary of the treasury in 1909. Thereafter, Hilles was frequently mentioned for the position of Republican state chairman in New York.

president, Representative Norris as vice-president, other leading progressives from the Senate and the House, and such noncongressional figures as William Allen White, Gifford Pinchot, James R. Garfield, Ray Stannard Baker, Frederick G. Howe, and Louis D. Brandeis.

There were comparable developments among the Taft leadership. Following a White House conference of New York leaders on January 18, 1911, an anti-Roosevelt leader, William Barnes, Jr., was elected Republican state chairman. Like his famous predecessor, Thurlow Weed, Barnes was publisher of the *Albany Evening Journal*. There were rumors that President Taft would replace acting National Chairman Hill with John W. Weeks of Massachusetts, but nothing came of this. Instead, Taft replaced his private secretary, Charles D. Norton, with Charles D. Hilles of New York, thereby putting Hilles in charge of his preconvention operations.

For his part, Roosevelt played his cards close to his chest. Speculation about his role in the forthcoming presidential election kept his name bobbing up constantly in the press. An old hand at political drama, Roosevelt, during March and April of 1911, conducted a tour of forty states to promote the New Nationalism, making speeches and holding informal conferences. According to Robert M. La Follette, it was on the basis of Roosevelt's findings during this trip that the former president began to think of making a presidential race in 1912.[19]

On April 30, 1911, leaders of the National Progressive Republican League met in a committee room at the Capitol and concluded that they should propose a candidate for the Republican presidential nomination, that La Follette should be their choice, and that this move had the general endorsement of former President Roosevelt. It was La Follette's personal belief that Roosevelt had clearly indicated, through Gilson Gardner, a political writer, that La Follette should be the progressive candidate.[20]

In July, La Follette headquarters were set up in Washington. This was followed by the Wisconsin senator's major attack on Taft's claim to the party's leadership. Despite the vigor with which La Follette's candidacy was launched, by late summer many progressive congressmen were still hesitant about endorsing him. A survey indicated that senators preferred Taft over La Follette by 3 to 1 and that representatives were for Taft 8 to 1.

Meanwhile, La Follette supporters were eager to get their campaign off the ground in the states. An initial step occurred in the Republican state convention in Nebraska where the progressives pushed hard, and with near success, for an endorsement of La Follette. National committeeman Rosewater met the challenge and skillfully maneuvered the proposal into a ratification of the Taft administration. The incident appreciably raised Rosewater's standing with the president.

3

Presidential activity was increased during the fall. In September and October, Taft again undertook a nationwide tour. At this time his distaste for partisan politics was revealed in a response he made to critics of the Supreme Court. On October 6, Taft commented, "I love judges and I love courts. They are my ideals on earth that typify what we shall meet in Heaven under a just God."[21]

Roosevelt, on the other hand, continued to be enigmatic. When a national conference of progressives from approximately twenty-five states gave La Follette its resounding endorsement on October 16, Roosevelt, in an editorial comment in the *Outlook* of October 28, suggested that this "endorsement is to be regarded as a recommendation rather than a committal of the movement to any one man."

During the fall of 1911, President Taft's feelings about the 1912 nomination hardened. In a conversation with his wife, as reported in the memoirs of Archie Butt, the president recalled that four years earlier he had thought there was little chance for his nomination, but subsequently he received it and the election. Replied Mrs. Taft: "Yes, but I was always hopeful then. I am not hopeful now. Things are different. I think you will be renominated, but I don't see any chance for the election." To which the president said: "Well, I am chiefly interested in renomination, so don't get disconsolate over that. If we lose the election, I shall feel that the party is rejected, whereas if I fail to secure the nomination, it will be a personal defeat."[22]

By the end of the year, Taft's self-confidence seemed to grow. Late in December he told Butt that he felt he would be renominated and re-elected. This attitude was in marked contrast with that of his cabinet, whose meetings, "once such cheerful sessions, became gloomy and futile."[23] In Taft's words:

> The only contingent which may block it [his own renomination] is the nomination of Roosevelt, and I don't believe he can be nominated. He will not dare to take it as long as I am in the field, for he will not underestimate my friends in this country. He will be forced to support me also. If he does not, he will be charged with my defeat in case I fail to be elected, and should I be elected he will get none of the credit for it.[24]

Several difficult issues confronted the meeting of the Republican national committee on December 12. Representing Taft was Presidential Secretary Hilles. The first issue the committee dealt with was the status of acting Chairman Hill. Rather than risk a major battle over the succession, the Taft people preferred to postpone the selection until after the national convention. Hill continued as acting chairman and appointed Victor Rosewater as vice-chairman. In view of the subsequent controversy over Rosewater, the new vice-chairman's description of the event is particularly interesting.

> Governor Hill, who had been in poor health latterly, advised me that he was naming me vice-chairman and would look to me to relieve him of some of the burdens of his position when convention day approached. The appointment, reduced to writing, was filed with Secretary [of the national committee] Hayward. Of course, the new chairman did not act in this wholly of his own motion—it was part of the understanding with Hitchcock who had made him vice-chairman, that this contingent authority be kept within the group which had cooperated all along and to which he satisfied himself my selection would be agreeable. Nothing then indicated, however, that my duties in connection with the convention would extend beyond participation in the work of the arrangements committee.[25]

A second issue before the committee was the problem of devising a new system of apportioning votes in the convention. The demands for a reduction of southern strength were becoming increasingly agitated, but the dependence of an incumbent Republican president upon the bloc of southern votes was an equally pressing consideration. A decision in the matter was again postponed.

Related to the apportionment issue was the squabble over the appointment of former National Chairman Harry S. New as chairman of the convention arrangements committee. Hilles presented New as the administration's choice. The southerners opposed New, ostensibly on the grounds that he had favored reduction of southern representation. Postmaster General Hitchcock supported the southern position. After conferences between Hitchcock and Hilles, New was named to handle the convention management. The decision, however, was not made without the president's personal intervention in New's behalf. Part of the arrangement was that New would appoint several of Hitchcock's "close friends" to the arrangements committee.[26] The incident left some doubt about Hitchcock's loyalty to Taft. In the words of Taft's biographer:

> The President, although he did not believe the rumors, was nonetheless apprehensive. Hitchcock was not an easy man to understand. He exchanged few confidences. He was inclined to brood by himself. At last, apparently in January, Taft . . . stood up, at the end of the Cabinet table, and pointed his finger at the postmaster general.
> "Frank!" he demanded, "Are you for me or against me?"
> Hitchcock, his face crimson, also arose from his seat. "I am for you, Mr. President," he said.
> Taft gave confidential assurances to the correspondents on January 23 that Hitchcock was loyal.[27]

A fourth difficulty was writing a convention call that could meet the requirements of new state primary laws governing the selection of delegates. Some fifteen states had enacted primary election laws. As a result, the fight for many delegation seats shifted away from state conventions into popular elections, necessitating a degree of preconvention public campaigning hitherto unknown in the presidential nominating process. Before the national conventions would meet in 1912, about three and a half million voters would participate in the primaries of thirteen states, electing delegations with mandates of varying force and clarity.

The arrival of the primaries did little to ameliorate the division in the Republican party. Despite its overwhelming popular majorities, three powerful Republican figures (Taft, Roosevelt, and La Follette), each with a substantial ego, were challenging each other, raising uncertainties far beyond the normal. This unstable situation was made possible by the popular role in the primaries and the ambivalent loyalties of state and local party leaders.

The defeat of a proposal by William E. Borah in the national committee on a matter concerning the primaries demonstrated that the Taft representatives were in control. The national committee then approved a call that sanctioned the election of delegates according to state primary law, instead of by convention, on condition that "the state committee of any such congressional committee so direct," subject to the further proviso "that in no state shall an election be so held as to prevent the delegates from any congressional district . . . from being selected by the Republican electors of that district."[28] At issue was the unwillingness of either faction to lose representation in a convention delegation because of an all-or-none statewide primary victory by an opposing faction.

4

January was a month of political declaration. On the first of the year, a convention of Ohio progressives, including such men as Garfield and Pinchot, declined to endorse La Follette's candidacy. The Ohio leaders hesitated to commit themselves before they could be certain what Roosevelt would do. On January 3, President Taft issued a fighting declaration of candidacy. By January 18, Roosevelt began setting the stage for an announcement of candidacy. The device he used was a letter from eight governors inviting him to declare. On February 24 he did so, with characteristic energy.

Before February had ended, La Follette's chances faded into the shadow of Roosevelt's candidacy. A Taft preconvention organization was set up, headed by Representative William B. McKinley of Illinois, who had just been re-elected chairman of the Republican congressional campaign committee. Both Taft and Roosevelt threw themselves into a hard personal campaign to win delegates in the primaries and the state conventions. The spectacle was an unfamiliar one for the country to behold: an incumbent president seeking renomination, but confronted by the active candidacy of a former president of his own party, in fact, by the man most responsible for the incumbent's first nomination.

By the end of March the two-pronged strategy of the Roosevelt managers became evident. First, the seating of Taft delegates would be challenged. Second, in many states the selection of national committeemen was now also subject to the primaries. There would be a drive to elect a majority of pro-Roosevelt national committeemen. A favorable national committee majority would not only give Roosevelt control of temporary and permanent chairmanships of the convention, but also enable him to have a substantial number of the contested delegation seats decided in his favor.

To implement the latter goal, the Roosevelt forces needed 27 of the national committee's 53 members. Of the 53, only 13 were anti-Taft (11 were for Roosevelt and 2 were for La Follette), 14 others from the South, Hawaii, the Philippines, and other territories were safely in Taft hands, about a dozen were uncommitted, and approximately 14 others were eventually defeated in the primaries. All 14 of the defeated national committeemen favored Taft. If their right to sit on the national committee prior to the convention could be challenged successfully, the committee would come under Roosevelt control.[29] On April 2, however, Hilles published an analysis that showed Taft in control of the national committee by a margin of 4 to 1.

Acting Chairman John F. Hill died on March 16, and Rosewater became acting chairman. The public announcement of the succession stated that "the appointment is in line with the precedent of long standing." It was a precedent, however, that would not go unchallenged.[30] Shortly after the acting chairman assumed his position, R.B. Howell, a Roosevelt supporter, defeated Rosewater in the Nebraska primary race for Republican national committeeman. The Roosevelt strategy was dramatized by the ensuing debate over Rosewater's status.

Howell planned to appear at the next meeting of the national committee and demand his seat at once. However, the custom had been for national committeemen to serve until the end of the national convention. There was also the precedent of 1908, which Rosewater cited, according to which a new national committeeman elected by primary vote in South Dakota was not seated until the establishment of a new committee at the end of the 1908 national convention. Howell finally dropped his proposed challenge, but not without casting doubt upon Rosewater's entitlement to the position of acting chairman as well as national committeeman.

When Rosewater arrived in Chicago for the committee's preconvention meeting during the first week of June, the suggestion was made that committee Secretary Hayward should take the gavel until Rosewater's formal election as national chairman. The explanation for this proposal sounded friendly enough. All that was under challenge was Hitchcock's original authority to name Hill as vice-chairman, since only the full national committee could choose its officers. When Hill followed the same procedure in naming Rosewater as vice-chairman, it was argued, an undesirable precedent was being established. Rather than challenge Rosewater's right to the position as acting chairman, would it not be technically appropriate to have the committee's secretary, as the ranking officer actually elected by the whole committee, call the opening session to order?

Rosewater had no intention of retreating. He pointed out that the forthcoming committee meeting was legal only because it was in response to an official call issued by him as acting chairman. In other words, the time to challenge his appointment as vice-chairman in the first place and his succession to the position of acting chairman subsequently had long since passed. In response to this argument, when the full national committee met on June 6, it elected Rosewater as chairman without opposition.[31]

5

To clarify matters, the national convention proceeded to adopt a series of rules that were, in effect, a constitution for the national committee. The rules set guidelines for the terms of service of members, procedure for filling vacancies caused by death or resignation, designation of the chairman, vice-chairman, treasurer, secretary, and "such other officers as the Committee may deem necessary" as the body of officers, authorization for the chairman to appoint an eight-member executive committee, and authorization for the executive committee to fill any vacancy occurring in these offices by majority vote, to be confirmed at the next full meeting of the national committee within sixty days.

Preconvention claims of delegate strength indicated how close the battle would be. One newspaper estimated that, of the 1,032 delegates, Taft had 472 and Roosevelt 439. Taft's spokesman, Congressman William B. McKinley, claimed 567, that is, 27 more than necessary. The searchers for a compromise candidate began to suggest Supreme Court Justice Charles E. Hughes, but, by June, Taft made it clear that there would be "no third alternative."

As the national committee decided contest after contest in favor of Taft delegations, Roosevelt, from Oyster Bay, kept up a tirade of charges against the committee. The committee eventually seated 233 Taft delegates and 19 Roosevelt delegates.

The next critical vote was taken on the temporary chairmanship. Elihu Root, Roosevelt's former close companion, was now a Taft supporter, and was elected over the progressive candidate by the narrow margin of 558 to 501. Over half of La Follette's Wisconsin delegation refrained from voting for either side's candidate. This, in effect, destroyed the Roosevelt strategy for defeating Root. This preliminary test and defeat of the Roosevelt forces was decisive. Writing from Washington, President Taft was candid about Roosevelt's dilemma and his own objectives.

> Chaos is still a proper term for conditions at Chicago. . . . Roosevelt is struggling to secure as many of his followers as possible to join him in a bolt, and it is their reluctance or refusal that makes the situation doubtful. He has given specific notice of his intention to bolt. If he does not do it at once, it will look like so many of his bluffs. . . . If I win the nomination and Roosevelt bolts, it means a long, hard fight and probable defeat. But I can stand defeat if we retain the regular Republican party as a nucleus for future conservative action.[32]

On the nominating ballot, Taft received 561 votes, Roosevelt 107, La Follette 41, Cummins 17, Hughes 2; 349 delegates refrained from voting.[33] Taft and the conservatives had succeeded in their main objective. In the words of Senator Murray Crane, "We are here . . . to defeat Roosevelt regardless of what happens anywhere or to anybody or to the party."[34]

Roosevelt was equally adamant. His followers rallied in Orchestra Hall where Roosevelt delivered a "Thou Shalt Not Steal" oration. He called for the formation of a new party and assumed he would be its nominee.

President Taft soon turned to the problems of organizing his campaign. The paramount difficulty was selection of a national party chairman. Speaker Joseph Cannon, Representative William B. McKinley, and Boies Penrose of Pennsylvania strongly urged the president to select William Barnes of New York. Taft rejected Barnes for fear that it would appear, as Roosevelt charged, that the party was in the hands of the state bosses.

Vorys of Ohio proposed Harry M. Daugherty, a rising Ohio politician who had worked hard for the Taft cause during the preconvention period. Taft and his advisers, however, had heard some unconfirmed rumors about Daugherty's honesty, but rejected his name ostensibly on the ground that he was not well enough known. Later, the president wrote Daugherty, "Personally, I should have been entirely willing to have you chairman, had it met with the views of those with whom I had to consult in making the selection."[35]

Taft finally turned to his personal secretary, Charles D. Hilles, as the only man on whom all the party factions could agree. Hilles accepted, reluctantly. Writing four years later, he reflected, "I have not relished the role of professional politician. I went into it because it was so hopeless that no one else would undertake it and because my affection for Mr. Taft left me no alternative."[36]

Hilles anticipated that a three-cornered presidential race would dry up the normal sources of Republican campaign finances. He was correct. As national chairman, he could not until mid-August find anyone to serve as party treasurer. After conducting an extensive search among such prospects as John Wanamaker and Charles G. Dawes, Hilles finally prevailed upon the incumbent, George R. Sheldon, serving since 1908, to stay on. Nonetheless, Hilles was compelled to conduct the campaign on less than $1 million as compared to the several millions that had been available in earlier years.

Hilles labored with other handicaps. The president spoke infrequently and, when he did, rather poorly and without heart. Relatively few speakers rallied to the Taft cause. Republican voters were further depressed by the death of Vice-President Sherman on October 30.

The Roosevelt campaign needed less organization. The former president made up his own mind on strategy and scheduled his own itinerary. There were fewer state campaigns to coordinate. Furthermore, several of the key campaign people in the Roosevelt camp had been functioning as such for some time. Senator Joseph M. Dixon of Montana arranged to issue a Progressive national convention call and chaired a provisional national committee. The call was signed by sixty-three individuals, many of them governors and senators, from forty states.

The Progressive national convention that selected the Roosevelt-Johnson ticket met in Chicago from August 5 to 7. At its conclusion, Senator Joseph M. Dixon became the party's national chairman. The chairman of the national committee's executive committee was financier George W. Perkins, who only two years earlier had withdrawn from the banking firm of J.P. Morgan and Company in order to devote his time to civic affairs. Other prominent Roosevelt managers were publisher Medill McCormick of the *Chicago Tribune* family, who served as vice-chairman in charge of the western headquarters, O.K. Davis, Washington correspondent for the *New York Times* and *Philadelphia Ledger*, who served as secretary of the national committee and director of publicity, and Francis W. Bird, former law partner of Elihu Root, Jr., and former appraiser of the port of New York, who concentrated on the New York campaign.

With Taft and Roosevelt intent upon defeating each other by splitting the normal Republican majority in the electorate, it was predictable that Woodrow

Wilson would win. In a retrospective letter some twenty-three years later, Charles D. Hilles reviewed the strategic character of the Roosevelt bolt:

> To plan for another party deliberately and cold-bloodedly is an enterprise on which experienced men do not embark. . . . Colonel Roosevelt could not have successfully set up a secessionist party in 1911 to resist the Republican party in 1912. His personal following was greatly augmented by his appeal to all Republicans before and during the selection of delegates in the spring of 1912. He had not defied in 1911 those who make a fetish of party regularity. His agents built up a case in the preliminary stages of the convention. He alleged that the party was imprisoned by its bosses and advised the people to strike for freedom. That movement, I say, could not have been brought into being by cold logic a year in advance of the convention. It may have been conceived conditionally late in 1911, but if it had been delivered then it would have had to be sent to an incubator.[37]

16 | Party Reunification, Permanent Headquarters, and a Popular Chairman

For the two losers in the 1912 presidential race, the real issue had been factional control of the Republican party rather than control of the national government. However, both men rationalized the defeat in other ways. Taft, of judicial mind, defended his "title" to party leadership; it had been bestowed upon him by the regular national nominating convention of the party.[1] Roosevelt charged Taft with having stolen a nomination. Roosevelt was explicit about his satisfaction in having denied the conservatives control of the national party. During a Chicago speech in which he lauded his Bull Moose followers and reviewed the outcome of the election, he said:

> We have accomplished more in 90 days than ever any other party in our history accomplished in such a length of time. We have forced all parties and candidates to give at least lip-service to Progressive principles. In this brief campaign we have overthrown the powerful and corrupt machine that betrayed and strangled the Republican party.[2]

Out-party status over the next eight years returned political reasonableness and reconciliation to Republicans and Progressives and to the Taft and Roosevelt factions, but not without the efforts of a skillful national chairman, Will Hays, and the failures of a stubborn Democratic president, Woodrow Wilson.

1

The overthrow of the Republican "machine," which Roosevelt declared as accomplished fact in his Chicago speech, was still a matter for the future. The problem of control of the Republican national organization was one that would have to be solved between the conservatives and those progressives who did not bolt. Of the eleven leading progressive insurgents in the Senate, only three had bolted to the Progressive party: Murdock, Poindexter, and Beveridge. Others, including La Follette, Borah, and Cummins, remained loyal to the regular organization.

Another consideration was the fact that the election left the Republicans in control of fifteen governorships and the mayoralties of twenty of the fifty-five largest cities in the nation. In a historically comparable situation, namely, the Whig-Republican split of 1856, the Whigs had no such solid base of political strength in state and local governments. As a consequence, the political impulse was for entire Whig state party organizations to march into the new Republican party. In 1913, however, the reverse was the situation. The long-established Republican organizations controlled state and local offices. It was up to the bolting progressives to build an entire third party from scratch, and they were therefore less likely to evolve into a second major party. The bolters would eventually have to find their way back to their Grand Old Party or complete their conversion to become Democrats.

Aside from the progressive bolt, one of the most serious issues within the Republican national organization continued to be the gross distortion of representation at the national conventions. Overrepresentation of the southern party organizations had clearly favored Taft. The close division in the convention vote and Roosevelt's charges of theft were likely to mar the legitimacy of future presidential nominations if the system of apportionment remained unchanged. Without a president in the White House to benefit from preservation of the status quo, it now seemed timely for party leaders to move on an issue that had troubled them for several decades. National Chairman Hilles therefore asked the members of his executive committee to meet in Washington to examine the apportionment problem.

Anticipating the meeting of the executive committee, scheduled for May 24, progressive Republicans called for a conference in Chicago on May 13, 1913. At the Chicago conference, the progressives declared that the only way the third-party movement could be ended would be for the regular Republican party to establish a new basis of organization. To this end, they recommended reducing southern delegate strength and convening a special reform national convention during the coming summer to implement this. The progressive conference also supported installation of new national committeemen before rather than after the national conventions in order to eliminate the "lame duck" influence of committeemen defeated in the primaries. From nearby Indiana, Speaker Cannon ridiculed the Chicago proposals and declared that the Republican national committee had no authority to call a special convention.[3]

At the executive committee meeting in Washington, the progressives made their proposals to a Committee of Conciliation. A split developed among the conservatives, particularly with respect to their proposal to call a special convention. William Barnes, Jr., of New York, Boies Penrose of Pennsylvania, and Charles F. Murphy of New Jersey joined Cannon in opposition. Many others, however, looked with favor upon the idea, according to Hilles' reports to Taft.[4] Some were uncertain and worried about the extent to which they could control a special convention. Others felt that a national convention in 1913 would be premature and could be more profitably held the following year. Most members of the executive committee did apparently agree that the proposed interim national convention would be a proper body for changing the apportionment rules of the party.

By a unanimous vote, the executive committee authorized the call for a meeting of the full national committee sixty days after the adjournment of Congress to consider whether to hold an extraordinary party convention or to determine on its own authority changes in the basis of representation. The executive committee also appointed a special Committee on Legal Matters to investigate the procedural issues involved in changing the apportionment rules. The chairman of the seven-man committee was Charles B. Warren of Michigan.

The executive committee considered two other significant pieces of organizational business: the establishment of a permanent headquarters and the appointment of a liaison committee to establish closer campaign cooperation between the national committee and the Republican congressional campaign committee. Action, if any, on the first issue was not reported in the press. The motion on the second point not only encouraged cooperation between the two committees, particularly in campaign management, but also recommended against combining the two or establishing a joint financial agency for them. Hilles appointed a three-man committee, headed by Senator Crane, to pursue improved liaison with the congressional campaign committee.[5]

After Congress adjourned, a meeting of the full national committee was scheduled for December 16. Two weeks before the meeting, Charles B. Warren, speaking on behalf of the Committee on Legal Matters, reported its opinion: that the national committee had no right of itself to change the basis of representation to the regular national convention, but that the national committee did have the right to call a special convention to consider the subject of reapportionment. Furthermore, the national committee was empowered to change the basis of representation to such a special convention.[6]

On December 11, the Committee on Conciliation announced that progressive Republicans would insist upon formal hearings before the national committee. A day later the Republican congressional campaign committee unanimously adopted a resolution favoring a special national convention and suggesting three alternative plans for reducing southern representation.

The full national committee met in an atmosphere of agreement that reform in the apportionment system was necessary. Voting 35 to 14, however, the committee rejected the proposal for holding a special national convention. The majority of members took the position that the national committee had the authority to change the apportionment rules. Then, by a vote of 38 to 6, the committee approved a subcommittee report setting forth a new basis for national convention representation to be incorporated in the call of 1916. The new apportionment would reduce the voting strength of the southern states by 82 delegates and that of the northern states by 8. The new plan would become effective only if endorsed by Republican state conventions in states making up a majority of the votes in the electoral college, such majority to be reached by January 1, 1915. This procedure was subsequently followed, and by October 1914, a sufficient number of state conventions had ratified the proposal to put it into force.[7]

2

The future of the Progressive party remained in doubt from fall of 1912 to the spring of 1914. Publicly, Roosevelt argued that only full adoption of the Progressive platform and retirement of the Republican "bosses" could pave the way for an amalgamation of the two parties. Privately, he expressed other views. Writing to Gifford Pinchot, he observed:

> It is a matter of incredible difficulty to shake loose from the old parties men who profess adherence to our principles. The strength of the old party ties is shown by the fact that although we carried the primaries two to one against Taft, at the polls about as many Republicans voted for him as for me. . . .
> [Looking to the future,] the great danger ahead of us is that with no clear-cut purpose and no adequate organization, our party may make so poor a showing in the local and state and congressional elections . . . as to be put out of the ring.[8]

The future of the Progressive party was further complicated by the belief among the electorate that a progressive administration (Wilson's) was actually in office.

Roosevelt's fears were well founded. As Progressive candidates for Congress came forward for the midterm races, there was evidence of a weak supporting organization, leading to incomplete slates in many districts. Upon his return from a trip to South America in May 1914, Roosevelt began to stress the importance of uniting in opposition to President Wilson.

In planning for the Progressives' future, Roosevelt told Hiram Johnson that account should be taken of the different types of groups within the Progressive party, that is, (a) those who had been "wild-eyed fanatics," (b) those who had rebelled at the abuses of the Republican politicians and bosses, and (c) those who were straight-out Progressives on principle. Fusion, Roosevelt thought, would have to come about under varying circumstances in different places.[9] Thus, in New York, Roosevelt recommended that the Progressives support a non-organization Republican for governor. In Pennsylvania, however, he would make a fight for a full-fledged Progressive.

The 1914 midterm elections proved disastrous for the Progressives. In the first popular election of senators under the new constitutional amendment, conservative Republicans won many major senatorial races. Elsewhere, progressive Republicans won. In some places, particularly the West, Progressives were only able to prevent Republican victories. Democrats continued to hold a working majority in the House, despite having lost some 60 seats. The Democrats also controlled the Senate, having beaten the Progressives in several places.

The plan for cooperation between the Republican national committee and the Republican congressional campaign committee met with very modest success. The conservatives who represented the national committee had to deal with Frank P. Woods of Iowa, a progressive Republican, resulting in much apprehension on both sides.[10]

Preparations for the 1916 nomination fight began to appear in spring of 1915. Taft offered an outstretched hand of welcome to returning Progressives. There was even talk of Roosevelt's reconversion. Penrose of Pennsylvania came out for Senator Elihu Root of New York for president; this had the support of William Barnes, Jr., of New York and National Chairman Hilles. Other conservative availables included former Senator Theodore E. Burton of Ohio and Senator J.W. Weeks of Massachusetts. On the Progressive side, Roosevelt's correspondence throughout 1915 mentioned such possible compromise candidates as Frank Knox of New Hampshire, Herbert S. Hadley of Missouri, Hiram Johnson of California, and possibly Charles E. Hughes, now serving on the Supreme Court.

On July 19, 1915, Roosevelt was reported as saying that the Progressives would support Hughes if he were nominated. Also favoring Hughes were former President Taft and Murray Crane. Taft himself was clearly out of the running and expressed regret that Chairman Hilles did not support Hughes, "Hilles' association with the national committee is such as to put him out of sympathy with the selection of a man like Hughes, who he anticipates will not recognize the workers in the party."[11]

Throughout 1915 Progressives and conservatives sought common ground on public issues. The sinking of the British liner *Lusitania*, in May 1915, shortly after the torpedoing of an American tanker, found Republicans and Progressives alike heaping abuse upon President Wilson's handling of these breaches of American neutral rights. They were also critical of his preparedness program.

Roosevelt was particularly vigorous in his criticism of the Wilson administration. "He was determined to do all he could to defeat Wilson, and the primacy of this goal fixed his course in a direction that made the continuation of the Progressive party less and less likely." Representing the regular Republican position, National Chairman Hilles, after the national committee meeting of December 1915, announced that the probable issues for 1916 would be the tariff, criticism of Wilson's foreign policy, the single-term plank in the Democratic platform of 1912, Democratic extravagance, and the shipping bill.[12]

The road to Republican-Progressive reunion was hardly smooth. Each side was adopting a posture from which to make its strongest bid. Some Progressives, leading among them Harold Ickes, favored another third-party ticket in 1916 in the hope that a second Republican defeat would shake the conservatives loose from control of the national party. This group strongly favored a second Roosevelt candidacy. Other Progressives—Medill McCormick of Illinois, Knox of New Hampshire, Miles Poindexter of Washington, and Johnson of California—promoted alliances with progressive Republicans in their respective states and regions, intending thereby to improve the chances for a progressive Republican candidate for the presidency. Still others considered a two-party Progressive-Republican alliance as the best way to beat Wilson. Working toward the latter goal was George W. Perkins, a wealthy New York Progressive. Perkins' plan was to hold a Progressive national convention simultaneously with the Republican, reiterate the Progressive platform, and offer to find a candidate agreeable to both parties.

Among conservative Republicans, the primary objectives were to retain control of the national organization and promote the candidacy of Elihu Root. As Progressives disbanded or formed alliances with Republicans during the 1915 fall elections and as the returns came in showing substantial Republican gains in local elections, the conservatives felt less and less inclined to compromise. As the months passed, Progressives continued to speak of another Roosevelt candidacy, progressive Republicans united behind Senator Albert B. Cummins, and conservatives stood pat with Root. All this pointed to the probability of a Hughes nomination.

Hughes was unwilling to leave the Supreme Court to reenter politics, except for a call to reunite the Republican party. His denials of candidacy fell short of complete withdrawal. When former National Chairman Frank Hitchcock assumed responsibility for a Hughes preconvention organization, the politicians knew that a serious bid would be made in Hughes' behalf. Hitchcock had the active support of Governor Whitman of New York as well as former President Taft and Murray Crane.

Early spring 1916 saw the alternatives clarified and the pressures mount. Roosevelt would veto Root's candidacy, but remain willing to accept Hughes. Taft was for Hughes. Progressive Republicans were for compromise. As Roosevelt became increasingly critical of Hughes, Hughes' chances improved. Conservatives refused to do business with Roosevelt, fearing that Hughes' candidacy would mean their sacrificing organizational control. The conservatives, therefore, were the ones under the most pressure if interparty and factional reunion were to be accomplished.

On March 31, 1916, newspapermen and politicians alike were startled by news of a luncheon that brought together three old friends who in recent years had parted company, socially as well as politically. Theodore Roosevelt, Elihu Root, and Henry Cabot Lodge, in the company of New York financier Robert Bacon, broke bread together and apparently set their signals straight regarding the 1916 presidential nomination. Root's supporters, particularly National Chairman Hilles, were caught completely unprepared to evaluate the development.

The Republican convention convened in Chicago on July 7. The new apportionment plan had the immediate effect of reducing the number of seating contests to a mere handful. The national committee was authorized to replace any member who refused to support the nominees of the convention. The largest bloc of votes—224 in a total of 987—seemed committed to Hughes. The conservatives scattered their support among three candidates—Root, Weeks, and Burton—for a total of 206 votes. The progressives supported Cummins and Roosevelt, for a total of only 149. Senator Warren G. Harding's election as temporary chairman prompted progressive charges that the Old Guard intended to boss the convention.

The Progressive party held its national convention in Chicago at the same time. The Republicans appointed a committee of five to negotiate with them. The first meeting of the conferees took place on June 8. The Progressives insisted that Roosevelt was the only possible choice. The Republican group replied that this was not acceptable. The Progressives offered no second choice. Since the Republican convention had not yet taken ballots, the Republican representatives could offer no alternative either. This negotiating situation changed when Hughes received $328^{1}/_{2}$ votes on the second ballot, with 494 needed to nominate.

When the conferees met again on the night of the 9th, the Progressives continued to offer only a single choice. The meeting broke up without an agreement. Nicholas Murray Butler, serving as chairman of the Republican conferees, proceeded to the Indiana delegation headquarters to meet with several of the conservative leaders. Butler informed them that George Perkins, the New York Progressive, had asked him whether he would be willing to talk with Roosevelt on the telephone. The leaders at the Indiana headquarters advised Butler to make the call. The conservative group decided that Butler should offer Roosevelt the names of Root, Knox, and Fairbanks in that order and ask whether he would be willing to urge the Progressive convention to support one of them. Butler was also to make it quite clear that Hughes was certain to be nominated by the Republicans unless Roosevelt supported some other name.

Butler went to Perkins' room and phoned Roosevelt. Roosevelt was unwilling to discuss Root and was ambiguous about his position on the other two. Roosevelt then inquired as to the prospects for General Leonard Wood or Senator Henry Cabot Lodge. Butler replied that the Republican convention would not welcome a soldier-candidate, but that he would refer Lodge's name to his colleagues. After the call ended, George Perkins expressed his own dissatisfaction with either Wood or Lodge. Butler reported all this to the conservative group.

The conferees met again the following morning, and the Republicans presented Hughes' name. Still no agreement was reached. Upon returning to their convention, the Republican representatives were handed a copy of a message from Roosevelt to the Progressive conferees in which the former president suggested the nomination of Senator Lodge. Just prior to the third ballot in the Republican convention, the delegates were informed of Roosevelt's preference for Lodge, the Republican conferees' support of Hughes, and the fact that the Roosevelt message on Lodge had been tabled at the Progressive convention. The result was that Hughes then received nearly all of the 987 votes in the Republican convention.

At the Progressive convention, meanwhile, the militants nominated Roosevelt over the objections of George Perkins. Almost as soon as the Progressive convention adjourned, Roosevelt issued a conditional refusal of the nomination. The situation now left Roosevelt with substantial leverage upon the course of the Republican campaign. Without committing himself to accept the Progressive nomination, he had it for the asking. He also had in the Republican nominee an acceptable compromise nominee. What remained was the need for assurances that the conservatives would not run away with the Republican organization and campaign, which is exactly what the conservatives proceeded to try to do.

The conservative leaders were intent upon preventing the selection of Frank Hitchcock, Hughes' preconvention manager, as national chairman. They favored the re-election of Hilles. Although Governor Charles S. Whitman of New York and other Hughes associates were working on behalf of Hitchcock, the former national chairman publicly expressed his disinterest in the position. "I would prefer to stand on my [past chairmanship] record."

At the national committee meeting of June 10, a motion was made to elect an executive committee of seven people with the power to select the officers of the new national commitee, including a national chairman, subject to the approval of Hughes. Vigorous objections were made on grounds that the executive committee would be usurping a basic power of the national committee. The proposal was finally abandoned, but a subcommittee was appointed to consult with the nominee on his choice of a campaign manager and the general management of the campaign. The seven-man subcommittee included five conservatives.[13]

Meanwhile, Hughes was moving ahead on his own initiative. Several associates from the days of the Hughes Alliance of 1908 established a personal campaign headquarters for him at the Hotel Astor in New York. The nominee checked in at this suite upon arriving from Washington, DC. During June and July, the national committee followed suit by establishing temporary headquarters at the Hotel Astor, but subsequently it moved to the Guaranty Building.

The Hughes Alliance had been a state organization set up in 1908 to help Hughes win the gubernatorial nomination over the objection of the regular Republican organization. At that time presidential nominee Taft and then National

William R. Willcox was fifty-three years old at the time he assumed
the chairmanship. He was raised on a farm and educated at the University of Rochester and Columbia Law School. He received his law degree in 1889. After several years as a school principal, he moved to
New York City to practice law. His first public appointment was as commissioner of parks in 1902 under Mayor Low. In that capacity he became closely associated with Jacob A. Riis and other city
philanthropists concerned with educational facilities for youths.

In private law practice at the time of his appointment to the chairmanship, Willcox had long been associated with both Roosevelt and
Hughes in New York Republican politics. President Roosevelt appointed him postmaster of New York City in 1905. When the New York
legislature reformed the state Public Service Commission in 1907 in
keeping with proposals submitted by Governor Hughes, Willcox was appointed as first chairman of the metropolitan branch of the new agency.
As in the case of the postmastership, direction of the New York Public
Service Commission carried with it control of extensive patronage.

Chairman Hitchcock gave substantial personal support to the Hughes campaign.
The revived Hughes Alliance now took on the shape of a national organization,
to work independently of the national committee, particularly in an effort to gain
the independent vote. Hughes had an arm's-length relationship with the national
committee in 1916, which was reminiscent of his relations with the state organization eight years earlier.

Almost three weeks after receiving the nomination, Hughes emerged from a
private dinner with Theodore Roosevelt to announce, among other things, that
William R. Willcox would be his "personal choice" for national chairman. The
selection had the approval of Roosevelt and was taken as a conciliatory gesture
to the Progressives.

Nicholas Murray Butler was particularly unhappy about Willcox's elevation
to the chairmanship. "He has no qualifications for the post except honesty and
good intentions." On another occasion Butler wrote, "He has no acquaintance,
no political sagacity, and nothing but good intentions and amiability to help
him."[14]

A further gesture to the Progressives was Hughes' appointment of a campaign
committee with greater authority than the executive committee of the national
committee. Six members of the campaign committee were Progressives; ten
were drawn from the national committee's executive committee. The conservatives objected strenuously to this arrangement. Nicholas Murray Butler reported
that "all the party workers in the West are up in arms . . . that the Progressives

William Harrison Hays' father was a prominent corporation lawyer of Sullivan County, Indiana, active in county and state Republican politics as delegate to and official of various party conventions. Will received the B.A. degree from Wabash College in 1900 and the Master's in 1904, for which he wrote a dissertation on the Black problem. He read law under his father's direction, and was admitted to the Indiana bar on his twenty-first birthday in 1900. Between 1900 and the time of his return to Wabash College for the Master's degree, he became a partner in his father's law firm and ran unsuccessfully as his party's nominee for prosecuting attorney in the Fourteenth Judicial District.

The Hays law firm specialized in railroad and mining businesses. Consistently active in party work, Hays became chairman of the Sullivan county committee by 1904 and chairman of his congressional district committee in 1910. A small man of some five feet, four inches, weighing about 120 pounds, Hays possessed an apparently inexhaustible supply of energy. When the national and state Republican organization split in 1912, Hays was offered the state party chairmanship, but declined in favor of the vice-chairmanship. When Taft became the regular party nominee for president, Hays put all his energies toward Taft's re-election. After the election, Hays went out of his way to cajole Progressive leaders back into the Republican party. By 1914, Hays was the logical man for state chairman.

In 1922, after serving as national chairman and postmaster general, he accepted the presidency of the Motion Picture Producers and Distributors of America, launching the famous Hays Office of the motion picture industry.

---

on the Campaign Committee are not procuring any money but are working night and day to strengthen their several Progressive organizations.''[15] By mid-August the conservatives began to suggest that Charles Warren of Michigan be placed in control of the national organization.

As the campaign progressed, it became increasingly noticeable that the conservatives were resisting Hughes' leadership. For example, John Wanamaker complained about the ''milk-and-water stuff'' coming out in the speeches and literature of the national committee.[16] Nicholas Murray Butler gravely predicted that the Democrats would carry all states west of the Missouri River. On his stumping tour of the West, Hughes found that the regular organization leaders were unenthusiastic and determined to complicate life for him. The most notorious instance, because of the subsequent impact of the California returns upon the outcome of the election, was the play given Hughes' so-called ''snub'' of Hiram

Johnson.[17] While campaigning in California, Hughes failed to pay his respects to Johnson, the leader of the California Progressives.

Despite his inexperience in the mechanics of political organization, National Chairman Willcox did much to revive the concept of efficiency (if not effectiveness) in Republican campaign management. Willcox was, interestingly enough, a former president of the Efficiency Society of New York.[18] In public interviews on the subject, he observed that there is no more room for inefficiency and haphazard methods in the work of a political organization than there is in any highly organized business enterprise. "It will be my effort to inaugurate methods where every ounce of work will bring its return."[19] Not many Republican state organizations emulated the Willcox creed, with the striking exception of Indiana.

The Indiana campaign brought to national attention the organizational achievements of Will H. Hays, the Republican state chairman. On good terms with both conservatives and progressives, Hays had sharpened the state organization sufficiently to carry the party from defeat in 1914 to victory in 1916. Reputed to know "more people by their first names than any other man in Indiana," Hays developed and operated an impressive state political machine by 1916. It consisted of more than 40,000 Republican workers, that is, between ten and fifteen workers in every precinct in the state. As soon as registrations for voting were completed in 1916, Hays conducted a poll that revealed the political leanings of every voter in every precinct. During the campaign, the state committee had a headquarters staff consisting of twenty-seven distinct bureaus; these included a "dissatisfied Democrats" bureau, a registration bureau, a "trouble" bureau, and many others, with remarkably little duplication of effort. The Indiana Republican organization became the subject of comment in the press across the nation.[20]

The presidential election of 1916 was close and critical. Wilson won by 277 electoral college votes to Hughes' 254 votes. The result hung on a few thousand votes in the late returns from California, presumably the consequence of Hughes' mishandling of relations with Hiram Johnson.

The 1916 presidential election ended the role of the Progressives as a near-major national party.

3

The election also established state presidential voting patterns that prevailed until 1928. Less than four percentage points separated the major party votes in fourteen states, five going Democratic, and nine Republican. California and New Hampshire went Democratic, and Minnesota, West Virginia, and Indiana went Republican by less than a percentage point each. Will Hays' organization in the latter state succeeded in carrying two United States senators, nine of the thirteen congressmen, and the entire state ticket into office. However, one-party and safe states continued to exist in most of the presidential arena.

National Chairman Willcox at once became the target of recrimination from the conservative wing. Some of the criticism went beyond mere complaint and included suggestions for organizational reform. Representative E.J. Hill of Connecticut, for example, called for consolidation of the national and congressional campaign committees, with one set of officers.

Senator John W. Weeks of Massachusetts said that any private business run as the national committee so frequently was would soon be in bankruptcy. He suggested that the national committee ought to be comprised of the chairmen of the party's state committees, with full power to select the campaign manager for the presidential race. He urged the establishment of a permanent, continuously active national committee headquarters that would be in the field the year around. Weeks further argued for closer coordination among the national, congressional, and new senatorial campaign committees.[21] His recommendations were endorsed by Barnes of New York and former National Chairman Hilles. Suggestions such as these paved the way for further formalization of the national chairmanship and for the efforts of Will Hays and his successors.

Many of the complaints included demands for Willcox's resignation. The New Hampshire *Manchester Union* not only suggested that Willcox retire, but that Hays of Indiana succeed him. Willcox was blamed for ineptitude and mismanagement. Former President Taft considered Willcox a "blunderhead."

Probably the most important factor in Willcox's status was the withdrawal of Charles E. Hughes from any activity that smacked of titular leadership. According to his biographer, Hughes "dropped the role of standard-bearer as completely as he had dropped the practice of law when he became governor and politics when he went to the Supreme Court." He never spoke as the leader of the opposition party, "thinking it absurd for a defeated candidate to retain any such prerogative."[22] Reluctant in the first place to leave the Supreme Court to accept his party's nomination, Hughes completely banished from his mind any idea of ever being president. He returned to the full-time practice of law. Later, in 1920, he firmly refused to deliver the keynote address of the Republican national convention and, when urged to become a candidate again, requested "that my name be not even mentioned."[23] With no political constituency of his own, it was just a matter of time before Willcox would depart the chairmanship.

The Progressives, on December 5, 1916, offered to return to the Republican fold if given a voice in party councils. To facilitate their return, the Progressives suggested continuation of the campaign committee on which ten regulars and six Progressives had served. The conservatives, on the other hand, were interested mainly in regaining full control of the national organization. At its January 1917 meeting, the executive committee of the national committee

Fifty-four-year-old John T. Adams was an Iowa sash and door manufacturer long active in Republican affairs. In 1908, he managed the Allison primary campaign for the United States senatorial nomination and,
in 1912, was a manager of the Taft forces in Iowa. He became a member of the Republican national committee in 1912.

re-elected Willcox as chairman but, in a surprise move, chose National Committeeman John T. Adams of Iowa to fill the vacancy of vice-chairman.

In order to end the practice of having the national chairman select his own
vice-chairman, the 1916 national convention had adopted a resolution formally
creating the office and giving the executive committee authority to select its
incumbent. Candidate Hughes left the matter of filling the position entirely up to
Willcox during the campaign. Willcox, in turn, intended that the position eventually should go to Alvin T. Hert of Kentucky, his western campaign manager.
Although Willcox tried to postpone the election of a vice-chairman, the executive committee voted to override him, and John T. Adams was elected.[24]

The conservatives buttressed their position further by appointing a subcommittee of three—Willcox, Adams, and Bliss, the national committee treasurer—
to pass upon all matters of publicity, finance, and expenditure. Chairman
Willcox was thus outnumbered. In a gesture of conciliation to the Progressives,
who had protested the election of Adams, the executive committee authorized
the establishment of a special advisory committee to the national committee to
include those members of the 1916 campaign committee not on the executive
committee, that is, the six Progressives—George Perkins, Jesse I. Straus, Harold
L. Ickes, Everett Colby, James R. Garfield, and R.B. Howell. Demands that the
full national committee be called to act on the vice-chairmanship continued long
after the January meeting, but Willcox declined to take further action.[25]

In response to demands for a better and more permanent organization, the
executive committee decided that permanent party headquarters should henceforth be maintained in Washington, DC. It also decided that the national committee should meet at least once a year, rather than wait until the eve of the national
convention. Will Hays' name again came up as a possible successor to Willcox.

Before the national committee met again, an entirely new political environment was created by the United States' entry into World War I. On April 2,
1917, President Wilson asked Congress for a declaration of war. By December,
the Republicans were ready to wage a midterm campaign focused on the problems arising out of the conduct of the war. They were also ready to select a new
national chairman to lead the way. On January 18, 1918, National Chairman
Willcox announced his resignation to accept one of the four seats on the wartime
U.S. Railroad Wage Commission.

Well before the national committee met in February, Vice-Chairman Adams was busy pursuing the votes needed to win the chairmanship for himself. Other candidates included John T. King of Connecticut, an associate of Penrose, and Will Hays of Indiana. Some of the older leaders were interested in reinstating Charles D. Hilles, but he would not think of it. Willcox's friend, Alvin T. Hert of Kentucky, considered by some to be a "dark horse" for the chairmanship, devoted his energies to collecting a majority of the fifty-three national committee votes for Hays. Hays himself remained absent in Indianapolis. It was generally expected that Hays would be a candidate for governor of Indiana in the fall, a factor that raised doubts about his availability for the chairmanship. The Progressives, led by Theodore Roosevelt and George Perkins, continued to be vociferously opposed to Adams; three of their number were present at the meeting as members of the special advisory committee.

As the national committee commenced its meeting, Adams seemed securely in the lead, claiming thirty-six pledged votes. Suddenly Senator Calder of New York made the charge that Adams had been pro-German before the war. It was a direct hit. A war party could hardly have a pro-German leader. Penrose won a few days postponement of the chairmanship choice. Frank Hitchcock, with twelve southern votes in his pocket, devoted himself to reestablishing harmony. Newspapermen counted twenty-one committee members pledged to Adams and sixteen to Hays, with the remainder uncommitted; Hitchcock's twelve were in the latter category.

The contest became bitter. Adams declined to withdraw in favor of a compromise. The Progressives refused to budge in their veto of Adams. Penrose and Hitchcock joined forces to work out a compromise.

The outcome involved several trade-offs. As a concession to Adams and the conservatives, eager to exclude George Perkins and the Progressives from party councils, the special advisory campaign committee was discontinued. As a concession to the Progressives, the old executive committee resigned in order to give the new chairman a relatively free hand. However, a new rule was adopted providing for the election of the executive committee by the whole national committee, thereby placing new limits on the appointment powers of the national chairman. The final element in the compromise was to allow Adams to continue in the vice-chairmanship and to elect Hays national chairman.[26]

4

Will Hays was a firm believer in organizational neutrality in factional and nominating battles. While a leader of the party in Indiana, he had declared:

> The slogan of the Republican state organization of Indiana is that we are organized to elect party nominees and not to nominate men to office. If I were to take sides one way or the other in this fight [between Taft and Roosevelt]

for delegates, I would first resign as district chairman and as vice-chairman of the Republican state committee. I would do this as a matter of principle. I am entirely conscientious in taking this stand.[27]

Hays plunged into the task of uniting and reorganizing the national party. He announced that he would attempt to apply the organizational and campaign methods he used so successfully in Indiana. Within a week after his election, he suggested a nationwide conference of all Republican national committeemen, state chairmen, senators, representatives, and governors to discuss the party's national affairs.

In New York on February 25, Hays gave a dinner in honor of all former national chairmen: Rosewater, Cortelyou, Hitchcock, Hilles, and Willcox. The following evening, Hays was the guest of fifty Washington correspondents representing various Republican, Progressive, and independent newspapers throughout the country. The evening after that, a reception in his honor was conducted by the Republican congressional campaign committee, which was attended by all factions, the most harmonious Republican gathering in years. Prior to the reception, Hays had wired the chairman of the committee, Representative Woods of Iowa, offering to work under his direction in the forthcoming midterm campaign. By midsummer, Hays had traveled over the entire country, interviewed practically every important Republican, and mediated innumerable differences between factions. Even in faction-torn Pennsylvania, Hays' efforts produced at least a temporary alliance between the Penrose and the Vare factions.[28]

Hays was an organizer and a manager. Over the next three years he developed an entirely new conception of the managerial functions of the national chairmanship. He prodded the national agencies of his party to a new level of integration and systematic effort. The organizational legacy that he left behind can in part be credited for carrying the Republicans through another Progressive defection in 1924 and the Al Smith threat of 1928.

Symbolic of the new national organization was an announcement on April 13, 1918, that a three-year lease, at a rental of $6,500 a year, had been signed for a permanent Republican national headquarters in Washington. A subheadquarters at Fifth Avenue and 40th Street in New York was set up at the same time, with others to be established in Chicago and San Francisco.[29] Hays appointed a personal representative, Ralph V. Sollitt, to manage the New York headquarters. On September 2, Hays convened the first meeting of the new Association of Republican State Chairmen.

Hays spoke and traveled incessantly. With no Republican titular leader active on the political scene, Hays' activities as national chairman were invariably newsworthy. He launched a verbal barrage against President Wilson and the Democrats, calling for an early victory in the war and for immediate preparations to meet the problems of the postwar period. To Wilson's statement of May 1918, that "politics is adjourned," Hays replied with a theme he had used in the 1914

Elected to Congress in 1912 while still president of Antioch College, Simeon D. Fess served in both capacities until 1917. The future national chairman was a native of Ohio, born there in 1861, graduating from Ohio Northern University, where he remained to teach American history. He received a degree from the Law Department of Ohio Northern University in 1894 and became dean of the College of Law in 1986. In 1902, he resigned as vice-president of Ohio Northern to become a graduate student and a lecturer at the University of Chicago. In 1907, he was chosen as president of Antioch College, a post in which he served for a full decade. He turned to elective politics in 1912 when he became vice-president of the Ohio constitutional convention. He sucessfully sought election to the House of Representatives. An interesting footnote to the 1918 campaign was Fess' attack on Herbert Hoover, then thought by many to be a Democrat because of his defense of Woodrow Wilson during World War I. A dozen years later Fess would become Hoover's choice for national chairman.

Indiana campaign, "What we need in this country is not less politics but more attention to politics. The man who has no time for attention to politics has no just complaints, whatever he may receive. He is riding on another's ticket." Hays defended "responsible party criticism":

> There must always be in American affairs at least two great parties. Our governmental organism cannot function healthily without the sturdy contest that inevitably arises when two strong political forces contend for mastery. This must and shall continue during the war, and it shall only be limited where it appears to be of any injury to the progress of the war.[30]

Combining patriotic and party goals, Hays committed the entire Republican organization, down to the smallest precinct, to assisting in the Liberty Loan drive of early fall. It was a patriotic opportunity to put party workers in touch with the voters. By June, Hays' position as his party's principal spokesman was well established.

Hays did not hesitate to intrude himself into congressional politics. He urged upon the leadership in the Senate and the House a more aggressive posture in their legislative agenda, particularly in support of the war. He also raised the question of having Frank Woods retired as chairman of the congressional campaign committee; Woods had voted against the United States' entry into the war. Hays was ready to press for Woods' retirement, but this proved unnecessary; Woods was defeated for renomination to his congressional seat in the Iowa primaries. At the end of August, Woods was succeeded by Representative Simeon D. Fess of Ohio as chairman of the Republican congressional campaign committee. Together, Hays and Fess planned and executed a hard-hitting congressional campaign.

National Chairman Hays gave strong personal leadership to the congressional campaign. He showed a willingness to confer with other Republican leaders regarding the party loyalty of all congressional candidates.

At one point Hays seemed interested in a proposal from George Harvey that at least one-half of the congressional contests be mutually conceded before election day, using majorities of three thousand votes in the previous two elections as the basis for selecting districts in which concessions would be made. The object was to reduce the number of contests from 435 to less than 100 as a demonstration of national unity. Harvey offered to arrange a meeting with the Democratic national chairman, but nothing came of the plan. Perhaps more significant than the proposal itself was the fact that it was initially addressed to National Chairman Hays rather than the congressional leadership.

On October 6, the German government sent a note to President Wilson requesting that steps be taken toward the arrangement of an armistice. There was an exchange of notes. Republicans, on the sidelines, were highly critical of peace proposals originating with Wilson. Theodore Roosevelt and Senator Henry Cabot Lodge were particularly severe in their reactions to Wilson's Fourteen Points.

On October 25, Wilson "reconvened politics" long enough to make his ill-fated appeal for a Democratic majority in Congress. The appeal provoked a strong Republican counterattack. Earlier in the campaign, Chairman Hays charged that Democratic leaders in Washington would go to any length, even ending the war with any kind of compromise, to ensure the continuance of the Democratic party in power. Now Hays charged that the president was playing politics despite his earlier declaration that politics ought to be adjourned for the duration of the war.

With exceptional daring, Hays proceeded, in a statement to the Republican electorate, to make the attack a personal one against Wilson, as follows:

> President Wilson has questioned the motives and fidelity of your representatives in Congress. He has thereby impugned their loyalty and denied their patriotism. His challenge is to you who elected those representatives. You owe it to them, to the honor of your party, and to your own self-respect, to meet that challenge squarely, not only as Republicans, but as Americans.[31]

This statement, a classic example of partisan rhetoric, received an unusual amount of publicity, provided a basis for bringing Republicans of all kinds and factions together, and, more than ever, confirmed Hays' position in the national leadership. Hays topped off the achievement by obtaining a joint statement from two former presidents, Roosevelt and Taft, urging the election of a Republican Congress.

President Wilson was thus confronted not only with his own contradictory statements and the combined prestige of his predecessors, but also with the historic tendencies of midterm congressional elections. The party controlling the White House almost invariably loses seats in Congress at the midterm. In 1918, this tendency produced a Republican majority of two in the Senate and forty-five in the House. Republicans were additionally jubilant over the Roosevelt-Taft reconciliation. This and the election returns brought further public recognition of Hays' leadership.

5

The peace negotiation was a victim of the bitterness of the campaign. Roosevelt and Lodge, old and skilled political infighters, joined forces in stubborn opposition to a League of Nations. Other Republicans took their cues from the League to Enforce Peace, a new and influential advocacy group headed by Taft. Ironically, Republican unity was reinforced by President Wilson, who came out of the campaign bitter against *all* Republicans and unwilling to deal with any of them in connection with the peace negotiations. President Wilson never made adequate use of the Taft group and failed to include prominent Republicans among his advisers on the peace mission. When Republican members of the Foreign Relations Committee met in December to plan Republican strategy, among those invited was Hays, whose role in the treaty and League of Nations fight was gaining in importance.

Theodore Roosevelt died on January 6, 1919. This removed him not only from the league fight, but also from the 1920 presidential race. Early in 1918, George Perkins and other Progressive leaders had announced plans to organize a draft-Roosevelt movement within the Republican party. It was generally believed that the sixty-year-old former president would be a factor in the election if not a candidate.

On his deathbed, Roosevelt expressed concern over the continuing clouds of dissension in the party. One of his last acts was to pen a memorandum to Hays, urging the national chairman to go to Washington for ten days to consult with the leaders in Congress and do all he could to prevent a split on domestic policies. The note, when made public, further enhanced Hays' already glowing prestige. When the Republican national committee met on January 10, it unanimously endorsed Hays' leadership and delegated to him authority to name new committees, including the executive committee.

In Minneapolis, on March 7, 1919, Hays formally opened the 1920 presidential campaign. Party and public were now becoming aware that Will Hays had turned the Republican national chairmanship into a full-time job. "Unprecedented," said the *New York Times*. "For the first time . . . the country has observed a chairman who works as hard between elections as he can do in the coming campaign. . . . Mr. Hays has invested the chairmanship with an entirely new authority."[32]

Hays brought further honor and homage to himself and the chairmanship when he declined the Republican nomination for governor of Indiana. This was considered a gesture of self-denial and a further indication of the new importance of the national chairmanship. At the December national committee meeting in 1919, several of Hays' admirers began a movement to have him retained as campaign manager by whichever candidate might be nominated. By April, all the major candidates for the Republican nomination agreed. Never before did all of the candidates for a party's presidential nomination pick the same man for the national chairmanship publicly and in advance of the national convention.[33]

Between spring of 1919 and the presidential election of 1920, Hays perfected the national committee's organizational structure and functions. The committee now had the appearance of its counterparts of half a century later. Foremost, Hays assumed duties that made him the national Republican organizational coordinator. He traveled and spoke constantly to local party organizations, to national and local interest groups friendly to the Republican cause, and to conferences of party officials. He gave particular attention to special social groups, for example, women and youth. With women's suffrage recently amended to the Constitution, he welcomed women into the Republican organization, creating a women's division at national headquarters to which he appointed a general chairperson, three vice-chairpeople, and a national women's council of a hundred. In a special gesture to young Republicans, he organized a platform-writing contest that received excellent publicity.

As national party spokesman, Hays made authoritative statements on the policy issues of the day. This frequently carried him into the corridors and offices of his party colleagues on Capitol Hill, either at their invitation or on his own initiative. He was asked to advise on problems of organizing Congress and on Republican legislative postures to be taken there.

In preparing for the 1920 convention, Hays set up a unique Advisory Committee on Policies and Platform. This committee consisted of 171 members, 19 of whom were women. The object was to hear the views of as representative a group of prominent Republicans as possible. On the committee were 12 national committeemen, at least 6 senators, about 14 members of the House of Representatives, such experienced talents as former National Chairmen Hitchcock, Rosewater, Hilles, and Willcox, and leaders of conservative and progressive views. Somewhat lost among the 171-member committee were former President Taft and former presidential nominee Hughes.

The large advisory committee established a distinguished executive committee with Ogden L. Mills, Jr., of New York as chairman. The operations of the advisory committee had Republicans talking to each other on public policy for months before the national convention, practically eliminating any prospect of unexpected or severe convention fights on the party platform. The possible exceptions were the planks on the League of Nations and the peace treaty issues. The advisory committee appointed twenty-one subcommittees, each handling a different subject matter. An extensive questionnaire on economic and political issues was distributed through the subcommittees, about 100,000 copies of the questionnaire eventually finding their way across the country. This technique for preparing for platform deliberations has since been used frequently by national chairmen of both major parties.[34]

Possibly among Hays' most impressive organizational achievements were the methods he developed for raising and dispensing funds. Sensitive to charges that Republican campaigns were financed by small groups of rich industrialists, Hays announced a $1,000 limit on individual contributions to the Republican national committee. Checks in excess of this amount were to be returned to the donor. This limitation, Hays believed, would not only help counter the image of the Republican party as beholden to the wealthy, but would also increase the interest of the rank and file. Hays' assumption was that an investor in an enterprise, even a small investor, is more deeply committed to its success than a noninvestor.

Hays also took a page from the fund-raising drives of the Red Cross and the Liberty Loan. He instituted a nationwide popular drive for Republican funds. A vast hierarchy of ways and means committees was created, reaching from counties and cities up through state and national headquarters. Paralleling these committees, both in function and geographical location, was an organization of hundreds of paid, professional fund-raising experts, or "money-diggers." These professional solicitors worked closely with the volunteer, unpaid party members of the ways and means committees, but had a primary loyalty to their employer, the Republican national committee.

Four distinct fund-raising drives were conducted. The first, during January 1920, was aimed at collecting relatively large sums from easily persuaded contributors, that is, amounts between $100 and $1,000. The second drive was along more popular lines, seeking smaller contributions, and was conducted in May 1920. Consequently, even before the national convention in June, the treasurer of the Republican national committee could report having received contributions totaling $1,835,353. This amount was contributed by 18,515 individuals. Two additional drives were conducted after the convention, in July and from September through election day.

The fund-raising plan enhanced the influence of the national chairman substantially. The huge field force of professional solicitors, because they were primarily loyal to the national chairman, were able to circumvent the countless pitfalls of local factionalism. The money raised gave the national chairman qualified but important control of the party's purse, with greater freedom regarding its allocation. The money raised and spent prior to the national convention permitted more thorough and earlier preparation for the ensuing national campaign, resulting in large economies of time and money. The single integrated national fund-raising drive did away with the need for many *ad hoc* appeals for money and permitted Hays to engage in politically meaningful financial negotiations with local, senatorial, and congressional campaign committees.

In addition, state fund-raising quotas were established on the basis of population, Republican vote, wealth, Red Cross quotas, and the value of industrial interests. Separate agreements were worked out with individual Republican state organizations to set the proportion of funds to be retained by the state party and by the national committee. Frequently, in order to obtain the best financial deal, a state organization would have to put its factional house in order and promise to cooperate with the national committee. Similar arrangements had to be worked out between the national chairman on the one hand and the senatorial and congressional campaign committees on the other. In this connection, the national chairman was able to guarantee the latter committees amounts sufficient for the congressional campaigns.

The Republicans reported a total of around $4 million expended by the national committee in the 1920 presidential campaign. The Democrats charged that the figure was closer to $15-$40 million. Before the campaign was over, Democratic nominee Cox and Republican Chairman Hays were conducting a dramatic altercation on the point, which later became grist for the mill of the Senate's Kenyon Committee investigating campaign expenses.[35]

Hays expanded the publicity operations of the national committee. Beginning long before the national convention, the publicity bureau was given a budget of nearly $1.5 million for the campaign proper. This was before the era of costly expenditures for radio and television time. The bureau developed a news service for Republican newspapers, produced boiler-plate releases (particularly for the intensively employed rural press), pamphlets, booklets, textbooks, lithographs, campaign buttons, billboards, and newspaper advertising. As early as May 1919, Hays was negotiating with motion picture companies to ensure fair treatment of the Republican candidate in the newsreels. As a result, the newsreel for the first time in 1920 became a major vehicle for political propaganda. In 1896, Mark Hanna had used an unprecedented number of speakers—1,400—to stump the nation. Hays had well over 15,000 speakers on the road.

As in the early days of the Republic, a national newspaper was established for the party. The *National Republican*, a Muncie, Indiana, newspaper, was moved to Washington and incorporated, its capital stock of $200,000 subscribed to by prominent Republicans in the East and Midwest. Ties between the *National Republican* and the national committee were informal but close. Hays encouraged the practice of having well-heeled Republicans give gift subscriptions to employees and less-well-off Republicans.

Still another innovation in the publicity department was the production of a Republican *Yearbook*, bound in imitation leather and profusely illustrated. Technically, this was not a national committee activity since it was prepared under the direction of William Barnes of New York. However, contributions to the *Yearbook* ranged from $500 to $2,500 per subscriber, and the subscribers were drawn from the nation's staunchest Republican families.

6

Throughout the preconvention period, National Chairman Hays received as much, if not more, personal publicity than the several contending presidential candidates. By inaugurating the practice of having the national committee conduct open meetings and by carrying on intensive full-time work at the Washington and New York headquarters, Hays' name and activities remained prominently at the forefront of national party news. This gave rise to persistent rumors that the national chairman was himself a dark-horse candidate for the nomination. Hays dismissed this prospect emphatically whenever questioned about it.

Nevertheless, Hays began to be sharply criticized by several of the candidates' managers when he called upon all candidates to send representatives to meet with him at regular conferences in the New York headquarters. Charges were made that Hays' oft-proclaimed neutrality was disappearing. In fact, the conferences were purely administrative in character, to set ground rules for the handling of various disputes at the national convention and to pave the way for efficient incorporation of the activities of the national committee into the campaign organization of the eventual nominee.[36]

For more than a year prior to the national convention, Chairman Hays, although holding no public office, was the principal Republican policy maker. He was particularly active in connection with the issues most likely to divide the party, namely, the peace treaty and the League of Nations. The Ogden L. Mills Advisory Committee on Policies and Platform did not include these issues in its list of policy problems on grounds that they would be handled by Republican leaders in Congress. As far as Hays was concerned, there were three Republican positions on the league that had to be reconciled: the anti-league stand of the Progressives, led by Senator Borah; the Lodge position seeking revision of particular sections of the treaty dealing with the league; and the pro-league position, whose spokesman was former President Taft.

When the proposed Covenant for a League of Nations was made public on February 15, 1919, just prior to the March adjournment of Congress, Senator Lodge arranged to have a Senate declaration issued over the signatures of a third or more of the members to the effect that the league in the form proposed was unacceptable. Of the forty-four Republican senators, thirty-three signed. A few days later this number was increased to thirty-nine, more than the one-third needed to veto a treaty.

In their constituencies, the legislators found it difficult to evaluate popular sentiment on the league. Chairman Hays concluded, after a trip through the West, that public opinion was pro-league, but not necessarily for the particular league being proposed. The situation was complicated by the fact that the Republicans held a slim forty-nine to forty-seven majority in the Senate. When Congress reconvened on May 19 for a special session, the Republican conservatives and progressives were able to unite long enough to organize the Senate. Within the month, they were again divided on what the party stand should be on the League of Nations.

Will Hays was invited to serve as mediator among the factions, an unusual request to a national chairman. He arrived in Washington on June 26 and spent several days trying to bring the various leaders together. Hays was indirectly aided by President Wilson's message to the American people on June 28 urging acceptance of the covenant. This brought pressure on Senate Republicans to unite.

Public demonstration of Republican unity was Hays' principal objective, regardless of the merits of the different positions. Thus, when former President Taft outlined a program upon which a certain number of Republicans and Democrats could agree, he urged Hays, to whom he addressed the proposal, to keep the plan from Lodge and Roosevelt on grounds that they might oppose it simply because it was advanced by a pro-league man. Hays would have no dealings with Democrats, and proceeded to inform Lodge and Roosevelt of the correspondence. The former president's efforts were completely negated when the confidential Taft-Hays correspondence suddenly appeared in the *New York Times* on July 24.

In September, President Wilson started an extended tour to carry his case for the League of Nations to the people, taking a thoroughly uncompromising tack. Taft was disheartened by Wilson's behavior and began to lose hope for the league.

> It is pretty hard when you are supporting a magnificent cause to find it to be imperiled by the attitudes and course of one's titular leader. It is impossible for him, schoolmaster as he is, to make speeches on the subject and explain the League without framing contemptuous phrases to characterize his opponents.[37]

By the time the treaty came to a vote in the Senate, Lodge and Hays had accomplished a rare unification of the party. President Wilson's version of the treaty failed to receive the necessary two-thirds vote. Fifteen Republicans who had been "mild reservationists," causing Lodge and Hays the most concern, had, in the showdown, voted with the party's majority in the Senate. Shortly afterward, Chairman Hays wrote a personal letter to the fifteen congressmen thanking them for their loyalty to the party. The party, however, did not rest easy with its victory.

Nor did the party approach the 1920 nominating contest with great assurance. The party's election prospects were excellent, but the choice of a nominee was not. With Roosevelt's death, two progressives scrambled to become heir to his following: Senator Hiram Johnson of California and Major General Leonard Wood of New Hampshire, an old and close friend of the deceased Roosevelt. Wood had the advantage of large financial resources and recent political martyrdom; President Wilson had refused to permit him to accompany his division to France for active duty in the field. The Johnson-Wood rivalry divided the progressive faction, which was further incapacitated by the postwar reaction against the growth of the federal government.

During the December 11, 1919, meeting of the national committee, there were rumors of a movement to head off the Wood campaign. Senator Warren G. Harding was mentioned as the most likely person behind whom the conservatives could unite. Harding's name had the cordial endorsement of two powerful colleagues in the Senate, Boies Penrose of Pennsylvania and Reed Smoot of Utah.

Other potential candidates included Governor Frank O. Lowden of Illinois, and Senators William E. Borah, Albert B. Cummins, Henry J. Allen, Irvine L. Lenroot, and James E. Watson. General Pershing made himself unavailable. William Howard Taft and Charles E. Hughes were frequently mentioned as compromise possibilities.

In July 1919, a poll of Republican governors, national committeemen, state chairmen, and editors showed that Wood, Lowden, Taft, Hughes, Harding, Johnson, Cummins, Allen, and Borah were preferred in this ranked order for the nomination. A poll taken in Congress in November showed Wood, Lowden, Harding, Watson, and Johnson as the top choices. Other names: William C. Sproul of Pennsylvania, to whom Penrose expected to retreat if his support of Harding faltered, Herbert Hoover, and Calvin Coolidge. Hoover was widely and favorably known for his outstanding public service in Wilson's wartime administration. Coolidge had just become governor of Massachusetts, where his great friend and backer was W. Murray Crane. Early in January of 1920, James B. Reynolds, also from Massachusetts, resigned as secretary of the national committee in order to manage Coolidge's preconvention campaign.

By 1920, some twenty states had presidential primaries of various types. Wood, Lowden, Johnson, Harding, Poindexter, and others entered primary contests with indecisive outcomes. The most conspicuous performances—and the most costly, according to the Kenyon Committee's investigations—were those of Wood, Lowden, and Johnson, who headed into a stalemate. At one point, Harding announced that he was not a candidate for the nomination.[38] A few weeks later, however, he threw his hat into the ring as part of a favorite-son strategy.

Harding did poorly in the primaries, receiving only part of the delegation of his own state. As the convention approached, the Wood-Lowden-Johnson impasse became fixed in concrete. The convention was ripe for a classic dark-horse decision. Repeatedly suggested for the compromise were Hughes, Harding, and Coolidge, the latter's availability now improved by his handling of a recent Boston police strike. Harding, in a negative way, seemed the most available.[39]

Harding had been a regular Republican throughout the years of the Progressive bolt. However, as keynoter of the 1916 national convention, his appeal for reconciliation left a favorable impression with the Progressives. He came from a pivotal state. He had voted straight down the line for the Lodge position in the recent Senate fight over the League of Nations. He had a bland personality that seemed admirably acceptable to the senators and the public, who were by now tired of activist presidents such as Roosevelt and Wilson. When the Kenyon Committee investigations cast unfavorable light upon the campaign methods of front-runners Wood, Lowden, and Johnson, by contrast Harding looked pure because of his very failures in the primaries. A further advantage was that he had one of the shrewdest managers in the business, Harry M. Daugherty. Above all, Harding was well known to and liked by the senators who constituted the principal leadership of the convention.

Many veteran politicians and analysts had doubts about the probable outcome of the convention. Typical was former National Chairman Harry New, who believed that there was little enthusiasm for any candidate and that "considerable balloting" would be required before a decision could be reached. "I have attended every Republican . . . convention since 1880," New told reporters, "and I have never known of a convention that is quite as uncertain as this appears to be."[40]

One other distinctive feature of the convention was the prominence of the senatorial leadership. The governor of Rhode Island expressed a widely held view when he said: "One would think that the gathering here . . . was to be a Senate caucus instead of a Republican national convention." National party developments had come full cycle, recognizing once again the doctrine of legislative ascendancy and the influence of its senators.[41]

On the first ballot, with 493 votes necessary to nominate, Wood received 287 1/2, Lowden 211 1/2, Johnson 133 1/2, Harding 65 1/2, and others received 286. Little changed through the fourth ballot. The convention adjourned, to return the next day for four more ballots. On the eighth ballot, Lowden was ahead with 307 votes, Wood 299, and Harding in third place with 133. Between the fourth and the eighth ballots the search for a dark horse proceeded both publicly and privately. Hughes, Harding, and Hays were the names most frequently mentioned. At one point, when an enthusiastic delegate from Oklahoma climbed up to the rostrum to try to stampede the convention to Hays, he was met by Hays himself, who quietly led him away.[42]

During the adjournment after the fourth ballot, the principal consultation was taking place in Suite 404 of the Blackstone Hotel, that is, George Harvey's headquarters. Discussion of the candidates went on without break. Senators of all factions wandered in and out during the night. Finally, it was strikingly clear that Harding offered the least common denominator. The Ohio senator was called in and told as much.

Harding evoked little enthusiasm, as reflected in the lethargic balloting from the fifth to the eighth roll call. The senators reconvened to review the candidate situation, at which time Will Hays' name was given more careful consideration. Hays was well known, acceptable to all factions, trusted by the senators, and a thorough-going organization man. To determine whether Hays had a chance, the leader of the Connecticut delegation, J.H. Roraback, was consulted. Connecticut's vote would be critical for starting a shift to Hays. Some members of the senatorial group went so far as to tell Roraback that there would be some 600 votes lining up for Hays.

The Connecticut leader responded that his delegation had decided to go for Harding on the next ballot. As others were called in to consider a move to Hays, it was realized that Harding votes were falling in line more readily than expected. In an interview thirty years later, Hays recalled that he had made emphatic protests against the mention of his name on grounds that as national chairman he had no right to use the organization as a springboard for his own advancement into higher office.[43]

In a taxicab winding up and down Chicago's streets another significant consultation was going on. Realizing that they were about to be eliminated from the race, General Wood and Governor Lowden discussed the possibility of breaking the impasse between them. The prolonged taxicab conference failed in its objective. Instead, it was the consultation in the "smoke-filled room" at the Blackstone that succeeded. Two ballots later, Harding received the nomination.

In view of their subsequent significance, the proceedings on the vice-presidential nomination were of particular interest. At the time, however, this hardly seemed the case. Vice-presidential nominating speeches began almost immediately after the presidential nomination. A great emotional letdown followed the prolonged effort to find a compromise for the presidency. Hiram Johnson, leader of the most determined faction in the convention, had declined to be placed in nomination. The senatorial group hastily agreed to support Senator Irvine L. Lenroot of Wisconsin, that is, a second from among their own number.

Only two others—Governor Henry J. Allen of Kansas and Henry W. Anderson of Virginia—were put forward. The confusion was ripe for exploitation by such experienced convention hands as W. Murray Crane and James Reynolds, two Massachusetts leaders intensely interested in Calvin Coolidge's future.

Coolidge's name went before the convention, accompanied by a wild and prolonged demonstration. "Silent Cal," whose national reputation was only eight
months old, received a majority on the first ballot.

As expected, Will Hays stayed on as national chairman. Harding's personal
manager, Harry Daugherty, took a place on the executive committee of the
national committee. Said Daugherty:

> After three days' conference with Chairman Hays, his assistants and the spe-
> cial committee to confer with Senator Harding, I can say that the organization
> which has been perfected under Chairman Hays will continue the good work
> which has been progressing for months.

Concerning his own status, Daugherty added:

> I consented to become a member of the executive committee at the request of
> Senator Harding and at the request of the entire committee. For reasons per-
> sonal to myself it was my desire not to become so active through the cam-
> paign, but I am interested in the cause of this party and in the success of the
> ticket.[44]

7

Chairman Hays continued to make news as he set in motion the Harding campaign. He took the appealing step of appointing seven women for the first time to
the executive committee and chose a woman to be its vice-chairman. He started
the third phase of his national fund-raising program. In view of the self-destructive divisions in the Democratic party's ranks, Hays was determined to recapture
the calm spirit of 1896 and 1900. Harding not only had a general physical
resemblance to McKinley, but also something of the late president's public
style—friendly and benign. The McKinley family flagpole was placed on the
Harding lawn as soon as it was decided that the nominee should conduct a front
porch campaign. To Chairman Hays' great satisfaction, Harding was able to
straddle the League of Nations issue satisfactorily. In a move to conciliate the
progressives, Hays expanded the campaign advisory committee to include forty
persons, many of them former Progressives.

The Republican victory was of landslide proportions. The women's vote—the
first in a presidential election—turned out to be predominantly that of upper-income Republicans. The Democrats had self-destructed in their own factional
chaos.

Once again in control of the presidency, Chairman Hays reminded the Republicans that certain organizational problems remained to be dealt with promptly.
Despite the great outcry about "the Republican campaign slush fund" during the
campaign, the national committee actually had an indebtedness of $1,600,000 as
of election day. Chairman Hays, maintaining the $1,000 per individual limit,

called upon his fellow partisans to help clean up the oversized debt.

Another pressing matter was the question of reform in the southern organizations. The delegation contests at the 1920 national convention had revealed the unsavory conditions prevailing in the Republican state organizations in the South. Chairman Hay's practice of conducting national committee meetings in open session threw the problem into the limelight and prompted the national committee to recommend a special investigation of the southern political situation. This resolution was confirmed at the national convention.

The national chairman was directed to appoint a special committee of three, with himself and the national committee secretary as ex-officio members, to study the entire political party environment in the South. When Hays selected three members to this Committee on Reconstruction, he added the comment that "this very likely may result in something of a revolution in the Republican Party organizations in the South." The size of the Republican presidential and congressional vote in the South had risen appreciably in 1920 over what it had been in 1916. The time seemed right for removing the artificial divisions between lily-white and black-and-tan Republican organizations. With a Republican in the White House, it also seemed feasible to review the 1916 rules of convention apportionment.

As the Committee on Reconstruction proceeded in its assignment, Charles D. Hilles of New York opposed further reduction of southern voting strength in the convention. Hilles proposed instead a system of bonus votes to be awarded to those states and districts where high Republican registration and voting occurred. A compromise apportionment formula was eventually worked out reducing the southern vote by about thirty delegates and raising the northern representation by approximately sixty. The South's representation was reduced as a last act of the Hays regime. At the same meeting, Hays resigned from the chairmanship, having three months earlier been appointed postmaster general in Harding's cabinet.[45]

Subsequently, with President Harding's public endorsement, the Committee on Reconstruction initiated steps to replace existing organizations in Louisiana, Georgia, and elsewhere with new ones made up of relatively prominent citizens, mostly white, to advise on the distribution of patronage. These efforts were very quickly frustrated by a Republican-Democratic alliance in the Senate, which approved appointments of several well-known spoilsmen.

In the discussions regarding Hays' successor as national chairman, three names were most prominent: Elmer Dover of Washington, former secretary to Mark Hanna; Joseph Kealing of Indiana, one of the promoters of Hays' original election to the chairmanship; and John T. Adams of Iowa, the incumbent vice-chairman of the national committee. The Adams and Dover supporters were the most active, with Adams receiving substantial support from party leaders in Congress. The matter was rapidly resolved when Harding passed word along that Adams was his own preference.[46]

Born in 1860 in Pennsylvania, the son of a Presbyterian farmer, Hubert Work spent most of his boyhood on his father's farm. He received some college training at Pennsylvania State Normal School and then moved on to the University of Michigan for his medical degree. He began his practice in Colorado where, about ten years later, he founded the Woodcroft Hospital for Mental and Nervous Diseases. In 1896, the same year that he founded the hospital, he was elected president of the Colorado State Medical Society. Almost as soon as he established his medical practice, Work became involved in Republican party affairs. He attended the national convention of 1908 as a delegate-at-large from Colorado, was elected Republican state chairman in 1912, and served as national committeeman from 1913 until his appointment to the Post Office Department. During the 1920 campaign, Work did yoeman service on Chairman Hays' executive committee: his specific assignment was to mobilize support in the farm areas. At the outbreak of World War I, he volunteered for service in the Army Medical Corps. He successfully acted as liaison officer between the surgeon general and the provost marshal in connection with the medical phases of the draft. He was president of the American Medical Association during 1921–22.

Work's subsequent career testifies to his skills as a politician and an administrator. He reduced the deficit of the Post Office Department from $81 million in 1921 to $24 million in 1923 without any increase in postal rates. When Albert B. Fall resigned as secretary of the interior in March 1923, President Harding asked Work to take on the difficult task of cleaning up the scandal-ridden department. In his first two years, Work turned back into the treasury approximately $35 million in unexpended budget allowances. President Coolidge kept him on as secretary of the interior. When Herbert Hoover consented to make the race for the presidential nomination in 1928, Dr. Work was the first member of the cabinet to declare his support.

In 1922, Hays accepted the presidency of the Motion Picture Producers and Distributors of America, the lobbying and self-policing organization of the movie industry. At about the time he resigned as head of the Post Office Department, two other men—both future national chairmen—also experienced job changes. Hays enthusiastically recommended to the president that Dr. Hubert Work, his first assistant postmaster general, be promoted to the cabinet position. Formerly a practicing physician, Work was a Colorado Republican leader of long standing, with administrative talents comparable to those of Hays. Harding needed a western man in the cabinet, and Work became postmaster general.

The second to change jobs was Simeon D. Fess, who was re-elected as chairman of the Republican congressional campaign committee and set in motion the machinery for the midterm campaign. Fess, however, resigned in June to devote full time to his campaign for the Ohio Senate seat, thereby escaping, as it turned out, responsibility for the party's subsequent loss of House seats to the Democrats and, if they could be counted as losses, to the progressives in the Republican party.

When he came into office, President Harding surrounded himself with what was for the most part a distinguished cabinet. The State Department went to Hughes, Treasury to Andrew W. Mellon, and Commerce to Herbert Hoover. Other strong appointments were John W. Weeks in War, James J. Davis for Labor, and Henry C. Wallace in Agriculture. The weak links were Harry M. Daugherty as attorney general, Albert B. Fall in Interior, and Edwin N. Denby for Navy. When Hubert Work, who succeeded Will Hays as postmaster general, became secretary of interior in 1923, former national chairman Harry S. New was called upon to take the Post Office Department. Possibly the weakest link of all was Harding himself, bland, affable, and vulnerable at the hands of his friends. It was also true that the fulcrum of power within the Republican party lay in the United States Senate, and would do so for the next decade.

Part V
Formalizing the
National Chairmanship

17 | Building a Foundation for a National Headquarters

Cox's defeat and Wilson's retirement in 1920 left a vacancy in Democratic titular leadership that would be filled only after a dozen years of severe factional controversy. William Gibbs McAdoo, Alfred E. Smith, the southern leadership in Congress, and Franklin D. Roosevelt were among the major actors in the slow-moving drama. The bitter convention of 1924 removed McAdoo from the play. The electoral defeat of 1928 put an end to Smith's prospects. Roosevelt's victory in 1932 was the beginning of the end for southern dominance. Amidst these scenes, the national committee and the national chairmen did what they could to hold the party together and to bring a modern national party headquarters into being on a permanent basis.

Complicating the struggle and possibly delaying its resolution were the large changes in the profile of the presidential electorate during the period of 1916 to 1932. According to one student of presidential elections, "The election of 1920 was unlike the three that preceded it and the three that were to follow it in this important particular—it did not present the familiar American alignment." The "normal" Republican voters who had been lost to the Progressives in 1912 and, in part, to the Democrats in 1916 were not the ones recovered by the Republicans in 1920.[1] Enough Progressives continued to be in and out of the two major parties to encourage the third-party La Follette candidacy in 1924. The women voters coming into the electorate added to the uncertainty, although most were initially Republicans. The nomination of a Catholic for the first time in 1928 also prevented the return to familiar alignments, even causing a breach in the Solid South. The final disturbance was the Great Depression, which led to an entirely new electoral pattern in its rejection of Hoover and Republicanism.

1

After the 1920 presidential election was over, Cox served out his term as governor of Ohio and then returned to his newspaper business. Having alienated the urban leadership by his strong pro-League of Nations campaign, he anticipated no major role for himself in national politics, least of all at the 1924 national convention. He, of course, watched closely as the 1924 battle took shape among the forces of McAdoo, Underwood, and Smith. Cox was opposed to McAdoo because he had gone "cold on the issue of the League of Nations for which his father-in-law, President Woodrow Wilson, had died. Besides, he remained silent at the sponsorship of his cause by the Ku Klux Klan. . . . The Klan was solidly behind him and the Anti-Saloon League forces as well."[2]

For William Gibbs McAdoo the period between 1920 and 1924 offered a "last chance" bid for the presidency. With his father-in-law no longer in the White House, McAdoo did not have to bear the crown prince stigma. By establishing residence in California, he avoided the risk of a fight with the New York organization. He also acquired some of the aura of a western candidate without losing the advantages of his old political friendships in the East and South. In 1924, however, McAdoo would be sixty-one years of age, his prospects for the presidential nomination declining with each passing year. He and his supporters, therefore, lost little time in seeking control of the national party. At a Jackson Day dinner in Los Angeles on January 8, 1921, McAdoo called for a reorganization of the party under a national chairman who could "devote all, or practically all, of his time to party affairs."[3] Blaming the recent defeat in part upon poor publicity and the inadequacy of the national organization, McAdoo made a strong appeal for building an efficient national headquarters:

> The officers of the National Committee are the business managers of the party, and political parties in these days require business management of the highest order. . . . The establishment and maintenance of permanent national headquarters with sufficient force to carry on its legitimate operations, the raising of necessary funds for this purpose, the educational work to be done through proper publicity, are all objects of the highest importance and should receive the whole thought and attention of the national officers.

Movement for reorganization of the national party also came from another leader. William Jennings Bryan and his brother, Charles, announced on January 20 that they were starting intensive organization work that would presumably reach every county and precinct in the nation. Their intention was to "educate" the voters on the progressive program.[4]

National Chairman White responded to these stirrings by appointing a committee of sixteen members to provide him with "counsel" on "an efficient organization of the National Committee." The move satisfied neither Bryan nor McAdoo. A few days after the appointment of the committee on reorganization, a petition signed by forty-nine members of the national committee was sent to White requesting that he call the full committee to meet in St. Louis on March 1. The petition concluded by wishing White "many years of happiness and added usefulness upon the retirement which he announced shortly after November 2 which his private interests will make it necessary for him to seek." The committeeman from Texas, Thomas B. Love, a McAdoo supporter, was largely responsible for obtaining the signatures. Suggested as possible successors to White were Daniel C. Roper, a McAdoo backer, and Thomas L. Chadbourne, a prominent New York attorney and political associate of Governor Smith.

With the "rough-and ready" language of his Klondike days, George White declared that he had no intention of retiring. To allegations that he was a part-time party official, he replied: "I now feel that I do not need to give my entire time to business and will be able to take care of the chairmanship." He later added, "I see no great haste for a reorganization meeting of the committee." In Washington, House Minority Leader Champ Clark and Representative Henry D. Flood, chairman of the Democratic congressional campaign committee, publicly reprimanded the McAdoo forces for their brash attempt to capture the national party machinery.[5]

As the day appointed for a meeting of the committee on reorganization approached, it became evident that the petition signers had not been of one mind regarding Chairman White's retirement. Several indicated that they had signed on the assumption that White was on the verge of resigning voluntarily. Carter Glass, Cordell Hull, and others prominent in the party indicated their personal support of White. Even the originators of the petition, Thomas B. Love and Robert W. Woolley, issued statements denying that any personal criticism of Chairman White was intended. The Democratic congressional campaign committee, upon Representative Flood's recommendation, adopted a resolution opposing an early meeting of the full national committee or any change in the national chairmanship. The resolution was an interesting intervention into the affairs of one national party agency by another.

At the reorganization committee's meeting, White's tenure was confirmed. He was authorized to appoint an executive secretary and other staff officers for national headquarters as well as to proceed with steps for paying off the campaign indebtedness.[6]

Within a few days, White accepted the resignation of W.R. Hollister as executive secretary and appointed in his place Burt New, who had been recommended by the Indiana leaders. New was to be in charge of the permanent headquarters then being set up in Washington. A director of publicity was shortly appointed, steps initiated to pay the debt of $267,000, and plans developed for the upcoming congressional campaign. Later that spring, White paid a visit to Woodrow Wilson to bring the ailing president up to date on party developments.[7]

White called for a meeting of the national committee on November 1, its first since the presidential campaign. The call revived rumors about the possibility of White's resignation, this time to become a candidate for governor of Ohio. Daniel C. Roper continued to be the chairmanship candidate of the pro-McAdoo members, but the Cox and Palmer members remained unalterably opposed to him. The candidates of the big-state organizations were Senator Carter Glass and Joseph P. Tumulty. White again announced that he did not plan to resign unless, he now added, a man could be found upon whom all could agree.

In discussions prior to the meeting, the names of former Assistant Secretary of State Breckenridge Long and ex-Representative Cordell Hull were offered as compromise candidates. Long's availability was contingent upon the resignation of the national committeeman from Missouri, who declined to do so. This left Hull, who was finally chosen as White's successor.

The selection of Hull was generally interpreted as a blow to the McAdoo forces. Democratic members of the House of Representatives, facing the 1922 midterm elections, were particularly elated to have the experienced collaboration of a former chairman of the congressional campaign committee and sent a special congratulatory resolution to the national committee.[8]

2

Hull was one of the most distinguished Border State politicians at the nation's capital. President Wilson considered him among those most acceptable for the vice-presidential nomination on the 1920 ticket. Cox hoped that Hull could become his national campaign chairman. When Hull was defeated for re-election to Congress in the 1920 Republican landslide, Wilson offered to nominate him to be Chief Justice of the Court of Customs. Instead, Hull preferred to return to Tennessee to practice law and mend political fences. He was particularly concerned with the new female vote; in 1920, he "noted the fact the Republicans got out their womenfolk to vote," whereas the Democrats failed in this regard.[9] Hull approached his new position with some trepidation. As he describes it,

> Having been on the Executive Committee for many years, I knew in detail the inside condition of the Democratic Party, both political and financial. From what I knew, I did not in the least hanker for the new chairmanship. Nevertheless, I was elected.
>
> With the Party out of power and in the minority in both Houses of Congress, whoever occupied the office of chairman of the National Committee was in the highest position of Democratic Party leadership in the nation. This post, which at all times ranks in the top in a Party hierarchy, is at the very top when a Party is in the minority.[10]

Hull's remarks are probably the first direct reference of a national chairman to his high position within his party. It is noteworthy that Hull recognized the seniority of the publicly elected party leaders in Congress when holding a majority there. Hull was also sensitive to his "superiors" in the titular leadership. At Wilson's request, he called upon the former president once or twice a month until the latter's death in February 1924. Hull frequently gave Wilson written reports on his organizational efforts, and Wilson gave advice freely, including comments on the various issues of the 1922 campaign.

During the spring of that year, a proposal for a midterm national party conference was made by the Woodrow Wilson Democracy, a party club in New York City. The midterm conference, whose membership was not indicated, was intended to "formulate a program and platform to serve as the basis for an appeal to the voters of the country."[11] All candidates for the Senate and the House of Representatives would be invited to subscribe to this program. When Wilson heard of the proposal, he wrote Hull, "Such a conference would lead to nothing but talk and outside rumors about it which would be misleading and hurtful to the party."[12]

Hull also had breakfasts every two or three weeks with another former titular leader, William Jennings Bryan, whom he regarded as "a magnificent orator" but whose judgment he found lacking at times.[13]

Hull's announced intention was to establish more responsible and stronger organizations in the states and counties. He proposed to maintain an efficient publicity bureau at national headquarters through which to voice criticisms about the shortcomings of the Harding administration. In this connection, he frequently turned over information relating to the Teapot Dome investigation to Senator Thomas Walsh, whose efforts led to the exposure of Secretary of the Interior Fall.

A more difficult aspect of Hull's job was liquidating the national committee's debt. He reports that most Democratic donors treated him "as if I had the smallpox." One of Hull's approaches to fund-raising was the formation of Victory Clubs, each club consisting of ten or more persons who had paid five dollars into the national party treasury. Hull soon paid off the full debt, leaving a surplus of $30,000.

A combination of personal qualities and political circumstances placed Chairman Hull in full charge of the 1922 midterm congressional campaign. Having been chairman of the congressional campaign committee, he knew its procedures and problems thoroughly. In addition, the campaign strategy was to focus on economic issues about which he was a specialist. "At the request of the chairman of the Democratic Congressional Committee, I conducted the combined campaign of the National and Congressional Committees."[14]

In the Democratic sweep that took place on election day, Hull was himself returned to his former congressional seat. The Democrats gained seventy-five seats in the lower House, reducing the Republican majority to eighteen. The party leadership throughout the nation applauded Hull's achievement. The Tennessee legislature urged the national party to nominate him for president. Hull discouraged such a boom, indicating that he had "consistently pursued the policy of making the party organization an agency in fact, as well as in name, for the entire party membership and of keeping it strictly aloof from elements, groups, factions, and individual contests for party nominations."[15]

Optimism regarding Democratic presidential prospects in 1924 was reflected in early and vigorous candidate activity. The titular leaders—Bryan, Wilson, and Cox—remained quietly but visibly in the background. Daniel C. Roper informally assumed charge of the McAdoo preconvention campaign early in 1923. A campaign biography of Henry Ford was issued in January; by June of 1923, Ford ranked second only to McAdoo in a *Literary Digest* poll of the preferences of 2,000 Democratic party leaders.

Oscar W. Underwood of Alabama, Democratic floor leader in the Senate, was the candidate of the congressional wing of the party. During the summer of 1923, Underwood became the first person to announce his candidacy. By October, he was conducting a frontal attack on the influence of the Ku Klux Klan in presidential politics, a reference to the Klan's open endorsement of McAdoo.

In New York, Governor Smith was coming to the end of the customary two terms in that office and was proposed for the presidency by Charles Murphy of Tammany. Tom Taggart of Indiana supported Indiana's Samuel M. Ralston. In November 1923 Murphy, George Brennan of Illinois, and James M. Guffey of Pennsylvania met at Taggart's French Lick Springs Hotel and agreed that they would oppose McAdoo to the bitter end. They did not, however, unite on any single candidate of their own.[16]

The stop-McAdoo combine was formidable. The French Lick Springs group comprising New York, Illinois, Indiana, and Pennsylvania forces controlled not only the convention votes of these four states, but also those of Ohio, Georgia, Alabama, and Missouri. The convention would have 1,094 votes in all; under the two-thirds rule, only 365 votes were needed to veto McAdoo or any other candidate. The French Lick Springs coalition could move at least 400 votes. The McAdoo leaders were aware of the threat. They came to the January national committee meeting advocating the abrogation of the two-thirds rule, a proposal that they unsuccessfully reiterated at the convention. No serious fight was made on the rule at the national committee meeting since so much of McAdoo's support came from the South, the major beneficiary of the rule.

McAdoo was not without opposition from another quarter: some of his former colleagues in Wilson's cabinet. Wilson's secretary of state, Robert Lansing, and secretary of war, Newton D. Baker, supported the favorite son from West Virginia, John W. Davis, solicitor general and ambassador to England under Wilson. Wilson died on February 3, 1924, leaving no clear impression whom he might have favored.

3

The scandals of the Harding administration, Harding's death, the elevation of the colorless "Silent Cal" Coolidge to the White House, and the congressional victories of 1922 gave Democratic leaders high hopes for 1924. Most hopeful was McAdoo, whose excellent organization carried him to victory over Ford in the South Dakota Democratic county meetings of late November 1923. On December 18, Henry Ford, until this time considered a Democrat, announced that he would not run for president because he felt "perfectly safe with Coolidge." The coast now seemed even clearer for McAdoo.

Somewhat overconfident, the McAdoo people approached the selection of a convention city rather casually. San Francisco, New York, Chicago, and St. Louis were among the competing cities. Now a Californian, McAdoo publicly expressed the hope that San Francisco would be chosen. Some of his supporters on the committee were wary of New York, where Tammany influence could make itself felt. New York had special appeal for Chairman Hull because its high bid of $205,000 exceeded all others and would help eliminate the committee's deficit. Moreover, Governor Smith was at this time merely a favorite-son candidate and not considered McAdoo's major opponent. McAdoo himself later indicated that he never opposed the selection of New York City since he doubted that any Tammany candidate would ever be acceptable to the national party. Thus, with the support of many McAdoo followers, Madison Square Garden in New York City was chosen as the site of the historic 1924 convention.

In February, McAdoo's name came up in connection with the Senate's investigation of Teapot Dome, during which he was identified as a former special counsel to Edward Doheny, the man who allegedly bribed Secretary of the Interior Albert B. Fall. Although McAdoo testified that he was not even remotely connected with the scandal, some of his leading supporters felt that his candidacy had been irrevocably impaired. Bernard Baruch advised him to withdraw. Senator Thomas J. Walsh, who headed the investigation, wrote McAdoo that "you are no longer available as a candidate."[17]

Two other issues began to put further obstacles in McAdoo's path. Underwood announced that he would propose to the national convention a plank condemning the Ku Klux Klan as an agency of intolerance in American life, organized as a secret society expounding white supremacy and nativism. Its activities, stimulated during the patriotic fervor of the First World War, attracted a membership of several millions, reaching into every state in the Union by 1923. In Texas, it dominated the Democratic organization; in Indiana, the Republican. During the 1924 primary elections, the Klan fought for and won control of several state party organizations. The McAdoo victory over Underwood in Georgia's March primary was considered a major advance in the Klan's march toward political power. The fundamentalist Protestantism of the Klan was particularly offensive in the multireligion regions of the country, that is, the Northeast, the West, and the urban centers. Underwood's stand against the Klan projected him beyond a regional candidacy.

The second issue was the Prohibition question. McAdoo was a pronounced

Dry, and the Anti-Saloon League mobilized its far-flung membership in his behalf. Thus, when Smith resoundingly defeated McAdoo in the April 1 Wisconsin primary, the result was widely interpreted as a strictly Wet-Dry division; neither candidate had campaigned extensively in that state. The Wisconsin outcome transformed Smith from a favorite son to a national candidate. The anti-Prohibition forces stood foursquare behind him. Smith next received the endorsements of the Rhode Island and Massachusetts organizations.

By the end of April, Franklin D. Roosevelt agreed to serve as Smith's pre-convention campaign manager. The prestige of the former vice-presidential nominee's name was the final boost that made Smith McAdoo's principal opponent.

After the defeat of the Cox-Roosevelt ticket in 1920, Roosevelt returned to business and practicing law in New York. Still new to national politics, Roosevelt kept his vice-presidential campaign staff in touch with each other through an annual dinner. The group came to be known as the Cuff Links Club when Roosevelt gave each member a set of initialed gold cuff links with his own initials engraved on one. Roosevelt succumbed to infantile paralysis on August 10, 1921. Not until the fall of 1922 did he recover sufficiently to contemplate a return to politics, encouraged to do so by his wife, Eleanor, and his political adviser, Louis McHenry Howe. Howe was a former political reporter who gave up his job in 1912 to manage Roosevelt's second campaign for the state senate. He later served as Roosevelt's secretary in the Navy Department and was his most intimate political confidante until his death. Management of the Smith campaign was Roosevelt's first formal step back on to the national scene and lent much drama as well as a Wilsonian tone to the Smith candidacy.

As contending candidates' forces gathered strength and momentum, National Chairman Hull was beset by reports and rumors concerning the role of national headquarters in the forthcoming battles. He finally issued a statement reiterating his conception of that role:

> I have constantly made plain to everyone that Democratic National Headquarters was not created for the purpose of either formulating a platform or nominating a candidate, but solely for the purpose of prosecuting educational and organization work. The great rank and file of the national democracy speaking through their chosen delegates at the next national convention, will write the Democratic platform and name the Democratic candidate.[18]

Hull reinforced this view with various general organizational activities: the establishment of a National School of Democracy to instruct Democratic women in public speaking and party administration, the promotion of fund-raising Victory Clubs, and other projects.

The two living former titular leaders assumed their divergent positions on candidates and issues. Bryan, now a resident in Florida, campaigned in Alabama and Florida against Underwood and continued to be a major defender of Prohibition. The Florida primary committed Bryan's own convention vote to McAdoo. Cox allowed the Ohio organization to use his name as a favorite-son candidate in order to forestall election of a McAdoo delegation, and the Cox slate won in the primary by a 5 to 3 margin. Elsewhere, the Underwood campaign was losing out against the opposition of the Klan. Favorite sons and dark horses were being suggested in growing number.

4

At Madison Square Garden, sixteen names were placed in nomination and some sixty individuals received votes before the nomination was made on the 103rd ballot. The atmosphere of the convention was dominated by the fact that the Ku Klux Klan—rural, Dry, nativistic, and Protestant—had established a conspicuous and noisy headquarters in urban, Wet, cosmopolitan New York, the home of the leading Catholic candidate.

As Underwood had promised, a platform plank condemning the Klan was introduced and became the first test of potential alliances in the fragmented convention. The McAdoo managers countered with the suggestion that the nomination be made before the platform was adopted in order to head off the expected bitterness over particular planks. They sought a recess before the platform was reported. The anti-McAdoo forces supported a motion to adjourn instead of recess and won, 559 to 513.

The platform was not presented until Saturday because of intense disagreement in the platform committee. The committee's majority offered a general plank upholding religious freedom. A minority proposed a plank specifically condemning the Klan for its efforts to arouse religious and racial dissension. In the convention's second test vote, the minority plank was defeated by the unprecedentedly narrow margin of $543^3/_{20}$ to $542^7/_{20}$.

The first presidential ballot gave McAdoo $431^1/_2$ votes, Smith 241, Cox 59, Harrison $43^1/_2$, Underwood $42^1/_2$, Davis 31, and scattered votes for over a dozen other candidates. On the sixty-ninth ballot McAdoo reached his highest number of votes: 530. By this time, it was more than clear that a stalemate had developed. After the seventy-sixth ballot, Tom Taggart proposed a conference of all leaders, but it failed to reach any conclusion. Several leaders then asked James M. Cox to come to New York to use his influence as titular leader to help bring the proceedings to an end. Cox, who had withdrawn his name in favor of Baker on an earlier ballot, performed yeoman service upon his arrival and is credited by many for the events that led to the nomination of John W. Davis and Charles W. Bryan.

Cox believed that the way out of the McAdoo-Smith deadlock was with Davis or Carter Glass. The Cox strategy was to urge the delegates to try out Davis and then Glass. The plan was to start being implemented on the 103rd ballot. When Ohio gave Davis 41 of its 48 votes, the reluctant Davis supporters, many of them leading Wilsonians, agreed to go along with the effort.[19]

On the ninety-third ballot, Franklin Roosevelt announced that Smith would withdraw his name immediately upon the withdrawal of McAdoo. McAdoo insisted upon remaining in the race until the end of the ninety-ninth ballot. It required another four ballots for the delegates to confirm Davis' nomination. With a Wall Street lawyer at the top of the Democratic ticket, the Bryan nomination for the second spot was intended to keep the midwestern progressives from departing for the La Follette Progressive party then being organized.

Any chance of uniting the Democratic party against Coolidge was destroyed by the protracted convention. Radio, for the first time reporting a national party convention, gave the public a vivid impression of Democratic factionalism and intransigence. One exception was noted by the New York *Evening World*, "No matter whether Governor Smith wins or loses, Franklin D. Roosevelt stands out as the real hero of the Democratic Convention of 1924."[20] A few days earlier the New York *Herald Tribune* had observed:

> While the results of the futile ballots were droned from the platform in the Garden yesterday, there sat in the exact center of the great hall the one man whose name would stampede the convention were he put in nomination. He is the only man to whom the contending factions could turn and at the same time save their faces and keep square with the folks at home. . . . From the time Roosevelt made his speech in nomination of Smith, which was the one great speech of the convention, he has been easily the foremost figure on floor or platform.[21]

The convention over, Chairman Hull asked the nominee to relieve him of his duties as soon as possible so that he might take a much-needed vacation. On July 19, John W. Davis announced that the "original Davis man," Clem L. Shaver, national committeeman from West Virginia, would be his choice for chairman at the national committee's meeting of August 11. Shaver took over command of the Washington headquarters on July 19.

As he left the convention city, Davis spoke cheerfully and hopefully about reuniting the party and carrying the battle to the enemy camp. Shaver announced plans for creating a special campaign advisory committee of such experienced strategists as Vance McCormick, Homer Cummings, George White, and Cordell Hull, that is, his predecessors in the chairmanship. Another Shaver plan was, if at all possible, to bring into the campaign all the managers of the preconvention candidates. There is no evidence that Shaver was able to organize either of these groups.[22] In fact, the division that so deeply split the convention carried over directly into the campaign.

At the very meeting at which Shaver was elected national chairman, a fight

John W. Davis' reference to Shaver as the "original Davis man" alluded to the fact that Shaver had been supporting Davis' political fortunes since 1910, when he put the latter's name in nomination for Congress. The two men had come to know each other while serving as Democratic county chairmen in the same congressional district in West Virginia. It was Shaver's firm conviction from the very first that Davis had the qualifications to be president "if people ever got to know him." A West Virginian by birth, Shaver attended a state normal school and early became active in Democratic politics. In 1893, while still in his mid-twenties, he went to Washington as a protégé of Representative William L. Wilson, obtaining a clerkship in the United States Weather Bureau and, in his spare time, studying law at what later became George Washington University. He completed his formal education in 1898, was admitted to the bar in West Virginia, and practiced without partners until his retirement in 1942. He had other business interests: farming, stock raising, and the sale of coal and timber lands. He served three terms in the West Virginia House of Representatives, where, in 1911, he was floor leader. He was chairman of the state central committee from 1912 to 1920, during which he managed a successful gubernatorial and two successful senatorial campaigns. Shaver was described in the press as "a sort of silent Tom Taggart, who makes no enemies, endeavors to keep his candidates from stepping on tender toes—then bides his time."[23] In West Virginia, he was familiarly known as "Shaver, the Sphinx" for his Coolidge-like reluctance to talk.

occurred over the appointment of the vice-chairmen. The convention had authorized three vice-chairmen. At the committee meeting, McAdoo supporters recommended the selection of four, two of whom would have been McAdoo men. Although their candidate had been defeated twice for the presidential nomination, the McAdoo men were reluctant to disband and thereby dissipate their collective influence.

Edmund H. Moore of Ohio raised a point of order, which Shaver sustained. The committee proceeded to elect the first two vice-chairmen without opposition. This left the two McAdoo candidates to contend for the third place. Debate was heated. Moore insisted that the rules of the convention be adhered to, and this was again sustained by Shaver, with a standing vote needed to sustain him. Shaver was supported by a vote of 27 to 26, boding little good for the future of the ticket.[24]

Shaver's management of the national headquarters produced little that was newsworthy. The Davis campaign dragged on. The talents of the various nomination candidates and other political figures were used poorly, if at all. Cox made campaign speeches in Ohio, Indiana, Kentucky, and Tennessee, enduring constant changes of tactics and itinerary.[25] Franklin Roosevelt withdrew to Warm Springs to continue his recovery. Smith, renominated for governor of New York, was thoroughly preoccupied by the state campaign. McAdoo's following made no secret of their expectation that Davis would be defeated and that their man would have another chance in 1928. Shaver put Daniel C. Roper in charge of the Washington headquarters and Thomas J. Spellacy in charge of the New York headquarters. This arrangement guaranteed constant strife between pro-McAdoo Roper and pro-Smith Spellacy.

Meanwhile, La Follette's third-party movement was gaining momentum. Political analysts generally anticipated that the Progressives would carry enough of the western states to prevent a majority in the electoral college, thus throwing the election into the House of Representatives. Writing from Warm Springs in October, Roosevelt observed:

> I have a hunch that Davis's strength is really improving, but I still think the election will go into the house. Anyway, I am philosophic enough to think that even if Coolidge is elected, we shall be so darned sick of conservatism of the old-money controlled crowd in four years that we [will] get a real progressive landslide in 1928.[26]

5

Election day brought dramatic changes in prestige and status among Democratic national leaders. Davis, thoroughly defeated, returned to his law partnership and corporate directorships. Shaver announced that Davis would not again be available as a candidate. Smith was the only candidate on the Democratic slate in New York to be elected. Shaver was criticized for having conducted a slovenly campaign. The McAdoo leaders in various states were accused of sitting out the election.

Almost immediately, the newspapers began to comment on the prospects of a Smith-McAdoo struggle for the 1928 Democratic nomination. There was much speculation about an early reorganization of the national committee and the party generally. One plan was to have a Democratic congressional conference called by the party steering committees in each house, a bicameral caucus procedure much like that of the pre-Jacksonian era.[27]

At national headquarters, Chairman Shaver had several postelection problems with which to deal: a $200,000 deficit, raising funds to maintain the permanent headquarters in Washington, and his own future as national chairman. By the end of February 1925, he was able to announce that the deficit was "no longer a serious problem." He also reported contributions sufficient for current headquarters operating expenses. He promised that "the Democratic National Committee will be in a position materially to aid, in a practical way, party candidates in the Congressional elections of 1926.''[28] On his retention of the chairmanship, Shaver said nothing.

The McAdoo supporters, however, had much to suggest regarding a new national chairman. Shortly after the presidential election, they began a semipublic search for a candidate for chairman upon whom they could unite: Colonel Samuel B. Amidon of Kansas, a vice-chairman of the national committee; Daniel C. Roper, McAdoo's preconvention campaign manager; J. Bruce Kremer of Montana, McAdoo's floor leader at the national convention; or Major John S. Cohen of Georgia. Any move by the McAdoo forces was expected to be countered by the Smith people who were uniting behind the candidacy of Mayor Frank Hague of Jersey City. In the event of a contest, many of the Davis committeemen were expected to line up on the Smith side. Another French Lick Hotel conference, including Smith, Brennan, and Taggart, was held in mid-November.[29]

On March 8, 1925, Franklin D. Roosevelt gave the press copies of an exchange of letters between himself and Senator Thomas J. Walsh, who had been permanent chairman at the Madison Square Garden convention, regarding the problems of national party organization. The interim organization of the national party was a long-time concern of Roosevelt.[30] Late in 1921, he had written to National Chairman Hull complaining that the party's machinery was archaic and urging that something be done. In December 1924, Roosevelt decided to bypass the national leaders and appeal directly to local leaders, particularly those who had been delegates to the national convention. In a letter that went out to 3,000 Democratic leaders, he invited their advice on improving the party organization.

In his letter to Senator Walsh, Roosevelt reported the general feeling expressed in several hundred replies. The respondents "overwhelmingly agree," he said, that the Democratic party must stand for progress and liberal thought. There was a need for a clearer distinction between national issues and "those matters of momentary or temporary nature which are principally of local interest." There ought to be an end to discussion of presidential candidates for the time being.

Roosevelt summarized the specific suggestions for immediate organizational reform. The national committee executive machinery should function "every day in every year." The national committee should be brought into closer touch with the state organizations. The permanent national headquarters should be put on a "business-like financial basis." Party information and publicity efforts should be greatly expanded. Party leaders from all sections should meet more frequently to plan for united action.

> Finally, a very large number of the delegates who have written to me offer the suggestion that a conference of representative Democrats from every State be called by the Chairman of the Democratic National Committee at some central

point this Spring, and that the primary purpose of this conference shall be to make recommendations to the National Committee, which, under the party rules, is the governing body between elections.[31]

On the same day that Roosevelt sent his letter to Walsh, a joint report of the National League of Young Democrats and the New York Democratic Club, submitted to National Chairman Shaver, assessed the causes of defeat in the recent election and suggested more frequent meetings of the national committee, biennial national party conventions, permanent divisional headquarters of the national committee to be established in Washington, Chicago, Los Angeles, and New York, and the creation of permanent bureaus for publicity, naturalized voters, labor, political statistics, and opinion trends.

Support for Roosevelt's off-year conference proposal was quick in coming, particularly from James M. Cox, John W. Davis, Cordell Hull, and Jonathan Daniels. Senator Walsh warmly endorsed the proposal.[32] Davis suggested a June date for the conference. Chairman Shaver preferred a fall meeting. The reaction of most Democratic leaders in Congress, however, was at best lukewarm. Some contended that even if the proposed conference confined itself to reorganization and permanent financing of the administration of the national party, it probably would be impossible to prevent discussions that would accentuate differences over public policy. Other critics were concerned with the selection of participants for the conference. The Roosevelt plan was thought to call for about 200 participants, yet there were 110 members of the national committee alone, not to mention state party officers and prominent senators and representatives in Congress.[33]

The Roosevelt-Walsh proposal very shortly became a bone of factional contention. William Jennings Bryan expressed the view that it was "too early" for a meeting of party leaders. The 1925 Jefferson Day dinner in Washington had to be called off because of suspicion that it would be converted into a midterm conference and because Bryan, Roosevelt, Daniels, and others declined to address it.

Roosevelt maintained his campaign for a reorganization conference throughout 1925. To avoid the impression that the conference was a pro-Smith or pro-Roosevelt maneuver, however, it would have been necessary for National Chairman Shaver to issue the call. Despite a variety of pressures from Roosevelt, Shaver refused to issue a call. The national chairman was obviously supporting the position of the Democratic leaders in Congress, many of whom were southerners with long tenure and seniority. In a midterm conference, these leaders would run the risk of having to share their policy-making prerogatives with noncongressional Democrats. By the end of 1925, the Roosevelt-Walsh proposal had, for all practical purposes, been "postponed out of existence."[34]

Meanwhile, rumors about the status of Clem Shaver as national chairman appeared frequently in the press. During the spring of 1925, there were only three persons working at the national headquarters in addition to Shaver. Shaver was devoting a large part of his time to fund-raising and was rarely present at headquarters. There were repeated rumors that Shaver was eager to resign, but would do so only if a replacement could be found who would placate both the McAdoo and Smith factions. Shaver issued several denials of plans to retire. In the wings, the McAdoo leaders were committing themselves to J. Bruce Kremer as their candidate for chairman. Others began suggesting the chairman of the Democratic congressional campaign committee, Representative William A. Oldfield, as a compromise. The Smith people refrained from suggesting anyone.

Between 1925 and 1927, the Smith faction gradually built its alliances in preparation for the 1928 convention. In the 1925 mayoralty fight in New York City, Governor Smith engineered the replacement of Mayor John Hylan by State Senator James J. Walker, thereby demonstrating his complete ascendancy in New York party affairs. In Connecticut, Homer S. Cummings, who had supported McAdoo, resigned as national committeeman after long years in that position, to be replaced by a pro-Smith man. Wet factions came into control of Democratic state organizations all along the eastern seaboard. The cause of the Drys was on the wane and so was enthusiasm for another McAdoo candidacy.

A critical source of McAdoo strength lay in the Democratic organizations of the South. As early as 1926, Governor Smith sent the charming Mayor Jimmy Walker on a tour to cultivate that garden. During 1927, the Smith people spoke frequently of making a strong fight to abolish the two-thirds rule, but retreated on this point as southern leaders became increasingly friendly. A final step in Smith's southern strategy was to advocate that the national convention be held in a city below the Mason-Dixon line. By late summer of 1927, McAdoo saw the handwriting on the wall. In September, he announced that he was no longer a candidate for the nomination. With McAdoo's withdrawal went nearly a score of favorite-son and dark-horse candidacies that had been anticipating another deadlocked convention.

6

The 1928 Democratic national convention was an Al Smith rally, with southern overtones. Smith votes on the national committee put the convention in Houston, Texas. There was no mention of the two-thirds rule. On the Wet-Dry issue, the party platform simply pledged itself to "an honest effort to enforce the Eighteenth Amendment." Franklin D. Roosevelt, who had publicly favored Smith's nomination earlier in the year, made another impressive nominating speech on behalf of the "Happy Warrior." The *New York Times* characterized the speech as "a gentleman speaking to gentlemen." There were approximately twenty seconding speeches. After Smith's nomination, the delegates balanced the ticket by selecting Senator Joseph T. Robinson of Arkansas as vice-presidential nominee. Robinson was a Dry, a Protestant, from a rural state, and the first southerner to appear on a national ticket since the end of the Civil War.

The ordeal of Chairman Shaver ended with the Smith nomination. Prior to McAdoo's withdrawal, Shaver was fearful of resigning lest he precipitate a battle royal. Nor was Shaver able to expand national headquarters: funds that he had so hopefully expected to raise were never forthcoming. However, when the national convention was held in Houston, home of Jesse H. Jones, director of finance of the national committee, the committee's deficit was quickly and happily turned into a surplus.

Governor Smith, the first Catholic to win nomination for the presidency, promptly attended to the organization of his campaign. His first choice for the national chairmanship was Franklin D. Roosevelt, who, commenting in a letter to his mother, reported, "I declined the National Chairmanship, and will decline the nomination for Governor [of New York]." Roosevelt felt committed to spending as much time as possible at Warm Springs, continuing his efforts to recover fully from polio.[35]

Despite an intense draft-Roosevelt movement, Roosevelt refused to yield to pressures that he run for governor. By October 1, Smith asked him to accept the gubernatorial nomination as a personal favor. Smith and his advisers felt that only a strong gubernatorial candidate could help the presidential nominee carry New York. The state convention nominated Roosevelt by acclamation, although he had not agreed to accept as recently as a conversation with Smith the previous day. In his acceptance speech on October 3, Roosevelt explained, "I was not dragooned into running by the Governor. On the contrary, he fully appreciated the reasons for my reluctance and was willing to give up such advantage as he felt my candidacy might bring him in deference to my wishes."

With Roosevelt out of the chairmanship picture, Smith turned to others. A leading possibility was George R. Van Namee, Smith's preconvention campaign manager and secretary of the New York Democratic state central committee. Another was J. Bruce Kremer, the former McAdoo leader who, by 1928, had moved into the Smith camp.

The man most persistently mentioned was Senator Peter G. Gerry of Rhode Island, descendant of Elbridge Gerry, signer of the Declaration of Independence. A millionaire who won his first election to the Senate in 1916 by successful appeals to the foreign-born of his state, Gerry had several qualities that could be helpful to Smith. An Episcopalian, he fit the decision of the Smith strategists that the national chairman must not be a Catholic. Not a New Yorker, Gerry would alleviate suspicion that the Smith campaign would be run by Tammany. A man of wealth, he would have access to campaign funds and perhaps even attract some leaders of the business community to the Smith bandwagon. Gerry's candidacy was debated among Governor Smith's advisers for over two weeks. The

Part Alsatian, part Irish, John J. Raskob was the son of an immigrant cigar maker who took up residence in Lockport, a town on the Erie Canal in New York. Even while in secondary school, Raskob had a reputation for being interested in making a great deal of money. He studied stenography and accounting in preparation for a business career. His father died in 1898 and, at the age of nineteen, young Raskob undertook the support of his mother, younger brother, and two sisters. His first job was as stenographer of the chief engineer of a subsidiary of the Washington Pump Company in Lockport. He advanced from a $5 per week salary to $7.50, but within two years began seeking better opportunities. A friend in Lorain, Ohio, informed him that Pierre S. du Pont, owner of a streetcar company in that community, was looking for a secretary. Raskob's new boss was one of three du Pont cousins who, in 1902, assumed control of the E. I. Du Pont de Nemours & Company of Delaware. Pierre du Pont became treasurer and Raskob accompanied him to Wilmington as assistant treasurer at a salary of $3,000 a year.

The First World War transformed the Du Pont Company into a major corporation and brought Raskob substantial wealth. In 1913, he somewhat casually invested in General Motors stock; by 1915, he and Pierre du Pont owned 3,000 shares. At this time, William C. Durant, founder of General Motors, was engaged in a bitter battle for control of the corporation. His opponent was a banking syndicate that had lent him large sums. The adversaries were evenly matched in voting strength and the outcome depended upon the relatively small number of pivotal Raskob-du Pont shares. Pierre S. du Pont was made chairman of the board of directors and Raskob became a member of the board. Thereafter, Raskob devoted himself to the expansion of the market for automobiles and to various financial coups that earned him and his associates many millions of dollars. He persuaded the executives of E. I. Du Pont de Nemours & Company to invest heavily in General Motors, enabling GM to become second only to Ford in the automobile industry. Raskob organized the General Motors Acceptance Corporation to facilitate the sale of cars on the installment plan. In 1923, he arranged for eighty senior and junior executives to organize the Managers Securities Corporation, which purchased $33 million of General Motors common stock. Four years later, these executives were known as "Raskob's Eighty Millionaires."[36]

Tammany advisers opposed Gerry, mainly because he was the choice of the non-Tammany group.

As the moment of decision approached, there was increasing agreement between anti-Tammany and Tammany advisers that the chairman be a businessman. Efforts were apparently made to recruit Melvin A. Traylor, president of the First National Bank of Chicago, or Owen D. Young, chairman of the board of directors of the General Electric Company, but with no success. As the national committee gathered in New York for its meeting on July 11, Tammany men were reported to be carrying on a quiet campaign among incoming committeemen in favor of the selection of "a businessman" whose identity they would not disclose.[37]

The next day the businessman turned out to be John J. Raskob, chairman of the finance committee of General Motors Corporation and long a personal friend of Governor Smith. The recommendation was decided upon only hours earlier, over the strenuous objections of many prominent Democratic leaders and several of the governor's own advisers. Raskob was clearly Smith's personal choice in a dramatic move to win the support of the business community.

Said Judge George W. Olvany, spokesman for Smith's Tammany advisers, "[Raskob's selection] will show the people throughout the country that big business need not be afraid of the Democratic Party, when the party is willing to leave its affairs in the hands of a man conspicuously identified with one of the biggest business corporations of the world."[38] With Andrew Mellon as the leading businessman behind Herbert Hoover's candidacy and a heady economic prosperity being widely credited to the talents of American business enterprise, the Smith leaders hoped that Raskob's chairmanship would not only reassure businessmen, but also bring them into support of the campaign.

Many of the party leaders had serious misgivings about the wisdom of choosing Raskob as chairman. He was inexperienced and himself acknowledged that "this was my first and only experience in political work."[39] He was a Wet activist as a director of the Association Against the Prohibition Amendment. His speech accepting the chairmanship made it clear that a change in the Prohibition law would be a major campaign issue as far he was concerned. Raskob attributed his acceptance of the chairmanship to the earnestness of Governor Smith's work for repeal.[40] Many Democratic leaders feared that the emphasis upon the liquor issue would prove costly in terms of southern and western support.

A third reason for concern was Raskob's membership in the Union League, a Republican stronghold. It was public knowledge that he had voted Republican—for Coolidge—as recently as 1924. Raskob responded that he also had voted for Woodrow Wilson and had no fixed party identification prior to his election as Democratic national chairman.

A fourth reason for concern was Raskob's reputation as a prominent Catholic, having presented a $1 million gift to the Diocese of Wilmington earlier that year. For those elements, particularly in the South, eager to raise the religious issue against Al Smith, Raskob afforded an easy secondary target. Franklin D. Roosevelt felt that a Wet, a Catholic, and a big businessman in the chairmanship would lose not only the Protestant South, but also the progressive elements in the Midwest.[41]

To deflect some of the anti-Raskob feeling, Smith created a special advisory committee to the national chairman, at the head of which he placed Senator Gerry of Rhode Island. Herbert H. Lehman, manager of Smith's 1926 gubernatorial campaign, served both on the advisory committee and as chairman of the finance committee. The forces stirred by Smith's candidacy were not that easily allayed. In Pennsylvania, former national chairman Vance McCormick bolted the ticket on the Prohibition issue. The factional difficulties in Connecticut compelled national committeeman Spellacy to resign. Anti-Catholic sentiment flared in the South. Wrote Walter Lippmann:

> There are passions at work this year which are capable of dissolving the political habits of very large numbers of people. These passions are most fiercely at work precisely in the States which have hitherto been most invincibly partisan. Both the Democrats and the Republicans are threatened in their own stronghold. If North Carolina is doubtful, so is Massachusetts; if Florida is doubtful, so is Rhode Island. The catalytic agent in this process of dissolution is, of course, Governor Smith.[42]

National voter turnout, normally low in years of economic prosperity, reached a record level in the presidential election of 1928. The turnout in the popular vote achieved the highest rate of increase over a previous election since 1856, with the exception of 1920 when women's suffrage went into effect. The vote for Smith pulled the Democratic party's percentage of the total popular vote up from 29 percent in 1924 to 41 percent. The Solid South was broken, with Florida, Texas, and states in the upper South going to Hoover. In the states where the Progressives had been strongest in 1924, Smith more than doubled the Democratic turnout. In large urban states he brought large segments of the working and recently naturalized immigrant population, many of them voting for the first time, into the Democratic column.

> Opinions can differ on whether or not the Smith nomination was a good thing for the Democratic party, but it would be difficult to argue that any other possible candidate could have increased the party vote so much in 1928, and especially in states where the party was so much in need of an increase if it was again to become competitive. The contrast is especially striking against the record of Smith's two immediate predecessors, Cox and Davis.[43]

For Smith, this was his last bid for public office. "I certainly do not expect ever to run for public office again. I have had all I can stand of it. . . . As far as running for office again is concerned—that's finished.''[44]

In his own state of New York, Smith was defeated by about 103,000 votes. Franklin D. Roosevelt, on the other hand, was elected by 25,000 votes, a handful in the total of 4 million. Roosevelt's victory and Smith's retirement immediately placed the new governor and former vice-presidential nominee in a position to become the Democratic presidential candidate in 1932. To letters of congratulations from across the nation, Roosevelt responded with appreciation and with "deep disappointment" over the defeat of Governor Smith. In the same letter, a first draft of which had been prepared by Louis M. Howe, he included the following:

> I am of course convinced that had we kept our national organization going between elections we should have done better and I hope that steps will be taken to have this carried out during the next three years. This is no time to discuss candidates but it is time for putting into effect a permanent working organization. I hope you will write me your views.[45]

Reporters sought out Roosevelt at Warm Springs, Georgia, to inquire if his survey was in any way related to his future candidacy for president. Roosevelt pointed out that he was simply following up an endeavor begun after the 1924 campaign when he performed a similar service for his party in calling attention to its organizational needs.

If Roosevelt was coy, several southern leaders were not; they were plainly suggesting that he be the 1932 candidate. At the same time, anti-Smith elements in the party announced their intention to remove "Raskobism" from the national chairmanship. One group that had supported Hoover and all Democratic candidates except Smith and Robinson called for an early convention to reorganize the party. M.D. Lightfoot, chairman of the National Constitutional Democratic Committee, declared:

> Six weeks before the election it was quite generally talked in the East that Mr. Raskob and those sympathizing with him were planning, in the event of Governor Smith's defeat, to use the machinery of the National Democratic Party to add prestige and dignity to the movement of the organization for the repeal of the Eighteenth Amendment.[46]

Dry Democrats in the South, prominent among them Bishop James Cannon, Jr., of the Southern Methodist Church, joined Lightfoot in demanding Raskob's retirement. Raskob in turn indicated that he would not return to his former position as chairman of the finance committee of the General Motors Corporation. Instead, he would serve out the "four-year term" for which he had been elected, transacting party affairs from the permanent headquarters in Washington.[47]

7

Early in December, Raskob announced that he planned to call a conference of party leaders, including Smith and several Democratic senators, after the Christmas holiday for a discussion of plans to strengthen the party and liquidate its $1.5 million deficit. Raskob expressed his intention to be an active national chairman in an active national headquarters.

A floor speech by Kentucky's Representative Ralph Kilpert and public statements by Senators Walsh of Montana, Caraway of Arkansas, and Swanson of Virginia heatedly articulated opposition to the conference and to Raskob's continuing at the national committee. The southern leaders referred to the proposed conference as a maneuver to put Smith at the head of the party again in 1932, Smith's retirement announcement notwithstanding.[48]

In anticipation of conversations with Smith and Chairman Raskob scheduled for mid-January, Governor Roosevelt issued a report on the survey he had been conducting among more than 3,000 Democratic leaders throughout the nation. A preponderant number of these, according to Roosevelt, felt that the Republicans had "cheated" in the campaign against Smith. These same respondents nevertheless currently had a genuine optimism about the party's prospects in the next elections. Roosevelt further reported "an unusual demand for immediate and continued national activity and a better organized and directed publicity."

> One of the structural faults of our national Democratic organization in the past, which has resulted from our previous practice of laying the national committee carefully away in cotton wool after each election, to be taken out and dusted off just before the next Presidential election, has been the lack of any central clearinghouse for exchange of ideas among the leaders, great and small, of our party. . . .
>
> One unanimous opinion . . . is that the crying need is publicity—publicity—publicity; that Democratic papers must be encouraged and increased in number; that the independent press of our country must be furnished with information and arguments as to the attitude of the Democratic Party on questions which are rightfully party questions.[49]

Smith endorsed the concept of a full-time national organization in a special radio broadcast a few days later. The great support given the Democratic party, he said, should "not be lost by failure to maintain an organization." This would require a national committee with "suitable and well-equipped offices" to provide a live point of contact for party members. He also called for thorough publicity and information services. These organizational goals and payment of the $1.5 million deficit made necessary a major fund-raising campaign; Smith asked his supporters to contribute to the best of their ability, promising those who gave $2 or more a volume of his campaign speeches. Some 32,000 persons had contributed about $495,000 between election day and the Smith broadcast, evidence of the intense loyalty of many of the nominee's supporters. The purpose of the broadcast was to further encourage this generosity.[50]

At the meeting between Roosevelt and Raskob in Albany, it was again asserted that the big organizational hurdle was money. Lieutenant Governor Herbert Lehman, who had been director of finance for the Democratic national committee until the time of his nomination for state office, attended the conference and made his advice available. Finances and organization were also the main reason for a conference of the executive and advisory committees in mid-April.[51]

Shortly after the executive and advisory committees met, Raskob conducted a series of unpublicized conferences with the party's leadership in the Senate and House of Representatives. Then, with an air of mystery, he called together some sixty newspaper correspondents on April 30, 1929, to announce: "I have succeeded in reducing the party deficit from over $1,550,000 to about $800,000 with every indication of a further reduction to under $500,000 within the next fortnight. . . . I have appointed today Mr. Jouett Shouse of Kansas City to be chairman of the Executive Committee, and he will immediately assume charge of the Washington Office."

Shouse was to have a "permanent and adequate headquarters" designed to "work 365 days in the year." Raskob expected Shouse to acquire a competent staff for organization, publicity, and research. The research bureau would not only furnish materials to the publicity bureau at national headquarters, but also to the members of Congress. Raskob expressed the opinion that perhaps "the senatorial and congressional committees would finally be brought into one organization."[52]

Shouse's appointment was well received. The chairman of the congressional campaign committee looked forward to a "harmonious coordination of effort on the part of the national committee and the Congressional and Senatorial committees" that would lead to a vigorous campaign in 1930. The Jefferson Democratic Association of Washington honored Shouse with a banquet at the Mayflower Hotel on June 10, and well over 300 party leaders, most of them from Congress, attended. It was a "love feast" that augured well for Shouse's future work.[53]

Shouse began at once to look around for competent staff. For director of publicity he sought out the chief of the *New York World*'s Washington Bureau, Charles Michelson. According to Michelson, the two men were "comparative strangers" at the time, Shouse knowing of Michelson mainly by reputation. In Michelson's words:

> On the fifteenth day of June, 1929, Jouett Shouse and I confronted each other across his broad desk of curly maple and attempted to survey the job that lay ahead of us. About us was a fine suite of vacant offices; and that vacancy was, it seemed to me, reflected in our own mental attitude. I, at least, had not the

slightest idea of how or where to begin my function of converting the country from a Republican to a Democratic frame of mind, and I thought there was no more of definiteness in the face across the desk than on my side. The conversation was desultory.[54]

By the end of 1932, many Democratic leaders were ready to credit Michelson rather than the depression or Franklin Roosevelt's campaign for the defeat of Hoover.

In assessing Raskob's motivation for setting up a permanent organization, Michelson noted that, financially, Raskob "had enough so that the pledge of a round million to finance the rejuvenation enterprise for three years was no great drain."[55] Michelson thought that Raskob was chagrined by the outcome of the 1928 campaign, the first failure of his career. In Michelson's opinion, Raskob believed that President Hoover would probably succeed himself for the usual incumbent's second term (this was before the stock market crash), that Roosevelt could well be the sacrificial lamb for the 1932 election, and that, by 1936, with an efficient organization, the Democrats might stage a comeback with Al Smith.

Shouse authorized Michelson to hire a director of research, and the latter "went around among my newspaper friends bidding ten thousand dollars a year and a cast-iron guaranteed three-year contract." Michelson never did find a person adequate to the job he had in mind and, as far as he was concerned, "we never missed a research director."[56] Shouse hired as his personal assistants former Governor Robert A. Cooper of South Carolina and Waller B. Hunt of Kentucky, the latter at a published annual salary of $27,000. Cooper usually assisted Michelson; Hunt worked directly with Shouse.[57]

Despite these achievements, or perhaps because of them, verbal attacks against Raskob continued throughout 1929. During the Virginia gubernatorial primary, Bishop Cannon, who headed the anti-Smith movement in the South in 1928, led Democratic anti-Smith elements into a coalition with the Republicans, making "Raskobism" the main issue of the state campaign. From Alabama, Senator Thomas Heflin increased the decibels of his usual opposition to the Smith influence. Anti-Catholics were joined by Drys, particularly Senator Furnfold Simmons of North Carolina.[58]

The assaults of the Drys reached their height in Senate speeches by Furnfold Simmons and Smith W. Brookhart of Iowa on April 7, 1930. Appearing before the Senate lobby investigating committee the following day, Josephus Daniels, former secretary of the navy and Franklin Roosevelt's old boss, reiterated the charges set forth in his Raleigh *News and Observer* that the anti-Prohibition activities of Raskob constituted a peril to the Democratic party. Daniel's editorial suggested that Raskob resign as national chairman. Several weeks later, returning from a trip abroad, Raskob denied that he was about to resign, reiterated that it was time for action on Prohibition, and reported his observations that there was growing sentiment abroad against American tariff policy.[59]

One of five sons of a Rockland County, New York, brick manufacturer, James A. Farley was born in 1888 of Irish antecedents. His father was one of the Democratic minority in the county. Son James was carrying Bryan-for-president torches at age eight. Farley was graduated from Stony Point High School in 1905 and, after studying bookkeeping at the Packard Commercial School in New York City, took a position as bookkeeper for a paper company at $8 a week. He next became bookkeeper for the Universal Gypsum Company, eventually becoming its sales manager. In 1912 he ran for town clerk of Stony Point. His surprise election was credited to his extensive use of postal cards during the campaign. He was re-elected three times with increasing majorities, at the same time developing an effective political organization in Rockland County. He became Democratic county chairman in 1918 and was among the first to get behind Alfred E. Smith for governor that year.

Governor Smith subsequently appointed Farley port warden for New York City. In 1920, Farley was elected supervisor of Stony Point and in two years won a seat in the lower house of the state legislature. He served a term, failed to be re-elected, and was appointed by Smith to be a member of the New York State Athletic Commission. He became chairman of the commission in 1925 and was the target of criticism for certain rulings he made for the fast-growing boxing industry. In 1926, Farley organized the James A. Farley Company, dealers in masons' materials. After several mergers, he built it into the General Building Supply Corporation, of which he remained president until 1933. He was elected secretary of the Democratic state central committee in 1928, put Roosevelt in nomination at the state convention that gave F.D.R. his first nomination for governor, and helped manage Roosevelt's campaign. In the course of these activities, Farley and Louis Howe found that they were an extremely compatible political team.

In the last days of the 1930 campaign, Raskob delivered a half-hour political radio broadcast on October 27 in which he again expounded upon his tariff views. He proposed to "take the tariff out of politics" by establishing a bipartisan tariff commission of about seven members appointed for life. This commission of experts was to make recommendations on what rates were fair, based on careful study, and forward the recommendations to Congress. This was a modification of Raskob's earlier high-tariff position, which had been the reason for the hostility of low-tariff Democrats.

Raskob also advocated such measures as holding a national referendum on Prohibition, empowering the Federal Trade Commission to permit certain business mergers, and instituting the five-day work week. Commenting on the deepening depression, Raskob made a prediction that could have easily been credited to President Hoover, namely, that by January 1931, the period of business depression would pass. "With the impetus the automobile industry is sure to provide starting with the January shows, we will . . . all be singing 'Happy Days Are Here Again.' "[60]

The Raskob broadcast was one of a series made available to the Democratic national committee by one of the radio chains. Among those invited by Jouett Shouse to speak in the series was Governor Roosevelt. Roosevelt declined because of previous engagements in his own campaign for re-election and because "as you know, one of the Republican pleas this autumn will be that a vote for F.D.R. will only build him up as an opponent of friend Hoover later on, all of which is pure rot but will catch some Republican voters if I show the slightest sign of national participation."[61]

8

During his 1930 gubernatorial campaign, Roosevelt gathered around himself a smoothly integrated team that later served him in his first campaign for president. Louis M. Howe was ever present. James A. Farley arrived on the scene, elevated, at Roosevelt's suggestion, from secretary to chairman of the New York Democratic state committee. Farley and Howe made weekly trips to Albany to review political strategy. Frank C. Walker and Samuel I. Rosenman were other key members of the group at this time.[62]

Probably the most eminent supporter of Roosevelt for president at this time was former National Chairman, now United States Senator, Cordell Hull. At first, however, Hull was more anti-Smith than pro-Roosevelt. In his own words:

> In the years following 1928 I strove hard but without particular publicity to organize members of the Democratic National Committee, and important Democratic leaders generally, against control of the Democratic Party by Governor Smith and his associates in 1932. I called on almost every National Committee member who came to Washington, and urged my views upon him. I wrote numerous letters and delivered a number of speeches. I antagonized the Smith group, of course, but I set forth my views to the country on both national and international policies.
>
> During the conversations I constantly had with Franklin D. Roosevelt when he passed through Washington, we covered the most important domestic and international points. I made clear to him my fight against the ideas of Governor Smith and his Democratic chairman. Mr. Roosevelt expressed himself as being as one with me on the necessity for lower tariffs and full cooperation with other nations. He seemed to me to be alert, serious, and aggressive. But since

he continued to be associated with the Smith organization, we did not discuss the plans I was formulating for a strong challenge to the Smith-Raskob leadership.[63]

When Roosevelt won his second gubernatorial term by a plurality of 725,000 votes, an Albany crowd of more than 5,000 persons greeted him, despite a rainstorm, as "the next president of the United States."[64] But support of Roosevelt's candidacy was hardly universal. Raskob and Shouse promptly did what they could to dim the spotlight on F.D.R. Their device was an open letter to President Hoover, pledging that the Democrats in Congress would not cause difficulty for the ailing business community by pressing for tariff revision at the coming session and promising cooperation with the administration in the interest of business recovery. The letter, published the day after the election, was signed by former presidential candidates Cox, Davis, and Smith, National Chairman Raskob, Headquarters Director Shouse, Senate leader Joseph T. Robinson, and John N. Garner, party leader in the House. Roosevelt's name was not among the signatories, and at this point, Roosevelt supporters became openly hostile to the leadership of the national committee.

On February 10, 1931, Chairman Raskob issued a call for a meeting of the national committee. Roosevelt supporters saw this as an opportunity to challenge the Smith-Raskob leadership. Raskob's call indicated that the purposes of the meeting would be: (1) "to receive reports of the splendid accomplishments secured during the past 18 months by the fine organization in Washington," (2) "to discuss plans and policies to govern our activities during the next 15 months," and (3) to hear the result of a two-months' survey by the John Price Jones Corporation of New York covering a comprehensive plan for soliciting funds to meet the deficit and carry on work both during and between national campaigns.[65]

The "plans and policies" part of the meeting referred to the Smith-Raskob desire to put forward a definite set of policy statements as a foundation for the platform in 1932. The proposal was in effect a repetition of one made by Smith at the 1928 Jackson Day dinner in Washington in which he suggested that the national committee tentatively draft platforms prior to national conventions. The proposal was probably in imitation of the successful 171-member Advisory Committee on Policies and Platform created by Republican National Chairman Will Hays in 1920. When the suggestion was made at the time, then Democratic National Chairman Clem Shaver did nothing to implement or even debate the suggestion.

The notion that the national committee should develop party platform positions was also resisted by Cordell Hull when he was national chairman and was again opposed by him in 1931. Hull issued a series of statements in February and March vigorously objecting to the Smith-Raskob plan. In the statement of March 1, he asserted that the Democratic national committee had no authority, express or implied, to prescribe issues for the Democratic rank and file of the Nation. To assert this authority would constitute a broader assumption of power by the committee than that of selecting Party candidates for the Presidency and Vice-Presidency.[66]

The national committee meeting was scheduled for March 5. On February 28, still working behind the scenes, Roosevelt addressed a letter to Smith, a copy going to Jouett Shouse in Washington:

> Dear Al:
>
> I have been trying to get you on the telephone. I do not know what the plans for next Thursday's meeting of the National Committee are, but the more I hear from different parts of the country, the more certain I am that it would be very contrary to the established powers and precedents of the National Committee, were they to pass resolutions of *any kind* affecting party policies at this time. This does not apply, of course, to any methods of financing, nor to any plan for building up organization work on a national basis.
>
> Historically, the National Committee has always recognized that in between conventions, the spokesmen on policy matters are, primarily, the Democratic Members of the Senate and House of Representatives, together with individuals high in the Party Councils, who, however, speak as individuals.[67]

Meanwhile, Senator Hull was lining up powerful supporters for what he called "the showdown": Senators Harry F. Byrd and Claude Swanson of Virginia, Joseph T. Robinson of Arkansas, and John S. Cohen of Georgia. On March 3, two days before the meeting, Hull received a long-distance telephone call from Roosevelt, "I just called to say that I want to get in and help you make that fight down there. The two national committee members from New York will support you, and I will send Jim Farley along with them to cooperate in every way." Farley sat next to Hull throughout the national committee meeting, leaving little doubt whose prestige was being tested.

Raskob opened the meeting with a long statement on party policy. He proposed that the states be allowed to control the manufacture, transportation, and sale of intoxicating liquors. He urged that business and trade be relieved of "unnecessary and unreasonable governmental restriction, interference, and manipulation." He repeated his plan for a tariff commission.

The Democratic leader in the Senate, Robinson of Arkansas, rose to deliver a blistering rebuttal on the Prohibition issue. Smith then chided those at any Democratic gathering who would "drag" and "kick around the lot" anyone expressing his own opinion.

By now, according to Hull's account, Raskob was convinced that he ought not create a test of strength in the committee. He therefore refrained from offering his resignation (presumably to be re-elected immediately) and from insisting upon a committee statement of party principles. The main formal business reduced itself to approval of the proposal to have a commercial firm raise funds for the 1932 campaign. The John Prince Jones Corporation was to create state, county, and ward fund-raising units with accompanying publicity in the mass media. A preliminary target of $1 million was set.

"Impartial observers," wrote Hull, "indicated very definitely that the prestige of the Smith-Raskob element in the Party had received a severe setback by the checkmating of their plans." This greatly "redounded to Roosevelt's advantage as the presidential race developed."[68]

Despite the setback, Raskob did not drop his efforts to survey party opinion in anticipation of the platform proceedings. On April 5, he sent out a letter to all members of the national committee asking them to send him their personal recommendations for the 1932 platform, especially on the Prohibition and economic measures he enunciated at the March meeting. On November 22, he went a step further and made a personal survey of 90,000 contributors to the 1928 campaign. The survey took the form of a questionnaire on specific public issues. All this seemed preparatory to another attempt to obtain a policy statement at the next meeting of the national committee. As New York state party chairman, Jim Farley issued a public statement regarding the national committee's traditional powers since its inception, raising questions about Raskob's attempted extension of those powers. The committee's powers, said Farley, include:

> first, to build up the party organization; second to raise the party finances; third, to choose the date and place of the next convention; fourth, to recommend the temporary organization for the next convention and suggest such changes in the procedure of the next convention as it sees fit. It seems a pity to confuse the powers of the national committee by seeking to create an issue or issues on which the national committee cannot by any strength of the imagination bind the party.[69]

When Governor Roosevelt declined to meet with Raskob in a "harmony luncheon" in December, it appeared certain that Roosevelt "had the votes" both in the national committee and in the forthcoming national convention. Such were the fruits of Farley's incessant efforts throughout the year, during which he conducted a tour of eighteen states to pin down promises of support.

A major concession to the Roosevelt movement came from Raskob himself at the end of December 1931. Speaking through Jouett Shouse, Raskob declared unofficially that he would voluntarily retire as chairman at the next national convention and that he had no intention of seeking re-election.

On January 22, Roosevelt formally declared himself a candidate for the presidential nomination. On February 8, Smith let it be known that he was willing to be a candidate. With Roosevelt clearly the front-runner, it was obvious that the Smith strategy was directed at vetoing Roosevelt's nomination under the two-thirds rule. It was to this problem that a group of Democratic senators addressed themselves at a Washington dinner honoring Homer S. Cummings, the former national chairman.

The group met on February 11. It included Cordell Hull, Thomas J. Walsh, Burton K. Wheeler of Montana, Hugo Black of Alabama, George McGill of Kansas, William J. Bulow of South Dakota, James F. Byrnes of South Carolina, and Josiah W. Bailey of North Carolina. The one private citizen other than Cummings was Daniel C. Roper, the former McAdoo manager. Cummings had himself been a McAdoo supporter in 1924 and 1928. At the conclusion of the meeting, Cummings agreed to served as informal liaison between the Farley-Howe operation in New York and the congressional leaders. Cummings subsequently also served as the contact with the various favorite-son movements developing in anticipation of a convention deadlock. One favorite son who immediately withdrew in favor of Roosevelt was Senator Hull. Cummings, however, was especially diligent in his talks with Senator Connally of Texas concerning the favorite-son candidacy of Speaker John N. Garner.

As the party faithful gathered in Chicago for the 1932 national convention, Roosevelt had a majority of the delegates pledged to him, but he was still short of the necessary two-thirds majority. In a final attempt to influence matters, Raskob had obtained an agreement with the Roosevelt leaders "commending" Jouett Shouse to be permanent chairman of the convention. As it later developed, Roosevelt's "commendation" was not exactly a "*re*commendation."

In the first test vote of the convention, the delegates cast 638¾ votes to 514¼ to seat Huey Long's pro-Roosevelt Louisiana delegation. A second credentials contest involving Minnesota was decided 658¼ votes to 492¾. These Roosevelt victories were followed by the committee on permanent organization's recommendation of Senator Thomas J. Walsh, not Jouett Shouse, to be permanent chairman. The Smith-Raskob charges of "double-cross" notwithstanding, Walsh was elected 626 votes to 528. There was enough bad feeling about the two-thirds rule to carry a motion requesting the 1936 national convention to consider rescinding the rule.

With 769 votes needed to nominate him, Roosevelt was not yet home safe. On the first ballot, Roosevelt had 666¼ votes to Smith's 201¾ and Garner's 90¼. By the third ballot, Roosevelt and Garner had gained slightly and Smith had dropped by about a dozen votes. The fourth ballot demonstrated the durability of old grudges. When California was called on the roll, William G. McAdoo rose to announce that California would give its 44 votes to Roosevelt. California had been committed to Garner. This was the move that ended Al Smith's career in the Democratic party. The Texas delegation followed suit by also giving its 46 votes to Roosevelt. When Garner received the vice-presidential nomination, it was evident to all that "an arrangement" among Farley, McAdoo, and Garner had been made and fulfilled.

Thus ended an era of Democratic disarray. Few anticipated the New Deal-Fair Deal era that would follow.

18 Maintaining National Headquarters under the New Deal

With Franklin D. Roosevelt in the presidency and James A. Farley in the Democratic national chairmanship, the concept of a permanent national headquarters was certain to be thoroughly implemented. Both men were devoted builders of party coalitions and institutions. The organization of the executive branch of the federal government, the national Democratic party, and the factional structure within the party was profoundly and permanently changed under their leadership.

1

Throughout most of Roosevelt's presidency, a principal source of loyalty and skill in the management of his and the Democratic party's interests was the group of men known as "the Friends of Roosevelt." On January 14, 1932, a five-room headquarters at 331 Madison Avenue was the scene of a birthday party for Louis Howe. The occasion also served as the start-up of Roosevelt's official preconvention campaign. As always, the prime mover was Howe himself, with the help of New York State Chairman Farley, New York's Secretary of State Edward J. Flynn, and lawyer-businessman Frank C. Walker, that is, the principal Friends of Roosevelt.

In many ways, these four men symbolized the functional specialization that had come to be associated with election campaigning in the United States. Howe, who remained close to headquarters as office manager, handled publicity: pamphlets about Roosevelt, a wide correspondence with political leaders, and press releases. Farley, the "outside" or field-working member, handled organizational relations with party leaders in other states. Flynn, boss of the Bronx, was skilled in dealing with the major centers of party power, particularly the city machines. Walker was treasurer and chief fund-raiser.

Frank C. Walker was born in Pennsylvania in 1886, and moved to Butte, Montana, with his parents while yet a boy. He received a law degree from Notre Dame in 1907 and joined his brother, State Senator T.J. Walker, in the practice of law at Butte. He became assistant district attorney of Silver Bow County for three terms and subsequently a member of the state legislature. This led to a political association with Thomas J. Walsh, with Walker serving as a leader in the legislative session that first elected Walsh to the U.S. Senate in 1913.

Senator Walsh's national reputation grew as a result of his work in the Wilson presidential campaigns and the investigation of the Teapot Dome scandal in 1923–24. As a colleague of Walsh, Walker, too, became increasingly drawn into national party affairs. In 1925, without resigning from his Montana law firm, Walker moved to New York City to act as general counsel of the real estate and theater interests of an uncle, M.E. Comerford, in Pennsylvania, New York, and New England. Following Walsh's lead in supporting of Roosevelt, Walker became a Friend of Roosevelt, contributing generously to its campaign funds. By 1931, he was helping Farley plan the strategy for Roosevelt's presidential bid.

When Al Smith was still in the nominating race, it was not easy to induce regular Democratic party contributors to place their bets with the Friends of Roosevelt. The early contributors, however, added up to an important roster of subsequent New Deal leadership: Walker, Henry Morgenthau, Sr., industrialist William H. Woodin, Jesse I. Straus of Macy's in New York, Henry Morgenthau, Jr., Lieutenant Governor Herbert H. Lehman, Joseph P. Kennedy, Joseph E. Davies, Laurence Steinhardt, and James W. Gerard were among those who backed the incumbent president.

It was an era in which urban political machines were at the pinnacle of their power. Anton Cermak ruled Chicago. Frank Hague held sway in Jersey City. Boston was dominated by Jim Curley. Tom Pendergast was at the height of his career in Kansas City and Missouri. John F. Curry was at the head of Tammany Hall, remembering many lost encounters with Roosevelt, particularly during the Wilson era. A major force in the New York City organization was Ed Flynn, whose Bronx Democratic majorities were larger than those in any other borough and whose commitment to Roosevelt was early and firm. Flynn was not only a major contributor of funds, but also of information and personal contact with the big-city leaders.

Born, raised, and educated in the public schools of the Bronx, Edward J. Flynn received a law degree from Fordham University in 1909, at the age of eighteen. It was necessary for him to wait three years before he could be admitted to the New York Bar. Shortly thereafter, he became a member of the firm of Goldwater and Flynn, with which he remained affiliated throughout his life. Flynn was elected to the New York State assembly in 1917 and served for three terms. In Governor Smith's 1921 effort to replace Mayor Hylan with James J. Walker, Flynn supported Smith and Walker, while he ran for sheriff of the Bronx. Walker later appointed Flynn city chamberlain. From 1922 on, his status as Democratic leader of the Bronx remained unchallenged. Flynn lent himself energetically to the first Roosevelt campaign for governor and was particularly active during the ballot-counting in that close election.

Farley's activities were the most public of the team. As formal head of the Democratic party in New York State, it was he who could most legitimately press the Roosevelt case with party officials and potential national convention delegates in other state organizations. In addition, Farley's incomparable "personal touch," his prodigious ability to remember thousands of names, and his outstanding organizational skills were major sources of strength. With Farley in the field and Howe at headquarters, there was little prospect that the unruly currents of nominating politics would sweep the wrong way for front-runner Roosevelt.[1]

Having received the nomination, Roosevelt broke precedent by flying immediately to Chicago to accept in person. This flight was the first of many precedents soon to be broken. After the vice-presidential nomination and Roosevelt's acceptance speech, the national committee met to elect Farley its new chairman. As the committee concluded the re-election of a Roosevelt supporter, Robert H. Jackson of New Hampshire, as secretary, Roosevelt entered the room. He warmly lauded the achievements of the retiring officials—Raskob, Shouse, and Michelson—to each of whom he referred as "my old friend." Roosevelt noted that something of a speed record was being set, "The new national committee is organizing and we start the campaign at 10 o'clock tonight." He then requested that the committee elect the retiring and venerable national committeeman from New York, Norman E. Mack, "a member emeritus for life." This unusual request was granted.[2]

The campaign had not only an early start, but also an unusual organization. In the pattern set by Friends of Roosevelt, Farley continued to deal with people and Howe with words and plans. Howe was to be in charge of headquarters operations. Charlie Michelson was kept on to handle publicity. The "Brain Trust," a small group of college professors and other experts who had been working on national policy matters with Roosevelt during most of 1932, continued under the general supervision of Raymond Moley, with Rexford Tugwell, Adolph Berle, Sam Rosenman, and Basil O'Connor as a nucleus. The Brain Trust was broadened into a large advisory committee of other experts as the campaign progressed.

The usual procedure for setting up regional headquarters was discarded. There was only one national headquarters, in New York City. State party organizations were made responsible for work in their own states. Farley was particularly careful in dealing with the regular organizations in the states, even those where the leadership had vigorously opposed Roosevelt. The standard procedure adopted was to place a Roosevelt campaign headquarters under the general direction of the state committee. Members of the national committee were, to a large extent, made responsible to these campaign committees for the conduct of the state campaigns. During August, Farley arranged to meet with state chairmen in groups of eight to ten a day. These conferences were prolonged and important exchanges of information. Financial capacities of state organizations were examined, requirements for campaign literature were noted, and preferences for nationally known speakers were stated.

At national headquarters, the division of labor moved ahead rapidly. Frank Walker was appointed national committee treasurer. Evans Woollen, a conservative Indianapolis banker, was chosen chairman of the finance committee. Former Governor Harry F. Byrd of Virginia became chairman of the executive committee of the finance committee. These appointments were interpreted as significant gestures to the conservative and southern wing of the party. A labor committee was established, with Daniel J. Tobin, former treasurer of the American Federation of Labor, as chairman.

There were stenographic and mailing departments created at headquarters. Foreign and veterans divisions were put into operation. Probably the largest and most effective headquarters bureau was the women's division, whose talented leaders were Eleanor Roosevelt and Mary W. Dewson. Robert H. Jackson was put in charge of the speakers bureau. Provision was carefully made to coordinate the Garner and Roosevelt campaigns. Speaker Garner's campaign manager was Representative Samuel Rayburn of Texas.[3]

In writing his own account of 1932, Farley underscored several aspects of the campaign as particularly significant. Observing that less than 10 percent of the campaign literature ordinarily found its way to the rank and file, he arranged to have these materials sent directly to county and precinct workers throughout the country. Thus, the usual hazards of delay or loss at intervening headquarters were eliminated. Farley found the women's division to be "the most effective innovation of the 1932 campaign." He developed a special corps of assistants-to-the-chairmen, many of whom had special knowledge regarding sectional problems. Among these were Senators John S. Cohen, Joseph C. O'Mahoney, and Arthur J. Mullen. Located in an office close to Farley's and frequently consulted was Senator Claude Swanson of Virginia, chairman of the senatorial campaign committee. One other assistant reflected the growing interest of party managers in the infant science of public opinion polling: Emil E. Hurja, a statistician, prepared special analyses of the major polls of the day, particularly those of the *Literary Digest* and the Hearst polls.[4]

2

Of the 44 million votes cast, Roosevelt won by 12 million. His landslide victory was accompanied by a less happy set of statistics: over 12 million people were unemployed in a labor force of about 50 million; there were massive farm foreclosures, exhausted relief funds, and unprecedented numbers of bank failures; and foreign nations, even the scrupulous British, were defaulting on payment of their World War I debts to the United States.

The uncertainties of the months between election and inauguration deepened the nation's paralysis. Under these circumstances, the estimated 75,000 patronage positions immediately available for distribution by the Roosevelt administration took on particular economic as well as party interest. This distribution was postponed, however, for as long as possible in order to give Roosevelt greater leverage with Congress during the critical first months of the New Deal. When the distribution of jobs did begin, "Farley conducted the largest, most systematic, and the most overt patronage operation in history."[5]

Emil Hurja administered "The System." The tests for office seekers were simple: personal qualifications for the job and loyalty to the party. Quotas were established for jobs to be allocated to states and, within states, to various factions. Special priority was given to persons and groups that had been "FRBC" (For Roosevelt Before Chicago). In his memoirs, Farley stoutly defends the efficiency and usefulness of the system. He also points out that most of the recommendations were subject to the keen and knowledgeable scrutiny of President Roosevelt, whose service in the Wilson administration had given him an excellent grasp of the requirements of federal service. Roosevelt's principal patronage advisers were, as might be expected, Howe, Farley, Flynn, and Walker.[6]

The cabinet appointments were a mixture of politics and expertise, mainly the former. Senator Cordell Hull, a major force in pushing the party toward Roosevelt, became secretary of state. William Woodin, one of the original contributors to Friends of Roosevelt, headed Treasury. Governor George Dern of Utah, one of the earliest Roosevelt supporters in the West, became secretary of war. Appointment of Senator Swanson of Virginia, formerly chairman of the senatorial campaign committee, to head Navy was a gesture to the South. Out of obligation to William G. McAdoo, Roosevelt appointed Daniel C. Roper, McAdoo's longtime campaign manager, as secretary of commerce. Looking for a progressive Republican to bring into his official family, Roosevelt found Harold L. Ickes for Interior. Among the experts was Henry A. Wallace as secretary of agriculture; a former Republican, it was Wallace's father who served in the same position under Harding. For the Department of Labor, Roosevelt brought in his commissioner of labor at Albany, Frances Perkins.

The way Roosevelt appointed his postmaster general was typical of his relations with Farley. There was a tendency to take Farley for granted—which Farley later interpreted as a "reluctance to praise."[7] Roosevelt never mentioned a cabinet appointment to Farley, although the press had him designated as postmaster general for more than two months. In the midst of a patronage discussion with Farley, the president-elect commented on the incumbent postmaster general's recent purchase of a high-roofed automobile to facilitate the wearing of high hats. Said Roosevelt, "I see your predecessor is having difficulty with his hat." The significant word for Farley was "predecessor," to which he replied: "Thanks. I accept."[8]

Another intimate who had difficulty adjusting to Roosevelt's new status and entourage of political associates was Louis Howe. Howe was, as he always dreamed of being, appointed secretary to the president. However, observers noted that he had "difficulty in becoming emotionally adjusted to the frequent intrusion of others on the presence of his idol."[9] Even more unfortunate was the decline in Howe's always precarious health. By fall of 1934 he was doing much of his work in his White House bedroom. He did not live to participate in the 1936 national convention.

Roosevelt launched the New Deal with an inaugural address that expressed the revitalizing belief "that the only thing we have to fear is fear itself." He ordered the banks closed for several days until the solvent ones could be identified and reopened. Congress was called into special session. A reassuring "fireside chat"—one of a long series—was delivered over radio. An economy bill reducing governmental salaries was jammed through Congress. The Volstead Act was amended to permit the sale of light wine and beer.

The legislative calendar was crowded with New Deal measures, many of which were hastily drafted and enacted: the Agricultural Adjustment Act, introducing price supports for farm products and procedures for crop reduction, an emergency farm mortgage financing plan, a securities exchange bill to compel full publicity of stock issues and other stock market transactions, and the National Industrial Recovery Act, providing for codes of fair competition in industry, for organized labor's right of collective bargaining, and for $3.3 billion in public works.

The public works legislation was part of a broad attack on unemployment. The intention was to bring immediate relief to the more than twelve million unemployed. Attention to the nation's natural resources was long overdue. The New Deal tied the needs of employment to those of conservation through the Civilian Conservation Corps, which at once recruited several hundred thousand young men for emergency work at more than a thousand campsites around the country. The Public Works Administration was created as a separate organization under the supervision of a cabinet committee eventually led by the irrepressible Secretary of Interior Ickes.

Because direct charity was considered degrading by most Americans, possibly the most difficult and controversial program was the one designed to handle direct relief to the starving and destitute: the Federal Emergency Relief Administration (FERA), with $500 million to distribute in grants to states and localities. It was similar to an unprecedented emergency relief program Roosevelt had pushed through the New York State legislature during fall of 1931, a program that called for an appropriation of $20 million to find work for the needy or to provide them with "food against starvation and with clothing and shelter against suffering." To run the federal program Roosevelt asked Herbert Lehman, now governor of New York, to release the man who originally ran the New York program as chairman of the state's Temporary Emergency Relief Administration, Harry L. Hopkins.

Iowa-born, Hopkins, a New York social worker who had become deeply involved in the problem of finding work for homeless, unemployed men, had worked swiftly and imaginatively in administering the New York program. He now accomplished a similar performance as Federal Emergency Relief Administrator, in which capacity he reported directly to the president.

FERA made outright grants for direct relief and work relief. These grants were distributed indirectly through state relief organizations as well as directly through FERA's own state and local programs. Hopkins authorized making payments in cash instead of grocery slips, for clothing, shelter, and medical care as well as for food. He articulated a relief doctrine that challenged long-held American attitudes and made him one of the most controversial figures in the New Deal. Relief, according to Hopkins, was a sacred right rather than an act of charity; an obligation of government to its citizens rather than an emergency alleviation of suffering in the form of alms.[10]

Giving away money can be an extremely difficult enterprise. With a half billion dollars to give away and with responsibility for developing meaningful work programs, Hopkins found himself running across the concerns of National Chairman Farley and state Democratic organizations on the one hand and Secretary of Interior Ickes' public works program on the other.

The patronage implications of the FERA relief program were quickly recognized by the party leaders. Although Hopkins' immediate organization—121 employees—remained relatively small, these positions were not classified under civil service. More potentially "political" were the judgments of local FERA administrators in applying standards of need to applicants. A zealous Democratic administrator could easily and informally interpose a party loyalty test. While Hopkins endeavored, as a professional social worker, to keep administrators and tests nonpartisan, he eventually found that any new organization develops loyalties of its own and grows into a political machine whether intended or not. Before he fully realized it, Hopkins, with cash resources that no political party manager had dreamed of before, found himself running a political machine similar and parallel to Farley's.

The political character of FERA was nowhere better illustrated than in the case of the federal unemployment director for Missouri, Judge Harry S. Truman. A presiding county judge since 1922, Truman had a statewide reputation for honesty and efficiency in the handling of public funds. The reputation was based upon his achievements in building county roads and other public improvements during a period in which the Tom Pendergast machine of Kansas City was emptying the public till for its own purposes. By 1931, Truman was known in Missouri as a politician friendly to, yet independent of, the Pendergast organization. Hopkins' search for a loyal but honest Democrat to administer relief in Missouri led to Truman, and the two men struck up a long and cordial friendship.

Both men were undoubtedly drawn to each other by their common origin in the Midwest, their reputations for honesty and efficiency, their talent for translating broad social objectives into meticulously administered programs, their scrappy postures in political battles, and their intense concern for the social and economic crisis brought on by mass unemployment. In their very first conversations, Hopkins explored with Truman ways in which to accomplish wholesale employment. Truman strongly endorsed proposals then developing in Hopkins' mind.[11]

As the biggest and fastest spender in Washington, Hopkins' activities were increasingly of concern to President Roosevelt. Roosevelt entrusted to Frank Walker the task of keeping an eye on Hopkins. The opportunities for waste and corruption were enormous. However, after a thorough personal investigation, Walker assured Roosevelt that criticism of Hopkins' management was entirely unfounded. Largely as a consequence of Walker's reports, Roosevelt came to consider Hopkins one of his most trusted associates.

The 1934 midterm election was the first in U.S. history in which the party of an incumbent administration gained rather than lost seats in Congress. Promptly after the election, Hopkins initiated plans for what became the Works Progress Administration (WPA). This was done in collaboration with Ickes. The Work Relief Bill called for an appropriation of $5 billion and contained provisions that brought Hopkins directly up against the facts of political life. All Works Progress administrators receiving a salary of $5,000 or more per annum were to be appointed by the president by and with the advice and consent of the Senate. This meant that senatorial courtesy and the recommendations of National Chairman Farley would have to be taken into account in building the new agency. Pondered Hopkins, "I thought at first I could be completely non-political. I found that was impossible, at least for me. I finally realized there was nothing for it but to be all-political." From 1935 on Hopkins became a major influence in the Democratic party. In 1940, he was among those most seriously considered by Roosevelt as available to be his successor in the presidency.[12]

3

By 1935, reaction to the New Deal set in. Unemployment and poverty were still very much in evidence. Conservatives, Democratic and Republican alike, were increasingly resisting the manner in which the Roosevelt administration seemed to be altering the traditional values of American society. The right to work, the right to receive emergency relief, the right to bargain collectively in industrial relations, governmental encouragement of industrial collusion under the National Recovery Administration (NRA), the payment of subsidies so that farmers would not produce—these and other principles seemed to be turning the American value structure upside down.

One response was the creation of the American Liberty League, organized during the fall of 1934 by former National Chairman Raskob, with Jouett Shouse as its director. It had the endorsement of former presidential nominees John W. Davis and Alfred E. Smith. A hard-hitting speech by Smith inaugurated the league's operations. A few days later, Senator Joseph T. Robinson of Arkansas made a nationwide radio address replying to Smith's charges. Farley turned the rhetorical artillery of national headquarters against the league, with instructions "to ignore the Republican Party." In this way, the public began to perceive the league as a millionaires' club and Smith's speeches as personal bitterness. Roosevelt referred to the league as evidence that concentrated wealth was the source of opposition to his programs.

Almost to the day of his death in April 1936, Louis Howe worried how the league's activities might influence the platform committee at the 1936 convention. He need not have been concerned. The platform draft that went before the committee was prepared by Sam Rosenman, under the president's supervision, in collaboration with William Bullitt, Donald Richberg, and Harry Hopkins.

There was little for the 1936 Democratic convention to decide. Despite the country's continuing economic problems, most of the opposition to Roosevelt was from Republicans or minor Democratic factions laying the groundwork for future battles. Within the party, Roosevelt, Garner, and Farley were about as popular as the top leadership of a party could be.

A real issue before the convention was the question of abrogating the two-thirds nominating rule. Even on this issue, the climate of opinion within the party was unusually favorable, making it possible to resolve the issue with minimum pressure. After token opposition by some southern delegates, the convention abolished what Farley called "the obnoxious two-thirds nominating rule, by means of which the party had on so many occasions in the past strangled itself into suicide." As a gesture to the southerners, the convention instructed the national committee to develop a plan of delegate apportionment that would take into account party strength and reward it by some bonus arrangement. The "ayes" and "nays" on the convention vote sounded about equal in volume, but Convention Chairman Joseph T. Robinson did not hesitate to declare the rule abrogated.[13]

The preparations for the 1936 election campaign had been long in the making. Despite instructions from Roosevelt in 1934 that the costs of national headquarters be cut in half, Farley maintained more than the usual off-year skeleton crew. From early in 1936, the national headquarters was occupied with updating contacts with state, county, and local organizations and with the campaign against the Liberty League. Farley made several trips around the country to pep up the organization and identify local problems. It was during one of these trips that he referred to Alf Landon as governor of "a typical prairie state." Roosevelt was quick to admonish Farley, sending a memorandum on the same day of the speech to say that "the word 'typical' coming from any New Yorker is meat for the opposition." The Republicans picked up the phrase and made much of it for nearly two weeks.[14]

It was Farley's intention that the campaign be a "one man show," which is as it turned out to be. Roosevelt's campaign train made a wide sweep across the country. With him was Sam Rosenman, handling nearly all of the on-the-spot speech writing. At Washington headquarters were other members of the speech team: Stanley High, a former Republican, and the soon-to-be-famous team of Corcoran and Cohen. The president was greeted everywhere by lively crowds.

An important appreciation from the businessman's point of view came from Joseph P. Kennedy's book *I Am For Roosevelt*, a widely distributed volume defending the New Deal, in which Kennedy revealed that "I am not ashamed to record that in those days (of the Depression) I felt and said I would be willing to part with half of what I had if I could be sure of keeping, under law and order, the other half."[15]

The 1936 campaign was also the occasion for strains in old political friendships and the intrusion of new ones upon the old. The president asked Eleanor Roosevelt to "look in" on the organizational activities of the national committee headquarters. On the basis of her conferences with Farley, Michelson, High, Early, and Miss Dewson, Mrs. Roosevelt prepared a lengthy memorandum covering the organizational problems she perceived. This was the kind of assessment that Louis Howe used to make orally rather than in writing. Farley, hurt by the implied lack of confidence in his work, prepared a reply that was twenty pages long.[16]

Farley did some assessing of his own with regard to Harry Hopkins' activities. He found an opportunity to tell Hopkins that 75 percent of the complaints received at national headquarters from party workers had to do with dissatisfactions caused by the WPA. Farley must have taken special pleasure in reporting to Hopkins that "the people had the impression he (Hopkins) was a spendthrift."[17] The complaints notwithstanding, Roosevelt was at this time, perhaps subconsciously, looking around for someone to succeed the deceased Louis Howe as political confidant and legman. This role eventually fell to Hopkins.

In the second volume of his memoirs, Farley refers to the 1936 campaign as the beginning of a "drifting apart" between Roosevelt and himself. During October "they"—presumably the president and his other advisers—suggested that Farley not appear with the president on the platform of the campaign train. Farley's personal popularity apparently distracted too much attention from Roosevelt.

> Looking back through the years, I find it hard to put the finger of memory on the beginning of the drift, so gradual was the process. Almost before I knew it, I was no longer called to the White House for morning bedside conferences. My phone no longer brought the familiar voice in mellifluous tones. Months dragged between White House luncheon conferences. Soon I found I was no longer being consulted on appointments, even in my own state. Then, too, I found I was as much in the dark about the President's political plans as the Chairman of the Republican National Committee. White House confidence on politics and policies went to a small band of zealots, who mocked at party loyalty and knew no devotion except unswerving obedience to their leader. . . . What few people realize is that relationship between Roosevelt and me had been basically political and seldom social. Strange as it may seem, the President never took me into the bosom of the family, although everyone agreed I was more responsible than any other single man for his being in the White House.[18]

Farley's excellent relations with the leadership and rank and file of the Democratic party brought him an unusual flow of information regarding the leanings of the voters. From reports and letters received at national headquarters, Farley was able to make a thorough analysis of the party situation in each state before election eve. On November 1, in the headquarters election pool, he bet as follows, "Landon will only carry Maine and Vermont. Seven electoral votes."[19] This was precisely the outcome, and Farley's reputation as a political seer was impressively confirmed.

4

The overwhelming popular vote of confidence gave Roosevelt a basis for launching a "second coming" of the New Deal. The nation's problems of 1932 were still tenaciously at hand, and the New Deal continued to test programs that might resolve them. But, in a series of recent decisions, the Supreme Court had invalidated many New Deal measures, bringing the president's program to a dead halt. In his second inaugural address, Roosevelt complained that he still saw "one-third of a nation ill-housed, ill-clad, ill-nourished." His annual message conveyed his concern over the impasse between the executive and judicial branches.

On February 5, 1937, Roosevelt sent to the Senate a series of recommendations for a general reorganization of the judiciary from the Supreme Court down to the district courts. The heart of the message was the proposal that whenever a judge reached the retirement age of seventy in any federal court, but refused to avail himself of the opportunity to retire on a pension, an additional judge should be appointed to that court by the president, with the approval of the Senate. The proposal would have resulted in the addition of six new members to "the Nine Old Men" then on the Supreme Court. The proposal was immediately denounced from many quarters as a "court packing plan."

Although the membership of the Supreme Court had been expanded several times by previous presidents under legislation passed by Congress, this time an increase was obviously little more than an attempt to strike back at an unfriendly Court. With dictators rising abroad and the separation of powers under the Constitution at issue, Roosevelt's proposal was politically vulnerable from the outset. In the retrospective opinion of his close adviser, Sam Rosenman, the plan "became the most controversial proposal Roosevelt ever made during his twelve years as President, and cost him much in prestige, particularly in party prestige."[20]

Roosevelt prepared the recommendation in great secrecy with the help of a few White House aides and Attorney General Cummings. It was released in part as a surprise attack and in part on the pretext that it was an ordinary proposal designed to relieve the congestion in the federal courts. Farley later complained to the president about this unusual procedure, particularly the lack of clearance with the party leadership in Congress. "Boss," he queried, "why didn't you advise the Senators in advance that you were sending the Court bill to them?" Roosevelt's reply was that he did not wish to have the plan leak prematurely to the press and that he was particularly concerned with its success.[21]

Senate Majority Leader Robinson carried the burden of the legislative campaign for the plan, assisted by Senator Pat Harrison of Mississippi and James F. Byrnes of South Carolina. The earliest opposition came from Democratic Senators Joseph Clark of Missouri, Burton Wheeler of Montana, and James F. Burke of Nebraska. The Republican strategy, developed by Senator William E. Borah, was simply to let Democrats lead the entire fight both for and against the proposal. What rankled Roosevelt most was that the principal opposition came from within his own party. The non-New Dealers in the party, particularly in the

Senate, were determined to demonstrate to the popular president that there were three, not merely two, branches in the national government.

Opponents of the bill adopted the strategy of delay. This was intended to allow public opinion to materialize and events, some quite unexpected, to unfold. During March and April, the Supreme Court began to reverse itself on New Deal legislation, upholding the minimum wage law for women, the National Labor Relations Act, and the Social Security Act. On June 2, Justice Van Devanter announced that, now seventy-eight, he planned to retire immediately; Van Devanter had been one of the most steadfast of the conservatives on the Court.

An unexpected political shock came with the sudden death of Majority Leader Robinson on June 13, depriving the president of his most effective representative in the battle. Even prior to Robinson's death, it had become evident that the Democratic majority in the Senate was thoroughly split on the issue.

The split continued to manifest itself in the fight over the selection of Robinson's successor. Pat Harrison of Mississippi and Alben Barkley of Kentucky were the principal contenders. Farley reports that Roosevelt told him to keep "hands off" this battle between two party stalwarts. However, Roosevelt himself addressed a famous note to "Dear Alben" and subsequently asked Harry Hopkins to help swing a few pivotal votes to Barkley.[22]

By July, the defeat of Roosevelt's proposal seemed inevitable. New Dealers, nevertheless, claimed victory in view of the reversal in Court opinions. They also were happy that the president would be able to choose a liberal to replace Van Devanter. The anti-New Dealers were pleased that the Senate's rejection of the Roosevelt plan on July 22 preserved the integrity of that institution. What the Court fight did disclose in all its depth was the existence of a factional split within the Democratic party, with anti-Roosevelt "headquarters" located in the U.S. Senate.

One of the principal incitements to division was Roosevelt's statement of March 4, 1937, delivered at a Democratic victory dinner, that he longed to turn over his office to a successor on January 20, 1941, "whoever he may be," with the assurance that he was turning over to him a nation that was at peace, prosperous, and ambitious to meet the needs of humanity. Talk of a third term for Roosevelt had begun almost immediately after his re-election the previous November. His March 4 announcement did not have the technical finality of a complete withdrawal, but it did come unusually early in the second term.

Jockeying among the presidential availables also began somewhat early. Crowding the field were Vice-President Garner, Speaker William B. Bankhead, Secretary of State Cordell Hull, Farley, Byrnes of South Carolina, Jesse Jones, and Harry Hopkins. Of these, Farley was by far the most popular among the party rank and file and, in many ways, the most available.[23]

The unabashed opposition of many major Democratic leaders to Roosevelt's Supreme Court plan in the spring of 1937, the severe split in the Senate leadership over the succession, and the defeat of the wages and hours and the administrative reorganization bills during the fall left Roosevelt keenly sensitive about the effectiveness of his own party leadership. By the end of the year, the problem of reasserting that leadership was paramount in his mind.

Roosevelt was also aware that the resources of the presidency for disciplining recalcitrant Democrats were extremely limited, particularly in a second, and presumably "lame duck," term. The usual presidential patronage was, by and large, disposed of or otherwise committed. The leverage afforded by the emergency programs had diminished. His own March statement appeared to undermine the third-term threat available to re-elected presidents.

One tactic never used was presidential endorsement of or opposition to candidates in Democratic party primary elections. One of the unwritten rules of American national politics had been the nonintervention of national leaders in the state and local contests among their fellow-partisans. At least, such intervention could not be overt. Indirect pressures, however, were assumed to be inevitable, and Roosevelt had not previously been reluctant to use such pressures. According to Farley, for example, Roosevelt tried to intervene in 1937 against the renomination of Ed Kelly for the mayoralty of Chicago, but had reversed himself when Farley informed him that Kelly could not be beaten.[24]

During 1938, Roosevelt considered a plan to intervene in certain Democratic primary elections, giving support to liberals wherever they stood out clearly against conservatives. Hopkins, Ickes, and Corcoran strongly urged this course. Farley took the position that such a procedure would be unwise in the interest of party unity and, further, that as national chairman, he personally would be technically prohibited from interfering in local fights. Farley had to and wanted to be neutral. Hopkins, recovering from surgery for cancer of the stomach, was compelled to take a backseat during his convalescence, leaving Corcoran to manage the Roosevelt endorsement tactic.

In a fireside chat on June 24, 1938, Roosevelt discussed the accomplishments and failures of the Seventy-fifth Congress. He closed the address with the following:

> As the head of the Democratic Party, however, charged with the responsibility of carrying out the definitely liberal declaration of principles set forth in the 1936 Democratic platform, I feel that I have every right to speak in those few instances where there may be a clear issue between candidates for a Democratic nomination involving these principles, or involving a clear misuse of my own name.[25]

Consequently, in the summer and fall, Roosevelt urged the nomination of Lawrence Camp over Senator Walter George in the Georgia primaries, David J. Lewis over Senator Millard Tydings in Maryland, James H. Fay over Representative John J. O'Connor in New York. The "purge," as his opponents called it, was a failure, although it set an important precedent regarding presidential involvement in primaries. Roosevelt won only in the case of O'Connor. The November returns added additional salt to Roosevelt's political wounds. Republicans gained eighty-two seats in the House and eight seats in the Senate.

The 1938 returns seemed to confirm the position taken by Garner and Farley, namely, that the New Deal needed to move to the right and that reconciliation with conservatives in Congress was necessary. Farley wrote to party leaders throughout the country, inviting their evaluations of the returns and explanations for the defeat. The replies, which Farley passed on to the president, were a catalog of conservative arguments: criticism of the spending program, complaints about CIO (Congress of Industrial Organizations) influence in the administration, low farm prices, dissatisfaction with the WPA program, business protest against regimentation, and the unfriendly press. Roosevelt thanked Farley for the letters on December 2, 1938, and suggested that "you ought to start a special division of the National Committee to begin giving the [newly elected Republican Governors] 'the works' as soon as they take office." The suggested bureau was never established. Meanwhile, opinion polls were showing Farley and Hull among the leaders most favored for the succession upon Roosevelt's retirement.[26]

The Farley report's reference to WPA reflected a general anti-New Deal campaign directed particularly at the relief agencies. For example, Representative Martin Dies, chairman of the House Un-American Activities Committee, was determined to root out of government such "subversives" as Harry Hopkins, Harold Ickes, Frances Perkins, and similar "Communists and fellow-travelers." The three individuals named were closely identified with the relief activities of the Roosevelt administration.

During 1938, Hopkins' personal and political life was undergoing substantial change. He left the Mayo Clinic in January and spent some time recuperating at the Florida home of Joseph P. Kennedy. He returned to Washington in time to work on the "purges." Then, during the spring, President Roosevelt and he had a long conversation about the 1940 Democratic nomination and election.

5

According to Hopkins' notes, Roosevelt did not rule out the possibility that he might seek a third term, particularly in the event of war. The president, however, did express strong personal and financial reasons for wishing to return to private life. Roosevelt then expressed opposition to Hull (too cold), Wallace, Ickes (too combative), McNutt, Governor Frank Murphy of Michigan, and Governor George Earle of Pennsylvania. Robert M. La Follette's name was mentioned in passing, but eliminated. Roosevelt considered Farley the "most dangerous'' and opposed the national chairman for his conservatism and his attitudes on foreign affairs.[27]

"Roosevelt expressed the belief that Hopkins could be elected (despite his recent illness and the circumstances of his divorce from his first wife) and would do the best job as President of any of those then in the running." The president then discussed strategy, concluding with the statement that he would appoint Hopkins as secretary of commerce. Roosevelt suggested that Hopkins "keep back a little" and apparently considered the transfer from relief administrator to secretary of commerce as a means of taking Hopkins out of the line of anti-New Deal fire. In December 1938, the president announced the appointment of Hopkins to the secretary of commerce post. Hopkins' confirmation by the Senate came only after lengthy debate. Roosevelt was taking his lessons about the succession from his cousin Theodore's experience and avoiding that of Woodrow Wilson.

As the Hitler machine drove the world toward war in 1939, Hopkins apparently set aside all his expectations of making a bid for the presidency. In June, he made his first public statement advocating a third term for Roosevelt. He and Eleanor Roosevelt engaged in a lively argument on the matter, with Mrs. Roosevelt taking the position that "the President has done his part entirely." During the summer, Hopkins again became ill, returning to the Mayo Clinic in August. The Germans attacked Poland on September 1. The Second World War was under way, and public discussion of a third term grew in intensity.

The public opinion polls, only in their third year of surveying presidential politics, but increasingly influential among politicians, began to show a rising popular acceptance of the third-term idea. The polls also showed Farley as a leading candidate among Democratic voters if the president decided not to run again. According to Farley, Cardinal Mundelein of Chicago spoke with him in July 1939, apparently at Roosevelt's suggestion, urging the postmaster general to withdraw his name. The cardinal feared that a Catholic would meet with the same fate that Smith had in 1928. Farley disagreed with this estimate of the situation and a year later found an opportunity to tell Roosevelt directly that a Catholic in the second spot on the ticket might even strengthen it. At no time, however, did Roosevelt consider Farley seriously for the vice-presidential nomination on a ticket with himself.[28]

In mid-December, Vice-President Garner announced his candidacy. Garner, the least vulnerable to presidential displeasure, intended to allow his name to become the rallying point for anti-third-term sentiment. When the convention was less than three weeks off, on June 28, Farley made up his mind that he, too, would allow his name to go before the convention. He resigned from the cabinet and the national chairmanship. A week later, on July 6, he and the president held a long conference at Hyde Park.

Farley frankly declared his views on the third term. "I was against it in principle and because the Democratic Party had always opposed it.'' Roosevelt offered pros and cons on the subject, then proceeded to review vice-presidential prospects and convention arrangements. Roosevelt asked Farley to urge Hull to accept second place, but the postmaster general declined to do so.

Farley then advised the president that he could "under no circumstances" run the campaign. Farley suggested Frank Walker, then treasurer of the national committee, as his successor in the chairmanship. Roosevelt agreed, and then asked if Senator Byrnes would be a good alternative. James F. Byrnes had for some time been a Roosevelt stalwart in the Senate and was under consideration by the president for either the vice-presidency or the national chairmanship.[29]

The Louis Howe of the 1940 Democratic national convention was Harry Hopkins. While still head of WPA, Hopkins had collected political IOUs from Democratic leaders and mayors of many of the major cities: Kelly of Chicago, Hague of Jersey City, Lawrence of Pittsburgh, and others. It was general knowledge that he, Ed Flynn, Frank Walker, and Kelly of Chicago made up the president's inner political council at this time. It was Hopkins who set up the Roosevelt convention headquarters at the Blackstone Hotel in Chicago and had a private telephone line leading from his hotel bathroom directly to the White House.

According to Hopkins' report to Sam Rosenman, the president wanted as his running mate Hull, Byrnes, or Wallace, in that order.[30] Hull steadfastly resisted presidential pressure in order to continue in his position as secretary of state "in the troublous days ahead."[31] Byrnes also resisted the honor that was offered to him about ten days before the national convention. He later wrote in his memoirs,

> In my opinion, the third-term fight would be a close one, and if Mr. Roosevelt should be defeated many would attribute his failure not to the real cause but to the fact that a South Carolinian had been selected as his running mate. It would then be many years before a national convention would again nominate a Southerner for either office.[32]

The choice for vice-president settled upon Wallace, whose record as secretary of agriculture and whose strong New Deal views on domestic and international matters appealed to the president. Despite Farley's comment that "the people look on him as a wild-eyed fellow," it was Roosevelt's opinion that Wallace would help the campaign in the farm states as well as the cities where he had the strong labor endorsement of the Congress of Industrial Organizations (CIO).

The national convention moved to its duties amid an undercurrent of uncertainty. The president confused the situation by communicating through Barkley that "all of the delegates to this convention are free to vote for any candidate." The moment this message had been read, however, the loudspeakers boomed "We want Roosevelt!" Mayor Kelly's "voice from the sewer" left no doubt which way the convention management wanted the delegates to vote.

Garner and Farley refused to withdraw. The vote was Roosevelt 946½ votes, Farley 72½, Garner 61, Tydings 9, and Hull 5. Garner's support came from Texas, as expected, Farley's from New York, Massachusetts, Alaska, Canal Zone, and scattered votes from elsewhere. His protest against the third term thus recorded, Farley moved to suspend the rules and make the nomination unanimous.

Trouble followed in connection with the vice-presidential decision. The anti-New Deal wing pressed for recognition. Their candidates were Jesse Jones, Speaker Bankhead, and Paul McNutt. Referring to Jones and Bankhead, the president told Rosenman, as they waited upon reports from Chicago, "I'm going to tell them that I won't run with either of those men or with any other reactionary." Over the telephone to Hopkins, Roosevelt reiterated his preference for Wallace at least three times.

McNutt mounted the rostrum to withdraw his name and support the choice (Wallace) of his commander-in-chief. Philip Murray of the CIO seconded Wallace's nomination, Congressman Sam Rayburn withdrew his name and became another Wallace second. The final move was the arrival of Eleanor Roosevelt to remind the delegates that "this is no ordinary time." Wallace was nominated, but over 40 percent of the convention's votes stubbornly voted for Speaker Bankhead and others. Wallace's nomination established a precedent: the naming of a vice-presidential candidate from the same wing of the party as the presidential nominee.[33]

To implement the instructions of the 1936 convention, this convention voted to establish a bonus vote system by giving two delegates-at-large to each state going Democratic in its presidential vote.

Farley's withdrawal from the national chairmanship left him in the New York State chairmanship, a position he had never relinquished. Roosevelt began the search for a successor. The first offer went to Byrnes, who declined on grounds that his duties in the Senate would have to come first. Byrnes proposed Joseph P. Kennedy, then ambassador to Great Britain. The president telephoned, but Kennedy also declined.[34]

Roosevelt retreated to two "old reliables": Frank Walker and Ed Flynn. Walker "felt that he was not sufficiently acquainted with the leaders and temperamentally was not suited for the arduous task involved." Flynn, considering himself too much the symbol of the political boss, declined no less than three times. The fourth offer came in a conference at Hyde Park with the president, Hopkins, and Walker present. Wendell Willkie's surprise nomination by the Republicans and his hard-hitting campaign meant that re-election was not yet a "sure thing" for Roosevelt. It was essential that someone who was already thoroughly acquainted with the Democratic organization throughout the country take the national chairmanship. Flynn reluctantly accepted.[35]

Roosevelt never lost interest in the organizational aspects of national headquarters. For example, in March 1940, he suggested that the records of the national committee during the period of his administration be deposited at the Hyde Park library. Writing to Mary Dewson of the women's division, he observed, "There are in existence, so far as I know, no records of Republican or Democratic National Committees in Presidential campaigns. Automatically, when a new Chairman takes over the old records have been destroyed." Preservation of such records, he thought, would be "of real historical importance."[36] Unfortunately, the preoccupations of the European war and the burdens of presidential duties never permitted Roosevelt to give the attention he wished to party organizational matters.

The national committee headquarters in 1940 went through a period of semiparalysis as the delicate transition from Farley to Flynn was being made. Farley remained at national headquarters for a month to help Flynn orient himself. As Charlie Michelson observed, "That was a trying time for us at headquarters. Flynn and Farley were old and intimate friends, and each was so fearful of treading on the other's toes that nothing was done during the joint incumbency . . . so a great friendship was preserved—and a month of campaign time was wasted."[37] From Flynn's point of view, "The national organization was a Farley organization, and as a new man on the job I had to exercise great tact and patience."[38]

Hopkins resigned as secretary of commerce in August because of ill health. By October, however, he had recovered sufficiently to move into a central staff position in the campaign. He and Rosenman recruited the playwright Robert E. Sherwood as part of a three-man speech-writing team that assisted the president for the remainder of the campaign. Hopkins served as chief of this informal group and, in Rosenman's opinion, established himself as "unquestionably the most influential of those who worked with (Roosevelt)" during the last five years of the president's life, "the most important years." Rosenman goes on to observe, "In many ways it was as strong as the earlier influence of Louis Howe; in many ways the two men were similar in character and in the way they worked. They were both extremely suspicious of people who sought access to the President, and jealous of almost anyone else who was close to him." As war approached, Harry Hopkins was invited to occupy quarters at the White House.[39]

As Flynn began to take full charge of national headquarters, he reappointed some of Farley's staff and brought in many new staff people. Oliver Quayle remained as treasurer and Charlie Michelson as director of publicity. In Flynn's words, "The actual mechanics of the campaign had, of necessity, to be in charge of a new group of men."[40] Edwin W. Pauley, an oil magnate from California, volunteered to help raise money in that faction-ridden state as well as nationally. Oscar Ewing, later vice-chairman of the national committee and federal security administrator, became an active headquarters aide.

One particularly difficult dilemma that confronted Flynn was dealing with an influential nonparty group, the National Citizens Political Action Committee (NCPAC), headed by George W. Norris and Fiorello La Guardia. The latter was a renegade Republican running for re-election as mayor of New York. NCPAC was organized to advance the liberal New Deal point of view during the campaign. Although La Guardia supported Roosevelt and the New Deal, the New York City contest was one in which Flynn had to join Farley in supporting the regular Democratic ticket.

Roosevelt's 5 million vote margin of victory over Willkie was less than the 11 and 12 million margins to which Roosevelt had become accustomed. Roosevelt himself enjoyed referring to the election as "close." The campaign for re-election over, Roosevelt now devoted his full energy to aiding the Western powers against the Axis. It was not easy to do this within the limits of American and international law.

In December, the president enunciated for the first time the concept of lend-lease. By May of 1941, he found it necessary to declare an unlimited national emergency. In August 1941, he and Winston Churchill propounded the Atlantic Charter. On December 7, the Japanese launched their surprise attack on Pearl Harbor. The United States was at war with the Axis.

War brought new assignments to Roosevelt's associates. Byrnes, who had been appointed to the Supreme Court, resigned in October 1942, to become director of economic stabilization. Half a year later, Byrnes was heading the Office of War Mobilization, a superagency intended as a mediator of interdepartmental disputes. In this job, Byrnes became known as "The Assistant President."

National Chairman Flynn waited patiently to be relieved of his duties. Flynn states in his memoirs:

> I had taken the position as National Chairman with the understanding that I would resign immediately after the election. I reminded Roosevelt of the understanding, and he agreed that we should do something about it. It was not easy to find a successor, however. Things drifted for some time. Meantime, as National Chairman I was the target for more than the usual amount of newspaper abuse. Over one case in particular [referring to the charge that he had used public materials—paving blocks—to have a parking space built at his Putnam County home] the press was especially vehement.[41]

As Flynn suffered through a prolonged period of unfavorable publicity regarding the "paving blocks scandal," national headquarters remained in a state of dormancy, with only a skeleton staff. Late in 1942, President Roosevelt asked Flynn to accept the ambassadorship to Australia, where he could perform double duty as ambassador-at-large for the South Pacific, a region about to become of major strategic significance. When he accepted the appointment, Flynn resigned his various party positions: leader of Bronx

County, national committeeman from New York, and national chairman.

Unexpectedly, the ambassadorial appointment, involving an old and trusted political friend of the president, provided a convenient target against which much pent-up hostility toward Roosevelt could be vented. After public hearings by the Senate Committee on Foreign Relations, it became apparent that the nomination could not be confirmed by the Senate without a rough battle. At Flynn's request, Roosevelt withdrew the nomination. Flynn was promptly re-elected Democratic leader of Bronx County and national committeeman from New York. He insisted that his resignation as national chairman stand.

At the time he announced his resignation as national chairman to accept the ambassadorship, Flynn arranged for a meeting of the national committee for January 18, 1943. This meeting took place several weeks before his nomination as ambassador was withdrawn. To serve as caretaker of the chairmanship, Roosevelt called upon Postmaster General Frank Walker. In a telegram to Edwin Pauley, secretary of the national committee, taking note of the Flynn resignation, Roosevelt half-facetiously said:

> I see by the papers that his [Flynn's] successor will probably be another very old friend of mine—one who has worked long and intimately with me in the cause of sound, liberal government. Please extend to the new chairman my best wishes for his usual success in whatever he undertakes.[42]

6

Walker accepted the position only to relieve the president of the immediate pressure to find a new chairman. With military and diplomatic developments consuming every moment of the president's time, the task of recruiting a chairman in time for the 1944 campaign eventually was undertaken without the president's direct participation.

Walker continued the policy of maintaining a tiny crew at headquarters. He put Assistant Postmaster General Ambrose O'Connell in charge of headquarters management and enlisted George E. Allen to serve as national committee secretary. In the belief that partisan politics was out of order during the war crisis, Walker suggested to Republican National Chairman Spangler that the 1944 national conventions be postponed until autumn in order to minimize the distractions of the fall campaign. The suggestion was not accepted.[43]

Meanwhile, both Flynn and Walker, keenly aware of the president's preoccupations, gave much of their attention to the search for a successor. Late in 1943, Mayor Kelly of Chicago proposed to Flynn the name of Commissioner of Internal Revenue Robert E. Hannegan. Hannegan, a former chairman of the St. Louis Democratic organization, was reputed to be one of the most astute and energetic of the younger party leader. Flynn thought it was a good suggestion, and in later years wrote:

> I had become acquainted with Hannegan when he was a candidate for the position of Internal Revenue Collector for the district of St. Louis, Missouri. Later I met him in connection with my work in the National Committee. When Guy T. Helvering retired from the office of Commissioner of Internal Revenue, I recommended Hannegan to the President as a successor, entirely because of the fine record he had made in Missouri.
>
> When I returned from Florida I spoke to the President about Hannegan as a suitable man for the chairmanship of the National Committee. After some consideration, Roosevelt agreed, and the National Committee elected Hannegan in January 1944.[44]

As national chairman, Hannegan went directly to work rebuilding national headquarters. He inaugurated a nationwide drive to help transient war workers register for the coming presidential election. He embarked upon a series of tours of the country to meet local leaders and precinct workers. He took careful soundings of factional difficulties in state and local organizations around the country and appraised organization opinion regarding a fourth nomination for Roosevelt. That renomination seemed inevitable.

The real issue before the 1944 convention, Hannegan found, would be the replacement of Henry Wallace as vice-president. Those most prominently mentioned for the vice-presidential nomination were Speaker Sam Rayburn, Senate Majority Leader Alben Barkley, Justice William O. Douglas, "Assistant President" James F. Byrnes, and Senator Truman. Truman had come into national prominence as head of the Senate committee investigating the management of the national defense program.

When Truman began his second term in the Senate in 1940, the United States was taking its first major steps toward the mobilization of its military and economic resources for national defense. Dramatic increases in defense outlays made possible all kinds of corruption and inefficiency in the handling of public funds. In February 1941, Truman put forward a proposal for creating a watchdog committee on defense spending.

Truman was knowledgeable about the conduct of similar committees during previous wars and appreciated the political implications of such investigations. He was aware how an unfriendly Committee on the Conduct of the [Civil] War, dominated by Radical Republicans, harassed President Lincoln. He was determined that his own committee would be friendly to the Roosevelt administration, yet in dead earnest about flushing out waste and corruption. On March 1, 1941, the committee was established with a fund of only $15,000. It evoked little interest on the Senate floor or elsewhere. Truman pulled together an investigating staff that included Hugh Fulton, Matthew J. Connelly, Fred Canfil, Colonel Harry Vaughan, and William M. Boyle.

Truman ran his committee with what was characterized as a "sort of unspec-

Robert E. Hannegan, born in 1903, was the son of a St. Louis police captain. Educated at St. Louis University, where he was active in athletics and in the organization of a student Democratic club, he received his law degree in 1925. Hannegan coached and played football and baseball for a short time as he established his law practice. For the next seven or eight years, he participated as an active worker for the Democratic party in the Twenty-first Ward of St. Louis and was elected ward chairman in 1933. Joining forces with Bernard F. Dickmann, mayor of St. Louis, Hannegan was elected chairman of the Democratic city central committee in 1933. In the factional struggles of 1935, Hannegan was temporarily deposed, but was promptly appointed by Dickmann as St. Louis' legislative representative at the Missouri General Assembly. He returned to the city chairmanship in 1936. The Dickmann-Hannegan machine prevailed in St. Louis over the next several years.

In Kansas City, meanwhile, the fabled Pendergast machine was falling upon evil times. Tom Pendergast was indicted in April 1939 for income tax evasion. The scandal not only undermined the Democratic organization in Kansas City, but in Missouri as well. These developments elevated the Dickmann-Hannegan organization to first place in the state, and a St. Louis man was nominated for the governorship for the first time in decades. In 1940, however, the entire state Democratic slate was in peril. The Republicans elected a governor, but Senator Harry S. Truman was narrowly re-elected by an 8,000-vote margin turned out for him in St. Louis by the Dickmann-Hannegan organization. When Dickmann failed in his bid for re-election as mayor in 1941, Hannegan turned his attention to his growing law practice.

Meanwhile, early in 1942, Senator Truman proposed Hannegan to Secretary of the Treasury Morgenthau for the vacancy occurring in the post of collector of internal revenue of the Eastern District of Missouri. The Missouri newspapers launched a campaign against the appointment, but Truman announced, "Hannegan carried St. Louis three times for the President and me. If he is not nominated there will be no collector at St. Louis. I think I have enough friends in the Senate to see that no other person gets the job."[45] Gaining a national reputation for his outstanding performance in reorganizing the Eastern District office, in 1943 Hannegan was chosen to be commissioner of internal revenue in Washington.

The Boyle family was living in Leavenworth, Kansas, when William Marshall Boyle, Jr., was born in 1902, one of a set of twins. The family moved to Kansas City, Missouri, where the elder Boyle engaged in the broomcorn business. Young William attended Kansas City Junior College. At age 16, he organized a Young Democrats' Club in the "silk stocking" ward of Kansas City and subsequently became a ward chairman. In 1922, he went to Washington, DC, to study at the Georgetown University law school, returning to complete his training at the Kansas City School of Law in 1926. While practicing law, Boyle served as leader of the Eighth Ward Democratic organization.

Boyle was appointed secretary to the director of police in Kansas City during the late 1930s, becoming acting director when the incumbent was indicted, along with Tom Pendergast, for income tax evasion. After several months as acting director of police, Boyle moved on to work in the prosecuting attorney's office. Boyle's family had come to know the Harry Trumans in the early 1930s. Boyle's mother was particularly helpful to the Trumans in 1934 when Judge Truman made his first campaign for United States senator. Truman invited Boyle to come to Washington in 1941 to serve as assistant counsel to the Truman Committee. After Truman's nomination at the 1944 national convention, Boyle assisted Hannegan at the national committee. Thereafter, he opened a law office in Washington, continuing as an informal but influential political adviser to Truman during the 1948 campaign and until his appointment as national chairman in 1949.

---

tacular competence," uncovering masses of detailed information about slovenly administration, incompetence, or dishonesty in spending in the factories, the military, and industry. Before its many years of work were ended, the Truman Committee was credited with having saved the federal treasury $15 billion.

Characteristically, Truman sent his reports to the parties most concerned before turning them over to the press. Although his name was constantly in the news, Truman never handled his findings in such a way as to embarrass President Roosevelt. Roosevelt was not unappreciative of this fact, nor was he unaware that Truman's Senate voting record was almost 100 percent in support of administration legislative proposals.

President Roosevelt at first considered Wallace, the incumbent, as the logical second man for the 1944 ticket. Wallace had the support of labor and the liberals in the party. The big-city leaders, however, felt that Wallace had antagonized enough party regulars and business interests to be a serious drag on the ticket.

Hannegan and Flynn openly committed themselves to the prevention of a Wallace renomination. It was National Committee Secretary Ed Pauley, however, who became the most active anti-Wallace organizer, or "conspirator," as he called himself.

Most of the alternatives to Wallace suffered one or another political debility. Rayburn could not go into the convention with a united Texas delegation. Barkley had just gotten into a serious altercation with the president over a veto message. Supreme Court Justice Douglas was an intellectual and liberal of the Wallace type, but without political support or organization. Byrnes was an ex-Catholic from the deep South. The only one without immediate political liabilities was Truman. Roosevelt found himself having to reject his political friends—Wallace, Byrnes, Douglas, and so on—for a relative stranger, Truman. He knew Truman mainly by reputation and voting record, hardly socially. The president, who could never say "no" to his friends, adopted the strategy of leaving the final decision up to the national convention.

Roosevelt wrote an open letter to the permanent chairman of the convention: "I like [Henry Wallace] and I respect him, and he is my personal friend. For these reasons, I personally would vote for his renomination if I were a delegate. . . . At the same time . . . the convention must do the deciding. And it should—and I am sure it will—give great consideration to the pros and cons of its choice." To Robert Hannegan, Roosevelt drafted an undated note, edited somewhat by Hannegan, saying, "You have written me about Harry Truman and Bill Douglas. I should, of course, be very glad to run with either of them and believe that either one of them would bring real strength to the ticket."[46] The note was read to the convention on July 20. Thus, Roosevelt made the question of Wallace's renomination an open one for the convention, at the same time indicating which two candidates would be most acceptable to him.

The outcome of Roosevelt's strategy was not at all certain. Wallace was the first choice of the labor delegates. Byrnes, until the very last, considered himself Roosevelt's first choice. Byrnes put in a direct call to the president and was unable to reach him. Byrnes withdrew his name. Truman's was placed in nomination and had the nomination on the second ballot.

Because of illness and frequent absences from Washington on missions overseas for the president, Harry Hopkins played a minor role in the 1944 convention, participating occasionally by long distance telephone from his Georgetown home. His later recollection, described to Robert Sherwood, provides evidence of Roosevelt's strategy.

> I'm pretty sure that Jimmy Byrnes and Henry Wallace and Harold Ickes are saying right now that they'd be President of the United States today if it weren't for me. But this time I didn't have anything to do with it. I'm certain that the President had made up his mind on Truman long before I got back to the White House last year. I think he would have preferred Bill Douglas,

because he knew him better and he always liked Bill's toughness. But nobody really influential was pushing for Douglas. I think he'd gone off fishing out in Oregon or some place. And Bob Hannegan was certainly pushing for Harry Truman and the President believed he could put him over at the Convention. So the President told him to go ahead and even put it in writing when Bob asked him to. People seemed to think that Truman was just suddenly pulled out of a hat—but that wasn't true. The President had had his eye on him for a long time. The Truman Committee record was good—he'd got himself known and liked around the country—and above all he was very popular in the Senate. That was the biggest consideration. The President wanted somebody that would help him when he went up there and asked them to ratify the peace.[47]

The 1944 Roosevelt campaign was possibly the least organized of his career. Even while the national convention was in progress, the president was on his way to Pearl Harbor and Alaska for conferences with military leaders about the forthcoming Pacific campaign. He indicated that he might be too busy to make many campaign speeches, and those that he made in the opening weeks were startlingly poor in content and delivery. The Republicans were declaring that "the Old Man is finished." The CIO Political Action Committee, under Sidney Hillman's leadership, was putting tremendous effort into the Roosevelt-Truman campaign, and Republicans were charging that the Democratic party was dominated by Hillman and a Communist element in the CIO.

Hannegan devoted nearly all of his attention to assuring a large voter turnout. He conferred with state and county party leaders about registration problems, particularly the registration of war workers, migratory workers, and Blacks. He pushed for simplification of ballot laws to enable absentee soldiers to vote, presumably in favor of their commander-in-chief. Finally, in August, the president announced that he was ready to open his campaign.

On September 23, before a convention of the Teamsters Union, he delivered his famous "Fala speech" in which he berated the Republicans for libelous statements about his dog, Fala. The speech gave the entire Democratic campaign a much-needed lift. On October 5, from the White House, he answered more directly Republican charges, particularly references to communism in the Democratic party. Even as Thomas Dewey, the Republican nominee, was criticizing the administration for the handling of the war, General Douglas MacArthur was landing at the head of American troops returning, as MacArthur had promised, to the Philippines. On election day, the second wartime election in American history, the voters returned their commander-in-chief to the task he seemed about to bring to successful completion.

What will undoubtedly remain a footnote in United States party history also occurred at about this time, namely, an indirect conversation between Roosevelt and Wendell Willkie, the 1940 Republican nominee. The communication between them held great but unfulfilled potential for a realignment of the national parties of the United States. Sam Rosenman was the principal intermediary and reports the details in a chapter of his memoirs.

During the last week in June, Roosevelt reported to Rosenman a conversation with Governor Pinchot. Willkie had suggested to Pinchot that the time seemed right for a new lineup of the parties. Defeated by the conservatives in his own party, Willkie seemed to be ready to encourage a coalition of liberals in both parties, leaving the conservatives in each party to join together if they wished. According to Rosenman, Roosevelt declared: "I agree with him one hundred per cent and the time is now—right after election. We ought to have two real parties—one liberal and the other conservative."[48] Roosevelt felt that, with work begun immediately after the 1944 election, it would be possible for Willkie and himself to bring together a liberal party in time for 1948.

Following the unfortunate purge of 1938, Roosevelt frequently spoke of the necessity for a new alignment of political parties in the United States. In Willkie, he thought, he had for the first time a Republican qualified to work with him on this most difficult undertaking. The president delegated to Rosenman the task of arranging a secret meeting with Willkie in New York City in order to communicate his interest. Such a meeting did take place on July 5. Willkie expressed great satisfaction and looked forward to meeting with Roosevelt after election day. After the two-hour conference between Willkie and Rosenman, the latter reported back to the president.

The project never got off the ground. By election day Willkie was dead and, five months later, so was Roosevelt.

In concluding his account, Rosenman observes:

> The project was never even discussed between them directly. It was a Herculean task that these two political leaders had thought of undertaking. No combination other than Roosevelt and Willkie could have done it. And 1948 would have been the most opportune time to do it. . . . Had Roosevelt and Willkie lived, their political alliance might have been so firmly cemented by 1948 that the great schism and realignment might have taken place that year.[49]

Possibly more significant than the realignment proposal itself was the implied characterization of American national politics held by its two great proponents. Roosevelt had spent a lifetime coping with factional considerations within his own party, whereas Willkie was a newcomer to factionalism. Given his unwillingness to compromise with the conservatives of his party, it is believable that Willkie felt he could lead a whole wing of his party over to another side. However, it is somewhat more difficult to believe that Roosevelt held a similar view, particularly since the Democratic party would have been the major beneficiary of a Willkie bolt. On the other hand, the unsuccessful purges of 1938, Roosevelt's need to insist upon having Henry Wallace as his running mate in 1940, and his growing impatience with Democratic conservatives do leave room for speculation about his judgment regarding the feasibility of a realignment.

19 | Another Presidential-Congressional Contest for the National Organization

The 1920 election opened another era dominated by Republican majorities. The large size of these majorities encouraged Republicans in Congress, particularly the Senate, to control the administrations of three Republican presidents. With the conservative wing in the saddle, the circumstances also led frustrated progressives into another bolt, this time behind the leadership of Robert M. La Follette. The severe fragmentation of the Democratic party, climaxed by a 103-ballot nominating contest in 1924, did little to constrain the influence and policies of the conservative Republican senators. Only the crash of 1929 and the Great Depression accomplished this.

1

The Harding administration came to power faced with a number of difficult national problems. The business boom of 1919–20 was followed in 1920 and 1921 by a depression, a decline in agricultural prices, over two million unemployed (a very high proportion of the labor force in that day), a number of violent strikes, and an intense national debate over the League of Nations covenant and the peace treaty. These problems notwithstanding, the administration's accomplishments were not inconsequential. The Budget Bureau and the powerful Veterans Bureau were established. The state of war with Germany and Austria was formally ended. Harding endorsed American participation in a World Court. The Washington Disarmament Conference produced an impressive treaty.

In the electorate, some former Progressives reaped the benefit of farm and labor discontent, defeating Old Guard leaders in several Republican primary elections. In Pennsylvania, Gifford Pinchot, who had followed Theodore Roosevelt into the Progressive party, defeated the machine candidate for the gubernatorial nomination. In Indiana, Albert J. Beveridge, another who followed Roosevelt, won election over Senator Harry S. New. When Farmer-Laborites

William Morgan Butler's father was a master mariner and, when he retired from the sea, a Methodist minister. His son was born in New Bedford and educated in its public schools. As a youth, Butler worked as a clerk in a shoe manufacturing firm, at the same time studying law at Boston University. He began his practice in 1884 in association with the New Bedford district attorney and two years later was elected to the community's common council. Butler was next elected for two terms to the Massachusetts House of Representatives and four terms to its senate. During this tenure, he became closely associated with the leading organization Republican of that state, W. Murray Crane. During Butler's last two terms in the senate, he was chosen its president. Butler left the state legislature in 1895 to establish a law firm in Boston, where he acquired a large and lucrative clientele that included industrial, public utility, insurance, and cotton mill interests. In 1902, he built his own mill and thereafter acquired other manufacturing properties. He relinquished his legal practice in 1912 in order to devote himself full time to his industrial interests. He maintained a close friendship with Senator Crane, serving as his legal counsel for many years. Butler also developed a friendship with another of Crane's protégés, Calvin Coolidge. Coolidge had advanced through Massachusetts politics along the same route as Butler, but continued on to the offices of lieutenant governor and governor. Butler was one of the very few people with whom Coolidge consulted in the handling of the Boston police strike.

and Democrats made substantial inroads into the Republican majority in both houses of Congress in the 1922 elections, the former Progressives became eager to go after larger prizes in the national arena.

Early in 1923 the nation began to hear first intimations that President Harding was surrounded by corruption. The head of the new Veterans Bureau resigned just prior to the exposure of graft in his agency. Three weeks later, his closest assistant committed suicide. Two months later, a notorious associate of Attorney General Daugherty also committed suicide. Gradually but inexorably the Teapot Dome oil scandal came into the open.

Secretary of the Navy Denby had urged the president to sign an executive order transferring control of the Naval Petroleum Reserves to the Department of the Interior. There, applying certain of Secretary of Interior Fall's prerogatives, augmented by several devious arrangements, leases were signed for the private exploitation of the public oil reserve lands. Secretary Fall was paid for his share in the scheme, and Attorney General Daugherty was involved in these and other connivances. President Harding must have been aware of the misdeeds of his old friends long before the Senate investigators, led by Thomas J. Walsh, exposed the tragic facts. His death on August 2, 1923, spared him further anguish.

Vice-President Coolidge was nowhere to be seen during these unhappy developments. Harding had taken the unusual step of inviting the vice-president to sit regularly with the cabinet and also frequently consulted with him. But Coolidge rarely participated in the cabinet discussions and never commented on them either publicly or privately. Coolidge did little beyond his constitutional duty to preside over the Senate. Although reluctantly attending the circuit of official and social luncheons and dinners in Washington, Coolidge conscientiously concerned himself with speaking engagements around the country. He maintained close touch with Massachusetts politics and was pleased when his good friend, William M. Butler, became the state's Republican national committeeman, succeeding Secretary of War Weeks. Butler, a textile manufacturer, had been one of Coolidge's closest advisers.

Coolidge took over the presidency under difficult circumstances. A Republican administration was falling apart under the weight of widespread corruption. An unfriendly Republican leadership in the Senate, having ignored him as their presiding officer for so long, was not going to change its attitudes.

The national party organization was in hostile and often foolish hands. National Chairman Adams, for example, had been using the chairmanship as a platform from which to castigate World War allies and oppose Harding's efforts to gain American participation in a World Court. There was strong objection to Adams' behavior, but, since only the national chairman could readily call a national committee meeting, it was difficult for Adams' critics to find an opportunity to demand his removal. Various expedients, such as widespread resignations among the national committeemen, were discussed, but eventually abandoned as impractical.

Another source of potential difficulty for Coolidge was the group around Harry M. Daugherty. This group had been readying itself to conduct a renomination campaign for Harding. As early as March 19, 1923, Daugherty had come forth with a semiofficial announcement that Harding would be a candidate. Democratic National Chairman Cordell Hull told reporters that the early timing rather than the content of the news was what was most surprising; apparently the president anticipated some difficulty in winning renomination.

Despite these and other difficulties, Coolidge succeeded in reviving rectitude and confidence to the United States presidency. He inaugurated a new era in open political communication. Ironically, it was "Silent Cal" who was the first major public figure to speak over the new radio broadcasting devices. On December 10, 1923, at the White House memorial service for Harding, Coolidge's nasal voice, penetratingly clear in its enunciation, spoke over the air. For at least the next half dozen presidential campaigns, radio was to be a major force.

2

With less than ten months to the next Republican national convention, Coolidge set about to mobilize support of his own for a presidential nomination. As his personal secretary, Coolidge appointed C. Bascom Slemp, a congressman and practical politician of long-standing and wide acquaintance in national politics. Slemp had been called "the Republican patronage boss of the South," and his selection at once made it clear that the new president was interested in southern delegates. William M. Butler was at hand as national committeeman, ready and willing to manage the president's preconvention campaign. Within a month after Harding's death, most of the cabinet made public statements favoring Coolidge's nomination in 1924. Furthermore, most of these cabinet officials were politicians who could deliver convention votes. The less savory members were on their way out; in time, Coolidge asked for and received Daugherty's resignation.

On December 8, 1923, the eve of a national committee meeting, Coolidge told a dinner group at the Gridiron Club that he was indeed in the race. A survey of the national committee members a few days later showed that forty-six of the fifty-three were for Coolidge. The committee proceeded to rescind the apportionment rule of 1921 and substitute a further compromise restoring much of the southern representation. The southern convention votes were readily available, a source of intraparty strength that no incumbent Republican president would willingly risk losing.

Coolidge allowed his name to be entered into most of the primaries. Only Hiram Johnson and Robert M. La Follette ran against him. The old Progressives, viewing the Democratic party as divided and ineffective, felt that discontent among farmers and laboring people ought somehow to be channeled into the Republican convention. For this, they had the organizational and financial support of the Railroad Brotherhood unions and certain farmer associations. Although entered in many primaries against Coolidge, Johnson won only in his own home state.

The progressive effort produced a mere 34 votes for La Follette and 10 for Johnson; over 1,000 votes on the first ballot gave the nomination to Coolidge. The only satisfaction the progressives had was the opportunity to present a complete minority platform, and even this was shouted down as soon as it had been read.

The convention majority did more than jeer and hoot at the progressives. Revival of the Roscoe Conkling loyalty pledge of 1880 was discussed, mainly as an instrument for ousting the pro-La Follette Wisconsin delegation. The convention contented itself with the 1916 rule authorizing the national committee to replace any member who refused to support the nominees of the convention, thereby making the Wisconsin committeeman and committeewoman responsible for their state party's conduct in the election campaign.

Butler managed the Coolidge preconvention organization with a tight hand. The *Literary Digest*, in a character sketch of Butler, noted that at times he was inclined to be dictatorial, made enemies easily, and was more disposed to use force than was Frank W. Stearns, Coolidge's other long-time friend and political adviser. In this vein, Butler somewhat abruptly informed the national committee that Cleveland, not Chicago, would be the convention city. Butler was undoubtedly instrumental in defeating National Chairman Adams' re-election to the national committee in early March; the same Iowa state convention unanimously endorsed Coolidge. Butler had Frank W. Mondell of Wyoming, a vociferous conservative, chosen permanent chairman of the national convention. The activities of the Massachusetts lawyer-industrialist particularly provoked the progressives, who charged that the Republican Senatorial Clique of 1920 was now being replaced by a "businessman's bloc" headed by Butler.

The president's personal representative ran into trouble in the course of the vice-presidential nomination. Butler made it known that Coolidge would consider William E. Borah acceptable as a running mate. Borah himself ridiculed the notion. At a late hour of the third day of the convention, Butler advised the principal leaders that Borah would accept. Several reminded Butler that the senator had already said many times that he would not accept. Butler indicated that he had been so informed by a "source close to Borah." Although Butler convinced most of the leaders that Borah would run, former Senator Beveridge found it difficult to believe and promptly telephoned Borah at his residence in Washington. Borah repeated his previous statements on the subject, and, in a later conversation, asked Beveridge to withdraw his name if it were presented.

The conservatives gathered their forces around Senator Charles Curtis of Kansas. Butler firmly asserted that the Kansas senator would not be acceptable. He then offered the name of William S. Kenyon of Illinois, but La Follette's support of Kenyon made this an unacceptable choice as well. Butler continued to insist that the president wanted Kenyon. By this time, opposition to Butler himself had grown to such proportions that many said privately that they would oppose any candidate Butler endorsed unless Coolidge made it unmistakably clear that he wanted that candidate.

The leaders of several of the large delegations conferred informally. Principally because Butler did *not* favor Lowden, the majority of these conferees agreed to support him for the vice-presidential nomination. Lowden had already declared that he was irrevocably disinterested, but the delegates on the second ballot gave him the nomination. Immediately following the motion to make the nomination unanimous, a letter from Lowden was read in which he thanked the convention for the honor and declined it. Since the letter was undated, the convention adjourned to allow the permanent chairman an opportunity to ask Lowden directly. Lowden's refusal was confirmed, and the delegates angrily reconvened for another try.

Butler was now less and less effective. He approached many of the delegates urging upon them Herbert Hoover as his latest choice. At the same time, Andrew Mellon and Bascom Slemp circulated among delegation leaders in support of Charles G. Dawes of Illinois. On the third ballot, Dawes had 682$\frac{1}{2}$ votes, Hoover 234, and the rest scattered. The Chicago banker accepted the nomination, the Senate leaders claimed his nomination as a victory for themselves, and the progressives were even more convinced that big business had completely captured the Republican party.

There was no doubt who would manage the Coolidge campaign. The president had indicated in May that he wanted William M. Butler as his national chairman. This arrangement, however, was not what Butler originally intended. Butler had expected to serve as Coolidge's personal representative in the preconvention campaign, then become a candidate for United States senator from Massachusetts. Frank Stearns, one of Coolidge's close advisers, wrote in December 1923, "We understand the present Chairman, Mr. Adams, does not wish to be Chairman in the campaign. Probably the right man will develop in the next six months."[1]

But the right man did not "develop," and Adams continued to estrange himself from the Coolidge administration as he had done under Harding. The situation was described by the *New York Times* as follows:

> The National Committee, which has been under the control of the so-called Senate oligarchy for years, has not been in harmony, in all respects, with either the present or the preceding Administration. Chairman Adams attacked the Harding Administration when President Harding made a speech indicating his predilection for an association of nations. Again he assailed the policy of Secretary Hughes in negotiating payment for the American troops on the Rhine. . . . President Coolidge does not agree with what is being done by the present officials of the National Committee . . . in investigating [Senator] Wheeler.[2]

Under these circumstances, the president resorted to a formal announcement of his intention to have the national committee make Butler its chairman. "President Coolidge, one of his advisers said tonight, had come to the conclusion that he must assume not only the titular but the actual leadership of the Republican party."[3]

In accepting the chairmanship, Butler at least temporarily gave up plans to make the race for senator. Butler's election as national chairman on June 13 took place in an atmosphere of deep resentment over his style and tactics. Had he not denied Senator Harry Cabot Lodge leadership of the Massachusetts delegation and the chairmanship of the national convention? Without consulting or seeking to assuage the older leaders, had he not brusquely named most of the convention officers? Whether intentionally or not, had he not made it evident that he little respected the advice of the national committee members and was less disposed to work on intimate terms with them? On June 14, 1924, the *New York Times* reported the obvious, "[I]t is no secret that Mr. Butler is extremely unpopular."

For vice-chairmen, Butler proposed former National Chairman Charles D. Hilles, Ralph E. Williams of Oregon, and Mrs. A.T. Hert of Kentucky. The number of vice-chairmen and the presence of a woman among them was evidence of two important changes in national committee structure. There would henceforth be more than one vice-chairman, with particular executive responsibilities assigned to each. In view of the fact that the 1924 national convention had adopted a rule under which each state was entitled to two members on the national committee, one a man and the other a woman, Butler selected Mrs. Hert to represent the women members themselves. Typically, he did so without consulting the women members. This, too, was resented.

Butler established national committee campaign headquarters in the Wrigley Building in Chicago and subheadquarters in Washington and New York. In contrast to the organizational arrangements of Will Hays four years earlier, it was Butler's plan to decentralize as many of the campaign activities as possible. For example, even before Butler moved into his office, the *National Republican* newspaper was detached from national committee operations. Similarly, Butler undertook no nationwide fund-raising, preferring that the state party organizations shift for themselves.

President Coolidge's personal campaign was intended to be a limited one. Coolidge was to make few public addresses and stay close to the White House. Butler hoped that most of the president's speech making could be accomplished over the microphones of the new radio broadcasting facilities. This was easier said than done. The broadcasters had strained every facility, including the full capacity of the American Telephone and Telegraph Company's long-distance lines, in order to transmit the proceedings of the two national conventions to as many as twelve cities across the country. Only a small number of speeches could be broadcast coast-to-coast, and even these limited efforts cost the national committee unexpectedly large sums of money.

Although intended to cut down the Republican margin in the electorate, the Progressive third-party campaign, even with the unprecedented official endorsement of the American Federation of Labor, failed to alter the outcome. Coolidge won handily. The Progressives made some inroads in the Midwest and New England, but these were areas in which most voters were solidly Republican and Republican victories were a foregone conclusion. The Democrats suffered losses to the Progressives where it hurt, that is, in the Mid-Atlantic states, the mountain states, and on the Pacific Coast.

3

Almost immediately after Coolidge's election to his first full term, the political trio that guided the campaign for nomination and election—Stearns, Butler, and

Everett Sanders was forty-three years old when he became presidential secretary. He was born and raised in Indiana on the farm of his father, a Baptist preacher. While at Indiana State Normal School, he met and married his first wife. Both taught school for a brief period before continuing their education at Indiana University. Sanders first practiced law at Terre Haute, between 1907 and 1917, building a large clientele and following. In an upset victory against a long-time Democratic incumbent, he won the Fifth District seat in the House of Representatives in 1917, and served continuously until 1925. He became a member of the powerful House Steering Committee and held other influential positions during his tenure. At the end of his fourth term, he announced that he did not intend to run again. At this time, William M. Butler asked him to manage the speakers bureau for the Coolidge campaign. Sanders, later to become Herbert Hoover's national chairman, planned to retire to his law practice at the end of the campaign, but Coolidge invited him to take on the presidential secretary position.

Slemp—moved on to other roles in the administration. Stearns, whom the president addressed as "Mr. Stearns" during the entire two decades of their intimate social and political friendship, continued in his accustomed role as occasional visitor and informal adviser.

Butler, who had been slated for a cabinet post, was instead appointed by Governor Cox of Massachusetts to fill out the term of Henry Cabot Lodge in the U.S. Senate; Lodge had died only a few days after the fall election. The appointment was the realization of Butler's cherished wish to succeed his friend, the late Senator W. Murray Crane. President Coolidge received the news with great satisfaction, for he would now have a trusted personal representative in the Senate.

The third of the trio, C. Bascom Slemp, announced his retirement as presidential secretary and was succeeded by Everett Sanders, a congressman from Indiana. Sanders had served as director of the speakers bureau of the Republican national committee during the 1924 campaign, and his selection indicated that the president intended to continue to run party matters through his personal secretary.

Senate Republicans offered little welcome to the newest of their number, William M. Butler. The older leaders, who had followed Henry Cabot Lodge over many legislative ramparts, found it extremely difficult to warm up to the man who had ignored them and humbled Lodge. That Butler should be the beneficiary of Lodge's death only added to the irony. Furthermore, when Coolidge succeeded Harding, Senate Republicans were thoroughly cut off from their influence upon the presidency. The glory of senatorial ascendancy in 1920 was too recent to be forgotten. Coolidge and Butler were bound to have trouble with Congress, and this was not long in coming. The 1924 Progressive bolt only complicated matters.

President Coolidge nominated Charles B. Warren of Michigan to be attorney general. Warren had long service as a Republican leader and served as chairman of the national convention platform committee in 1924. It was the platform committee that dealt so sternly with the planks of the Republican progressives. Senate Progressives and Democrats at once joined hands to defeat the Warren nomination, and succeeded by a 41 to 39 vote. Vice-President Dawes had absented himself, returning too late to break what might otherwise have been a tie. Not since President Andrew Johnson had the Senate turned down a presidential cabinet nomination.

Senator Butler was, during his very first days in Congress, embroiled in the difficult task of selecting its Republican leadership. The Republicans had a slim margin in the Senate and a relatively substantial one in the House. Representative Nicholas Longworth, son-in-law of Theodore Roosevelt, was elected Speaker, but twelve Progressives were denied places on important committees as punishment for their 1924 defections. The Republicans held the Senate by a majority of only six votes, but only if they included in that number eight Progressives and independents.

Shortly after election day, the White House indirectly made known its support of the action of the Republican conference in declaring Senators La Follette, Ladd, Frazier, and Brookhart ineligible for their regular committee assignments because of their activities in the third-party movement. Coolidge was prepared to end all consultation with these senators in matters of patronage. On March 5, when the Republican committee assignments in the Senate implemented the disciplinary action against the four insurgents, the Progressives retaliated by opposing the Warren cabinet appointment. Despite Butler's protests, the Republican leadership promptly made concessions, giving the insurgents the usual Capitol patronage and agreeing not to bind all members of the Republican conference to mutual action. Several of the Old Guard Republicans seemed unusually willing to help the insurgents humiliate the White House's spokesman in the Senate.

When asked whether or not Butler, as a senator, would eventually resign from the national chairmanship, the president observed that a law of physics seemed relevant: a body at rest remains at rest, and a body in motion continues to move forward in a straight line until acted upon by some outside force. Such a law, the president indicated, is applicable to officeholders. Coolidge obviously intended that Butler should be his Mark Hanna.

Butler's retention was also widely interpreted as an indication that Coolidge would again seek the presidency in 1928. Butler, meanwhile, told reporters that the national committee headquarters would be maintained in skeleton form over the next four years. The campaign had ended with a surplus in the committee's coffers, permitting Butler to maintain some of the publicity activities as well as to cooperate with the congressional campaign committee in the forthcoming midterm elections.[4] As his assistant to handle press and other releases at national headquarters, Butler appointed L. White Busbey, later succeeded by Washington correspondent Arthur J. Dodge.

In the McKinley tradition, Coolidge avoided the appearance of being partisan. He was the very antithesis of such vocal and activist presidents as Roosevelt and Wilson. Political observers of the period often reiterate the opinion that much of Coolidge's success among the voters rested upon his ability to defeat the "evil forces of politics." Had he not reestablished public confidence in the presidency after the scandals of the Harding administration? Did he not oust the Senatorial Clique from its seats of influence? Had he not surrounded himself with solid businessmen as advisers, and were not these men the architects of the unprecedented prosperity that existed under Coolidge?

Coolidge had been in politics too long to leave his political future to chance. He clearly recognized and confronted the political character of the presidency. His observations merit lengthy quotation:

> Under our system the President is not only the head of the government, but is also the head of his party. The last twenty years have witnessed a decline in party spirit and a distinct weakening in party loyalty. While an independent attitude on the part of the citizen is not without a certain public advantage, yet it is necessary under our form of government to have political parties. Unless someone is a partisan, no one can be an independent. The Congress is organized entirely in accordance with party policy. The parties appeal to the voters in behalf of their platforms. The people make their choice on those issues. Unless those who are elected on the same party platform associated themselves together to carry out its provisions, the election becomes a mockery. The independent voter who has joined with others in placing a party nominee in office finds his efforts were all in vain, if the person he helps elect refuses or neglects to keep the platform pledges of his party.
>
> Many occasions arise in the Congress when party lines are very properly disregarded, but if there is to be a reasonable government proceeding in accordance with the express mandate of the people, and not merely at the whim of those who happen to be victorious at the polls, on all the larger and important issues there must be party solidarity. It is the business of the President as party leader to do the best he can to see that the declared party platform purposes are translated into legislative and administrative action. Often times I secured support from those without my party and had opposition from those within my party, in attempting to keep my platform pledges.
>
> Such a condition is entirely anomalous. It leaves the President as the sole repository of party responsibility. But it is one of the reasons that the Presidential office has grown in popular estimation and favor, while the Congress has declined. The country feels that the President is willing to assume responsibility, while his party in the Congress is not. . . .

Under our system it ought to be remembered that the power to initiate policies has to be centralized somewhere. Unless the party leaders exercising it can depend on loyalty and organization support, the party in which it is reposed will become entirely ineffective. A party which is ineffective will soon be discarded. If a party is to endure as a serviceable instrument of government for the country, it must possess and display a healthy spirit of party loyalty. Such a manifestation in the Congress would do more than anything else to rehabilitate it in the esteem and confidence of the country.[5]

The policy postures of the Coolidge administration were typical of that day. Unemployment, child labor, old-age pensions, and slum clearance were deemed concerns of local, not federal, government. Coolidge stood for economy, tax reduction, observation of the spirit of the Prohibition laws, and participation in the World Court. When Secretary of the Treasury Andrew W. Mellon in 1924 suggested that the federal treasury could afford tax reductions amounting to $300 million, Congress proceeded to reduce tax rates considerably. The national debt at the end of 1926 stood at $19.3 billion, some $7 billion less than in 1919. Industrial profits reached all-time highs.

There was also the darker side of the coin. Under the eyes of the "Puritan in Babylon," as William Allen White called Coolidge, the nation was passing through one of its wildest orgies of gambling and lawbreaking. Farm prices and income dropped as farm surpluses multiplied. An agrarian rebellion was in the making, particularly after Coolidge and Mellon came out against the McNary-Haugen Bill proposing federal purchase of farm surpluses in order to stabilize farm prices.

Two senatorial elections excited particular interest in 1925 and 1926. In the Wisconsin Republican primary of September 1925, Robert M. La Follette, Jr., entered in the hope of succeeding his father in the U.S. Senate. In view of his father's bolt in 1924, at issue immediately was the younger La Follette's party regularity. Senator Butler did not hesitate to express an opinion on this subject, his own and on behalf of the national committee. Butler was emphatic. In his opinion, those who joined with the late Senator La Follette in his campaign to defeat President Coolidge and were currently seeking to elect a senator from Wisconsin on a platform made up of La Follette's principles had no place in the Republican party and could not expect to receive the support of its national committee. "I am, of course, simply giving my private opinion," Butler declared.[6] Ordinarily, he continued, the national committee does not take any part in a primary campaign and was not participating directly in this one. Nonetheless, it was apparent that the Coolidge leaders on the committee were hopeful that Roy Wilcox, La Follette's opponent, would be the victor. But the younger La Follette won and, after some doubt and contention, was assigned to Senate committees as a regular Republican.

The other interesting senatorial contest was National Chairman Butler's. His opponent was a very popular Democratic ex-senator, David I. Walsh, who had been defeated by only 18,000 votes in 1924 when Coolidge carried Massachusetts by 400,000 votes. Furthermore, former Lodge adherents in Massachusetts were still rankled over the rebuff Butler had dealt their deceased leader. President Coolidge did not hesitate to intervene actively to help his national chairman and friend, making special efforts to conciliate the Lodge followers. From a distance, a *New York Times* editorial on June 27, 1925, observed, "Mr. Butler's political manners have given deep offense. Such is the penalty of zeal. . . . [The president's] task is to convince a large number of Coolidge Republicans that they must be Butler Republicans. This may be difficult." And indeed it was difficult.

Butler campaigned hard, but his opponent was both popular and skillful. Walsh particularly hammered away at doubts that Butler could serve the interests of Massachusetts in the Senate so long as he retained the position of national chairman. Walsh argued that the chairmanship obliged Butler to have national considerations in mind to the detriment of what might be best for his own state. The Butler men worried increasingly about the outcome, calling upon numerous public figures to endorse Butler. Secretary of Commerce Herbert Hoover wrote a public letter of high praise. Henry Cabot Lodge, Jr., working as a newspaper correspondent in Washington, returned to Massachusetts to speak for Butler.

The big endorsement was the letter in which President Coolidge asked the voters of Massachusetts to re-elect Butler. The letter, released on October 24, 1926, was Coolidge's first and only utterance in behalf of any Republican candidate during the midterm election campaign. Butler promptly asked the voters "to stand by the President," in effect making the Massachusetts senatorial election a test of Coolidge's status as a national leader. Butler was neverthless defeated by approximately 50,000 votes. To add insult to injury, the Massachusetts electorate gave the Republican candidate for governor a majority of almost 200,000 votes.[7]

During the summer Republican primaries, friends of the administration were defeated by Progressives and Republican insurgents in Iowa, Illinois, and North Dakota. Midwestern isolationism was having great success opposing American participation in the World Court. Demands for farm relief were growing louder daily. The Republican primary in Pennsylvania provided a preview of what would happen in Massachusetts in the general election: the Vare faction undercut Senator Pepper's bid for renomination. In Oregon, Illinois, and New York, Republican independents were creating three-cornered senatorial fights.

There was widespread complaint in Republican ranks that the national leaders were neglecting their duties in the campaign. With the exception of his letter on behalf of Butler, the president refused to take the stump. Butler was thoroughly preoccupied with his own campaign in Massachusetts and was particularly blamed for his failure to deal with factional differences in Oregon, Illinois, and New York. The national committee headquarters limited itself mainly to a nationwide turnout drive, under the direction of Simon Michelet, a Washington lawyer.[8]

The Republicans lost 7 Senate and 20 House seats. Pointing to the fact that only one-third of the Senate membership had been up for election, Coolidge cited the House returns, where the Republicans held a safe majority of 40, as the true national test of popular support for the Republican party. He called it a Republican victory. Republicans held 54 Senate seats, to 40 Democratic and 1 Farmer-Laborite, but the Senate majority included 5 Republican insurgents (Norris, Howell, Nye, Frazier, and La Follette) who voted consistently with the Democrats. Thus, the Republican majority was really 49, and this only if such former Progressives as Borah of Idaho, Johnson of California, and Couzens of Michigan remained in line.

President Coolidge looked on the bright side regarding the future status of National Chairman Butler. News of Butler's defeat in Massachusetts gave rise to reports that he would resign from the chairmanship. The president, however, took the position that Butler would now be free of his "time consuming duties" in the Senate and better able to devote great energy to matters of national party organization. Said Butler himself, "I never had any purpose other than to retain the chairmanship of the national committee unless I was elected."[9] With Butler in the chairmanship, talk of Coolidge's plans for the 1928 presidential race now became of special interest.

4

The new party alignments in Congress put pressure on the lame-duck session meeting in February 1927. The McNary-Haugen Bill was finally passed by both houses, but within a week vetoed by Coolidge. This prompted Senator La Follette to introduce a joint resolution against third terms in the presidency, but the move was tabled. Soon the Republican right began joining the Republican left on the third-term issue. In late February, President Nicholas Murray Butler of Columbia University, long a conservative spokesman in Republican presidential politics, added his judgment that Coolidge ought not and would not be a candidate in 1928. Two months later, Senator Norris of Nebraska referred to a third term as a long step toward monarchy, "The fact that a President has succeeded to an office by the ascendancy from the Vice Presidency is absolutely immaterial."[10]

Precedents, however, were relevant. Before Coolidge, five vice-presidents had succeeded to the presidency upon the death of the incumbent. Four of these—Tyler, Fillmore, Johnson, and Arthur—unsuccessfully sought nomination for a full term. Only Theodore Roosevelt, the most recent case, succeeded in winning nomination and election to a full term. Roosevelt handled the problem of a second full term by actively supporting his own choice, Taft, for the succession.

Coolidge could seek the nomination for a second full term, actively support another candidate, or stand aside and let party's factions find their own solution.

William Butler and Frank Stearns proceeded during the early part of 1927 on the assumption that Coolidge would run. The president, however, in his fifty-fifth year and somewhat concerned over his own and Mrs. Coolidge's health, chose the last alternative. He was undoubtedly also sensitive to the political implications of the anti-third-term movement in Congress. On August 2, 1927, the fourth anniversary of his assumption of the presidency, Coolidge announced, "I do not choose to run for President in nineteen twenty eight."[11]

The announcement caught the country, and particularly Republican leaders, by surprise. Even Butler and Stearns were without prior knowledge. During the preceding February and March, Charles D. Hilles, as vice-chairman of the national committee, had spent a month traveling from New York to the Pacific coast, including a great part of the South, to ascertain party and popular sentiment regarding the nomination of the president. During April, National Chairman Butler made a similar tour, reporting highly favorable findings at a breakfast with the president and other administration leaders on May 6. Butler, Hilles, and the national committeeman from Virginia, C. Bascom Slemp, had been actively lining up southern delegations. In view of these activities, Coolidge's withdrawal and his untraditional choice of words in doing so proved extremely unsettling to Republican leaders.

There is reason, however, to accept Coolidge's own explanation as the most accurate analysis:

> I had never wished to run in 1928 and had determined to make a public announcement at a sufficiently early date so that the party would have ample time to choose some one else. An appropriate occasion for that announcement seemed to be the fourth anniversary of my taking office. . . .
>
> While I am in favor of continuing the long-established custom of the country in relation to a third term for a President, yet I do not think that the practice applies to one who has succeeded to part of a term as Vice-President. . . .
>
> It is difficult for men in high office to avoid the malady of self-delusion. . . . They live in an artificial atmosphere of adulation and exaltation which sooner or later impairs their judgment. They are in grave danger of becoming careless and arrogant. The chances of having wise and faithful public service are increased by a change in the present Presidential office after a moderate length of time.
>
> It is necessary for the head of the nation to differ with many people who are honest in their opinions. As his term progresses, the number who are disappointed accumulates. Finally, there is so large a body who have lost confidence in him that he meets a rising opposition which makes his efforts less effective. . . . An examination of the records of those Presidents who have served eight years will disclose that in almost every instance the latter part of their term has shown very little in the way of constructive accomplishment. . . .
>
> In making my public statement I was careful in the use of words. There were some who reported that they were mystified as to my meaning when I said, "I do not choose to run."

Although I did not know it at the time, months later I found that Washington said practically the same thing. Certainly he said no more in his Farewell Address, where he announced that "choice and prudence" invited him to retire.

There were others who constantly demanded that I should state that if nominated I would refuse to accept. Such a statement would not be in accordance with my conception of the requirements of the Presidential office. I never stated or formulated in my own mind what I should do under such circumstances, but I was determined not to have that contingency arise.

I therefore sent the Secretary to the President, Everett Sanders, a man of great ability and discretion, to Kansas City with instructions to notify several of the leaders of state delegations not to vote for me. Had I not done so, I am told, I should have been nominated.[12]

His contemporaries did not take the Coolidge statement at face value. For months, Republican leaders speculated about his real wishes, his attitudes toward the activities of other possible candidates, and his probable action if finally confronted with the convention's nomination. Senator Simeon D. Fess of Ohio, one of the president's staunchest supporters, had a three-hour personal meeting with the president and came away convinced that Coolidge did not wish another term. Somewhat later, however, Fess suggested publicly that the president nevertheless should be compelled to run. Fess was called to the White House and told to desist in this kind of statement. When the Republican national committee met at the White House on December 6, 1927, the president made a surprise supplementary statement urging the party to seek another candidate from among the many "distinguished men available."

The "distinguished men available" no longer restrained themselves. Secretary of Commerce Hoover, a prospect since 1920, had an extensive preconvention organization waiting in the wings until the president's withdrawal was positive. Vice-President Dawes, after making known his own unavailability, announced that he planned to support former Governor Frank O. Lowden of Illinois. Lowden was a leading supporter of the McNary-Haugen Bill; his nomination would probably diminish Coolidge's gratitude for the "privilege, after seeing my administration so strongly endorsed by the country, to retire voluntarily from the greatest experience that can come to mortal man."[13] Lowden's campaign was less organized and financed than the one he conducted in 1920. He had the further difficulty of coping with a host of favorite-son candidacies coming out of the Midwest. Looking back over the nominating events, Coolidge commented in his memoirs:

A strong group of the party in and outside of the Senate made the mistake of undertaking to oppose Mr. Hoover with a large number of local candidates, which finally resulted in their not developing enough strength for any particular candidate to make a showing sufficient to impress the convention.[14]

At the December 1927 national committee meeting in Washington to select a convention city, Chairman Butler, evidently no longer in the president's confidence on matters of the nomination, was obviously as much taken by surprise as the other committeemen when the president asked them to seek a candidate from among other party leaders. Butler, in fact, had given the press the opinion that the president would probably not elaborate upon his "I do not choose to run" statement. Butler nevertheless went to the national convention at the head of the Massachusetts delegation insisting upon a "draft Coolidge" strategy.

The national committee embarked upon a prolonged squabble over the choice of convention city, the object of which was primarily to discredit Butler. Butler had declared himself for Kansas City. On the first ballot, the vote was San Francisco 40, Kansas City 34, Detroit 16, Cleveland 3, Chicago 4, Philadelphia 2, and San Antonio 2. Since Hoover was a Californian, his supporters on the committee favored San Francisco as Hoover territory. By the time a decision was made on the twentieth ballot, it had become clear that something more than Hoover's presidential aspirations was involved. Kansas City finally won with a vote of 58 to San Francisco's 39, 5 votes going to other cities. Administration leaders insisted that a national convention in the Midwest was an important gesture to the discontented in the farm states.[15]

5

A few months after Coolidge's "I do not choose to run" statement, a hostile Senate added its gratuitous farewell. Robert La Follette's anti-third-term resolution was passed on February 10, 1928, with an overwhelming vote of 56 to 26. Two days later, Walter F. Brown, former political boss of Toledo and currently Hoover's assistant secretary of commerce, entered his chief's name in the Ohio primary. This was the first formal step in Hoover's candidacy.

Secretary of Commerce Hoover was in a favorable position from the very first. Mentioned at two previous conventions as a possible presidential candidate, his name was widely known throughout the country. President Coolidge at no time raised objections to having a member of his cabinet engage in preconvention campaigning. This hands-off policy gave substance to the impression that Hoover was the favorite of the Coolidge administration.

Former National Chairman John T. Adams opened Washington headquarters for Hoover. The former congressman from Iowa, James W. Good, who was for some time in charge of a Washington committee for Hoover, took on the difficult job of organizing the Midwest. Claudius H. Huston, formerly chairman of the ways and means committee of the national committee under Adams and at one time Hoover's assistant secretary of commerce, joined the group, his expertise suggesting that he would handle fund-raising. Colonel Horace A. Mann, working with Huston, concentrated on bringing southern Republicans and anti-Smith

Claudius H. Huston was at all times a behind-the-scenes political operator. Born in Indiana in 1876, he was educated at Valparaiso University and the Chattanooga Normal University. He began his work career as a college instructor, but at twenty-five entered the manufacturing business at Chattanooga. In a few years he became chairman of the Transcontinental Oil Company and a director in many other companies. For his civic efforts on behalf of business during this period, he was elected president of the Chattanooga Manufacturers Association and, at another time, the Chattanooga Chamber of Commerce. During 1920, he became chairman of the campaign and advisory committees of the Tennessee Republican state committee and was entrusted with raising funds for the 1920 presidential campaign in Tennessee by another Hoosier, Will Hays, the national chairman. Huston's success as a fund raiser was striking and be became better known throughout the national party. He was among those mentioned for secretary of commerce under Harding, but that post went to Hoover. Huston became assistant secretary of commerce from 1921 to 1923. It was during this period that he served as chairman of the national committee's ways and means committee. He returned to his business enterprises, particularly Transcontinental Oil Company, in 1923, but remained a devoted political supporter and adviser to Hoover.

---

southern Democrats behind the Hoover movement. The senior public official to join the Hoover cause in its earliest stage was Secretary of Interior Hubert Work.

The press and the pundits never doubted that Hoover could defeat Lowden and the many favorite sons at the convention. There was doubt, and for some Republican leaders hope, that Coolidge could be drafted. Several of the northeastern leaders—Secretary of the Treasury Mellon of Pennsylvania, National Chairman Butler of Massachusetts, and National Committee Vice-Chairman Hilles of New York—were determined to keep alive the Coolidge possibility by holding their delegations uncommitted and working to keep the southern vote unpledged.

At Kansas City, it was the general impression that only Secretary of the Treasury Mellon could stop the Hoover forces. As political analyst Arthur Krock observed, "If Mellon would say one favorable word about any candidate, Kansas City would break open with excitement."[16] There was, in fact, great excitement when, at 8 P.M. on June 11, the night before the convention opened, Mellon issued a statement "suggesting" that the Pennsylvania delegation vote for Hoover on the first ballot.

The initial test vote in the convention was on the seating of Texas delegates opposed to Hoover. The Hoover side won in a vote of 659½ votes to 399½. During the nominating roll call, a letter was read announcing Lowden's withdrawal. Hoover's nomination followed.

Writing years later, Hoover referred to the 1928 nomination fight in words that support President Coolidge's intimation that most of the opposition to Hoover was from the Senate leadership. Hoover reviewed his own "restricted" preconvention efforts, noting that the other leading candidate was Lowden of Illinois. He then observed:

> But the active candidate was most of the United States Senate. They wanted neither Lowden nor me. For the first time in many years they had elected one of their members directly from the Senate to the Presidency in the person of Mr. Harding, and they liked the idea. The Senatorial group could not agree upon any one of its members but was resolved to keep control by setting up "favorite sons" in the primaries of various states with the hope of another stalled convention and a "smoke-filled room." Some pretended that they favored renominating Coolidge. The great majority of the House of Representatives under the leadership of Congressman Burton, supported me. . . .
>
> There were over half a dozen candidates from the Senate. . . . The favorite among them, if there was one, was Senator Curtis, the Senate Republican leader. . . .
>
> The Senate created a committee to investigate the pre-convention expenditures of candidates. The committee devoted most of the investigation to my friends.[17]

Hoover's nomination did not discourage the senators, who kept themselves mobilized to influence the vice-presidential choice. In this, conservatives and progressives cooperated. One surprise suggestion for the second spot, perhaps in recognition of the fact that Calvin Coolidge still held the presidency, was Presidential Secretary Everett Sanders. Speaker Longworth and Senator Gillette proposed Sanders' name to Secretary of War John Weeks of Massachusetts. Weeks cleared the suggestion with Postmaster General New, inquiring about the probable reaction of the leadership in Sanders' home state of Indiana.

New reported that it was highly probable that Indiana's Senator James E. Watson, the anti-Hoover leader of Senate conservatives since the early twenties, would vigorously oppose any effort by the Hoover people to give recognition to a Coolidge colleague. Nevertheless, the following day Andrew Mellon informed New that New York and Pennsylvania were ready to vote for Sanders. When this word reached Watson, he "plunged through the hall to Mellon and in the most violent terms opposed Sanders." Sanders name was never placed in nomination.[18] Instead, progressive Senator William E. Borah placed in nomination Charles Curtis, the Senate's majority leader. By the time the vote began, every vestige of opposition to Curtis had disappeared.

The Hoover leaders were still eager to establish some kind of symbolic connection with the Coolidge administration. They had for some time been trying to induce Butler to continue in the chairmanship should Hoover receive the nomination. Butler, however, announced three weeks before the convention his intention to step down from the chairmanship and to serve simply as Massachusetts' national committeeman.

The search for a Hoover national chairman led to several logical candidates: Secretary of Interior Work, Assistant Secretary of Commerce Brown, former Congressman Good, National Committeeman Ralph Williams of Oregon, and others of the preconvention Hoover movement. There were several days of consultation. The national committee, in something of a "show-of-force," created a Special Committee of Twenty-four to consult on the chairmanship. Before long, Secretary Hoover, Senator Curtis, and the special committee reached a series of decisions on personnel. Work would be national chairman. The vice-chairmen would include Ralph Williams of Oregon, Daniel E. Pomeroy, a retired New Jersey banker, and Mrs. Alvin T. Hert of Kentucky.

With the announcement of his selection, Work indicated that he would resign as secretary of the interior within two weeks and that, as far as he was concerned, the campaign was "already under way." He announced further that main headquarters would be in Washington, with branches in New York and Chicago. The new national chairman expected the campaign to be "quiet, dignified, instructive, and educational." Secretary Hoover's name is a "household word," he remarked; there would be no need for an aggressive campaign.

A "quiet" campaign against the Democrats' Al Smith was unthinkable to all who appreciated Smith's hard-hitting style. Dr. Work very shortly became a subject of concern to the Hoover campaigners. When Hoover appointed Senator Henry J. Allen of Kansas as director of publicity in Washington, Work appointed his own publicity man and practically ignored Allen. Hoover put New Hampshire's Senator George H. Moses, permanent chairman of the 1928 national convention, in charge of New York headquarters. Difficulties that arose between Moses and Work continued until the former threatened to resign, staying on only after Hoover's personal intervention. James W. Good was in charge of what became the key headquarters of the campaign in Chicago.

As the contest progressed, Hoover became increasingly his own campaign manager, circumventing Work whenever possible. Work in turn began to absent himself more and more from headquarters, frequently represented at conferences by James F. Burke of Pittsburgh, general counsel of the national committee.[19]

This was the first presidential campaign in which national radio hookups played a major part. Hoover, whose name was indeed a household word, made only seven major campaign speeches, all over radio. President Coolidge remained almost entirely in the background, allowing himself to be photographed with Hoover at the White House, and, on election eve, making a radio speech in behalf of the full Republican ticket.

Coolidge could afford to husband the popular goodwill that he enjoyed. Contrary to the generally held view that Coolidge was a failure as a president, at least one notable contemporary—Alfred E. Smith—disagreed with this impression. The contrast between Coolidge's personality and the social milieu of the 1920s was a rare and fortunate coincidence, according to Smith:

> [Coolidge's] great task was to restore the dignity and prestige of the Presidency when it had reached the lowest ebb in our history, and to afford, in a time of extravagance and waste, a shining public example of the simple and homely virtues which came down to him from his New England ancestors. These were no small achievements.[20]

The Hoover election victory was not without its drawbacks. Republican majorities in both houses of Congress were large, creating an environment once again congenial to factionalism. The Senate consisted of 56 Republicans and 39 Democrats. Among the Republicans, there was the Old Guard and those progressives whom Senator Moses referred to as "sons of the wild jackass" [alluding to their affinity for going along with Democrats, whose popular cartoon symbol is the donkey]. In the House, the Republican margin was 254 to 143.

George H. Moses of New Hampshire became president pro tem of the Senate, James E. Watson of Indiana was chosen Republican floor leader, and Simeon D. Fess of Ohio, former chairman of the congressional campaign committee, was made Republican whip. Together with Reed Smoot of Utah, these men were the backbone of the conservative wing. Leading the Republican insurgents were George W. Norris, who had opposed Hoover in the campaign, and Robert M. La Follette, Jr. William E. Borah of Idaho was now the elder statesman of the Republican progressives and their nominal leader.

6

President Hoover found himself with a party situation in Congress similar to President Taft's: an actively hostile, uncompromising progressive faction on the one hand and an immoderate conservative majority on the other hand. The latter faction was constantly calling for assertions of senatorial ascendancy. In the House, as in the Senate, few party leaders felt a personal loyalty to Hoover. Hoover in turn could neither placate nor develop an effective alliance with one or the other of the contending factions. Hoover's main difficulties, however, were with the Senate.

In 1928, as in other years, politicians linked the tariff by some obscure causal chain to various economic woes of the day. Thus, the American Farm Bureau Federation and the midwestern progressives led by Senator Borah blamed the chronic agricultural depression of the 1920s on the lack of adequate protection against foreign competition. Manufacturers complained to their representatives in Congress that costs of production at home and abroad should be "equalized" with foreign production costs and that a higher tariff would accomplish this. Labor leaders, interested in protecting employment and wage levels from cheaper labor forces abroad, were willing to join with the manufacturers' recommendation.

During the campaign, both candidates had promised early action on the tariff problem. Hoover went so far as to promise a special session of Congress. The special session met in April 1929. So certain were Democratic leaders that Hoover would have severe factional difficulties that they issued a postelection statement promising him their cooperation on the tariff issue.

Congress sweltered over the tariff from April to November and adjourned without passing a bill. It reconvened in December and struggled on through June 1930. The final product was the highest tariff in U.S. history; the Hawley-Smoot Tariff Act passed by a 49–47 vote. The rest of the world assessed this action as a supremely isolationist move that would exacerbate the existing grave international economic crisis. Like Taft in 1910, Hoover was in the position of having to put the best possible face on the legislation. At the time the tariff was adopted, the catastrophic significance of the stock market crash of October 29, 1929, was just beginning to be understood.

Hoover had even less success with the Congress elected in 1930. John N. Garner of Texas took the Speaker's gavel as the Democrats organized the House for the first time since 1919. Congressman Fiorello H. La Guardia of New York led a small group of Republican insurgents in an effort to control the swing votes between the two parties. There was almost complete paralysis in the Senate. Each party controlled forty-eight seats, and Hoover suggested to Senator Watson that the Democrats be permitted to organize that body.[21] A battle developed over the election of president pro tem. When Republican insurgents threatened to oppose Senator Moses for re-election, Moses in turn threatened to vote with the Democrats in selecting committee chairmen. After several ballots, Moses regained the position.

The national chairmanship became another pawn in this antagonistic presidential-congressional environment. Chairman Work, who had earned the hostility of Senator Moses and others during the campaign, was ready to resign on inauguration day. He was prevailed upon not to do so on the very first day of the new administration. Instead, he addressed the members of the national committee, convened for the inauguration, on plans for what he called "the Republican forces in times of passivity."[22] Between elections, he urged, the national organization should be kept ready for action at any moment's notice. Democrats were creating a permanent organization under John Jacob Raskob, and the Republicans needed to do so as well. With particular lack of foresight, the *New York Times* editorialized:

> While no one would put anything in the way of Chairman Work's innocent magnifying of his own office, in these days when political amusement is rare,

it must be said that his vision of a party organization maintaining itself in great activity throughout the four years between Presidential elections is certain to prove unsubstantial in the light of common day. . . . As for the general public, it will speedily forget that there was such a thing as a national committee or that it had an illustrious Chairman.[23]

Hoover's unprecedented success among the voters of the South revived Republican interest in that region to an extent that had not existed since Reconstruction days. Within three weeks of inauguration, Hoover warned southern Republicans that they might not be recognized in party and patronage matters if they did not reorganize themselves and their leadership. He made particular reference to recent revelations of abuses in recommendations for federal positions by leaders in South Carolina, Georgia, and Mississippi.

Hoover modified the usual procedure of clearing patronage appointments through southern senators and national committeemen. Instead, he created a special committee to clear problems of southern patronage, appointing to it Postmaster General Brown, Walter F. Newton, one of his personal secretaries, and James F. Burke, counsel of the national committee. The patronage at the disposal of the group was to be substantial, not only postmasterships but also appointments of census workers for the 1930 survey. In order to handle some of the complexities of clearance at the state level, Hoover reestablished the old referee system.[24]

Along with aggressive plans for reorganization in the South, Hoover attended to the difficulties at national headquarters. To reward and retire Dr. Work, he offered the national chairman the ambassadorship to Japan, which was declined. In June, Work simply announced his resignation, effective in the fall.[25]

For weeks the newspapers speculated about which of the president's former campaign associates would be chosen as Work's successor. James Good was now in the cabinet as secretary of war and not likely to step down to become national chairman. Good recommended George Woodruff, the Chicago banker, but federal banking law prevented officers of banks from serving on political committees. The names of the secretary of the national committee, Congressman Franklin Fort, and the treasurer, J.R. Nutt, came up. From among the president's intimates such names as Raymond Benjamin of California and Claudius Huston of Tennessee were identified as prospects. Others were Postmaster General Brown, National Committeeman Ralph Williams, and James F. Burke, the national committee counsel.[26]

At the beginning of August, Senate Republicans selected the senatorial committee for the midterm election campaign, with Senator Moses to be its chairman. In announcing the new campaign committee officers, Senator Watson, the Republican floor leader, noted with some satisfaction that Claudius Huston was under serious consideration for the national committee chairmanship. Watson also noted that Huston had recently expressed to him high regard for the leadership of Senator Moses.

At the national committee meeting in September, it was learned that Huston was indeed the president's choice. To work with him as national headquarters manager, with title of executive secretary and duties similar to those of Jouett Shouse at Democratic headquarters, the committee chose Representative Albert F. Dawson, an Iowa banker. Plans were made to house in one building the national, senatorial, and congressional campaign committees and to provide all three with a well-balanced clerical force on a permanent basis. Later staff adjustments, however, shifted Dawson to the position of executive secretary to the senatorial campaign committee rather than the national committee.[27]

The selection of Huston was evidence of Republican recognition of the changing South. Not only was Huston from Tennessee, which the press too readily considered part of the South, but, more pertinently, he had been mainly responsible for the "Hoovercrat" campaign in that region during the previous fall. One of the first announcements made by Huston as national chairman concerned the enlarged apportionment of national convention delegates to southern states for 1932 and the intention of the national party to work assiduously in that region to help overcome its racial and organizational difficulties.

Hardly in the chairmanship a few months, Huston was himself beset by a problem not easily disposed of. In March 1930, it was revealed before a Senate lobby investigating committee that Huston had for several years been a paid lobbyist against federal development of the Muscle Shoals power project on the Tennessee River and that he had at one time used lobby funds to finance personal speculations on the New York Stock Exchange. Huston asserted that he was innocent of any unethical or criminal act. However, Senate Democrats and Republican insurgents were not about to drop the matter. Demands for Huston's resignation were repeated at every opportunity during Senate business and in the midwestern press.

Huston indicated that he did not intend to resign under fire. Senators Moses and Watson conferred with President Hoover and expressed the hope that Huston would stay on. Western and midwestern members of the national committee, on the other hand, proceeded to explore ways of compelling the resignation. Aside from a voluntary resignation, the only means open was to have President Hoover personally request Huston to resign or to hold a special meeting of the national committee. The president was not disposed to make such a request. The special meeting would have to be called either by the chairman or at the request of a majority of the members.

As pressure upon Huston mounted during June and July, he continued to function as though he intended to remain in office for some time. He consulted frequently with Senator Moses and Representative Wood on strategies for the midterm campaign. He addressed a letter to each member of the national committee explaining in detail the charges against him and offering his explanations.

On July 6, Huston and President Hoover had an hour and a half conference at the White House in anticipation of a meeting of the national committee's officers four days later. The meeting spurred another flurry of newspaper speculation on whether or not the president would directly request a resignation.

The national committee officers met jointly with representatives of the senatorial and congressional campaign committees. At the close of these meetings, Huston told the press that further statements on his status would be withheld until after adjournment of the Senate two or three weeks later. Finally, at the August 7 meeting of the executive committee of the national committee, Huston formally offered his resignation, declaring that

> no man in political life has ever been subjected to more unjust and unwarranted attacks. . . . In the past it has been the policy of the party leaders to maintain a solid front when under the enemy fire, but as this has not been the policy in the present case, I have reached the conclusion . . . that I should tender my resignation.[28]

The conservatives retained control. Huston's successor, selected by the executive committee, was Senator Simeon D. Fess, Republican whip and a leader of the Old Guard. Fess' background as a former chairman of the congressional campaign committee as well as his senior status among Senate conservatives left no doubt that the management of the midterm congressional campaign would be carried on smoothly during its few remaining months.

As additional assurance that the operation of the national committee would be handled efficiently, the executive committee chose Commissioner of Internal Revenue Robert H. Lucas of Kentucky as its executive director. Apparently one of Senator Fess' requirements for accepting the chairmanship was that "all detailed work would be taken off my hands [to] leave me free to outline plans to be carried out by [a headquarters manager]."[29] Fess originally intended that Lucas be chairman of the executive committee, as in the case of the Democrats' Jouett Shouse. However, the executive committee decided that it had no authority to elect Lucas to its chairmanship since the national chairman normally held that position ex officio. The executive committee suggested making Lucas "executive assistant to the chairman," but Fess wished to give him a more dignified title. Lucas' salary was reported to be about $25,000 annually.

There was some question whether the executive committee had the authority to accomplish these changes in permanent organization. President Hoover raised these questions and was assured that the executive committee had full power. Senator Fess himself made it clear that his duties as Ohio's representative precluded his remaining as chairman for very long or giving it his full time. This explained, he said, the selection of a salaried executive director.

The Senate's Republican insurgents clearly scored a point by compelling the resignation of Huston. However, they did not win the game since Fess was an Old Guardsman to whose appointment President Hoover had acquiesced. The insurgents were outraged, recalling that Fess had recently characterized them as "pseudo Republicans."[30] Since there was not much they could do about the selection of Fess, several indicated that they would be conducting their own re-election campaigns without the aid of the various campaign committees.

Hoover's difficulties with his national chairmen—Work and Huston—led to costly delays in implementing plans for a Republican revival in the South. Even as Senator Fess was being chosen chairman, one of the Hoover's erstwhile southern campaign managers, Colonel Horace A. Mann, was in Savannah conducting a convention of Republicans from nine southern states in order to bring pressure on the administration regarding patronage policies for the South. As Colonel Mann put it, the new organization would not permit "designing political hijackers to invade the Southland every four years and rob her of the right to a legitimate representation at Republican National Conventions." The southern revolt was short-lived, submitting to pressure from Postmaster General Brown.[31]

Senator Fess' assumption of the national chairmanship gave him only three months in which to organize a midterm campaign. The returns on election day brought a Democratic majority into the House and an even split in the Senate. As Fess rationalized in his postelection statement,

> Even without such a disturbing factor as the economic depression, it was to have been expected that the Republicans would lose approximately thirty-five seats in the House, as this is about the average that the party in power loses in off-year elections, particularly after landslides in presidential contests of the proportions that attended the election of President Hoover. While this number [thirty-five] has been exceeded, it hasn't been exceeded by an overwhelming margin.[32]

The assumption had been that Senator Fess would retire from the chairmanship after the midterm election and that Executive Director Lucas would succeed him. Shortly after the election, it was Lucas, not Fess, who led a group of national committee officers to the White House to review with the president the requirements for maintaining a permanent headquarters. Shortly thereafter, Lucas announced a new agricultural division at national headquarters, with the main office in Des Moines. Hoover had concluded that the growing farm revolt in the Midwest would be his major hurdle in making another bid for the presidency in 1932.[33]

Eager to retire from the chairmanship, Fess shortly found himself in a predicament similar to that of his predecessor, Huston. Chairman Fess was by reputation as Dry on the Prohibition question as Democratic National Chairman Raskob was Wet. Although both parties were split on the Prohibition issue, the two national chairmen symbolized the difference. The Wets had the votes on the Democratic side and the Drys were ascendant among the Republicans. Republican Wets called for Fess' resignation because of his outspoken support of the

Eighteenth Amendment. The pressure to resign did not disturb Fess as it had Huston. Fess' difficulty was the sudden demise of Robert Lucas as his presumed successor.

In December 1930, the Senate committee investigating campaign practices drew from Lucas the admission that he had circulated campaign cartoons against Senator Norris of Nebraska. Lucas acknowledged doing so at a personal expense of $4,200 on grounds that he considered Norris "no Republican." There were immediate demands from the party's progressive wing for Lucas' resignation.[34]

Once again speculation in the press began regarding the chairmanship. Former California State Chairman Raymond Benjamin, a personal friend of the president, was again thought to be a likely national chairman. Western and midwestern Republicans suggested Ambassador Charles G. Dawes. Secretary of War Patrick J. Hurley was popular in some quarters. However, Postmaster General Brown of Ohio was considered the most probable prospect. Brown had not only the support of Senate leader Watson but also of many progressive leaders who recalled that Brown had managed the Roosevelt campaign in Ohio in 1912.

Senator Fess, however, was prevailed upon to hold the chairmanship until the end of the national convention, thus avoiding a third turnover in the position in the space of two years and delaying any fight over Fess' successor.[35]

7

President Hoover's renomination was a certainty, but it also was the occasion for manifestations of dissent. Republican progressives spoke again of a third-party movement, but the Senate progressives acknowledged that they would be unable to offer Hoover a serious challenge in the presidential primaries. Despite early attempts to revolt, southern delegations were considered safely in the president's hands as the result of adjustments made in the distribution of patronage. Some of the opposition to Hoover boosted Dwight Morrow, former ambassador to Mexico under Coolidge. Coolidge's death in October 1931 put an end to this effort as well as to a "draft-Coolidge" movement. In fact, the former president had already publicly advised Republicans everywhere to give their solid support to Hoover.

Another manifestation of factional dissatisfaction was the endless speculation about who would become national chairman in Hoover's second campaign. The list was long: Lawrence C. Phipps of Colorado, recommended by western conservatives; Henry M. Robinson of Los Angeles, personal friend of the president and author of the famous Young Plan; former National Chairman Butler, mentioned during the "draft-Coolidge" boom; Secretary of War Hurley; Ambassador Walter E. Edge; and James R. Garfield of Ohio, scheduled to be chairman of the platform committee at the national convention. The matter seemed settled when there were reports that Senator Watson had urged the president to appoint Postmaster General Brown, and that Brown had agreed to take the job.[36]

It was not a year in which Republican politicians eagerly sought the privilege of guiding their party's campaigns. Economic statistics showed 45 percent unemployment among factory workers, an 86 percent decline in residential building since 1929, and a 75 percent drop in steel production for the same period. In May of 1932, the Bonus Expeditionary Force arrived in Washington to demand increased veterans' benefits; some 700,000–800,000 veterans and dependents were among the most economically destitute in the country. On July 28, President Hoover authorized Secretary of War Hurley to disperse the bonus marchers. General Douglas MacArthur, whose junior officers included Dwight D. Eisenhower and George B. Patton, led several tanks and cavalry into the unpleasant undertaking.

It was also the year of the Samuel Insull and Ivar Kruger scandals which destroyed the last shred of popular confidence in American business leadership and in an administration that had identified itself conspicuously with business enterprise.

Renomination of the Hoover-Curtis ticket drove many Republican progressives into Franklin D. Roosevelt's campaign. Among the more prominent were George W. Norris, Bronson Cutting, Donald Richburg, Harold L. Ickes, Robert M. La Follette, Jr., Hiram Johnson, Smith W. Brookhart, and Gerald P. Nye. To help cope with the party's disintegrating midwestern leadership, Hoover called upon Everett Sanders of Indiana to serve as national chairman.

Political commentators generally interpreted the selection of Sanders as an effort to symbolize the regularity and prestige of the Coolidge following and the importance to be given to rural-agricultural interests in the Midwest. A letter from Coolidge to Sanders reveals that the former president had been consulted. "Some time ago, in discussing who ought to be Chairman of the National Committee, I said that you were the best man I could think of for the place. I am very glad that you found it possible to take it."[37]

Sanders was not only expert in midwestern political problems, but also had politically less to lose than some of the others mentioned for the chairmanship. After retiring as Coolidge's secretary, Sanders joined the law firm of James W. Good, later Hoover's secretary of war. Good handled Hoover's midwestern political affairs and was among the closest of his advisers. When Good died in November 1929, Sanders took over many of his late partner's Republican party obligations.

Sanders maintained continuity of personnel in national headquarters by appointing Robert Lucas as his assistant and reappointing former Senator Henry J. Allen as director of publicity, the position held by Allen in the 1928 campaign. To further demonstrate Republican concern with the Midwest, the principal campaign headquarters was set up in Chicago. General campaign strategy, however, emanated from President Hoover himself.[38]

The Republican electoral situation was hopeless, as Hoover later admitted in his memoirs. The desperation of some in the party is illustrated by the behavior of the Republican leaders in Indiana who were frantically trying to stem the tide. At stake was not only President Hoover's re-election, but also that of Old Guardsman James E. Watson. The state party leadership sent out an urgent call to former National Chairman Will Hays, still handling public relations for the motion picture industry, to return from Hollywood and help with the Indiana campaign. Even President Hoover joined in the request. But the political magic of 1918–20 was hardly available to Hays in 1932. The electorate swept aside not only President Hoover, but also some of his principal senatorial adversaries.

The 1932 election marked the end of a cycle in the struggle between presidential and congressional Republicans. The senatorial ascendancy represented by the nomination of Harding had been staunchly resisted by Coolidge. Hoover's efforts to straddle the conservative-progressive division brought little success and eventually became a matter of collaboration-in-distress between Hoover and the Old Guard. In later years, the rivalry would emerge again, in the contests between Senator Robert A. Taft of Ohio and Governor Thomas E. Dewey of New York.

20 | Organizing a Loyal Opposition in a New Deal Era

The Franklin D. Roosevelt landslide and the New Deal coalition that followed would hold Republicans at bay for more than a generation. "Hoover's Depression" remained the ultimate Democratic campaign slogan, akin to the "bloody shirt" cry of Republicans in the 1870s and 1880s. With their progressive wing co-opted by Roosevelt, the more realistic among the Republican leaders looked forward to many years as a loyal opposition tending to grass roots, looking for new constituencies, recruiting unhappy Democrats, and searching for exciting presidential candidates. "Alf" Landon and Wendell Willkie were the best candidates they could get under the circumstances, and, surprisingly, each made a positive contribution to the party. Landon helped bring in astute national chairmen and Willkie attracted Democrats ready to switch parties.

1

The Depression and the Republican defeat were blamed on Hoover and all who were associated with him. Next to the rejected president himself, the first to feel the heat was National Chairman Everett Sanders who, within three weeks after the election, found it necessary to issue a denial of any intention to resign his position. Robert Lucas did resign within the month.

Sanders' statement did not stop the rumors about the chairmanship. One rumor reported that Presidential Secretary Lawrence Richey would be assigned the task of reorganizing the party for the 1934 and 1936 contests. Another rumor suggested the early application of a new rule, adopted at the 1932 national convention, that permitted calling a meeting of the national committee by written petition of sixteen or more members representing not less than sixteen states. This was a measure apparently promoted by New York National Committeeman Charles D. Hilles, the former national chairman.

More fact than rumor was news that Old Guard senators were proposing their recently defeated leader, James E. Watson of Indiana, for the chairmanship. The New Deal landslide had carried sixty Democrats into the Senate, leaving thirty-five Republicans, most of them old-line holdovers from safe Republican states. Determined to diminish the Hoover influence in the party, the Old Guard advanced the Watson candidacy aggressively; Watson had the solid support of fully one-fourth of the members of the national committee.

President Hoover, however, held a majority on the national committee, his own man in the chairmanship, and had the responsibility for liquidation of more than $200,000 in campaign debts. Even before he departed from the White House, the defeated president acted as though he did not intend to abdicate his involvement in the national party's affairs. There was, after all, the possibility that Hoover might be a candidate for renomination in 1936.

Chairman Sanders, on the other hand, was in poor health, concerned about the condition of his law practice, and generally unable to give the necessary attention to the dormant national headquarters. It was only a matter of time before he would resign. He continued to be blamed for the 1932 defeat, although that campaign had largely been managed by Hoover and his undersecretary of the treasury, Ogden L. Mills. Throughout 1933 and early 1934, Republican leaders in Washington discussed the problem of finding a successor with the desired qualifications.

What remained of the party's progressives wanted a young liberal, preferably from the West or Midwest. The Old Guard sought a man loyal to the Senate leadership, for example, James E. Watson of Indiana, George H. Moses of Maine, or Charles D. Hilles of New York. Because Hoover was from the West and most of the Republican senators from the East, it seemed to some that the national chairman should come from "neutral" territory in the Midwest. Many Republican leaders hoped that a skillful organizer could be found to do the kind of interim party-building that Will Hays did so well from 1918 to 1920, the last time the Republicans were the out-party.

Preparation for the 1934 midterm campaign brought on the first overt conflict. In February, the chairmen of the Senate and House campaign committees announced that they would conduct a joint campaign independently of the national committee. This would end a practice of several decades according to which the three committees cooperated during off-year campaigns. Republican legislators reported that they had been unable to agree upon a fund-raising plan with Chairman Sanders, whose main concern continued to be his own committee's $200,000 debt. It soon appeared that there were also factional as well as managerial considerations. The Senate campaign committee chairman announced that Senator Arthur Capper of Kansas, a Hoover man, would not be reappointed to its executive committee. The chairman also announced that the congressional campaign effort would be a substantial one, with a $400,000 budget, a publicity bureau, and a bureau of economic research.

John D.M. Hamilton was the protégé of conservative David W. Mulvane, who, with the exception of eight Progressive years between 1912 and 1920, had been Kansas national committeeman and state party boss since 1900. Hamilton was chosen to succeed to the national committee post upon Mulvane's death in 1932. Hamilton was born in 1892 in Fort Madison, Iowa, where his father became mayor. During Hamilton's youth, his father's duties as lawyer for the Santa Fe Railroad required that the family move to Topeka, Kansas. Hamilton was subsequently sent to Phillips Academy at Andover, Massachusetts, and then to Northwestern University to study law. After a brief practice in Kansas City from 1916 to 1918, Hamilton returned to Topeka to form his own law partnership. Shortly after, running as an independent, Hamilton beat David W. Mulvane's candidate for the position of probate judge. This victory brought Hamilton a $250 monthly income plus fees, but, above all, the respect and friendship of Mulvane. Meanwhile, his law practice expanded, and Hamilton developed a specialty in the field of insurance law. He became a member of the Kansas House of Representatives in 1925 and its speaker in 1927–28. He received some renown at this time as a result of his controversy with the Kansas Ku Klux Klan. In 1928, he ran in the Republican primary for governor and lost. His opponent's campaign manager was Alfred M. Landon, with whom Hamilton struck up a close political friendship. In 1930, Hamilton was elected chairman of the Republican state committee and was part of the campaign effort that elected Landon governor in 1932 in the face of the Roosevelt landslide nationally. As governor-elect, Landon strongly endorsed Hamilton for the position of national committeeman.

Several weeks later, while hospitalized, Sanders gave out word that he would resign at the next meeting of the national committee for reasons of health. As speculation once again began, National Committeeman Hilles predicted that ability and geography would be the major considerations in the choice of a successor. Much attention was given to two young and energetic leaders of the Hays type: William B. Harrison of Kentucky and John D.M. Hamilton of Kansas. Both had recently conducted impressive, although unsuccessful, campaigns for governor in their respective states. Harrison had been mayor of Louisville and Hamilton was currently speaker of the Kansas House of Representatives.

Just prior to the national committee meeting in June, former President Hoover told several of his political friends—former Postmaster General Walter F. Brown, George F. Getz, national committee treasurer, and Senator Arthur Capper—that he would not be a candidate for renomination in 1936, but that he

Henry P. Fletcher was born in Pennsylvania in 1873 and was given his early education at private schools. After receiving his degree from Lafayette College, he studied law under the preceptorship of D. Watson Rowe, winning admission to the bar in 1894. Fletcher became Rowe's law partner in 1896, at the same time continuing his duties as official reporter of the Thirty-ninth Judicial District in Pennsylvania, a position he held from 1891 to 1898. With the outbreak of the Spanish-American War, Fletcher enlisted as a private and served with Roosevelt's Rough Riders. After the war, he reenlisted to serve in the Philippines. Fletcher entered the diplomatic service in 1902 as a legation secretary in Peking, later serving in similar capacities in Lisbon and Havana. He was promoted to minister to Chile in 1909, becoming the first ambassador to that country. His diplomatic career was at all times distinguished, and President Wilson kept him on as ambassador to Mexico during the entire period of strained relations with that country. President Harding appointed Fletcher as undersecretary of state. He later served as ambassador to Belgium and Italy, resigning from the latter position in 1929. In 1931, President Hoover called Fletcher back to the public service as chairman of the Tariff Commission. Much of Fletcher's involvement in party organization was apparently on the fund-raising side. In 1932, he became Hoover's chief money raiser in the East. With the national committee debt still standing at about $200,000, Fletcher's access to sources of funds was undoubtedly a factor in his selection.

would continue to exert his influence in party affairs and its campaigns. Hoover suggested that the national committee seek a chairman from outside the leadership of his administration, preferably someone from the Midwest with practical organizational experience and a capacity for fund-raising.[1]

Hoover's job description fit John Hamilton, who also had the active support of a number of younger Republican leaders. As their "younger man," the Old Guard, led by Hilles, favored Walter S. Hallanan of West Virginia, although Hallanan was probably second to their preference for former Senator Watson.

Two or three other names were proposed as possible compromise candidates during the days just before the committee's meeting. Many expressed a desire to make a compromise choice, which would postpone the fight for control of the national organization until after the 1936 nomination. Among those suggested as a compromise were National Committee Vice-Chairman Ralph E. Williams of Oregon and Henry P. Fletcher of Pennsylvania, the latter having served as chairman of the eastern finance committee in the campaign of 1932. Fletcher, Hamil-

Son of a farmer-politician, Spangler was born on an Iowa farm in 1879, of Dutch and Scotch descent. After serving as a private in the Spanish-American War, Spangler undertook the study of law at the University of Iowa, receiving the degree and entering the bar in 1905. He joined a firm in Cedar Rapids in 1907 and the following year campaigned to elect James W. Good to Congress. A doorbell-ringing Republican for his father, Spangler worked his way up through the precinct and county organizations in Iowa, the only break in his regularity occurring when he supported Roosevelt in 1912. By 1930, he was elected chairman of the state central committee and in 1931 was appointed national committeeman. He served as a member of the executive committee of the national committee in 1932.

---

ton, and Hallanan were formally placed in nomination. Upon the advice of Hilles, Hallanan withdrew. Walter Brown, as spokesman for the former president, endorsed Fletcher, who received 68 votes to Hamilton's 24.

The spirit of compromise—or postponement—prevailed during most of the national committee meeting. In recognition of the younger leaders, John Hamilton was chosen general counsel at a salary of $15,000.

A midterm declaration of policy, similar to the one issued during Will Hays' regime, was produced by a committee of nine under the chairmanship of Charles D. Hilles, in consultation with Senators James Reed and Ogden L. Mills. The document was a composite of eastern and western policy positions, an obvious attempt to reestablish the national committee as an influential participant in the midterm campaign. Adoption of the policy statement received high praise from former President Hoover, whose comments also included his conception of the role of the party when in opposition:

> The firm declaration by the Committee of Republican Principles and Purposes will hearten not only Republicans but the whole country, for even those who disagree with us will realize the vital importance of scrutiny and constructive debate of all proposals, and opposition to those which will hurt the progress and welfare of the country.
>
> In order to accomplish this service to the nation, vigorous party organization is essential.[2]

The fall election gave the New Deal an increased majority in Congress, the first time in over a hundred years that the party controlling the presidency gained rather than lost seats. The principal Republican victory occurred in Kansas where Governor Landon was re-elected at the end of a vigorous campaign managed by John Hamilton.

2

As the ranking state Republican party in the nation, the Kansans felt ready to take initiatives in national organizational affairs. In January 1935, John Hamilton said as much. He proposed a Republican "Grass Roots" convention in the Midwest. This gathering would be, he declared, a first step in reviving the national party. To advance this enterprise he had the help of Harrison E. Spangler, Iowa's national committeeman and state chairman.

Some six thousand delegates from ten midwestern states gathered in Springfield, Illinois, during June 1935, in response to Hamilton's call. The convention generated much rank-and-file enthusiasm and received favorable coverage by the press. When the national committee's executive committee met for a business meeting three months later, it was agreed that the Midwest organizing effort begun by Hamilton and Spangler should be continued. Spangler was put in charge, and he carried it forward by inaugurating Grass Roots Clubs, encouraging Young Republican Clubs, and endorsing women's organizations. The executive committee also created a Young Republican division for the national committee, as suggested by Hamilton many months earlier.

The optimism and dynamism emanating from the Kansas organization was in striking contrast to the Republican party elsewhere. The crushing congressional defeat of 1934, the mounting recovery successes of the New Deal, and Franklin D. Roosevelt's popularity left most Republican leaders in a mood to skip the 1936 election. The party's morale was so low and the organizational machinery so battered that a substantial element in the party decided to create its own anti-New Deal organization. They found willing allies among conservative Democrats, with whom they founded the Liberty League.

In the opinion of Frank Knox, the Liberty League held promise of becoming a third-party movement. "I expect it will . . . eventuate in the formation of an independent democratic group like the Palmer-Buckner ticket in 1896 of Gold Democrats."[3] With this kind of movement in mind, the December meeting of the Republican national committee adopted an unusual resolution inviting all "Jeffersonian Democrats" to join the Republicans in restoring representative government. In response to this development, the Democrats, under Chairman James A. Farley's direction, adopted the tactic of concentrating their campaign attacks against the Liberty League's unvarnished conservatism. Farley and President Roosevelt seemed to enjoy acting as though the Republican party no longer existed.

Progressive Republicans, increasingly isolated from their own party by these conservative maneuvers, began to complain publicly of Chairman Fletcher's exaggerated anti-New Deal stance. They worried that the influence of the Hoover moderates was receding and that the Old Guard was coming into full control of the national organization. Republican liberals became particularly aroused when, during the winter of 1935, Charles D. Hilles unsuccessfully attempted to have a new plan of national convention apportionment adopted. Just as aggravating was Chairman Fletcher's announced organization of the national convention; key positions were to go almost exclusively to conservative leaders.

From a managerial point of view, neither liberals nor conservatives could complain very much. By April 1936, Fletcher had raised enough money to change the national committee's red ink of $200,000 to some $250,000 in the black. With the help of his general counsel, John Hamilton, Fletcher was actively encouraging the organization of Young Republicans. In November 1935, young Republicans from twenty-one states founded the Young Republican National Federation. Its elected chairman became ex officio director of the new youth division at the national committee. By February, this division was producing a monthly magazine called *The Young Republican.*

Another national committee innovation was the creation of a research division. The new division was headed by Dr. O. Glenn Saxon, professor of economics at Yale. Saxon, a former Democrat, had substantial experience in the preparation of testimony for congressional and other governmental committees. He mobilized the research division so that it could contest statements made by New Deal agencies, prepare its own reports of economic trends, and provide speakers' materials for Republican orators. Before the 1936 campaign had ended, Dr. Saxon had the help of an advisory board of nine college professors and some forty to fifty research assistants.

Chairman Fletcher also called in Bruce Barton, partner in one of the country's major advertising agencies, to evaluate the publicity going forth from national headquarters.

One particular development brought home to Fletcher the difficulty of out-party management. President Roosevelt had announced that he would deliver his annual message to Congress during evening hours in order to enable the new national radio networks to carry his speech at prime time. Fletcher called the annual message a "political" speech and demanded equal radio time for a reply, even indicating that the Republican national committee would be willing to pay for the air time. The networks were willing to grant free time, but unwilling to sell time for political broadcasts until after the regular national conventions.

While the weeks passed in negotiations about this issue, the Republican headquarters produced a series of dramatic skits for broadcast. Network executives refused to consider the president's address as anything but an official event and, further, found the skits objectionable on editorial grounds. Fletcher called the networks' objections censorship and threatened to bring suit. Without an identified opposition spokesman, Republican leaders became painfully aware of the difficulty of capturing the same popular attention that a presidential statement does. The *New York Times* succinctly summarized the dispute as follows,

Joseph W. Martin, Jr., was the first of eight children born to a North Attleboro, Massachusetts, blacksmith. Born in 1884, Martin spent much of his childhood as an enterprising young newspaper peddler. While in high school, he found employment in various jobs at local newspaper shops and at night as a telephone operator. He also found time to do well scholastically and to become captain of the baseball team. Declining a scholarship to Dartmouth, he went to work as a newspaper reporter for the next six years. In 1908, he and several others purchased the North Attleboro *Evening Chronicle*, which eventually became a fully owned Martin family enterprise.

After managing the campaign of a friend running for state legislature, Martin, in 1911, decided to make his own race. He was elected and served in the lower house for three years, after which he retired to manage an insurance agency he had just purchased. He remained active in party affairs and, in 1917, was chosen chairman of the Republican legislative campaign committee. In 1922, he was drafted by Massachusetts Republican leaders to serve as executive secretary of the state committee and to take on the difficult task of restoring peace between the quarreling Lodge and Crane factions. In 1924, Martin ran his own campaign for Congress and was elected and re-elected continuously thereafter. By 1929, he was serving on the House Rules Committee and, in 1933, he was appointed assistant to the Republican floor leader. At the 1936 national convention, he served as Landon's floor leader. In later years, Martin rose to be minority leader and Speaker of the House of Representatives, permanent chairman of the Republican national convention, chairman of the Republican congressional campaign committee in 1938, and, in 1940, Republican national chairman.

"Under our system of government the Administration is bigger news than the Opposition. . . . It is the Opposition's hard luck."[4]

Finding a Republican presidential nominee in 1936 was no simple enterprise. Former President Hoover had bowed out privately, but never publicly or categorically. In his case, the party was not likely to turn to a loser, particularly one so tarnished by the depression. Senator Borah was actively interested, but too far to the left and handicapped by his failure to support the ticket in 1932. Newspaper publisher Frank Knox launched a campaign in his own behalf that met with little response.

Governors Styles Bridges of New Hampshire and Alfred M. Landon of Kansas were among the very few recently successful Republican candidates for elective office. Polls of Republican party workers during late 1935 and early

1936 showed Landon, Knox, and Borah as the top preferences. More strictly in the favorite-son category were Arthur Vandenberg of Michigan and Robert A. Taft of Ohio, son of the late president.

During the spring of 1936, John Hamilton resigned as general counsel of the national committee in order to manage Landon's preconvention campaign. In April, Hamilton went to New York to open an eastern headquarters. Preconvention work proceeded smoothly. Hamilton traveled widely, and the Hearst newspaper and magazine chain lost no opportunity to give Landon favorable publicity.

As the convention approached, Landon ran into problems with respect to the platform. While the platform committee accepted most of the planks recommended by Landon, under pressure from the eastern wing, it, however, rejected other of Landon's positions. Thus, the platform committee declined to favor state control of minimum wages and hours for women and children, place the Post Office under civil service, or endorse reciprocal tariffs. While the convention was in progress, Landon wired it a message, read by John Hamilton, reasserting his position on the three planks. This disagreement was the full extent to which a liberal-conservative split appeared. The convention proceeded to nominate Landon, the only candidate formally placed before it. The vice-presidential place went to Knox by acclamation.

3

As expected, unity prevailed at the meeting of the national committee. Hamilton was elected to succeed Fletcher and immediately appointed Fletcher as the new general counsel. Hamilton then chose as his executive committee and special assistants a new generation of younger leaders: for the executive committee, men like Earl Warren of California and Robert Burroughs of New Hampshire; to run eastern headquarters, Joseph Martin, Jr.; as personal assistants, such men as Spangler of Iowa and MacVeagh of New York.[5]

In the election campaign, Landon and Hamilton put on a two-man show, only rarely consulting with the national committee or national headquarters. Landon worked out his own itinerary and speeches and conducted himself with dignity and moderation. Landon confided to oil magnate Joseph Pew during the campaign that he realized he was a sacrificial lamb for the party, that beating Roosevelt was hardly in the cards in 1936.[6] John Hamilton, on the other hand, conducted himself as though he himself were the nominee for president. The campaign, he felt, was a precious opportunity to rebuild the debilitated national party. Win or lose, Hamilton was considering the need for a strong interim organization, for which he paved the way during the campaign months.

Two weeks after he assumed charge of national headquarters, Hamilton was off for a campaign tour of New England. After returning from New England, he chartered a plane for a tour, accompanied by twelve assistants, which took him over 6,500 miles through the Midwest and West. He conferred with state and local party leaders. He gave speeches attacking New Deal policies, particularly the Social Security Act. He caused much political heat when he called labor leader David Dubinsky a "Red." By mid-October, Hamilton joyfully applauded the *Literary Digest* opinion poll predicting that Landon would win. His own forecast gave 302 electoral votes to the Republican nominee.

Preoccupied with travel and speeches, Hamilton neglected the executive management of national headquarters. The national committee offices had been divided into several bureaus for the purposes of the campaign: organization, publicity, public relations, research, and editorial, as well as various bureaus for particular groups—youth, minorities, women, etc. A feud developed between the journalists of the publicity bureau and the academicians of the research bureau. Complicating matters further were the efforts to introduce modern advertising techniques, with at least three bureaus designing and producing propaganda. Even more serious was the uncertainty about policy positions, particularly as these positions became increasingly conservative toward the close of the campaign.[7]

Several innovations were made and some records were broken during this campaign: spot radio announcements were introduced; 2,000 broadcasts utilized 250 stations; innumerable films and newsreels were produced; 361,000 press releases were turned out; and, in all, some 310 million pieces of campaign literature mailed from national headquarters.

To grapple with the difficulties, Hamilton appointed Harrison Spangler executive vice-chairman for headquarters operations. In addition, he hired Arthur A. Ballantine as a special coordinating assistant. Hamilton then returned to the campaign trail.

Before the campaign was over some $9 million were officially expended through the national committee. This compared to $5 million spent by the Democrats. The campaign was vigorous and expensive, but no match for the overwhelming tide favoring the New Deal. Landon carried only Maine and Vermont against yet another Roosevelt landslide. This was the election in which the Democrats became the "normal majority" in the electorate.

The character of the defeat moved Republican leaders to an unusually open discussion of their party's predicament. Typical was Senator Arthur Vandenberg's article in the *Saturday Evening Post* on "How Dead is the GOP?" Implying that interim party leadership would come from Congress, Vandenberg declared that "sentry-service" would be "the function of the direct opposition."[8] Others recommended changing the party's name, adhering more closely to its traditional conservatism, forming a coalition with conservative Democrats, etc.

In Hoover and Landon, the Republican party now had two titular leaders, one of whom had actually served in the presidency. In John Hamilton, it had a national chairman who represented a new generation and whose enthusiasm for the party's future remained undiminished in defeat. Despite a million dollar campaign deficit, Hamilton placed his tenure as national chairman on the block at a special meeting of the national committee called for December 1936.

Only fifty-nine members were present, plus twenty-four who came as proxies. Hamilton submitted his resignation, explaining that this was only proper in view of the electoral disaster. In his statement he recommended that the party look seriously to the establishment of a year-round national organization. After some debate, the national committee, in an overwhelming majority, declined to accept his resignation.

4

Hamilton now held the chairmanship in his own right, without the endorsement of a presidential nominee. In fact, during the meeting, evidence of a rift between Landon and Hamilton could be detected. A telegram from Landon was read praising the efforts of the national committee, but failing to mention the work of Hamilton. The rift widened with the passing months, particularly as Hamilton struck out more and more on his own. In later years Landon recalled that his support of Hamilton was tacit but nonetheless real, "John and I never did agree, particularly, on our political philosophy. But I felt that, with the collapse of the Republican organization all over the country, that we needed a good cavalry leader . . . to roam over the country and pep up the state organizations."[9]

Hamilton at once offered the national committee his plans for a permanent national headquarters. He recommended the creation of a full-time, salaried chairmanship. The committee concurred. Hamilton's salary was set at $15,000 a year, plus $10,000 as fixed allowance for expenses. Hamilton proceeded to establish a permanent headquarters in Washington and appointed several staff persons: two assistants to the chairman, a secretary, a director of publicity, a director of research, and a librarian. There followed a rush of headquarters activity that lasted until the next national convention. For many old-timers, it seemed a return to the busiest days of the Will Hays regime.[10]

Hoping to make the concept of a full-time headquarters more palatable to his fellow-partisans, Hamilton went to England during the summer of 1937 to observe the operations of the major parties in that country, particularly the Conservative's national headquarters. He reported his findings, without recommendations, to all members of the national committee. Hamilton himself recalled that no "specific action was taken based on the Report," but that one effect was to lift the morale of the headquarters staff who were happy to find support for "organizational politics as a career."[11]

Hamilton's achievements as national chairman from 1937 to 1940 were notable and possibly more enduring than those of his redoubtable predecessor, Will Hays. In the words of one student of that period:

> It can be argued that the fortunes of the Republican party had reached such a low ebb in 1936 that any Chairman could only have improved its standing. The claim can further be made that the establishment of a permanent and energetic national staff, along with the other changes instituted by Hamilton, was inevitable and necessary. The fact remains that most of the operating divisions of the Republican National Committee had their precursors in similar organizations established by John Hamilton.[12]

One of Hamilton's major concerns was establishing closer contact between the national and local organizations. At first a headquarters newspaper, later a newsletter, were among the devices created to promote this contact. Hamilton personally visited thirty-seven states during 1937 and 1938 to describe national headquarters activities to the local people, encourage local activity, and stimulate their fund-raising efforts.

Relations with Republicans in Congress were another of his primary concerns. Staff for legislators and congressional committees were not yet a large part of the operating scene on Capitol Hill. No longer in control of the resources of the federal bureaucracy and the minority party in both houses of Congress, Republicans on Capitol Hill found themselves painfully short-handed and ill-staffed for carrying on political opposition. Hamilton reappointed Dr. Saxon as director of the national committee's research division, expanded its staff, and made it available to Republicans in Congress.

To coordinate legislative-headquarters research and policy, Hamilton established the "weekend conference," a series of Saturday meetings to put congressmen and national committee staff into a close working relationship, develop policies and strategies, and, generally, to familiarize all concerned with Republican views on complex legislation. Usually each conference dealt with a particular subject for which the research division had prepared documents in advance. Eight to ten congressmen, Hamilton, Saxon, and special experts invited for the weekend, spent the full day in analysis and discussion. Although a simple technique for communication among national leaders, the weekend conference was a marked advance over the ad hoc and practically nonexistent leadership consultations that had taken place previously. The conferences became the Republican opposition's equivalent of President Franklin D. Roosevelt's weekly meetings with his official party leaders in Congress that he inaugurated in 1937.

Hamilton gave special encouragement to headquarters divisions dealing with special groups. The Young Republican magazine was revived. An oratorical contest was sponsored through the youth division. In 1938, the National Federation of Republican Women was established, and Miss Marion E. Martin provided leadership of women's activities for nearly a decade thereafter. The problems of various ethnic groups were given continuing attention by special individuals at headquarters.

Financial matters were also approached systematically. A finance division was created under the direction of Carlton G. Ketchum. A program of sustaining memberships and an extensively organized soliciting campaign were inaugurated. Membership cards were given to each contributor. Members were encouraged to pledge specific amounts to be donated in later years. By 1938, there were approximately 6,400 sustaining members. Persistent efforts were made through state and local finance committees to attract additional contributors.

Reporting to the national committee in 1939, Hamilton revealed that joint solicitation arrangements with the state organizations in 1937 resulted in contributions of approximately $400,000 from eighteen states and $31,000 from all the others. In 1938, these same eighteen states contributed $700,000 and the others $14,000. At the end of 1939, the national committee deficit stood at $655,000. A special committee headed by George W. Pepper, former senator from Pennsylvania and in later years a senior law partner of Hamilton, was able to eliminate this deficit within two months, leaving the national committee treasury in the black at the end of Hamilton's tenure.

Another financial innovation in 1938 was the creation of joint fund-raising machinery for the national, senatorial, and congressional campaign committees. This was an arrangement that had been discussed in previous years, but never before put into operation. Hamilton set fund-raising goals of $500,000 for the House and $175,000 for the Senate campaigns and achieved substantial success in reaching these goals. The 1938 midterm election was in general a successful one for the Republicans; it put into the Senate and governors' mansions Republicans who would play a major part in national politics for the next two decades, for example, Robert A. Taft of Ohio, Harold Stassen of Minnesota, Leverett Saltonstall of Massachusetts, Alexander Wiley of Wisconsin, and others.

The headquarters staff numbered about forty persons during most of Hamilton's tenure. Morale was consistently high and a spirit of professionalism flourished. To add a semblance of economic security to this precarious type of political employment, Hamilton considered, but never formally proposed, a pension plan for the regular employees.[13]

Most of the staff worked under Dr. Saxon's supervision in the research division. A library of more than six thousand volumes was collected. In addition to its work for Republican congressmen, this division also produced a loose-leaf handbook of background materials for campaigns, speeches, and policy reports. Called *The Republican Reporter*, some two thousand paying subscribers regularly received its inserts as they were published. The energies of the research division were particularly called upon in two connections: the Supreme Court fight of 1937 and the work of the Glenn Frank program committee.

President Roosevelt's apparent reluctance to run for a third term was encouraging news to Republicans as well as to the anti-New Deal elements within the Democratic party. The 1937 Supreme Court fight gave Republicans further cause for rejoicing: Democrats were seriously divided on the issue. This battle gave John Hamilton his first real experience with the difficulties of maintaining a Loyal Opposition, in the British sense, based at an American national party headquarters during nonpresidential election years.

Hamilton was scheduled to address a group of Pittsburgh businessmen on the evening after Roosevelt's announcement of his court-packing plan. He was at first inclined to take a vigorous stand against the plan. During the meal prior to the speech, Hamilton received a telephone call from Senator Vandenberg in Washington telling him of a meeting of three Republican Senate leaders that afternoon. The three leaders—Charles McNary, the Senate minority leader, William E. Borah, and Arthur H. Vandenberg—had agreed that the only way Roosevelt's court-packing plan could succeed would be to make it a party issue. Vandenberg told Hamilton that there were enough Democratic votes to kill the proposal and that the decision had been made to let Democrats lead the opposition. Vandenberg asked Hamilton not to mention the Court plan in his speech that evening and further asked the national chairman to make no public mention of the Court plan "until further notice." Hamilton saw no alternative but to agree.[14]

The "strategy of silence" devised by the three Senate leaders had to be sold to other Republican leaders in and out of Congress. They were able to convince Landon, who was on the point of devoting a Lincoln Day address to the Court proposal, to ignore the issue entirely. The strategists were more circumspect in approaching former President Hoover, who, despite all their efforts, spoke at length before the Union League of Chicago on the topic "Hands Off the Supreme Court."

The different degrees to which party leaders deferred to the Senate leaders were of particular interest. The closer a party leader was to political "practicalities," the greater his deference.

> The effort of Senators McNary and Vandenberg to silence Mr. Hoover was not successful, and there is little indication that the public felt Hoover spoke for the party. But the episode demonstrates the jealousy of incumbent legislators, who feel that the definition of the opposition attitude is their exclusive responsibility. Governor Landon, partly because of his unprecedented defeat in the electoral college, received no allegiance as party spokesman; indeed, he chose to be guided by the judgment of the "strategists of silence."
>
> The Chairman of the National Committee, the sole elected leader of the national party, finds himself in grave difficulty if he presumes to speak for the party. Party members in Congress regard the National Committee as a source of rival definition of party attitudes. They fear that such a definition may alienate supporters in their own districts. Mr. Hamilton dared not oppose the wishes of the party leaders in the Senate when they announced the "strategy of

silence," and he could not win complete approval of the resumption of partisan activities three months later.[15]

Silence did not mean inactivity. The Republican national committee served as a key coordinating agency in the fight against the Roosevelt Court plan. The research division prepared data and speeches for Republicans and Democrats alike. Materials going to Democrats were channeled through Senator McNary, who acted as the principal link between congressional Democrats and Republican national headquarters. National headquarters worked closely with the Washington office of the American Bar Association in organizing the witnesses appearing before the Senate's Committee on the Judiciary.

The national committee also became a secret clearinghouse for funds distributed to pressure groups opposing the Roosevelt bill. Requests for financial help came to Hamilton either through Senator McNary on behalf of various legislators or directly from interest organizations. After investigating the trustworthiness of the "applicant," Hamilton went to regular Republican contributors for funds. These funds were usually forthcoming, although sometimes they meant a sacrifice to the regular Republican fund-raising drives. Several religious organizations were particularly active in the opinion-creating undertaking and were directed by the Reverend Theodore Graebner of St. Louis and Dr. Ralph E. Nollner, a Methodist. According to Hamilton, some $250,000 were handled in this manner.

Throughout, Hamilton resisted the "strategy of silence" for fear that a Democratic faction would win public credit for defeating a piece of legislation that had almost united the Republican opposition. Furthermore, in his fund-raising for the national committee, Hamilton was constantly confronted by the inquiry, "What is the party doing?" Unable to point to the committee's role in the Court fight, Hamilton at last decided to inaugurate a series of political radio broadcasts in May of 1937.

The broadcasting plan met with opposition immediately. Senate Republican leaders solicited Landon's help in an attempt to have Hamilton abandon his radio plan. Hamilton agreed only to exclude the Court plan from among the topics. After the first of four talks had been broadcast, Landon wrote to Hamilton again questioning the wisdom of the series. Hamilton's reply was pragmatic, "Something [should] be done to show some life upon which our solicitors can base their work."[16]

5

Probably the most controversial undertaking of the Hamilton tenure was the proposal for a midterm national convention. This was the first serious effort on the part of the leadership of either national party to convene such a convention on a regular basis. The proposal was caught in a multidirectional crossfire:

between presidential and congressional party leaders, between Hoover and Landon supporters, and between national and local party interests. The proposal also suffered from poor presentation to the public.

The 1935 Grass Roots Convention called by Hamilton in the Midwest had been so successful that, in 1936, Hamilton spoke of a similar type of convention at the national level. Hamilton's interest in a midterm convention was further stimulated by his trip to England in 1937, where he learned of the annual conferences of the major British parties. During the early summer of 1937, Hamilton conversed privately with various national leaders about the possibility of having a midterm convention. He won the support of Walter E. Edge and the national committeeman from Texas. Former President Hoover was enthusiastic, apparently having previously given such a convention much thought.

The matter came before the public prematurely in June when Hoover's former Secretary of Agriculture Arthur Hyde reported that Hoover favored a national party meeting to promulgate a statement of creed on behalf of the entire party. Hyde coupled this news with a recommendation that the party draft Hoover for the 1940 nomination.

Landon supporters saw in the Hoover proposal an attempt to regain active control of the party. Landon was personally skeptical about the proposal, anticipating that it hardly could do more than compose broad generalizations and would at all times run the risk of reviving factional conflicts. Furthermore, because the proposal implied that the Republican party had no program during a congressional election year, Landon urged that no action be taken without close consultation with the Republican members of Congress.[17]

In September, Hoover published a detailed statement of his plan. It called for a full-dress convention of those delegates who attended the previous two Republican national nominating conventions. The proposed convention would meet for the purpose of issuing a thorough statement of the party's program and philosophy.[18]

Hamilton brought up the Hoover proposal at the September meeting of the executive committee, revealing that the plan originally was his own, not Hoover's. Joseph Martin, Jr., expressed doubt that any such convention could be worthwhile since any principles adopted would necessarily be vague and perhaps academic. Harrison Spangler, on the other hand, supported the plan, reporting that he had recently conducted a survey among 11,000 Republican leaders with responses showing that 94 percent of those replying favored a special convention. The executive committee postponed further discussion until the meeting of the full national committee in November.

The midterm convention plan was widely discussed by party leaders and received much attention in the press. Hoover made a special effort to win over the elder statesmen in the party, taking the opportunity to mention that he had no future presidential aspirations. This seemed to allay the suspicions of such men as Lowden, Landon, and Knox. It was Knox's belief that any midterm declaration should be issued after the midterm elections.

Hamilton also solicited support for the plan, but less successfully. Landon took the view that new blood was needed at such a convention, not old-timers from the previous two national nominating conventions. Former National Chairman Fletcher, Senator Vandenberg, and Senator Townsend, chairman of the senatorial campaign committee, expressed fear that such a convention would jeopardize the party's chances in November. Senators Borah and Capper anticipated discord resulting from the struggle for control of the party machinery that would take place at such a convention. Others replied that if a fight were to develop, it would be better to have it sooner, in 1938, rather than later, in 1940, a presidential year.

The compromise worked out at the November national committee meeting drew from the precedent set by Will Hays in 1919. A program committee of one hundred was established to prepare the way for the work of the platform committee of the 1940 national convention. This program committee would presumably define the party's stand on national issues and report its recommendations to the national committee sometime before the 1940 convention. The appointment of program committee members was left to Chairman Hamilton and the executive committee.

The executive committee subsequently met and found before it a list of 1,250 names from which to choose the 100. There was prolonged and vigorous debate over the size of the committee and the criteria of selection. It was finally decided to enlarge the committee to 200; the number eventually grew to approximately 250. To make the program committee broadly representative, it was agreed that at least 55 members be drawn from among labor leaders, editors, social workers, farmers, and professional people. Women were to be given 65 places, Blacks 8, Jews 16, and Catholics 25.

The committee that was finally appointed included 52 lawyers, 27 businessmen, merchants, and manufacturers, 25 farmers and farm leaders, 23 housewives, 15 editors and publishers, 10 educators and college presidents, 7 bankers, 6 insurance company presidents, 4 labor leaders, 2 doctors, 2 clergymen, and miscellaneous members of other occupations. Herbert Hoover and Charles G. Dawes accepted positions on the committee. Knox and Landon declined. Dr. Glenn Frank, former president of the University of Wisconsin, was named chairman. Dr. Thomas H. Reed was appointed director of studies.

The first meeting of the program committee took place in March 1938 in Chicago. Subcommittees were established for specific topics such as security, government activities, foreign policy, and many others. Membership on these subcommittees was arranged to form nine regional groupings for the purpose of representing Republican opinion throughout the nation. Subject-matter experts were consulted and extensive public interviews conducted. Findings were reported to drafting committees for each region. When draft reports had been prepared in platform style and form, they were transmitted to national headquarters where they were consolidated and edited. The national staff, under Frank's direction, then incorporated all the materials into a single, final document.

As the committee's work progressed, Republican congressmen, as well as other Republican officeholders running for re-election in 1938, began to indicate that they would not be bound by any pronouncements of the Frank group. To avoid such disavowals, the committee's press releases during the midterm campaign were predominantly anti-New Deal in content. Even after the election, however, Republican legislators continued to refer negatively to the work of the Frank committee. Dr. Frank himself expressed the belief that "the custodians of party policy in the interims between National Conventions are the Republican members in the Senate and the House when, as now, the party is not in power."[19]

The final report of the program committee was a document of over 33,000 words, entitled *A Program for a Dynamic America*, issued on February 16, 1940. The report declared it the duty of an opposition to "appraise the policies of the party in power and, where basic disagreements exist, to restate the principles upon which, in its judgment, effective national policies must be based."

Major themes of the report were overcentralization and overspending by the New Deal. In a more affirmative tone, the program committee urged a return to American free enterprise as the best way to achieve full employment. It objected to the creation of the Tennessee Valley Authority as unfair governmental competition with private enterprise, an issue that acquired particular and unexpected significance when Wendell Willkie entered the 1940 nominating race. A major weakness in the document was its inadequate treatment of the spreading war in Europe; much of the Republican leadership at this time maintained a noninterventionist posture.

The program committee report did much to start Republicans talking with each other. It was useful in the preparation of the 1940 platform. But, like the platform, it had little impact on the political developments of the day. Furthermore, the report was quickly lost in the rapid flow of the 1940 presidential candidacies. Hoover, Knox, and Landon were no longer in the field. New, available presidential candidates included Senator Robert A. Taft of Ohio, New York District Attorney Thomas E. Dewey, Senator Arthur H. Vandenberg, and Senate Minority Leader Charles McNary. Favorite sons included Arthur H. James of Pennsylvania, Styles Bridges of New Hampshire, and Joseph W. Martin of Massachusetts. A self-selected candidate was publisher Frank E. Gannett.

For one reason or another each of the front-runners was a doubtful prospect. Senator Vandenberg, the eldest of the candidates, seemed to have been too long at the forefront of Republican conservatism and isolationism, hence he was a poor match for the New Deal or the problems emerging from the European war.

Dewey's racket-busting successes as district attorney gave him a place as one of the most popular of Republican leaders, but he was little known to the party outside of the East and, in 1938, had suffered a hairbreadth defeat in the gubernatorial race against Herbert Lehman.

Robert A. Taft was heir to one of Ohio's most honored political families and at the 1936 national convention had been Ohio's favorite son. Although a freshman senator in 1939, Taft held seats on three of the most powerful Senate committees: appropriations, banking and currency, and labor. He emerged from his first session in Congress a serious presidential prospect. Since much of his political support came from the same wing of the party as Vandenberg, Taft at this time consistently deferred to the seniority of the Michigan senator.

In sum, as 1940 approached, the Republicans had many older leaders who were committed to particular factional interests and many younger men not yet "ripe" for the main prize. One other factor cooled the enthusiasm of the Republican candidates: the growing likelihood that the race would be against "The Champ" himself. Franklin D. Roosevelt was gearing up to run for an unprecedented third term. The Republican nominating situation therefore remained fluid and open to new personalities.

6

Just such a personality appeared in the person of Wendell Willkie. During the 1920s, while still counsel and junior partner in the Ohio Edison Company, Willkie devoted much energy to civic affairs and Democratic party activities. As late as 1935, after establishing residence in New York, Willkie was an elected member of the Tammany county committee in the Thirty-seventh Election District of the 15th assembly district. His fellow committeemen included James A. Farley and Frank C. Walker, Democrats of note.

Willkie's Republicanism began with his 1936 vote for Landon. His national renown came as a result of his fight against the Tennessee Valley Authority. In 1929, Willkie had became legal counsel to the Commonwealth and Southern Corporation, a utility holding company. By 1933, he was the company's president. Throughout the seven years of his presidency of Commonwealth and Southern, Willkie waged a vigorous battle against public ownership of utilities. He carried on the fight in the courts and the mass media. These activities won favor in the business community, and, between 1937 and 1939, he was occasionally mentioned as a potential presidential candidate. Arthur Krock, the well-known political commentator, described Willkie as outstanding presidential material in his column as early as February 1939. Added support for this suggestion came from a disaffected New Dealer, General Hugh S. Johnson, in his syndicated column in November 1939. Russell Davenport, managing editor of *Fortune*, also became interested and invited Willkie to prepare a statement of his political views. The statement appeared in the April 1940 issue of *Fortune* and has been credited with placing Willkie directly in the running as a candidate.

Meanwhile, National Chairman Hamilton was solidifying his own leadership position, mainly by his handling of national headquarters and his hard-hitting criticism of the Roosevelt administration. Although his relations with Landon supporters continued to be strained, particularly with those who sought his resignation during 1938, the national chairman was able to establish himself as an organization man acceptable to all factions.

Many Republican leaders recalled the party's gratitude to Will Hays for his rebuilding efforts in 1918–20. They also remembered the agreement among the 1920 presidential aspirants that Hays would remain as national chairman regardless of which of them became the nominee. Several sought to arrange a similar recognition for John Hamilton. Various leading Republican contributors were particularly interested in such an arrangement and were able to obtain assurances from all the major candidates for the 1940 nomination, including Willkie, that Hamilton would be retained. Hamilton maintained a fair impartiality among the aspiring candidates until early 1940. At this time, eastern industrialist Charlto MacVeagh convinced him that Willkie was probably the closest thing to a winner then available to the party. Hamilton thereafter became a partisan of the Willkie cause.[20]

The Willkie preconvention campaign consisted of three organized movements. The first was the Associated Willkie Clubs of America, inaugurated by a young lawyer, Oren Root, Jr. Root started by mailing out $40 worth of petitions to be signed in support of the Willkie candidacy. In short order, more than 3 million signatures were collected. Some 500 Willkie clubs were in operation by mid-June. When the presidential campaign got under way after the conventions, about 700 Willkie clubs were on hand to help. At mid-campaign, the Associated Willkie Clubs of America numbered 4,000, with an estimated membership of over 500,000. The Willkie clubs eventually became so numerous and widespread that they found themselves competing with regular local Republican organizations where these existed and functioning as the Republican party where the regulars did not have an organization. The clubs were not only a nettle in the sides of the Republican regulars, but also a magnet for the younger talent that might otherwise have come into the Young Republican National Federation.

A second Willkie movement took place among businessmen, financiers, and publishers. A host of editors, advertising executives, and corporation officials took leaves of absence to contribute time, experience, and funds to the Willkie candidacy. Initiated in the mass circulation magazines, such as *Fortune* and *Saturday Evening Post*, this movement finally infiltrated the large-circulation newspapers, particularly after the Cowles brothers added the resources of their chain.

The third movement was the Democrats-for-Willkie organization, established by former Director of the Budget Lewis Douglas, president of the Mutual Life Insurance Company. To regular Republicans this movement was a reminder of Willkie's recent origin as an active Democrat. Later, during the presidential campaign, Democrats-for-Willkie became a refuge for many Democratic defectors protesting Roosevelt's third-term nomination. The 1928 Democratic nominee, Alfred E. Smith, took his famous "walk" to Willkie, as did former Democratic National Chairmen Vance McCormick and George White.

Thus, during his preconvention candidacy Willkie's supporters were creating the organizations that would eventually lead to his isolation from the regular Republican party. Although largely responsible for Willkie's nomination, these three movements never became an integral part of the official Republican effort to win the election. Operating independently of the regular organization during the fall campaign and independently of each other as well, the three Willkie groups competed with the regular party personnel for campaign workers, funds, and influence in the nominee's inner circle.

These movements were at their most effective during the preconvention months. In March of 1940, the Gallup poll showed Willkie to be the preferred candidate of less than 1 percent of its sample. In early May, this percentage rose to 3 percent of the Republican voters, that is, excluding the "undecided" vote. By June 12, Willkie was in second place behind Dewey; Dewey had the imposing margin of 52 percent and Willkie 17 percent. In the eyes of professional politicians, Willkie's rapid rise was a most impressive development.

The Germans invaded Poland in August of 1939. By the spring of 1940, there was a general war in Europe. The gravity and immediacy of the problem of aiding the Allies at the risk of involvement in the war confronted American leaders in both parties. These problems were the background of the Republican national convention in June. Further confounding the Republicans was President Roosevelt's appointment of two Republican elder statesmen, Henry L. Stimson and Frank Knox, to his cabinet on the eve of the Republican convention.

Perturbed by the president's attempt to dampen party enthusiasm even before it could be expressed at the national convention, Chairman Hamilton rejected Roosevelt's bid for an "adjournment of partisanship" and practically read Stimson and Knox out of the Republican party, declaring them unqualified to speak as Republicans any longer. Ironically, Roosevelt's appointments gave a substantial boost to Hamilton's own candidate, Wendell Willkie. All contenders except Willkie had already taken antiwar or isolationist positions. Only Willkie had announced himself in support of aiding the Allied cause. By accepting places in the cabinet of a Democratic president at a time of international crisis, Stimson and Knox literally made it unpatriotic for the Republican delegates to consider the antiwar or isolationist candidates.

By convention time John Hamilton had accomplished a great deal for the Willkie cause. He had managed to have Philadelphia, a hotbed of Willkie enthusiasm, chosen as the convention city. Despite substantial national committee support for Glenn Frank to serve as temporary chairman of the convention, Hamilton was able to have his own preferred person, Governor Harold Stassen, selected. After delivering the keynote address, Stassen caused a sensation by coming out for Willkie; he was at once invited by the candidate to serve as floor leader.

Most important, Hamilton, acting through Representative Charles A. Halleck of Willkie's home state, organized a strategy committee of about sixteen party leaders to function in Willkie's behalf at the convention. The strategy group met secretly in Hamilton's hotel suite the night before the convention and convinced favorite-son Governor Baldwin of Connecticut to second Willkie's nomination and deliver Connecticut's solid vote.

A major weakness in Willkie's armor was the stubborn resistance of Republican congressmen to his candidacy. In the Senate, too, the colleagues of Senators Charles McNary, Arthur Vandenberg, and Robert Taft derided the intrusion of this political novice. A few days before the national convention, Representative Usher Burdick of North Dakota aimed a blistering attack against Willkie's backers. Later, about forty members of the House and five senators, equalling more than two-thirds of the states having Republican representation in Congress in 1940, conducted a conference opposing the nomination of Willkie. Eight of those attending issued a long statement urging the national convention delegates to nominate a man whose views were in harmony with the Republican record in Congress.

To counter these congressional maneuvers, two of Willkie's backers, Sam Pryor of Connecticut and Sinclair Weeks of Massachusetts, flew to Washington to enlist the support of Minority Leader Martin. Martin, who had been chosen to serve as permanent chairman of the convention, expressed his conviction that a Willkie nomination could never come out of a convention with so many strong Republican regulars in attendance.

Dewey received 360 of the convention's 1,000 votes on the first ballot, Taft 189 votes, Willkie 105, Vandenberg 76, and the rest was scattered in a field of about nine candidates. By the fourth ballot Dewey had lost enough support to put him out of the race; Willkie had moved into second place ahead of Taft. Between the fourth and fifth ballots Willkie and Taft gained 123 votes each, the count standing at 429 for Willkie and 377 for Taft. Willkie's biggest gains thus far had come from Massachusetts' third ballot switch from favorite-son Joseph Martin and Kansas' switch from Dewey on the fifth ballot. On the sixth and final ballot, Vandenberg released his Michigan delegates, who cast most of their votes for Willkie. This started the bandwagon.

Throughout the balloting, each delegation in the hall received hundreds of thousands of letters, postcards, and telegrams supporting Willkie. In the packed galleries, a booming "We Want Willkie" chant could be heard during almost every moment of the proceedings. Thus, "the party of Harding, Coolidge, and Hoover, over the objection of its congressional wing and many local bosses, accepted a former Democrat, a corporation president, and political maverick."[21]

The choice of a vice-presidential nominee was Willkie's first gesture of reconciliation with the congressional wing. Willkie asked Joseph Martin to extend the invitation to Senator McNary, who immediately accepted. McNary received the nomination on the first ballot.

7

The arena of factional accommodation and campaign coordination next moved to the national committee where a subcommittee of eleven, representing diverse interests, was appointed to consult with Willkie. The subcommittee's chairman was Walter J. Hallanan of West Virginia. Among its members were Harrison Spangler of Iowa, William Knowland of California, and Werner Schroeder of Illinois. General Counsel Henry Fletcher served the subcommittee in an advisory capacity. Hallanan later described as a "refreshing experience" Willkie's willingness to "sit around the table with the national committee" to discuss the organization of the campaign.[22]

Willkie's first inclination was to establish a three- or five-man committee to direct the campaign organization. This was apparently designed to circumscribe the influence of the regulars and the conservatives. Willkie intended John Hamilton and Russell Davenport to serve on this committee. Immediately after his nomination, Willkie spoke of his plan to Raymond Moley, a personal friend. Moley's opinion was that such a committee would be disastrous. Moley asked Willkie to seek the advice of former Chairman Will Hays, and it was Hays who persuaded Willkie to abandon the committee structure for his campaign organization.[23]

Having dropped the idea of a campaign "board," Willkie announced the appointment of a personal advisory committee. The twelve-member group, later expanded to twenty-two, included the two congressional campaign committee chairmen as well as the preconvention managers for Dewey and Taft; it was an attempt to bring as many views as possible to bear upon the operation of the campaign. As is the case with all committees of this size, it was rarely convened or otherwise employed.

Willkie was even less fortunate in his handling of the selection of a national chairman. From his approach to the various committee structures, it could be inferred that Willkie considered the national chairmanship a political plum to be given in exchange for support. Accustomed to organizational models for corporations, Willkie apparently viewed the national chairmanship as similar to the presidency of one company within a larger holding company complex. He showed little appreciation of the significant managerial functions that John Hamilton had so recently built into the office.

Since the chairmanship "belonged to the party people," Willkie must have reasoned, it should be filled by the senior man in the party. The senior man holding public office was Minority Leader Martin. Disregarding his pledge to keep John Hamilton as chairman, Willkie offered the place to Martin. Martin retreated to Massachusetts to "think it over," meanwhile expressing sincere reluctance. After several days, Martin agreed that if "the boys in Washington approve" he would accept. Congressional Republicans were enthusiastic, and Martin was selected. John Hamilton remained with the committee as its executive director at a salary of $15,000 and an expense account of $10,000. Fletcher also continued as general counsel.

In later years, Hamilton's demotion and Martin's selection were frequently discussed by the principals and among party leaders. The discussion was usually stimulated by recollections of the rapidity with which Willkie's campaign organization fell apart and the bitter hostility toward Willkie that resulted among Republican leaders. In the words of one scholar, "the removal of Hamilton . . . was a crude error in practical politics." It was an error that Willkie himself subsequently admitted in writing to Hamilton. "It deprived the party of a seasoned politician who had formed an effective party machinery and who represented the best liaison between the nominee and a rather hostile National Committee." The appointment of Minority Leader Martin was a second miscalculation. Martin could hardly do justice to either of his political obligations—as leader in the House or as national chairman responsible for conducting a presidential campaign.[24]

During July and August other errors were made, aggravating organizational problems. Willkie permitted the Associated Willkie Clubs of America and the Democrats-for-Willkie to continue functioning as independent organizations during the campaign, accountable only to their own leadership and in charge of their own fund-raising. The more than 700 Willkie clubs were presumed to provide a channel to independent voters and the Democrats-for-Willkie to attract the anti-New Deal Democrats.

The nominee traveled according his own schedule, accompanied by his own staff of advisers. Two autonomous campaign organizations were in the field. The party regulars, still quite skeptical about Willkie's "regularity," were without an attentive leader. Given these circumstances, Martin and Hamilton found it difficult to mobilize what had become the normal activities of national headquarters. When headquarters did begin full-scale operation, numerous discords and encounters with the Willkie clubs and Democrats-for-Willkie threatened campaign chaos.

Relations among organizations became tense enough to prompt Willkie to call in Senator Taft's law parter, John B. Hollister, to help establish a liaison system.

On September 6, Willkie held a special meeting with eighty party leaders in an attempt to achieve greater coordination among the campaign organizations. The meeting reportedly was a success. Shortly thereafter, Oren Root issued a statement that the Willkie clubs would disband on election day. Root's statement was interpreted as an assurance to the regular party workers that the clubs would not disturb normal party operations in any lasting way.

Willkie's personal campaign was a dynamic one. He covered 19,000 miles in fifty-one days. His audiences were generally enthusiastic. But his ad-libbing and repeated failure to follow the text of his speeches kept the press and his staff in a constant state of turmoil. His repeated stands contrary to the Republican position on issues before Congress compelled Joseph Martin to come to his defense more times than Martin thought wise. Although the Hatch Act of 1940 was passed during the campaign, setting limitations upon campaign contributions and expenditures, funds flowed generously into Republican coffers to the point of becoming an embarrassment to Willkie.

In the electorate of 1940, Willkie appealed to independent voters and proved to be acceptable to anti-New Deal Democrats. Students of the election were particularly impressed by the striking clarity of its division of income classes between the two parties. Voters in the upper-income group (that is, families earning more than $50 a week) favored Willkie 71–29; middle-income people supported him 53–47; but less than a third of the lower income and relief families favored him over Roosevelt.[25] Although he was defeated in the election, Willkie's candidacy dramatically shifted the presidential electorate from its one-sided preference for Roosevelt in 1936 back to a more competitive pattern.

Part VI
Bureaucratizing the
National Committee

21 | Constitutional Crisis in National-State Party Organization

Over the New Deal and Fair Deal years, the Democratic national party agencies—convention, committee, and chairman—became increasingly organized and concerned with issues of representativeness and party loyalty. A century earlier the question for the nation was whether a state could secede from the Union with which it had a solemn constitutional contract. A Civil War resolved that question. By the late 1940s and early 1950s, a comparable issue, arising in part from the abolition of the two-thirds nominating rule, gave rise to a less violent "civil war" within the Democratic party. May a state party organization "secede" from the national party in whose decisions it has participated? Party leaders sought to resolve this question through loyalty pledges and new rules of representation. It was a time of constitutional change for the Democratic party.

1

In the eighty-two days that he served as vice-president, Truman's major political assignment from President Roosevelt was to see that Henry Wallace's nomination as secretary of commerce went safely to confirmation by the Senate. As presiding officer of that body, Truman had to break two ties to get Wallace confirmed. Meanwhile, Roosevelt was out of the city nearly all the time, at Yalta or Warm Springs.

Roosevelt's death came as a national shock on April 12, 1945. It fell to the former senator from Missouri, described in the press as "just an average American," to carry the country to the victorious conclusion of a global war, help build the foundations of a world organization capable of guaranteeing the peace, direct the reconversion of the nation from a highly controlled wartime economy to a free but stable peacetime one, and accustom the people of his country to a new brand of political leadership in the wake of a dozen years under the cultured patrician of Hyde Park. Politician and citizen alike, in appeciation of Truman's overwhelming responsibilities, initially offered wholehearted cooperation. In a typically American way, the offer was for a very short term.

The partisan honeymoon lasted long enough to help bring the war to its conclusion. The Germans surrendered unconditionally a month after Truman assumed the presidency. On July 16, Truman, Churchill, and Stalin met at Potsdam to coordinate Pacific strategy and lay the groundwork for peace negotiations. Even as the conference proceeded, a British national election produced a Labor government, and Clement Atlee took Churchill's place at the conference table. During the conference, news came to President Truman of the first successful detonation of an atom bomb by American scientists. Truman made the decision that led to the atom bombing of Hiroshima on August 5. Three days later the Soviet Union belatedly declared war against Japan. The following month the Japanese surrendered.

The last gun had hardly ceased firing when Truman's political troubles began and continued at a pace that might have caused even a Franklin D. Roosevelt some misgivings. As a popular ex-senator, President Truman lunched and conferred frequently with his former legislative colleagues. His store of goodwill enabled him to win several encounters on Capitol Hill. The honeymoon ended with the delivery of his September 6 message to Congress, in which he reaffirmed Roosevelt's economic bill of rights of 1944 and the New Deal was officially replaced by the Fair Deal. Conservatives in both parties did not like what they heard. What followed were several years of kaleidoscopic shifts and adjustments in the relations between Truman on the one hand and New Deal liberals, organized labor, and southern Democrats on the other hand.

Truman started his administration with most Democratic factions represented in his cabinet, particularly in the persons of Henry Wallace and James F. Byrnes. Wallace had been confirmed for secretary of commerce. Byrnes, however, had resigned from the government five days before Roosevelt died. As soon as he became president, Truman offered him the position of secretary of state in time for Byrnes to lead the delegation at the San Francisco conference establishing the United Nations. Truman's subsequent difficulties with these two cabinet officials had much to do with the fact that each, recalling the circumstances of the 1944 national convention, felt that he rather than Truman should now be president. Byrnes eventually resigned in January 1947, as the preliminary peace treaties were being completed.

In view of the leftward thrust of the Fair Deal and the resignation of the leading southern member (Byrnes) of the administration, the South's Democratic leaders in Congress and in the states began to consult with each other. They publicly reminded the president that without their support he would not have been nominated to the 1944 ticket. Despite the looming factional clouds, in December 1946, Truman appointed a Committee on Civil Rights to examine the constitutional and practical issues associated with race relations throughout the nation. Senators Richard Russell of Georgia and Tom Connally of Texas, neither a firebrand, took strong exception to the inquiry. Three months after the committee rendered its controversial report on October 29, 1947, the president sent a bill asking Congress to implement many of its recommendations.

The South, thoroughly provoked, took up political arms. A mid-February conference of southern governors appointed a delegation, headed by Governor J. Strom Thurmond (then a Democrat) of South Carolina, James F. Byrnes' home state, to present demands to the president. On February 20, some fifty-two House Democrats issued a manifesto condemning the Truman civil rights program. In March 1948, within a week after Truman announced his candidacy for the presidential nomination, a meeting of southern governors embarked upon plans to deprive him of electoral college votes if he were to become the party's nominee.

Truman's trouble with Henry Wallace had similar factional consequences. Although secretary of commerce, Wallace, during 1946, made several foreign policy statements that cut the ground out from under Byrnes' peace treaty negotiations, causing confusion about administration policy. Wallace urged a policy of close friendship with the Soviet Union, ignoring the fact that Soviet leaders were breaking agreements made at Yalta and Potsdam. The embarrassment to the president became personal when, in a September 12 speech, Wallace described the president as "neither anti-British, nor pro-British—neither anti-Russian, nor pro-Russian." On September 20, President Truman dismissed Wallace from the cabinet.

The New Deal wing, whence Wallace drew much of his following, fell into a brief period of confusion. This passed quickly with the founding of the Progressive Citizens of America (PCA, a play on the acronym of the New Deal-led NCPAC, National Citizens Political Action Committee). The PCA organization led to the founding of the Progressive party in December 1947, with Wallace as its spiritual leader and, subsequently, nominee for president. Other New Dealers, wishing to distinguish between Democratic liberalism and the Wallace brand of progressivism, founded Americans for Democratic Action (ADA).

Truman's troubles with labor were even more complex and confusing, particularly since the labor movement had become a major pillar of the party's electoral fortunes. In the spring of 1946, with the war still in progress, the miners, led by John L. Lewis, and the railroad brotherhoods, led by Alfred F. Whitney, went on strike over wage demands. Given the wartime circumstances, the president struck back, proposing a draft-labor law. Organized labor became thoroughly agitated by the showdown. Then, in a spirit of compromise, the strikes were ended and the draft-labor bill withdrawn. Truman was able to reestablish good relations with his old friends in the railroad brotherhoods, but continued to have difficulty with Lewis' mine workers. This culminated in a court-ordered contempt fine of $3,500,000 levied against the United Mine Workers.

The 1946 election of the Eightieth Congress put the Republicans back in control of both houses of Congress. Labor legislation was their first order of business, and the Taft-Hartley Act emerged. Labor considered the act's provisions highly punitive. When Truman vetoed the bill, the same labor leaders who condemned him several months earlier now praised him without qualification. The veto, however, was overridden.

A second piece of significant and controversial legislation was the Full Employment Act, which made full employment a responsibility of the federal government. Truman's support of this bill brought organized labor solidly into his corner. Organized labor was now eager to exert its best campaign efforts on Truman's behalf in 1948.

While domestic difficulties kept Truman's popularity ratings fluctuating, his moves in the foreign policy field brought him relatively stable popular support. His appointment of General Marshall to succeed Byrnes as secretary of state gave the administration the benefit of the universal esteem in which the general was held. As relations with the Soviet Union deteriorated, American firmness in negotiations with the Communists hardened. Containment of communism began to take form as a national policy, leading in 1947 to the Truman Doctrine of aid to Greece and Turkey. In June 1947, the Marshall Plan for emergency economic and technical assistance to Europe's devastated countries, particularly those threatened by communism, was proclaimed.

These moves were not made without being challenged. The Soviet Union's occupation forces held Eastern Europe tightly under their control. The Chinese Communists were driving the Nationalists off the Asian mainland to Formosa, later known as Taiwan. The external threat of Communist expansion and evidence of Communist spying within the governmental bureaucracy led the president to ask for $29 million for the conduct of loyalty checks of federal employees, inadvertently setting the stage for the Communists-in-government witchhunt that consumed the McCarthy era soon to follow.

2

National Chairman Hannegan succeeded Frank Walker as postmaster general when Roosevelt's fourth term began. Thoroughly exhausted by his work in the presidential campaign, Hannegan was at this time particularly concerned about his long-standing problems with high blood pressure. At each advancement in his political career, Hannegan complained to friends, "I'm just killing myself." Although only forty-five years old at the time, he was therefore unable to give much energy to the 1946 midterm campaign. Because he was generally blamed for the disastrous Democratic defeat in the congressional returns, Hannegan finally concluded that his failing health demanded complete retirement from politics.

In order to ease the transfer of national headquarters to a successor, Hannegan created the position of executive director and appointed his second assistant postmaster general, Gael Sullivan, to fill it. Forty-three years old, Sullivan had been a resident of Chicago for two decades, a college instructor who became administrative assistant to Mayor Ed Kelly, and eventually a Kelly protege. Sullivan was appointed as Hannegan's second assistant in the Post Office Department in 1945.

As executive director at national headquarters, Sullivan was charged with direction of "all matters of policy and operation of the Democratic National Committee."[1] With headquarters management thus taken care of, Hannegan resigned as postmaster general and national chairman on November 25, 1947. This news was accompanied by the announcement that he had purchased a major interest in the St. Louis Cardinals baseball club. Hannegan died in 1949.

Sullivan made national headquarters a beehive of activity, in part to prepare for the 1948 presidential contest and in part to demonstrate to the president and party leaders that he could be a worthy successor to Hannegan. His efforts were not uncontested. Secretary of Agriculture Clinton Anderson had a lively interest in the national chairmanship. Others mentioned for the post were Undersecretary of the Interior Oscar Chapman, New York State Chairman Paul Fitzgerald, and William M. Boyle, Jr., the president's former secretary.[2]

Sullivan's chairmanship aspirations were ill-fated. A few weeks after his appointment, he appeared as the guest of the television program "Meet the Press" and was asked how Democratic national headquarters planned to deal with Henry Wallace and Senator Claude Pepper. Wallace was not yet a third-party nominee and Pepper had severely criticized the president's program in the Senate a few days earlier. Sullivan responded that he would not ask for either Wallace's or Pepper's support in the 1948 campaign.

Immediately, Senate Minority Leader Barkley and others in Congress objected to Sullivan's presumptuous reading of a United States senator out of the party and demanded that Sullivan apologize publicly to Senator Pepper. After intervention by third persons, including Mayor Kelly, Sullivan apologized to Pepper privately and the matter was settled. President Truman called Sullivan in to urge better coordination with the White House.

A second misadventure occurred during late summer when Sullivan became involved in an automobile accident in which the local police charged but never proved him guilty of drunken driving. The press and Sullivan's rivals made much of the incident. This ended his availability for the chairmanship.[3]

Rhode Island's Senator J. Howard McGrath was President Truman's solution to the problem of finding Hannegan's successor. As governor of Rhode Island, McGrath seconded Truman's vice-presidential nomination in 1944 and delivered one of the few solid delegations. In the Senate, McGrath was a down-the-line Fair Dealer. Together with his senior colleague, Theodore Green, he was one of

James Howard McGrath, born in 1903, was the son of an Irish immigrant whose first employment in this country was as a knitter, later as an insurance company manager. McGrath first came to the attention of a Democratic politician when, as a boy, he won a newspaper subscription contest whose sponsor was Senator Peter G. Gerry. While attending Providence College and Boston University, where he received his law degree in 1929, McGrath was employed by Senator Gerry as a junior assistant. Still a law student, McGrath, with the help of the senator, became vice-chairman of the Democratic state central committee. He was president of the state's Young Men's Democratic League from 1924 to 1928. From 1930 to 1934, he served as city solicitor of Central Falls. In 1932, he became a law partner of Theodore F. Green. Two years later, McGrath was appointed United States district attorney for Rhode Island, an office he held for six years. During these years, he accumulated a substantial personal fortune in real estate, insurance, banking, and manufacturing enterprises. McGrath was elected governor in 1940, and re-elected in 1942 and 1944. He received the nomination for United States senator in 1946 and, despite the Republican landslide elsewhere, was elected, serving as the junior senatorial colleague of his senior law partner.

a tiny handful of staunch Truman supporters in 1947. His reputation as a rebuilder of the Rhode Island Democratic organization seemed particularly pertinent to the task confronting national headquarters in anticipation of 1948.

Senator McGrath was a childhood friend of Gael Sullivan. Both men attended La Salle Academy in Providence for their secondary school education. It is possible that Sullivan suggested McGrath's name to the president; it is certain that the selection of McGrath alleviated some of his own disappointment. McGrath was elected national chairman in October 1947 and declined to accept the resignation of his friend, Gael Sullivan. McGrath intended to continue many of Hannegan's organizational policies and wanted to retain Sullivan and other national headquarters staff to help.

One major feature of the Hannegan strategy had been to keep hitting hard at the Republican record being made in Congress, particularly in the Senate, under the leadership of Robert A. Taft. Although the 1948 Republican nominee was expected to be Governor Dewey, it was inevitable that Dewey would have to run on the Taft congressional record. That record, according to Hannegan and his associates, was vulnerable. Both Hannegan and McGrath assumed that President Truman would be the Democratic nominee.

With the approach of spring, Chairman McGrath began to run into problems.

Sullivan resigned to accept a lucrative position with a private interest group. The certainty that Truman would be nominated diminished as liberals, big-city leaders, and southerners began a movement to draft General Dwight D. Eisenhower, the hero of the European front. Eisenhower had resigned as army chief of staff in February 1948 to become president of Columbia University.

Uncertain that Truman could handle the Palestine crisis and the civil rights controversy and worried that urban Democrats might suffer a loss in their Jewish and Black constituencies, Jake Arvey, chairman of the Cook County Democratic Committee, Mayor William O'Dwyer of New York City, Leon Henderson, speaking for Americans for Democratic Action, and, subsequently, James Roosevelt of California, inaugurated a "dump-Truman" collaboration. The original suggestion to give the Democratic nomination to Eisenhower came from Senator Richard Russell of Georgia, whose surprise was genuine when his proposal was endorsed by the liberal northerners.

Truman was less upset about the Eisenhower movement than his national chairman. In his memoirs, Truman reports that he had Eisenhower's personal assurances that he was not a candidate, confirming a letter released by the general in January. Wrote Truman:

> The President is traditionally the leader of his party. He has great influence with the National Committee, and usually the party will nominate a chairman of the convention who is friendly to the President and who needs the approval of the Chief Executive. No matter how many detractors there may be, the chairman controls the organization of the convention. The convention will operate in the manner in which the chairman and the President want it to....
>
> In 1948, I was in a position to control the nomination. When I had made up my mind to run, those in the party who turned against me could do nothing to prevent it. For this reason, Thurmond and Wallace had to bolt the Democratic Party and stir up their own following. If Eisenhower had gone after the Democratic nomination, there would have been a four-way split in the party, but otherwise, the situation would have remained unchanged. Presidential control of the convention is a political principle which has not been violated in political history.[4]

By March, McGrath was sufficiently concerned over the Eisenhower movement to ask the president to announce his candidacy a few days earlier than planned. The president obliged, and this helped clear the air, at least for the party regulars.

3

Hostile strategies were being developed in the South. In February, the special Thurmond committee representing the southern governors met with Chairman McGrath. The meeting lasted for about ninety minutes. Assuming that the proceedings would have many public interpretations, McGrath had a corps of stenographers present to produce a transcript. At the conclusion, there was no agreement. Two of the governors remarked to the press that McGrath had been most cordial. Thurmond, as spokesman for the group, said that the South had only one recourse, "direct action."

Such action was initiated in the Virginia state legislature, which banned the names of the national Democratic nominees from the ballot, thereby enabling the presidential electors to cast their votes for whomever they chose. In Mississippi, Louisiana, and South Carolina, steps were taken to place the national party's ticket under a ballot symbol different than the regular one, in effect, presenting the national party as a third party. In early May, Alabama Democrats chose eleven presidential electors who were pledged not to cast their votes for any presidential nominee committed to a civil rights program. On May 10, a conference of southerners was held in Jackson, Mississippi, during which it was tentatively decided to hold a separate national convention in Birmingham immediately after the Democratic convention if Truman were nominated. Meanwhile, for their participation in the Democratic national convention, the South planned to unite behind a single sectional favorite-son candidate.

The public opinion polls were no help to the Truman candidacy. The polls reported Truman to be hopelessly behind various Republican candidates in popular support. "In order to circumvent the gloom and pessimism being spread by the polls and by false propaganda in the press," reported Truman in his memoirs, "I decided that I would go directly to the people in all parts of the country with a personal message from the President."[5] In June, the president made a cross-country tour to report on the record of the Eightieth Congress. The "do-nothing Eightieth Congress" became a theme that the president carried into the campaign in the fall. The trip was successful and lifted Truman's rating in the polls several points.

Another development late in June lifted the ratings even higher. The Russians sealed off highway, rail, and river traffic in and out of Berlin in an effort to force the Allies out of the city. Truman's response was the Berlin airlift. This move was dramatic, symbolic of Western resistance to Soviet encroachments, and effective in reopening normal routes of entry into Berlin. Truman's leadership impressed the electorate as well as the Western allies.

The delegate mood was an uneasy one as the 1948 national convention opened. Instead of attacking Truman, the northern liberals and the southerners concentrated fire upon each other. The first liberal move was a minority report from the credentials committee demanding that the Mississippi delegation be denied seats. The Mississippi state convention had pledged the delegation would withdraw from the national convention if a states' rights plank were not specifically incorporated into the platform. The state convention also denied the delegates the power to bind the Mississippi party to the support of any nominee favoring Truman's civil rights program. These provisions were incorporated in the credentials of the Mississippi delegates. The minority report lost on the voice vote, but several delegations asked to go on record as favoring the minority report. It was found that there were 503 such votes, very close to the 618 needed for a nominating majority.

The southerners prepared a minority report in the rules committee proposing to reinstate the two-thirds nominating rule. This report was rejected by a voice vote. It now seemed that there was no firm majority on either side.

Southerners next presented three separate minority reports in connection with the work of the platform committee, all directed at watering down the civil rights plank. From the convention floor, northern liberals, led by Mayor Hubert H. Humphrey of Minneapolis and Andrew J. Biemiller of Wisconsin, introduced a plank stronger than that of the majority in the platform committee. The Humphrey-Biemiller plank specifically endorsed Truman's civil rights program. Their amendment was passed by a vote of $651\frac{1}{2}$ to $582\frac{1}{2}$. This was the firmest evidence of a Truman majority in the convention.

At the end of the vote on the Humphrey-Biemiller plank, thirteen members of the Alabama delegation withdrew from the hall. Mississippi refused to vote on the presidential nomination. In the nominating ballot, Truman received 926 votes and Senator Richard Russell, the South's candidate, 266. A minor shifting of votes gave Truman a final tally of $947\frac{1}{2}$. When Senators Russell and Alben Barkley were placed in nomination for the vice-presidential place, a Russell spokesman withdrew the Georgian's name. Barkley was nominated unopposed.

The Truman campaign was run from two centers: national headquarters under Chairman McGrath and a small group that handled the campaign train operation under William Boyle's direction. The two teams worked in a well-coordinated fashion. McGrath had his hands full grappling with technical ballot problems created by the Progressive candidacy of Wallace and the Dixiecrat candidacy of Thurmond. Pro-Truman state organizations were endeavoring to keep Wallace off the ballot. The anti-Truman southern organizations either kept Truman off the ballot entirely or gave Thurmond the regular Democratic ballot symbol.

National headquarters encouraged the establishment of Truman-Barkley Clubs for independent voters. McGrath coordinated national, state, and local campaign efforts, raising and allocating the somewhat limited funds. Contributors were skeptical. The national headquarters staff tried a few new propaganda gimmicks: a pro-Truman comic book, a daytime soap opera aimed at women listeners, and a special motion picture documentary about Truman's life. There were also the usual press, radio, and pamphlet efforts. To symbolize Truman's civil rights program, McGrath ended the unofficial racial segregation that existed on the national committee staff by declaring that Blacks were eligible for senior staff positions.

The final pre-election Gallup and Crossley public opinion polls predicted over

49 percent of the popular vote for Dewey and only about 44 percent for Truman. On the basis of research at national headquarters, McGrath pointed out that the Gallup poll made errors favoring the Republicans by 2.4 percentage points in 1940 and 2.8 percentage points in 1944. "This historical error in favor of the Republicans mirrors the reluctance of some polltakers to go into factory and poor areas," he telegraphed Dr. Gallup in mid-October.

The political pundits nevertheless believed the polls and predicted a Dewey victory. What the forecasters failed to take into account, in addition to normal margins of polling error, were last-minute turnout and switching factors in voting behavior, about which very little systematic knowledge was available in 1948. Truman's personal appearances in carefully selected communities affected Democratic turnout in ways impossible to measure through national polls.

The presidential campaign train, which eventually covered 31,700 miles, was managed by several fellow-Missourians: William Boyle at the central headquarters in Washington, Clark Clifford on the train itself, and Donald S. Dawson handling community relations along the route. By his own count, Truman delivered 356 prepared speeches and 200 extemporaneous ones. Because of his astute selection of issues and localities to be visited, Boyle won a reputation as an outstanding campaign strategist.

Truman pitched his campaign appeals to four audiences: labor, farmers, Blacks, and consumers. Organized labor was angry about the Taft-Hartley legislation. The farmers were up in arms about the continuing decline in farm prices. Blacks were impressed by Truman's civil rights policies, particularly after the bolt of the Dixiecrats. Finally, consumers, struggling with the rising cost of living, were ready to blame someone, and Truman pointed to the Eightieth Congress. Truman's colorful and hard-hitting speeches were filled with statistical data compiled by the research division at national headquarters, a staff contribution that left a strong impression on the president. Truman's specificity was in sharp contrast to Dewey's ambiguity.

Liberals and labor, despite their prenomination resistance, closed ranks behind Truman. The New York Liberal Party and Americans for Democratic Action endorsed the Truman ticket. CIO's Political Action Committee and the A.F. of L. Labor League for Political Education organized massive turn-out-the-vote campaigns in Democratic strongholds.

A by-product of Truman's aggressive campaign was its impact on Democratic party workers. What did it matter if "Harry can't win," was he not making "the good fight"? The mood filtered up to the leadership in the South. Senator Russell and others gave up their tacit support of the Dixiecrat cause and endorsed Truman.

The Thurmond-Wright States' Rights slate was the Democratic ticket in only four states: Alabama, Louisiana, Mississippi, and South Carolina. In these states, the traditional Democratic emblem, the rooster, was placed over the Thurmond-

Wright electors; voters casting their ballots for the Democratic party had no choice but to vote for Dixiecrats. In three of these states, Truman electors could be found elsewhere on the ballot; in Alabama, Truman electors were completely left off the ballot.

Despite factional defections and discouraging opinion polls, President Truman led Dewey by 2 million votes in the 49 million cast. The combined popular votes of the Progressives and States' Righters came to less than 3 million.

In evaluating the election, analyst Samuel Lubell identified several tendencies that made this a period of realignment of party preferences among the voters. Components of political transformation included the urban minorities, a new middle class, the migrating Blacks, the South in economic revolution, the isolationists, the farmers, and organized labor. Whereas Dewey's response to these changes was inertia, Truman's was "hectic, even furious, activity."[6] The changes were also having consequences for the factional composition within the Democratic party.

4

Having achieved an electoral mandate in his own right, President Truman turned his attention to problems of national party organization in characteristic fashion. His carrot-and-stick approach, particularly in disciplining the southerners, was exemplified by the hard line taken by National Chairman McGrath and the soft line adopted by McGrath's successor, William M. Boyle, Jr.

Shortly after inauguration, McGrath announced that he had proposed to the president a policy of awarding patronage positions only on the basis of "the appointee's record and an estimate of his future value to the party." McGrath took pains to point out that there could be no "future value" to the party for a Democrat who did not support the party's nominees or platform. It followed, therefore, that the Dixiecrats would have no future in the party.

McGrath's declaration came as an explanation of a press conference statement by the president, who had observed that Democrats are those people who support the Democratic platform, a document that Truman regarded as the law of the Democratic party. Asked whether he would consider congressional voting on repeal of the Taft-Hartley law as one of the tests of party loyalty, the president replied that he certainly would. In response, southerners in the House of Representatives charged the president with demanding support on legislation in exchange for patronage.

Several months later, Truman carried the testing of party loyalty a step further in the nomination of Leland Olds for a third term as federal power commissioner. A substantial number of Democratic senators opposed the Olds nomination, but the president was determined to push it through as a "party matter." At a press conference during the first week of October, Truman referred to the Olds nomination as a party matter. It was Truman's opinion that an impending political decision becomes a party matter only by the president's fiat at some moment in advance of the decision. As party leader, the president could exercise this prerogative unilaterally and whenever he chose. Having identified a party issue, the president could properly expect that, in the interest of party discipline, all members of his party in Congress would support his position. This was possibly the strongest and clearest affirmation to date of presidential prerogatives as party leader.[7]

President Truman made less public moves to strengthen the national organization. Having blossomed and survived in the machine politics of Missouri, the president never took matters of party organization for granted. As Chairman McGrath returned to his duties in the Senate and prepared for a cabinet appointment, the president asked William Boyle to leave his Washington law practice to take over the administration of headquarters as executive vice-chairman. It was the position that Gael Sullivan had filled.

Boyle began serving as executive vice-chairman on a part-time basis, without pay, for a short period during February 1949, as he concluded arrangements to turn over his law practice to an associate in his firm. He transferred some twenty-three of his cases for a fee of $150,000. As it later turned out, eight of these twenty-three cases involved representations before federal agencies.

At national headquarters, Boyle began to tighten up the loosely coordinated bureaus: the women's division, publicity department, treasurer's office, and political organization bureau. On the president's recommendation, Boyle also began to look into setting up a competent research division.

In August 1949, Truman nominated McGrath to be attorney general. The national chairman called the national committee together to choose a successor. The press noted two "unusual" features of McGrath's committee call: first, he specifically recommended a successor, William Boyle, and secondly, he pointedly did not invite "members of the national committee of record in the states of Mississippi or Louisiana, because in my judgment, by their several actions at the convention and subsequently in the campaign they have left the Democratic party."[8] Thus, McGrath carried a hard line against the defecting Dixiecrats. He also anticipated a credentials fight on this matter in the national committee.

The credentials contests materialized. Trumanite Democrats, designated by loyal state conventions in 1948, laid claim to the vacant Mississippi and Louisiana seats. A somewhat more difficult contest emerged from South Carolina where the Truman people argued that the same state party body that had instructed the 1948 presidential electors to vote against Truman had just chosen that state's new national committeeman, Senator Burton H. Maybank. The South Carolina Trumanites wished to carry the test of party loyalty beyond the immediate acts of national committee members into the acts of the state party selecting these committee members. A Texas contest was more strictly a factional fight involving no technical issue of party self-government.

An old political friend of the president, National Committeeman Frank McHale of Indiana, held the difficult chairmanship of the credentials committee. McHale's committee turned for guidance to the *Democratic Manual*, an unofficial compilation of rules of the national convention compiled by Clarence Cannon, and found in Section 11 the power they needed. Based upon national committee action taken in 1896, when it expunged from its rolls the names of two members who bolted from the Bryan ticket and attended another national convention, the rule empowered the national committee "to expel members for cause." On this basis the credentials committee recommended, and the national committee approved, expunging the names of five of the Dixiecrat committeemen.

Having boldly asserted the McGrath hard line, President Truman himself swung in an opposite direction. On the same evening of the expulsion ruling, the president dined with members of the national committee. In his address he invited the States' Righters and other dissidents to return to the party "as loyal Democrats." This was Truman's soft line which Boyle was expected to implement. Truman further declared that the Democrat party was "a national party and not a sectional party any more."

As a new and salaried national chairman, Boyle adopted an economizing approach to the reorganization of national headquarters. The staff was reduced in size. Hoping to reduce rental costs, Boyle initiated negotiations for the purchase of a six-story building across from the Mayflower Hotel in Washington.

Most headquarters attention went into preparations for a large Democratic conference in Chicago during May of 1950. This conference was pictured by the press as virtually a midterm national convention, attended by national committee members, state chairmen, and state vice-chairmen. The conferees were to hear a major address by President Truman. As late as September, Boyle arranged for the appointment of Senator Clinton P. Anderson of New Mexico as executive vice-chairman for the congressional campaign. Senator Anderson was already chairman of the senatorial campaign committee. The Democrats had been on the defensive throughout the year, and the Anderson appointment was a belated attempt to strengthen the poorly financed and poorly coordinated midterm effort, which by now had become a normal part of national headquarters business.

5

The attacks on Democratic policies and leaders were of more than ordinary severity in 1950. The investigation of Alger Hiss, which Truman had called a "red herring," culminated in a verdict of guilty on charges of perjury in a trial that ended in January 1950. One consequence was the popular impression that the federal bureaucracy was peppered with espionage agents of international communism and that the Democratic leaders were either dupes or themselves conspirators. On February 9, Senator Joseph R. McCarthy of Wisconsin announced in a startling public address that he knew of 205 Communists in the State Department.

Thus began an era of spy-hunting that bears the senator's name. In tune with this Communists-in-government theme was the Republican contention that the Truman-Acheson policies had "lost China" to Communist leader Mao Zedong. Public confidence in the Truman administration was further unsettled by the discovery of "influence peddling" in high places close to the president. In response to these attacks, Truman conducted a "non-political" tour of the country during the spring and made known his intention to participate actively in the fall campaign. The North Korean invasion of South Korea in June, however, put an end to these plans. Events compelled the president to leave the defense of his administration to national party headquarters.

With respect to headquarters operations, Truman reiterated his interest in developing a research division that could effectively produce the facts and organize the arguments with which to reply to Republican charges. His suggestion was in line with recommendations made by the Committee on Political Parties of the American Political Science Association. This committee's report was published in September and received a great deal of attention from practicing politicians as well as academicians. One of its major recommendations was the creation of a "stronger full-time research organization adequately financed and working on a year-in, year-out basis." The president heartily agreed.

Truman disapproved of the committee's recommendation regarding the establishment of a party council of fifty members to handle the larger problems of party policy and management. He doubted that this could be a useful vehicle of presidential leadership and anticipated that such a council could readily become a rival to as well as a distraction from presidential leadership of the party.[9] He later changed his mind when the Democrats were the out-party.

In Korea, General MacArthur's United Nations forces were driving the North Koreans back toward the Chinese border. In October, the Chinese Communists twice warned that they might intervene in the Korean conflict if the 38th parallel were crossed by the UN troops. In the United States, the congressional elections took place as the nation speculated about Chinese intentions. The election returns allowed the Democrats to retain control of the Senate, 49 to 47, and the House, 235 to 199, but at the cost of a Republicans gain of 5 Senate seats and 28 House seats. The most prominent returns were those in Ohio, where Robert A. Taft won an overwhelming victory, in California, which returned Richard M. Nixon to the Senate, and in Maryland, where Senator Millard Tydings, a Democratic conservative, was unseated in a campaign that employed the tactics and staff of Senator McCarthy. McCarthy's influence and activities had thus inaugurated an era.

Politicians and commentators turned to the prospects for the 1952 presidential race. The Twenty-second Amendment limiting presidents to two terms was a new consideration. Technically, Truman did not come under the restriction. Although in 1949 Truman had hinted that he would probably not run again, he never made a firm declaration on the subject. During 1951, there was much doubt about his intentions. Further, the entry of the Chinese Communists into the Korean conflict made it uncertain how long that war would last; in the past, the electorate tended to be disinclined to change presidents in the middle of a war.

An initial probe of Truman's intentions came in the form of criticism of National Chairman Boyle. In August 1951 the *St. Louis Post Dispatch* charged Boyle with having received a fee of $8,000 for inducing the Reconstruction Finance Corporation to lend $565,000 to the American Lithofold Company of St. Louis while Boyle was serving as an official of the Democratic national committee. Senator Harry F. Byrd of Virginia followed up with a demand for Boyle's resignation or dismissal.

Boyle denied having anything to do with the application for a loan, reported that the firm had given him $500 a month in legal fees for two and a half months' service early in 1949 before he became a full-time official of the national committee, and expressed his expectation that he would serve out his full term as national chairman. After conducting an independent investigation of the circumstances surrounding the loan, Truman supported Boyle's statements and expressed full confidence in his national chairman.

The anti-Truman leaders did not drop the matter. To them, the retention of so close a Truman associate as Boyle in the national chairmanship was evidence that the president would seek another nomination. A Senate investigating committee called Boyle before it for questioning. Senator Nixon of California assumed the role of prosecutor and inquired in detail about the twenty-three legal cases that Boyle had turned over to his associate. Among these were eight cases dealing with matters before federal agencies and representing potential fees of $158,500, according to Nixon. Boyle acknowledged that these facts were true. Further evidence was offered that Boyle had arranged an appointment for the president of Lithofold with the chairman of the RFC board three days before the first loan was authorized. Two weeks later, claiming that he had been cleared by the Senate investigation, Boyle offered his resignation as national chairman and defended his conduct while an official of the Democratic party. The president accepted the resignation.

A few days later, Truman mentioned during a press conference that he had a list of as many as thirty prospects for the national chairmanship. His own first choice was former Secretary of the Navy John L. Sullivan, an old political friend and possibly New Hampshire's best known Democrat. Sullivan declined because he felt that it would be impossible for him to give up his District of Columbia law practice. A second choice was the acting national chairman, Mrs. India Edwards, regularly vice-chairman in charge of the women's division. For per-

At the time of his selection for the chairmanship, Frank E. McKinney was vice-president of the United States Pipeline Company, president for seventeen years of the Fidelity Trust Company of Indianapolis, president of an Indianapolis radio station, a holder of investments in baseball clubs, and treasurer of the Indiana Democratic state central committee. Because the pipeline company then had a routine application before a federal agency, McKinney announced that he would resign as its vice-president.

McKinney was the son of a city fire chief. He began his work career as a bank messenger. Extension courses at Indiana University and a degree from the LaSalle Institute of Accounting qualified him to become a bookkeeper. By the time he was old enough to vote, McKinney was a bank cashier and a regular in the Indiana Democratic party. He rose to the presidency of the Fidelity Trust Company in 1935. He was at the same time elected treasurer of Marion County, having already served as treasurer of the Democratic city committee of Indianapolis and of the Democratic central committee for the county. In 1936, he served as subtreasurer of the national committee in charge of Indiana. In the 1940 campaign he was vice-chairman of the national committee's finance committee. Commissioned a major in World War II, McKinney served as a finance officer in the procurement division of the army.

---

sonal reasons, and possibly because a first woman national chairman at this time might have complicated organizational politics even more, Mrs. Edwards also declined.

For several days the names most seriously discussed were those of Senator Anderson of New Mexico, Michael V. DiSalle of Ohio, director of price stabilization, and Wilson Wyatt of Kentucky, former federal housing administrator. Anderson was in poor health and could have given only part of his time away from his senatorial duties. DiSalle was needed in the price stabilization job. Wyatt preferred to keep himself free to work for a particular candidate in 1952.

Frank McHale, the national committeeman from Indiana who had so skillfully handled the Dixiecrat seating contests, had a candidate who seemed to meet most of the qualifications: Frank E. McKinney. Wealthy, a leader of the pro-Truman faction in the Indiana party, a skillful fund raiser, McKinney became the choice. Although the chairmanship carried with it $35,000 a year in salary and expenses, McKinney was able to decline all remuneration.

In his acceptance speech, McKinney stated several principles that would guide him, a statement intended to leave the impression that the new headquarters regime would be "clean" and free of "influence peddling." McKinney declared that no headquarters employee would be permitted to accept "favors, gifts, fees, emoluments or remunerations of any kind, from outside sources for intercession, influence or services rendered, while receiving a salary from the national committee."[10]

McKinney required every headquarters employee to file a written statement with him within two or three days describing "what his duties are, what his present salary is, what it was when he first went with the committee, and who sponsored him."[11] The following day McKinney took another step to remove the "corruption" stigma. He publicly recommended to President Truman to bring internal revenue collectors, then political appointees, under civil service. Truman responded by stating that he would recommend such a step to Congress.

In response to the president's desire to create a competent research division, McKinney sought funds and personnel. To direct the division, he recruited Bertram M. Gross, executive secretary of the president's Council of Economic Advisers and a professional political scientist. To "maintain liaison with Democratic members of Congress" in the manner developed by the Republicans in 1945, McKinney appointed Col. Lawrence Westbrook, an Arkansas engineer with substantial administrative experience in the federal government, as assistant chairman. The headquarters staff expanded rapidly in size and output.

6

As the presidential year opened, there continued to be great uncertainty among Democratic politicians regarding the president's intentions. Wishing to capitalize on his recent renown as an investigator of crime and corruption and, despite expected resistance from the president and organizational leaders, Senator Estes Kefauver announced his candidacy on January 23. Kefauver in fact premised much of his campaign upon criticism of the Truman administration's handling of the corruption issue. On February 6, Senator Robert S. Kerr of Oklahoma announced his candidacy, indicating that he would step aside if President Truman became a candidate.

Meanwhile, the president was searching for a candidate of his own. Chairman McKinney had the difficult task of feigning ignorance of the president's plans while keeping a lid on the factional situation. An early miscalculation allowed Truman's name to be filed in the New Hampshire preference primary. The poll in that state gave Kefauver, the only other candidate, an impressive victory over the president.

Another disturbing activity was southern preparation for the convention. In February, Georgia adopted legislation that allowed the omission of all names of candidates for president and vice-president from the November ballot, giving state party leaders extensive discretion in the handling of ballot arrangements.

Dixiecrat strength was still great in five other southern states: South Carolina, Louisiana, Mississippi, Texas, and Virginia. In each of these, procedures were being developed for the instruction of delegations to the national convention and the handling of the November ballot. On February 28, 1952, Senator Richard B. Russell of Georgia, Truman's main adversary in the 1948 convention, announced his candidacy ostensibly in the belief that President Truman would not seek re-election.

The president's search for a successor led him to Governor Adlai E. Stevenson of Illinois, who carried that state by a half million more votes than he had in 1948. A successful Democratic governor of a large and pivotal state, a moderate liberal, Stevenson seemed to have all the requisites of availability. On January 22, while Governor Stevenson was in Washington on other business, Truman invited him to the White House for a private conversation. In his memoirs, Truman reports:

> I told him that I would not run for President again and that it was my opinion he was best-fitted for the place. He comes from a political family, . . . had served the country in the State Department and the United Nations, . . . had made an excellent Governor of Illinois. . . . I asked him to take it and told him that if he would agree he could be nominated. I told him that a President in the White House always controlled the National Convention.[12]

Stevenson immediately said "no" to the president. An announced candidate for re-election as governor, he insisted until the very eve of the national convention that this was the only office he sought. As the months passed, Stevenson continued to disclaim his presidential candidacy in what seemed an infinite variety of ingenious turns of phraseology. He urged national committeeman Jacob Arvey of Illinois and other political friends to restrain themselves from doing anything for him in connection with the presidential race. A group of leaders of Independent Voters of Illinois established an Illinois Stevenson for President committee in February, which grew to be a national movement distinguished by the meticulous care with which it avoided contact with its candidate.

On March 18, Chairman McKinney asked California Democrats to withdraw the president's name from the June 3 primary. On March 29, at a Jefferson-Jackson Day dinner in Washington, President Truman announced that he was not a candidate for re-election: "I do not feel that it is my duty to spend another four years in the White House." His search for a successor continued. Professional politicians, accustomed to the highly organized exertions necessary for winning presidential nominations, began to take Stevenson at his word and to look elsewhere. Chairman McKinney, too, became convinced that Stevenson had taken himself out of the picture.

The president and the chairman undertook an examination of other possibilities. There was some difficulty in each case: Kefauver, because of his attacks on the administration and his alienation of the regular organization; Russell, a southerner who opposed the civil rights stand of the administration; Kerr, who had represented oil and gas interests in the Senate in support of legislation vetoed by the president; Averell Harriman, despite his wide experience in the federal government, had yet to run for an elective office; Vice-President Barkley, whose personal popularity was unquestioned, was seventy-five years old and uncertain of labor's endorsement. With Stevenson still their first choice, Truman and McKinney made Barkley their second choice, with concern about the caretaker aura of the Barkley candidacy. Determined though he was to retire, Truman himself was under heavy pressure to become a candidate in order to avoid a leadership vacuum. In view of the uncertainties, the president and McKinney urged their party allies to keep their delegations uncommitted or behind favorite sons.

Observers estimated that the president could swing about 400 votes to any candidate who had other support in the convention and about 200 votes to a candidate that the convention did not like. On July 19, the Associated Press reported Kefauver in the lead with $257^1/_2$ committed delegates, Russell with $161^1/_2$, Harriman $112^1/_2$, Kerr $45^1/_2$, Stevenson $41^1/_2$, others $231^1/_2$, and as many as 380 votes undecided, uncommitted, or in dispute (including 52 from Texas and 18 from Mississippi). The vote needed to nominate was 616.

With General Eisenhower as the Republican nominee, the southerners in the Democratic party were substantially strengthened. In one way or another, six southern state parties left the way open for a possible bolt from the national ticket. The failure of the third-party strategy in 1948 and the withdrawal of Truman as a candidate in 1952 reduced the need for a bolt. In addition, the nomination of Eisenhower gave southern leaders an acceptable alternative to any Democrat who might be nominated by their own convention. "The result was something in the nature of a constitutional crisis within the Democratic party—a crisis that was to dominate and complicate every aspect of the convention of 1952."[13] The man upon whom the strain of the convention was probably heaviest was Chairman McKinney, who labored heroically to keep the party from flying apart.

In platform developments, Americans for Democratic Action (ADA) claimed the support of 654 convention votes for a civil rights plank more far-reaching than the one in 1948. McKinney never left the middle of the platform struggle. At 5:30 A.M. of the morning on which it was to report, the civil rights subcommittee of the platform committee was still locked in disagreement over a plank calling for a new cloture rule in the Senate that would eliminate the filibuster, a principal hurdle to civil rights legislation. McKinney called the subcommittee to his office and worked out a compromise that left the strong civil rights plank intact, but put the antifilibuster demand into less offensive language in another plank calling for efforts to "improve Congressional procedures so that majority rule prevails."[14]

Paul M. Butler was at this time a forty-seven-year-old corporation lawyer from South Bend, Indiana. Born in that city in 1905, he received a law degree from the University of Notre Dame Law School in 1927 while working as a part-time reporter for the South Bend *Tribune*. Thereafter, his legal practice and party activities consumed most of his time. In 1938, he managed the unsuccessful congressional campaign of a friend. After serving as president of the South Bend Young Democrats, he became Democratic chairman of the Third District organization. Developing a close political and personal friendship with Henry F. Schricker, Butler became a leader of the intraparty contests that paved the way for Schricker's election as governor and for his own selection in 1952 as Indiana's national committeeman.

In the credentials committee, the issue was party loyalty, resulting in a recommendation that the national committee place the States' Rights delegations from Texas and Mississippi on the temporary roll and that the national convention adopt a resolution "that the honorable course of every delegate who participates in its proceedings is to support the majority decisions of the convention here and hereafter." As time passed and tempers heated, the loyalty pledge question completely overshadowed the civil rights issue, creating confusion among candidate supporters. McKinney called numerous meetings of factional leaders in search of some solution.

In the candidate race, McKinney—and his chief in the White House—had a first-choice commitment to Barkley, whose availability disappeared on the morning that the convention opened when the leadership of the American Federation of Labor and the CIO Political Action Committee announced that they would be unable to support the vice-president. Barkley immediately withdrew his name. Elsewhere, the Stevenson "noncandidacy" was in hands of politicians who could hardly be considered representatives of the White House. The Walter Johnson committee was by now serving as the communications center for a draft- Stevenson movement.

At conferences convened by Johnson, steps were taken to select a Stevenson floor leader and a man to place him in nomination. On July 20, the evening before the convention, one such conference was attended by Pittsburgh's Mayor David Lawrence, former Pennsylvania Senator Francis J. Myers, Philadelphia leader James Finnegan, and Indiana's Governor Henry F. Schricker. Schricker was accompanied by Paul M. Butler, who had recently won the state's seat on the national committee in a bitter factional contest with the McKinney-McHale forces. Myers was chosen floor leader, and Schricker agreed to lead off the nominating speeches.

In the credentials fight, the ADA-liberal leaders asked the convention to adopt a pledge resolution that required that

> no delegate shall be seated unless he shall give assurance to the Credentials Committee that he will exert every honorable means available to him in any official capacity he may have, to provide that the nominees of the convention for President and Vice President, through their names or those of electors pledged to them, appear on the election ballot under the heading, name or designation of the Democratic Party.[15]

If adopted, it was explained, any delegate in the present convention refusing to make the necessary certification would not be seated. Many southern delegates, bound by instructions from their state parties, vociferously opposed the resolution, but the liberal version was adopted on a voice vote.

The critical practical test of the loyalty pledge involved the seating of the Virginia delegation. When the credentials committee made its report, it became apparent that Virginia, South Carolina, and Louisiana had not submitted the written assurances required by the new rule. Senator Byrd of Virginia simply announced, "We're just going to sit here and maybe they'll have to throw us out."

Under these circumstances, the temporary chairman, Governor Dever of Massachusetts, ruled that the three states did not have the privilege of voting in the convention. Shortly thereafter, McKinney called Senator Byrd and the governors of the three states into his office behind the rostrum. It was subsequently rumored, and substantiated by the events, that McKinney had assured the southerners that means would be found for seating their delegations eventually. An opportunity for doing so presented itself during the roll call for nominating speeches. When Louisiana was reached, it yielded to Virginia for a "parliamentary inquiry" as to whether Virginia was entitled to full participation in the activities of the convention. The permanent chairman, Speaker Rayburn, held that they were not so entitled since the delegations from the three states had not complied with the rules, and ordered the roll call to continue.

Then, with a precision that suggested careful preparation, Rayburn recognized Representative Sasscer of Maryland, who moved that Virginia be seated in view of the "substantial compliance" of the loyalty pledge contained in certain conciliatory statements by the governor of Virginia and leaders of the other delegations involved. Rayburn interpreted this as an appeal from his previous ruling on Virginia, and the matter was eventually taken up as the subject of a roll call vote. Thus, McKinney and Rayburn injected the question of what to do with the southern dissidents directly into the nominating situation.

The ensuing ballot on seating Virginia required two hours, with delegations passing, changing votes, and generally in great confusion about the relationship between their vote on the seating issue and the prospects of their favored candidate for president. Delegate eyes were fastened on the Illinois delegation for some clue as to the wishes of the Stevenson supporters. Illinois voted 45 to 15 against seating Virginia. This was soon followed by the Pennsylvania vote of 57 to 13 in favor of seating Virginia; this was the delegation whose chairman was the unofficial Stevenson floor manager. Disorder reigned in the convention hall until Illinois changed its vote to 52 to 8 in favor of seating. The final tally seated the Virginia delegation. Loss of the South was thus prevented under conditions that brought credit to the skills of Chairman McKinney and the Stevenson leadership.

In allowing his name to be placed in nomination, Stevenson had consulted by telephone with the president to see if it would now cause Truman any "embarrassment." The president had his first-choice candidate, but only when Stevenson decided to run. In his memoirs, Truman reports that he replied favorably to Stevenson's inquiry "with a show of exasperation and some rather vigorous words."

The seating of the three southern delegations removed any prospect that the South, by walking out, would leave the convention in Kefauver's hands. In the balloting, Kefauver and Russell cancelled each other's chances. On the third ballot the favorite sons and uncommitted votes shifted to Stevenson, and he was nominated. As a gesture to both liberals and southerners, Senator John Sparkman of Alabama was nominated for vice-president.

7

Having received the nominating without obligation to the incumbent president, Stevenson now had the problem of conducting his own campaign without offending his well-meaning supporter in the White House. How could Stevenson run a campaign based on his own record rather than Truman's? How could Stevenson integrate the party organization, particularly at national headquarters, into his campaign without becoming a prisoner of the policy positions and propaganda line of the organization people, most of them Truman appointees? How could Stevenson symbolize his friendly independence of the White House at the same time escaping Republican charges of corruption and communism that were being levied against the administration?

In his first interviews with the press, Stevenson indicated that he planned to run his own campaign from Springfield where he continued to have duties as governor of Illinois. Springfield also afforded physical distance from Washington and the White House. He expressed some hope about having a "say" in President Truman's campaign plans. Stevenson was not certain whether he would invite McKinney to stay on as national chairman. Meanwhile, he began pulling together a personal staff at Springfield, with Wilson Wyatt, former housing administrator and former mayor of Louisville, as campaign manager.

Iowa-born, the forty-nine-year-old Stephen A. Mitchell was a practicing lawyer in Chicago at the time of his selection. He had attended Creighton University and had earned his livelihood as assistant credit manager in an Iowa dry-goods company during 1920 and 1921 and credit manager for the General Motors Acceptance Corporation from 1924 to 1928. During this period, he studied for his law degree at Georgetown University, which he received in 1928. Thereafter, he served as a legal adviser to the General Motors Acceptance Corporation in New York. In 1932, he took up practice with a Chicago law firm.

Active in civic affairs, Mitchell met Stevenson in 1937 when both were members of the Committee to Defend America by Aiding the Allies. The two men became close personal friends and shared common interests in public and party activities. From 1942 to 1944, Mitchell served in the French division of the Lend-Lease Administration. Later, for a year or so, he was adviser on French economic affairs for the State Department. In 1947, he and other friends formed a Stevenson-for-Senator Committee and this led to Stevenson's first nomination for public office as Democratic candidate for governor of Illinois. In 1952, Mitchell was chief counsel for the House Judiciary subcommittee investigating irregularities in Truman's Justice Department. Stevenson reportedly chose Mitchell as chairman from a list of twelve or fourteen possible candidates.

Party professionals and Truman supporters urged Stevenson to keep McKinney in the chairmanship. McKinney had campaign experience and had won great admiration for his skillful work at the national convention. In addition, national headquarters had been fully staffed and readying itself for the campaign since the beginning of the year and was accustomed to working with McKinney. Stevenson, however, was determined not to carry the burden of defending the recently investigated Democratic city machines and the Truman administration. To underscore the "new look" in Democratic party leadership, Stevenson chose his close friend Stephen A. Mitchell to be national chairman. Mitchell was a "clean amateur" in politics. Truman called it "firing" McKinney.

Having avoided the Truman embrace in filling the chairmanship, Stevenson and Mitchell were quick to demonstrate public deference to the president as "the head of the Democratic party." The president, Mitchell declared, would be consulted continuously regarding the conduct of the campaign and other organizational problems. Mitchell denied that he was taking on the job of chairman in order to liquidate national headquarters. He indicated that he would retain the three vice-chairmen who had served with McKinney: Mrs. Edwards, Senator

Green of Rhode Island, and Representative Dawson of Illinois. Mitchell also pointed out that the Springfield campaign headquarters would not be considered a separate organization, but rather "the Springfield office of the Democratic National Committee," that is, an integral part of the national committee's payroll.

Despite Mitchell's good intentions, the problem of coordinating the Springfield and Washington headquarters was never resolved. Upon retiring, McKinney observed that only one man could lead a campaign, namely, the individual chosen to be the national chairman. Wyatt, the Springfield campaign manager, added, diplomatically, that Governor Stevenson would be the man to run his own campaign. Publicly and privately, party professionals expressed unhappiness over having the leadership of the national party placed in the hands of a man without previous experience in national campaigning.

The media echoed the party professionals in referring to the Stevenson organization as a two-headed campaign. Even as Stevenson spoke of his own record as governor of a major midwestern state, President Truman carried on a vigorous campaign defending his own record in Washington. When a newspaper editor in Portland, Oregon, asked Stevenson how he proposed to deal with "the mess in Washington," Stevenson's response implied that it was a valid problem on which he intended to act. The president was offended and later observed in his memoirs: "How Stevenson hoped he could persuade the American voters to maintain the Democratic party in power while seeming to disown powerful elements of it, I do not know." Truman was convinced that Stevenson would have received at least three million more votes than he did if he "had accepted in good faith the proposition I made to him on January 30, 1952 (sic) and enabled us to make the proper build-up."[16]

As weeks passed, McKinney appointees at national headquarters departed. In the closing days of the campaign, Mitchell dramatically dismissed Colonel Westbrook, the assistant for congressional relations, upon learning that Westbrook had helped negotiate a government contract for a Portuguese tungsten firm while on the national committee staff. Denying that Westbrook had engaged in "improper activity," Mitchell explained his action as indicative of his determination to maintain the rule that committee staff not make representations to the government. However, party bureaucratization had grown to the point where it was becoming increasingly difficult to draw the line between party staff work on the one hand and lobbying public officeholders on the other hand.

On election day, with the Eisenhower landslide, another line was drawn between an outgoing New Deal-Fair Deal era and an era of Republican presidencies.

22 | Nationalizing the Party Structure

The 1950s found the Democratic national committee and national chairman in out-party status for the first time in twenty years. The New Deal coalition continued to prevail and to give the national party a liberal orientation. Factional conflicts were mild compared to those of the self-destructive 1920s. Adlai Stevenson and the national chairmen who served at this time devoted themselves to building an organization that could, to some extent, function as the seat of a loyal opposition. The institutional odds were against them.

1

The day after the election President Truman passed the mantle of titular leadership to Stevenson in a telegram in which he expressed the hope that ''you may see your way clear as the head of our party to initiate steps as soon as possible to revitalize the national committee and set the wheels in motion toward a victory in 1954.''

Stevenson delayed public comment on his new party status until he completed his term as governor of Illinois. From his many consultations with National Chairman Mitchell and Campaign Manager Wyatt, it could be inferred that Stevenson would play an active role. One unusual and serious proposal made to Stevenson was that he assume the office of Democratic national chairman in order to have a formal position from which to speak out. He rejected the proposal.

Mitchell told reporters that he expected to stay on as national chairman, serving under Stevenson. He referred to Stevenson as the party's leader, but acknowledged that the Democrats in Congress were ''a major party power.''[1] Observing that national headquarters had become ''quite abundant'' in personnel, Mitchell indicated that staff would be reduced to ''financial realities.'' Headquarters would have to adjust to its status at the head of the minority party and move ahead on such matters as improved relations with congressional leaders. Mitchell virtually disbanded the research division, a step that was opposed by Truman elements. Political observers began to predict that future battles over control of the national committee would be waged between "the amateurs" and "the old pros."

The Democrats were a minority by one vote in the Senate and by less than a dozen seats fewer than the Republicans in the House, that is, "out" in all branches of the federal government. These circumstances gave the national chairman the appearance of special seniority in the party since even the titular leader had a dubious authority. Senator Russell of Georgia, in fact, took pains to point out that "titular" meant "title without authority." There would be no question, he said, that Stevenson was titular head of the party; on the other hand, Democratic policy would be set in Congress during the next four years.

The leadership of the Democratic minority in the Senate was in the hands of Lyndon B. Johnson of Texas, a political protégé of the minority leader on the House side, Sam Rayburn. In a public comment on the election of Johnson to the leadership post, Stevenson anticipated that Johnson would succeed in bridging the North-South split in the party. Stevenson added his hope that northerners like Senator Humphrey of Minnesota and southerners like Senator Russell of Georgia would keep the different wings of the party working with each other.

In February 1953, Stevenson completed his duties as governor. During a long vacation on Barbados in the British West Indies, according to his biographer, "he resolved, there in the golden sunlight, to play out the role assigned to him with more planned consistency than most, if any of his predecessors in that role had done."[2] Fully aware of the political and organizational difficulties of his position as titular leader, Stevenson wrote in the published collection of his speeches in 1956:

> In our country this role is a very ambiguous one. . . . The titular head has no clear and defined authority within his party. He has no party office, no staff, no funds, nor is there any system of consultation whereby he may be advised of party policy and through which he may help to shape that policy. There are no devices such as the British have developed through which he can communicate directly and responsibly with the leaders of the party in power. Yet he is generally deemed the leading spokesman of his party. And he has—or so it seemed to me—an obligation to help wipe out the inevitable deficit accumulated by his party during a losing campaign, and also to do what he can to revise, reorganize, and rebuild the party.[3]

In another place, Stevenson observed "that opposition leadership rests in the Congress, except that it is assumed by individuals for the most part ambitious to be heard."[4]

Chairman Mitchell took energetic and sometimes provocative measures to deal with the organizational aspects of Stevenson's titular leadership. To coordinate the work of the publicity, research, and speakers bureaus in handling statements and other political information from Stevenson and Truman sources, Mitchell named as his deputy chairman Clayton Fritchey, a former Truman aide who had worked closely with the Stevenson staff in Springfield during the campaign. Fritchey also served as editor of the *Democratic Digest*, a monthly political magazine made up of reprints of newspaper articles and cartoons presenting a Democratic point of view. The *Digest*, an experimental party magazine, was never financially solvent despite a paid circulation of 20,000–70,000 during its lifetime.

Mitchell not only cut back staff, but also moved the national headquarters to a new location to save about $20,000 annually in rent. He then focused on three fund-raising objectives: payment of the $200,000 campaign deficit; provision of a regularized income to support national headquarters on a year-round basis; and preparation for the midterm campaign of 1954. Mitchell hoped to raise $750,000 annually. His specific goal for 1953 was $1,000,000 and, for 1954, $1,250,000. A substantial part of this money was to come from $100-a-plate Jefferson-Jackson Day dinners. Another source was to be the regular party faithful.

A unique fund-raising device was the establishment of an advisory council to the national committee. The advisory council consisted of about 380 units throughout the country, each unit made up of five fund raisers whose goal would be $2,500 annually. For example, New York State had 32 unit leaders working with 128 associate members, all striving for a state goal of $80,000. Certificates were awarded to units achieving their quotas. Chairman Mitchell felt that the advisory council system would facilitate the recognition of contributors and party workers who were not regular party officials, broaden the working base of the party, and otherwise provide a channel through which Democrats could offer ideas and advice to the national leadership.

Mitchell also concerned himself with the organizational structure of the national party. In this he had the assistance of the national committeeman from Indiana, Paul M. Butler. At the April 1953 meeting of the national committee's executive committee, Butler offered a proposal for a midterm national convention to be held in 1954 to help Democrats regain control of Congress. Butler argued that such a convention would enable the party to explore major areas of internal disagreement long before the 1956 election and give it time to perfect its national machinery for the next presidential contest. To avoid unnecessary intraparty wrangling, Butler further suggested that this midterm national convention be held in August or September after party primary contests were over. The executive committee authorized Mitchell to appoint a committee to investigate the Butler plan.

The committee on the midterm convention, consisting of representatives from Congress, the national committee, and state and local organizations, reported the following September. It concluded that an official midterm convention would be inadvisable because of cost and the impediments presented by many state laws and party regulations. Instead, the national committee approved a proposal made by House Minority Leader Rayburn that a committee be established to look into the rules of the regular national convention, including, of course, the loyalty pledge. Such a rules committee was established in September 1953, with instructions to report to the national committee in time for a presentation of the findings to the 1956 national convention. As an alternative to the Butler midterm convention, the executive committee encouraged the national chairman to arrange for a series of regional conferences of party leaders during the midterm campaign.

Meanwhile, the titular leader was making arrangements for an active exercise of his ambiguous responsibilities. Stevenson opened a small office in Chicago, which, two years later, became his law office. From this office, he maintained close contact with the men who aided him in his presidential campaign. An informal advisory group began to meet with Stevenson at irregular intervals to discuss public issues. The group included Thomas K. Finletter of New York, former secretary of the air force, historian Arthur Schlesinger, Jr., Harvard economist Seymour Harris, Harvard economist Kenneth Galbraith, Chester Bowles, former ambassador to India, and W. Willard Wirtz. Other policy experts frequently joined their discussions.

In March 1953, Stevenson set out for a tour of the Far East, returning through the Middle East and Europe. His arrival back to Chicago was scheduled for mid-August. Chairman Mitchell arranged that a mid-September national conference of Democratic leaders serve as a welcome-home rally for Stevenson. This September conference was in fact the occasion for meetings of several party groups: the executive committee, the full national committee, the advisory council, and a $100-a-plate fund-raising dinner. The research division prepared a large compilation of data on "unkept Republican promises" for distribution at the conference. Stevenson was to present a nationwide radio and television talk as the major event of the gathering.

At the Chicago conference the national committee disposed of Butler's midterm national convention proposal and set up a special committee to examine the rules of the convention. As a step toward the reconciliation of northern and southern interests, the northern leaders conceded that the rules—particularly the loyalty pledge—adopted in 1952 had lapsed and that it would be up to the next convention to adopt its own regulations. In other words, the issue of party loyalty was once again open to debate and negotiation.

At this same conference the national committee voted an annual salary of $25,000 a year for Mitchell, retroactive to January. There was some discussion of a proposal to have a national political meeting through closed circuit television, a further indication of the extent to which the new technologies of communication were nationalizing the party's operations. A number of fund-raising dinners earned a profit of over $100,000.

During the first week of October, Frank McKinney spread word that former President Truman and others were suggesting that he return to the national chairmanship. Shortly after, Mitchell announced that he would be resigning after the 1954 congressional elections. It was his belief that a national chairman should be neutral on the matter of the presidential nomination, and he clearly could not be. He was still 100 percent for Stevenson.

Throughout the months of the 1954 campaign, one name after another was publicized as a possible successor to Mitchell. The southerners were interested in Leslie Biffle, former secretary of the Senate. The Truman leaders preferred either former Secretary of the Interior Oscar L. Chapman or former Price Administrator Michael V. DiSalle. A group of Senate Democrats was lining up support for Senator Earle C. Clements of Kentucky, chairman of the Senate campaign committee since 1952. Party leaders in the Northeast made James Finnegan of Philadelphia their candidate. From the Midwest the name of Paul M. Butler of Indiana was suggested.

2

Stevenson, recovered from recent surgery, began an extensive series of public appearances to help pay off the clinging 1952 campaign debt and to lend a coattail to those midterm congressional candidates who invited him to speak on their behalf. In Washington, his friend Stephen Mitchell was running into controversy over his exercise of the prerogatives of the national chairmanship during the midterm campaign.

During April, in response to the California national committeeman's request for financial aid to that state's candidates for Congress, Mitchell called attention to "the unusual circumstances presented by the candidacies of Robert Condon in the Sixth and James Roosevelt in the Twenty-Sixth District."[5] Condon had been denied access to the Nevada testing grounds by the Atomic Energy Commission on grounds that he was a security risk. Roosevelt's wife had accused him of adultery in a divorce proceedings. Both men were asking their constituents to vindicate them. In Mitchell's opinion, the circumstances "will bar any financial support in those contests."[6]

Writing in his capacity as national chairman, but without authorization by the executive or the national committee, Mitchell told the California national committeeman, "Mr. Condon's misfortune and question of innocence or guilt should not be the burden of the Democratic party—they are personal to him."[7] Referring to the Roosevelt case, Mitchell said, "Here again a Democratic primary or a Congressional election is not the proper forum to render a verdict on private litigation relating to a man's domestic affairs."[8] Concluded Mitchell, "The right and privilege to determine how [the national committee's] available funds will be spent are ours, and in these cases we will exercise our right to withhold support."[9]

This intervention by a national party leader into local party contests on grounds of personal guilt or morality provoked a furor that sounded much like the reaction to Franklin D. Roosevelt's purges of 1938. Mitchell came out of the situation somewhat less scarred than Roosevelt since the executive committee endorsed his decisions. Subsequently, the full national committee took no formal action, but did urge the Mitchell committee to consult its members more carefully before making high policy decisions for the party.

The Democrats regained control of both houses of Congress in 1954: 231 seats to 204 in the House, and 48 to 47 in the Senate. This returned Sam Rayburn to the speakership and elevated Lyndon B. Johnson to three posts: chairmanship of the Democratic conference, chairmanship of the Democratic Policy Committee, and majority leader. With the party in control of Congress, Chairman Mitchell was beginning to feel reluctant about retiring to his law practice.

Between election day and the meeting of the national committee early in December, some ten individuals were in the running for the chairmanship, including Paul Butler, James E. Finnegan, Michael V. DiSalle, former Governor Elbert N. Carvel of Delaware, former Under-Secretary of the Army Archibald S. Alexander of New Jersey, and F. Joseph Donohue, a commissioner of the District of Columbia. Senator Earle C. Clements was "ineligible" in view of the preference for a full-time chairman. Mitchell was, for all practical purposes, Butler's campaign manager. Mayor David Lawrence of Pittsburgh enlisted several big-city leaders for Finnegan.

Butler seemed in the lead. Former President Truman, still loyal to the McKinney-McHale leadership in Indiana, thought someone other than Butler could be found, but did not actively oppose him. Butler had important support not only from the incumbent national chairman but also from the chairman of the House congressional campaign committee, Mike Kirwan. Stevenson took no public position.

In a final effort to find a compromise candidate, Truman, after consulting with Stevenson, asked his former secretary of the air force, Thomas K. Finletter, to take the position. Finletter had not only served Truman well, but was part of Stevenson's unofficial policy seminar. Finletter, however, declined, and the contest remained centered around Butler, Finnegan, and DiSalle.

Butler was by no means passive. Prior to the national committee meeting, he made long-distance telephone calls to 93 of the 105 national committee members. His campaign arguments were the following: (a) he was the only member of the national committee being considered for the chairmanship, and (b) he promised to hold himself responsible to the national committee members only, and not to any single political sponsor such as Truman (who now favored DiSalle's candidacy), Stevenson (whose Illinois committee members eventually voted for Finnegan), or Kefauver (whose candidate was Donohue).[10] Some leaders now turned to a strategy of postponement, urging Mitchell to stay on as national chairman in order to prevent an open split at the national committee meeting. Speaker Rayburn particularly supported this strategy, but Mitchell reiterated his intention to resign.

The national committee gathered to hear some good news as well as to deal with the chairmanship. As a result of the work of Senator Humphrey of Minnesota and former Governor Battle of Virginia, it was agreed that the loyalty oath, so objectionable to the South, would be radically altered or dropped at the 1956 national convention.

The election of a national chairman required a roll call vote. Butler received 70 votes, DiSalle 18, Finnegan 16, and Donohue 1. Butler's election was accomplished over the opposition of the committeemen of Pennsylvania, New York, Illinois, and Massachusetts, who voted solidly for Finnegan. The outcome was hailed as a victory for Stevenson, but closer observers gave most credit to Mitchell.

Wrote columnist Arthur Krock: "No more unlikely figure [than Mitchell] has appeared in professional politics for a long time or has more thoroughly disproved the rule that this is not a business for amateurs."[11] Krock reviewed the Mitchell record in the chairmanship: reconciliation of the South by extensive travel there and by discarding the loyalty pledge; naming of his successor despite the opposition of the "city bosses," thereby keeping the national chairmanship in pro-Stevenson hands; lending prestige and competence to official party journalism by the creation of the *Democratic Digest*, with a particularly competent journalist as its editor; the elimination of the 1952 campaign debt; and retaining for himself the chairmanship of a special committee on national convention rules and procedures, in which capacity he intended to prevent a recurrence of the loyalty pledge fight and to help streamline the proceedings in keeping with the requirements of television.

At the conclusion of the national committee meeting on December 4, 1954, Stevenson told the assembled leaders that "as in the past I have no political ambitions." Having for more than two years sought to discharge his obligations to the party and to his fellow Americans, he said, he now felt it imperative that he devote most of his time to his personal and professional affairs.[12] At a later time, Stevenson spoke of this announcement as a withdrawal from political life. "Actually, it was no such thing. What it did do was give party leaders an opportunity to withdraw support from him, should they choose to do so, while encouraging his supporters to express their wishes."[13]

3

The new national chairman began his duties, making serious moves toward party unity. Butler visited President Truman in Missouri shortly after the New Orleans meeting, and Truman publicly promised his cooperation and support. With regard to the 1956 nomination, Butler, a thoroughgoing Stevenson man in 1952, declared his neutrality. At a later time he simply observed that if Stevenson wanted the nomination he would have to fight for it. At national headquarters, Butler kept the Mitchell staff.

Two problems particularly preoccupied Butler during most of 1955: the work of the Mitchell committee on convention rules, and relations between the presidential and congressional wings of the party. In keeping with his previous proposal for a midterm national convention, Butler was eager to improve coordination of the organizational arrangements of the semiautonomous agencies of the national party. With respect to national headquarters staffing, Butler sought to reduce personnel turnover in the postconvention period, a time when experienced hands could mean greater efficiency during the short and intense period of the campaign. With this in mind, but anticipating that "this appointment would probably draw fire from some quarters," Butler selected as his administrative assistant Dr. Paul Willis, a political science professor from the University of Indiana.[14] To assist the Mitchell committee in its research and decisions, Butler made available the services of the national committee's counsel, Harold Leventhal.

The Mitchell committee submitted its report to the national committee in mid-November 1955.[15] The most significant rule change it proposed concerned the loyalty oath. Under the pledge adopted in the 1952 convention, each head of a delegation was obligated to state in writing that every delegate would use every honorable means to provide that the convention's nominees would be placed on the state's ballot under the Democratic symbol. The proposed new rule would provide that, by its election of national convention delegates, a state party organization automatically assumed an obligation to assure that the convention nominees would appear on the ballot under the Democratic symbol; individual delegates, however, would not be bound to support the nominees. Members of the national committee, however, would have an affirmative duty to declare openly their support of the nominees. A national committeeman failing to do so could possibly have his seat on the committee declared vacant. Other proposed rules, subsequently adopted, dealt with polling delegations during roll calls, filling vacancies on the national ticket if any should occur, appointing the four major convention committees prior to the national conventions, and other procedural matters.[16]

Relations with the party's leadership in Congress were a more difficult matter. Speaker Rayburn and Senate Majority Leader Johnson were a close team whose political strategy consisted of "responsibility in opposition," that is, congressional Democrats would work with President Eisenhower as much as possible. Butler considered it "folly" for Democrats to support the Eisenhower program. Democratic strategy, he thought, should emphasize the existence of the party's own national program since the 1956 contest would have to be fought in terms of the Eisenhower record versus the Democratic record. Butler therefore began urging Democratic congressional leaders to prepare a distinctly Democratic program on all issues on which there existed substantial agreement within the party, leaving aside for the moment such divisive issues as Taft-Hartley and the Fair Employment Practices Committee (FEPC).[17]

Adlai Stevenson was in substantial agreement with Butler. Stevenson's underlying philosophy about the role of an opposition is stated in a volume of his public addresses:

> It should not surprise anyone to discover that this is primarily a book of criticism. If "the duty of loyal opposition is to oppose," I cannot see how one can offer effective opposition without giving reasons for it and these reasons are, of course, criticisms.
>
> Yet I very well know that in many minds political "criticism" has today become an ugly word. It has become almost lèse-majesté. And it conjures up pictures of insidious rascals hacking away at the very foundations of the American way of life. It suggests nonconformity and nonconformity suggests disloyalty and disloyalty suggests treason, and before we know where we are, this process has all but identified the critic with the saboteur and turned political criticism into an un-American activity instead of democracy's greatest safeguard.
>
> The irony of this position—so often held by people who would regard themselves as most respectably conservative—is that it is nowhere more ardently embraced than in Moscow or Peiping. There the critic really is a conspirator and criticism is genuinely an un-Russian or un-Chinese activity.
>
> In fact, if I were asked to choose a single principle which underlies more than any other the difference between the Communist and the free philosophy of government, I would be inclined to single out this issue of criticism, which we in the West not only tolerate but esteem. . . .
>
> For, paradoxical though it may seem, free criticism can flourish only in a society where mutual trust is strong. The spirit of criticism shrivels when the citizens distrust their neighbors and the give and take of confidence gives place to the silence of suspicion. The neighborliness, the charity, the very goodness of a society, can best be measured by the freedom with which men may honestly speak their minds. Criticism is therefore not only an instrument of free society. It is its symbol and hallmark as well.[18]

Stevenson and Butler were eager to formalize the activities of the Finletter seminar as a device not only to create a distinctive Democratic program, but also to help in communication between the leadership in and outside of Congress. Throughout 1954 the Finletter policy advisory group, or "brain trust," had worked on policy development with both Stevenson and Butler's predecessor, Mitchell. After Butler assumed the chairmanship, discussions continued on how to make the informal group into a policy planning staff "to mobilize the best brains in the party." Mentioned as a possible chief for such a staff was Paul

Nitze, former head of the State Department's policy planning staff. Nitze had been an active member of the Finletter seminar.

The crisis in the Far East in March 1955 revealed how little the Democratic leaders in Congress would take Stevenson into their confidence. The Chinese Communists were threatening the offshore islands of Quemoy and Matsu. President Eisenhower requested and received from Congress advance authorization to do whatever in his judgment was necessary in the event of a full-scale attack against the islands. Speaker Rayburn and Senate Majority Leader Johnson cooperated actively with the president in obtaining this special authorization. Stevenson was not consulted at all, although, as titular head of his party, he received an impressive volume of telephone calls, letters, and telegrams urging him to speak out on the Quemoy-Matsu issue. Stevenson was not even given official information about the crisis.

This failure to inform the titular leader of the opposition party was in contrast to the Truman administration's dealings with the Republican titular leader, Thomas E. Dewey, between 1945 and 1953. From time to time, Governor Dewey's counsel was sought by Secretary of State Dean Acheson, with John Foster Dulles serving in a liaison capacity. Even more painful to Stevenson than Republican disregard was that of his Democratic colleagues on Capitol Hill.[19]

One political commentator commented on "the information gap" and commiserated with Stevenson:

> [Stevenson] insists on applying reason to politics, a remarkable innovation. He does not like to improvise. He thinks the party's legislative program and its political strategy should be coordinated, and though he doesn't complain about it, he does wonder why men who say they are for him [for president in 1956] feel that he should be kept in his present isolated role.[20]

Stevenson's isolation, however, was not that difficult to understand. He and the national chairman of his choice were committed to the composition of a distinctive "Democratic program." The Democratic leaders in Congress, on the other hand, were committed to a strategy of cooperation with the Republican president's legislative requests. Congressional-presidential cooperation would be seriously hampered if the Democratic presidential wing were consulted. Furthermore, any show of deference to Stevenson as titular leader would reinforce the prospect that he would again receive the nomination in 1956, and there were those in Congress who had presidential aspirations of their own. Prominent among these were Senators Estes Kefauver and Lyndon B. Johnson.

As of June 1955, the next presidential contest seemed destined to be another Eisenhower-Stevenson encounter. By September, however, the political situation was substantially altered. Senator Johnson suffered a heart attack in July, and this was expected to remove him as an influence at the national convention. In the same month, Stevenson was stricken by a severe case of viral pneumonia, but recovered quickly enough to attend the August Governors' Conference during which most of the Democrats governors present in one way or another indicated their support of him for a renomination. In September, Stevenson journeyed to Johnson's ranch in Texas for a visit during the latter's convalescence. Sam Rayburn's presence made the occasion undeniably political and presumably aimed at discovering any sources of congressional opposition to Stevenson's renomination. Reassured, Stevenson began to gather his staff in preparation for an announcement of his candidacy in November.

4

On September 23, President Eisenhower suffered a heart attack, which seemed to put him out of future presidential politics. The stock market suffered a $12 billion decline in prices the following day. While it was soon established that the president would be physically able to complete his term in office, his capacity to deal with a second nomination remained in doubt. The easy Democratic renomination that Stevenson anticipated now became a hot race.

The value of the Democratic nomination rose with every bulletin on Eisenhower's health. Kefauver stepped up preparations. Harriman, now governor of New York, became noncommittal about his earlier endorsement of Stevenson. Truman expressed hope for an "open convention." Governor Williams of Michigan and Senator Humphrey of Minnesota began to be mentioned as worthy candidates.

Stevenson was irrevocably committed to making the race, but he now reluctantly reviewed strategy with his campaign staff. The manager of that staff was James Finnegan, secretary of the Commonwealth of Pennsylvania. His principal aide as executive director was Hyman B. Raskin, Stephen Mitchell's law partner and former deputy chairman of the national committee under Mitchell. On November 15, Stevenson announced his candidacy. A month later Senator Kefauver formally entered the arena. Governor Harriman made no announcement until about a month before the national convention.

The hazards of the presidential primary system in nineteen states, Alaska, and the District of Columbia, soon pressed on Stevenson, who had been spared these tests in 1952. Nevertheless, Stevenson was willing to accept the inevitability of campaigning hard in several primaries. The sole other entry, Kefauver, began by making a respectable showing in the New Hampshire poll on March 13. The two men faced each other for the first time in the Minnesota primary of March 20. Stevenson agreed to make this race at the invitation of Governor Orville Freeman and Senator Humphrey, who controlled the state party organization. Stevenson failed to anticipate two pitfalls: Kefauver's energetic campaign and the open primary system that enabled Republicans to cross over into the Democratic contest. Kefauver won heavily in Minnesota and nearly put Stevenson out of the race.

Stevenson again faced Kefauver in Oregon, Florida, and California, winning handily in each. After the California primary, Stevenson seemed so clearly in command of the field that Butler went to Chicago to confer with him directly about plans for the postconvention campaign. Regarding his personal future, Butler inquired "whether he should plan on going back to the private practice of law or whether, as he much preferred to do, he should plan on remaining as national chairman. Stevenson replied that in the event of his own nomination, he wanted Butler to remain as chairman and to manage the Presidential campaign."[21]

Meanwhile, Governor Harriman mobilized his forces offstage in anticipation of a deadlocked convention. He expected to have former President Truman and former National Chairman Frank McKinney in his corner. On June 9, Harriman announced his candidacy, only to have it crowded out of the headlines by news of a second Eisenhower illness requiring surgery for ileitis. Even former President Truman's dramatic endorsement on the eve of the convention failed to shore up Harriman's position.

On July 6, President Eisenhower told politicians and public alike that, despite his temporary incapacity, he expected to be fully ready for the fall campaign if renominated. This statement led Kefauver unexpectedly to announce his withdrawal on July 31, and he asked his supporters to give their votes to Stevenson. On the first and only ballot, Stevenson received $905^1/_2$ of the 1,372 votes of the convention, Harriman 210, Johnson 80, and $176^1/_2$ went to others.[22]

This convention produced one of the rare spectacles in national politics: a serious contest for the vice-presidential nomination. At least three candidates made organized efforts in the preconvention period: Senator Hubert H. Humphrey, who went so far as to make a formal announcement of his candidacy; Senator John F. Kennedy of Massachusetts, who took pains to cultivate the southern delegates; and Mayor Robert Wagner of New York City. Tennessee produced two available but unannounced candidates: its junior senator, Albert Gore, to whom its delegation was formally committed, and Senator Kefauver, whose supporters began to promote him for the vice-presidency shortly after he stepped aside in favor of Stevenson.

Kefauver, Humphrey, and Kennedy were well known to the delegates. Kefauver had caused the party regulars no small discomfort by his aggressive campaigns in 1952 and 1956. Humphrey was an established leader of the liberal wing and, together with former Governor Battle, was responsible for the skillful handling of the loyalty pledge problem. Kennedy, coming from one of Massachusetts' best-known political families, had been conspicuous in this convention, placing Stevenson in nomination and narrating a documentary film. Kennedy also had the backing of Senate Majority Leader Johnson.

Since any one of these men would have been an acceptable running mate, Stevenson, as did William Jennings Bryan in 1896, decided to do nothing to influence the convention's choice. Speaker Rayburn, Senator Johnson, and Chairman Butler argued vigorously with Stevenson, for fear that the convention would be deadlocked or that commitments to television and other mass media would fail to be met. Stevenson prevailed, and the ensuing contest brought home to the viewing public the seriousness of the vice-presidential nomination, particularly in the light of President Eisenhower's repeated illnesses.

The first ballot resulted in the following tally: Kefauver $483^1/_2$, Kennedy 304, Gore 178, Wagner $162^1/_2$, Humphrey $134^1/_2$, the remaining votes scattered. The surprise was the size and distribution of Kennedy's support. It would be expected that Massachusetts and neighboring Connecticut would support a favorite son. It was not expected that Georgia, Louisiana, and Virginia would give their full vote to a liberal northerner of Catholic faith. Senator Johnson was widely credited with having orchestrated this feat. Johnson's own Texas delegation, however, gave its 56 votes to Senator Gore on the first ballot. New factional alignments appeared to be in the making.

The second ballot was marked by confusion, caucusing, and all the excitement of a photo-finish horse race. With each increment in the Kefauver vote, a counterbid was made by the pro-Kennedy delegations. A major block of votes went to Kennedy from the New York delegation when Wagner supporters were released. When Texas' turn came, it shifted its 56 votes from Gore to Kennedy. Several other states made minor switches. At the end of the second ballot the tally gave Kennedy 618 votes and Kefauver $551^1/_2$, with $686^1/_2$ needed to nominate.

At this point the convention's permanent chairman, Speaker Rayburn, was beset by delegations calling for recognition to shift their votes. At the high point of his strength, Kennedy had 656 votes and Kefauver 632. Missouri, which had passed in order to be polled, added 36 votes to the Kefauver column, placing him ahead. After further switching and confusion, the official count gave Kefauver $755^1/_2$ and Kennedy 589. Political commentators later speculated whether Kennedy might not have gotten the nomination if Speaker Rayburn had recognized the convention delegations in some other sequence.

Chairman Butler had accomplished a great deal toward preparing national headquarters for the election campaign. He had carried on a poll of party officials and Democrats in public office to ascertain their conception of the principal issues. During June, he had an extensive conference with the managers of the three announced candidates for the presidential nomination to determine to what extent the national headquarters could prepare for the election campaign of any one of them, particularly with respect to the use of television, radio, and transportation facilities. Few Democratic national chairmen in recent decades had taken the office as seriously as Butler, a factor that won for him the esteem if not the support of nearly all of the principal leaders.

Determined to avoid the "two-headed" organization that plagued him in 1952, Stevenson planned to put James Finnegan, his preconvention manager, into the national chairmanship to coordinate the entire election campaign. Butler became aware of Stevenson's desire to replace him with Finnegan on the evening before the national committee was to meet. A few minutes before the national committee was scheduled to meet on the morning of August 17, Stevenson invited Butler to his room, spoke to the national chairman about Finnegan's great contribution to the Stevenson preconvention campaign, but did not go so far as to ask specifically for Butler's resignation. Butler in turn reminded Stevenson that they had come to an agreement in mid-June on the matter of the chairmanship, and Butler had based all his personal plans on that agreement. Stevenson had yet to reach a decision when Butler departed to open the meeting of the national committee.

Pressed by the members of the committee to report on his interview with Stevenson, Butler gave all the details. On hand and listening was Speaker Rayburn, who had been impressed with Butler's energetic handling of the national headquarters and with the warm endorsement given Butler by Mike Kirwan, chairman of the congressional campaign committee. Rayburn left to talk with Stevenson in Butler's behalf. Meanwhile, a series of speeches on Butler's merits as national chairman led to a resolution adopted, with few dissents, urging Butler not to resign under any circumstances. A few minutes later Stevenson sent word of his decision to keep Butler as chairman and to appoint Finnegan as his personal campaign manager.[23] To avoid the organizational divisions of the 1952 campaign, Finnegan's office was established next door to Butler's.

The design of the Stevenson campaign was straightforward. Finnegan planned that the nominees concentrate in those counties where a relatively slight shift might make the difference between an Eisenhower or a Stevenson victory. To provide a contrast with the ailing president, Stevenson was to carry on an intensive stumping tour. But the public opinion polls gave the Stevenson managers little grounds for hope; the popular president led Stevenson in the polls throughout the campaign. On election day Eisenhower's share of the popular vote was larger than in 1952.

5

Even more impressive than the Eisenhower landslide were Democratic successes in the congressional races. The Democrats retained control of the Senate, 49–47, and won a House majority of 233–201. For a landslide winner in the presidential race to fail to carry with him both or at least one house of Congress for his party was still a rare event in national politics. The cause seemed to be a combination of Eisenhower's personal popularity and the wisdom of the Rayburn-Johnson strategy of "responsibility in opposition." In a perverse way, congressional Democrats had benefited from the Eisenhower coattail.

As for Stevenson's second round as titular leader, congressional leaders, particularly in the Senate, minimized his future influence. In a published interview, Stevenson recalled the importance he had placed on the programmatic aspects of the recent campaign, "We must maintain the dialogue of democracy to do justice to our system of Government. . . . While we lost the election, I have no doubt at all that many of the views and ideas I have tried to express will ultimately prevail."[24] Stevenson then indicated that he was "not going to wash his hands of the party or any obligations he has, but that he must also turn to the business of earning a living again."[25] Hubert Humphrey predicted that party leadership "will be essentially Congressional." Majority Leader Johnson observed, "Mr. Stevenson can speak for himself."[26]

Senator Johnson was not without challenge in his own bailiwick. His status as majority leader rested upon a coalition of southern and southwestern senators. Anticipating re-election, Johnson predicted a continuation of the "responsible opposition" strategy of the previous Congress. "We are a good and reasonable group of men working for the good of the country without parties, labels, or cliques." On the matter of developing a distinctive Democratic program, he said, "No, we'll wait for the President. We'll support him when he's right and oppose him when he's wrong."[27]

Liberal Democrats from the Northeast, upper Midwest, and the Far West disagreed. Led by Senators Humphrey and Paul Douglas of Illinois, this minority developed plans for carving out a distinctive Democratic program, particularly in the civil rights field. As a necessary step toward civil rights legislation, the liberals announced a full-scale campaign against the filibuster rule. When this was interpreted as part of a plan to remove Johnson from the leadership, Senators Kennedy and Humphrey issued emphatic denials, hailing Johnson as the only man skillful enough to lead the party in the Senate.

The presidential election outcome brought challenges to another Democratic leader: National Chairman Butler. Illinois' National Committeeman Jacob Arvey suggested that there was need for "a few new pass catchers" on the Democratic team.[28] Elsewhere the suggestion was made that James Finnegan replace Butler. But Butler's wide support among national committee members was not easily upset. Butler carried little of the onus of defeat in 1956 for he had hardly been consulted by Stevenson and Finnegan. For those national committee members whose political influence derived in part from the survival of a national headquarters, there was no alternative to Butler's strong management.

Secure in the chairmanship, Butler turned to the tasks that would occupy him for the next three and a half years: a million dollar campaign debt remained. To raise money Butler inaugurated a series of $100-a-plate dinners, another series at lower prices, and a direct-mail solicitation. Costs at headquarters were cut by reducing the staff from 180 to 50.

The format of the *Democratic Digest* was revised. Popular among intellectuals in the party, the *Digest*'s circulation never reached beyond 70,000. The change in format was designed to lower production costs and subscription prices, and, because of its house-organ content, broaden its audience to include more of the party rank and file. The sustaining membership "dues" were given renewed attention. By 1958, more than 35,000 Democrats were making regular annual contributions of $10 or more. This money provided the hard core of operating funds for the national headquarters, including Butler's annual salary of $25,000 plus expenses.

To bridge the political distance between national headquarters and precinct organizations, Butler appointed six regional representatives to work regularly on coordination of national, state, and local organizational, campaigning, recruiting, and training programs. A precinct workers' training program was inaugurated, which eventually reached some fifteen thousand party workers in more than thirty states.[29]

The most famous and controversial of Butler's organizational innovations was his attempt to establish a consulting committee that could coordinate the policy and strategy decisions of the party leadership in the Senate, the House, state houses, city halls, state organizations, national headquarters, and the private sector. Butler's interest in such a coordinating committee came as no surprise. He had sponsored the plan for a midterm national convention during Mitchell's chairmanship and was familiar with the American Political Science Association's recommendation for a party council of fifty. Butler expressed a special frustration over the frequency with which party leaders communicated with each other through the newspapers, particularly in view of the typical press inclination to magnify disagreements. Butler's consulting committee plan was itself drawn by the press into the ongoing battle over the filibuster and civil rights legislation.[30]

On November 27, 1956, the executive committee of the national committee approved plans to create a high-level advisory board to shape legislative proposals in keeping with the party's "progressive, forward-looking platform."[31] A board that gave only advice rather than directives would also prevent infraction of the Hull-Farley rule against the national committee taking formal public policy positions of its own. The executive committee members most strongly endorsing the plan were Mayor David Lawrence of Pittsburgh, National Committeeman Paul Ziffren of California, and Jacob Arvey of Illinois. Chairman Butler was authorized to appoint a board of not more than seventeen senior Democrats whose function would be to "coordinate and advance efforts in behalf of Democratic programs and principles."[32]

A week later, on December 3, 1956, Butler announced the names of twenty party leaders who had been "invited" to serve on the new Advisory Council. Butler explained to the press that he had tried to name members "on the basis of their familiarity with the great problems that will come before this committee, rather than on the basis of their representation of any particular interest, group or program." He also told reporters that the invitations were "obviously" a formality since acceptances had been assured by prior inquiry.

The roster of members that he gave out was a significant portrait of the structure of influence among leaders in the national party as seen by the presidential wing:

—*Members-at-large:* Adlai E. Stevenson, Harry S. Truman, Mrs. Franklin D. Roosevelt, Senator Estes Kefauver, Speaker Sam Rayburn, Senator Lyndon B. Johnson, Governor John S. Battle of Virginia, Governor Averell Harriman of New York, Governor G. Mennen Williams of Michigan, Mayor Raymond R. Tucker of St. Louis, Luther Hodges of North Carolina, and Ernest W. McFarland of Arizona.

—*Senate Members:* Mike Mansfield of Montana, the party whip, George A. Smathers of Florida, chairman of the senatorial campaign committee, Hubert H. Humphrey of Minnesota, and John F. Kennedy of Massachusetts.

—*House Members:* John W. McCormack of Massachusetts, majority leader, Carl Albert of Oklahoma, party whip, Michael J. Kirwan of Ohio, chairman of the congressional campaign committee, and Edith Green of Oregon.

Butler was able to announce during this same press conference eight acceptances: Truman, Stevenson, Harriman, Williams, Kefauver, Humphrey, Tucker, and Green. In Chicago, Adlai Stevenson commented on his membership on the Advisory Council with an announcement of his own: He would not run again for president. He added: "The greatest service the Democratic party can now render is a strong, searching and constructive opposition." Newspaper commentators noted the heavy northern liberal composition of the Council, the speed with which noncongressional individuals had accepted their places on it, and the opportunities it would afford Democratic leaders such as Stevenson to be heard on national policy issues.

The congressional leaders suspected a trap. There was a week of private conversations. On December 9, Speaker Rayburn wired Butler from Texas that he had consulted with Representatives McCormack, Albert, and Kirwan, and on behalf of all four, Rayburn declined membership on the Advisory Council. In Rayburn's opinion it would be "a mistake" for these party leaders to accept a place on a noncongressional policy-making body. The Speaker thought that the 233 party members in the House would undoubtedly resent it if the four leaders were to develop legislative policies on any committee outside of the House.

A few days later, on December 12, former Governor Battle declined to serve. Senator Johnson announced his declination on December 13, saying that "legislative processes are already very difficult, and the necessity of dealing with an additional committee not created by Federal law before taking action would only cause delays and confusion." Johnson, as had Rayburn, expressed his willingness to consult informally with the Advisory Council.

Having announced the creation of the Advisory Council with such fanfare and having been publicly rebuffed by the congressional leaders, Butler retreated on December 18, but with care lest he diminish the prestige of those who had accepted. He called the declinations from the congressional leaders "regretful," insisted that the purpose of the Advisory Council had been misrepresented, and declared that there had been no intention to dilute the powers of the leaders in Congress or to question their responsibilities in legislative action.

On December 19, Butler announced that the Advisory Council would be retained as an adjunct of the executive committee of the national committee, but that no effort would be made to fill vacancies on it by appointing congressional replacements. Instead, new members would be drawn from among Democratic governors and mayors. The Council, he said, would hold its first formal meeting on January 4, 1957.

In making this announcement, Butler explained the functions intended for the Advisory Council. The Advisory Council would give "some form of national representation to the millions of Democrats who are not represented" by a Democratic senator or representative. It would function as a clearinghouse for the analysis of the problems of the state organizations, contributing "a great deal toward organizational planning and strategy" for future campaigns and for the resolution of "such inside-the-family problems as national committee rules and fund-raising." Butler expected the Council to provide "progressive and effective political leadership . . . by a continuing study of the inter-convention problems that are constantly arising and [by] suggesting programs to deal with them."[33]

Stevenson endorsed Butler's explanation, adding that the Democratic party "to be an effective opposition . . . must have a broader base than the Democrats in Congress." Democrats in Congress, said Stevenson, should welcome the ideas of party leaders outside Congress. On the other hand, he added, Democratic governors, mayors, officials, and party workers throughout the country must be kept informed about party policy at the national level.[34]

Five members of the Advisory Council met with eleven members of the national committee's executive committee in Washington on January 4. The five included Truman, Stevenson, Mrs. Roosevelt, Humphrey, and Kefauver. The group issued a statement that day declaring that the party's platform would be its guide, but that the further deliberations of the Advisory Council would "enable our party on a national basis to present new programs to meet problems which arise during the periods between conventions." Chairman Butler noted that the national committee had in the past avoided policy-making declarations, but that the new committee could make such declarations "on an advisory basis."

Butler also reported that the Advisory Council would become a permanent agency of the national party. He had been authorized to employ a staff including an executive director, legal counsel, and individuals to lead task forces studying specific policy problem areas. Butler continued to hope that he might persuade congressional leaders to permit the chairmen of the two congressional campaign committees to become members of the Advisory Council in their formal capacities.

The following morning, in a grand display of party harmony, Speaker Rayburn, Senate Majority Leader Johnson, and House Majority Leader McCormack breakfasted with the members of the Advisory Council. Former President Truman led the discussions and warmly thanked the congressional leaders for meeting with them. On their part, the congressional leaders agreed to consult with the Advisory Council. The extent of Truman's endorsement of the Advisory Council as an instrument of party policy making was impressive and in contrast to his skepticism about proposals for such a council while he was the occupant of the White House.

On February 16, the executive committee of the national committee met, gave Butler a vote of confidence, and endorsed the creation of the Advisory Council, on which its fourteen members were given ex officio positions. The following day the full Advisory Council issued its first official statement. It urged Congress to enact strong civil rights legislation, recommended statehood for Alaska and Hawaii, and deplored Eisenhower's foreign policy. Butler was authorized to appoint a five-member steering committee to direct the Council's organization and staffing. He chose Stevenson, Harriman, Williams, Ziffren, and the national committeeman from Louisiana, Camille F. Gravel, Jr., who also was chairman of the southern conference of national committee members. The steering committee was authorized to establish task force committees for each public policy field, to be made up of policy experts within the party and possibly some nonpartisan advisers. A few weeks later Charles Tyroler II, of New York, was appointed executive director. A former Defense Department official, Tyroler had been campaign manager for Senator Kefauver in 1956.

The executive committee action came before the full national committee on May 4 and was challenged by the southern members. The national committeeman from Georgia moved that the Advisory Council be required to receive advance approval of the full national committee before declaring party policy. The motion was defeated 65 to 26. At the end of the May 4 meeting, the Advisory Council issued its second series of policy statements calling the Eisenhower foreign policy a form of "appeasement," asking for tax reductions in the low income categories, and opposing federal right-to-work legislation.

Southerners were not the only ones dissatisfied with the form in which the Advisory Council had emerged. Some liberals, including former Senator Herbert H. Lehman of New York, felt that although they supported it, the Council was "not enough."[35] Lehman in particular urged the Democratic party to hold a national convention once a year, as do the British parties, to decide policy and plan legislative programs. Lehman thought that the main problem in creating such national conventions would be the procedures for choosing the delegates.

Reacting to the Lehman proposal, Tammany leader Carmine De Sapio thought that national conventions would involve the party in unnecessary expense and "bickering." Instead, De Sapio proposed a more intensive use of the national committee for policy making, perhaps through monthly meetings. Lehman's comments, however, carried particular weight in view of his senior status in the party. He became an influential member of the Advisory Council a few weeks later.

During 1957, the Advisory Council issued some twenty-three statements on national policy. Some of these were the product of task-force committees headed by eminent specialists within the party. Others were drafted by the Council staff and approved by Council members. Typical of the latter was the statement of November 1957 in reply to two major addresses by President Eisenhower. The statement was prepared by the staff so as to make a speedy retort.

The task forces were numerous, often with a dozen or more members led by a chairman and a vice-chairman. For example, the Advisory Committee on Foreign Policy was headed by former Secretary of State Dean Acheson and had as its vice-chairman the former head of the State Department's policy planning staff, Paul Nitze. The Advisory Committee on Economic Policy had as its chairman Professor John K. Galbraith of Harvard and consisted mainly of lawyers and economists. The Advisory Committee on Political Organization was led by Michigan's State Chairman Neil Staebler. This committee came up with such fund-raising recommendations as a Democratic Party Night, a national event built around $5 box suppers; a national door-to-door solicitation called Dollars for Democrats Day; a sustaining membership drive; a Democratic Trust Fund, for Democrats wishing to make provision for the party in their wills; a direct-mail solicitation; and regional fund-raising dinners. There was also an Advisory Committee on Urban and Suburban Problems headed by Mayor Richard C. Lee of New Haven, whose work on urban redevelopment for his city had received favorable national attention.

In February 1958, the Advisory Council set an important precedent by issuing its own "State of the Union Message" at the same time that members of Congress gathered for the new session. In December 1959, as part of the preparation for the platform work of the 1960 national convention, the Advisory Council issued a ten-thousand word policy statement consisting of twenty-two "chapters." This pronouncement was issued dramatically at a party dinner in New York City at which all the party leaders mentioned for the 1960 nomination, with the exception of Senator Johnson, delivered addresses.

Shortly after the Advisory Council meeting of October 19 and 20, 1957, the Council's staff evaluated what public attention was being given its activities and statements. They found that news stories on the Council's statements were carried on the front pages of virtually every major newspaper in the country and that well over 75 percent of the smaller papers also gave front-page attention. In the opinion of an independent research agency, the Advisory Council achieved "saturation coverage" in the press, usually matched only by major policy statements of the president himself.[36] The press association services referred to the Advisory Council with such phrases as "the Democratic party high command," "the agency that is spokesman for the National Democratic Party," "the policy-making voice of the Democratic party," etc.

Columnists took particular note of the Advisory Council. Commentator Arthur Krock observed how "brilliantly composed" were the Council's tracts, pointing out that some of them were written by authors of no small fame: Dean Acheson, Paul Nitze, John Galbraith, etc. It was Krock's opinion that these policy statements held a "monopoly" of "the political publicity market" because the Republicans had nothing comparable, an observation that implied that President Eisenhower was not exercising his full prerogative in this respect.[37] Another commented: "The need for a party voice between conventions and elections is as old as the system. If the Council can be made to serve that function, it can become a useful instrument of party policy."[38]

6

During the first year of Eisenhower's second term there was mounting criticism of the president's failure to reciprocate the Truman policy of occasional consultation with the titular leader of the out-party. Reacting to this criticism, the president invited Stevenson to serve as consultant on the administration's North Atlantic Treaty Organization plans. It was to be Stevenson's duty to study the new program and to comment freely on it without assuming any responsibility for the acceptance or rejection of his comments or suggestions.

Stevenson referred to this arrangement as a step toward "nonpartisanship" rather than "bipartisanship." He conferred widely with the Democratic national leadership before accepting. In November 1957, he did take on the status of consultant on NATO problems. The implications abroad were more significant than at home, in the opinion of the *New York Times:*

> Stevenson's influence abroad is probably greater than it is at home. Here he's still the twice-defeated Democratic candidate, and there he's the Leader of the Opposition. Here he's the titular head of the Democratic party, and not more than that; there—because European constitutional systems are so different from ours—he's billed in the popular mind as the official spokesman for the party of Roosevelt and Truman, the party that has traditionally had the more sympathetic approach to foreign affairs and America's relationship to Europe. Here he is a respected figure whose political future is at best highly precarious; there he's a powerful representative of a major segment of public opinion.[39]

This analysis was underscored by Stevenson's own view of his status at home. Asked by a newspaperman during a television interview how far his influence extended as titular head of the Democratic party, Stevenson replied that he thought it extended about five yards, no farther.[40]

Although the Advisory Council and Stevenson's prominence as titular leader earned the presidential wing of the party an unusual amount of attention, Democratic activity in Congress also received more than ordinary attention. Legislative strategies continued to be directed by Rayburn and Johnson, who were credited for the landslide victory in the midterm election of 1958. This election produced the largest Democratic majority in the Senate since 1940 (62 to 34) and the greatest lead in the House since 1936 (282 to 153).

Eyes were particularly focused upon the Senate, where a large number of Democrats were making themselves available for the 1960 presidential nomination. Washington had in these years become so much the media center of the world that aspiring senators enjoyed great new advantages in achieving renown whereas governors, mayors, and others outside of the nation's capital were beginning to complain that the news "black-out" in their state capitals and city halls hampered their chances.

As keeper of the Senate's timetable and image, Lyndon Johnson distributed ample opportunity for public display and legislative achievement among his more presidentially inclined colleagues, keeping a good portion for himself and sharing in the glory of Senate Democrats as a whole. For example, in 1957 Hubert Humphrey led the liberal attack on the filibuster as part of the strategy to pass civil rights legislation. Humphrey was given every opportunity to make his case. It was Johnson, however, who received the lion's share of the credit for the compromise that came out of the North-South negotiations. The first civil rights legislation to be passed in eighty-five years came forth, but the filibuster rule remained intact. This legislation placed Humphrey among the leading liberal candidates. Johnson also used the occasion to assure many that he was more a westerner than a southerner.

Similar opportunities were afforded Senators Stuart Symington and John F. Kennedy. With the contemporary world's most famous military figure in the White House, Symington's criticisms of Eisenhower's military policy and requests for defense outlays had particular point. Symington fought to increase military appropriations above amounts requested in the Eisenhower budget.

Kennedy's opportunities for broadening his appeal to those constituencies suspicious of his wealth came in connection with labor legislation. A Kennedy bill in 1959 was intended to raise the minimum wage. Kennedy-led investigations of corruption and racketeering in certain labor unions brought proposals for restrictive union legislation. Offered as anticorruption rather than antiunion legislation, a Kennedy-Ervin bill nevertheless became encumbered by a series of antilabor amendments as it was processed through the Senate. Johnson stepped in to arrange various compromises to water down the punitive character of some of the amendments. In the end, it was passed by a vote of 47 to 46, with Johnson sharing Kennedy's achievement. From the House of Representatives, however, came the heavily punitive Landrum-Griffin bill, which had 229 to 201 support on a test vote. Kennedy's work in arranging further compromises in conference committee were lauded by labor leaders as giving the unions the best they could get in the current session. The son of one of the nation's wealthiest men, Kennedy's attitudes toward labor, not previously tested, were thus able to remove any suspicions that liberal and labor leaders may have had, thereby improving his availability for the presidential nomination.

As competition for the nomination increased, Chairman Butler was making headlines in his own right, but under circumstances that brought charges of incompetence and partiality in the exercise of his duties. To criticisms made during 1957, Butler offered a response in a Los Angeles speech on August 10, 1957.[41] He accused some leaders in the party of wanting to disband the national headquarters simply because it had a deficit of $700,000. "Already, at the national level, we are witnessing the beginnings of efforts by a little group of men to capture control of our party's national convention and dictate the nomination of our presidential and vice-presidential candidates," he charged. "These are the very men who would weaken the prestige and influence of the office of National Chairman in order to gain their ends."

Washington observers, unable to learn the identity of the "little group of men" from Butler directly, assumed that he was referring to the efforts of former National Chairman McKinney to promote former Senator Earle Clements of Kentucky, now executive director of the Democratic congressional campaign committee, as Butler's replacement.

In 1958, the factional split on the issue of school integration was aggravated by the role of Governor Orval E. Faubus' segregationist conduct in the Little Rock school crisis. Chairman Butler called Faubus an "unworthy Democrat," and the Advisory Council issued a statement denying that Faubus' views were also those of the national Democratic party.

Another controversial southern development occurred in the Louisiana state central committee, which, in early October, voted 69 to 30 to remove Camille F. Gravel, Jr., as that state's national committeeman. A moderate on civil rights, Gravel had been working on Butler's executive committee and Advisory Council as a key representative of the southern view. Gravel announced that he would carry the fight for his seat to the national committee.

The following day Chairman Butler stated that the national committee "is the judge of its membership, not a state committee or a state convention." Butler added that a national committee member could be removed only if "proper grounds" were brought against him. To Butler's chagrin, a vote of two-thirds of the members present at the next national committee meeting approved of Gravel's removal.

Butler, in a television interview, pledged that the national party would not compromise on "the moral issue of racial integration." If southerners did not like the party's official stand in favor of integration, he said, they could find asylum either with the Republicans or in a third political party. Coming on the eve of the midterm elections, these statements and southern reactions caused concern among some Democratic leaders. Senator George A. Smathers of Florida suggested that Butler remain silent on the civil rights issue and more profitably concentrate on electing Democrats to Congress in November.

The full national committee came into the fray some weeks after the election. A resolution emphasizing the need for a strong civil rights stand was endorsed, 79 to 27. Butler was commended for his conduct of the chairmanship, 84 to 19. National Committeeman Gravel was permitted to keep his seat as Louisiana's representative, 91 to 15. The steering committee—now called the Administrative Committee—of the Advisory Council was reconstituted to include Butler as chairman, Thomas K. Finletter, Philip B. Perlman, Charles S. Murphy, and Henry H. Fowler, giving northeastern liberals even more representation in the future of the Council.

Possibly the noisiest of the Butler encounters was his altercation with party leaders in Congress during 1959. Again, in a television interview, Butler observed that "quite a few Democrats around the country are unhappy about the progress that has been made" in the current session of Congress.[42] Senator Johnson later observed that Butler's dissatisfaction was akin to that of his opposite number as the head of the Republican national committee. "Mr. Butler and Morton are both entitled to their opinions," said Johnson.[43]

Senate Democratic Whip Mansfield spoke more directly, "I think it would be far better for the Democratic national committee and its leadership to get behind the responsible leadership shown by Senator Lyndon B. Johnson in the Senate and Speaker Sam Rayburn in the House and remember that the same factors will decide the elections in 1960 that decided the elections in '54, '56 and '58."[44] Continued Mansfield, "The record on which the Democratic party will run next year, as in other years, will be the record of the Democratic party in Congress." Joining this commentary was Senator R. Vance Hartke, a member of the anti-Butler faction in Indiana. Hartke made an elaborate speech supporting "the Johnsonian concept of [a] responsible Congress."[45] Speaking as a member of the national committee and a much esteemed elder statesman, Senator Green of Rhode Island also reprimanded Butler.

Butler responded by charging that certain elements in Congress were seeking to replace him with a western senator, but that the move was meeting little success because of the reluctance of the unnamed senator. Butler expressed the hope that his successor would not even be a member of Congress, because "the chairmanship of a national party is not a part-time job."[46] In a more conciliatory gesture, Butler asked Speaker Rayburn to call a meeting with Senator Johnson in

Rayburn's office. The three men consulted together alone for a full hour. When they emerged, the Speaker reported that all three placed full blame on "press misrepresentation" for their alleged disagreements.

Meanwhile, the Democratic Advisory Council was gaining in prestige and authority as the voice of the presidential wing. Prior to summer of 1959, the Council included among its members at least four presidential candidates: Stevenson, Humphrey, Kefauver, and Governor Williams of Michigan. In July, Governor "Pat" Brown, California's favorite son in 1960, joined. In November, two other presidential prospects became members: Kennedy and Symington.

7

The shape of Democratic nominating politics was somewhat different than what it had been three years earlier. During 1957 it was assumed, even by the pollsters, that Stevenson was out of the running. During 1958 Kefauver, the vice-presidential nominee of 1956, ran ahead of Kennedy, his erstwhile opponent, in the polls. When Stevenson's name was reintroduced into the polls this same year, he led the other two by a substantial margin. From mid-1958 to late 1959 Stevenson and Kennedy were the leading preferences of Democratic voters, according to the Gallup poll; running third was Senator Johnson.[47]

Stevenson declared that he would not be the nominee in 1960. Aware of invidious comparisons between himself and three-time loser William Jennings Bryan, Stevenson found himself in as ambivalent a personal situation as in 1952. Stevenson supporters rallied behind Eleanor Roosevelt, whose preferred candidate he was, yet the former nominee could hardly erase the record of two defeats. Stevenson kept himself available, but immobile. Many less tenacious Stevenson supporters were being recruited by Kennedy and Humphrey organizations.

Kennedy's obstacles were his youth and religion. Humphrey was too closely identified with a particular faction. Despite his efforts to the contrary, Johnson continued to be classified as a southerner. Kefauver's supporters were more nostalgic of 1952 than hopeful for 1960. Symington's candidacy could only come to life in a deadlocked convention. All were burdened by the fact that Stephen A. Douglas in 1860 was the most recent presidential nominee of the Democratic party to come directly out of the Senate.

> The Kennedy strategy was to seek victories in the primaries to impress the delegates selected elsewhere and the leaders by whom they were influenced or controlled. . . . The general result was a gathering consensus in which Kennedy became progressively stronger both in voter support and in delegate support, but without being able to demonstrate conclusive majorities in either case.[48]

As Kennedy and Humphrey campaigned in Wisconsin and West Virginia during March, a "high Democratic source" reportedly predicted that Kennedy would beat Humphrey in Wisconsin and possibly in West Virginia. This same "source" predicted that if Kennedy failed in West Virginia, Symington—not Humphrey—would have the next best chance for the nomination. Although he never acknowledged or denied that he had been the "high source," it became known that the predictions were those of Butler during a briefing session with newspapermen.

Humphrey, facing a difficult contest in Wisconsin, angrily called for Butler's resignation. Butler expressed regret over Humphrey's attack and added that he would resign under the conditions announced the previous December, that is, after the 1960 national convention; he would not be a candidate for re-election as chairman under any circumstances.

Butler was involved in two other disputes during March 1960. One resulted from his implied charge that President Eisenhower, using a navy band for entertainment during an official visit to Brazil, shared responsibility for the tragic death of twenty-five navy men in an air accident during transport of the band. Reaction was sharp; the charge seemed in bad taste. Butler insisted that his remarks had been distorted. He nonetheless apologized to the president for the implications of the distortion.

The second battle was the perennial one with the southern delegations preparing for the national convention. The convention call mentioned the "good faith" with which all delegates were expected to participate and stated that members of the national committee would have to "declare affirmatively" for the nominees at the risk of having their seats declared vacant. To get around this, in at least six southern states a "free elector" movement was under way to allow presidential electors chosen under the Democratic symbol to be independent decision-makers in the final voting. Butler threatened to challenge the credentials of delegations from such states and to encourage the loyalist factions to send competing delegations.[49] These threats and counterthreats failed to materialize as realities.

Just prior to the national convention, Butler was attacked from an unexpected quarter on an unexpected charge. Former President Truman, supporting the candidacy of Symington, announced that he would "boycott" the convention to which he had been chosen as a delegate because Butler was rigging it in favor of Kennedy. As stated by Mrs. India Edwards on behalf of the Johnson forces, the charge left the implication that Butler was to be "paid off" with Kennedy family legal business. Butler dismissed the charge as "ludicrous" and hoped Truman would reconsider the boycott.[50]

Meanwhile, the national chairman continued to push ahead on rules changes designed to strengthen the national organization. One rule, adopted at the national committee meeting of September 16, 1959, gave each national committee member one-half vote which, when cast, would not be bound by the voting of their respective state delegations. The rules committee of the convention, although allowing the one-half vote, made it subject to the instruction practices that applied to state delegations generally.

Another rule adopted by the national convention gave the Advisory Council official status and authority in the national party. The specific language: "Be it further resolved, that the Democratic National Committee . . . is hereby authorized and directed to take whatever action may be advisable and necessary to continue the services of the Democratic Advisory Council, and its various advisory committees under the present plan of operation, or, as may be revised from time to time by the Democratic National Committee."

A somewhat radical proposal, opposed by Butler, came from National Committeeman Arvey of Illinois. His proposal would give the more populous states greater proportionate representation on the national committee, based on a formula similar to that applied in distributing votes to the national convention.

On the weekend before the convention, the Associated Press reported that 546 votes were committed to Kennedy, 235 to Johnson. Needed to nominate were 760 votes. The Kennedy strategists aimed for a first-ballot nomination. The informal Stevenson group, led by James Doyle of Wisconsin, worked for postponement of the nominating decision until a later ballot. Stevenson was the second choice of many Kennedy delegates; Kennedy was the second choice of many Johnson supporters. Uncertainty reigned until the presidential ballot itself, on which Kennedy received 806 votes to Johnson's 409.

On July 14, as the vice-presidential nomination was about to take place, Kennedy announced that he thought "it would be the best judgment of the convention to nominate Senator Lyndon B. Johnson of Texas for the office of vice-president." Thus, not one, but two senators emerged as the 1960 Democratic ticket.

The senatorial leaders were also involved in the selection of a national committee chairman. Even before his nomination, Kennedy indicated that he would consult Johnson and Rayburn on the selection of a national chairman. In other press interviews prior to the presidential nomination, certain of Kennedy's aides let it be known that, if nominated, the senator would not make Al Smith's mistake of selecting a Catholic (Raskob) as national chairman for a ticket headed by a Catholic.

These aides speculated openly about Kennedy's "requirements" for a national chairman. The new national chairman would have to contribute to party unity, an indirect reference to Paul Butler's embattled incumbency. He would have to be a non-Catholic. He would also have to organize the national headquarters in such a way that the Kennedy preconvention team could readily be incorporated into it, thus avoiding the dual headquarters arrangements of 1952 and 1956.

Among those considered, it was reported, were Leonard Reinsch, an Atlanta radio and television executive who was handling media relations for the 1960

Fifty-four years old, John M. Bailey had been state chairman for four-teen years. He received the bachelor's degree from Catholic University in 1926, where he achieved some prominence as an athlete. He gradua-ted from Harvard Law School in 1929 and returned to Hartford, Connect-icut, to establish his practice. He began his party career as a precinct and ward leader and as a political apprentice to Hartford "boss" Thomas J. Spellacy. In 1933, Bailey was appointed local police court judge upon the recommendation of Spellacy. He ran for probate judge of Hartford in 1940 and was defeated; this was the only race for elective office that he ever ran. Bailey became a member of the Democratic state central committee, Connecticut statute revision commissioner, and, in 1946, Democratic state chairman.

Bailey formed a close and effective association with Abraham A. Ribicoff, another Hartford leader who eventually received the gubernato-rial nomination in 1954. In 1956, Ribicoff and Bailey performed much of the legwork involved in the Kennedy candidacy for the vice-presidential nomination. During the four years thereafter, Bailey continued as the key party official advancing the Kennedy cause among party officials throughout the country.

national convention, and Senator Clair Engle of California. Ineligible because of the religious requirement were the principal leaders of the preconvention cam-paign: the Senator's brother, Robert F. Kennedy, and Connecticut State Chair-man John M. Bailey.

The North-South complexion of the slate made it particularly important to find a prominent westerner to give the appearance of regional balance to the leadership of the party. Still another requirement implicit in the makeup of the group consulting on the chairmanship—Kennedy, Johnson, and Rayburn—was that the man be well known and acceptable to the congressional leadership, effectively narrowing the search to the membership of Congress.

The combination of qualifications reduced the list of prospects to Henry M. Jackson: a Lutheran, a senator who had won a national reputation for his role in the highly publicized Army-McCarthy hearings and for his support of the contro-versial Admiral Rickover, and one of the most popular young westerners in the Democratic party.

Jackson accepted the chairmanship on a temporary basis, that is, until the end of the presidential contest, after which he intended to return full-time to his senatorial duties. That Jackson would serve in a symbolic and spokesman's role could be inferred from the composition of the rest of the campaign organization.

Robert F. Kennedy was named campaign manager and Lawrence F. O'Brien,

Of Norwegian immigrant parents, Henry M. Jackson was born in Washington in 1912. His father was a building contractor of limited means. The young Jackson had to earn his tuition in order to obtain a college education. He attended Stanford University, but took the bachelor's and law degree at the University of Washington, the latter in 1935. Jackson practiced law until he was elected county prosecutor of Snohomish County in 1938, in which he built a reputation as a racket-buster. In 1940, at the age of twenty-eight, Jackson was elected to the House of Representatives, where he served for six terms.

In Congress, Jackson became a member of the Joint Congressional Committee on Atomic Energy and an expert on atomic and missile developments. In 1952, he ran for the Senate, defeating Republican Harry P. Cain despite the Eisenhower landslide in that state. He later was one of three senators who resigned from the Senate Permanent Investigations Subcommittee in protest against its chairman's tactics; the chairman was Senator Joseph McCarthy of Wisconsin. In 1958, he was re-elected by one of the largest majorities in the state's history.

---

a Massachusetts public relations man who had been on the Kennedy staff for some time, became executive director of the national headquarters staff. It was understood that O'Brien would be in line to succeed Jackson.[51] Senator Jackson also agreed to serve without pay. The press releases announcing Jackson's selection heralded the fact that the West had in this way been given important recognition in the national party.

The 1960 presidential campaign demonstrated strikingly the nationalizing influence of various technological changes upon the political parties. Jet airplanes brought the most distant boundaries of the nation within a few hours of each other and were used frequently by the candidates, particularly during their final drives in all the marginal communities. The four televised debates between Kennedy and Nixon were without precedent in national party history and were subsequently credited with being a decisive factor in what turned out to be the closest presidential election in American history.

In the field of social science technology, the Kennedy strategists had available the findings and projections of Simulmatics Corporation, a group of social scientists who had developed a mathematical model of the U.S. electorate. Encouraged by Paul Butler and the Democratic Advisory Council, the Simulmatics group was able to process over six million pieces of information about American voters drawn from the findings of sixty-six nationwide public opinion surveys conducted since 1952. The findings were particularly useful with respect to Kennedy's handling of the religious issue.[52]

The special involvement of the congressional wing of the party—if not already evident from the presence of three senators in positions of titular and formal leadership—was indicated by the convening of a special session of Congress after the national conventions. Speaker Rayburn and Senate Majority Leader Johnson, with substantial majorities in their respective houses, had arranged for the special session in advance of the conventions. Vice-President Nixon, in his official capacity as presiding officer of the Senate, was thereby put in a position of playing a passive role in legislative activity dominated by Majority Leader Johnson's agenda. With Senator Kennedy leading the fight for legislation on the minimum wage, care for the aged, public housing, and other measures, the public was able to witness a confrontation of its presidential nominees as dramatic as the televised debates.

The outcome of the election was so close that speculation about what might take place in the electoral college continued until the day that body recorded its official decision. In a total vote of more than sixty-eight million, Kennedy received a popular plurality of approximately 100,000. With six Alabama electors unpledged, eight Mississippi electors uninstructed, and questions of local voting frauds raised against the Democrats by Republican National Chairman Morton, some analysts went so far as to speculate how the idiosyncracies of the electoral college system might give the presidency to Senator Johnson. In the actual event, Kennedy received 303 of the 537 electoral votes.

Several national committee organizational developments took place almost immediately. As arranged, Senator Jackson resigned from the national chairmanship after the election. The national committee met on January 21, 1961, to install his successor, John M. Bailey, who had served as Kennedy's liaison with state and national party officials during the campaign. Bailey served without pay and, as in the case of James A. Farley, retained his position as Connecticut state party chairman.

Bailey, in accepting, indicated that he hoped to "revitalize" the executive committee of the national committee and direct his attention to local party activities aimed at winning the next midterm elections to Congress and the state legislatures. Introduced to the national committee by Bailey, President Kennedy spoke of his national chairman as "a man from the field who knows what's wrong in Washington."[53] On this decentralizing note, Bailey proceeded to his work of reorganizing the national headquarters.

The Democrats had emerged from the campaign with a debt of $3,800,000. Given recent dissatisfaction of Democratic leaders in Congress with the activities of national headquarters, the debt became the justification for a drastic staff retrenchment. Regional field service organizers were dropped. Publication of the *Democratic Digest* was terminated. The financial operations of the national, senatorial campaign, and congressional campaign committees were merged; the national committee tentatively agreed to provide the congressional committees with more than half a million dollars through election day, 1962, for operating and campaign costs.

Disbanding the Democratic Advisory Council in March 1961 was probably the most symbolic evidence of the promotion of the Democratic party from "out" to "in" party status. In announcing the Council's end, Chairman Bailey acknowledged that it had served "a function" while the party was out of power, but that henceforth policy would have to come from the White House.

Having served as something of a shadow cabinet through which titular leader Stevenson and others of the presidential wing could make known their policy positions, the Advisory Council, as an organizational device, had been caught up in a set of unusual political coincidences that perhaps inevitably led to its demise. It was gestated during a period when the Democratic leadership in Congress was winning electoral majorities even as the titular leader was suffering his second electoral defeat. A device intended at minimum to coordinate the lines of communication among the several agencies of the national party, it ran into the presidential aspirations of several senators who could little serve their own causes by giving comfort to such a competitor for public attention.

During the Kennedy-Johnson campaign, Chairman Jackson relegated Advisory Council staff and publications to the background. Between election day and inauguration, President-elect Kennedy organized a series of his own policy task forces intended to help orient the new administration in its policy positions. The personnel of these task forces were, to large degree, recruited from the membership of the Advisory Council task forces. When the time arrived for appointments in the Kennedy administration, thirty-two of the first seventy-eight major appointees had been members of the Advisory Council committees or staff.

Significantly, the Advisory Council was never a pro-Kennedy group and did not aid in his receiving the nomination. The Council and its task forces were primarily agencies for leadership communication and consultation, for permitting policy specialists to become visible and establish party credentials, and for keeping the electorate aware of the presidential wing's policy positions in national affairs at a time when it was the out-party. The sheer technicality of national policy problems and the multiplicity of available candidates for the Democratic nomination in 1960 made the existence of the Council important. President Kennedy's appointments from its membership confirmed that importance.

Again in the White House, Democrats had little reason to anticipate the political and social turbulence of the 1960s and the intensive nationalization process that lay ahead for their national committee and national chairmanship in the 1970s. It was sufficient to appreciate how much had changed since 1848.

It was also worth noting what had worked and what had not with respect to the Stevenson era's experiment in providing the nation with a coherent loyal opposition leadership. The national chairmen of both major parties had by now acquired substantial experience with this enterprise.

23 | Bureaucratizing the Loyal Opposition's National Headquarters

During the 1940s, the New Deal became the Fair Deal, and the Republican party made a generational change from an older leadership to a younger one. The followers of Hoover, Landon, and Willkie rearranged themselves to become the followers of Robert A. Taft and Thomas E. Dewey. By and large, the national chairmen devoted themselves to building and managing a national headquarters whose personnel were employed semipermanently and who could serve the needs of all Republicans. Headquarters began to acquire a bureaucratic look.

1

Following their defeat in November 1940, the Republicans counted three men who could claim to be their titular leadership: Hoover, Landon, and Willkie. Each was interested in maintaining some measure of active influence. Hoover still had a band of followers who reacted loyally and volubly every time Democrats spoke of "Hoover's Depression." Although not a candidate for renomination in 1940, Landon continued to speak freely on public and party matters, his political friends widely spread among the party's officialdom. Two brief months after Willkie's defeat, for example, Landon commented, "If Mr. Willkie had revealed [his unequivocal support of Lend-Lease] before the Republican national convention, he would not have been nominated."[1]

Willkie had the freshest claim to the titular leadership. After election day, tens of thousands of letters and telegrams urged him to remain active. Believing that the Republican party needed revitalization, new blood, and new symbols, Willkie decided to grasp the leadership role firmly. On November 11, over the combined radio networks of the country, he gave his "Loyal Opposition" speech.[2]

Willkie called for American unity, invigorated by a loyal and public-spirited party opposition. He made recommendations for a less restrictive economy and a more integrated foreign policy. Without naming the Associated Willkie Clubs of America, he asserted that it was entirely appropriate for his supporters to remain active if they felt so inclined. Thus, Willkie did what no other defeated Republican candidate had ever done, namely, assert his status as a titular leader and spokesman for the party. In marked contrast to Charles E. Hughes' retirement in 1916, Willkie's persistence probably paved the way for the party's readiness in 1948 to make its first renomination of a defeated titular leader, Thomas E. Dewey.

Republican reaction to the Willkie speech ranged from enthusiastic endorsement by Kenneth F. Simpson, New York County Republican leader, to biting skepticism from Clarence Budington Kelland, the national committeeman from Arizona, who argued that no opposition could be loyal, particularly to the New Deal. National Chairman Martin took a position near the middle, "I believe . . . [Willkie] is on honest and sound ground when he says democracy needs a strong opposition party."[3]

Two days later, Oren Root announced that the ten thousand Willkie clubs would continue in operation. Simultaneously with Root's announcement came Joseph Martin's that he was planning to resign as national chairman in January. Shortly after, Democrats-for-Willkie disbanded as a national organization; state and local affiliates were invited to make their own decisions regarding their future.

Willkie's Loyal Opposition speech and Martin's imminent resignation provoked discussions about national party leadership that dealt with every difficulty faced by an out-party in the United States. There was the immediate question of the formal leadership, that is, the national chairmanship. As usual, different factions had different candidates. Taft supporters favored Taft's former law partner, John Hollister, or Ohio National Committeeman David S. Ingalls. Willkie followers suggested Bruce Barton, the advertising executive. Walter S. Hallanan of West Virginia was mentioned as a compromise. Several congressional Republicans were mentioned.

Journalist David Lawrence made the suggestion that Willkie himself take the chairmanship. Lawrence's argument touched upon all the major weaknesses of the out-party, which presumably would be resolved by having Willkie as national chairman. Lawrence pointed out that Willkie as chairman would provide a powerful voice for the national party, enable a prospective president (Willkie) to acquire greater familiarity with national affairs, and set in motion conferences that would eliminate Republican policy contradictions both in and out of Congress. Martin endorsed Lawrence's proposal, as did many of Willkie's friends. Others of Willkie's advisers contended that the duties of the national chairmanship "would work against his interests if he planned to seek the presidential nomination in 1944."[4] Landon preferred to have Martin retain the chairmanship in order to forestall a party split. Willkie agreed and convinced Martin not to resign until March in order to allow time to discover a "good liberal" as a replacement and to keep the "reactionaries out."

Republican hostility toward Willkie was stirred by his endorsement in January of President Roosevelt's lend-lease plan to render aid to the Allies. Landon condemned the lend-lease bill as a step toward war. Several congressional Republicans such as Henrich Shipstead and Hamilton Fish expressed no interest in Willkie's views and denied that Willkie spoke for the party.[5]

A Gallup poll in January, however, revealed that 62 percent of those who had voted Republican in November approved of the lend-lease bill in principle. These findings and the overt factional debate led to a publicity slowdown at Republican national headquarters. The staff retreated for several weeks from the lend-lease issue, waiting to see whether the Landon-Taft or the Willkie position would prevail. Martin, in the middle of the cross fire, was more than happy to call a national committee meeting for March to offer his resignation.

Republicans all over the country waited for Willkie to prove that he could maintain actual as well as titular leadership.[6] At the beginning of February 1941, for example, a conference in Omaha, Nebraska, of Midwest party chairmen from sixteen states was the occasion for much criticism of Willkie. With regard to the reconstitution of the national party organization, one of the conference leaders claimed that, since the main strength of Republicanism lay in the Midwest, the initiative should come from that region. Lobby conversation among the leaders in Omaha also dwelt upon Willkie's stand on lend-lease. Said the national committeeman from Nebraska, "Willkie is not going to get a grip on the party organization. You can bet your bottom dollar on that. He was a Democrat before he came into the party and I'm not so sure he still isn't a Democrat." On February 2, 1941, the Omaha conference adopted resolutions commending two Republicans in Congress, Representative Joseph W. Martin, Jr., and Senator Charles McNary; no mention was made of Willkie. State chairmen agreed that the national committee should do all it could to obtain an experienced political organizer rather than an amateur for its chairmanship.

In Des Moines at this same time, the Young Republican National Federation met and prepared resolutions criticizing Willkie's leadership. Chairman Martin stated that he would regret any serious attention the federation might give to such resolutions. The Des Moines meeting satisfied itself with a resolution criticizing independent organizations, that is, the Willkie clubs.

These open and organized demonstrations of hostility toward Willkie were part of a factional struggle begun several weeks earlier. In a Lincoln Day address in Virginia, Senator Taft denied that Willkie did or could speak for the Republican party. Taft saw "no justification in precedent or principle for the view that a defeated candidate for President is the titular leader of the party."[7]

He specifically took Willkie to task for his interventionism. Taft's position was supported by other noninterventionists such as Senator Nye, Representative Fish, and Clarence Budington Kelland. In an effort to straddle the issue, Governor Dewey said he favored a lend-lease plan "in a form that Republicans can support."

Taft's declarations notwithstanding, Willkie was by most measures still the top Republican leader in the nation during the spring and summer of 1941. A Gallup poll taken shortly after Willkie's return from a trip to England as President Roosevelt's representative showed him even more popular than he was at the height of his election campaign. A survey of over seven thousand Republican party officials, conducted by the Young Republicans, showed Willkie far ahead in popularity among party workers, leading with 51 percent of the votes cast, followed by 16 percent for National Chairman Martin. In the congressional test of Willkie's position on lend-lease, an overwhelming majority of Republicans in the House of Representatives voted for passage. In the Senate, however, only a small group of Republicans supported the Willkie position.

The March national committee meeting convened after the lend-lease vote in Congress. To maintain some semblance of party harmony, Willkie, with the help of Will Hays, succeeded in convincing Martin to remain on as national chairman. Martin requested appointment of a headquarters manager who could give full time to grass-roots organization. To the surprise of many observers, the national committeemen, in private conversations, expressed a willingness to regard Willkie as titular head of the party.[8] Willkie, however, rejected all suggestions of a second nomination in 1944. Talk of partisan politics and candidates, he declared, were very much out of order in the light of the great national and world crisis.

This overt premeeting harmony, however, concealed a great deal of turbulence and discussion. One of the principals was former National Chairman Hilles of New York, whose correspondence on the issues was authoritative and revealing. Writing in February, Hilles expressed the view that "if the party must have a bitter contest over the Chairmanship—if such a contest concededly is unavoidable—it would be better to have it next month than next year and let the healing streams abound for a full year."[9] Hilles saw Harrison Spangler and Werner Schroeder as the leading candidates for the position. Willkie, according to Hilles, tendered the chairmanship to John Hollister of Ohio over the telephone, but Hollister declined because of his commitment to work for the presidential candidacy of John Bricker. Willkie and Sam Pryor, the national committeeman from Connecticut, then agreed on Raymond Baldwin, the former governor of Connecticut, who was willing. There was opposition to Baldwin on grounds that he had demonstrated certain inadequacies in campaign management and, when elected governor, had been only a minority winner. Schroeder's name was proposed by Governor Dwight Green of Illinois, without enthusiasm on Schroeder's part. Green felt that Schroeder could strengthen him in downstate Illinois where Green's support was weakest.

Hilles summed up the selection problem as follows:

> If they in the middle west will not go for Spangler—and Landon would, I presume, say they are "cock-eyed" and thence resist the proposal; if Schroeder's involuntary entry should be scratched; if Hollister is irrevocably opposed to even a draft; and if Ingalls' selection would be an embarrassment to Taft, then Baldwin alone of the field thus far trotted out will remain. In that case the indications are that a majority of the members of the Committee will vote to continue Martin.[10]

Hilles went on to discuss the relationship between titular leaders and the chairman:

> Those who have written to me—say nine members—think the Committee in choosing an interim Chairman should not be subjected to outside pressure. Two members pointed out the fact that we now have three "titular leaders." . . . We all agreed, and have always agreed, that the nominee of a National Convention must have a pretty free rein and with it the right to use the whip and the spur. The candidate and the Chairman must enjoy each other's complete confidence. After a successful issue, the Chairman must be the liaison officer between the President and the organization. But the functions of a Chairman who serves the party in opposition are very different from those of a Chairman who serves in the shadow of the White House. The former must recruit and organize and finance and direct strategy; the latter has only the duties of a loyal and discreet top-sergeant.[11]

Then, commenting on the fact that Joseph Martin was holding down two major leadership positions in the party at the same time, Hilles wrote:

> I agree with you that the old rule under which the Committee and Congress were regarded as separate and distinct entities had much to support it, a statement that is not a reflection upon either body. The functions are quite different; the meetings of the one frequently conflict, in point of both time and place, with the other; and a member of Congress who also serves on the National Committee is given an advantage over colleagues from his own state, a fact that has created embarrassments on many occasions and generated friction on other occasions. The principal objection, however, relates to the allocation of party funds in lean years in close campaigns. Members of Congress who feel a sense of insecurity press for all-out aid to the "ins," to the exclusion of potential "outs." The problem is forced upon a Chairman and he should be as nearly free from bias as may be. He would have a sense of balance and of proportions, and should be free to use party funds wisely to attack districts represented by Democrats who are vulnerable. Otherwise there is an ingrowing condition and a narrowing of party direction and control. But Congressmen feel a proprietary interest in the Committee and the old rule has been more honored in the breach than in the observance.[12]

2

The following month Willkie joined a law firm, but continued to make news with his pronouncements about foreign policy. These were invariably provocative and tended to accentuate the growing internationalist-isolationist factionalism within the party. In one such speech Willkie urged Americans not only to produce goods for her allies, but also to deliver them by whatever means could be most effective. This was a position more radical than the president's. From the Midwest came a manifesto in response, signed by such Republican elder statesmen as Lowden, Landon, Hoover, MacNider, Dawes, Robert Hutchins of the University of Chicago, and former National Chairman Fletcher, insisting that the party stand by its noninterventionist positions. The America First Committee, the *Chicago Tribune*, and hero Charles A. Lindbergh used the occasion to reiterate their isolationism.

During the fall, Willkie provoked further division within the party by stating that he would take an active part in the 1942 midterm elections on behalf of candidates supporting internationalist policies. Under current international conditions, an isolationist Republican party, he said, would be an open invitation for the founding of a new national party.

The reaction of House Republicans came on November 2 in a movement to read Willkie out of the party. Charles Halleck of Indiana and Dewey Short of Missouri led the group, whose goal was designation of Representative Martin as the party's spokesman. Three days later, Short delivered a vehement anti-Willkie speech on the floor of the House, an address that obviously had been cleared with Minority Leader Martin.

The following January, in his capacity as national chairman, Martin appointed Clarence Budington Kelland, a vocal isolationist, to be publicity director for national headquarters. Martin had appointed Kelland without clearing it with Willkie. Said the Republican, internationalist *New York Herald Tribune*, "The Republican party has faced a lot of hard luck in its day but Mr. Kelland is just too much."[13]

Such were the isolated, embittered, and ultimately effective first steps in the factional movement to retire Willkie. Willkie helped his adversaries by neglecting party organizational matters and by his style of argument on the issues. His policy admonitions often came at inopportune times. For example, at the April 1942 meeting of the national committee, Willkie asked for endorsement of a resolution committing the party to assume new international responsibilities, immediately and after the war. John Hamilton, Robert Taft, and other anti-interventionists introduced their own resolutions and were ready for a battle.

Chairman Martin attempted to bury all the resolutions in a subcommittee. The compromise resolution that came out of the subcommittee was generally considered a Willkie victory. Declared Willkie, "The next job for Republicans to do is to see to it that in the coming primaries candidates are nominated not alone for Congress but for other positions of public influence who have the courage to declare and who believe sincerely these principles and their necessary implications."[14] Senator Taft, on the other hand, asserted that the national committee had no power to commit the party to a postwar program.[15] Taft also noted that the subcommittee had managed to "draw the teeth" out of the Willkie resolution; no one could take exception to the language finally used.

By declaring himself in favor of the internationalists in all the Republican primaries, Willkie, a titular leader without portfolio, went out on a longer limb than President Roosevelt had in his 1938 Democratic party "purges." But Willkie failed to follow up this endorsement with active campaign support. This failure cost him whatever loyalty remained among party regulars. After belatedly removing himself from the New York governorship race, Willkie did not endorse Dewey until well into October. During the last week of August, at President Roosevelt's request and as his personal representative, Willkie departed upon his famous "One World" trip. Republican candidates for Congress were crushed by Willkie's timing and his gross neglect of their campaign needs. The party was without a popular titular head at the height of an off-year election campaign. In the words of one congressional leader, "After the campaign of 1942, not five members in the House were willing to follow his leadership."[16]

Willkie made headlines as he sped around the world on the presidential mission. Returning in mid-October, he made a nationwide broadcast to report on his tour. He called for a second front in Europe and improvements in the conduct of the war. He concluded by urging that planning for the postwar adjustments begin immediately lest the peace once again be lost.

Even without aid from its titular leaders, the Republican party gained forty-four seats in the House and nine in the Senate. Among the winners were several presidential aspirants: Thomas E. Dewey in New York, John Bricker in Ohio, Harold E. Stassen in Minnesota, and Leverett Saltonstall in Massachusetts. The election over, Chairman Martin announced his irrevocable intention to resign in order to tend to his duties as minority leader in the House of Representatives.

As they had been in February 1941, the major prospects to succeed Martin were Werner Schroeder of Illinois and Harrison Spangler of Iowa. Willkie seemed not to have a candidate of his own, although he did say that he wanted a man who believed in the "principles of the Republican Party . . . regardless of whether he was an isolationist before Pearl Harbor. And I want a fellow who is a liberal on the economic front." Schroeder, who had an excellent reputation as a fund raiser and party organizer, was a conservative from the isolationist Midwest. Supported by Hoover and Taft elements, Schroeder decided, despite his earlier reluctance, to make a fight for the chairmanship. Claiming 55 of the committee's 106 votes, Schroeder declined to withdraw in the interest of party unity when requested to do so by Martin. Lem Jones, Willkie's secretary and representative at the national committee meeting, also claimed 55 votes.

The national committee meeting tried unsuccessfully for a compromise. Among those suggested were Barak Mattingly of Missouri, Frank Gannett of New York, and John Townsend of Delaware. Unexpectedly, one of the pro-Willkie committeemen nominated Frederick E. Baker, a thirty-five-year-old businessman from the state of Washington. When Schroeder's name was placed in nomination, a supporting speech was made by Senator Taft. Spangler, Gannett, and Mattingly were also nominated.

Baker and Schroeder each received 40 votes, Harrison E. Spangler 15, Gannett 3, Mattingly 1, and 2 abstentions. A recess gave Joseph Martin an opportunity to arrange a compromise.

Several hours were necessary for the arrangement. When the national committee returned, Baker and Schroeder walked in "arm in arm" to withdraw in favor of Spangler. Spangler was elected unanimously. Spangler himself recalls that Senator Taft was privately for him and that several representatives of both the Willkie and Schroeder sides had asked him to remain in the race as a possible compromise candidate. Spangler had supported Taft in the 1940 convention (and would do so again in 1948). Nevertheless, the Willkie people spoke of Spangler's election as a victory over the interests represented by Schroeder. Crowed the *Chicago Tribune*, "Nobody here has any thought that Harrison Spangler will be found among the Willkie backers in 1944."[17]

Recalling the selection of Spangler at a later time, the national committeeman from Connecticut, Sam Pryor, a staunch Willkie supporter, felt that it was a costly defeat for Willkie. Had Willkie been more active in party functions after his trip to England, the chairmanship fight would never have come up, in Pryor's opinion.

> I suggested to Wendell that he go out and raise money to help the party to hold the meeting and also to reacquaint himself with the party leaders so that he could have an important role in the selection of a new chairman who would be favorable toward him. Willkie, at this time, felt that he had the party solidly behind him; I knew that he didn't. Willkie stayed at home and did not raise the necessary money, and Harrison Spangler, an anti-Willkie man, was chosen. Willkie should have worked vigorously at this point to elect a chairman who was in tune with him, but he didn't and his leadership was further impaired.[18]

Spangler began his incumbency close to the middle of the road within the party. His early press statements seemed at once to reject isolationism—to the satisfaction of the Willkie supporters—and to support completely anti-Roosevelt stands—to the satisfaction of conservatives. His true leanings became more evident when he appointed James P. Selvage, a former director of public relations for the National Association of Manufacturers, as his publicity director.

The national committee began to pour out anti-Roosevelt releases. Spangler talked of building a grass-roots organization. In preparation for the 1944 platform committee, on May 31, 1943, he announced creation of a Post-War Advisory Council of forty-nine members to write "a realistic peacetime program for American progress." The group was chosen from the top elective representatives of the party: twenty-four governors, five senators, twelve representatives, the chairmen of the senatorial and congressional campaign committees, and six members of the national committee. Willkie, Landon, and Hoover—the titular leaders—were kept out of the picture. The selection procedure gave the noninterventionists the greatest weight in the group.

To work for an internationalist plank in the 1944 platform, a Republican Post-War Policy Association was formed by Deneen Watson, a Chicago lawyer and former campaign manager for Governor Dwight Green. The association's meetings were dominated by Willkie supporters. This movement, which disbanded before the year was out, was widely credited with compelling Spangler to create the national committee's Post-War Advisory Council.

The advisory council conducted a major conference at Mackinac Island, Michigan, on September 6 and 7. In view of the procedure for selecting council members, Willkie was not present. Governor Dewey was, however, and he made the most of the occasion. In a newsworthy statement, he advocated a postwar alliance that would include Great Britain, China, and Russia. Thus, Dewey launched his first major effort to claim Willkie's foreign policy positions. The conference produced a "procollaboration" statement dealing with postwar relations with the Allies. Willkie approved it as "a move in the right direction."

A week later, writing for *Look* magazine, Willkie announced his willingness to seek the 1944 nomination on a "liberal" platform.

The candidates' maneuvers had been going on throughout the year. Early in December 1942, Senator Taft announced that he would not be a candidate. Instead, Taft indicated that he would support the aspirations of Governor Bricker of Ohio. Bricker considered himself a serious candidate, and Taft went to great lengths to avoid a split in the Ohio organization. A week or so later, Senator Vandenberg withdrew his name in the expectation that the nominee would come from "the new timber" in the party. By May of 1943, a full-blown campaign organization had developed, without the charismatic general's approval or disapproval, on behalf of General Douglas MacArthur. Harold Stassen, about to resign from the governorship of Minnesota to go on active duty with the navy, issued innumerable statements about the postwar world in which he saw a United Nations and effective world government.

Public opinion polls gave little encouragement to Willkie supporters. The Gallup poll for November 1942 showed 49 percent of the national sample looking with favor upon Willkie, but as many as 38 percent with strongly unfavorable reactions. Dewey appeared to be better liked than any other Republican: 53 percent of the sample preferred him. Trailing were Stassen, Bricker, and Taft. In

Herbert Brownell, Jr., was a native son of Nebraska. He was born in Peru in 1904, but his family moved to Lincoln when he was young. His father was a member of the University of Nebraska faculty. Brownell received his bachelor's degree from the University of Nebraska in 1924 and a law degree from Yale in 1927. After two years of service as a law clerk in a New York City firm, he became a member of the firm Lord, Day, and Lord. His first efforts as a party worker were in the Tenth Manhattan Assembly District, which housed the headquarters of Tammany Hall. Working with Brownell as election district captain for a neighboring district was Thomas E. Dewey. The two men became close friends.

When Brownell ran for election to the New York State assembly in 1931, Dewey served as his campaign manager. Their assault on Tammany's stronghold was not an easy one. The young men adopted several campaign innovations, including distribution of a phonograph record with music, an introduction by Dewey, and a speech by Brownell, which went to every voter in the district. Losing in 1931, Brownell repeated the race in 1932 and was elected. He served five one-year terms in the state assembly before returning to his law practice in 1937. His friend Dewey, on the other hand, had by this time achieved national repute for his racket-busting investigations begun in 1935. By 1938, Dewey's popularity made him the unanimous choice of the Republican state convention for the gubernatorial race against Herbert Lehman. Losing a close race to Lehman, Dewey's name was advanced by state leaders for the 1940 presidential nomination. At about this time, Herbert Brownell began again to take part in Republican party affairs, managing the successful campaign of the party's nominee for Manhattan borough president in 1941. In the next two years Brownell ran two other major campaigns successfully: Dewey's for governor in 1942 and Hanley's for lieutenant governor in 1943.

March of 1943, Republican voters were in favor of Dewey by a very impressive margin: 69 percent favorable against 13 percent unfavorable and 18 percent no opinion. Only 49 percent spoke favorably of Willkie and as many as 43 percent unfavorably. Surveys of Republican members of the House of Representatives, Republican state legislators, and Republican voters revealed that Dewey was firmly in the lead. Not even the April publication and sale of over a million copies of Willkie's *One World* could improve support for Willkie.

A few organization Republicans were among the last to harbor Willkie sentiment. National Chairman Spangler, in appearing to become more and more neutral about the aspiring candidates, was less and less for Willkie by doing so. The facilities of national headquarters were increasingly in anti-Willkie hands.

Former Chairman John Hamilton, now a partner in the law firm of former Senator George Pepper in Philadelphia and counsel to Joseph Pew's Sun Oil Company, undertook a tour of seventeen states to sound out the preferences of organization people. Hamilton urged each state to develop "favorite sons" in order to assure a wide open convention. In some places he reportedly recommended supporting Governor Dewey. At the end of the trip he did report that Governor Dewey had substantial strength in all the communities he visited. Elsewhere, Alfred E. Landon made the strikingly correct prediction that Willkie would be out of the running before June and that Governor Dewey would be the choice of the national convention by the second ballot.

3

In Albany, Governor Dewey was biding his time and stepping on as few toes as possible. The Dewey forces avoided active part in the national chairmanship fight of December 1942. Dewey still enjoyed substantial political capital carrying over from the 1940 convention in which he had the support of several southern delegations (Florida, Georgia, and South Carolina), Idaho, Washington, and Wisconsin. There were a substantial number of Dewey votes from Illinois, Oklahoma, Maryland, New Jersey, and New York, but these had been willing to shift to Willkie as a second choice. Dewey now had the added status and resources of the governorship of New York from which he could effectively nurture former alliances. There was also the possibility that Dewey would inherit much of the Willkie delegate strength, particularly from the eastern states.[19]

Dewey gathered together a powerful team of political strategists: New York's National Committeeman J. Russell Sprague, Republican State Chairman Edwin F. Jaeckle, and campaign manager Herbert Brownell, Jr.

Dewey was reticent. Willkie was willing. At the January 1944 meeting of the national committee, it was announced that Willkie would enter the Oregon and Wisconsin primaries. Dewey, meanwhile, continued to deny any desire to be a candidate and sought to withdraw his name from the Wisconsin primary, scheduled for April 4. Soon after, General MacArthur's supporters, hoping to capitalize on the fact that Wisconsin was the general's home state, placed his name on the primary ballot. Another entry, bidding for the same sources of support as Willkie, was Harold Stassen, expecting to do well in a state neighboring his own Minnesota. Despite the confusing multicandidate primary, Willkie publicly chose to make the Wisconsin primary the crucial test of his cause. Speaking in Milwaukee, he said:

> Here is a Midwest state with an established leadership that holds views opposite to the views that I have on domestic and international affairs. . . . I look upon this as a good state for me to make a test and I am anxious to make it. I

believe that the rank and file of Republicans should determine who is to be the Presidential nominee. . . . Wisconsin is one of the most difficult states for me to make such a test.[20]

National opinion polls showed a continuing decline in Willkie's popularity and a rise in Dewey's. The Wisconsin party organization, which favored Dewey in 1940, and the state's Republican delegation to Congress, which had voted against nearly every measure supported by Willkie, remained solidly opposed to the titular leader. The ineptness of Willkie's manager further weakened his cause. Practically no Wisconsin campaign organization was established. Local pro-Willkie leaders were poorly coordinated. Willkie's field organization was negligible; he personally constituted almost the entire campaign operation. By the time he returned to Wisconsin in the closing weeks of March, the test that Willkie had set for himself was even more precarious than he had anticipated.

During his two weeks in the state, he traveled nearly fifteen hundred miles and spoke until he was physically exhausted. The odds against him were consistently overwhelming. His defeat in the primary was decisive. Fifteen of the national convention delegates elected were pledged to Dewey, who had hardly lifted a finger to campaign; Stassen received four delegates, MacArthur three, and Willkie none.

The following day Willkie issued a formal withdrawal from the presidential race. The road was now wide open for Dewey's nomination, which he received without further opposition. Even Governor Bricker joined the roster of Dewey seconds at the convention and himself received the vice-presidential place.

Two former titular leaders participated in the national convention: Hoover giving a convention address and Landon as a delegate from Kansas. Willkie was uninvited and absent. According to National Chairman Spangler, after the Wisconsin primary, he had inquired of several of Willkie's friends whether the former nominee would or would not support the party's choice. Willkie refused to commit himself, and Spangler decided to avoid bringing the unpredictable Willkie before the convention delegates. "Willkie had practically seceded from the party," said Spangler. Even Willkie's attacks in the press on the convention's foreign policy plank went unheeded.[21]

The national committee appointed a subcommittee of five to meet with Governor Dewey on problems of organizing for the campaign. The Dewey preconvention campaign team had been so tightly integrated that there was some speculation about which member would become national chairman. National Committeeman Sprague, having served as Dewey's preconvention manager in 1940, seemed to have seniority. State Chairman Jaeckle had organizational experience, but, according to some, was too important in his positions as New York State and Erie County chairman, both important in carrying this pivotal state. Herbert Brownell was the youngest and perhaps the most energetic of the trio. His successes in two difficult New York campaigns in the two preceding years qualified him for the difficult campaign ahead.

Brownell was chosen. The new set of vice-chairmen included Werner Schroeder, Mrs. Horace Sayre, and Ezra Whitla, all for Dewey in 1940 and 1944, and Mrs. Katharine Kennedy Brown, pro-Taft in 1940 and pro-Bricker in 1944. Spangler replaced former National Chairman Fletcher as general counsel, following the precedent established for Fletcher. According to one knowledgeable observer, "the shake-up was intended in part to correct a geographically unbalanced official staff that was appointed in 1940. At that time, New England held not only the balance of power but the lion's share of it."[22] Noting that his foe Schroeder had been named a vice-chairman and that his friend Sinclair Weeks has been dropped as treasurer, Wendell Willkie stoically commented, "They're making it complete, aren't they?"[23]

Establishing principal campaign headquarters in New York City, Brownell held the limelight as Governor Dewey retreated to his official duties in Albany. One of Brownell's principal themes was the charge that the "Communist-led CIO" was dominating the Roosevelt campaign. This was a theme that would appear in Republican campaigns over the next decade. Dewey, for his part, remained relatively preoccupied in Albany, taking time for a 6,700-mile campaign tour by train to the Pacific Coast in September. The *New York Times* referred to this phase of the Dewey campaign as "sedate." In October, however, Dewey began pounding away at New Dealers and Communists.

One of Brownell's most difficult tasks was to bring into the camp Wendell Willkie and his followers. Willkie's followers were easier to win over than the former nominee. Brownell made place for Sinclair Weeks and other Willkie leaders in the Dewey campaign organization. Willkie, on the other hand, withheld his endorsement in the express hope of compelling Dewey to take a more outspoken position in the field of international affairs. On October 8, when Willkie died suddenly after a series of heart attacks, he had not yet spoken in support of the New York governor.

Dewey could not overcome President Roosevelt's popularity. The forty-two-year-old governor was no match for the experienced war leader who at that very moment was taking his country to victory over the Axis. After the election, Republican leaders around the country commended Dewey's defeat as an "honorable" one and Brownell's work in the campaign as "outstanding."[24] Unlike Willkie, Dewey concluded his first presidential campaign with a substantial store of good will among the party leaders. Given Dewey's youthfulness and the probability that he would be re-elected governor of New York in 1946, few commentators doubted that he would once again make a presidential bid in 1948. If he did, however, he would have to buck a long-held Republican tradition that discarded presidential losers. Dewey would also have to overcome the eager candidacies of Governor Bricker, Harold Stassen, and Senator Taft as well as the hero-worship of General MacArthur.

4

One month after the election, Republican congressional leaders took the initiative for keeping together a strong, full-time national party headquarters to prepare for the 1946 and 1948 campaigns. Senate Minority Whip Kenneth Wherry of Nebraska reported this wish of his colleagues. National Chairman Brownell, returning from a vacation in the Southwest, was gratified by the news and told of plans for a series of conferences with congressional and state leaders regarding the future of national headquarters. Brownell, however, was uncertain about his own status. He had assumed the chairmanship for the campaign period only. Without a salary for his duties as national chairman and with a lucrative law practice awaiting his attention, he was ambivalent about staying at the post.

Brownell called a meeting of the national committee for January 22, to consider "a vigorous progressive, all-year program of party activity." With $300,000 left over from the campaign, headquarters had a strong financial start on interim operations. Brownell offered an eight-point program which was unusual in its clarity and directness, stating some of the most fundamental organizational problems of the national party.

The Brownell program called for: (1) a national organization to function on a full-time, all-year-round basis, with an enlarged and trained staff; (2) close working relations with the Senate and House party organizations; (3) staffs equipped for research, investigation, and publicity to serve party members in Congress as well as the national committee; (4) a vigorous program of cooperation among the national committee, House and Senate party members, the party's governors, and state organizations; (5) integration of the activities of the national committee with those of state and county committees; (6) more active participation by individual members of the national committee in the development and execution of a party program; (7) a broadened basis for contributions to the party treasury; and (8) cooperation between the national committee and the House and Senate organizations during congressional campaigns. Brownell's eight-point program was a careful articulation of most of the organizational objectives initiated by John Hamilton. It was a fair statement of the kinds of organizational arrangements that national chairmen of both major parties would henceforth seek.

The national committee gave overwhelming support to the plans for a full-time headquarters. However, significant points of disagreement were raised in the discussions. Some committeemen insisted that the chairmanship be considered a full-time job; Brownell would only agree to give it the "time it needs." A proxy-holder from Minnesota argued that the national chairman should not come from a state with a potential 1948 presidential candidate. This argument pressed home the conception of a "neutral" national party bureaucracy and meant that at that time no national chairman could come from New York (Dewey), Ohio (Bricker), or Minnesota (Stassen). The Minnesotan expressed what was on the minds of many: whether Brownell's continued incumbency in the chairmanship would pave the way for another Dewey effort. Brownell answered the argument only by restating his interest in hiring a purely professional staff. A third point of contention concerned the propriety of the national committee's making foreign policy declarations; the Republican senators present argued that this should be left entirely to the party leadership in the Senate.

With the authority to do so, Brownell embarked upon the task of recruiting qualified staff. Significantly, he went to the congressional leaders first for specific suggestions. His talks with Senators Arthur H. Vandenberg, William Allen White, Robert H. Taft, Warren Austin, and Kenneth Wherry also touched on his own future role. Senator White expressed the expectation that eventually a paid, full-time executive assistant to Brownell would be chosen.

Brownell inaugurated several innovations. He turned to former Senator John Danaher of Connecticut for advice regarding the problem of liaison with Congress. Brownell agreed that party leaders in both houses had responsibility for making policy and that the task of the national committee was essentially one of translation and publication. Brownell suggested creation of the position of "legislative counsel" at the national headquarters. Danaher objected on grounds that this implied advice or dictation to Congress. Brownell then suggested the title "congressional aide" and convinced Danaher to take on the responsibilities of this new staff position at a salary of $20,000 a year.[25] Another innovation was the creation of a full-time foreign affairs section at national headquarters. For this position Brownell was able to recruit Hugh R. Wilson, former ambassador to Germany and a former assistant secretary of state.

Brownell established a system of fund-raising quotas for each state party, based largely upon size of Republican vote cast. Responding to the growing interest in issuing midterm programmatic declarations, Brownell appointed a Special Committee on Development of National Policy, with Barak Mattingly of Missouri as its chairman. The committee was instructed to work out its statement in consultation with congressional leaders. Working through Danaher, Brownell reestablished the practice of periodic conferences with congressional leaders in the manner of John Hamilton's Weekend Conferences.

In February 1946, Brownell informed congressional leaders that national headquarters organization was completed and that he would shortly be retiring to his law practice. To minimize the factional juggling over a successor, Brownell declared that Governor Dewey had no personal choice for a national chairman. Brownell only hoped to find a man who could work hard on the 1946 campaign and remain fully committed to the maintenance of a year-round headquarters. Regarding the institutional development of the nation's party system, Brownell spoke out for change or abolition of the electoral college system. He was possibly the first national party chairman to do so, and his comments revealed a belief that almost any change would strengthen the national agencies of the parties.

A direct descendant of one of the first settlers of the region that became Tennessee, Brazilla Carroll Reece was born in that state in 1889,
one of thirteen children. He received his schooling in rural public
schools, Watauga Academy, and Carson and Newman College in Tennessee. An articulate activist in high school and college, he was class
valedictorian in both. He played football and basketball and was elected
to a number of top offices in student government. After receiving his
bachelor's degree in 1914, he was appointed principal of a local high
school. A year later he began graduate study at New York University in
economics and finance, receiving a master's degree. From 1916 to
1917, he was an instructor in economics at New York University, taking
a leave of absence for military service in World War I. His heroism as
an infantry lieutenant won for him the Distinguished Service Cross, the
Distinguished Service Medal, the Croix de Guerre with palm, and the
Purple Heart. Returning from Europe in 1919, Reece became Director
of the School of Commerce, Accounts and Finance at New York University, but again took a leave of absence in 1920 to run for Congress from
the First District of Tennessee. This district was one of two Tennessee
districts that had been traditionally Republican. At thirty years of age,
he entered Congress and served continuously thereafter. While in Congress, he passed law examinations admitting him to the Tennessee
and District of Columbia bars. He also became involved in the banking
business. Defeated only once, in 1930, Reece became a House expert
on economic legislation, particularly in the securities, monopoly, and
consumer fields. In 1939, he was elected national committeeman for
Tennessee and came to be regarded as the head of the Republican
party in the South. He served on the executive committee of the congressional campaign committee from 1937 to 1939 and again from
1939 to 1941, acquiring invaluable experience in the problems of national campaigning.

Of the dozen names suggested for chairman, the real candidates were soon
reduced to John Danaher and Representative Carroll Reece of Tennessee. Neither Danaher nor Reece had enough votes to win outright. Danaher had performed well as congressional aide and was popular among congressional
Republicans. It also became evident that Danaher was the candidate of the
Dewey people.

Reece had the advantage of long experience on the executive committee of
the House Republican campaign committee. His campaign manager for the
chairmanship was Walter Hallanan of West Virginia. Reece was also the leading

southern Republican in Congress and was planning to make a bid for the U.S. Senate in 1948. His support came primarily from pro-Taft members of the national committee.

A third contender for the chairmanship was suggested by former Willkie supporters: John W. Hanes, a New York banker. The Willkie people, many looking to Harold Stassen for leadership, were determined to defeat Danaher and reduce Dewey's influence in the national committee. The three-way division forced a roll call vote. On the first ballot Reece fell 7 votes short of a majority, Danaher was runner-up, with Hanes trailing him closely. The second ballot remained about the same. On the third, a number of the Hanes votes shifted to Reece, giving him a majority of 59 votes to Danaher's 22 and Hanes' 21.

The committee appointed Reece's campaign manager, Walter Hallanan, to the executive committee. A $2 million budget for the 1946 campaign, which included the requirements of the national, senatorial, and congressional campaign committees, was discussed. Reece invited Danaher to remain at headquarters as congressional aide, but Danaher declined.

Reece led a successful midterm campaign. As U.S. relations with the Soviet Union deteriorated, more and more Republicans injected the issue of communism into their oratory. Charging that the CIO-PAC and the Democratic party were guided by Marxist principles, Reece endeavored to simplify the choice into one between communism and republicanism. "Labor bosses" and "Labor Reds" were terms frequently heard from Republican headquarters. The election returned both houses of Congress to Republican control for the first time in many years. A by-product of the campaign was that the Red issue remained a durable component of Republican campaign strategy.

The year 1947 was one of buildup for the major presidential protagonists in the Republican party. Governor Dewey's second term was newsworthy; a friendly New York legislature put through one after another of his administration's bills. Senator Taft became chairman of the new Republican Policy Committee in the Senate. This committee was created by the 1946 Legislative Reorganization Act as an important recognition of the role of political parties in Congress. Senator Taft set out to make his new position one of major significance in the leadership of the out-party. As a result of his activities in this office, he came to be known as "Mr. Republican," spokesman for the party in opposition.[26]

Chairman Reece was willing to follow Taft's lead in most national party matters. Reece's record revealed sympathy for Taft's presidential aspirations and policy positions. Although he made public statements to the effect that the national committee was not interested in infringing upon the prerogatives of Congress, he made a special point of placing national headquarters at the disposal of the Republican majorities in Congress.

The Dewey managers—Brownell, Sprague, and Jaeckle—became increas-

Leonard Hall was born to Republicanism in Nassau County, New York, in 1900. His father was a coachman for Theodore Roosevelt and subsequently a White House librarian. Hall received his law degree from Georgetown University at nineteen and immediately plunged into Nassau County Republican politics. Two years later he was able to begin practice as a lawyer in New York City. When President Coolidge appointed New York State Assemblyman Davison as assistant secretary of war, the Republican organization nominated and elected Hall as his successor. Hall served three terms in the assembly, then agreed to run for sheriff in 1928 as a compromise candidate. After a term as sheriff of Nassau County, Hall returned to the assembly for terms from 1934 to 1938. In the latter year, he was elected to the House of Representatives where he served until 1952. Shortly after entering Congress, Hall began to devote his efforts to the revitalization of the Republican congressional campaign committee, of which he was a member. He then became a Dewey supporter for the presidential nomination and served as the manager of Dewey speakers bureau during the 1944 campaign.

ingly concerned about the pro-Taft complexion of the national party agencies. When a small group of Republican liberals squabbled with Chairman Reece, the Dewey cause was a beneficiary. Freshman Senator Raymond E. Baldwin of Connecticut wrote Reece complaining that Senate newcomers were being ignored by the party's leadership during the development of a legislative program. Reece recommended patience. When the liberals charged Reece with having precisely the same political views as Taft, the national chairman replied that his job was mainly one of developing the party's organization and selling the party's policies "as developed by the Republican Congress on the basis of the broad principles enunciated by the Republican National Convention."[27] At one point Senator George Aiken of Vermont demanded that Reece resign from the chairmanship. The pressures compelled Reece to issue almost as many "party unity" statements as anti-Truman releases. The publicity tended to improve Reece's chances of becoming U.S. senator from Tennessee in 1948.[28]

The Dewey leaders did not fail to challenge Taft's domination of the congressional party. Two politically agile New Yorkers lined up Dewey support: freshman Senator Irving Ives, who had earned a reputation as a spokesman for Republican moderates, and, in the House, Representative Leonard Hall, respected for his work as a member of the executive committee of the congressional campaign committee. Ives and Hall served as liaison between the Dewey team in Albany and members of Congress in Washington. In March 1947, Hall was elevated to the chairmanship of the congressional campaign committee, a position he held until he became national chairman in 1953.

The Republican leadership interpreted the 1946 election returns as a mandate for new legislation in the labor field. One of the most publicized pieces of legislation during the session was the Taft-Hartley Bill, strenuously opposed by the unions. The product of many authors, the Taft-Hartley Bill was eventually credited to the senator from Ohio. Significantly, however, the bill did not pass until it had the acquiescence of Senator Ives of New York, an expert in the labor field before he entered Congress.[29]

5

The presidential year 1948 began with Taft and Dewey at a standoff as front-runners. Several favorite sons were in the background: Stassen, MacArthur, and, from several states, Dwight D. Eisenhower. Stassen was considered a good bet as a compromise, but disqualified himself by entering and losing primaries in Ohio to Taft and in Oregon to Dewey.

In the last days before the convention, about a third of the delegates seemed committed to Dewey and another third to Taft. Several delegations held back behind favorite sons. Pennsylvania's seventy-three convention votes were a special case. Governor James Duff and Senator Edward Martin were factional rivals in the state organization; each controlled a substantial portion of that delegation. Martin was pro-Dewey; Duff was pro-Taft. The two had apparently agreed on a strategy of holding for favorite-son Martin, then moving to Vandenberg on an early ballot. Working closely with Duff, but in Taft's corner, was former National Chairman John Hamilton, who had been a Dewey supporter in 1944.

A dramatic boost to the Dewey cause came just prior to the convention when Martin withdrew as Pennsylvania's favorite son and announced his willingness to second the Dewey nomination. The withdrawal gave Dewey forty-one of Pennsylvania's votes and led several other favorite sons onto the Dewey bandwagon. John Hamilton's penthouse apartment at the Drake Hotel became the scene of secret conferences among stop-Dewey forces. Taft emerged from several of these conferences with words of encouragement to his followers, but without the necessary votes.

Dewey had 434 votes on the first ballot, Taft 224, Stassen 157, with several others following. Dewey's vote went to 515 on the second ballot, with 548 needed to nominate. He received a unanimous vote on the third ballot. After prolonged conferences with representatives of all factions, Dewey recommended Earl Warren of California as his running mate.

Brownell, Sprague, and Jaeckle were expected to continue as Dewey's intimate advisers, but these men favored the selection of someone outside their group for the national chairmanship, possibly someone from the Midwest to

---

Hugh D. Scott was born in Fredericksburg, Virginia, in 1900, from a line of early settlers. Part of his ancestry traced back to President Zachary Taylor. Scott's elementary and secondary education came from the public schools of Fredericksburg and his bachelor's degree from Randolph-Macon College. He received his law degree from the University of Virginia in 1922, and shortly thereafter began the practice of law in Philadelphia. He became a regular party worker at about this time and, in 1926, assistant district attorney for the City of Philadelphia, a position he held until 1941. Scott won in his first race for Congress in 1940, took a military leave of absence for active duty as a naval officer and returned to his congressional duties late in 1942 when he was re-elected for a second term. Scott served other tours of active military duty during 1944 and in 1945–46. He did not run for Congress in 1944, but was re-elected regularly thereafter.

---

balance the East-West composition of the ticket. However, the one political obligation of overriding importance to Governor Dewey was the contribution that Senator Martin had made to his nomination; the Martin-Grundy faction in Pennsylvania had run substantial political risks to provide Dewey with timely support. This wing needed to be strengthened, particularly against the Duff-Pew faction. Governor Dewey decided to reward Senator Martin by allowing him to name the national chairman.

Martin proposed Representative Hugh D. Scott, one of the rising young leaders among his Pennsylvania associates. The chairmanship was expected to help build Scott up for higher office; he eventually did become U.S. senator from Pennsylvania. At the time, as Pennsylvania's member on the Republican congressional campaign committee working alongside Leonard Hall of New York, Scott probably had enough national campaign experience to qualify for the chairmanship on the basis of competency alone.

When he accepted the chairmanship, Scott announced that Herbert Brownell would serve as campaign manager. Scott was to follow the lead of Dewey's personal campaign team, devoting his own talents to liaison work with congressional Republicans and therefore stationing himself chiefly at Washington headquarters. During August, the national chairman made a twenty-eight-state speaking tour in which he gave principal attention to the Communists-in-government issue.

In addition to Brownell, Sprague, and Jaeckle, Dewey's campaign strategy board included Elliott V. Bell, New York superintendent of banking, Representative Leonard Hall, John Foster Dulles, Allen Dulles, Senator Henry Cabot Lodge, Jr., and Representative Everett Dirksen, who advised on midwestern and agricultural problems. The weak link was Bell, whose information proved to be inadequate or misleading. According to one analyst, "If anyone can be tagged as the architect of the [election day] disaster, it is Bell." Dewey and the others reached similar conclusions.[30]

With the governors of the two most pivotal states, New York and California, on the Republican ticket and with President Truman's party coping with Dixiecrat and Progressive bolts, the Dewey strategists found it easy to agree with the political pundits who described 1948 as a certain victory for the Republicans. The main problem for the Dewey campaign, therefore, was to keep from alienating elements of support. The basis for this tactic were Bell's evaluations of the 1944 Dewey campaign against Roosevelt.

According to Bell, Dewey's aggressiveness in that campaign alienated a substantial number of political moderates. In addition, Bell suggested, Dewey then sounded so much like a Willkie liberal that many conservative Republican regulars were also disenchanted. Thus, Dewey's 1948 campaign emphasized caution and ambiguity in style and speech; "unity" became the basic theme.

As the campaign progressed, President Truman used the Republican-controlled Eightieth Congress as the whipping boy of his hard-hitting speeches. From his posture of statesmanlike aloofness, Dewey began to see his lead slipping away during the last weeks of the campaign. Subsequent research suggests that had the election taken place two weeks earlier than it did, or two weeks later, Dewey would probably have been elected president. As it happened, election day came at the high tide of Truman's whirlwind effort.[31] Among the losers was former Republican National Chairman Reece, whose opponent for senator, Estes Kefauver, enjoyed a two-to-one margin of victory.

When it was all over, Chairman Scott wrote some 180,000 party workers asking for their explanations of the defeat. Their views, he said, would be important in planning a more effective midterm campaign for 1950. The rank-and-file replies were fairly explicit: 38 percent said, "No fight"; 27 percent, "Me too"; 13 percent blamed lack of local organization; 10 percent, overconfidence; 4 percent Dewey, the man.

With defeat came the inevitable flurry about changing the party's officials. Dewey told the press, "Never again!" His withdrawal presumably left the 1952 nominating race wide open. Representative Scott received a large share of blame for "mismanagement" of the campaign, although insiders knew that he had relatively little to do with it. Leonard Hall, who had been chairman of the congressional campaign committee during the contest, was particularly critical of the unaggressive character of the campaign and placed the blame directly on Dewey and Brownell, leading to an estrangement that took on significance in later years. Some Republicans suggested that it was time for Vandenberg and Taft, who had done little for the Dewey cause, to step down from their posts in the Senate. Possibly the only national leader to escape condemnation was House Minority Leader Martin.

6

As 1949 began, the shape of Republican factional politics stabilized. Senator Taft continued as chairman of the Republican Policy Committee in the Senate, as "Mr. Republican," and as one who faced a hard campaign for re-election in Ohio in 1950. A landslide victory in that race held promise of placing Taft in an almost unassailable position for the 1952 presidential nomination.

Governor Dewey, at the age of 46, seemed unlikely to withdraw from an active role in Republican affairs. True, according to Chairman Scott, Dewey "should not, could not and will not be a candidate in 1952."[32] Dewey nevertheless referred to himself as "titular head" of the party and as a comparatively young elder statesman.[33] Whenever an opportunity presented itself, he offered a glowing comment about General Dwight D. Eisenhower who, upon appointment to the presidency of Columbia University in 1948, had become a citizen of New York. Whether or not Dewey would again head a New York delegation to the national convention remained a subject of speculation. Much depended on whether the governor would run in 1950 for another four-year term in Albany.

Thus, Taft and Dewey were ensconced in their public offices, their factional supporters not about to disband. Factional considerations began to swirl around National Chairman Scott. Taft observed that Scott was holding down two full-time jobs as a member of Congress and as national chairman, and suggested that the Pennsylvanian resign from one or the other. Former National Chairman Carroll Reece recalled how *he* had resigned from the House in order to devote full-time to the chairmanship. When Scott reorganized his executive committee shortly after the election, he was charged with loading it with Dewey supporters. Another former national chairman, Harrison Spangler, joined Taft and Reece in what shortly became a well-organized movement to replace Scott.

Chairman Scott was not without his own resources. His first reaction to Senator Taft's suggestion that he resign was to declare that he had a four-year term that he had every intention of serving out. The headquarters money left from the 1948 campaign gave substance to Scott's plans to strengthen national headquarters, plans that sounded very much like the eight-point program set down by Herbert Brownell in 1945. All that Scott added was a proposal for a national party policy conference in 1950. He expected to appoint about ten subcommittees to work with the executive committee on national policy positions for the party.

Scott manifested little concern about the movement to remove him from the chairmanship, claiming the support of 68 of the 105 votes on the national committee. The anti-Scott group, on the other hand, claimed 57 signatures on a petition to declare the chairmanship vacant, 4 votes more than a majority of the committee. This group, made up mainly of Taft, Vandenberg, and Stassen supporters, indicated that they would be able to unite behind a candidate, namely,

Guy George Gabrielson was born on an Iowa farm in 1891. His father was a Sioux Rapids banker. After attending the public schools of that city and the University of Iowa, Gabrielson went to Harvard for a law degree, which he received in 1917. During the First World War, he entered the army as a private and was commissioned a second lieutenant in the air service. Settling in New Jersey after the war, he was admitted to the bar of that state in 1919 and, by 1931, had extended his practice to New York City as well. Gabrielson was elected to the New Jersey assembly, where he served from 1926 to 1930, in 1928 as its majority leader and in 1929 as speaker. Meanwhile, he became a director on the boards of several mining, pharmaceutical, and chemical firms, president of a Quebec mining company, and president of the Carthage Hydrocol Company, a patent medicine producer in which he also held the position of chief counsel.

Roy Dunn of Minnesota, a "lukewarm" Stassen follower.

Scott called a meeting of the national committee for January 26, 1949, to consider his proposals for headquarters reorganization. The movement for the ouster quickly took precedence over all other business. The national committee chose a "peace committee" to explore the prospects for a compromise on the chairmanship. Three of the seven committee members—G. Mason Owlett of Pennsylvania, Harry Darby of Kansas, and Ezra Whitla of Idaho—strongly favored retaining Scott. National Committeeman Schroeder of Illinois was the leading member opposing Scott. The committee heard the case against Scott from the lips of someone outside its membership, i.e., from Harrison Spangler. The other "peace committee" members included Ralph Cake of Oregon, Ralph Gates of Indiana, and Guy Gabrielson of New Jersey.

The efforts of the peace committee failed. When the full national committee met, the member from Maryland moved that the chairmanship be declared vacant. There followed four and a half hours of intense debate. Finally, in a motion to lay the Maryland proposal on the table, the Scott forces triumphed 54 to 50. As a step toward reconciliation, Scott altered the composition of the executive committee, replacing four incumbents with Gabrielson of New Jersey, B. Carroll Reece of Tennessee, Mrs. Margaret A. Rockwell of Arizona, and Mrs. Maude Hickman of Iowa.

Scott again took up his proposal for a midterm national policy conference and looked to the mobilization of headquarters for the 1950 campaign. However, he soon found that an unfriendly congressional leadership could make his incumbency in the national chairmanship meaningless in more ways than by removal. In the House of Representatives, the Republican minority, on the very day that

Arthur E. Summerfield was born in Michigan in 1899. He completed his formal schooling at the end of the seventh grade. At thirteen, he started his work life in a Chevrolet, later a Buick plant. From 1922 to 1929, Summerfield was engaged in real estate. Although he lost substantial assets in the stock market crash of 1929, he formed the Summerfield Oil Company as a distributor for Pure Oil, a business upon which he concentrated until 1937. In 1930, he became the Chevrolet dealer for Flint, Michigan, subsequently taking over dealerships in other Michigan communities. In time he was reputed to be the largest Chevrolet dealer in the world. Summerfield's career in Michigan Republican politics moved along simultaneously with his business activities. In 1942, he sought, but failed to receive, the party's nomination for Michigan secretary of state. In 1943, he was appointed chairman of the finance committee of the state central committee. At the end of a sharp factional contest in 1944, he was elected national committeeman and re-elected in 1948. In recognition of his fund-raising skills, he became regional vice-chairman of the national finance committee for the North Central states in 1946.

the national committee was voting to retain Scott, established a committee on public information through which to place its record before the electorate. The Senate Republican Policy Committee, meeting the day after Truman's inauguration, began to draw up its own plans for the 1950 election. With Senators Taft and Vandenberg playing lead roles, the meeting appointed four senators to attend the national committee meeting to urge caution in accepting Scott's proposal for an interim conference.

To deal with the party's separation-of-organizations, Senator Margaret Chase Smith of Maine proposed formation of a national policy committee that would consist of three senators, three members of the House, three governors, and two members of the national committee. In a variation of the Smith proposal, Chairman Scott appointed a strategy committee for the 1950 campaign. This was a twenty-one-member group, with representatives from national, state, House, and Senate Republican organizations. Scott served as chairman, appointing Thomas E. Coleman, Wisconsin state chairman, as vice-chairman.

The drive to remove Scott continued. On July 8, a secret meeting of some twenty-five members of the national committee took place in Pittsburgh to discuss further plans. The conference consisted mainly of Taft and Stassen supporters, with former Chairmen Spangler and Reece carrying the initiative. A few days before the Pittsburgh meeting, as part of the anti-Scott maneuver, Thomas E. Coleman resigned as vice-chairman of the strategy committee. Scott repeated his "four-year term" stand and denied that he would resign "unless, and until, a man can be found who can bring the desired harmony and cohesiveness to the party organization."[34] Seeking middle ground, Scott resigned from the strategy committee, a concession to match the Coleman resignation. The national committeeman from Michigan, Arthur E. Summerfield, was designated as the new chairman and went directly to work trying to coordinate the 1950 campaign effort.

The chairmanship difficulties finally led Senator Taft and Governor Dewey to consult together in New York on July 15, 1949. Each was now planning his own 1950 re-election campaign. Neither relished the prospect of a distracting struggle for control of the national party, for this would be likely to have repercussions on factional alignments and fund-raising efforts in their respective states and possibly dire consequences for their re-election prospects. Four days after the Taft-Dewey conference, Scott announced that he would resign.

Former Chairman John Hamilton, one of the principals in the anti-Scott movement, took advantage of the announcement to press home the point that the chairmanship was a full-time job meriting a full-time salary. Speaking from his long experience on the national committee, Sinclair Weeks of Massachusetts suggested that the Republican members of Congress participate overtly and directly in the selection of a new national chairman. He specifically recommended that the national chairman, four members of the executive committee of the national committee, the party leader in the Senate, the leader in the House, and the chairman of the two congressional campaign committees meet to nominate someone to the national committee. Under this procedure the most interested and influential elements presumably would be directly represented. Senator Taft was skeptical about the plan's feasibility.

Names for the chairmanship began to circulate in what the press described as a Taft-Dewey-Stassen free-for-all. Stassen, now president of the University of Pennsylvania, was still considered a factor in Republican presidential politics. Among those mentioned by Senator Taft as "acceptable" were John Danaher of Connecticut, Guy Gabrielson of New Jersey, Nebraska State Chairman A.T. Howard, and J. Edgar Chenoweth of Colorado. Carroll Reece was recommended by the *Chicago Tribune*. Arthur Summerfield of Michigan was mentioned as a middle-of-the-roader. Danaher withdrew because of responsibilities to his law practice.

Within a few days, Gabrielson and Howard were counted as the front-runners, Gabrielson campaigned actively, and Taft's friends began to consolidate behind Gabrielson in the belief that the usual close ties between New Jersey and New York Republicans would make Gabrielson acceptable to the Dewey people. Dewey followers, uneasy about accepting a pro-Taft easterner, were busy looking for a pro-Dewey westerner. In a telephone conversation on July 28, Taft and Dewey seemed to agree only that an open fight should be avoided.

As the national committee gathered, J. Russell Sprague of New York and G. Mason Owlett of Pennsylvania worked furiously to find a candidate of their own since Harry Darby of Kansas and Charles A. Halleck of Indiana had declined. The Dewey people finally settled on Axel J. Beck of South Dakota. With such old hands as Spangler and Reece managing his campaign, Gabrielson claimed a comfortable majority. Just prior to the vote, Beck rose to invite Gabrielson to withdraw with him in favor of a compromise. Gabrielson did not budge from his seat. In the vote, Gabrielson received 52 to Beck's 47; 1 vote went to Howard of Nebraska.

In what was becoming standard procedure for reorganizing national headquarters staff, Chairman Gabrielson authorized the preparation of an organizational study. This survey included an evaluation of functional operations, personnel, and costs. To the surprise of no one, the study revealed "overlapping and waste." National headquarters, which had been operating at a cost of $70,000 a month, would have to be reorganized on a "business-like basis." Change would begin with the appointment of Albert B. Hermann, former administrative assistant to Senator H. Alexander Smith of New Jersey, as $20,000-a-year executive director. Chairman Gabrielson referred to Hermann's appointment as the "opening gun of the 1950 campaign."

Other major staff changes were made. Reflecting the party's commitment to the Taft-Hartley Act and to cope with organized labor's overwhelming endorsement of the Democrats, Gabrielson appointed a special adviser on labor affairs. This adviser was to interpret Republican positions to the rank and file of labor and encourage them to find a place within the Republican party. Gabrielson later claimed that his staff's work among labor people was one of the principal achievements of his regime.

Another major concern was the development of a network of effective precinct-level organizations throughout the country. The particular device chosen was an itinerant "School for Politics." National headquarters hired and trained a team of professional organizers sent, with the consent of state and county chairmen, into states and congressional districts where Republican candidates had lost or won by a 5 percent margin or less in 1948. The national headquarters team trained local teams on Republican policy positions, registration techniques, and turnout problems. The national training team was to move on to less competitive districts after covering the marginal ones, depending upon invitations and the extent to which local organizations were willing to help finance costs.

Probably the most difficult matter before Chairman Gabrielson was financial. The $500,000 surplus with which national headquarters had begun 1949 dwindled to $90,000 by the end of the year. The figures soon moved to the red side of the ledger and reached a $500,000 deficit before spring 1950. Gabrielson sought to raise a $2 million midterm election fund. His solicitation gave large contributors an opportunity to express their views on public policy, with respect to which the press began to report conservative pressures on the national chairman to end the "me-tooism" of Willkie and Dewey.

Within days after taking over the chairmanship, Gabrielson consulted with Taft's Senate Policy Committee regarding the mechanics of drawing up a statement of party principles in time for the 1950 campaign. Although the congressional leadership had objected to Scott's activities in this connection, it remained an inescapable problem for the national chairman as principal coordinator of the midterm effort.

The strategy committee under Arthur E. Summerfield, to which Gabrielson had fallen heir, had been established to produce such a statement of principles. Although Summerfield was personally a vocal opponent of "me-tooism," he had supported Dewey in the recent chairmanship contest. His committee had a strong representation of Dewey followers. Gabrielson tried to terminate the strategy committee, by acting outright at first, then by denying it funds and attention. He next created a separate policy committee from the membership of the national committee to prepare the midterm statement in cooperation with the Senate Policy Committee and the Senate and House campaign committees. By January 1950, a small drafting subcommittee of Gabrielson's policy committee submitted its work to the Senate and House policy committees, which had been working on statements of their own. The final amalgam was the Republican *Restatement of Principles and Objectives.*

Publication of the *Restatement* in February provoked an intraparty squabble because of its attack on "socialism" in government and the welfare state and its support of the investigative activities of Senator Joseph McCarthy. Senator Margaret Chase Smith and others wrote their own *Declaration of Conscience.* Others in the party declared that the national committee had no business planning policy for the party. Another view, held particularly in Congress, repeated the standard argument that an opposition's record must be made in Congress and could not be produced by fiat of the national committee. National Committeeman Summerfield resigned from the chairmanship of the strategy committee in the midst of the campaign, complaining that Gabrielson had allowed it to "die on the vine." Gabrielson retorted that the purpose of the strategy group had been superceded by the regional conferences being conducted around the country.

Possibly the two most significant midterm contests were those in Ohio for U.S. senator and in New York for governor. Senator Taft wanted a landslide victory in order to impress his party with his vote-getting ability, particularly against a candidate known to be the choice of Ohio's labor leaders. Dewey sought not only the governorship, but also a base from which to influence the choice of the next presidential nominee. His own choice, whose name and popularity he was not adverse to mentioning during his own campaign, was clear. In a television interview on October 15, Dewey observed:

We have in New York a very great world figure, the president of Columbia University, one of the greatest soldiers of history, a fine educator, a man who really understands the problems of the world and, if I should be re-elected governor and have influence with the New York delegation, I would recommend to them that they support General Eisenhower for president if he would accept the draft.[35]

7

The Korean War had begun, and its disillusionments and uncertainties were being felt across the nation. Senator McCarthy of Wisconsin had become the principal Republican spokesman on the Communists-in-government issue. McCarthy and his associates gave particular attention to unseating conservative Democratic Senator Millard Tydings of Maryland by suggesting that the senator had links with Communists, an attack that produced one of the major upsets of the year.

The returns brought substantial Republican gains in the House, but the party still remained short of a majority. There were moderate Republican gains in the Senate. Four contests were of particular importance. The Democratic leadership in the Senate lost its majority leader (Lucas) and one of its longest tenured members (Tydings). In Ohio, Senator Taft received his landslide victory, leading by more than 400,000 votes. Dewey was re-elected governor.

The Republican gains were credited to National Chairman Gabrielson, who was now expected to remain at national headquarters through the presidential nominating contest. Gabrielson's opportunities to help one or another presidential aspirant were not lost upon those who perceived him as a Taft man. The current tribulations of Democratic National Chairman Boyle in connection with legal services he rendered the Lithofold Corporation, which eventually led to Boyle's resignation, suggested to anti-Taft Republicans that Gabrielson's extensive business interests might be similarly tarnished.[36] With the investigation of Boyle holding public attention, Republican Senator John J. Williams of Delaware revealed that Gabrielson was in fact still representing a private company in loan negotiations with a federal agency. Senator Williams pointed out that the Carthage Hydrocol Corporation, of which Chairman Gabrielson was president and chief counsel, was at that time petitioning the Reconstruction Finance Corporation for a postponement of payment on loans totaling $18,500,000. The youngest Republican in the Senate, Richard M. Nixon of California, immediately called for Gabrielson's resignation if the charges were true.

The pressures for Gabrielson's resignation were compelling. Republicans did not wish to be tainted by the same corruption brush being administered to the Democrats. Chairman Gabrielson was fortunate in two respects: first, as he pointed out, his company's petition was turned down by the RFC; secondly, his was not the party in power, hence it could not be expected that his access to the executive branch would have significant influence. Gabrielson weathered the storm. Within a month of the initial charges, he received an informal vote of confidence from the executive committee of the national committee. Gabrielson also ran into factional difficulties in connection with his reorganization proposals. It was his judgment that the functions and staffs of the national, senatorial, and congressional committees might profitably be consolidated and handled from a single, permanent national headquarters. His view was opposed by Leonard Hall and Charles Halleck. The latter position prevailed when the joint finance committee for the three party agencies authorized a regular, full, and separate campaign budget for each of the congressional committees.

Despite his reputation as "Mr. Republican" and his supporting majority in the national committee, Senator Taft's presidential candidacy faced many hurdles. One of these developed unexpectedly when President Truman dismissed General Douglas MacArthur from his command in the Far East on April 11, 1951. A national military hero of long standing, MacArthur's name was now actively proposed in many quarters as a possible Republican dark horse for 1952. A serious MacArthur candidacy was expected to eat into a significant part of the Taft support. However, by his choice for another military post, President Truman removed one of Taft's most serious potential competitors; in December, 1950, he designated General Eisenhower as supreme Allied commander in Europe.

In the latter part of 1951 there were various announcements of and denials of candidacy. After several months of highly publicized speculation about General Eisenhower's party affiliation, and following a stream of Republican politicians visiting Eisenhower at his headquarters in Paris, Governor Sherman Adams on October 30 announced that Eisenhower's name would be entered in the New Hampshire Republican presidential primary. By the end of December, Senator Henry Cabot Lodge, Jr., spokesman for an Eisenhower-for-president organization, announced that the general had given him personal assurances of his life-long Republicanism and assured him that his name would be allowed to stand in the New Hampshire primary.

Meanwhile, on October 16, Senator Taft announced his own candidacy and plans to enter the Wisconsin and Ohio primaries. On November 14, Governor Earl Warren of California reported that he was in the running. On December 27, Harold E. Stassen, still president of the University of Pennsylvania, offered himself as a prospective nominee. There was some speculation that the Stassen candidacy might serve as a stalking-horse for Eisenhower.

By March, the Taft preconvention organization, headed by David Ingalls, was claiming 579 votes on the first ballot, only 25 short of the number needed to nominate. The Eisenhower organization, under Lodge, estimated 549 for their candidate.

As the presidential primaries and state conventions began to choose delegations, the Taft campaign got off to a vigorous start in the Wisconsin and Nebraska primaries of April 1. On April 2, General Eisenhower asked to be relieved of his European command, effective June 1. Former National Chairman Brownell assumed a leading role in the Eisenhower movement during April, by which time it was fairly clear that 1952 was in many respects another Taft-Dewey battle. Delegate selections seesawed between Taft and Eisenhower supporters all through April and May. The Iowa delegation unexpectedly split. The Idaho group went entirely for Taft. Eisenhower carried Kansas. Taft won in Kentucky. And so it went.

In three states, developments carried the seeds of substantial threat to Taft's chances. In Michigan, the state convention chose seven Eisenhower delegates, six for Taft, and, after some maneuvering by National Committeeman Summerfield, held thirty-three delegates uncommitted. In New Jersey, Governor Driscoll announced for Eisenhower; Taft immediately charged him with breaking a pledge to remain neutral. Taft attempted, unsuccessfully, to withdraw from the state's preference primary, which Eisenhower carried. Most of the delegation, although unpledged, was known to favor Eisenhower.

In Texas, anti-Truman Democrats and a minority faction in the Republican party merged into an Eisenhower-for-president club that spent an estimated $3–6 million in organizational work aimed at capturing the Texas delegation from the dominant Zweifel faction. Jack Porter's grass-roots Eisenhower movement invaded precinct meetings and county conventions, overwhelmed the Taft forces in some and bolted to rump, i.e., dissident, conventions in others. At the Texas state convention on May 27, the Taft-Zweifel leadership was in control and selected thirty-eight pro-Taft delegates. The Eisenhower-Porter representatives bolted, held their own state convention, and selected a contesting delegation. The Michigan and Texas outcomes would prove to be critical at the national convention.

8

Returning from Europe, General Eisenhower made his first political speech in his home town of Abilene on June 4 and then retired to his Morningside Heights residence at Columbia University to conduct a front-porch preconvention campaign. Elsewhere, Taft managers were claiming 588 firmly committed votes and continued to exercise a decisive influence in the national committee. Eisenhower supporters in the New Jersey delegation spoke threateningly of replacing Gabrielson as national committeeman. Walter S. Hallanan, the Taft leader in West Virginia, was selected to serve as temporary chairman of the national convention under a special arrangement permitting General MacArthur to be guest keynote speaker. With 96 seats in contest, it was widely expected that the pro-Taft decisions of the national committee would seat enough Taft delegates to give the nomination to the senator.

The Dewey-Brownell strategists launched their heavy artillery during June and the first week of July. The press was filled with charges from Eisenhower supporters concerning the "Texas steal." From the 1952 annual Governor's Conference being held in Houston, Governors Dewey, Adams, and McKay sent a message to the national committee urging that the pro-Eisenhower Porter delegation from Texas be seated.

From this same Houston conference came "the governors' manifesto," signed by twenty-three of the twenty-five Republican governors present, proposing that contested delegations should not be allowed to vote in the national convention until after contests had been settled, the so-called "fair play" rule. In previous conventions, all delegates on the temporary roll, contested or uncontested, could vote on any question except in seating contests involving themselves. In the 1952 situation, the contested Taft delegates from Louisiana and Texas, for example, could have voted to seat the contested Taft delegates from Georgia, etc. The governors' manifesto was difficult for the Taft managers to handle. Further, it confronted the national party with a constitutional crisis: Who at the grass roots could be considered a Republican? What delegations to the national convention had a legitimate right to vote in its proceedings?

National Chairman Gabrielson responded to the manifesto with a full statement of the historical precedents. Ironically enough, these included the judgments made in the Taft-Roosevelt struggle of 1912. In that convention, the followers of President Taft, the present senator's father, ruled against the Roosevelt proposal that contested delegations be denied the privilege of voting on any question until their own status had been determined. The Roosevelt proposal was substantially the same as the governors' "fair play" proposal in 1952. Referring obliquely to the Dewey leadership, Chairman Gabrielson concluded his statement, "It is difficult for me to understand why some of those who controlled the Republican National Conventions of 1944 and 1948 did not seek such a rule then, but demand it now."[37]

There were other party nationalizing pressures for Republicans during 1952. Republican state chairmen were particularly hopeful of expanding their influence in national party affairs. The Midwest and Rocky Mountain Republican State Chairmen's Association, representing twenty state organizations, at its January meeting, passed resolutions demanding that the national committee be reorganized so as to award extra seats to those states going Republican in their votes for president, governor, or the state's congressional delegation.

National Committeeman Clarence Budington Kelland of Arizona, recalling how it had become "an unpleasant job" to get rid of a losing candidate's national chairman and eager to strengthen the committee's own integrity in national party affairs, proposed that in 1952 the national committee refuse to give the nominee his traditional right of picking his own national chairman.[38] Still other national committeemen, angry over committee decisions favoring

Taft, pressed for a new rule that would permit a state committee to declare a vacancy in its representation on the national committee, thus enabling it to remove a lame-duck committeeman about to be replaced at the next national convention.

Over the objection of Gabrielson, women members, and southern members, the national committee adopted and the convention approved the bonus seat proposal of the state chairmen. The Kelland and lame-duck proposals were not acted upon. In another rule, the Republican national committee authorized its chairman, if requested by a majority of the committee, to appoint an advisory committee composed of state chairmen, members of Congress, and others.

On the convention floor, Governor Arthur B. Langlie of Washington sponsored the pro-Eisenhower "fair play" proposal. The Taft floor leaders objected to any proposal that would change the rules in the middle of a contest. After prolonged debate, the test vote came on a pro-Taft amendment to the Langlie motion. The Taft position was defeated 658 to 548. The Langlie rule was passed and control of the convention shifted to the Dewey-Eisenhower side.

The contesting forces now focused attention upon the 115 uncommitted votes, including approximately 33 in Michigan and nearly the same number in Pennsylvania. These were the votes that could give the nomination to either Taft or Eisenhower. Activity in the Michigan delegation, led by National Committeeman Summerfield, was particularly intense. Summerfield had organized a "Delegate Contact Operation" to keep himself thoroughly informed of attitudes and decisions going on in other delegations. The Michigan party leadership was not going to be caught on the wrong horse. Observers noted that a struggle between the titans of the automobile industry was also being enacted in microcosm in the Michigan delegation. Henry Ford II and his associates were working on behalf of Eisenhower and most of the leadership of General Motors Corporation was behind Taft.

The roll call revealed 35 of Michigan's 46 votes supporting Eisenhower and 53 of Pennsylvania's 70 also in the general's corner. Before delegation switches began, the tally stood 595 for Eisenhower, 500 for Taft, 81 for Warren, 20 for Stassen, and 10 for MacArthur. With 604 needed, most of Stassen's 19 votes in the Minnesota delegation broke to Eisenhower, giving him the convention's majority. California's 70 votes stood firm for Warren. The final official vote: Eisenhower 845, Taft 280, Warren 77, MacArthur 4.

Herbert Brownell promptly called a conference of leading Republican governors and state party officials to discuss balancing the ticket and other considerations involved in the choice of a vice-presidential nominee. No offer, perfunctory or real, was made to Senator Taft. Instead, the conferees, with Governor Dewey among them, after reviewing a list of names, decided to recognize Republican youth and the West by recommending Senator Richard M. Nixon to General Eisenhower. Informed by Brownell of this recommendation, the general approved.

C. Wesley Roberts was born into a Kansas newspaper family in 1903. He attended Kansas State College as a journalism major, leaving college in 1926 to become coeditor and copublisher, together with his father and a brother, of three weekly newspapers. These were part of a small chain that had grown from a weekly founded by his grandfather. Ten years later Roberts became active in Republican party affairs as the manager of an unsuccessful gubernatorial campaign. The following year he became executive secretary of the Republican state committee and, from 1939 to 1943, served as secretary to Governor Payne Ratner. During World War II, he served as a major in the Marine Corps and an officer in a bomber squadron that saw action in the Far Pacific. His first postwar political position was as publicity director of the Kansas State Highway Commission. From 1947 to 1950, he was Republican state chairman, managing the campaign of Senator Frank Carlson in the latter year. Roberts also headed a public relations firm operating near Topeka.

Speculation about Eisenhower's choice for the national chairmanship was brief. In view of his contribution to the Eisenhower nomination, his status on the national committee, and his established fund-raising record, Arthur E. Summerfield was the first preference of the general's advisers. Summerfield would also add a midwestern representative to the East-West ticket. Summerfield accepted the post for the duration of the campaign.

After an extended conference with Brownell, the general announced other appointments to his campaign staff: Senators Frank Carlson of Kansas and Fred A. Seaton of Nebraska as his personal advisers; Arthur H. Vandenberg, son of the late Senator Vandenberg of Michigan, as his executive assistant in charge of his personal campaign staff; as appointment secretary and press secretary, Thomas E. Stevens and James C. Hagerty, respectively, both Dewey aides; his preconvention campaign manager, Senator Lodge, preoccupied with his own campaign for re-election, as chairman of a campaign advisory committee. Brownell returned to his New York law practice, but maintained close touch with campaign developments on an unofficial basis. General Eisenhower chose Governor Sherman Adams of New Hampshire as his personal liaison with national and state party officials.

Taking office with Summerfield were thirty-two new ex officio members of the national committee, i.e., state chairmen assuming bonus seats. Within a fortnight, Summerfield recruited the public relations director of the Republican congressional campaign committee, Robert Humphreys, as his publicity director. To replace Albert Hermann, Gabrielson's executive director, Summerfield chose the

Wisconsin state chairman, Wayne J. Hood. A former state chairman, C. Wesley Roberts of Kansas, was made director of organization. A coordinating board, including Senator Everett Dirksen and Representative Leonard Hall, chairmen of the congressional campaign committees, was created.

Chairman Summerfield moved slowly in making appointments to a new executive committee; selections were delayed for a full month. This and other evidence suggested that direction of the Eisenhower campaign was coming from outside national headquarters, but without challenges to the management of the headquarters.

From the conclusion of the two national party conventions, public opinion polls showed Eisenhower with a two-to-one lead over Adlai Stevenson. The Republican campaign themes concentrated on the alliterative trilogy of corruption, communism, and Korea. The corruption theme capitalized on the charges of "influence peddling" that had been leveled against many of President Truman's political associates and self-appointed friends. The pre-1952 campaigns of Senators McCarthy and Nixon paved the way for the Communists-in-government attack. The war in Korea had become stalemated and was the source of great popular frustration, particularly among the families of men in the military services. During the closing days of the campaign, General Eisenhower underscored his special competence in bringing wars to a successful conclusion by offering, if elected, to "go to Korea."

Two potential difficulties for the Eisenhower campaign were successfully avoided. The first, incorporating the Taft following, was handled by a well-publicized meeting and "pact" between Taft and Eisenhower at the latter's Morningside Heights residence. The second difficulty was the revelation that Senator Nixon had been in part maintained by a special private fund to cover some of his expenses as a senator. The Republicans' corruption theme and vice-presidential nominee seemed about to go by the board. Nixon met the challenge in a remarkable televised explanation that included humble references to his wife's cloth coat and his dog, Checkers.

The contest ended with Eisenhower receiving over 55 percent of the popular vote, pulling support from every segment of the American electorate, and carrying several states of the Solid South, including Florida, Virginia, and Texas. The extremely narrow Republican majorities in Congress suggested that the election was more of a personal than a party victory. Another interpretation was that "Eisenhower Democrats" had taken their first step across party lines to become more permanent members of the Republican party-in-the-electorate.

24 Rebuilding the Party and Electorate around a Modern Military Hero

The Eisenhower era began the long process of dismantling the New Deal-Fair Deal coalition. His election resulted in much more than another military hero in the White House. The Solid South was no longer to be solidly Democratic; it was now populated in large and lasting measure by "Eisenhower Democrats" en route to the Republican party. The "military-industrial complex" about which Eisenhower warned was well on its way to becoming a major economic and political force in the nation. His vice-president was Richard M. Nixon, a partisan whose party and public career would leave many historic marks on both his party and his country.

1

President Eisenhower lost no time in recognizing the men who made his nomination and election possible. Herbert Brownell was appointed attorney general. National Chairman Arthur Summerfield became postmaster general. These two would handle the principal sources of patronage. A long-time colleague of Governor Dewey, John Foster Dulles, became secretary of state. The cooperation of the Taft wing was rewarded by appointment of such cabinet officers as Charles E. Wilson of General Motors, Sinclair Weeks, and Ezra Taft Benson.

Eisenhower deferred from the very beginning to those masters of congressional politics: Senator Taft and Speaker Martin. Taft continued to have independent strength in the party and in the Senate. If implemented in the extreme, the Morningside Heights Agreement would have given the senator the role of a prime minister without portfolio. Vice-President Nixon, in his capacity as president of the Senate, assumed a traditionally passive role. Former Governor Adams eventually became The Assistant to the President and headed a White House staff that soon resembled the hierarchical structure of a military or business organization.

Eisenhower placed himself behind and above this hierarchy; access to him was carefully managed by Adams and Press Secretary Hagerty. During his first year, the president was visibly uncomfortable in his first elective office, despite his great earlier successes as a military politician. He never fully acknowledged that he was leader of a political party and often made statements implying that politicians were a separate breed. In the tradition of General Washington, Eisenhower preferred to remain "above politics." As a consequence, many of the legislative prerogatives of the executive branch rested with the congressional leadership, and Taft and Martin willingly accepted them.

Republican national headquarters were handled by the president as though it were a highly specialized technical agency with only an occasional bearing upon the operation of the presidency. Eisenhower often permitted the prerogatives of titular leadership to reside with others; with Vice-President Nixon during national campaigns and with the national party chairman during other times. In the view of one student of the presidency:

> Dwight D. Eisenhower's great strength as President was as a unifier of the nation, an accommodator rather than a provoker of controversy, a man of decency and dignity, a man who blurred issues, a tranquilizer rather than a stimulant. . . . Without Eisenhower as the head of the Republican party, the venom that disgraced Democratic politics in the closing years of Truman's presidency would have been rife in the nation.
>
> He purged national life of rancor. And by presenting himself continuously as standing at the moderate and reasonable center of American life, he was able to tune in on the deepest instincts of the people, who, at this stage of their history, desired pause, comfort, and repose; a mood which reflected the spectacular expansion of the middle class base of American life.[1]

The commitment to "communism, corruption, and Korea" as campaign themes carried over into the Eisenhower administration. Eisenhower went to Korea; soon after, negotiations were begun to bring an end to the hostilities. A new security clearance program for government employees was undertaken and became a device for removing many Democrats who had been brought into the civil service by Truman executive orders. Writing in *Look* magazine, Senator Taft, shortly after the presidential election, discussed "What the G.O.P. Must Do To Win in 1954."[2] Taft's recommendation was to continue heavy fire on the Truman administration and the things it stood for. In a subsequent interview, Taft said that the investigating committee headed by Senator McCarthy would have the principal job of turning up information the Republicans could use.

On the corruption theme, the Eisenhower administration proceeded to envelop itself in an aura of purity, often at great expense in personnel. A charge of dubious relationships leveled against members of the president's administration came to be sufficient to compel "voluntary" resignations. The first case occurred in connection with the appointment of Summerfield's successor to the national party chairmanship, Wesley Roberts.

Summerfield had been explicit and clear about serving as chairman only for the duration of the 1952 campaign. In anticipation of Summerfield's resignation, Republican leaders were busy publicizing their candidates: Thomas E. Coleman, who had served as Taft's floor manager at the convention; David Ingalls, Taft's campaign manager; Walter Williams, chairman of the Citizens for Eisenhower Committee; Senator Fred A. Seaton, whose switch from Stassen to Eisenhower had come at a critical time; and John Minor Wisdom, who had served actively in the Eisenhower campaign in the South. The Republican politicians of Kansas, however, made the case for their nominee most effectively: Wesley Roberts, director of organization at national headquarters during the campaign.

Kansans had been among the first to launch the Eisenhower bandwagon, according to National Committeeman Harry Darby, but Kansas, Eisenhower's home state, had yet to be recognized in the cabinet or elsewhere in the administration. Kansas' Senator Frank Carlson, who had been an adviser on Eisenhower's personal campaign staff, lent his full support to their claims. Furthermore, Roberts had performed well during the campaign, successfully coordinating the activities of party regulars with those of National Citizens for Eisenhower and Nixon.

Summerfield appointed a special five-member nominating committee, headed by Harry Darby of Kansas, which met, considered only Roberts' name, and consulted with the president-elect. Eisenhower took the position that the election of a chairman was "of course" the province of the national committee and not of the president-elect. However, he did express pleasure over the nomination of Roberts as a way of giving recognition to his home state. The following day the new executive committee met to provide for a salary of $32,500 for Roberts.

In taking over the reins on January 17, 1953, Roberts pointed to the difficult tasks before the national party: strengthening the organization in the South and extending the party's majorities in both houses of Congress. Roberts did not mention the difficulties of distributing patronage among party leaders who had been out of power for two decades, particularly since not much patronage seemed available. To complicate matters, there was a strong predisposition to reward Eisenhower Democrats in the South rather than Republican regulars there.

Less than a month later, on February 10, a group of Kansas state legislators brought charges against Roberts for evasion of the Kansas Lobbying Act. According to the charges, Roberts had failed to register as a lobbyist during the 1951 state legislative session. At that time he participated in the sale of an insurance company's sanitarium to the state; the company had built the sanitarium on state property. The sale was consummated at a price of $110,000, for which Roberts received $10,750 for his part. Governor Arn, an associate of Roberts, found it necessary to select an investigating committee to examine the evidence. Among those pressing the charges were members of another

Republican faction led by Lieutenant Governor Fred Hall.

To the surprise of all, the investigating committee, on March 27, reported "that while there is doubt that there was a violation of the letter of the law, the committee is firmly convinced that there had been a violation of the spirit of the law, and the protection which it was designed to afford the people of this State was deliberately and intentionally frustrated by Wes Roberts."[3] In view of the Eisenhower promise to "clean up" Washington, Roberts had no alternative but to resign immediately. In doing so, he charged that "a carefully contrived and thinly veiled plot, growing out of a fierce factional fight in Kansas state politics, has destroyed my usefulness as national chairman."[4]

The following day, at a banquet honoring former Congressman Leonard Hall, Speaker Joseph Martin announced his candidate for the national chairmanship. The party would be "wise" to choose Hall, he said to an audience that included Vice-President Nixon.

Looking to the 1954 midterm congressional campaign, Martin argued that Hall's many years as chairman of the congressional campaign committee particularly qualified him for the job at national headquarters. Martin obviously did not want the initiative in the selection of a national chairman to slip away again from Capitol Hill.

In 1952, Hall had retired from the House of Representatives to run for surrogate in New York, a position paying $25,000 a year. Probably one of the reasons for Hall's withdrawal to the security of a judgeship was the expectation that he would have little influence in an administration in which Governor Dewey had the ear of the president. One of Dewey's inner circle during the 1948 campaign, Hall had been publicly critical of the management of that campaign. When New York's National Committeeman J. Russell Sprague expressed his desire to resign from the national committee in 1951, he recommended to Dewey that Hall be his successor. Dewey preferred to appoint someone other than Hall, whereupon Sprague decided to stay on in the position. Hall reportedly later broke with Sprague as well as Dewey. In reply to inquiries about this rift, Speaker Martin simply observed that Hall "does not need local endorsement" to become national chairman.[5]

The White House had its own reservations about choosing Hall. Eisenhower advisers were somewhat wary of putting another New Yorker in a key political post in Washington. They had in fact turned to the Midwest twice for a national chairman. There was the further prospect that Hall might still be considered a "Dewey man," raising objections in certain factions of the party. Although admitting to the press that he expected to have influence and responsibility in the selection of a chairman, President Eisenhower thought that this was a job for the national committee itself to take "with the utmost seriousness."[6] Eisenhower expressed as his main personal concern that a man be chosen who commands the "highest respect in every way."[7]

Meanwhile, various elements in the party leadership were making known their views about Hall. Forty-seven Republican congressmen met with a White House aide to urge Hall upon the president. The chairman of the Republican congressional campaign committee, Richard Simpson, added his support. Then, unexpectedly, National Committeeman Sprague announced his support. Sprague and Hall flew to Albany for a conference with Governor Dewey, which ended with an announcement of the latter's endorsement. The Dewey statement said, "We believe that Judge Hall has unique qualifications for the office of National Chairman by reason of his long and successful experience as chairman of the Republican Congressional committee."[8] After discussing the matter with the president, Senator Taft indicated that he had no choice of his own and that Hall would be acceptable, as would be "a number of others who have been proposed."[9] Following Taft's statement came Nixon's favoring Hall as the best possible choice.[10]

Although the duties of the national committee's nominating committee were presumed to be perfunctory, the group nonetheless conferred with Hall and asked for assurances that he would give national committee members a greater voice in clearing the patronage appointments of the Eisenhower administration. Hall gave these assurances. Hall also indicated that he would serve without pay in view of the "comfortable law practice" he expected to maintain in Oyster Bay.[11]

Chairman Hall's first administrative move was to appoint a special three-man committee of "outsiders" to study the structure and staff of national headquarters. The committee included a New York lawyer, an officer of the American Research and Development Corporation, and an officer of the Owens-Corning Fiberglass Corporation. The latter, David Baumhart, after the report had been submitted, became Hall's headquarters executive director. Hall also asked all employees at headquarters to submit their resignations so that he might have a free hand in the reorganization.

That reorganization came within a month. In May of 1953, Hall announced that about forty headquarters employees would be dismissed and that this would result in a savings of approximately $100,000 a year. The remaining staff of approximately a hundred were placed under three officials: an organization director, handling campaign and party organization, patronage, southern activities, and field services; a public relations director, in charge of the press, publications, TV-radio, films, the speakers bureau, research, and the library; and an executive director, who would not only manage the entire headquarters, but also serve as chairman of a "Special Activities Board" dealing with women, youth, minorities, farm groups, labor, veterans, and other special groups.

Hall expressed the hope that he might find government jobs for those national committee staff being dismissed. Before long, Hall acknowledged that patronage distribution was one of his biggest problems. The party faithful, meanwhile, were grumbling more and more loudly over the slowness of appointments. There were reportedly more than 300,000 jobs available outside the civil service, but "outside" did not really mean "available."

Almost 250,000 of the 300,000 positions were technical jobs in various agencies and overseas operations. Many thousands were "Schedule A" positions—noncompetitive but protected from removal for political reasons. It was to Schedule A positions that Hall referred when he charged the outgoing Truman administration with blanketing into civil service thousands of Democratic politicians. In the last analysis, probably less than 15,000 positions were "easily available" to the new administration for patronage appointments. At the time Hall became chairman, little more than a fourth of the more than 12,000 Republican applications had been "processed" by the patronage division of the national committee for referral to appropriate party leaders in the federal agencies. A further complication was the decision to employ patronage to build up the party in the South, which meant that antiquated Republican party organizations were to be circumvented.[12]

The Republican ranked second only to Eisenhower in the planning of appointments, policies, and legislative program was Senator Taft, "Mr. Republican." Taft was determined that Eisenhower's assurances regarding domestic policy and recognition of his followers, received at the Morningside Heights conference, would be met. However, when cabinet appointments were made, Taft found that only one appointee had been on his recommended list. He accepted the others in good spirit, but openly regarded the appointment of Martin Durkin as secretary of labor as "incredible."

2

Relations between the president and the senator remained uncertain. The administration had relatively little success on Capitol Hill whenever Taft withheld his endorsement. Although there is some evidence that personal rapport between the two men improved as the new administration settled down, it was hardly a settled matter whether Taft could or would have become an administration spokesman. Taft died on July 11, 1953, leaving a great void in the Republican leadership.

> Taft's absence made a subtle but significant change in Eisenhower's relations with Congress and the conservative Republicans generally. It introduced a new element of contingency, for without the Senator's powerfully supporting, restraining, and at times protecting influence, the administration was thrown more on its own resources. None of the remaining legislative leaders could speak with Taft's authority at the White House, or command the influence Taft had in Congress. The administration now had more freedom both to follow its own impulses and to make its own mistakes.[13]

Senator William Knowland of California was chosen to succeed Taft as chairman of the Republican Senate Policy Committee, but other avenues to and from the White House now opened up. Vice-President Nixon became a more active behind-the-scenes intermediary. Speaker Martin mediated between Eisenhower Republicans in the House and the right wing. The more moderate Taft followers remained leaderless for the time. Senator McCarthy hoped to become heir to the Taft following and stepped up his investigative and other activities. Whereas Taft in 1954, as in previous midterm elections, would probably have been the principal caller of campaign signals, this responsibility now fell to National Chairman Hall.

At the beginning of 1954, Hall acknowledged McCarthy's popularity as a speaker, indicated that the senator would be an asset in the midterm campaign, and anticipated that the national committee would pay his travel and speaking expenses. Within three months, Hall felt compelled to reverse his willingness to go along with the leader of the radical right. It was announced that the national committee would neither seek nor accept McCarthy as a speaker. Responsible for Hall's reversal were the commotion caused by McCarthy's efforts to set the tone of the campaign, the Mundt committee investigation of the Army-McCarthy controversy, and the Watkins committee examination of a motion in the Senate to censure McCarthy. At no point did President Eisenhower descend into the political pit to engage McCarthy directly; he left this task to competent "specialists," that is, Vice-President Nixon and National Chairman Hall.

The president was eager to have a Republican Congress, but in October 1953 and again in February 1954, he spoke publicly of his intention to take no personal part in the campaign. Instead, he designated Vice-President Nixon as his "personal representative" in the campaign. Nixon later explained that Eisenhower, by abstaining from the midterm contests, was seeking to avoid the mistakes of Roosevelt and Truman under similar circumstances, that is, personal involvement in local fights for congressional seats. Nixon referred to this as "a correct role," although at a later time he found it necessary to assure party officials that the president stood behind every Republican nominee against every Democratic one. By October, however, as Republican prospects seemed to be dimming, President Eisenhower reluctantly allowed himself to be drawn more and more into the campaign.

The national, senatorial, and congressional campaign committees, under Hall's leadership, planned and executed a $4 million campaign effort. They were aided by a revived Citizens for Eisenhower Campaign Committee that devoted its attention to the "independents," with well-publicized plans to raise $500,000 for work in 111 congressional districts. Republican orators claimed that their leaders had been "makers of peace" in Korea, removers of subversives from government, and cleaners of the atmosphere of corruption in Washington. By October, the national committee had nearly 150 speakers in the field, but none as hard-working and effective as Vice-President Nixon.

Nixon was unquestionably the workhorse of the campaign. His stumping tours covered nearly the entire nation. He visited thirty-one states, gave an average of three speeches and three press conferences a day, moved an average of five hundred miles between dawn and dusk, and hammered hard at the issues of communism, corruption, and Korea. At workshops of party leaders, he admitted that the party was trailing, but argued that there was some basis for hoping that 1954 would be as unusual as 1934 in that the party in the White House would gain rather than lose seats in Congress.

As prospects grew slighter, however, the vice-president and the national chairman were compelled to draw upon the Eisenhower glamor. The president agreed to make several television and radio addresses during October. He and his cabinet spread out in various directions across the country for a special push in the last days. The Democrats nevertheless carried election day, winning 17 additional House seats for a majority of 232 and taking the Senate by 48 to 47. Senator Wayne Morse of Oregon took the opportunity to leave the Republican party and place himself in the strategic role of an independent.

The national committee next turned to preparations for 1956. Early in 1955, the committee voted to have a late nominating convention, probably in August. The assumption was that Eisenhower would again be the nominee and would require very little campaigning. It was also true that a short presidential campaign would place a premium on keeping an experienced team together, specifically, Vice-President Nixon and National Chairman Hall.

Hall and his staff worked closely with Sherman Adams and the White House staff on all aspects of presidential and party publicity. In January 1955, another step in the nationalization of party leadership took place. For the first time the presidential press conference was filmed for rebroadcast over television. The Eisenhower smile and informal style were now visible under everyday circumstances in the homes of most Americans. At every opportunity, Nixon, Hall, and Dewey, now as ex-governor, expressed their hope that the president would again run for office.

3

On September 24, the president suffered a coronary thrombosis while in Denver, Colorado. There followed five months of high political suspense, at first concerning Eisenhower's personal survival and recovery, then concerning his capacity and willingness to make another race for the presidency. The president's name appeared almost daily in headlines and over the airwaves. The additional good will generated by his illness practically turned his popular support into unanimous endorsement. Statements by his physician, White House spokesmen, and national party headquarters tended to maintain the suspense.

On January 13, 1956, the convalescing president, confronted by the practicalities of a presidential year, called together a private gathering of his advisers. These included the "political" members of his cabinet, Brownell, Dulles, Humphreys, and Summerfield, five former or present presidential assistants, former Senator Lodge, National Chairman Hall, and the president's brother, Dr. Milton Eisenhower. All agreed that Eisenhower was the American who could contribute most to world peace and to the unity of the American people. Further, it was agreed that another Eisenhower victory would give the Republican party the time it needed to modernize itself. There was no qualm expressed regarding Eisenhower's physical capacity to serve out another full term as president.

Six days later, the president, without admitting "any final decision on my part relative to a candidacy for a second term in office," raised no objection to having his name entered in the New Hampshire primary. On February 29, at a press conference and later over a nationwide radio and television hookup, President Eisenhower announced that he would seek another nomination.

The state of Eisenhower's health lent particular significance to the vice-presidential candidacy. The spotlight had been blazing upon the vice-president throughout Eisenhower's incapacity, and Nixon had meticulously avoided any act that would give the impression that he was other than a member of a team holding the fort for the bedridden president. Nevertheless, Eisenhower's illness provided an opening for proposals to replace Nixon on the 1956 ticket. The replacement mentioned most often was Governor Christian A. Herter of Massachusetts, an eastern liberal. The president was asked whether he was interested in having Nixon as his running mate again. His reply was, "I have not presumed to tell the Vice President what he should do with his own future. . . . The only thing I have asked him to do is to chart out his own course and tell me what he would like to do." Not until the national convention did the president explicitly state a favorable attitude.

Others, however, were less ambiguous. Chairman Hall repeatedly and emphatically predicted an Eisenhower-Nixon slate. Receiving an astonishing number of write-in votes for vice-president in the New Hampshire primary, Nixon visited with President Eisenhower and on April 26 announced that he would "be honored" to receive a second nomination. The situation was further complicated and the significance of the vice-presidency further heightened by the occurrence of another Eisenhower illness.

On June 9, only six weeks before the Republican convention, President Eisenhower underwent surgery for ileitis. Again the president's health commanded the nation's attention, much to the frustration of the two Democratic gladiators—Adlai Stevenson and Estes Kefauver—then battling their way through the Democratic presidential primaries. During this crisis, Chairman Hall and members of the White House staff kept a firm hand on party decisions. On July 23, however, Harold Stassen, then serving as the president's

Hugh Meade Alcorn, Jr., was the national committeeman from Connecticut, born in that state in 1908. His father was state's attorney in Hartford and the Republican nominee for governor in 1934, a race that he lost. The younger Alcorn was a Dartmouth Phi Beta Kappa and track star who went on to take his law degree at Yale, passing his bar examination in 1933. At the same time that he joined his father's law firm, he also entered Republican politics as a town committeeman. In 1936, Alcorn was elected state representative, and then re-elected in 1938 and 1940. In 1939, he was chosen House majority leader and, in 1941, Speaker. The following year he succeeded his father as state's attorney and served as a member of the state central committee. In 1948, Alcorn received his party's nomination for lieutenant governor, but was defeated by approximately five thousand votes. Early in 1952, he assumed the chairmanship of Connecticut Citizens for Eisenhower and became national committeeman in 1953. A close friend of another New Englander in the Eisenhower administration, Sherman Adams, Alcorn kept himself available for any service to the administration and the national party. Chosen to handle the 1956 national convention arrangements, his performance favorably impressed many state leaders throughout the country.

disarmament adviser, publicly proposed that Nixon be replaced by Governor Herter.

The timing of the Stassen statement was intended to head off an invitation to Herter to make the speech putting Nixon into nomination at the national convention. Herter agreed to postpone a decision on the nominating speech until Stassen had an opportunity to discuss the matter with President Eisenhower. The president told Stassen that he could not dictate to a convention that had not yet given him its nomination. He declined to foreclose anyone's vice-presidential aspirations. Stassen interpreted this as encouragement to proceed with his "dump Nixon" movement. Chairman Hall reiterated his expectation that Nixon would be on the ticket with Eisenhower and, within two days, had Governor Herter's agreement to nominate Nixon at the convention. The Eisenhower illness continued to be handled gingerly. At no time was there an expression of anything but complete confidence that the president would regain his health shortly and be ready for the campaign and further public service.

In addition to his involvement in the news about the Eisenhower illnesses and the moves in the Nixon renomination problem, Hall was busy with the ordinary duties of preparation for the national convention. In this he had the able assistance of H. Meade Alcorn, Jr., vice-chairman of the arrangements committee.

Chairman Hall's three principal political problems during the preconvention period were the uncertainties of President Eisenhower's surgery in June, the stubborn but diminishing anti-Nixon maneuvers of Stassen, and the preparation of a review of the Republican record for the presidential campaign. The second Eisenhower convalescence was handled, as various press analyses implied, with calculated nonchalance.[14] On July 10, the president casually confirmed what many had suspected for weeks; that he had found it unnecessary to reconsider his availability for renomination. National Chairman Hall had been saying for three weeks, "You can paste the names of Eisenhower and Nixon in your hats. That will be the ticket. . . . Len Hall is speaking."[15]

The Stassen campaign was tenacious. A series of Stassen statements reported opinion survey findings that presumably demonstrated how much Nixon would weaken the ticket. The Stassen campaign continued into the second day of the national convention. Meanwhile, Chairman Hall and Presidential Assistant Adams made certain that Stassen would not have access to the president except to express a willingness to second the Nixon nomination. This is precisely what happened on the third day of the convention. The president came out of a private conference with Stassen to report that Stassen found no further basis for opposing Nixon and would in fact second his nomination.

The third difficulty confronting Hall was the Rayburn-Johnson strategy of "responsible opposition." That strategy called for legislative cooperation between the Democratic congressional leadership and the White House. Just as Democratic National Chairman Paul Butler argued to have his fellow-Democrats in Congress shape a "distinctive" Democratic program, so did Chairman Hall seek to show that the Democratic leadership in Congress was "ditching" the president's program. It was a difficult argument to make, for much of the president's program was being successfully processed by the Democratic-controlled legislature.

The national convention performed as expected, renominating the Eisenhower-Nixon ticket. With a short campaign before it and preparations almost entirely completed under Hall's direction, the national committee met on August 23 to re-elect its incumbent chairman. Two weeks later, the White House announced that Hall would serve as campaign manager as well as national chairman. To serve as Hall's vice-chairman, the national committee chose H. Meade Alcorn, Jr., of Connecticut. Former National Chairman Hugh Scott, Jr., who had been serving as general counsel, was re-elected.

The Republican campaign featured "Truth Squads," a "new Nixon," and concern over the problem of winning a Republican majority in Congress. The Truth Squads were teams of Republican senators and representatives who traveled behind major Democratic speakers, issuing rebuttals to Democratic allegations as soon as they were made.

The "new Nixon" was projected as a dignified public servant with maturity and statesmanlike qualities needed for the vice-presidency, and possibly the presidency. This was a direct rejoinder to Democratic references to "Tricky Dick" and to Nixon's reputation as a campaign "hatchet man." The vice-president had to overcome not only the issue of being such a young person in high public office (he was forty-three), but also the fact that he was the target of some of the heaviest Democratic attacks. The latter problem arose, of course, from the special attention being given to the vice-presidency in the light of President Eisenhower's health problems. Adlai Stevenson, in his election-eve speech, went so far as to say, "I recoil at the prospect of Mr. Nixon as custodian of this nation's future, as guardian of the hydrogen bomb, as representative of America in the world, as Commander in Chief of the United States armed forces."[16]

From the Republican point of view, however, Nixon was again the workhorse of the party's national campaign. He conducted no less than three swings around the country. The first of these took him over fifteen thousand miles to thirty-two states, in the company of his wife, numerous staff personnel, and nearly three dozen newspapermen. His standard speech was a model of partisan restraint, taking the form of a public report on the president's achievements in bringing peace, prosperity, and progress to the country. The second campaign tour covered ten thousand miles and fourteen states, concentrating on seven of the largest, pivotal states. The third tour narrowed to Michigan, Ohio, Indiana, and Illinois, where the contest seemed the closest.

National Chairman Hall, Vice-President Nixon, and the members of the White House political staff were less optimistic than ordinarily about the prospects of winning congressional majorities on Ike's coattails. Much of the campaign bore the appearance of a midterm contest, with Eisenhower and Nixon itineraries being scheduled so as to help particular embattled Republican candidates. The Eisenhower coattail, however, failed; Republicans suffered a net loss of two seats in the House and a continued failure to gain control of both houses, despite a landslide victory in the presidential race.

Apart from the excitement of the presidential campaign, two minor changes in the formalization of the national party agencies occurred. One was something of a retrogression: Rule 30 providing for an advisory committee to the national chairman was rescinded by the national convention, reflecting the party-in-power's disinterest in such an organizational device. The second development seemed to be conclusive evidence that national headquarters staff professionalization and tenure had arrived. A retirement system for all employees of the national, senatorial, and congressional campaign committees was put into force in August.

With victory came speculation about National Chairman Hall's reward for the conduct of so successful a presidential campaign. Early in January 1957, Hall announced plans to retire as national chairman, effective February 1. The retirement came, however, before Hall's next job had been firmly arranged. Some sources reported evidence that he would receive a high position in the federal government. Others indicated that he was making plans to run for governor of New York in 1958. Adding to the confusion were the many names being circulated in the press as prospective successors in the chairmanship. Hall himself offered a list of eight possibilities, including former Senator Harry Darby of Kansas, National Committee Vice-Chairman H. Meade Alcorn, New York State Chairman L. Judson Morhouse, Ohio State Chairman Ray C. Bliss, Arizona's former Governor Howard Pyle, and others.

The national committee met, appointed the usual nominating committee to consult with the president, and awaited developments. There was every indication that Presidential Assistant Sherman Adams and Chairman Hall had strongly recommended to the president the appointment of Meade Alcorn. At the national committee meeting, Carroll Reece offered a motion to have the president make three recommendations rather than the usual single name; the motion was shouted down.

There was discussion of a telegram hoax of the previous week. Some forty-four telegrams had been sent to Republican leaders around the country urging that Alcorn be elected in order to "keep the future of the country safe from the Nixons and Knowlands"; they were signed "Harold E. Stassen." The telegrams were sent from Stamford, Connecticut, by "two well-dressed men," whose identity was never ascertained. Stassen denied having anything to do with the crude hoax. Furthermore, at the time that it was sent, Alcorn's selection as national chairman was fairly certain.

On January 22, Alcorn was named as the president's "personal choice." Conservative members of the national committee expressed misgivings about having so complete an Eisenhower Republican in the office, particularly in view of the fact that the Twenty-second Amendment made Eisenhower a two-termer. These conservatives spoke pessimistically about having to win in 1960 without the Eisenhower name at the head of the ticket.

Vice-President Nixon took his own steps to head off factional juggling and to stake out his own claims for 1960. One move that put politicians on notice that Nixon expected to be the next presidential nominee was taken on inauguration day. In an unusual press conference at his residence just prior to the ceremony, Nixon indicated that he had learned much in his years in Washington and that he expected to assume a much larger role in the affairs of the second Eisenhower administration.

4

Factionalism could hardly be expected to subside during the final term of a two-term president. The two-term limit set by the Twenty-second Amendment automatically created a "lame duck" in the White House and was bound to invite challenges to Eisenhower's party leadership, legislative program, and influence over the succession. A consequence of the Twenty-second Amendment was that it was likely to wed second-term presidents to their most probable successors, in part to outweigh the weaknesses of lame-duck status. In the case of President Eisenhower it was particularly convenient to have on Capitol Hill a vice-president who was experienced in party leadership, skilled in legislative management, and available for nomination as his successor. But party factions are not instruments of convenience, and those in the Republican party at this time were laying their own plans for future presidential nominating contests. The Republican right began to develop a hero in Senator Barry Goldwater of Arizona. The party's liberals turned to Nelson Rockefeller, encouraged by his election in 1958 as governor of New York.

President Eisenhower responded to the need for leadership of the party to a greater degree than previously. During April and May of 1957, National Chairman Alcorn conducted six regional conferences to examine why the party had done so poorly in the 1956 congressional elections and to prepare for 1958. Among the most serious complaints was one concerning the president's budget; in the opinion of many party leaders, it was too large. Alcorn reported these findings to President Eisenhower, who tackled the complaints about his legislative program at a press conference the following day.

The president told the complainers to consider what the budget might have been had he not exercised a restraining influence. On other aspects of his program, he declared that Republican leaders in and out of Congress were obligated to support the party's 1956 platform or "the entire concept of party responsibility . . . collapses." Eisenhower was then asked to elaborate on his conception of the role of a president as the leader of his party. To this he replied:

> He is the leader not of . . . the hierarchy of control in any political party. What he is is the leader who translates the platform into a legislative program. . . . And after that . . . I think it is his duty to use whatever means he deems most effective in order to get that program . . . translated into law.[17]

Thus, for the first time President Eisenhower made clear the assumptions that underlay his dealings with the formal party organization. His position of titular leadership did not include, in his opinion, the management of party organizational affairs. Rather, titular leadership in the presidency was primarily obligated to facilitate a lawmaking function, namely, the translation of the party platform into legislation.

The president's general attitude toward the party, coupled with control of Congress by a Democratic leadership willing to support most of his program, complicated matters for National Chairman Alcorn, particularly in connection with producing a strategy for the 1958 midterm campaign. Eager to advise the president on the potential impact of many legislative and administrative matters on the party

Alcorn soon found that his job as representative of the party's interests was frequently confounded by an administrative arrangement which treated party affairs as a functional subdivision of the administration's responsibilities, comparable to agriculture or commerce.

Just as farm problems were expected to be handled by the Department of Agriculture, which in turn was not expected to interfere with other departments' programs, so Republican party affairs were expected to be handled by National Committee headquarters, which was not expected to concern itself with decisions on administrative policy. Since virtually everything the administration did had implications for the party, this arrangement proved extremely frustrating to Alcorn; his efforts to overcome it met only limited success.[18]

By normal standards, Alcorn assumed the national chairmanship under relatively favorable circumstances. His party held the presidency. Leonard Hall had accumulated a substantial surplus in the treasury, freeing Alcorn of the usual pressing financial worries. Hall also left a talented and well-integrated headquarters staff, between 80 and 120 persons, most of whom Alcorn kept on. For the position of executive director, Alcorn rehired A.B. Hermann, who had served in that capacity under Guy Gabrielson.

Circumstances also favored other activities suggested by Alcorn. President Eisenhower, one of the oldest men to hold the presidency, warmly endorsed Alcorn's creation of the Senior Republican Clubs, a practical response to an aging electorate. Eisenhower's continued popularity among southern voters also enabled Alcorn to work effectively toward building the party organization in the South. To do this, he inaugurated "Operation Dixie," headed by a five-man subcommittee under the leadership of Virginia State Chairman I. Lee Potter.

There were also unfavorable circumstances. An all-out Eisenhower supporter, Alcorn was kept at arm's length by the party leadership in Congress. He took special pains to overcome this difficulty, maintaining close ties with the congressional campaign committees and conducting a series of evening meetings with Republican legislators in an effort to demonstrate how useful national headquarters could be to party members on Capitol Hill. Alcorn also had his staff produce a new publication, *Battle Line*, a two-page newsletter distributed four times each week while Congress was in session. *Battle Line* was widely quoted by Republican legislators on the floor of Congress and in their newsletters to constituents.

Another source of difficulty was the distribution of patronage. A second-term administration usually has less to distribute than a first-term administration. In addition, Alcorn found that much of the available patronage was being channeled through cabinet members, very often without informing or seeking the advice of national headquarters. In this way many positions went to less ardent Republicans and even to independents, undermining Alcorn's relations with the Republican state organizations.

Nor did international, economic, and other events help Alcorn make a case for his party. The launching of Sputnik by the Russians raised doubts about the Eisenhower administration's commitment to the conquest of outer space. An economic recession set the Democrats to recalling the "Hoover Depression." The crisis over school desegregation in Little Rock threatened to undermine "Operation Dixie," especially when Virginia State Chairman Potter made quotable prosegregation comments to a local audience in his home state. When a congressional investigating committee revealed that Presidential Assistant Adams had engaged in activities of dubious political morality on behalf of industrialist Bernard Goldfine, the pristine image of the Eisenhower team seemed in jeopardy. As the Adams-Goldfine furor grew, Republican leaders throughout the nation complained to Alcorn that Adams was a serious liability to the party. It became Alcorn's unpleasant duty to convey these complaints about his friend, Adams, to the president. Adams announced his resignation on September 21, but, as far as the Democrats were concerned, the incident did not end there.

With justifiable trepidation, Alcorn confronted the probability of the usual midterm losses in congressional seats suffered by the party in the presidency. With the Eisenhower legislative program faring relatively well in a Congress under Democratic leadership, White House staff advisers, with problems of their own in the Adams-Goldfine case, did not view the midterm contest with any sense of urgency. Former Governor Howard Pyle, now a presidential assistant, was appointed as the administration's representative in the campaign. This was in contrast to the performance of this function by a person of the rank of Vice-President Nixon in 1954. Pyle soon discovered that many leading members of the Eisenhower cabinet and administration had decided to refrain from participation.

Even the participation of Vice-President Nixon was significantly reduced. As always, Nixon was active in the 1958 campaign, but less involved in its management and covering less ground in his itineraries than in previous years. The language of his speeches was more moderate and his predictions of legislative gains significantly tied to the contingency that economic conditions remain stable. Nixon was not without his personal dilemmas. His party and he needed midterm victories in order to maximize election prospects in 1960. Yet the probability of these victories in 1958 was poor. Nixon could little afford to carry the blame for defeat. National Chairman Alcorn, very much in the limelight, was more expendable, and the Eisenhower administration still had enough political capital to be able to absorb a midterm defeat without catastrophe.

Another Nixon dilemma related to campaign style. Any Republican nominee in 1960 interested in holding the Eisenhower electorate would have to recognize that a significant part of that support came from normally Democratic voters. Robert A. Taft's intense partisanship may have earned him the title "Mr. Republican," but not the presidential nomination. Vice-President Nixon intended to avoid Taft's experience.

As National Chairman Alcorn struggled against the midterm tide, his predecessor Leonard Hall found rough swimming in other waters. Rumors that Hall would receive a high federal post upon retirement from the national chairmanship proved false; in President Eisenhower's words, "there was no suitable vacancy."[19] Having said this, the president noted that he had been reading in the press about the possibility that Hall might run for governor of New York. While presidents do not interfere in the political affairs of the separate states, remarked Eisenhower, if Hall should run for governor, he would most assuredly have a "booster" in Eisenhower.[20]

Within two weeks the president had to modify these remarks. Republican leaders in New York were having slate-making headaches. In the state legislature, Speaker Oswald D. Heck and Senate Majority Leader Walter J. Mahoney were the main contenders for the gubernatorial nomination; Hall's entry, not yet announced, was bound to rock the boat. President Eisenhower's clarification was that his praise of Leonard Hall did not mean "that I am going to enter a New York primary fight among Republicans."[21] Even more humbling to Hall, however, was the contender still standing in the wings, who in the end ran off with the gubernatorial prize: Nelson A. Rockefeller. The Rockefeller entry proved Hall's undoing.

Few American families have given as much to the Republican party as the Rockefellers. Nelson Rockefeller served in appointive offices under several administrations: Roosevelt's, Truman's, and Eisenhower's. He left Washington early in 1956, somewhat critical of developments in the Eisenhower administration. Despite efforts of New York party leaders to have Rockefeller accept the Senate nomination, he campaigned vigorously across the state to win support for the gubernatorial nomination. Once nominated, he conducted an astute campaign, coming from behind to win the governorship by an overwhelming 570,000 votes. A landslide victory in a New York gubernatorial race, in either party, makes the victor immediately "available" for the next presidential nomination. In Rockefeller's case, wealth and previous public service made him particularly available.

5

The Republican congressional defeat in 1958 was overwhelming. The Democrats received their largest majority—62 to 34—in the Senate since 1940, making it reasonable to predict that the Democrats would retain control of the Senate in 1960. The House divided 282 to 153, the largest margin for the Democrats since 1936. Only Senator Goldwater performed a feat comparable to Rockefeller's by winning in Arizona on the basis of a conservative antilabor campaign.

"Alcorn, who presided over the worst licking the GOP has taken in years, ordinarily would be expected to bow out and let another man rebuild on the

Thruston Ballard Morton, born in 1907, was a seventh-generation Kentuckian. Upon graduation from Yale in 1929, he entered the family grain and milling business in Louisville, eventually becoming the company's president. He served in the navy from 1941 to 1946. Upon his return to Louisville, he was elected representative to Congress. Serving in public office was part of the Morton family tradition; Morton's grandfather had been elected lieutenant governor of Kentucky in 1919. Morton entered Congress in 1947, the same year in which Richard M. Nixon of California took his seat; the two men became close friends. In 1952, the controlling faction in Kentucky Republican politics strongly favored Taft for the nomination. The pro-Eisenhower opposition was led by Morton and a group of young Republicans in Louisville. Of the twenty Kentucky delegates to the national convention, Morton was the only Eisenhower supporter. During the campaign that year, Morton became campaign manager for the entire Republican ticket in Kentucky and his brother served as finance chairman. The entire ticket was successful and Morton gained a reputation for his campaign skills. Morton served in the House of Representatives until 1953, when he retired to become assistant secretary of state for congressional relations. While assistant secretary of state, he was chairman of the platform subcommittee on foreign policy in the 1956 Republican convention. In that year he was elected, along with Senator John Sherman Cooper, to the United States Senate. Most observers considered Morton to be a firm Nixon supporter and a moderate liberal in his Senate role.

ruins," wrote one political observer.[22] However, no one in the party leadership seemed interested in making Alcorn the scapegoat. Instead, Alcorn was encouraged to remain in office and to take steps in preparation for 1960. He conducted an intensive survey among national committee members and others to determine the causes of the 1958 defeat. Out of this research he developed an extensive proposal for reorganization at national headquarters.

In its prepublication draft, the reorganization plan included such recommendations as the addition of at least forty field staff members to the national headquarters, expansion of the committee's public relations staff, publication of a monthly party magazine, sponsorship of a weekly television program to be called the "Republican Forum of the Air," creation of an advisory committee to the chairman which would meet every sixty days, systematic recruiting of the strongest possible candidates, and year-round fund-raising designed to put the party headquarters on a firmer financial basis. The final version of these proposals was presented to the national committee meeting of January 22, 1959.[23]

Another Alcorn proposal called for the establishment of a study committee, the Committee on Program and Progress, to reexamine the party's philosophy and policies. Headed by Charles H. Percy, youthful president of the Bell and Howell Corporation, the study committee issued four "task force reports" in October under the title *Decisions for a Better America*. Percy subsequently became chairman of the platform committee at the 1960 national convention.

Despite the support of the party leadership, Alcorn decided to resign as of April 1, 1959. His announcement spoke of "compelling personal reasons unconnected with politics." Alcorn had been serving without salary and his absences from Hartford placed a substantial burden on his law partners. Subsequently, except for a brief period as general counsel to the national committee from July to December in 1960, Alcorn did retire from all his national and Connecticut party positions, waiting only as long as necessary to find replacements to carry on his various responsibilities.

On March 20, eleven days before Alcorn announced his resignation, the president consulted with Senator Thruston B. Morton of Kentucky and invited him to serve as national chairman. Morton was eventually selected, but not without some objections from conservative elements in the party.

Ostensibly, the conservatives' objection to Morton was that he would be a part-time national chairman. The conservatives' objection was voiced by Representative Richard Simpson, chairman of the congressional campaign committee, who spoke on behalf of himself and Senator Barry Goldwater, chairman of the senatorial campaign committee. Morton had indicated that he would not resign from the Senate and that he would serve only through the national convention. Then, "if the nominee wanted me, I would continue through the election."[24] Up for re-election in 1962, Morton assumed that his own race would take all of his attention after 1960.

Simpson gained little support for his opposition to Morton. The supporters of Nelson Rockefeller were consulted and raised no objection, leaving the national committee free to formalize the choice on April 11, 1959. To underscore the attention that he thought party affairs should receive in the conduct of the presidency, Senator Goldwater recommended at the same meeting that the national chairman sit in on all cabinet meetings. Chairman Alcorn had done so from time to time, and Senator Morton agreed to pursue the suggestion.

The midterm election results indicated that Governor Rockefeller would be the only significant threat to Vice-President Nixon's chances for the 1960 nomination. Senator Goldwater's supporters spoke of him as presidential material, but there was a greater probability that the Arizona senator would be the spokesman for the conservative wing rather than a national nominee. Goldwater was heir to much of the late Senator Taft's following and attracted a number of southern Democrats seeking an ally in the Republican party.

Vice-President Nixon began 1960 preparations in December 1958. At that time he met with Leonard Hall and a young California lawyer, Robert H. Finch. These two men were to serve as Nixon's principal managers throughout the preconvention and election campaign periods. Although Hall had been pro-Nixon for some time, his present role undoubtedly had additional satisfactions; his erstwhile opponent for the gubernatorial nomination, Nelson Rockefeller, was now the only other potential contender for the presidential nomination. The Nixon-Hall-Finch consultations concluded that the vice-president held such an advantage among the organization people around the country that he could afford to remain "above" the factional battle until Governor Rockefeller had defined his position with respect to the nomination. A small Nixon staff, under Hall, Finch, and Herbert Klein, a California public relations man, was established early in 1959 in Washington. The national party headquarters, under Senator Morton, remained in safe and responsible hands.[25]

By the fall of 1959, the time had arrived for Governor Rockefeller to evaluate his position with respect to the 1960 national ticket. Collecting a staff of some seventy persons, he undertook "one of the most extensive and highly organized preannouncement campaigns of modern times."[26] Rockefeller's research undoubtedly revealed that the organization people involved in choosing convention delegates through the state convention system were overwhelmingly committed to Nixon. To challenge Nixon by way of the presidential primaries was likely to take the New York governor into early primaries in states where little support could be developed, foreclosing any possible impression that a grass-roots tidal wave was behind his candidacy.

In December 1959, Rockefeller issued the announcement that he would not run for the presidency. Said he, "I believe . . . that the great majority of those who will control the Republican convention stand opposed to any contest for the nomination. . . . I am not, and shall not be, a candidate for the nomination for the Presidency."[27] This announcement notwithstanding, Rockfeller decided to retain much of the preannouncement staff for the remainder of the preconvention period.

Although the task force reports prepared by the Percy committee concluded most of the preparatory work for the 1960 Republican platform, Rockefeller and Goldwater forces continued to try to influence the final version of the party's policy statement. The debate was reported as a left-right factional controversy, putting Vice-President Nixon even more securely in the position of the party's middle-of-the-road candidate. In a dramatic gesture of conciliation with Rockefeller, Nixon flew from Washington to New York on the Friday before the opening of the national convention for a secret meeting. After unsuccessfully trying to induce Rockefeller to accept the vice-presidential nomination, Nixon agreed to issue a joint statement with Rockfeller on certain platform issues. This statement complicated the platform committee's activities, particularly on the matter of civil rights, but succeeded in removing the principal obstacles to a united presidential campaign.

With Rockefeller and Goldwater no longer the major prospects for second place on his ticket, Nixon said in press interviews that he would be happy to have as his running mate Ambassador to the United Nations Henry Cabot Lodge, Jr., Secretary of the Interior Fred Seaton, or Senator Thruston B. Morton, the national chairman. The alternatives were reduced to Seaton, who was popular among the farm states, and Lodge, who symbolized Republican achievement in the foreign policy field. The final choice was Lodge.

Nixon then retained Morton as national chairman and Seaton as his principal adviser on agricultural policy. The Nixon-Lodge campaign organization was headed by Leonard Hall as general manager and Robert Finch as campaign director. Senator Morton placed himself and national headquarters entirely at their disposal. All the critical decisions, however, were made by Nixon himself.

Nixon's campaign dilemmas were those usually associated with the differences between presidential and congressional election contests. With three out of five potential voters identifying themselves in public opinion polls as Democrats, Nixon could ill-afford the intense Republican partisanship that he had customarily displayed in congressional contests. Such a degree of partisanship would not only activate many Democratic voters otherwise likely to stay at home, but might also alienate those Democrats willing to cross party lines. Nixon's decision to remain "above politics" during the campaign was a continuation of his preconvention strategy to remain above the factional strife within his party. In both instances, this stance also communicated the qualities of maturity and statesmanship.

The strategy was suitable to Nixon's position as president of the Senate during the special session following the convention. Sitting at the head of the Senate, Nixon could portray judicious calm while his Senate colleagues carried on the partisan battle against the Johnson-Kennedy leadership of the opposition. Nixon's "above politics" posture during the television debates with John F. Kennedy was less impressive; he, in fact, came across as aloof and condescending. Kennedy later asked, "Why had Nixon talked down to the people?"[28]

Another Nixon dilemma was the fact that the White House was occupied by the incumbent titular leader of the Republican party, President Eisenhower. How much of the Eisenhower popularity and statesmanship was transferable to Nixon's candidacy?

6

The election was close, won for Kennedy by several thousand votes in Chicago that gave him Illinois' electoral votes. The closeness of the outcome in many states led Republicans to cry "fraud" and "recount." As national party chairman, Senator Morton called for further information on returns in as many as eleven states. The problem of handling recounts, if any, was left entirely to Morton, but at no point did the national chairman contend that the Democrats had lost or that recounts would upset the Kennedy victory. At most, Morton predicted that the issue of election fraud might be introduced into the campaigns of 1962 and 1964.

The Republican party again found itself the out-party. In 1960, there were several important differences from earlier out-party periods. Nixon had lost in a contest so close—the few thousand votes in Illinois—that his defeat was deemed politically honorable. There was evidence that he had provided many Republican candidates for Congress with a helpful coattail, again ingratiating him with the party regulars.

From President-elect Kennedy, Nixon received recognition as leader of the opposition. Kennedy sought and held a conference with Nixon in Florida during November. After the conference, Kennedy observed: "Mr. Nixon has a definite responsibility as leader of his party, and I think perhaps he can answer how he would define that responsibility more satisfactorily than I can." In a separate press conference, Vice-President Nixon added this observation:

> As the Senator indicated, I have a responsibility as the leader of the opposition at this time, and I would like to say that as the leader of the opposition it is my responsibility to see that our opposition is constructive, that we support those policies which we believe are in the best interest . . . of the nation, . . . whenever the Administration advocates such policies, but that where the new Administration advocates policies that we disagree with, that it is our responsibility vigorously to oppose them."[29]

There were those who demurred on granting the title of titular leader to Nixon. During a November 29, 1960, press conference regarding his own candidacy for re-election as governor in 1962, Nelson Rockefeller observed, "I consider Mr. Nixon one of the vital forces in the Republican party, but I don't think frankly, between elections, when a party loses the Presidency, that the party has an actual head. The only real head is the national chairman."[30] Elsewhere, Senator Goldwater took the position that as far as he was concerned, Nixon would have to be elected to some public office such as governor or representative before he could exert further leadership in the party.[31]

The outgoing president had a word of his own to add. At a White House dinner for members of his cabinet and other administration leaders, President Eisenhower, using the device of a dinner toast, wished Nixon well and added, "The Vice-President will be the head of the Republican party for the next four years, and he will have my support and the support of all those who are here tonight."[32] Thus, in a somewhat unusual manner, the transfer of party leadership from one titular leader to another was accomplished.

The following day Governor Rockefeller, although expressing no wish to debate with the president on the matter, reiterated his previous statement that the national chairman is the "only real head" of the Republican party. Rockefeller did acknowledge that Nixon could be considered the titular head of the party, but preferred to consider the party as having a "collective leadership" for the next four years. On the importance or unimportance of the titular leadership, Governor Rockefeller simply observed that this depended "on what's made of it."[33] The following morning Rockefeller was Nixon's breakfast guest, at which time the two men were reported to have discussed the future of the party.

A few days later, Senator Kenneth E. Keating of New York urged the formation of a thirty-five-member "All-Republican Committee" to serve as a high-level policy planning committee and to advise on the formulation of party programs, as he put it, to shape but not dictate party policy. The membership of the committee, proposed Keating, would be ten senators, ten representatives, ten public members, and, finally, President Eisenhower, Vice-President Nixon, former President Hoover, 1960 vice-presidential candidate Lodge, and the national party chairman. The Keating plan was similar to that of his New York colleague, Senator Jacob Javits, who had recently suggested the creation of a Republican "shadow cabinet" to set the tone and direction of his party's opposition to the new administration.[34] Inevitable comparisons were made to the Democratic Advisory Council of recent years, but Keating preferred to compare his proposed committee with the Percy group that operated prior to the 1960 national convention.

Republican congressional leaders were opposed to the Keating plan, but did acknowledge that something similar to the weekly meetings of the top party leadership at the White House under Eisenhower would have to be arranged. At the January 1961 meeting of the national committee it was agreed that the party's congressional leaders and the national chairman should continue to meet at weekly intervals after January 20.

The first of these meetings was held in the office of Senate Minority Leader Everett M. Dirksen on January 25, and thereafter every Tuesday. Following these conferences, Senator Dirksen and House Minority Leader Charles A. Halleck issued joint statements. Emerging out of these weekly Republican leadership conferences was a weekly televised news conference featuring Dirksen and Halleck, intended to match President Kennedy's televised news conferences. The Republican conference came to be known as the "Ev and Charlie Show," the first of which was televised on June 11, 1961.

The upshot of Republican conversations regarding the titular leadership was that the out-party more than ever before was examining its leadership predicament in a conscious and deliberate manner. In a public lecture in March 1961, Senator Morton, referring to Nixon's status as titular leader, said, "His role as the party's titular leader is a personal role, arising out of tradition, it is true, but

William E. Miller was born in New York in 1914. His father was a janitor, his mother the operator of a millinery store. From these lower class beginnings, Miller earned his bachelor's degree at the University of Notre Dame and law degree from the Albany Law School. He entered the army in World War II as a private in 1942 and terminated service as a first lieutenant in 1945. He served as an assistant to Justice Robert A. Jackson in 1945 during the Nuremberg trials. In 1948, Governor Dewey appointed Miller district attorney of Niagara County to fill a vacancy. Miller was elected to this position in the fall and in 1950 was elected to the House of Representatives. There he became a friend of Representative Nixon. Miller became the second Catholic to hold the Republican national chairmanship.

entirely dependent on the activities of the incumbent in the role for whatever content it may achieve."[35] Characteristically, the congressional leadership and the men who, like Governor Rockefeller and Senator Goldwater, might be available for the next presidential nomination raised questions about the "unity" of the out-party's titular leadership. In many respects, the Ev and Charlie Show was to become a two-headed response to the apparent Republican national leadership needs of the time.

As 1961 opened, Senator Morton found the job of national chairman an exhausting one. His approaching 1962 senatorial contest in Kentucky left little alternative but to seek a successor. The two most prominent prospects were Ohio State Chairman Ray Bliss and Representative William E. Miller of New York, chairman of the congressional campaign committee.

According to press reports, Bliss was reluctant to take on the national chairmanship. Miller was supported by Senator Styles Bridges of New Hampshire, chairman of the Senate Policy Committee. Some midwesterners again raised the objection of part-time service in the chairmanship. Miller agreed, if chosen, to decide by January or February 1962 whether or not he would resign from his House seat.

Miller had another influential supporter in Senator Goldwater, with whom he had worked in their respective capacities as chairmen of the party campaign committees in Congress. There was some question of whether Miller's policy conservatism would be acceptable to the liberal elements in the party. Miller had joined the Nixon forces early in 1960 and was the first of the New York delegation in Congress to do so despite Governor Rockefeller's interest in the nomination. Speaking for the Rockefeller forces on the national committee, Senator Keating raised no objection to Miller's selection. On June 2, 1961, Miller was chosen national chairman and agreed to serve without salary.

Before the end of 1961, Miller expressed his unwillingness to use the national committee as a source of party policy guidance, preferring to leave that function to the congressional leadership, already manifest in the Dirksen-Halleck joint statements noted earlier. Before long, the Republican national committee became occupied with the production of the series of television broadcasts called, significantly enough, "The Loyal Opposition," and, less respectfully, as the aforementioned "Ev and Charlie Show."

Nixon returned to a partnership in a Los Angeles law firm where, characteristically, he found himself on the horns of several dilemmas. Should he operate as titular leader from his law office, as Adlai Stevenson had done with such difficulty? Would this help make him the Republican nominee again in 1964? What kind of presidential year would 1964 be: a re-election of a young and active Democratic incumbent, or another close encounter as in 1960? Was it possible to dodge the 1964 test in an honorable way without foregoing the possibility of another nomination in 1968? Should he run for election to the governorship of California in 1962, thereby providing himself with a powerful political base? Or was a race against the incumbent Democratic governor, Edmund (Pat) Brown, too risky to undertake?

Nixon chose to risk the race, and lost. He now shared the lot of many out-party titular leaders before him. He was a defeated senior party leader without office or rostrum from which to exercise the functions and responsibilities of a leader of the loyal opposition.

The relative calm of the 1950s was soon swept aside by the turbulence of the 1960s. Vietnam, the civil rights movement, urban riots, political assassinations, and nuclear missile crises were among the tragic events that weighed upon the national spirit and stretched the integrative capacities of the political parties. The ideological extremes of the parties' factions would thrust national chairmen into the roles of mediators and managers as never before. And the long-term developmental processes would assure the continued nationalization of party structures.

Part VII
The Long View:
Processes and Problems

25 | Conflict and Developmental Patterns: The Investiture and Socialization Processes

Political conflicts have developmental consequences for the organized groups between or within which they occur. These consequences may contribute to the organization's growth and integration or lead to its disintegration. To recognize which kinds of conflict tend to promote integration would presumably enable organization leaders to manage conflicts and the development of their organization, for example, a political party, more deliberately and positively. This seems particularly important and true if we accept the position that (1) the essential activity of politics is the management of conflict and (2) the most significant outcome of democratic or constitutional politics is the socialization of conflict.[1]

Even friends fight from time to time. It is a well-known experience among friends that a "good fight" may indeed settle some issues and improve the cohesiveness of the friendship. Similarly, some kinds of conflict seem to integrate and strengthen cooperation among fellow partisans whereas other kinds of conflict lead to organizational disintegration and demise. How exactly is conflict associated with such integrative or disintegrative tendencies in organizations?

Organizational consequences of conflict processes

According to Chester A. Barnard, an organization comes into being when there are persons able to communicate with each other who are willing to contribute their effort to accomplish a common purpose.[2] Thus, the principal structural components of an organization are (1) the tasks that, when successfully performed, are expected to lead to the common goal, (2) the persons whose individual training and socialization enable them to perform the tasks, and (3) the organization's method of putting a person and a set of task expectations together. The sets of task expectations are the *positions* and offices in the organization. The person's performance may be called *role behavior*. When person and position come together, the result is an *incumbency*.

More specifically and technically, a *task-expectation* is a description or explicit conception of a human activity (a) by one or more organizational members, (b) assumed to contribute to implementing an organizational goal, and (c) regularly associated with a named position or office in the organization. A position consists of a set of task-expectations. Task-expectations are usually set forth in job descriptions, constitutions, regulations, and directives of an organized group or its executives.

Task-expectations tell the incumbent of a position what he or she should be doing. This raises several questions. Are these expectations being stated by all or a significant component of the organization? Have the prescribed job activities been or are they intended to be an enduring feature of the position involved? In conflicts about task-expectations, do the parties argue about the relevance of the prescribed tasks for the achievement of the organization's goals?

Role-behavior is a pattern of personal activities, verbal or physical, performed by individuals who, in their own minds, believe that these activities fulfill the cultural or organizational expectations for the identified position, office, or status. Each pattern of actions is usually a consequence of the individual's role learning or socialization. A set of learned roles that are consistently associated with each other may be called the "role-structure" of the person and, from a psychological view, may be considered that individual's personality.

A task-expectation is a prescription. A role-behavior is an action. How are the incumbents of an organizational position actually behaving? Do incumbents carry on this conduct as though they believe it to be appropriate to the position held? In conflict situations, do the parties to the conflict address this regularly performed role-behavior? Does the outcome of the conflict modify the actual behavior of the incumbent?

An *incumbency* is an explicit consensus among the members of an organization that a particular person is to be accountable for the performance of the task-expectations of a particular position. Usually the beginning or the conclusion of an incumbency is made explicit by some overt procedure or act that provides evidence of the consensus, such as, election, appointment, hiring, impeachment, firing, etc.

If there is conflict about incumbency, it may deal with such questions as the following: has the person actually been elected or otherwise selected for the position? Has a ceremony, certification, or other ritual been conducted to make known the fact that this person is formally in office? Have the rules of selection or removal of incumbents been disputed or modified? What, if any, is the usual path of recruitment or advancement into the position?

To describe an organization as integrated is essentially a way of commenting on the condition of its *structure*.[3] Therefore, it is appropriate that a theory of organizational conflict ought to concern itself with the effect of particular conflicts upon structural components of the organization.[4] The analytical scheme guiding this inquiry focused on the three structural components just defined: organizational positions (the national chairmanships), particular persons and personalities (the chairmen), and the circumstances of incumbency of these persons in the chairmanships.

Time is, by definition, a critical factor in the study of organizational development, particularly in tracking the cycles or episodes of conflict that take place within the broader framework of cooperation. For purposes of developmental analysis, then, we may refer to historical sequences of conflict episodes as conflict processes. A distinct conflict process is essentially a sequence of contests and decisions that relate to each of the aforementioned structural components.

The sequence of events that culminates in a positional consequence, as in the case of specifying or circumscribing a national chairman's duties, may be called a *formalization* process. If the consequence results in a modification of the role-behavior of a particular officeholder (again, a chairman), the process may be called *socialization*. Finally, if the conflict leads to a modification in the *incumbency* situation that ties a particular person to a particular position, this may be considered a phase in the organization's *investiture* process.

There is rarely a total and conclusive termination of an episode of political conflict. However, there is usually a time when the adversaries decide that they have expended enough or more than enough on the conflict in progress. This decision, which is usually signaled by a willingness to negotiate or otherwise communicate with the adversary, will usually be expressed cautiously and tentatively since neither side wishes to appear weak on the basis of a willingness to conclude the conflict. The observer may have to look hard for evidence of a willingness to communicate and negotiate about the issues. In the case of factional conflicts, this evidence, as we have seen, could appear in correspondence, public statements, committee meetings, test votes on minor issues, and similar actions. An action that is the concluding event of the conflict episode is of special interest if it has consequence for the structure of the organization, that is, for task-expectations, role-behaviors, and/or incumbencies.

The three conflict processes—formalization, socialization, and investiture—may produce not only changes in the structure of an organization, but may also have consequences for the integration of the organization, for example, those factional conflicts that have advanced the development of the party national committees. Integration may result from changes in the rules or practices (a formalizing outcome) according to which actors (the chairmen) are expected to carry on their duties. Outcomes that affect the role performance of one or more parties to the conflict (a socializing outcome) may also influence the degree of integration of the organization. Finally, an investiture process outcome may determine what persons may become incumbents of the organization's offices, resulting as well in integrative effects.

Conflict processes and the national chairmanships

By the 1960s, the variety and scope of the work of the party national committees and chairmen would certainly have astounded even the prophetic Thomas Jefferson amd his adversary, Alexander Hamilton. These organizations and offices have performed political functions that continue to grow in scope, volume, complexity, and political significance, particularly as secular trends continue to point toward greater nationalization of the parties.

If this inquiry reveals anything, it is that factionalism has been a constant in the internal affairs of both major parties. Factional conflict has influenced who would be the party's nominees and officers, whether their personal backgrounds would serve them well in their party roles, and to what extent party decision rules and administrative functions would become increasingly explicit, detailed, and bureaucratized. Perhaps most importantly, the existence of factions as significant informal organizations within each of the parties has, for the most part, been a natural and salutary aspect in the maturation of the party system.

What may be said with confidence is that the national chairmanship has been at the center of national factional developments throughout the history of each major party. Factional conflict has had much to do with the manner in which individuals have been chosen for or removed from the office, the qualities of the persons who have been its incumbents, and the kinds of job descriptions and expectations held for the office. The investiture, socialization, and formalization processes have had discernible developmental patterns.

With respect to the selection of national chairmen and headquarters staff (investiture process), the more recent tendency has been to choose factionally neutral or centrist persons. This tendency seems to be associated with the growing need for managerial skills and various types of expertise in the daily operations of national headquarters as the senior unit in a large-scale organization. It is no longer enough to be the personal friend or colleague of the titular leader; such an individual can be recognized in some other way, perhaps as campaign manager, general manager, or another special title. Nor is a particular faction's total capture of the chairmanship any longer an objective worth the cost. Furthermore, for those wishing to control political organization, the means for circumventing or opposing such factional conquests through independent club movements, etc., are available.

The investiture process appears increasingly to resemble the recruitment of chief executive officers in other large organizations in society. Professional avenues of recruitment have begun to overtake factional affiliation. Factional leaders have become more willing to negotiate the selection of a chairman, particularly since the outcome of a contested election is inevitably interpreted by political observers as a "victory" of one faction over others, thereby potentially producing changes in the balance of power within the party.

The chairmanship and national headquarters were well on their way toward bureaucratization by 1960. There was interest in purchasing headquarters buildings on Capitol Hill in Washington. Both chairmen and staff became full-time and salaried. Congress was considering and subsequently authorized public funding of activities in which national party headquarters have a major role, namely, the conduct of the national nominating conventions and the presidential election campaigns. Liaison with congressional policy and campaign committees, governors' conferences, associations of state and regional party officials, various leadership councils, organized interests groups, and friendly media increasingly absorbed a major portion of the time and energy of headquarters personnel. However, possibly the best evidence that the formalization process was advancing inexorably was the recurrent rule-making that specified changes in national party operations. Such were the subsequent reports of the McGovern-Fraser, O'Hara, Mikulski, Sanford, and Winograd commissions on the Democratic side and the Delegates and Organization Committee and the Rule 29 Committee on the Republican side. Each formalizing rule change was, of course, leavened by factional debate.

With respect to the socialization of chairmen, those who offered themselves as candidates were increasingly from among experienced political professionals, with expertise in one or more of the essential headquarters functions, for example, mediating skills, management of media relations, opinion polling, election analysis, fund-raising, etc. As in earlier times, much of the professional experience continued to be gained from participation in the management of a presidential candidacy or from service as a party officer in a highly competitive state. Factional affiliation was, of course, relevant in both circumstances.

A more detailed summarization of the investiture, socialization, and formalization trends follows.

The investiture process

How have contests and choices related to incumbency in the chairmanships been resolved? What have been the circumstances, rules, and patterns of selection and removal of national chairmen?

Technically, all national committee chairmen have been elected to or confirmed in that office by the full membership of the national committee. Most committee votes have been by acclamation (often after factional negotiations), a few have been warmly contested. Some chairmen have been re-elected for second and third terms, but, normally, chairmen leave office at the succeeding national convention although there have been cases of resignation and death. In short, many factors, most prominently factional considerations, have governed the chairmanship's investiture process.

Factions, as we have seen, have been organized around particular candidates, controversial issues of the day, competing senior party leaders, and/or a desire to control the resources of national party offices or organizations. The summaries below will remind the reader of the major factional considerations associated with each party and with particular chairmen. The rosters also allude to major selection factors when they were present: personal friendship or close political association with the titular leader, various types of balance and representativeness within the presidential party leadership, financial contributions or fund-raising, concession to an opposing faction, reward for an allied faction, extreme or moderate policy or ideological posture, managerial or other professional competency, victory in a national committee chairmanship contest, a strategy of keeping the chairmanship out of the hands of an opposing faction, etc.

The Democratic experience

The Democrats were the first to establish a national committee and a national committee chairmanship, thereby setting precedents for the Whigs and the Republicans in later years.

Benjamin F. Hallett. A founder of the Anti-Masonic party, later the leader of the Massachusetts Democratic party. Delivered critical convention vote to nominee Cass, hence won Cass support for chairmanship. Hunker* moderate on slavery but able to deal with both factions on this issue.

Robert M. McLane. Enjoyed a family connection with the Jackson administration; a supporter of General Pierce, whose nomination was intended to revive the Jacksonian image. Recommended by vice-presidential nominee, who was a close friend.

David A. Smalley. New England leader and lifelong friend of Senator Douglas, who lost nomination to Buchanan. Selection was a Buchanan effort to conciliate the Douglas faction.

August Belmont. New York political and financial leader. Long-time supporter and contributor to Douglas presidential aspirations. War Democrat. As major financial contributor, held chairmanship for twelve years.

Augustus Schell. New York political leader and financial contributor to Greeley. With Greeley, an advocate of postwar reconciliation with Southern Democrats.

Abram S. Hewitt. Long-time personal friend, contributor, and New York political associate of Tilden.

William H. Barnum. Major Democratic financial contributor. Close ally of Tilden and, subsequently, Cleveland. A moderate tariff protectionist.

Calvin S. Brice. Important Democratic financial contributor and member of

---

*The Hunkers were a pre-Civil War Democratic faction, mainly in New York, willing to accept proslavery policies. Their abolitionist opponents charged them with doing so out of "hunger" for federal job patronage.

national committee executive committee. Originally thought to be neutral on tariff issue, but eventually turned out to be protectionist and opposed to Cleveland's renomination.

William F. Harrity. Colleague and successor to William L. Scott of Pennsylvania, who was principal Cleveland spokesman on national committee. As leader of pro-Cleveland gold standard faction in Pennsylvania, Harrity worked closely with William C. Whitney, Cleveland's preconvention manager. Elected chairman after Whitney declined.

James K. Jones. A principal free-silver leader whose selection was Bryan's recognition of older silver faction leadership.

Thomas D. Taggart. Member of an increasingly powerful coalition of state party bosses. Campaigned strenuously for the chairmanship.

Norman E. Mack. New York state leader, associated with the Hill-Parker faction that won the nomination. Factional moderate.

William F. McCombs. Prenomination campaign manager for Wilson. Maintained liaison with, and later supported by, state party leaders, much to Wilson's displeasure.

Vance C. McCormick. Wilsonian progressive; Pennsylvania state leader who held critical delegation for Wilson's first nomination.

Homer S. Cummings. Wilsonian progressive; Connecticut state leader.

George White. Preconvention manager of Cox candidacy; anti-McAdoo.

Cordell Hull. Southern Wilsonian; experienced and popular chairman of congressional campaign committee.

Clement L. Shaver. A leader of Dry faction; Davis' long-time friend and campaign manager.

John J. Raskob. Wealthy Catholic contributor to Smith candidacy. Supporter of Wet faction. Established and financed permanent national headquarters.

James A. Farley. New York State leader and Roosevelt preconvention manager.

Edward J. Flynn. New York leader and member of Roosevelt inner circle.

Frank C. Walker. Early Roosevelt associate and financial contributor.

Robert E. Hannegan. Missouri leader and Truman supporter.

J. Howard McGrath. Truman supporter and adviser.

William M. Boyle, Jr. Truman protégé and adviser.

Frank E. McKinney. Leader of midwestern Truman faction.

Stephen A. Mitchell. Stevenson friend and political associate. Projected "clean politics" image.

Paul M. Butler. Pro-Stevenson; campaigned for chairmanship.

Henry M. Jackson. Reward to an allied faction; represented western Democrats during campaign.

John M. Bailey. Kennedy supporter.

Table 2 provides an impressionistic summary of the Democratic investiture process experience.

Table 2

Selection Factors in Investiture Process: Democrats

Chairman	ASSOC	BAL	FIN	REW	OPCAN	OPPOL	MOD	MGR	WIN	PREV
Hallett		x		x			x			
McLane	x	x								
Smalley				x	x			x		
Belmont	x		x							
Schell	x		x							
Hewitt	x		x							
Barnum	x		x							x
Brice							x			
Harrity								x		
Jones, J.K.				x	x					
Taggart									x	
Mack							x	x		
McCombs	x							x		
McCormick	x		x							
Cummings	x									
White								x		
Hull								x		
Shaver	x									
Raskob		x								x
Farley	x							x		
Flynn	x									
Walker	x	x								
Hannegan	x							x		
McGrath	x									
Boyle	x									
McKinney	x							x		
Mitchell	x									x
Butler, P.									x	x
Jackson		x								
Bailey	x							x		
	18	5	4	4	2	0	3	11	2	3

Key:
ASSOC—close associate or personal friend of titular leader
BAL—balances (regional, religious, etc.) presidential party leadership
FIN—major financial contributor or fund-raiser
REW—reward for pivotal support in nominating process
OPCAN—representative of opposing candidate faction
OPPOL—representative of opposing policy faction
MOD—a moderate, centrist, or compromise leader
MGR—managerial or other professional competency
WIN—winner in a contested chairmanship election
PREV—prevents control of chairmanship by opposing factions

As the historical record reveals, the factional and candidate loyalties of Democratic chairmen played a major part in their election. Some chairmanship selections took into account regional balance (Smalley, Jackson). Some occupied the chairmanship to prevent an opposing faction from taking it over (Barnum, Raskob). In a few instances, an apparent centrist was chosen because factional affiliation was ambiguous or unrevealed (Brice). In more recent years, particularly during periods of out-party status, national chairmen moderated their factional affiliations and emphasized their managerial talents in the interest of party unity. At times, the chairmanship election was an opportunity to test the support for presidential candidates or titular leaders.

The source of chairmen was at first from among leaders of critical state delegations or regional coalitions (Hallett, Smalley, etc.). This was followed by a series of large financial contributors who, in time, became party elder statesmen (Belmont, Schell, Hewitt, Barnum). Then came managers of preconvention nominating campaigns (Harrity, McCombs, Shaver, Farley). More recently, some were chosen for demonstrated executive competence (Hull, McKinney, Butler).

The Republican experience

With a fairly direct heritage from the Federalist, National Republican, and Whig parties of earlier decades, the Republicans became a nationally organized party in the mid-1850s. The predecessors of the modern Republican party, it will be recalled, had difficulty facing up to the national-level organizational needs of their parties. Hamilton could not get his Federalist colleagues to participate in grass-roots or other levels of organization-building; they, in fact, refused to consider themselves a political party. John Quincy Adams railed against parties generally, discouraging any realistic organizational work among the National Republicans who supported him. The Whigs fell into a long tug-of-war between Henry Clay and Thurlow Weed regarding the mobilization of party support. Clay focused on Congress; Weed gave his energies to state and local rank-and-file organizations. Weed's approach prevailed. It was Weed, an inveterate party founder, who brought his experience to the founding of the Republican party, which included the creation of a national committee and the selection of a close colleague, Edwin D. Morgan, as the first Republican national chairman.

Edwin D. Morgan. State chairman of the Whig party in New York (the state with the largest number of votes in the electoral college) and a major financial contributor to the Weed-Seward faction. Participated in the Weed-Seward strategy to make Fremont the first Republican presidential nominee in 1856. Remained in national chairmanship after 1860 following Weed and Seward reconciliation with Lincoln.

Henry J. Raymond. Protégé of the Weed-Seward-Morgan leadership in New York and editor of the *New York Times*. All four were Lincoln supporters by

1864 under the Union party banner. Delivered New York delegation to Lincoln. Wrote platform and a Lincoln biography.

Marcus L. Ward. Distinguished Republican governor of New Jersey, who joined Radical Republicans in order to recapture Republican national organization from National Chairman Raymond and to forestall President Johnson's efforts to keep the Union party label alive. Radicals sought to capitalize on Ward's prestige and status as a moderate.

William Claflin. Leading Free Soiler prior to becoming head of the Massachusetts Republican organization. Intermediary between conservative and Radical factions. After Grant's nomination as Radicals' candidate, helped swing New England's national convention vote to a midwestern moderate for vice-president to balance the ticket. As chairman, Claflin added regional balance and factional moderation to the ticket.

Edwin D. Morgan. Second incumbency. Now considered an experienced and wealthy party elder with friendly ties to both Stalwart and liberal factions.

Zachariah Chandler. One of the principal early leaders of the Radical Republicans. A leader of the Stalwart faction at the time, he brought this faction behind Hayes' nomination. In a divided national committee vote, Chandler beat Hayes' preferred candidate for chairman. Did not have the unanimous support of the Stalwarts on the national committee. Died while incumbent in chairmanship.

James D. ("Don") Cameron. Pennsylvania's Republican boss and a member of a pro-Grant coalition of Republican state bosses—Conkling, Cameron, and Logan. Elected to complete Chandler's chairmanship term, winning by a bare majority of national committee votes. Supported by Grant and Sherman committeemen, defeating the Blaine candidate. In the 1880 convention, Cameron and the Grant coalition vetoed a Blaine or Sherman nomination by supporting Grant's renomination for a third term.

Marshall Jewell. Former member of Grant's cabinet, but opposed to a third term for Grant. While governor of Connecticut, viewed as a moderate. An experienced member of executive committee of national committee, acceptable to nominee Garfield and various factions eager to prevent Cameron's re-election without alienating the Conkling-Cameron-Logan coalition. Jewell died while incumbent in chairmanship.

Dwight M. Sabin. President Arthur's preferred candidate for chairman was not likely to win against the candidate of the Blaine-Logan-Southern coalition. Arthur committeemen proposed Senator Sabin from Minnesota, who was not identified with any faction, but who had served on executive committee of national committee and was a compromise acceptable to Logan's coalition.

Benjamin F. Jones. A wealthy iron manufacturer and long-time personal friend of nominee Blaine. Major financial contributor to campaign. Jones also favored protective tariff, now an important factional issue.

Matthew S. Quay. Pro-Sherman leader of dominant faction in Pennsylvania, whose reluctant shift to Harrison came late in the convention. Closely associated with several Republican state bosses whose support was essential in the election campaign. Forced to resign in 1891.

James S. Clarkson. Vice-chairman of national committee who succeeded to chairmanship through approval of executive committee rather than entire national committee, an unprecedented formal selection procedure. Authority of executive committee to name national chairman later came into question. Pro-Blaine in 1884 and again in 1888, although apparently eager to bring President Harrison's and Blaine's supporters together.

Thomas H. Carter. A leading silver Republican from the Northwest and a Harrison manager at the 1892 convention. Although not a member of the national committee, he was chosen to be its secretary under Chairman William J. Campbell, the latter having been elected as a conciliatory gesture to the Blaine faction. However, when Campbell resigned within a few weeks, the executive committee elevated Secretary Carter to the chairmanship. The following year the full national committee declared the executive committee decision out of order and elected Carter in proper fashion despite his continued nonmembership on the national committee. The first "outsider" to become chairman.

Marcus A. Hanna. Long-time supporter of Ohio's Senator Sherman's candidacies. With McKinley as Sherman's successor in Ohio politics, Hanna served as preconvention manager of McKinley's 1896 nominating campaign. Wealthy and widely recognized as an outstanding campaign manager and party organizer. Became senator from Ohio and re-elected national chairman for McKinley's campaign in 1900. Died while incumbent in chairmanship.

Henry C. Payne. Manager of Harrison's midwestern campaigns in 1888 and 1892 and vice-chairman of national committee at time of Hanna's death. Despite ill health, became acting chairman until end of 1904 national convention.

George B. Cortelyou. Presidential secretary and adviser to Harrison, Cleveland, and McKinley. Extremely talented administrator and knowledgeable about party personnel and factional conditions. Appointed secretary of commerce and labor, a new federal department, by Roosevelt. Was Roosevelt's personal choice for chairmanship. Subsequently, prominently mentioned for the presidency.

Harry S. New. A Cortelyou protégé and vice-chairman of the national committee. Assumed acting chairmanship when Cortelyou resigned to become postmaster general. Later confirmed as chairman by full national committee.

Frank H. Hitchcock. Another Cortelyou protégé and aide in the Commerce and Labor and Post Office Departments. Assumed management of Taft's preconvention campaign, sponsored by Roosevelt and Cortelyou. In a numerous field of candidates for the chairmanship, Rosewater (see below) organized a national committee petition to Taft favoring Hitchcock, who was selected.

John F. Hill. A long-time friend of Hitchcock, a former governor of Maine, and a manager in the Taft preconvention campaign, Hill was appointed by Hitchcock to be vice-chairman of the national committee. Hill became acting chairman when Hitchcock was appointed postmaster general and was confirmed for the chairmanship at a later time. Hill died while incumbent in the chairmanship.

Victor Rosewater. Another Hitchcock associate (see above). National committeeman from Nebraska and a member of the executive committee of the national committee during the 1908 campaign, Rosewater was appointed vice-chairman by Hill when the latter was still acting chairman, but in too poor health to handle all the preparations for the 1912 convention. Upon Hill's death, Rosewater became acting chairman. Although his incumbency was challenged on procedural grounds, Rosewater was elected chairman prior to the convention.

Charles D. Hilles. President Taft's personal secretary and personal choice for the chairmanship after others had declined.

William R. Willcox. An associate of Hughes and Roosevelt in New York politics for many years. After conferring with Roosevelt, Hughes recommended Willcox as his personal choice. Willcox's selection was also seen as a friendly gesture to the Roosevelt Progresssives and as a mediator of conservative and progressive factions.

William H. Hays. Indiana state chairman on excellent terms with conservatives and progressives. Outstanding Republican party organization in Indiana established his reputation nationally. Willcox, blamed for Hughes' defeat in the close election of 1916, resigned, and it was expected that he would be succeeded by his vice-chairman, John T. Adams. Adams was vetoed by the progressives. In a compromise arranged by Hitchcock, Hays, who was favored by both conservatives and progressives, was chosen chairman and Adams remained as vice-chairman.

John T. Adams. Elected chairman upon Hays' resignation to become postmaster general in Harding's cabinet. Strongly endorsed by Republican party conservatives in Congress, who were interested in extending their influence to the national committee.

William M. Butler. National committeeman from President Coolidge's home state of Massachusetts and manager of his preconvention campaign in 1924. Coolidge's personal choice for national chairman. In accepting chairmanship, Butler set aside plans to run for United States senator.

Hubert Work. Coolidge's secretary of interior and the first cabinet officer to endorse Hoover's declaration of candidacy for president. The national committee set up a Committee of Twenty-four to consult with Hoover on the choice of chairman. Hoping to establish some strong symbolic connection with the popular Coolidge presidency, Hoover and the special committee agreed on Secretary Work, who accepted for the period of the election campaign.

Claudius H. Huston. Assistant secretary of commerce to Secretary Hoover from 1921 to 1923 and a Hoover enthusiast thereafter, Huston was an unusually successful fund raiser for the national committee. He was Hoover's personal choice to succeed Work, but only after Senate Republicans also expressed their satisfaction with him. From Tennessee, Huston was expected to take advantage of Hoover's strong support in the southern presidential electorate in 1928 to reorganize and build the party organization there. However, he was compelled to resign under allegations of lobbying improprieties in earlier years.

Simeon D. Fess. The executive committee, controlled by the Senate Old Guard, sponsored Fess, the Republican whip in the Senate and a leading conservative. The principal rationale was presumably Fess' ability, as former chairman of the congressional campaign committee, to carry on the 1930 midterm campaign. The appointment infuriated Republican insurgents.

Everett Sanders. Renominated in 1932, President Hoover asked Sanders, a party leader under Coolidge, but now practicing law in Indiana, to serve as chairman in order to strengthen the party organization in the Midwest where progressive defections to Roosevelt were decimating the leadership. Hoover campaign headquarters were set up in Chicago as further indication of the importance of the Midwest in the Hoover strategy. Resigned in 1934 because of ill health.

Henry P. Fletcher. A Hoover associate and important fund raiser, whose selection was in part motivated by the probability that he could find money to pay off the Hoover campaign debt. Won in a divided committee vote, 68 to 24, over John Hamilton. The division was also seen as a generational split, with Hamilton representing the younger leadership.

John D.M. Hamilton. Successfully managed the Landon campaign for governor of Kansas in 1932. Considered one of the party's outstanding organizers in the Hays tradition. Served as general counsel of the national committee under Fletcher. The re-election of Landon in 1934, managed by Hamilton, was the principal Republican victory nationwide in that year. When Landon was nominated for president in 1936, Hamilton was his personal choice for chairman.

Joseph W. Martin, Jr. Disregarding his promise to keep Hamilton as chairman and believing that the chairmanship belonged to "the party people," Willkie asked Minority Leader Martin to take on the chairmanship. Willkie assumed that this would satisfy the party regulars while the main thrust of his campaign would be carried on through the Willkie clubs.

Harrison E. Spangler. Iowa state chairman, a former member of the executive committee of the national committee, and an associate of John Hamilton when the latter was endeavoring to rejuvenate Republican organizations in the Midwest. Spangler was considered a middle-of-the-roader—an internationalist as well as a conservative—in the altercations between Willkie and the party regulars. In the candidate factionalism, Spangler regularly favored Taft.

Herbert Brownell, Jr. A friend of Dewey since the late 1920s, Brownell managed Dewey's successful campaign for governor of New York in 1942 and was the most energetic of the trio handling Dewey's preconvention campaign. He was nominee

Table 3

Selection Factors in Investiture Process: Republicans

Chairman	ASSOC	BAL	FIN	REW	OPCAN	OPPOL	MOD	MGR	WIN	PREV
Morgan		x	x				x			
Raymond							x	x		x
Ward							x		x	x
Claflin		x					x			
Morgan			x				x			
Chandler				x				x	x	
Cameron					x				x	
Jewell							x			x
Sabin							x		x	
Jones, B.F.	x		x							
Quay					x					
Clarkson					x		x			
Carter						x		x		
Hanna	x		x					x		
Payne								x		x
Cortelyou	x							x		
New								x		x
Hitchcock									x	
Hill										x
Rosewater									x	x
Hilles	x									
Willcox	x						x			
Hays							x	x	x	
Adams						x				x
Butler, W.	x							x		
Work		x			x					
Huston	x	x	x							
Fess								x		x
Sanders		x						x		
Fletcher	x		x						x	
Hamilton	x							x		
Martin		x				x				
Spangler							x		x	x
Brownell	x							x		
Reece					x				x	x
Scott	x							x		
Gabrielson					x				x	x
Summerfield			x	x						
Roberts								x		
Hall	x							x		
Alcorn	x									x
Morton	x						x			x
Miller	x	x			x			x		
	15	6	7	2	7	3	12	17	11	14

Table 3 *(continued)*

Key:
ASSOC—close associate or personal friend of titular leader
BAL—balances (regional, religious, etc.) presidential party leadership
FIN—major financial contributor or fund raiser
REW—reward for pivotal support in nominating process
OPCAN—representative of opposing candidate faction
OPPOL—representative of opposing policy faction
MOD—a moderate, centrist, or compromise leader
MGR—managerial or other professional competency
WIN—winner in a contested chairmanship election
PREV—prevents control of chairmanship by opposing factions

Dewey's personal choice. Resigned in 1946 to return to law practice.

B. Carroll Reece. Long experience on the executive committee of the party's congressional campaign committee; a leading southern (Tennessee) Republican in Congress; supported by the pro-Taft members of the national committee.

Hugh D. Scott, Jr. Obligated to the Edward Martin faction in Pennsylvania for giving him the winning vote in the national convention, Dewey asked Senator Martin to name the national chairman. Martin named Scott, a protégé among his younger associates in Pennsylvania. A campaign to remove Scott, a Dewey supporter, from the national committee led to his resignation in 1949.

Guy G. Gabrielson. Pro-Taft national committeeman from New Jersey. Won by 52 to 47 in a Taft-Dewey test vote in the national committee.

Arthur E. Summerfield. National committeeman and effective fund raiser. The critical votes of his Michigan delegation put Eisenhower instead of Taft over the top for the 1952 nomination. He was rewarded with the chairmanship. Resigned at end of campaign to return to his business.

C. Wesley Roberts. A former Kansas state chairman. Director of organization at the national committee under Summerfield, with responsibility for coordinating efforts of Republican regulars with those of Citizens for Eisenhower. Recommended by a five-member nominating committee of the national committee. Forced to resign when Kansas state legislators charged him with failure to register as a lobbyist under Kansas law.

Leonard Hall. Former chairman of the House congressional campaign committee, manager of the Dewey speakers bureau in the 1944 campaign (but with whom he later had strained relations), and strongly recommended by Speaker Joseph Martin, who was also interested in having an experienced national committee chairman in place for 1954 midterm elections.

H. Meade Alcorn, Jr. Connecticut national committeeman and friend of President Eisenhower's White House chief of staff, Sherman Adams. Recommended to Eisenhower by Adams and Chairman Hall.

Thruston B. Morton. A moderate liberal and strong Senate supporter of

Nixon. Opposed by conservatives, it was agreed that he would serve part-time and only until the end of the campaign, particularly in view of his own upcoming re-election campaign in Kentucky.

William E. Miller. An early Nixon supporter in New York, in opposition to prospective candidacy of Governor Rockefeller. Chairman of the House congressional campaign committee, in which position he became friends with Senator Goldwater, chairman of the Senate campaign committee. Recommended by conservative Senator Bridges, chairman of the Senate Republican Policy Committee. Elected chairman without objection from the Rockefeller supporters on the committee.

Table 3 provides an impressionistic summary of the Republican investiture experience.

Several generalizations, in rough quantitative terms, may be made about the investiture patterns that prevailed in the selection of Republican chairmen. In nearly two-thirds of the cases, the choice of a chairman was the result of a factional victory to one degree or another. In these instances, the candidate winning the presidential nomination would recommend a "personal choice," most often a manager of his nominating campaign, a senior factional colleague, an old and trusted friend, or a personal secretary or adviser. Similarly, when the Republicans were the out-party, a dominant faction whose base lay in Congress or in a particular presidential candidacy would choose as chairman an ally already on the national committee.

About a fourth of the time, the chairman elected was a compromise choice, that is, a moderate or middle-of-the-road leader during a time of intense factional strife, usually a skillful broker among the contending leaders. These chairmen tended to be senior leaders, the elder statesmen of the party, or someone who had demonstrated great success at bringing the factions together at the state level or in the Congress.

The fewest cases were those in which the chairmanship was used as a reward to a leader whose help, for example, a swing vote in the national convention, had been invaluable to the leader of the dominant faction or whose factional support had been important in the presidential campaign.

In addition to factional considerations, the other stepping-stones to the national chairmanship have been fairly constant: service as a successful fund-raising manager, chairman of a congressional campaign committee, vice-chairman or member of the executive committee of the national committee, or preconvention campaign manager for a candidate.

Table 4 offers a comparison of the investiture factors of the two parties.

While personal association with the titular leader has been a major factor in chairmanship selection in both parties, it has been much more so among the Democrats. Reward for pivotal support has been somewhat more important in Democratic selections, undoubtedly a function of the two-thirds nomi-

Table 4

Percent of Each Selection Factor Present in Both Parties*

Party (N)	ASSOC	BAL	FIN	REW	OPCAN	OPPOL	MOD	MGR	WIN	PREV
Democrats (30)	60	17	13	13	7	0	10	37	7	10
Republicans (43)	35	14	16	5	16	7	28	40	26	33

*Percentages are derived from the number of instances each factor was found in the total number of chairmanships for each party, for example, 18 cases of close association in the 30 Democratic chairmanship cases equals 60 percent.

Key:
ASSOC—close associate or personal friend of titular leader
BAL—balances (regional, religious, etc.) presidential party leadership
FIN—major financial contributor or fund-raiser
REW—reward for pivotal support in nominating process
OPCAN—representative of opposing candidate faction
OPPOL—representative of opposing policy faction
MOD—a moderate, centrist, or compromise leader
MGR—managerial or other professional competency
WIN—winner in a contested chairmanship election
PREV—prevents control of chairmanship by opposing factions

nating rule that often required coalition building or the "purchase" of swing voting blocs. Negotiation and compromise seem to have been a frequent part of Republican chairmanship selection, as evidenced by the proportion of factional victories in contested elections (26 percent) and the frequency with which factional centrists and chairman candidates of opposition factions have been chosen, 28 percent and 16 percent, respectively.

In some respects over the decades, the investiture factors have been roughly the same for both parties. Wealthy contributors filled the chairmanships at first. Then came preconvention managers of major presidential candidates. Most recently, organization managers, election campaign experts, and other political professionals have been the most frequent choices.

The socialization process

How have personal backgrounds and role performances of the chairmen changed over the course of this office's history? Biographical details about each chairman may be found throughout the text of this book and may be summarized as follows.

The Democratic experience

Thirty men held the position of Democratic national chairman between 1848 and 1961. What were their general social attributes as a group? Only a few generalizations will be ventured.

These men, on the average, were forty-eight years old at the time of their election to the office, about four or five years younger than their Republican counterparts. Among the oldest were Schell (60) and Barnum (58). At the youngest end of the scale were McCombs (36) and McLane (37). Most could be considered to be in political mid-career.

At least seven were born and raised in New York. In other words, most of their political experience was gained in the state most vigorously contested by the parties during this entire period. New York Democrats had the additional special experience of contending with the powerful and wily Tammany organization. Other chairmen came mainly from Pennsylvania, Delaware, and other eastern seaboard states.

About half the Democratic chairmen were members of Protestant religious denominations, slightly fewer were Catholics, and only one was of Jewish affiliation. This contrasted with the Republicans, whose chairmen were nearly all Protestants. The Democratic party has, of course, been a major avenue of upward social mobility for Catholics, particularly the Irish, as reflected in the nomination of two Irish Catholics for the presidency: Alfred E. Smith and John F. Kennedy.

The greatest number of Democratic chairmen came from families in which the father was an owner or executive of a business. The next major occupation among the fathers was farming; a few others were professionals. Their sons, that is, the chairmen, were predominantly business executives, professionals (mainly lawyers), and public officials. Most Democratic chairmen were college graduates, having earned law degrees or having read law. Only one chairman did not complete elementary school.

Nearly all the chairmen were long-time participants in Democratic party organizational affairs. For many, the chairmanship was a stepping-stone to higher public office, notably postmaster general. For almost a third, the chairmanship was the highest and last significant party or public office held. None was nominated for president, although a few were in contention at some point during or immediately following their service in the chairmanship: Hewitt, Barnum, Brice, Hull, Farley, and Jackson.

This brief collective profile fails to identify trends and changes in the types of persons who have held the office. Such patterns are difficult to quantify. However, a few characterizations may be permissible.

The first Democratic chairman, Hallett, was particularly interesting in that he was almost a mirror image of the political profile of the Democratic party during the period of his participation in politics. From northeastern abolitionist, Hallett moved gradually toward a role as national broker in the rivalry between the abolitionist and proslavery factions, North and South. His search for a middle ground led him—and the Democratic party—to ambiguous platform language and support for "Northern candidates with Southern principles." His performance while chairman and later gave practical meaning to the chairman's responsibility as a mediator-broker trying to hold the party together. In 1860, the party's failure was also his.

Place of residence and personal friendships had particular meaning for McLane and Smalley. Each man lived in a state—Maryland and Vermont—that added an element of geographical balance otherwise missing from the national tickets they served. Each was also well-connected: McLane through his father's service in Andrew Jackson's cabinet and Smalley as a lifelong friend of Senator Stephen A. Douglas. Their performances as chairmen were less than interesting.

An era of wealthy and politically influential chairmen followed. Their wealth meant major contributions to the national presidential campaigns. Belmont, Schell, and Hewitt had the added qualification of New York residency, the state with the largest electoral college vote and the most closely contested party battles. The three men—together with Samuel J. Tilden—were also veterans of battles to reform Tammany Hall. In the case of Barnum, the factor of wealth was significant, but not much more so than strong personal loyalty to Tilden. Brice's main attributes appeared to be his wealth and, although based in Ohio, his excellent political and social connections in New York.

At about this time, wealth ran a close second to factional and state leadership considerations. At the height of the gold-silver debate, Harrity and Jones were experienced and respected factional leaders, Harrity in his native state of Pennsylvania and Jones in the U.S. Senate. They were succeeded by a pair of senior state party leaders: Taggart, boss of the Indiana party, and Mack of upper New York State. Managerial skills appeared to be gaining in importance.

The next era brought a series of Wilsonian progressives into the chairmanship: McCombs, McCormick, Cummings, and Hull. In McCombs' case, his background as a former student of Wilson and his efforts to mediate between Wilson and state leaders proved to be his undoing. McCombs, White, and Shaver also shared the role of preconvention manager of the candidates they helped to nominate.

Raskob, like Barnum before him, held the chairmanship largely because he was a major financial contributor. For him, the office was also a holding operation on behalf of Al Smith, his candidate for president. A successful corporate executive, Raskob supervised a thorough reorganization of national headquarters, converting it to a permanent operation. Farley's great achievement was his superb performance not only as preconvention manager but also as national chairman.

The Roosevelt era saw two loyal political associates—Flynn and Walker—

take on the chairmanship duties as a favor to their old friend in the White House. The chairmen who followed—Hannegan, McGrath, Boyle, McKinney, Mitchell, and Butler—could be generally characterized as political managers of various styles. Jackson and Bailey were respected senatorial colleagues who were recruited to lend a certain importance and balance to the top of the presidential ticket, albeit in the role of party chairman.

Many of the above observations may be excessively general and do injustice to some of the chairmen. Nevertheless, they do reveal long-term patterns in the socialization of Democratic national chairmen, including the important role of factional influences in that development.

The Republican experience

Forty-two different men held the Republican national chairmanship between 1856 and 1960, one of these—Edwin D. Morgan—twice. When compared to the 3.9 year average tenure of Democratic chairmen, the 2.5 year average for the Republicans reflects a higher turnover and, as the investiture data suggest, perhaps a lesser career interest in the office than that found among Democrats.

A collective profile of Republican chairmen indicates that the average age of Republican chairmen, upon assuming that position, was about 52 to 53 years old, somewhat older than among Democrats. The mode for Republicans lay between 56 and 63 years. The two oldest chairmen were Simeon D. Fess (69) and Hubert Work (68); the youngest were Will Hays (38), Thomas H. Carter (39), Dwight M. Sabin (40), and Herbert Brownell (40). The oldest Democrats were 58 and 60 and the youngest 36 and 37. These comparisons would seem to support the observation that Republican chairmen, because they were older and closer to retirement years, were less interested in the career aspects of the chairmanship.

As in the case of the Democrats, most Republican chairmen were residents of the competitive and pivotal state of New York. Close second and third place states were Pennsylvania and Massachusetts, normally Republican during the periods covered. Chairmen also came from other Republican-leaning states: Indiana, Iowa, and Ohio. Democratic chairmen, it will be recalled, came mainly from New York and Pennsylvania. The state origin of chairmen was undoubtedly related to the facts that these states were also major sources of presidential candidacies, state party influence at the national conventions, and, in victory, major recipients in the distribution of federal patronage.

The concern has often been expressed that national chairmen coming from major competitive states may not be factionally neutral because of association with an active presidential candidate from the same state. The historical odds seem to make it difficult for matters to be otherwise, since the politics of major competitive states provides excellent preparation not only for presidential candidates but also for party chairmen who must deal with intense party competition at the national level.

The Republican chairmen have reflected the predominantly Protestant character of the population of the United States. Nearly all were Protestants. More specifically, about a fourth were Presbyterians and over 10 percent were Methodists. Only one or two were of either the Catholic or Jewish faiths. This, of course, contrasts with the high proportion of Catholic chairmen on the Democratic side.

About half of the Republican chairmen came from families in which the father was either the owner of a farm or a business enterprise. Another fourth of the fathers were in professional occupations. The chairmen themselves were almost equally distributed among business, the professions, and public offices as their principal occupations. About half the Republicans were trained as lawyers, almost the same number as the Democrats. Unlike the Democrats, Republican chairmen included two physicians and one Ph.D. among their number. A substantial proportion—one-fourth—had completed their formal education at the secondary school or business college level.

Although difficult to measure comparatively, participation in party organizational affairs was as pervasive among Republican as among Democratic chairmen. Although many were men of wealth who made large financial contributions, money was a less significant factor in their participation than for the Democrats, particularly during the earlier periods. Republican chairmen tended to be senior state party officials, governors, congressmen, senators, and senior officers in Republican administrations both before and after their incumbency in the chairmanship. Prior to 1960, the only chairmen to be considered seriously for the party's presidential nomination were Jewell, Quay, Hanna, Cortelyou, Hays, and Hamilton.

In general, Republicans, somewhat more so than Democrats, seem to have selected party chairmen with organizational and managerial skills and experience. These individuals have been recruited from such positions as state party chairmen, chairmen of congressional campaign committees, national committee staff and membership, and corporate executives. Republicans have manifest a concern, particularly after the Hanna and Hays regimes, for "business-like" efficiency at national party headquarters. Accordingly, Republicans have also given particular attention to the formalization process, that is, organizational development of the national committee, the chairmanship, and the operation of national party headquarters, as will be described in the following chapter.

26 | Conflict and Developmental Patterns: The Formalization Process

How have the task expectations, that is, the functions and duties, of the national chairmanship evolved? The early national chairmen would undoubtedly recognize many of the job specifications for the contemporary chairmanship: campaigner, publicist, fund raiser, factional mediator, etc. However, they would be amazed by the extent of the modern organization, the number of personnel, the size of the budgets, the scope of the communications media, the multiplicity of organized interest groups to be dealt with, and the changing relationships between national and state party organizational units.

The contrasts are even more striking when we recall that national party organization in the United States began with the correspondence of Thomas Jefferson and the congressional caucusing of James Madison on the Democratic-Republican side and the correspondence of Alexander Hamilton on the Federalist side. These one-man "national headquarters" were aided by little more than the two leading party newspapers: the Democratic-Republican *National Gazette* and the Federalist *Gazette of the United States*.

The Democratic experience

Several factors paved the way for establishment of the first Democratic national committee, for example, the need of party leaders from different regions to consult and contest presidential candidacies, public policies, and election campaign strategies. For these purposes, the unofficial congressional nominating caucuses of the Jefferson-Madison-Monroe era had sufficed. These caucuses usually arranged to have a resident committee, that is, resident in the nation's capital, prepare a platformlike "address to the people" and encourage congressional and state leaders to support the ticket. Congress was, after all, the hub of national politics. By 1824, however, the congressional caucus fell into disrepute and, additionally, became organizationally a poor channel to the party-in-the-electorate.

556

The idea of conducting national nominating conventions to select presidential slates began to gain currency during the 1820s. In 1831–32, all three major parties of that day—Anti-Masons, National Republicans, and Democratic-Republicans—held their first national conventions. The Democratic-Republicans were the only one of the three to survive to hold further quadrennial meetings. These early conventions also arranged for resident committees to coordinate the presidential campaign, but failed to create any other permanent organization to conduct party business between conventions.

Andrew Jackson's Kitchen Cabinet was a first attempt to give organized and sustained attention to national party affairs. Led by Martin Van Buren, the Kitchen Cabinet included several functionally relevant specialists: a congressional party leader, journalists, a state party boss, etc. The task of getting out the vote was left to regional political machines in Richmond, Nashville, Albany, New York, and elsewhere, for example, the Albany Regency and Tammany Hall in New York. When President Van Buren failed to be re-elected, he used his residence as the national party headquarters and acted in a manner appropriate to a leader of the loyal opposition.

By 1844, the nation consisted of thirty states, and the national parties reached into most of them. National party politics had settled into a contest between Democrats and Whigs. The Democratic national convention had become sufficiently institutionalized to produce the first "dark-horse" nominee, James K. Polk. Running a presidential campaign had outgrown the capacities of small resident committees and long-distance correspondence among a few party leaders.

Polk's nomination was the work of several master politicians, particularly Robert J. Walker of Mississippi. For the campaign, the 1844 convention created a fifteen-member central committee, a model for the first full national committee established four years later. The central committee, led by Walker, devoted itself mainly to negotiations among factional leaders, particularly with President Tyler's following, and the preparation and distribution of campaign tracts.

The next formalizing step came with the creation of the first national committee in 1848. All state parties were represented and membership on the national committee was to be continuous between conventions, linking convention to convention.

Along with Benjamin F. Hallett as the first Democratic national chairman, two national committee secretaries were chosen, one residing in the North and the other in the South. The secretaries were to serve as regional communication centers during the 1848 campaign and were to keep a sharp eye out for "enemy duplicity." In addition to his duties as chairman of the Massachusetts Democratic party, Hallett gave his principal attention to writing and distributing campaign literature for the national effort. Four years later, while opening the 1852 national convention, Hallett introduced several enduring procedural duties for national chairmen.

In contrast to Hallett, the next chairman, McLane, spent most of his time making speeches in his home state of Maryland, which caused some dissatisfaction among his colleagues on the national committee. They clearly expected McLane to prepare and distribute campaign literature, and when he did not they organized a resident committee in Washington to perform these duties.

Smalley performed a much larger role, particularly as a factional broker who helped put together a balanced North-South ticket, that is, Buchanan from Pennsylvania and Breckinridge from the South. In 1852, the now-customary resident committee was given the job of writing and distributing campaign literature, with the added responsibility of maintaining a speakers bureau. The first executive committee was established, primarily for fund-raising purposes. Reaching the more than 3 million voters across forty states was beginning to cost more money than any nominee could gather from a few of his friends.

Belmont became chairman of the pro-Douglas or regular national committee when the party split in 1860. He was assisted by three national secretaries, a seven-member executive committee, and a seven-member resident committee. There was never any doubt that Belmont would be the principal contributor and fund raiser: his links to the banking and commercial communities in New York, Philadelphia, and Boston were critical for the three presidential campaigns during which he served. Given the circumstances of the Southern wing of the Democratic party during the Civil War, Belmont had the additional responsibility of keeping alive the party's image as a distinct, viable, and patriotic organization.

This was not readily accomplished, given the defection of the Southern Democrats and President Lincoln's strategy of running for re-election on a Union party ticket with a War Democrat as his running mate. In addition, western Democrats were thinking in secessionist terms of forming a "Northwest Confederacy," hardly a patriotic thought.

In 1872, when the party refrained from making a presidential nomination of its own, it endorsed the Liberal Republican nominee, Horace Greeley. The new chairman, Schell, was compelled to grapple with difficult interparty negotiations between Democrats and Liberal Republicans as well as with factional relations. He and Greeley also sought to open channels for the return of Southern Democrats to national politics and the national party.

National committee functions and organization continued to expand. During campaigns, the three national committee secretaries hired assistant secretaries. A separate office of treasurer was established after 1880. The executive committee grew from seven to twenty-five members by 1888 in order to provide representation to the new states of the West. During the years of Tilden's influence, the resident committee was replaced by a literary bureau, a speakers bureau, and a bureau of correspondence. The emergence of a congressional campaign committee in its modern form took place during the years from 1878 to 1882 and required a coordinating mechanism between the two committees; this led to the formation of the advisory committee.

During the disputed election of 1876, Chairman Hewitt, who was a leading member of Congress at the time, was thrust into a major public role as defender of his party's interest before the Special Electoral Commission chosen by Congress to judge the returns. No other party officer could have conducted the exhausting negotiations. The outcome gave the presidency to Hayes, ended Republican sway over southern reconstruction, but also destroyed Hewitt's lifetime friendship with Tilden.

Another major contributor of funds, Barnum, was the first to assume the tasks of field inspector of state party organizations and campaigns. Interim meetings of the national committee increased in order to hear his reports and deal collectively with matters of party tactics. By 1884, the now-powerful executive committee was appointing several subcommittees from among its members. One such subcommittee, chaired by Senator Gorman of Maryland, was the principal distributor of the vast federal patronage when the first Democratic administration in a generation took office in 1884. Another subcommittee—a nine-member campaign committee led by Brice—was in charge of presidential campaign management in 1888. By 1892, the campaign subcommittee was assisted by its own advisory committee.

The proliferation of functions and committees was compounded during the William Jennings Bryan era, to the point of blurring all semblance of systematic organization around the chairmanship. Chairman Jones was called upon to coordinate several free-silver parties—Silver Republicans, Populists, and National Silver party—with the Democratic campaigns, a responsibility that was burdened by the factionalism within each party. Party management was not Senator Jones' forte, nor did nominee Bryan, a loner on the campaign road, do much to help. Even a special Joint Campaign Committee, established for the 1900 campaign, failed to maximize the efforts of the unruly coalition of parties. Poor national committee management between 1896 and 1904 was in stark contrast to the unprecedentedly successful organization of the Republican national committee by their chairman, Mark Hanna.

Although there was no permanent Democratic party headquarters between 1896 and 1900, there were party debts and expenses being incurred during the interim between national conventions. To meet these needs, Chairman Jones appointed a five-member ways and means committee in 1898 to raise the necessary funds. Preoccupied with his Senate duties, Jones also established the first national committee vice-chairmanship in 1899.

As the twentieth century opened, the work of the Democratic national committee and chairmanship appeared to be fairly well institutionalized. The national committee, its executive committee, and the various subcommittees and advisory committees were providing representation to factional as well as geographical interests within the party. Factional tests and contests most often manifest themselves in disputes over the size of representation on various committees, strategic instructions to chairman or subcommittees, and the selection of time, site, and other arrangements for a forthcoming national convention. A major exception to this trend was Woodrow Wilson's insistence that only men loyal to himself should be seated on the various committees, a view that gave rise to profound disagreements between himself and his protégé, Chairman McCombs.

Often jointly with the chairman of the congressional campaign committee, the national committee chairman now tried to remain knowledgeable about state and local party affairs, particularly in those localities that could have consequences for the national campaigns. While campaign literature was expected to reflect the views of the nominees and the dominant faction of the moment, political pamphlets and other campaign documents also endeavored to avoid alienating minority factions or interests whenever possible.

Media relations were becoming increasingly complex and compelling. Fundraising for rent and staff expenses was becoming more difficult and always urgent. It was no longer possible to rely on a few major contributors, and new fund-raising methods were constantly being tested, for example, mass appeals for small contributions. Relations between the national chairman and state party officers were intensifying, with coalitions of state leaders increasingly interested in exercising influence upon and through the national chairmanship. To deal with these trends, a substantial number of new national committee rules of organization and procedure were proposed in 1900, but few were adopted.

With the passage of time, the national committee was assigned or assumed additional duties and constraints. In 1904, the national convention authorized the committee to fill any vacancy on the national ticket that occurred between the end of the convention and the election. In 1908, at Bryan's behest, the committee agreed to make public all financial contributions and to accept none from corporations.

The need for a permanent national headquarters was first given substantial attention during the McCombs chairmanship. McCombs insisted that "we should be in thorough cooperation all the time."[1] The national committee agreed to maintain headquarters offices in both New York and Washington. This was in part a response to McCombs' alienation from President Wilson and Wilson's refusal to conduct party business in a friendly manner with the leading state party organizations. Wilson, whose concept of the function of parties was primarily legislative, abhorred the prospect of putting himself under obligation to party bosses. By 1916, this disaffection reached such intensity that many national committee members tried to turn over all responsibility for the presidential campaign to Wilson personally. This proposal was rejected, and national headquarters staff rose to one hundred persons during the 1916 campaign, many of whom were retained after the election to help with the committee's campaign to sell war bonds.

From the early 1920s, the size, maintenance, duties, and organization of a Democratic national headquarters were the subjects of review, debate, and revision among the members of the national committee. Two prominent Wilsonians—Franklin D. Roosevelt and William Gibbs McAdoo—raised questions with particular force and frequency about national committee organization. Reorganization proposals were inevitably reflections of factional or candidate concerns. Headquarters offices did not always exist or, if they existed, were not well staffed. The prerogatives of the national chairman were often at issue. Funding became a chronic problem, needed to pay off indebtedness from past campaigns or to prepare for future ones. Not until John J. Raskob assumed the chairmanship was the national headquarters well financed.

The election of Franklin D. Roosevelt and the inauguration of the New Deal-Fair Deal era assured sustained and significant attention to the development of an adequately staffed permanent national headquarters. Chairman Farley elevated national and state party relations to a new level of cordiality and efficiency. He converted the party organization into a powerful source of political intelligence and created a system of patronage distribution that served the party effectively and honorably. His personal relationships with congressional leaders and rank-and-file party members were the envy of many, including the president himself.

By 1948, a century after the first Democratic national committee had been created, the party's national committee, national chairmanship, and national headquarters were at last institutionalized as permanent features of the party structure. The formalization process had produced both a representative national committee and a bureaucratic headquarters. The chairmanship itself became a full-time, paid position for most incumbents.

But the development process had only begun. The 1950s and subsequent decades were yet to add demanding new responsibilities: arranging elaborate national conventions; managing the demands of the new media of radio, television, and international press; responding to the countless interest groups that comprise the Democratic coalition; preparing platform drafts for consideration by the national convention; designing ever-changing rules of representation and procedure at both the national convention and on the national committee; managing massive fund-raising solicitations; maintaining contact and coordinated relations with the congressional leadership; directing vast registration and get-out-the-vote drives, to mention some of the more conspicuous duties. Unquestionably, more functions, more institutionalization, and more bureaucratization were yet to come.

The Republican experience

When the Republican party was founded in 1854, the Democrats and the Whigs had already established national committees to serve as the interim agencies of their national conventions. Therefore, a national committee was an integral part of the initial Republican structure. Several of the new Republican leaders were in fact experienced party organizers who had served on the Whig national committee: Thurlow Weed, for example, was at the center of the establishment of the Anti-Masons, the National Republicans, and the Whigs, Horace Greeley was an old hand at composing party platforms and campaign literature, Edwin D. Morgan was Whig state chairman in pivotal New York, and Abraham Lincoln was the Whig national committeeman from Illinois. There were others.

The principal initiatives for incorporating a Republican party came from the New York leaders. An outstanding interparty negotiator, Morgan, in his role as the first Republican national chairman, did what he could to bring the North American party ("Know-Nothings") and the Fillmore Whigs of New York into the Republican coalition. Also, fund-raising and political brokerage were clearly to be among the essential duties of Republican national chairmen over future generations.

Committees and subcommittees very soon became the organizational means for providing representation of state, sectional, and factional interests and for sharing the workload among political leaders, most of whom were usually engaged in occupations elsewhere—as members of Congress, in private businesses, as public officials in the states, etc. Thus, between 1856 and 1860, the national committee created an executive committee of from five to seven members to be readily available to advise and otherwise help the national chairman, a national committee secretary, and a six-member executive congressional committee. The general executive committee concentrated on fiscal operations and factional coordination. An executive congressional committee, in the fashion of the old resident committees, took charge of propaganda and its distribution.

National level organization became particularly vulnerable to factional battering during the Lincoln and Johnson presidencies. As President Lincoln sought to entice War Democrats into his camp under a Union party banner, Republican conservatives and radicals struggled for ascendancy, particularly in Congress. When the executive congressional committee added the prefix "Union" to its name in keeping with Lincoln's strategy, Republican Chairman Morgan left the national committee to move into the congressional committee chairmanship in an effort to conciliate the Radicals and the unhappy Fremont supporters.

Henry J. Raymond took over as national committee chairman and treasurer, assisted by a small executive committee and an advisory committee. In 1866, when Raymond participated in a pro-Johnson midterm national convention on the uncertain grounds that the Union party designation would be perpetuated, the Radicals declared his actions equivalent to a defection, took control of the Republican national committee, and left Raymond with the remnants of the Union national committee.

The Radicals also supplanted the Union executive congressional committee with a Union Republican congressional committee that served as their anti-Johnson campaign vehicle. Its objective was to elect Radical rather than pro-Johnson members of Congress in the 1866 midterm elections. After 1868, the two congressional committees evolved into the modern Republican congressional campaign committee and became increasingly independent of the national committee. In 1880 and later, it was often necessary to create a special subcommittee of the national committee to maintain liaison between the two committees.

Having recaptured the chairmanship in 1866, the Radicals returned the party to its original Republican designation, put Marcus Ward into the chairmanship, and appointed a new seven-member executive committee. At the 1868 national convention, the Radicals had the organizational rules amended to prohibit interim conventions (such as the pro-Johnson midterm convention) and quorumless national committee coups of the kind they themselves had perpetrated against Chairman Raymond just two years earlier.

In the 1868 Grant campaign, the national chairman's principal activity was fund-raising in Boston and New York, the country's major commercial centers. The national committee now had "outside" and "inside" tasks, and the latter—headquarters administration—were assigned to the secretary, William E. Chandler. Campaign direction and national committee communication were distributed among an elaborate committee structure: a central executive committee in New York, a western executive committee, a southern executive committee, and a Pacific Coast executive committee. In 1872, these committees were consolidated into a single fifteen-member executive committee. The national chairman, once again Edwin Morgan, pursued funds while William Chandler again ran headquarters.

National committee functions and management expanded in various ways in 1876 under the leadership of the most fiery of the original Radicals, Zack Chandler. With the presidential electorate evenly divided between the parties and with much political heat being generated by the issue of continued federal military occupation of several Southern states, Chandler led a hard-hitting "bloody shirt" campaign against Samuel J. Tilden. Two national headquarters were maintained. Particular attention was paid to balloting in the South.

When the returns were contested in three Southern states, Chandler sent an army of Republican investigators to protect the party's interests in each of these states. He led Republican efforts to influence the outcome of the investigations of the Special Electoral Commission created by Congress. In all, it was an especially busy season for Republican headquarters and its chairman. An unofficially negotiated outcome gave the presidency to Hayes and the withdrawal of federal troops from the South to the Democrats.

When Don Cameron became national chairman and tried, unilaterally, to reestablish unit rule voting by national convention delegates, he found himself threatened with removal by the national committee for exceeding his prerogatives. Committee members turned to the sergeant-at-arms, a leader of the Grant faction, for a ruling on their authority to depose a chairman. The sergeant-at-arms ruled that it was within the national committee's power to remove its chairman. Factional conflict was indeed formalizing the prerogatives of the chairman and the operations of the committee.

By 1880, the Grant Stalwarts and the reformist factions were again locked in a bitter struggle. The consequence at the national committee was an organizational arrangement for shared control. The two factions divided national committee offices between them: the chairmanship going to the reformers (Jewell) and the secretaryship to the Stalwarts (Dorsey). The executive committee was expanded to twenty members to accommodate factional representation. This permitted creation of a subcommittee to operate the Chicago headquarters and another—an eight-member advisory subcommittee—to deal with finance.

Unfortunately, the creation of an advisory committee was not enough to diminish the factional battles. In 1888, the office of national committee treasurer was established. However, shortly afterward, John Wanamaker, chairman of the fund-raising advisory committee, refused to turn over funds to the party treasurer for allocation. Wanamaker was a leader of the reformers whereas the treasurer was affiliated with the rival Stalwarts.

An important issue in the factional affairs of the national committee became salient in the 1880s. It was becoming clear that the South would be voting solidly Democratic in future years and that Republican state parties in that section would be chronically weak, surviving only on presidential patronage. As a consequence, these states would become heavily overrepresented in delegation strength at the Republican national conventions. Acting as a bloc, southern delegations at the conventions and their representatives on the national committee could exercise factional influence well beyond their numbers. Republican presidents, using patronage astutely, could assure themselves, as several did, of the complete support of this bloc. What to do about this power aberration absorbed the attention of Republican leaders for years.

Factional influence at the national committee increasingly manifest itself in the subcommittee structure and assignments. Factional representation on all committees was careful arranged. Chairman Jones, for example, maintained liaison with the protectionist faction, whose constituency included the iron and steel industry of which he was part. The Blaine campaign was in the hands of a five-member subcommittee of the executive committee rather than a single person.

In 1888, with duties growing in number and complexity, the national committee established the offices of vice-chairman and treasurer on a permanent basis. A smaller executive committee took on the duties of running the presidential campaign; membership on the committee could now come from outside the national committee. This was a major step toward making available "outside" skills and influence. The vice-chairman (James S. Clarkson) became President Harrison's first assistant postmaster general and directed the distribution of what had grown to be an enormous postal patronage. This close connection between the national committee and the Post Office Department led to the practice of rewarding successful national chairmen with the postmaster generalship.

When Clarkson was elevated to the chairmanship, he combined his national committee responsibilities with those of president of the newly organized National Republican League, a network of local clubs. Much of this work was carried on during the interim between national conventions and consisted of building up the regular party machinery, local clubs, and support for the Republican position on the tariff issue. Clarkson's successor was Thomas H. Carter, the first nonmember of the national committee to become national chairman. Carter, in 1892, was preoccupied with factional negotiations while his advisory committee handled fund-raising. His executive committee managed campaign literature and speakers.

Mark Hanna brought the Republican chairmanship into the modern era. He was given full responsibility for selecting the secretary, the treasurer, the executive committee, and all other officers and staff. He established two headquarters and several bureaus: press, speakers, special distributions. He absorbed the staff of the National Republican League into the party structure and inaugurated the practice of using commercial auditors to tighten fiscal accountability for the committee's income and expenditures. His propaganda and fund-raising operations were of unprecedented scope by several orders of magnitude.

In the twentieth century, major steps in the formalization, even bureaucratization, of the chairmanship and the party's national headquarters took place during the incumbencies of George Cortelyou, Will Hays, John Hamilton, Herbert Brownell, Hugh Scott, Leonard Hall, and Meade Alcorn. A brief comment about each may suffice to identify how the formalization process changed and expanded task expectations over the years.

Cortelyou ended the practice by which national committee bureau chiefs let contracts for supplies and services; the practice made it easy to arrange for kickbacks. He made the executive committee responsible for accountability in all financial transactions. He made it a basic principal of operations to arrange for fair factional representation in the subcommittee structure. He planned the Roosevelt presidential campaign in meticulous detail and at minimum cost.

Hays gave new meaning to the concept of factional neutrality at national headquarters. He used conferences of party officials, precinct and district polls of voters' leanings, celebrity receptions and dinners, and personal travel as tools of recognition and reconciliation of party leaders and factions. Hays never hesitated to broker factional disputes in state organizations and even in Congress.

Hays' fund-raising drives imitated the Liberty Loan drives of World War I.

He introduced fund-raising quotas for the party's state organizations. He leased a permanent headquarters office in Washington. He expanded the publicity operations of national headquarters, introducing the use of film and newsreels. He issued questionnaires to thousands of Republicans across the nation to determine their views on current public issues. These findings aided the deliberations of the 1920 national convention platform committee. He arranged for the equivalent of a national party newspaper. In sum, Hays carried the national organization at least a generation forward from its development under Mark Hanna.

Sixteen years later, Hamilton repeated the Hays achievements and went steps beyond. He was responsible for establishing a research division at national headquarters, producing a national monthly magazine, using film and radio as never before, converting the chairmanship into a full-time salaried position, building a full-time permanent headquarters organization, providing representation at headquarters for special constituency groups (women, youth, etc.), proposing a midterm national convention, and other innovations.

After Thomas E. Dewey's defeat in 1944, Brownell announced an eight-point program of reorganization that is described in detail in an earlier chapter. His plan built upon Hamilton's work. One of the main thrusts of Brownell's plan was closer coordination of the activities of the party's several committees: national, state, and congressional. He also sought more expert headquarters staff and greater participation by national committeemen in the committee's programs. The contributions of Hamilton and Brownell were the bases for the subsequent organizational efforts of Chairmen Scott, Hall, and Alcorn.

Factional conflict and administrative development

By the 1960s, the basic organizational functions and duties of the Democratic and Republican national committees, chairmen, and headquarters were fairly well defined and stabilized.

As the interim organization of the quadrennial national nominating conventions, the national committee from the outset bore several convention-related administrative duties: issuing the call for the next convention, after deciding time and place; making arrangements for the convention hall, seating, and related needs of the attending delegations and often deciding how these arrangements could favor one faction or another; recording and publishing the convention proceedings; and maintaining contact with state parties through each state's national committeeman.

Since parties are political, it did not take long for these apparently simple duties to acquire various kinds of political (read "factional") significance. Decisions to select the convention date and host city became occasions for testing factional or leadership clout. Seating and hotel arrangements favored some delegations, hence the factions with which they were associated, over others. The language of the convention calls, particularly the apportionment rules, was subject to factional battles. The degree of national committee contact with state organizations often depended upon which was the dominant state faction.

From the beginning of the national convention system in 1832, several essential functions had to be performed to implement the decisions of the conventions. These administrative duties were assumed by the national committees. The most important was undoubtedly providing coordination for the election campaigns of the national tickets that had just been nominated. When Congress passed the law scheduling the selection of all presidential electors on the same day in November (previously chosen on a schedule that stretched over several months), nationwide campaign coordination became a pressing need best handled by the national committees. National committee members were expected to help reach the electorate in each state in a timely fashion. In time, national campaign coordination became contingent upon the degree of factional cooperation among the state representatives on the committee.

A second function was to prepare an "address to the people," campaign literature, and articles for the party press. These were the "literary" part of the campaign, initially performed by central committees and resident committees. The membership of these committees tended to be drawn mainly from Congress, the geographical hub of national politics in a world of slow communication and transportation. These committees were conveniently located in Washington, where the party's policy positions in Congress were best understood and where communication with state and local leaders—many of whom were members of Congress—was relatively direct. The literary products for the campaign were usually prepared by one or two congressional or newspaper staff persons talented in rhetoric and propaganda. Since factional differences over public policy and party program were directly pertinent to addresses to the people, these talents necessarily included the ability to circumvent or remain ambiguous about factionally controversial issues, a talent still in demand.

A third function involved grass-roots research and organization to survey voter preferences and to get the party's supporters to the polls. Senators, who were then elected by state legislatures and therefore necessarily informed about state and local politics, and party newspapers were the principal voting analysts and forecasters. The task of assessing national election trends on the basis of information from these sources became an early duty of the national committees. Given the great subjectivity of these assessments in times before public opinion polls, the national committees often had to rely more heavily than they wished upon the reports of state organization leaders, some of whom were leaders of dissident factions or state party machines.

These same campaign activities—disseminating the party platforms, preparing campaign materials for different media, and assessing the extent of voter support—are a familiar part of national committee administration to this day.

The national committee has also devoted major resources to voter registration and turnout campaigns, in past generations sometimes skirting the fringes of legality in doing so.

The judicial functions of the national committees have gradually become more formal and comprehensive. At first, the national chairman and the presidential nominee were the ultimate judges or mediators of campaign-related disputes, particularly in connection with drafting or intepreting the party platform. The standing committees of the national conventions as well as the conventions as a whole were not long in assuming major decision-making roles in conflicts pertaining to party rules, platform planks, disputed credentials, and related matters. In time, the national committees began to make first attempts at settling convention credentials, rules, personnel, and programmatic controversies, or, failing to do so, prepared the dispute for consideration by the appropriate committee in the convention. The national committees also served as the repository of parliamentary and other rules for the convention's and the committee's parliamentarians. Needless to say, most legal and parliamentary disputes have been spawned as a consequence of factionalism.

Thus, from small and simple beginnings, the administrative activities of the national committees have grown to include, with different emphases at different times, national convention management, coordination of national-level party agencies, fund-raising and accounting, research and electoral assessment, patronage distribution, candidate recruitment, volunteer supervision, media relations, platform preparation, defense of party policy positions, and civic education. One of the committees' most controversial activities has been their occasional role as the rostrum of the loyal opposition.

The special problem of formalizing titular leadership

The 1930s and 1940s were a time when national headquarters in both major parties became permanent. Often, major progress in chairmanship and headquarters development occurred when the party was not in control of the presidency. Under this circumstance, developments tended to be a response to the question of an appropriate role for the out-party in a presidential system in which the separation of powers is a fundamental principle of governmental organization. The United States has no office such as the British Leader of the Loyal Opposition.

It is a distinctive anomaly of the U.S. party system that there is no formal organizational status for the titular leaders of the presidential parties. The president and his most recently defeated opponent enjoy formal membership in their respective parties only because they have enrolled as such when registering to vote. Incumbency in the presidency or recent selection as the party's presidential nominee bestows no formal or special organizational status beyond election day. The party's presidential nomination is nothing more than a short-term contract:

"Be our nominee within the constraints of our platform and rules, and we'll give you our organizational support and the good will that is attracted by our party name."

Yet, these individuals—president-elect and defeated opponent—are generally perceived as the principal leaders of their respective parties and are expected to exercise influence. The president, in Woodrow Wilson's view, has no choice. He must operate as leader of his party if he is to accomplish anything. To this end, his governmental status provides him with resources that could benefit his constituencies and fellow partisans, from whom he must draw political strength.

The titular leader of the out-party has neither governmental nor any other official status (except as the official loser of a recent election), nor does he have resources, a predicament commented upon by several out-party leaders. This titular leadership anomaly is in marked contrast with the leadership arrangements in modern parliamentary systems where the victorious party's leader becomes prime minister and the principal opponent assumes the official status of Leader of the Loyal Opposition.

Further confounding matters is the ambiguity of the terms *majority party* and *minority party* in the American system. To be the nation's majority party, a national party must have majority status in at least four places simultaneously: (1) the electoral college, derived from pluralities in a sufficient number of states, that is, the party-in-the-electorate; (2) the presidency; (3) the Senate; and (4) the House of Representatives. Even when these numerical requirements are met, a party with majority status faces problems of coordination among its many semi-autonomous national-level party agencies, not to mention its various factions.

The national chairman is usually the most motivated to coordinate; leaders in the other party agencies are more likely to be separatists, protective of their constitutional prerogatives. From the perspective of resources, however, the national chairman is the weakest link in this chain. To illustrate: the president's chairman is usually his ally and servant. There are, of course, exceptions, when a chairman, in alliance with other powerful party leaders, is able to exercise political independence from his president, e.g., McCombs during the Wilson presidency. Normally, however, when president and national chairman have a falling out, it is the chairman who submits.

In the case of the out-party national chairman, who may be referred to as the residual chairman, quite different conditions usually prevail, accompanied by different approaches to titular leadership, dilemmas of various kinds, and frustrations almost always. Technically, after election day the out-party national chairman is the chief formal executive of the presidential wing of his party. In the public mind, he is a peer of the leader of his party-in-the-Senate and a peer of the leader of his party-in-the-House. Among these three, the residual chairman is burdened by important handicaps. He lacks a formal place in the constitutional system and the legislative resources enjoyed by the other two. Further, he has been associated with a lost cause, the electoral defeat of his party's presidential nominee. He is usually further burdened by campaign debts and surrounded by factional leaders either eager to take over his job or jockeying for intraparty advantages aimed at winning the next presidential nomination. Perhaps the residual chairman's most delicate problem is deciding how to relate to the recent loser, nominally the out-party titular leader, particularly if that person aspires to lead in the role of a loyal opposition.

The Democratic experience

Among Democrats, Jefferson, Madison, and Van Buren had no problem with titular leadership. Their party's national agencies were either nonexistent or in a formative stage. They were their own national party organization and, consequently, its titular leader. Chairman Hallett was the first residual national chairman for a party whose defeated nominee retreated to his previous political status as a U.S. senator. Thus, Hallett was free to function organizationally in any way he wished. He chose to serve as a mediator in what proved to be vain efforts to bring the factions together on the slavery issue.

In his turn, Belmont was another out-party chairman without a defeated nominee seeking to be a leader of the opposition; Douglas died, McClellan went off to Europe, and Seymour retired. Schell's nominee (Greeley) also died. These residual chairmen were truly the formal and titular chief officers of the presidential wing of the party. With Democrats in the minority in both houses of Congress, these chairmen were also cast in the role of leader of the loyal opposition.

Tilden was the first Democratic titular leader who actively maintained an influential, albeit a relatively low profile role in national party organizational affairs. He accomplished this in part through control of the national chairmanship, a position held by his colleagues Hewitt and Barnum over the years from 1876 to 1889. Tilden was able to pass the torch of party titular leadership on to his protégé, Grover Cleveland, who was twice elected president. As it turned out, Cleveland was not particularly attentive to party organizational matters, nor were his chairmen: Barnum in his declining years, Brice in his incompetency, and Harrity in a junior status among Cleveland's advisers. Even during those years 1887 to 1893 between his terms in the presidency, Cleveland remained quiescent about most party organizational issues.

The Bryan era introduced an entirely new approach to Democratic titular leadership. From his defeat in 1896 until his national convention switch to Wilson in 1912, the young and energetic Nebraskan was a declared and activist titular leader, performing this role in almost total disconnection from the national committee or other party agencies. Bryan published his own newspaper, wrote his own political tracts, and carried on an endless series of speaking tours. He was a master of national convention strategy and a self-declared spokesman for the progressive wing of his party. Bryan viewed the national chairmanship as a resource with which to give recognition to important elements in the party: to Jones as the senior among the older Silverite leaders and to Taggart and Mack as representatives of an increasingly powerful coalition of state and urban machines. Otherwise, Bryan had relatively little to do with party officials.

The next Democratic titular leaders—Cox, Davis, and Smith—were nominees whose defeats by landslide margins left them with little influence in party organizational affairs. The residual chairmen of the period—White, Hull, Shaver, and Raskob—became deeply absorbed in the problems of factional reconciliation and the establishment of a permanent national headquarters. They were encouraged not by their nominal titular leaders, but by two leading contenders for a future presidential nomination, Roosevelt and McAdoo. Under the circumstances, these chairmen met obstacles and contention at almost every step of the way.

The New Deal-Fair Deal era ended with Adlai Stevenson's defeat in 1952. Encouraged to do so by President Truman, Stevenson decided to conduct himself as the party's titular leader and pursue a revitalization of the national committee as a significant rostrum to articulate party policies. For a time there were proposals that Stevenson assume the national chairmanship in order to have a formal position from which to speak out. (The same proposal had been made to Wendell Willkie on the Republican side in 1940.) He declined to follow this approach. Instead, Chairman Mitchell began to refer to him as "the Party Leader," a mode of address that quickly drew criticism from party leaders in Congress. Nevertheless, Mitchell, and subsequently Butler, joined with Stevenson in a commitment to give the Democratic out-party a potent voice in national affairs.

Stevenson initiated the process in Chicago by bringing together an informal group of policy advisers who came to be known as the Finletter Seminar, after its host, former Secretary of the Air Force Thomas K. Finletter. When Butler was elected national chairman, he formalized the arrangement by creating the Democratic Advisory Council. The Stevenson-Butler collaboration represented a unique convergence of titular and formal leadership energies. Their principal difficulties arose from the reluctance of their party peers in Congress—Speaker Rayburn and Majority Leader Johnson—to join the enterprise. Rayburn and Johnson led the majority party in their respective houses and were unwilling to share power with a weaker party agency. The Democratic Advisory Council functioned impressively through an array of policy task forces, but was inevitably disbanded when Democrats returned to the White House under President Kennedy.

With the arrival of the 1960s, the development of the Democratic national committee and its chairmanship remained on a plateau. As always, the national party experienced the tribulations of coordinating the multiplicity of semiautonomous national-level agencies. At times, the national chairmen served a less than interested Democratic president and at other times as the chairman of a headless out-party.

The Republican experience

For the Republican party, the problem of out-party leadership was, in large measure, formulated during the era of Henry Clay's leadership, first when he was Speaker of the House of Representatives and, later, in the Senate, when he was a perennial Whig presidential candidate. Clay's coalitions, legislative skills, and policy initiatives left little doubt that he conceived of legislative leadership in Congress as the appropriate locus of a loyal opposition.

In the mid-1850s, as the Republican party was coming into being, William H. Seward, Thurlow Weed's colleague, became the chief Republican voice in the Senate during the Buchanan administration, viewing himself as titular leader for a brief time even after Lincoln was elected president. The principle of legislative supremacy was carried to an extreme when Radical Republicans came close to removing President Johnson, a former Democrat, from office.

In control of the presidency until 1884, the Republicans gave little thought to problems of opposition. Blaine's defeat and subsequent retirement left the party in the hands of potent state organizations whose leaders were either governors or U.S. senators. President Harrison's retirement after his defeat in 1892 allowed the party's leadership to remain in the hands of the state leaders.

Hanna and Cortelyou gave new stature to the national chairmanship, but they did so at times when the Republicans were either coming into or already holding the presidency. It was Will Hays who first handled the chairmanship as though he were the official leader of a loyal opposition.

Hays launched a barrage of criticism against President Wilson and the Democrats regarding the conduct of the war. He gave the chairmanship his full time. He declined to run for governor of Indiana in order to continue in the chairmanship. He made policy statements in his many speeches and in his counseling of congressional leaders and gave campaign advice to the Republicans in Congress. In the congressional, state, and local factional fights, Hays intruded himself as a peacemaker frequently, energetically, and successfully.

In preparation for the 1920 national convention, Hays addressed another duty of opposition leadership, namely, building a platform. The party's program of public policies was in need of composition and coordination. Hays therefore set in motion an Advisory Committee on Policies and Platform. The committee had 171 members: national committeemen, senators, representatives, women, a former president (Taft), a former nominee (Hughes), several former national chairmen, and others. Hays described the committee as follows:

> The purpose of this committee is to invite the advice and cooperation of the ablest men and women from all groups, sections, industry, business, profes-

sions, and interests of the nation; to gather pertinent facts and data; to study intensively the larger problems confronting us, and to offer the result of their efforts as suggestions to the [national convention] Resolutions Committee.[2]

Ogden L. Mills, Jr., of New York served as chairman of the executive committee of the advisory committee. Twenty-one subcommittees were established, each dealing with a different policy area. The Mills Committee had national headquarters send out 100,000 questionnaires asking the party faithful for their views on policy issues. The procedure soon had Republicans throughout the country talking to each other about party program. It was a major undertaking and a precedent for similar efforts in both parties in later years. However, the press and the congressional leadership were unimpressed. After several months, Everett Colby of New Jersey took Republican leaders in Congress to task for giving the Mills Committee "the cold shoulder."[3] When the committee sent a report to the national convention's resolutions committee, it received no notice in the press.[4] The programmatic consultations of a loyal opposition did not seem to be exciting news.

A similar midterm policy effort was made in 1934 when a small committee of nine, under the leadership of former Chairman Hilles, prepared a statement that was adopted by the national committee. This received the enthusiastic endorsement of former President Hoover, who emphasized the importance of maintaining an opposition. At this particular time, however, Republicans had little enthusiasm for loyal opposition; the New Deal was reaching the height of its popularity.

The mood changed in 1937, even though the Landon defeat pushed the Republican presidential party further out of office than it had ever been before. With former titular leaders Hoover and Landon looking over his shoulders, Chairman John D.M. Hamilton endeavored to make the national committee the rostrum for a loyal opposition. It was not easy. For example, during the fight over President Rooosevelt's Supreme Court packing proposal, Senate Republicans insisted that Hamilton remain silent and work in secret to help those Democrats and others opposing the proposal. Silence was hardly appropriate conduct for a loyal opposition.

When Hamilton proposed an interim national convention on party program and policy, his suggestion was soon submerged by a Hoover-Landon factional tug-of-war over principles of apportionment of representation and provisions for congressional participation. He was eventually able to establish a two-hundred-member Committee on Program. The committee held a five-day midsummer conference and prepared a thirty-thousand-word report over the signature of its chairman, Dr. Glenn Frank. Little else was heard of the committee and its product.[5]

The next effort followed upon Wendell Willkie's defeat in 1940. In what came to be known as his "Loyal Opposition" address, Willkie announced his intention to be active as an opposition leader. Editor David Lawrence went so far as to propose that Willkie assume the national chairmanship in order to have a formal position from which to speak. As it turned out, international crisis and war in Europe led Willkie to work closely with rather than against President Roosevelt in the foreign policy field.

Taking an approach similar to Hays' and Hamilton's, Chairman Harrison Spangler sponsored a Post-War Advisory Council meeting in 1943 at Mackinac Island, Michigan, which produced an unremarkable and uninfluential statement.[6]

By 1947, the Senate created new standing committees, one for each major party, namely, the Senate Policy Committees. These had the potential for providing an official and permanent rostrum for opposition leadership. This, in many respects, was the outcome of Senator Robert Taft's management of the Republican Policy Committee in the Senate when he became its chairman. It was in this position that Taft soon became known as "Mr. Republican." In the light of this development, even Chairman Brownell, a Dewey ally, acknowledged that Republican policy was made in Congress and that the job of the national committee was to translate and disseminate that policy to the citizenry. Brownell's observation notwithstanding, the Senate Policy Committees have yet to become the official locus of a leader of the loyal opposition.

In 1950, Chairman Gabrielson brought together reluctant representatives of the national committee, the Senate, and the House of Representatives to draw up an interim platform. As this was completed, Governor Dewey announced his intention to draft his own separate policy statement. Other Republicans did the same. Rather than provide a unified voice, Gabrielson's endeavor opened up the battle royal that would engage the Taft and Dewey-Eisenhower forces in 1952.[7]

The century of Republican experience with out-party status and the performance of an opposition role confirmed the difficulty of the problem.

E Pluribus Unum?

Should the party losing the presidential contest have a formal spokesman and recognized leader, or must the out-party remain voiceless or exhibit a cacophony of many voices? This has been a recurrent question about which numerous analyses and proposals have been offered.[8]

The question has been complicated by constitutional factors such as separation of powers and the federal structure of the governmental system; institutional developments such as a decentralized two-party system and a pervasive interest-group politics; and the personal ambitions and claims of party leaders, whether in office—the Speaker in the House, the majority leader in the Senate, a leading governor of a pivotal state, etc.—or out of office, such as defeated presidential candidates. Even a defeated former president, e.g., Herbert Hoover or Jimmy Carter, may also have a claim to the role of opposition leader.

At times the residual chairmanship of the out-party is proposed as the logical place to find the opposition leader, but this suggestion, among numerous others, invariably runs into objections from many quarters. The more general subject of titular leadership, but particularly in the out-party, arises with increasing frequency, but is more likely than not to be tabled in frustration or for lack of apparent urgency.

The problem is formulated in a number of ways. The absence of a designated leader of the loyal opposition or a significant residual chairman of the out-party is deemed wasteful of the judgment, talent, knowledge, and experience of some of the best national leaders of the out-party, particularly the losing presidential nominee. In an epoch of increasing executive power, there is no one to question the president of the U.S. except the members of the press, who do so primarily at the presidential press conferences. The president is not balanced, checked, and continuously debated by an adversary with the stature of an official leader of the opposition. Congressional leaders may, but more often do not, occasionally serve in this role. But the adversary of the minority leader of the Senate is the majority leader, not the president; the same is generally true for leaders in the House of Representatives. To rectify this imbalance in national leadership, it is suggested that the leader of the opposition needs official status, salary, a forum, and regular occasions for questioning and debating with the president.[9]

The problems of leadership structure in the out-party may be analyzed in more general terms.[10] Difficulties arise from internal factionalism, which, as this book describes, may be an indispensable feature of competition and democracy within the parties. But factional conflict may destroy any possibility of a united voice in the loyal opposition. Other difficulties would arise if opposition leadership were to reside solely in the congressional leadership. The electorates and party support systems of the members of Congress are quite different from those of the presidential electorate. Taken collectively, the constituencies of Congress, either as individual members or as separate houses, are different from those of the president, both by constitutional design and by well-tested institutional practice. In short, an opposition voice originating in Congress is likely to convey quite different messages from one reflecting the concerns of the presidential wing of the party.

The trials and tribulations of out-party titular leaders and residual chairmen as individual leaders have been amply described throughout this book. The same may be said of the various experiments in collective leadership, such as the Democratic Advisory Council of the Stevenson years. Sound working arrangements for collective leadership tend to be resisted by those party leaders whose political exposure derives largely from their incumbency at the head of one of the semiautonomous national agencies of the party. Factional leaders, particularly those with prospects for presidential nomination, tend to shy away from the constraints of collective leadership.

Then there are those who argue that the absence of a specific position of opposition leadership is a good thing. Such a void presumably leaves open many opportunities for factional adjustments and many avenues for the emergence of a fresh leadership in the out-party. Others make the case that there really are not so many factional accommodations to be made—unless, of course, a faction is preparing to bolt. Another often overlooked fact, they claim, is the dearth of leaders of presidential caliber and political availability; openness at the top of the out-party increases the chances of finding presidential talent.

To repeat, the constitutional and institutional context for this problem of leadership of the loyal opposition is the combination of a federal system of government and a system of separation of powers among the branches of government. If the major parties of the United States fell along the lines of the neat organizational pyramid of the textbook charts, the national chairman would be the chairman of the party's senior board of directors or its chief executive officer, the party's state central committees would be lined up fifty abreast in equal subordination to the national committee, and the organizational charts would show party units descending down the hierarchy to the precinct captain and precinct committees. But there is no party organizational hierarchy. The national committee is only one of several semiautonomous national agencies of the party. The route down to the precinct is a zigzagging and broken path, not a straight avenue.

Should the leadership of the opposition be explicitly assigned to the Speaker of the House of Representatives or his opposite number, the minority leader? Should the responsibility reside in the Senate with the majority leader or the minority leader, or possibly with the chairmen of the Senate Policy Committees? Should both houses be involved, as in the case of the "Ev and Charlie Show"? Perhaps the need could be filled by a newly structured national party chairmanship, whose incumbents are chosen by miniconventions, such as the Democratic national committee itself has become. Or should the status quo—no designated leader of the loyal opposition—continue?

The questions are not likely to rest or disappear. The trends in the party system are constantly evolving in ways that assure further formalization in the out-party. Among the relevant trends is, first, the increasingly evenly matched national competition between the parties. Second, there is the continued centralization and nationalization of the major parties, that is, growth in size, permanence, functions, and political importance of their national agencies. Third, intensified ideological orientations are complicating as well as compelling improved coordination of party policy positions. Fourth, there is a tendency toward more direct and sustained contact between the national party agencies and the national electorate by way of the media, direct mail, computerized data-gathering, and other means, all of which may enable the national committees to provide more of the precinct-type services of earlier eras. Fifth, the stabilization of factionalism within each of the parties may compel the national chairmen and national headquarters more into the mold of factionally impartial service agencies.

All of these tendencies are likely to make the void in the leadership of the loyal opposition institutionally less and less tolerable. However, a sixth factor may be perhaps the most important of all. Belated on-the-job training of the presidential leaders of a minority party that may become a majority may be too costly and too risky, given the accelerated pace and unpredictability of modern politics. A designated leader of the loyal opposition may well be an essential component for preparing and maintaining a minority fit to govern.

Notes

Preface

1. For a definition and typology of factionalism, Mark N. Hagopian, *Regimes, Movements, and Ideologies* (New York: Longman, 1978), pp. 323–26. Also, Giovanni Sartori, *Parties and Party Systems* (Cambridge: Cambridge University Press, 1976), chap. 4.

2. "Intensity, Visibility, Direction and Scope," *American Political Science Review*, vol. 51 (December 1957), pp. 933–42 passim.

3. Ralph M. Goldman, "A Theory of Conflict Processes and Organizational Offices," *Journal of Conflict Resolution*, vol. 10 (September 1966), no. 3, pp. 328–43.

Chapter 1

1. Roy Franklin Nichols, *The Disruption of American Democracy* (New York: Macmillan, 1948).

2. Jackson to Randolph, November 11, 1831, Andrew Jackson Papers, Library of Congress (hereafter referred to as L.C.).

3. Charles M. Wiltse, *John C. Calhoun, Nullifier, 1829–1839*, 3 vols. (Indianapolis: Bobbs-Merrill, 1949), vol. 2, pp. 16–18.

4. Lewis to Kendall, May 25, 1831, in "Origins of the Democratic Convention," *American Historical Magazine and Tennessee Historical Quarterly* (July 1902), pp. 267–73.

5. John Spencer Bassett, *The Life of Andrew Jackson* (New York: Macmillan, 1928).

6. Letter of February 12, 1832, quoted by Bassett, *ibid.*, p. 543.

7. *Proceeding of Convention of Republican Delegates, Baltimore, 1832* (Baltimore: 1832); for the version of the New York delegation, *Proceeding of a Convention of Republican Delegates at Baltimore, May 1832* (Albany: 1832).

8. Leon W. Cone, Jr., "Martin Van Buren: The Architect of the Democratic Party, 1837–1840" (Ph.D. dissertation in History, University of Chicago, 1950), pp. 85–86.

9. *Autobiography of Martin Van Buren*, ed. by John C. Fitzpatrick, 2 vols. (New York: Da Capo Press, 1973); quoted by Cone, "Martin Van Buren," pp. 124–25.

10. *Niles' Weekly Register* (Baltimore), May 23, 1835.

11. *Ibid.*, May 30, 1835; Erik McKinley Eriksson, "Official Newspaper Organs and the Presidential Elections of 1828, 1832, and 1836," *Tennessee Historical Magazine*, vols. 8–9 (1927–1928), part 3, p. 7.

12. Cone, "Martin Van Buren," p. 92. The discussion of events in the Van Buren administration is based in large part on Cone.

13. *Abridgement of the Debates of Congress, 1788–1856* (New York: D. Appleton and Co., 1857–1861).

14. *Ibid.*, vol. 13, p. 567.

15. *Ibid.*, p. 568.

16. Cone, "Martin Van Buren," p. 275.

Chapter 2

1. Leon W. Cone, Jr., "Martin Van Buren: The Architect of the Democratic Party, 1837–1840" (Ph.D. dissertation in History, University of Chicago, 1950), pp. 193–94.

2. Letter of November 7, 1840, in John Spencer Bassett, ed., *The Correspondence of Andrew Jackson*, 7 vols. (Washington, DC: The Carnegie Institution of Washington, 1926–1935), vol. 6, p. 81.

3. James C.N. Paul, *Rift in the Democracy* (Philadelphia: University of Pennsylvania Press, 1951), p. 25.

4. For some time the only full biographical account of Walker was a typewritten manuscript in the Library of Congress, under the custody of Emil Hurja: William E. Dodd's address at Randolph-Macon Women's College, entitled "Robert J. Walker, Imperialist" (April 15, 1914). George W. Brown's *Reminiscences of Governor R.J. Walker* (Rockford, IL: Printed by the author, 1902) is of little value. A doctoral dissertation on Walker is James P. Shenton, "The Complete Politician—The Life of Robert John Walker" (Ph.D. dissertation in History, Columbia University, 1955).

5. Denis T. Lynch, *An Epoch and a Man; Martin Van Buren and His Times*, 2 vols. (Port Washington, NY: Kennikat Press, 1971 [1929]), pp. 477, 479, 483.

6. A substantial part of the account that follows is based upon Robert S. Lambert, "The Democratic Party, 1841–1844" (Ph.D. dissertation in History, University of North Carolina, 1950).

7. Green to Calhoun, November 10, 1842, Calhoun Papers, Library of Clemson Agricultural College, South Carolina.

8. Cass to Green, January 29, 1844, Green Papers, Library of Congress, Box 1, Folder E, cited by Lambert, "The Democratic Party," p. 92.

9. Letter #25, May 13, 1844, James K. Polk, *Letters of James K. Polk to Cave Johnson* (Nashville: Tennessee Historical Magazine, 1915).

10. *Baltimore Sun*, May 28–31, 1844; *Niles' National Register* (Baltimore), June 1, 1844. Compare *Richmond Enquirer*, June 4, 1844, which reported that "Mr. Walker moved the appointment of a Central Committee of sixteen—which was agreed to. The Committee will be announced hereafter."

11. Samuel H. Laughlin to Polk, June 11 and 18, 1844, Polk Papers, L.C. Regarding the precedents set by the 1844 central committee, see James A. Farley, "History and Functions of the National Committee," Address delivered before the American Political Science Association, December 29, 1933 (Washington, DC: U.S. Government Printing Office, 1934). Even during the 1844 campaign, the novelty of having a national central committee resident in Washington caused some public confusion about the difference between the Democratic Central Committee and the District of Columbia Democratic Association. The latter was concerned with local aspects of the party's affairs. See District of Columbia Democratic Association, *Address* (Washington, DC: September 20, 1844).

12. Eugene I. McCormac, *James E. Polk; A Political Biography* (Berkeley, CA: University of California Press, 1922), p. 285; Dorothy C. Fowler, *The Cabinet Politician; The Postmasters-General, 1829–1909* (New York: Columbia University Press, 1943), p. 54;

Lyon G. Tyler, *Parties and Patronage in the United States* (New York: G.P. Putnam's Sons, 1891), pp. 83–84.

13. Walker to Polk, June 18, 1844, Polk Papers, L.C.

14. Walker to Polk, July 11, 1844, Jackson to Polk, July 26, 1844, Polk Papers, L.C.

15. William E. Dodd, "Robert J. Walker, Imperialist." April 15, 1914, Typewritten copy of address given at Randolph-Macon Women's College, L.C.; *National Intelligencer* (Washington, DC), October 3 and 29, 1844; *Globe* (Washington, DC), October 3, 1844; William E. Cramer to Polk, October 4, 1844, Polk Papers, L.C.

16. Roy Franklin Nichols, "The Democratic Machine, 1850–54" (Ph.D. dissertation in Political Science, Columbia University, 1923; New York: AMS Press, 1967), p. 2.

17. Fowler, *op. cit.*, Appendix 3.

18. Andrew Jackson to Francis P. Blair, February 8, 1845, cited in letter by Dr. James W. Smith in *New York Magazine* (October 9, 1955).

19. Milo Milton Quaife, *The Diary of James K. Polk*, 4 vols. (Chicago: A.C. McClurg, 1910), vol. 1, pp. 235, 264–65, 362.

20. *Ibid.*, vol. 1, p. 266, vol. 3, pp. 448ff.

21. *Ibid.*, vol. 2, p. 347.

22. *Ibid.*, pp. 306–7, 392.

23. *Ibid.*, vol. 3, pp. 256–57.

24. Johnson to Buchanan, October 14, 1849, December 13, 1850, and later correspondence between the two men, James Buchanan Papers, Historical Society of Pennsylvania.

25. McCormac, *James E. Polk*, p. 715.

26. "Selection of Candidate for President in 1848," Memorandum in Gideon Welles Papers, L.C.

27. *Ibid.*

28. *Union* (Washington, DC), January 25, 1848. The *Union* was the Polk newspaper in Washington.

29. According to the delegate list in the *The Campaign* (Washington, DC), May 31, 1848, Toner Collection, L.C., Senator Bright was an alternate delegate to the convention. *The Campaign* was a campaign weekly issued by the Democrats.

30. Different versions of this final resolution appear in the *Proceedings of the Democratic National Convention, 1848* (Washington, DC: Blair-Rives, 1848), in *The Campaign* (Washington, DC), and in *National Intelligencer*, May 27, 1848.

31. *Ibid.*

32. *Ibid.*

33. Text in *The Campaign* (Washington, DC), October 20, 25, 1848.

34. *The Campaign* (Washington, DC), June 21, 1848; Gideon Welles, "Memorandum on Election of 1848" (written about 1855), Welles Papers, L.C.

Chapter 3

1. Letter to Bushrod Washington, November 15, 1786, in J. C. Fitzgerald, ed., *The Writings of George Washington*, vol. 29 (Bicentennial Edition, Washington, DC: U.S. Government Printing Office, 1940), p. 67.

2. Letter to Bayard, April, 1802, in John C. Hamilton, ed., *The Works of Alexander Hamilton* (New York: John F. Trow, 1851), vol. 6, pp. 540–43.

3. John S. Murdock, "The First National Nominating Convention," *American Historical Review*, vol. 1 (July 1896), p. 680; Samuel E. Morrison, "The First National Nominating Convention, 1808," *American Historical Review*, vol. 17 (July 1912), p. 744.

4. Florence Weston, *The Presidential Election of 1828* (Washington, DC: Ruddick Press, 1938), pp. 99–103, 113–14, 155, 159.

5. Samuel R. Gammon, Jr., *The Presidential Campaign of 1832*, Johns Hopkins University Studies in Historical and Political Science (Baltimore: Johns Hopkins Press, 1922), vol. 40, pp. 45–52; *Proceedings of the Second United States Anti-Masonic Convention, Baltimore, September, 1831* (Boston: Boston Type and Stereotype Foundry, 1832).

6. Clay to B.W. [Heyb?], December 22, 1824, Henry Clay Manuscripts, New York Public Library.

7. Henry Adams, *The Degradation of the Democratic Dogma* (New York: Macmillan, 1920), p. 85.

8. *Autobiography of Thurlow Weed*, ed. by Harriet A. Weed and Thurlow Weed Barnes, 2 vols. (Boston: Houghton Mifflin Co., 1884), vol. 1, p. 180.

9. E. Malcolm Carroll, *Origins of the Whig Party* (Durham, NC: Duke University Press, 1925), p. 20.

10. *The Memoirs of John Quincy Adams*, ed. by Charles Francis Adams, 12 vols. (Philadelphia: J.B. Lippincott, 1876), vol. 6, p. 296, vol. 7, pp. 468–69.

11. James Truslow Adams, *The Adams Family* (Boston: Little, Brown, 1930), pp. 177, 179, 197.

12. Webster to Clay, May 29, 1830, cited by Carroll, *Origins of the Whig Party*, p. 68.

13. Erik McKinley Eriksson, "Official Newspaper Organs and the Presidential Elections of 1828, 1832, and 1836," *The Tennessee Historical Magazine* (1827–28), part 3, pp. 38–42.

14. Irving Stone, *They Also Ran* (Garden City, NY: Doubleday, Doran, 1954), p. 52.

15. Bernard Mayo, *Henry Clay, Spokesman of the New West* (Hamden, CT: Archon Books, 1966), pp. 383, 423; George D. Prentice, *Biography of Henry Clay* (New York: J.J. Phelps, 1831), pp. 80, 162, 168.

16. Another reason for lagging grass-roots organization by the Whigs may have been that, according to Glyndon G. Van Deusen, "Whig leadership in the Jackson period was too realistic to oppose universal manhood suffrage, but its acceptance could scarely be termed enthusiastic." "Some Aspects of Whig Thought and Theory in the Jacksonian Period," *American Historical Review* (January 1958), p. 309.

17. Jabez D. Hammond, *The Political History of New York*, 4th ed., 2 vols. (Buffalo: Phinney and Co., 1850), vol. 2, p. 419.

18. Carroll, *Origins of the Whig Party*, pp. 31–33.

19. Gammon, *Campaign of 1832*, p. 60.

20. *Journal of the National Republican Convention, December 12, 1831* (Washington, DC: Office of the National Journal, 1831).

21. Weed was never a national committee chairman. However, he was in many respects a long-time equivalent of one, although a poorly remembered figure in the development of the United States party system. Hence, his brief biographical sketch is included here.

22. Glydon G. Van Deusen, *Thurlow Weed: Wizard of the Lobby* (Boston: Little, Brown, 1947), pp. 66–69.

23. Eriksson, "Official Newspaper Organs," part 2, p. 1.

24. Horace Greeley, *Recollections of a Busy Life* (New York: The Tribune Association, 1873), p. 111.

25. *National Intelligencer* (Washington, DC), July 8, 1835.

26. Freeman Cleaves, *Old Tippecanoe; William Henry Harrison and His Times* (New York: Scribner's, 1939), p. 299.

27. Carroll, *Origins of the Whig Party*, pp. 128–29.

28. *National Intelligencer* (Washington, DC), December 24, 1835.

29. Carroll, *Origins of the Whig Party*, pp. 157–58; Van Deusen, *Thurlow Weed*, p. 110; Clay to Colonel A. Hamilton, August 28, 1838, Henry Clay Manuscripts, New York Public Library.

30. Greeley, *Recollections*, pp. 133–34.

31. George R. Poage, *Henry Clay and the Whig Party* (Chapel Hill: University of North Carolina Press, 1936), pp. 18–19.

32. Robert J. Morgan, *A Whig Embattled; the Presidency under John Tyler* (Lincoln: University of Nebraska Press, 1954), pp. 18ff.

33. *Ibid.*, pp. 40–43.

34. *Ibid.*, p. 158.

35. *Ibid.*, p. 159.

36. Proceedings of the Whig national convention reported in *Niles' National Register* (Baltimore, MD), May 4, 1844.

Chapter 4

1. Weed to Patterson, April 9, 1848, quoted in Holman Hamilton, *Zachary Taylor; Soldier in the White House*, 2 vols. (Indianapolis: Bobbs-Merrill, 1941–1951), vol. 2, p. 74.

2. Arthur C. Cole, *The Whig Party in the South* (Washington, DC: American Historical Association, 1913), pp. 128–29.

3. George R. Poage, *Henry Clay and the Whig Party* (Chapel Hill: University of North Carolina Press, 1936), p. 169.

4. *Ibid.*, p. 179.

5. Hamilton, *Zachary Taylor*, pp. 88–89.

6. Harry J. Carman and Reinhard H. Luthin, "The Seward-Fillmore Feud and the Disruption of the Whig Party," *New York History* (April-July 1943), pp. 163–84, 335–57.

7. Hamilton, *Zachary Taylor*, pp. 168–71, 207ff.

8. Ulrich B. Phillips, "The Southern Whigs," in Guy Stanton Ford, ed., *Turner Essays in American History* (New York: Henry Holt, 1910).

9. Poage, *Clay and Whig Party*, pp. 266–75.

10. *Baltimore Sun*, June 22, 1852; *National Intelligencer* (Washington, DC), June 23, 1852.

11. Horace Greeley, *Recollections of a Busy Life* (Port Washington, NY: Kennikat Press, 1971), p. 285.

12. James A. Rawley, *Edwin D. Morgan, 1811–1883; Merchant in Politics* (New York: AMS Press, 1968).

13. William E. Smith, *The Francis Preston Blair Family in Politics*, 2 vols. (New York, Macmillan Co., 1933), vol. 1, pp. 320–21; Roy Franklin Nichols, *Franklin Pierce; Young Hickory of the Granite Hills* (Philadelphia: University of Pennsylvania Press, 1931), pp. 446–48; Gordon S.P. Kleeberg, *The Formation of the Republican Party as a National Political Organization* (New York: Moods, 1911), pp. 23–26.

14. Jeter A. Isely, *Horace Greeley and the Republican Party, 1853–1861* (Princeton: Princeton University Press, 1947), pp. 158–59, 163, 166; Russell Errett, "The Republican Nominating Conventions of 1856 and 1860," *Magazine of Western History* (July 1889), p. 262; William E. Smith, *The Blair Family*, pp. 331, 342–43; Ruhl Jacob Bartlett, *John C. Fremont and the Republican Party*, Contributions in History and Political Science (Columbus: Ohio State University, ca. 1930), pp. 15–16. According to Errett, it was

Weed who "fathered the movement for Fremont." It seems that the Chase supporters were the only major group without direct representation at this conference.

15. *Proceedings of the First Three Republican National Conventions* (Minneapolis: C.W. Johnson, 1893).

16. Isely, *Horace Greeley*, p. 152, and Andrew W. Crandall, *The Early History of the Republican Party, 1854–1856* (Boston: Richard G. Badger, 1930), pp. 50–53, both agree that the Pittsburgh convention was at first a pro-Chase meeting.

17. *Proceedings of the First Three Republican National Conventions*, p. 7.

18. Roy F. Nichols, "Some Problems of the First Republican Presidential Campaign, *American Historical Review*, 28 (April 1923), pp. 492–96; James A. Rawley, "Financing the Fremont Campaign," *Pennsylvania Magazine of History and Biography*, 75 (January 1951), pp. 25–35; I.T. Martin, *Recollections of Elizabeth Benton Fremont* (New York: Frederick H. Hitchcock, 1912).

19. Rawley, "Financing the Fremont Campaign."

20. Morgan to Welles, May 22, 1858, Gideon Welles Papers, L.C.

21. David M. Potter, *Lincoln and His Party in the Secession Crisis* (New Haven: Yale University Press, 1942), p. 30; Alexander Hawley to Chandler, May 19, 1859, Zachariah Chandler Papers, L.C.

22. William Baringer, *Lincoln's Rise to Power* (Boston: Little, Brown, 1937), p. 131; William E. Smith, *The Blair Family*, vol. 1. p. 473.

23. Baringer, *op. cit.*, pp. 127, 248, 278.

24. *Caucuses of 1860* (Columbus: Follett, Poster, 1860), pp. 121 ff.

25. Baringer, *Lincoln's Rise to Power*, p. 238.

26. *Autobiography of Thurlow Weed*, ed. by Harriet A. Weed and Thurlow Weed Barnes, 2 vols. (Boston: Houghton Mifflin, 1884), vol. 2, p. 264.

Chapter 5

1. Roy Franklin Nichols, "The Democratic Machine, 1850–1854" (Ph.D. dissertation in Political Science, Columbia University, 1923; New York: AMS Press, 1967), pp. 26–29. The Union party idea did not take hold until the Republicans adopted it in 1864.

2. Nichols, "The Democratic Machine," pp. 52–55, 82, 90, 124–25, 126–27, *passim*; Roy Franklin Nichols, *Franklin Pierce; Young Hickory of the Granite Hills* (Philadelphia: University of Pennsylvania Press, 1931), pp. 188, 190–91.

3. Robert M. McLane, *Reminiscences, 1827–1897* (privately printed, 1903), p. 106.

4. Burke to Pierce, June 24, 1852, Pierce Papers, L.C.

5. July 13, 1852, Pierce Papers, L.C.

6. Burke to Pierce, June 6, 24, 1852, Pierce Papers, L.C.

7. Letter to Isaac Davis, July 5, 1852, Isaac Davis Papers, American Antiquarian Society.

8. McLane, *Reminiscences*, p. 124; Nichols, "The Democratic Machine," pp. 147–48, 161–62; Nichols, *Franklin Pierce*, p. 214; Grant Green to J.C. Breckinridge, July 30, 1852, Breckinridge Family Papers, L.C.; J.S. Thomas to Marcy, July 19, 29, 31, 1852, Marcy Papers, L.C.

9. Buchanan to Marcy, August 23, 1852, Marcy Papers, L.C.

10. August Belmont to Buchanan, March 5, 1853, Buchanan Papers, Historical Society of Pennsylvania.

11. Allan Nevins, *Ordeal of the Union*, 2 vols. (New York: Charles Scribner's Sons, 1947), vol. 2, p. 453; Nichols, *Franklin Pierce*, p. 451.

12. Nichols, *Franklin Pierce*, pp. 454, 457, 464; Roy Franklin Nichols, *The Disruption of American Democracy* (New York: Macmillan, 1948) p. 12; John Bassett Moore,

ed., *The Works of James Buchanan* (Philadelphia: J.B. Lippincott, 1900–1911), vol. 10. p. 8; Nevins, *Ordeal of the Union*, vol. 2, pp. 453, 456; Louis M. Sears, *John Slidell* (Durham, NC: Duke University Press, 1925), pp. 122–23.

13. *Proceedings of the National Democratic Convention, held in Cincinnati, June 2–6, 1956* (Cincinnati: Enquirer Steam Print Co., 1856).

14. *Ibid.*

15. Nichols, *Franklin Pierce*, pp. 464, 466–69, Nichols, *Disruption of American Democracy*, pp. 17, 49–50; *New York Times*, June 11, 1856; Nevins, *Ordeal of the Union*, vol. 2, pp. 458–59.

16. *Union* (Washington, DC), July 10, 1856.

17. C.L. Ward to Buchanan, June 28, 1856, Buchanan Papers, Historical Society of Pennsylvania.

18. Charles Faulkner to Buchanan, July 4, 1856, Buchanan Papers, Historical Society of Pennsylvania.

19. Glancy Jones to Buchanan, June 30, July 10, 20, 1856; Howell Cobb to Buchanan, July 14, 1856; C.L. Ward to Buchanan, July 20, 1856; Buchanan Papers, Historical Society of Pennsylvania.

20. Ward to Buchanan, July 23, August 27, 1856, Buchanan Papers, Historical Society of Pennsylvania.

21. Nichols, *Disruption of American Democracy*, pp. 57, 62–63, 285–86; Sears, *John Slidell*, pp. 138–39, 148–49, 159–60; Reinhard H. Luthin, "The Democratic Split During Buchanan's Administration," *Pennsylvania History* (January 1944), pp. 13–35; Allen Johnson, *Stephen A. Douglas; A Study in American Politics* (New York: Macmillan, 1908), pp. 325, 334.

22. This endorsement was not hastily given, for it was under consideration by the Republican national committee as early as 1857. William M. Chance to Welles, November 3, 1857, Gideon Welles Papers, L.C.

23. Lawrence T. Lowrey, "Northern Opinion of Approaching Secession," *Smith College Studies in History* (July 1918), pp. 241, 257. For insight into the character of the Southern secessionists, see Ralph A. Wooster, "The Secession Conventions of the Lower South: A Study of Their Membership" (Ph.D. dissertation in History, University of Texas, 1954). Wooster studied the social attributes of the 948 delegates to the first seven secession state conventions, and concluded that these delegates did represent "a popular movement." Wooster found that ten former United States senators and twenty-four former representatives were among the 948 delegates.

24. Ollinger Crenshaw, *The Slave States in the Presidential Election of 1860* (Baltimore: Johns Hopkins Press, 1945).

25. *Congressional Globe* (May 17, 1860), p. 2152.

26. Emerson D. Fite, *Presidential Campaign of 1860* (New York: Macmillan, 1911), pp. 207, 225. Written on June 29, 1960, the Pierce letter was reported in the *New York Times* of July 18, 1960.

27. *Ibid.*, p. 225.

28. Elbert J. Benton, *The Movement for Peace Without a Victory During the Civil War*, 99 (Cleveland: Western Reserve Historical Society Collections, December 1918).

29. *Ibid.*

30. August Belmont, *Letters, Speeches, and Addresses* (Privately printed, 1890), p. 24.

31. Perry Belmont, *An American Democrat; The Recollections of Perry Belmont*, 2d ed. (New York: Columbia University Press, 1941), p. 76.

32. August Belmont, *Letters*, pp. 35, 40, 41, 45–50.

33. William Starr Myers, *General George Brinton McClellan* (New York: D. Appleton-Century, 1934), pp. 425, 444.

34. August Belmont, *Letters*, p. 116.

35. *New York Times*, November 1, 2, 1864

Chapter 6

1. John Bigelow, *Letters and Literary Memorials of Samuel J. Tilden*, 2 vols. (New York: Harper and Bros., 1908), vol. 1, pp. 218, 233–36.

2. The pervasive significance of the money question for factionalism in both parties is carefully analyzed by Robert P. Sharkey, *Money, Class, and Party* (Baltimore: Johns Hopkins Press, 1959).

3. *Official Proceedings of the National Democratic Convention, held in New York, July 4–9, 1868* (Boston: Rockwell and Rollins, 1868).

4. *New York Times*, July 10, 1872. The committee vote was reported in *New York Times*, July 11, 1972.

5. Francis Schell, *Memoir of Augustus Schell* (New York: Privately printed, 1885).

6. October 5, 1872.

7. *New York Times*, November 13, 1872.

8. Allan Nevins, *Abram S. Hewitt* (New York: Harper and Bros., 1935); Allan Nevins, *Selected Writings of Abram S. Hewitt* (New York: Columbia University Press, 1937).

9. *New York Times*, March 12 and December 7, 1875, January 29, 1876; Randolph to Marble, April 7 and 10, 1876, Manton Marble Papers, L.C.

10. Orin G. Libby, "A Study of the Greenback Movement, 1876–1884," *Transactions of the Wisconsin Academy of Sciences, Arts and Letters*, vol. 12, part 2 (1899).

11. Pelton to Marble, April 1, 1876, Marble Papers, L.C.

12. Nevins, *Hewitt*, p. 307.

13. Nevins, *Writings of Hewitt*, pp. 159ff.

14. *New York Times*, August 3, 1876; Nevins, *Writings of Hewitt*, pp. 159ff.

15. Alexander C. Flick, *Samuel Jones Tilden: A Study in Political Sagacity* (New York: Dodd, Mead, 1939), pp. 303, 316, chap. 25 passim.

16. Nevins, *Hewitt*, pp. 214–315; Nicholas Murray Butler, *Across the Busy Years*, 2 vols. (New York: Scribner's, 1935), vol. 1, pp. 306–7. According to Butler, Hewitt recounted the story in 1891 as part of an explanation of how Grover Cleveland came to be in the White House instead of Hewitt himself. Hewitt was one of the few national chairmen seriously rated as presidential timber.

17. Flick, *A Study*, pp. 324–25. Greater detail may be found in Leon B. Richardson, *William E. Chandler, Republican* (New York: Dodd, Mead, 1940), pp. 184–88.

18. Letter to Governor Hayes, December 12, 1876, cited in Hodding Carter, *The Angry Scar* (Garden City, NY: Doubleday, 1959), pp. 330ff.

19. C. Vann Woodward, *Reunion and Reaction* (Boston: Little, Brown, 1951).

20. Nevins, *Hewitt*, p. 390.

21. *New York World*, March 5, 1877; *Daily Free Press and Times* (Burlington, VT), March 6, 1877.

22. *New York Times*, May 12, 1876, October 19, 1882.

23. *Ibid.*, September 25, 1879, May 10, 1880.

24. Nevins, *Hewitt*, pp. 391–98.

25. *New York Times*, July 1, 1880.

26. *Ibid.*, September 14, 15, 16, 1879; Mark D. Hirsch, *William C. Whitney, Modern Warwick* (New York: Dodd, Mead, 1948), pp. 149–54.

27. *New York Times*, May 9, 1880.

28. *New York Tribune*, June 12, 1880.

29. Reverend Herbert J. Clancy, *The Presidential Election of 1880* (Chicago: Loyola University Press, 1958), pp. 143–44.

30. Manton Marble Papers, vol. 53, no. 248.

31. Quoted by Clancy, *The Presidential Election*, p. 144 fn. For one observer's interpretation of Tilden's intent, William C. Hudson, *Random Recollections of an Old Political Reporter* (New York: Cupples and Leon, 1911), p. 110.

32. Smith M. Weed to Tilden, June 25, 1880, Tilden Manuscripts, New York Public Library.

33. *New York Times*, June 30, July 1, 5, 12, 13, 14, 1880.

34. John Hunter to Bayard, July 13 and 17, 1880, Thomas F. Bayard Manuscripts, L.C.

35. Nevins, *Hewitt*, p. 185.

36. *Ibid.*, pp. 435–37; Robert G. Caldwell, *James A. Garfield, Party Chieftain* (New York: Dodd, Mead, 1931), pp. 308ff.; *New York Times*, October 31, November 3, 1880, March 7, 1881.

37. Almira Russell Hancock, *Reminiscences of Winfield Scott Hancock* (New York: C.L. Webster, 1887), p. 175.

38. Hirsch, *William C. Whitney*, pp. 160–73, 180–86.

39. *New York Times*, May 10, 1884.

40. Although never national chairman, Gorman's influence in the party led many to believe over the years that he had held that office. Gorman knew the halls of Congress well. At thirteen he had been a page in the House, transferred to the Senate upon the request of Senator Stephen A. Douglas. In the Senate, he rose to the office of postmaster, was removed in 1866, and immediately appointed as collector of internal revenue in his home state. He advanced rapidly in Maryland politics, becoming speaker of the state House of Delegates and a state senator. He was elected president of the Chesapeake and Ohio Canal Company in 1872. When elected to the United States Senate in 1881, he was thoroughly in control of the state's Democratic organization and recognized as a political campaigner of no ordinary talent, well fortified by a large personal fortune.

41. *New York Times*, July 19, 22, 24, 1884; Marvin H. Bovee to Vilas, July 19, 1884, quoted in Dorothy G. Fowler, *The Cabinet Politician; The Postmasters-General, 1829–1909* (New York: Columbia University Press, 1943), p. 189.

42. Allan Nevins, *Grover Cleveland: A Study in Courage* (New York: Dodd, Mead, 1932), p. 163.

43. Whitney to Cleveland, December, 1884, Cleveland Papers, L.C.

44. Gorman to Manning, January 5, 1885, Cleveland Papers, L.C.

45. At the New York state convention of 1885, Cleveland supporters tried without success to block Hill's nomination for governor. Hill never forgave Cleveland's opposition.

Chapter 7

1. Burton J. Hendrick, *Lincoln's War Cabinet* (Boston: Little, Brown, 1946), pp. 113–23; for Seward's views on presidential-cabinet relations, pp. 80–81.

2. *Detroit Post and Tribune, Zachariah Chandler; His Life and Public Services* (1880); Wilmer C. Harris, *Public Life of Zachariah Chandler, 1851–1875* (Lansing: Michigan Historical Commission, 1917).

3. Philip S. Foner, *Business and Slavery; The New York Merchants and the Irrepressible Conflict* (Chapel Hill: University of North Carolina Press, 1941), chap. 14.

4. Hendrick, *Lincoln's War Cabinet*, p. 356.

5. *Ibid.*, pp. 331–47.

6. *Ibid.*

7. William A. Dunning, "The Second Birth of the Republican Party," *American Historical Review*, 16 (October 1910), pp. 56–63.

8. Glyndon G. Van Deusen, *Thurlow Weed, Wizard of the Lobby* (Boston: Little, Brown, 1947), p. 320.

9. Hendrick, *Lincoln's War Cabinet*, pp. 404–5.

10. *Ibid.*, p. 421. Ruhl J. Bartlett, *John C. Fremont and the Republican Party* (New York: Da Capo, 1970), chap. 7.

11. Augustus Maverick, *Henry J. Raymond and the New York Press for Thirty Years* (Hartford, CT: A.S. Hale, 1870); Ernest Francis Brown, *Raymond of the Times* (Westport, CT: Greenwood, 1970); Greeley letter, June 1864, Abraham Lincoln Papers, L.C.

12. *Proceedings of the First Three Republican National Conventions of 1856, 1860, and 1864* (Minneapolis: C.W. Johnson, 1893). There were twenty-seven Republican national committee members chosen at the 1860 national convention. Only sixteen of this original group were still members at the February 22, 1864, meeting, seven others were new, and four states—Virginia, Missouri, Texas, and Oregon—were unrepresented. The national committee had apparently used its power to fill vacancies where unsympathetic state organizations refused to send representatives.

13. Frederick C. Meyer, chairman of the executive committee issuing the convention call, to Lincoln, June 7, 1864, Lincoln Paper, L.C.

14. Van Duesen, *Thurlow Weed*, pp. 307–8; Ward Lamon to Lincoln, June 7, 1864, Lincoln Papers, L.C.; George B. Lincoln to Johnson, June 11, 1864, Andrew Johnson Papers, L.C.

15. *Proceedings of the First Three Republican National Conventions of 1856, 1860, and 1864; New York Times*, June 9, 11, 1865.

16. Raymond to Cameron, August 19, 21, 1864, Cameron Papers, L.C.

17. The election of 1864 is examined in detail by William F. Zornow, *Lincoln and the Party Divided* (Norman: University of Oklahoma Press, 1954).

18. *Twenty Years of Congress*, 2 vols. (Norwich, CT: Henry Bill, 1886), vol. 2, pp. 118–21.

19. Harriet A. Weed and Thurlow Weed Barnes, eds., *Autobiography of Thurlow Weed*, vol. 2, pp. 450–52 (Boston: Houghton Miffin, 1884).

20. William E. Smith, *The Francis Preston Blair Family in Politics*, 2 vols. (New York: Macmillan, 1933), vol. 2, p. 329.

21. Weed and Barnes, eds., *Autobiography*, vol. 2, pp. 450–52.

22. H.W. Raymond, "Extracts from the Journal of Henry J. Raymond," *Scribner's Monthly Magazines* (June 1880), pp. 275ff.

23. Simon Cameron to C.A. Dana, August 12, 1866, Cameron Papers, L.C.; Samuel Purviance to Ward, August 20, 1866, Marcus L. Ward Papers, New Jersey Historical Society.

24. *National Intelligencer* (Washington, DC), August 16, 17, 1866.

25. Purviance to Ward, August 20, 1866, Ward Papers, New Jersey Historical Society.

26. *New York Times*, August 25, 1866; Ward to Defrees, August 25, 1866, Raymond to Ward, August 29, 1866, Ward Papers, New Jersey Historical Society.

27. *New York Tribune*, September 4–6, 1866; Howard K. Beale, *The Critical Year; A Study of Andrew Johnson and Reconstruction* (New York: Harcourt, Brace, 1930), pp. 184–87; Blaine, *Twenty Years of Congress*, vol. 2, p. 224.

28. *New York Tribune*, September 4, 1866; *New York Times*, September 4, 1866, January 18, 19, 1867.

29. *New York Tribune*, September 3, 4, 1866; Greeley to Ward, September 13, 1866, Ward to Defrees, September 14, 1866, Ward Papers, New Jersey Historical Society.

30. *The English Constitution*, rev. ed. (New York: D. Appleton, 1903), pp. lx-lxi.

Chapter 8

1. Gordon S.P. Kleeberg, *The Formation of the Republican Party as a National Political Organization* (New York: Moods, 1911), pp. 204–5. There is also circumstantial evidence that Lincoln in 1860 and again in 1864 was consulted and his views taken into account.

2. *New York Times*, September 10, 1868; Louis T. Merrill, "General Benjamin F. Butler and the Campaign of 1868" (Unpublished Ph.D. dissertation in History, University of Chicago, 1936), pp. 216–17; Claflin to Ward, September 28, 1868, Ward Papers, New Jersey Historical Society.

3. See chapter 6.

4. Leon B. Richardson, *William E. Chandler, Republican* (New York: Dodd, Mead, 1940), p. 128.

5. Earle D. Ross, *The Liberal Republican Movement* (New York: Henry Holt, 1919), chap. 7.

6. McCormick to Hayes, July 26, 1876, quoted in Dorothy G. Fowler, *The Cabinet Politician: The Postmasters-General, 1829–1909* (New York: Columbia University Press, 1943), p. 162.

7. Quoted in Claude G. Bowers, *The Tragic Era: The Revolution After Lincoln* (Boston: Houghton Mifflin, 1929), p. 485; *New York Times*, July 9, 13, 1876.

8. H.J. Eckenrode, *Rutherford B. Hayes: Statesman of Reunion* (New York: Dodd, Mead, 1930), p. 307.

9. Richardson, *William E. Chandler*, p. 247.

10. *New York Times*, May 10, 1878.

11. *Ibid.*, December 15, 17, 1879.

12. *Ibid.*, December 16, 18, 1879, March 26, 1880.

13. *Ibid.*, June 1, 2, 1880; Richardson, *William E. Chandler* (1940), pp. 249–53; William Starr Myers, *The Republican Party* (New York: Century Co., 1931), pp. 253–54; S.P. Brown to Chandler, May 29, 1880, Blaine to Chandler, June 1, 1880, William E. Chandler Papers, L.C.; *Proceedings of the Republican National Convention held in Chicago, June 2–8, 1880* (Chicago: J.B. Jeffrey, 1881).

14. Letter to George O. Odlin, April 14, 1880, William E. Chandler Papers, L.C.

15. Chandler to Garfield, June 14, 1880, William E. Chandler Papers, L.C.

16. *Ibid.*

17. Jewell to Chandler, June 15, 1880, William E. Chandler Papers, New Hampshire Historical Society.

18. Forbes to Garfield, June 20, 1880, copy of which was sent to Chandler, June 26, 1880, William E. Chandler Papers, L.C.

19. *New York Times*, June 22, July 1, 1880; Jewell to Chandler, June 24, 1880, William E. Chandler Papers, New Hampshire Historical Society.

20. Hale to Chandler, June 27, 1880, Forbes to Chandler, June 26, 1880, William E. Chandler Papers, L.C.; Jewell to Chandler, June 15, 1880, William E. Chandler Papers, New Hampshire Historical Society.

21. Forbes to Chandler, June 28, 1880, William E. Chandler Papers, L.C.

22. Forbes to Chandler, June 25, 1880, William E. Chandler Papers, L.C.

23. Blaine to Chandler, July 1, 1880, William E. Chandler Papers, L.C.

24. Theodore Clark Smith, *The Life and Letters of James Abram Garfield*, 2 vols. (New Haven: Yale University Press, 1925), vol. 2, pp. 999–1000.

25. *Ibid.*

26. *New York Times*, July 2, 3, 1880; Richardson, *William E. Chandler*, pp. 258–59; Smith, *Life of Garfield*, vol. 2, p. 1012; George F. Howe, *Chester A. Arthur; A Quarter-Century of Machine Politics* (New York: Dodd, Mead, 1934), p. 117.

27. McCormick to Chandler, August 13 and October 5, 1880, William E. Chandler Papers, L.C.

28. Jewell to Garfield, September 7, 1880, Garfield Manuscripts, L.C.

29. Jewell to Garfield, September 14, 1880, Garfield Manuscripts, L.C.

30. Jewell to William E. Chandler, March 22, 1881, Chandler Papers, New Hampshire Historical Society.

31. Vincent P. De Santis, *Republicans Face the Southern Question; The New Departure Years, 1877–1897* (Baltimore: Johns Hopkins Press, 1959).

32. *New York Times*, December 13, 1883.

33. *Ibid.*, December 12, 13, 14, 1883.

34. *Ibid.*, June 3, 1884.

35. Edmund M. Smith to Chandler, June 8, 1884, William E. Chandler Papers, L.C.; cf. Howe, *Chester A. Arthur*, p. 261.

36. *New York Times*, December 18, 1883, June 8, 1884.

37. *Iowa State Register* (Des Moines), July 1, 1884, quoting press opinion in other parts of the country.

38. Howe, *Chester A. Arthur*, pp. 279–80; *New York Times*, December 3, 1886.

39. Richardson, *William E. Chandler*, p. 354; *New York Times*, December 3, 1886.

40. *Iowa State Register* (Des Moines), November 22, 1884.

41. David S. Muzzey, *James G. Blaine: A Political Idol of Other Days* (New York: Dodd, Mead, 1934), p. 326.

Chapter 9

1. Allan Nevins, *Grover Cleveland: A Study in Courage* (New York: Dodd, Mead, 1932), pp. 371–82.

2. Whitney to Cleveland, December 11, 1887, Cleveland Papers, L.C.

3. *Official Proceedings of the National Democratic Convention, held in St. Louis, June 5–7, 1888* (St. Louis: Woodward and Tiernan, 1888); *New York Times*, February 23, 24, May 16, 1888.

4. *New York Times*, June 6, 1888.

5. Robert McElroy, *Grover Cleveland: The Man and the Statesman*, 2 vols. (New York: Harper and Bros., 1923), vol. 1., pp. 290–91. The implications of this account are accepted by Nevins, *Cleveland*, p. 401.

6. Cleveland to Bissell, June 17, 1888, Cleveland Papers, L.C.

7. *New York Times*, June 27, 1888.

8. *Proceedings of the National Democratic Convention, 1888*.

9. Scott to Lamont, July 9, 1888, P.W. Dawson to Cleveland, July 12, 1888, Cleveland Papers, L.C.

10. William C. Whitney to his wife Flora, July 17, 1888, Whitney Papers, L.C.

11. Barnum to Lamont, July 12, 1888, letterhead, Barnum to Lamont, September 25, 1888, Cleveland Papers, L.C.; Nevins, *Cleveland*, p. 416; *New York Times*, July 18, 1888.

12. Sheerin to Lamont, July 18, 1888; Brice to Lamont, August 4, 16, 1888; Chairman of New Canaan, Connecticut, Democratic Club to Lamont, August 8, 1888; Cleveland Papers, L.C.; *New York Times*, August 19, 1888; Albert Small to Harrison, July 20, 1888, Benjamin Harrison Papers, L.C.

13. Parker to Lamont, August 18, 1888, Brice to Lamont, August 18, September 11, 1888, Cleveland Papers, L.C.

14. B.S. Johnston to Cleveland, May 14, 1889, Cleveland Papers, L.C.

15. *New York Times*, May 10, 11, June 12, 1889.

16. *Cincinnati Commercial Gazette*, June 16, 1890.

17. Nevins, *Cleveland*, p. 697.

18. *Ibid.*, pp. 467–69.

19. *Ibid.*, pp. 475–76.

20. *New York Times*, November 9, 1890; Al Carlile to Cleveland, April 5, 1892, Cleveland Papers, L.C.

21. *New York Times*, January 17, 1892.

22. *Ibid.*, October 1, 23, November 5, 1891, January 15, 16, 17, 21, 1892.

23. Cleveland to Whitney, March 19, 1892, Whitney Papers, L.C.

24. Charles Tracey to Whitney, June 9, 1892, Whitney Papers, L.C.

25. Harrity to Whitney, May 25, 26, 27, 28, 1892, Whitney Papers, L.C.

26. Dickinson to Whitney, June 1, 1892; Whitney's list of invitees, June 3, 1892, Whitney Papers, L.C.

27. Estimate sheet, item 13254, Whitney Papers, L.C.; Dorothy G. Fowler, *The Cabinet Politician: The Postmasters-General, 1829–1909* (New York: Columbia University Press, 1943), p. 226.

28. W.D. Chipley to Whitney, July 8, 1892, Whitney Papers, L.C.

29. Cleveland to Bissell, June 30, 1892, Cleveland Papers, L.C.

30. Vol. 68, Whitney Papers, L.C.

31. Holmes Cummins to Whitney, July 14, 1892, B.B. Smalley to Whitney, June 26, 1892, Whitney Papers, L.C.; Vilas to Dickinson, July 18, 1892, Dickinson Papers, L.C.

32. Jones to Dickinson, July 13, 1892, Dickinson Papers, L.C.

33. Harrity to Whitney, July 2, 8, 10, 14, 1892, Brice to Whitney, July 9, 1892, Cleveland to Whitney, July 9, 1892, Pattison to Whitney, July 11, 1892, Whitney Papers, L.C.

34. Mark D. Hirsch, *William C. Whitney, Modern Warwick* (New York: Dodd, Mead, 1948), p. 401.

35. Josiah Quincy to Whitney, October 13, 1892, Whitney Papers, L.C.

36. Whitney to Cleveland, July 10, 1892, Cleveland Papers, L.C.

37. Irving Stone, *They Also Ran* (Garden City, NY: Doubleday, Doran, 1954), p. 43. Bryan was born in Salem, Illinois, on March 19, 1860. In 1887, while traveling through Iowa and Kansas, Bryan stopped off at Lincoln, Nebraska, to visit a law school classmate who promptly offered him a partnership in a new law firm. Three years later, he was elected to the House of Representatives. Bryan was appointed to the powerful Ways and Means Committee while still a freshman as a consequence of his support of William Springer against Charles Crisp for the speakership. Bryan received the committee appointment as part of the compromise that elected Crisp. He quickly gained national prominence for his floor speeches in favor of tariff and currency reform.

38. George H. Knoles, *The Presidential Campaign and Election of 1892* (Stanford: Stanford University Press, 1942), p. 225.

39. *Ibid.*, pp. 246–47.

40. Nevins, *Cleveland*, chap. 31.

41. McElroy, *Cleveland*, vol. 2, pp. 113–14.

42. *New York Times*, August 15, 16, 18, 1895; Stone to Bryan, August 26, 1895, Tillman to Bryan, December 7, 1895, Towles to Bryan, March 26, 1896, Bryan Papers, L.C.

43. Cleveland to Dickinson, March 25, 1896, Grover Cleveland Manuscripts, L.C.

44. *Omaha World-Herald*, February 24, 1896.

45. Marion Butler to Bryan, January 8, 1896, George P. Keeney to Bryan, January 3,

1896, L.W. Rissler to Bryan, May 16, 1896, James B. Weaver to Bryan, December 31, 1895, January 3, May 29, 1896, William Jennings Bryan Papers, L.C. Elmer Ellis, "The Silver Republicans of the Election of 1896," *Mississippi Valley Historical Revew* (March 1932), pp. 519–34.

46. Altgeld to Bryan, June 12, 1896, Bryan Papers, L.C.

47. William Jennings Bryan, *Memoirs* (Chicago: John C. Winston Co., 1925), pp. 109–10.

48. Wayne C. Williams, *William Jennings Bryan* (New York: G.P. Putnam's Sons, 1936), p. 137.

49. *Ibid.*

50. Farrar Newberry, *James K. Jones; The Plumed Knight of Arkansas* (n.p.: Siftings-Herald, 1913), pp. 329–30.

51. Stone to Bryan, July 14, 1896, Bryan Papers, L.C.

52. Teller to Bryan, July 18, 1896, Bryan Papers, L.C.

53. C. Vann Woodward, *Tom Watson; Agrarian Rebel* (New York: Macmillan, 1938), pp. 289, 294–301, 315; James K. Jones to Bryan, July 21, 1896, Bryan Papers, L.C.

54. *New York Tribune*, July 27, 1896.

55. Allan Nevins, *Letters of Grover Cleveland, 1850–1908* (New York: Da Capo, 1970), p. 457; Cleveland to Judson Harmon, September 13, 1896, Cleveland Manuscripts, L.C.

56. W.D. Bynum to M.L. Crawford, November 18, 1896, W. D. Bynum Manuscripts, L.C.

57. William Jennings Bryan, *The First Battle* (Chicago: W.B. Conkey, 1896), pp. 385, 601.

Chapter 10

1. Sewall to Bryan, December 3, 1896, Tillman to Bryan, November 4, 1896, Bryan Papers, L.C.

2. *Detroit Tribune*, November 9, 1896, quoted by Joseph Schafer, Jr., "Presidential Election of 1896" (Ph.D. dissertation in History, University of Wisconsin, 1941).

3. St. John to Bryan, December 4, 8, 1896, Bryan Papers, L.C.; Wayne C. Williams, *William Jennings Bryan* (New York: G.P. Putnam's Sons, 1936), pp. 201, 204, 206.

4. Rosser to Bryan, November 2, 1896; Washburn to Bryan, November 4, 1896, January 8, 1897, Bryan Papers, L.C.

5. Mather Vrooman to Bryan, May 30, 1897, Jones to Bryan, April 21, 1900, Bryan Papers, L.C.

6. Jones to Bryan, December 19, 1896, Bryan Papers, L.C.

7. *New York Times*, October 4, 1898.

8. Harvey to members of the Ways and Means Committee, March 27, 1899, Bryan to Hearst, July 22, 1899, M.F. Dunlap to Bryan, December 1, 1899, Bryan Papers, L.C.; *Official Proceedings of the Democratic National Convention held in Kansas City, July 4–6, 1900* (1900); *New York Times*, May 25, 26, June 13, July 13, 17, 20, 21, 1899.

9. Bynum letters to L.C. Krauthoff, December 21, 1896, George Foster Peabody, December 12, 1896 and April 30, 1897, John P. Frenzel, June 30, 1897 and July 29, 1897, W. R. Shelby, July 3, 1898, William C. Whitney, August 24, 26, 1898, Charles J. Canda, August 25, 1898, Bynum Papers, L.C.; *New York Tribune*, July 15, 26, 27, October 6, 1900.

10. Mack to Bryan, July 19, 1900, Bryan Papers, L.C.

11. Thomas M. Patterson to Bryan, June 9, 1899, W.H. Thompson to Bryan, November 23, 1899, James Creelman to Bryan, April 22, 1900, John H. Girdner to Bryan, April

21, 28, May 29, June 16, 1900, Bryan Papers, L.C.; *New York Times*, July 4, 6, 7, 1900.

12. Jones to Bryan, February 1, 1898, Bryan Papers, L.C.

13. Jones to Bryan, January 17, 24, 30, 1899, Bryan Papers, L.C.

14. Jones to J.G. Johnson, May 3, 1900, Bryan Papers, L.C.

15. Sulzer to Bryan, April 2, 1900, Bryan Papers, L.C.

16. W.H. Thompson to Bryan, April 26, 1898, Jones to Bryan, April 29, May 9, 1898, D. Woodson to Bryan, May 2, 1898, Stone to Bryan, May 11, 1898, Thomas D. O'Brien to Bryan, May 13, 1898, C.S. Thomas to Bryan, May 18, 1898, John Gilbert Shanklin to Bryan, May 3, 1898, Joseph Howley to Bryan, May 4, 1898, Guffey to Bryan, May 14, 1898, Bryan Papers, L.C.; *New York Times*, June 7, 1898.

17. *New York Times*, July 24, February 22, 1899; Farrar Newberry, *James K. Jones; The Plumed Knight of Arkansas* (n.p.: Siftings–Herald Printing Co., 1913), p. 222; W.F. Sapp to Bryan, May 30, 1900, John W. Tomlinson to Bryan, June 28, 1899, Stone to Bryan, April 10, 1899, Bryan Papers, L.C.

18. *New York Times*, May 25, 26, June 13, 1899.

19. *Ibid.*, July 13, 17, 20, 21, August 31, 1899; Bryan to Hearst, July 22, 1899, M.F. Dunlap to Bryan, December 1, 1899, Bryan Papers, L.C.

20. *Official Proceedings of the National Democratic Convention, July 4–6, 1900* (Chicago: McLellan, 1900); *New York Times*, February 23, 24, 1900; *New York Tribune*, February 23, 1900; W.H. Thompson to Bryan, November 9, 1899, S.E. Morss to Bryan, February 17, 1900, James K. Jones to Bryan, December 18, 1899, Bryan Papers, L.C.

21. Girdner to Bryan, April 21, 1900, Jones to Bryan, April 26, 1900, Bryan Papers, L.C.; *New York Tribune*, May 11, July 2, 1900.

22. *New York Times*, January 5, 1900; Pettigrew to Bryan, June 9, 1900, Morss to Bryan, June 29, 1900, Bryan Papers, L.C.

23. Jones to Bryan, April 27, 1900, Bryan Papers, L.C.; *New York Times*, July 5, 13, 24, 1899.

24. *New York Times*, June 29, 1900.

25. *Ibid.*, September 1, October 9, 1900; Willis J. Abbot, "The Management of the Democratic Campaign," *American Review of Reviews* (November 1900), pp. 556–62; C.E. Jones to Bryan, January 10, 1900, Hearst to Bryan, May 19, July 4, 1900, Creelman to Bryan, May 24, June 6, 1900, Bryan Papers, L.C.

26. Jones to Bryan, August 3, 1900, Bryan Papers, L.C.

27. Jones to Bryan, December 1, 1900, Bryan Papers. L.C.

28. Homer S. Cummings to Bryan, November 8, 1900, Bryan Papers, L.C.; *New York Times*, February 14, 1901.

29. *New York Journal*, November 8, 1900.

30. *New York Tribune*, July 31, 1901.

31. William Jennings Bryan (ed.), *The Commoner Condensed* (New York: Abbey Press, 1902), vol. 2, p. 25.

32. *Ibid.*, vol. 1, pp. 21–23.

33. *Ibid.*, vol. 3, pp. 383–84.

34. *Proceedings of the Democratic National Convention, 1904.*

35. *New York Times*, January 13, 27, February 18, 1904.

36. *Ibid.*, January 14, February 26, 27, April 20, June 4, 5, 28, July 3, 4, 27, 1904.

37. *Proceedings of the Democratic National Convention, 1904.*

38. *Ibid.*

39. *Ibid.*

40. *Ibid.*

41. *New York Times*, July 11, 1904.

42. *Ibid.*, July 20, 1904.

43. Circumstances surrounding the national committee meeting are described in the *New York Times*, July 4, 5, 7,11, 19, 20, 21, 26, 1904.

44. *Proceedings of the Democratic National Convention, 1904.* See minutes of national committee meeting.

45. *Review of Reviews* (September 1904), p. 260.

46. J.P. Hornaday, "Taggart and the Democratic Campaign," *Review of Reviews* (September 1904), pp. 289–93.

47. *New York Times*, October 9, 1904.

Chapter 11

1. *New York Times*, December 9, 1887, February 10, 12, March 23, 25, May 19, 1888.

2. Vincent P. De Santis, *Republicans Face the Southern Question; The New Departure Years, 1877–1897* (Baltimore: Johns Hopkins Press, 1959), pp. 184–86.

3. Marcus A. Hanna, "Industrial Conciliation and Arbitration," *Annals of the American Academy of Political and Social Sciences* (July 1902), pp. 21–26.

4. Harrison to Wharton Barker of Philadelphia, November 25, 1886, Wharton Barker Manuscripts, L.C.

5. Elkins to Michener, March 21, 1888, Louis T. Michener Papers, L.C. See also Elkins to Michener, March 26, June 7, 10, 1888.

6. Elkins to Harrison, February 27, 1888, Benjamin Harrison Manuscripts, L.C.

7. Michener and John B. Elam to Harrison, June 17, 1888, Benjamin Harrison Papers, L.C.

8. Unsigned letter to Thomas M. Boyne, June 23(?), 1888, Benjamin Harrison Papers, L.C.

9. Elkins to Harrison, May 2, 1888, Harrison Manuscripts, vol. 29, p. 5891, L.C.

10. Medill to Gresham, May 21, 1888, Walter Hugh Gresham Manuscripts, vol. 30, p. 6894, L.C.

11. Sherman to Mark Hanna, telegram, June 1, 1888, John Sherman Manuscripts, vol. 446, p. 223, L.C.

12. Sherman to Hanna, telegram, June 19, 1888, Sherman Manuscripts, vol. 449, pp. 231–33.

13. Sewell to Harrison, June 29, 1888, Harrison Papers, L.C.

14. Smith to Harrison, July 9, 1888, Harrison Papers, L.C.

15. J.N. Huston to Harrison, July 8, 1888, M.G. McLain to Harrison, July 8, 1888, Edwin H. Terrell to Harrison, July 9, 1888, Harrison Papers, L.C. For public speculations, see the *New York Times*, July 11, 1888, in which New, Dudley, Quay, Hyde, Sanborn, Hobart, and Conger are mentioned.

16. Gordon S.P. Kleeberg, *Formation of the Republican Party as a National Political Organization* (New York: Moods, 1911), pp. 210–13. Clarkson's account was given in an interview with Kleeberg almost twenty years after the event.

17. Memorandum, 1888, Michener Papers, L.C.

18. Clarkson to Harrison, July 21 and 25, 1888, Harrison Papers, L.C.

19. Allan Nevins, *Grover Cleveland: A Study in Courage* (New York: Dodd, Mead, 1932), pp. 436–37; *New York Times*, November 4, 1888.

20. Nevins, *Cleveland*, pp. 437–38.

21. Alexander K. McClure, *Old Times Notes of Pennsylvania*, 2 vols. (Philadelphia: John C. Winston, 1905), vol. 2, p. 573.

22. Thomas C. Platt, *Autobiography*, ed. by Louis J. Lang (New York: B.W. Dodge, 1910), p. 206.

23. Clarkson to Michener, February 16, 1889, Michener Papers, L.C.; John S. Wise to Harrison, August 3, 1891, G.M. Dodge to Harrison, June 28, 1892, Hamilton Disston to Harrison, June 26, 1892, and W.O. Bradley to Harrison, June 22, 1892, Harrison Papers, L.C.

24. Clarkson to Michener, May 29, 1890, Michener Papers, L.C.

25. Dorothy G. Fowler, *The Cabinet Politician; The Postmasters-General, 1829–1909* (New York: Columbia University Press, 1943), chap. 11 and p. 307.

26. De Santis, *Republicans Face the Southern Question*, chap. 5.

27. *Ibid.*

28. *New York Times*, July 19, 20, 27, 29, 1981.

29. *Ibid.*, April 24, 1891.

30. Clarkson to Harrison, July 22, 1891, Harrison Papers, L.C.

31. *New York Times*, July 30, 31, 1891; Michener to E.W. Halford, July 30, 31, 1881, Michener to his father, July 30, 1891, Michener Papers, L.C.; Clarkson to Harrison, August 7, 1891, Harrison Papers, L.C.

32. The description of the convention is based upon a memorandum written in 1892, Michener Papers, L.C.; Hanna to John Sherman, June 14, 1892, John Sherman Papers, L.C.; *Proceedings of the Tenth Republican National Convention, held in Minneapolis, June 7–10, 1892.*

33. Michener to Foster, June 7, 1892, Harrison Papers, L.C.

34. *Ibid.*; Michener memorandum on Republican national convention, 1892, Michener Papers, L.C.

35. Platt, *Autobiography*, p. 219.

36. Michener to Halford, June 9, 1892, and Michener to Foster, June 7, 1892, Harrison Papers, L.C.

37. *Ibid.*

38. Nicholas Murray Butler, *Across the Busy Years*, 2 vols. (New York: Scribner's, 1935), vol. 1, pp. 221–22.

39. Michener memorandum on the organization of the national committee, 1892, Michener Papers, L.C.

40. Hobart to Michener, June 13, 1892, Michener Papers, L.C.; *New York Times*, June 27, 28, 1892; Quigg to Harrison, June 18, 1892, Harrison Papers, L.C.

41. G.M. Dodge to Harrison, June 28, 1892, A.A. Bateman to Harrison, June, 1892, Harrison Papers, L.C.; *New York Times*, June 24, 1892.

42. Harrison to Depew, June 27, 1892, Michener to Halford, June 27, 1892, Harrison Papers, L.C.; *New York Times*, June 26, 1892.

43. Clarkson to Harrison, June 25, 1892, Harrison Papers, L.C.

44. *New York Times*, June 30, 1892.

45. Copy of statement dictated by T.H. Carter, July 5, 1892, Harrison Papers L.C.; *New York Times*, June 28, 29, 30, July 4, 6, 1892.

46. *New York Times*, July 8, 14, 15, 16, 1892; S.N. Chambers to Halford, July 12, 1892, R.R. Shiel to Harrison, July 12, 1892, Michener to Halford, July 2, 1892, Sawyer to Payne, July 13, 1892, Halford to Spooner, July 13, 1892, Spooner to Halford, July 14, 1892, Payne to Halford, July 22, 1892, Harrison Papers, L.C.

47. *New York Times*, July 17, December 6, 8, 14, 1892; January 22, May 11, 1893.

48. Whitelaw Reid to Harrison, August 5, 6, 1892, Frank Hiscock to Harrison, August 13, 1892, Harrison Papers, L.C.; George H. Knoles, *The Presidential Campaign and Election of 1892* (Stanford: Stanford University Press, 1942), pp. 145–49; *New York Times*, October 26, 27, 1892.

49. Harrison to Platt, August 17, 1892, Harrison Papers, L.C.

50. Platt to Harrison, August 22, 1892, Harrison Papers, L.C.

51. Harrison's commentaries are in his *This Country of Ours* (New York: Scribner's, 1897), and *Views of an Ex-President* (Indianapolis: Bowen–Merrill, posthumous, 1901).

52. Harrison to Michener, November 12, 1894, Louis T. Michener Papers, L.C. Michener's assessment is in Michener letter to E.G. Hay, July 25, 1894, E.G. Hay Manuscripts, L.C.

53. At Republican ratification meeting, New York, August 27, 1896, italics added.

54. Platt, *Autobiography*, p. 331.

55. Harold F. Gosnell, *Boss Platt and His New York Machine* (Chicago: University of Chicago Press, 1924), pp. 114–17.

56. Butler, *Across the Busy Years*, vol. 1, pp. 222- 23.

57. Elmer Ellis, "The Silver Republicans of the Election of 1896," *Mississippi Valley Historical Review* (March 1932), pp. 519–34.

58. *New York Times*, June 20, 1896.

59. For example, Herbert Croly, *Marcus Alonzo Hanna* (New York: Macmillan, 1912) and Thomas Beer, *Hanna, and the Mauve Decade* (New York: Alfred A. Knopf, 1941).

60. *New York Times*, July 21, 1896; William M. Osborne to McKinley, August 11, 1896, McKinley Papers, L.C.

61. Joseph Foraker, *Notes of a Busy Life* (Cincinnati: Stewart and Kiss, 1916), vol. 1, p. 498.

62. Beer, *Hanna*.

Chapter 12

1. Margaret Leech, *In the Days of McKinley* (New York: Harper, 1959), pp. 67–69.

2. Thomas E. Felt, "The Rise of Mark Hanna," (Ph.D. dissertation in History, Michigan State University, 1960), pp. 235–36.

3. Leech, *In the Days of McKinley*, pp. 99–102.

4. Dorothy G. Fowler, *The Cabinet Politician; The Postmasters-General, 1829–1909* (New York: Columbia University Press, 1943), pp. 247–49.

5. *New York Nation*, May 5, 1898.

6. Fowler, *The Cabinet Politician*, pp. 254–55.

7. Thomas Beer, *Hanna, Crane, and the Mauve Decade* (New York: Alfred A. Knopf, 1941), p. 576.

8. *New York Times*, December 1 and 2, 1899.

9. Leech, *In the Days of McKinley*, p. 533. There is evidence among the Hanna Papers, particularly among the observations of Hanna's political friends Charles Dick and E. Dover, that President McKinley was prepared to drop Hanna had the latter's friends not promptly come to his support.

10. Charles G. Dawes, *A Journal of the McKinley Days* (Chicago: Lakeside Press, 1950), May 31, 1900.

11. Nicholas Murray Butler, *Across the Busy Years*, 2 vols. (New York: Scribner's, 1935), vol. 1, pp. 226–29; Harold F. Gosnell, *Boss Platt and His New York Machine* (Chicago: University of Chicago Press, 1924), pp. 119–22.

12. Leech, *In the Days of McKinley*, p. 537.

13. Dawes, *Journal*, pp. 233, 369.

14. William H. Allen, "The Election of 1900," *Annals of the American Academy of Political and Social Sciences* (January 1901), pp. 53–73.

15. McKinley Papers, October 12, 29, 1900; Herbert Croly, *Marcus Alonzo Hanna* (New York: Macmillan, 1912), p. 333.

16. Leech, *In the Days of McKinley*, p. 575.

17. Dawes, *Journal*, p. 207.

18. *New York Times*, June 10, 1901.

19. May 29, 1902.

20. Mark Sullivan, *Our Times*, 6 vols. (New York: Scribner's, 1928–1935), vol. 2, pp. 447–48.

21. Letter to Clarkson, March 13, 1903, Theodore Roosevelt Papers, L.C., quoted in Fowler, *The Cabinet Politician*, p. 265.

22. This exchange between Hanna and Roosevelt is reported in Henry L. Stoddard, *Presidential Sweepstakes*, ed. by F.W. Leary (New York: G.P. Putnam's Sons, 1948), pp. 126–27.

23. *New York Times*, November 5, 1904; Dawes, *Journal*, pp. 370–71.

24. May 28, 1904.

25. Dawes, *Journal*, pp. 370–71.

26. Fowler, *The Cabinet Politician*, pp. 272–78.

27. Dawes, *Journal*, pp. 473–76; *New York Times*, June 16, 18, 20, 21, and 24, 1904.

28. For Cortelyou's role at the convention, see Albert Halstead, "Chairman Cortelyou and the Republican Campaign," *American Monthly Review of Reviews* (September 1904), pp. 294–98.

29. Dawes, *Journal*, p. 383.

30. Halstead, "Chairman Cortelyou," pp. 297–98; Fowler, *The Cabinet Politician*, pp. 281–83.

31. Fowler, *The Cabinet Politician*, pp. 278–81, reports this exchange between Roosevelt and Cortelyou.

32. *Ibid.*, pp. 283–85; *New York Times*, November 1, 4, 5, and 6, 1904.

33. Dawes, *Journal*, pp. 396, 403.

34. Fowler, *The Cabinet Politician*, pp. 287–88; *New York Times*, January 8, 1907.

35. Howard K. Beale, *Theodore Roosevelt and the Rise of America to World Power* (Baltimore: Johns Hopkins Press, 1956), p. 448.

Chapter 13

1. *New York Tribune*, June 8, 1906.

2. *New York Times*, August 7, September 15, 1906.

3. *New York Tribune*, July 8, 1906, quoted by Paxton Hibben, *The Peerless Leader, William Jennings Bryan* (New York: Farrar and Rinehart, 1929), p. 269.

4. *Ibid.*, p. 270.

5. *Ibid.*, p. 274.

6. *Ibid.*, p. 279.

7. *Ibid.*, p. 255; also, Perry Belmont, *An American Democrat* (New York: Columbia University Press, 1940), p. 482.

8. *Proceedings of the Democratic National Convention, 1909.*

9. Victor Rosewater, "Bryan's Stories," *Philadelphia Bulletin*, March 19, 1935.

10. *New York Times*, December 26, 1932.

11. This account of the Foraker-Haskell episode is based upon Wayne C. Williams, *William Jennings Bryan* (New York: G.P. Putnam's Sons, 1936), pp. 298–301.

12. *New York Evening Post*, April 10, 1909.

13. Arthur S. Link, *Wilson: The Road to the White House*, 3 vols. (Princeton: Princeton University Press, 1947), vol. 1, chap. 6. Among the most important Wilson biographies, of which there are many, are the memoirs of Joseph P. Tumulty, *Woodrow Wilson as I Know Him* (Garden City, NY: Doubleday, Page, 1921) and the four volumes of *Intimate Papers of Colonel House* (Boston: Houghton Mifflin, 1926–1928), edited by

Charles Seymour. Tumulty was Wilson's private secretary and House his intimate adviser. Tumulty's memoirs contain extensive comments on Wilson's handling of party matters, particularly the national chairmanship, as does the volume by William F. McCombs, *Making Woodrow Wilson President* (New York: Fairview, 1921), which describes in detail the difficulties that arose between Wilson and National Chairman McCombs. For a succinct review of Wilson's emergence as a party leader, see Laurin L. Henry, *Presidential Transitions* (Washington, DC: Brookings Institution, 1960), part 2.

14. Hibben, *Peerless Leader*, p. 296.

15. *New York Times*, June 18, 1916.

16. House to C.A. Culberson, April 23, 1912, and to Mary Baird Bryan, June 22, 1912, Edward M. House Papers, quoted by Link, in *Wilson: The Road to the White House*, vol. 1, pp. 422–23.

17. *Memoirs* (Port Washington, NY: Kennikat Press, 1971), p. 160.

18. The story of Wilson's reply to Bryan is told in Tumulty, *Woodrow Wilson*, p. 111 and McCombs, *Making Woodrow Wilson President*, p. 122.

19. *Proceedings of the Democratic National Convention, 1912.*

20. *Ibid.*

21. Josephus Daniels, *The Wilson Era: Years of Peace, 1910–1917* (Chapel Hill: University of North Carolina Press, 1944), p. 65.

22. *Proceedings of the Democratic National Convention, 1912.*

23. Wayne C. Williams, *William Jennings Bryan*, p. 327–28.

24. The controversy is fully described by Link, *Wilson: The Road to the White House*, vol. 1, p. 451, n. 99.

25. McCombs, *Making Woodrow Wilson President*, pp. 161–62. The only other direct evidence is in Bryan's memoirs, edited by his wife, in which the Nebraskan told his wife that only on the condition that the convention was hopelessly deadlocked and only if he could unite the party would be accept a fourth nomination. *Memoirs*, pp. 334–35.

26. Daniels, *The Wilson Era*, pp. 68–70. This account of McCombs' election as national chairman is based upon Link, *Wilson: The Road to the White House*, vol. 1, pp. 480–81; McCombs, *Making Woodrow Wilson President*, pp. 180–88; and Maurice F. Lyons, *William F. McCombs, The President Maker* (Cincinnati: Bancroft, 1922), pp. 109ff.

27. Lyons, *William F. McCombs*, p. 129.

28. Among the more valuable assessments of Wilsonian theories about parties are Austin Ranney, *The Doctrine of Responsible Party Government* (Urbana: University of Illinois Press, 1954); Earl Latham (ed.), *The Philosophy and Policies of Woodrow Wilson* (Chicago: University of Chicago Press, 1958); the biographical volumes of Arthur S. Link; Laurin L. Henry, *Presidential Transitions*; and Alexander L. and Juliette L. George, *Woodrow Wilson and Colonel House* (New York: J. Day, 1956), pp. 144–54.

29. *Colonel House*, p. 318.

30. The summary, quotations, and analysis that follow are based on George and George, *Woodrow Wilson*, chap. 8, and Latham, *Philosophy and Policies*, pp. 60–70.

31. McCombs, *Making Woodrow Wilson President*, pp. 208–9.

32. Wilson is quoted by Henry, *Presidential Transitions*, p. 47, in an analysis of Wilson's cabinet appointments.

33. *Ibid.*, pp. 52–53.

34. *Ibid.*, pp. 80–83; A.S. Link, "Woodrow Wilson and the Democratic Party," *Review of Politics* (April 1956), pp. 146–56.

35. George and George, *Woodrow Wilson*, chap. 8.

36. Henry, *Presidential Transitions*, pp. 54–56.

37. McCombs, *Making Woodrow Wilson President*, p. 220.

38. *Ibid.*, pp. 222–23.

39. *New York Times*, March 6, May 18, 1913.

40. McCombs later charged the president with having failed to fulfill any part of this arrangement. McCombs, *Making Woodrow Wilson President*, pp. 224–25.

41. *New York Times*, January 11, 12, 28, February 10, 11, March 8, May 15, and June 28, 1914.

42. McCombs, *Making Woodrow Wilson President*, p. 261.

Chapter 14

1. *New York Times*, July 28, October 1, 6, 1914.

2. *Ibid.*, February 14, April 1, December 8, 1915.

3. *Ibid.*, April 15, June 6, 8, 17, 22, 31, and August 31, 1915.

4. *Ibid.*, April 26, 27, June 9, 10, 14, 1916.

5. Josephus Daniels, *The Wilson Era; Years of Peace 1910–1917* (Chapel Hill: University of North Carolina Press, 1946), pp. 452–55.

6. Ray Stannard Baker, *Woodrow Wilson, Life and Letters* (Garden City, NY: Doubleday, Page, 1937), vol. 6, pp. 252, 258.

7. *New York Times*, June 13 and 16, 1916; Daniels, *The Wilson Era*, p. 460; Alexander L. and Juliette L. George, *Woodrow Wilson and Colonel House* (New York: J. Day, 1956), p. 155.

8. *New York Times*, June 28, August 6, September 2, 1916.

9. *Ibid.*, August 27, November 27, 1916; Daniels, *The Wilson Era*, pp. 460–69.

10. *New York Times*, November 18, 22, 1916, February 28 and May 15, 1917.

11. The description and assessment of the 1918 congressional campaign and the quotation of Wilson's statement are from Herbert Hoover, *The Ordeal of Woodrow Wilson* (New York: McGraw-Hill, 1958), pp. 14–17.

12. George and George, *Woodrow Wilson*, p. 322.

13. *New York Times*, May 29, 1919.

14. *Ibid.*, March 13, May 29, July 29, September 26, 1919.

15. *Ibid.*, September 28, 1919.

16. *Ibid.*, January 9, 1920; see also, *Ibid.*, December 15, 1919, January 5, 1920.

17. This account of the 1920 Democratic preconvention and convention developments is drawn from T. William Goodman, "The Presidential Campaign of 1920" (Ph.D. dissertation in Political Science, Ohio State University, 1950).

18. According to Josephus Daniels, Wilson considered McAdoo unfit for the office. *The Wilson Era: Years of War and After* (Chapel Hill: University of North Carolina Press, 1946), p. 553.

19. Rixey Smith and Norman Beasley, *Carter Glass* (New York: Da Capo, 1972), pp. 207–8.

20. *New York Times*, June 20, 22, 1920.

21. Daniels, *Wilson: Years of War*, pp. 555–57.

22. Goodman, "Presidential Compaign," p. 191, n. 26. David Lawrence letter to T. William Goodman, August 11, 1949, is quoted *ibid.*, p. 208.

23. Cummings to Wilson, July 10, 1920, Wilson to Cummings, July 12, 1920, in Cummings' File, Ray Stannard Baker Papers, L.C.

24. *New York Times*, July 25, 1920.

25. James M. Cox, *Journey Through My Years* (New York: Simon and Schuster, 1946), pp. 238–39; *New York Times*, July 19, 1920.

26. Cummings Memorandum, July 26, 1920, in Cummings' File, Ray Stannard Papers, L.C.

27. Cox, *Journey*, p. 243.

28. *New York Times*, November 3, 1920.

29. *Ibid.*, July 23, 25, 26, 29, 30, 1920.

30. *World's Work* (September 1920), pp. 425–26.

Chapter 15

1. Letter to William H. Taft, March 15, 1906, *The Works of Theodore Roosevelt*, Memorial edition, 24 vols. (New York: Scribner's, 1923–26), vol. 24, p. 118.

2. Henry F. Pringle, *The Life and Times of William Howard Taft*, 2 vols. (New York: Farrar and Rinehart, 1939), vol. 1, pp. 236, 242, 248–49, 251–52, 264–65, 268.

3. *New York Times*, January 5, 6, 14, 1907.

4. Dorothy G. Fowler, *The Cabinet Politician; The Postmasters-General, 1829–1909* (New York: Columbia University Press, 1943), pp. 290–92; *New York Times*, December 7, 8, and 12, 1907; *New York Evening Post*, October 31, December 7, 12, and 13, 1907.

5. For analysis of convention vote on apportionment, Richard C. Bain, *Convention Decisions and Voting Records* (Washington, DC: Brookings Institution, 1960), pp. 173–74.

6. Victor Rosewater, *Backstage in 1912* (Philadelphia: Dorrance, 1932), pp. 22–23.

7. Fowler, *The Cabinet Politician*, pp. 296–97; *New York Evening Post*, June 27, 1908.

8. Oscar Straus, *Under Four Administrations, from Cleveland to Taft* (Boston: Houghton Mifflin, 1922), pp. 253–54.

9. Fowler, *The Cabinet Politician*, pp. 297–99; *New York Evening Post*, September 21, 1908.

10. Fowler, *The Cabinet Politician*, p. 299. Fowler observes that this connection between the national chairmanship and the postmaster generalship was becoming established, ironically, at a time when the postal system was being divorced from the party machinery as a consequence of civil service reform.

11. Victor Rosewater, *Backstage in 1912*, pp. 22–23.

12. *New York Times*, March 4, 1909.

13. Pringle, *Life and Times*, vol. 1, pp. 354–55.

14. Letter from Taft to Roosevelt, quoted in Herbert S. Duffy, *William Howard Taft* (New York: Minton, Balch & Co., 1930), p. 220. The second letter is quoted *ibid.*, p. 226.

15. Pringle, *Life and Times*, vol. 1, pp. 404–7.

16. *New York Evening Post*, June 18, 1910.

17. Archibald W. Butt, *Taft and Roosevelt*, 2 vols. (Garden City, NY: Doubleday, Doran, 1930; Port Washington, NY: Kennikat Press, 1971), vol. 1, pp. 416, 418.

18. Henry F. Pringle, *Theodore Roosevelt* (New York: Blue Ribbon Books, 1934; Harcourt, Brace, 1956), pp. 543ff.

19. Robert M. La Follette, *Autobiography* (Madison, WI: Robert M. La Follette Co., 1913), p. 511.

20. *Ibid.*, p. 512.

21. *Chicago Record Herald*, October 7, 1911.

22. Butt, *Taft and Roosevelt*, pp. 767–68.

23. Pringle, *Life and Times*, vol. 2, pp. 762–63.

24. Butt, *Taft and Roosevelt*, vol. 2, pp. 802–3.

25. Rosewater, *Backstage in 1912*, p. 37.

26. *Ibid.*, pp. 35–36. Significantly, Rosewater included himself among Hitchcock's "close friends" in this context.

27. Pringle, *Life and Times,* vol. 2, pp. 763–64.

28. *New York Times,* December 12, 13, 1911.

29. *Ibid.,* March 17, 1912; Rosewater, *Backstage in 1912,* pp. 80–85, discusses the strategy in some detail.

30. *New York Times,* March 17, 1912.

31. Rosewater, *Backstage in 1912,* pp. 87–88.

32. Taft to M.T. Herrick, June 20, 1912, quoted by Pringle, *Life and Times,* vol. 2, p. 808.

33. Because of its drama, the Republican national convention of 1912 is one of the most commented upon in party history. Excellent and authoritative analyses may be found in Bain, *Convention Decisions,* pp. 178–84, and Rosewater, *Backstage in 1912.* Pringle's biographies of Taft and Roosevelt offer the perspectives of the two major contestants.

34. James Watson, *As I Knew Them* (Indianapolis: Bobbs–Merrill, 1936), p. 150.

35. Taft to Daugherty, July 17, 1912, quoted in Pringle, *Life and Times,* vol. 2, p. 828.

36. Hilles to Butler, June 27, 1916, Nicholas Murray Butler Papers, Columbia University.

37. Hilles to James M. Beck, August 21, 1935, Butler Papers, Columbia University.

Chapter 16

1. One political commentator, writing years later on Alfred E. Smith's status as Democratic party leader after his defeat in 1928, credited Taft with introducing the term "titular leader" into the political vocabulary of national politics. Richard V. Oulahan, in *New York Times,* November 18, 1928, wrote:

> Under a definition offered by William H. Taft, a candidate for President of the United States is the "titular" head of his party. When James M. Cox addressed the Madison Square Garden convention in 1924, four years after his defeat, he so described himself. Even without the titular position conferred by his nomination at Houston, Governor Smith has an actual leadership conferred, for one thing, by the support he received from more than fourteen million members of the electorate. . . . With his retirement from public office in January, and perhaps from future political candidacy, as he indicated immediately after his defeat, he will not be in a position to point the way to party procedure through official recommendations.

A search of Taft's writings failed to uncover the original occasion at which he used the term in remarks about the divided Republican convention. As chairman of the committee notifying Taft of his nomination by the regular Republican convention, another eminent legalist, Senator Elihu Root, began by saying: "Your title to the nomination is as clear and unimpeachable as the title of any candidate of any party since political conventions began."

Taft again referred to titular leadership in his James Stokes Lectures at New York University in 1921. In this instance, however, Taft referred to the president rather than the nominee as "titular head of the party."

> With the necessity for parties in order to secure effective action according to the will of the people, the President, who is the titular head of the party that elected him, should work in unison with the majority of his party in each House. This is essential not only in party success but to real efficiency in the public interest. If he has successful elements of leadership, the people look to him as responsible for legislation.

2. December 10, 1912, *The Works of Theodore Roosevelt*, Memorial edition, 24 vols. (New York: Scribner's 1923–26), vol. 19, p. 473.

3. *New York Times*, May 12, 13, 14, 1913.

4. Howard S. Greenlee, "The Republican Party in Division and Reunion, 1913–1920" (Ph.D. Dissertation in History, University of Chicago, 1950), p. 60.

5. *New York Times*, May 25, 1913.

6. *Ibid.*, November 12, December 5, 1913.

7. *Ibid.*, December 17, 18, 1913, October 26, 1914.

8. Letter to Gifford Pinchot, November 13, 1912, Theodore Roosevelt Manuscripts, L.C.

9. Roosevelt to Hiram Johnson, July 30, 1914, Roosevelt Manuscripts, L.C.

10. For Woods' views, *New York Times*, August 30, 1913. For Hilles' views, letter from Hilles to Taft, May 27, 1913, Taft Manuscripts, L.C.

11. *New York Times*, April 26, May 23, July 16 and 20, September 13, 1915; Taft to G.J. Karger, May 22, 1916, Taft Manuscripts, L.C. In 1913, Taft accepted an appointment as professor of law at Yale. He considered his retirement from elective and party politics permanent and even declined an offer of membership on the Republican national committee. Henry P. Pringle, *The Life and Times of William Howard Taft*, 2 vols. (New York: Farrar and Rinehart, 1939) p. 863.

12. Greenlee, "The Republican Party," pp. 128, 144.

13. *New York Times*, June 11, 13, 18, 1916.

14. Letters to Senator W. Murray Crane, August 14 and 28, 1916, Nicholas Murray Butler Papers, Columbia University.

15. Letter to Crane, August 28, 1916, Butler Papers, Columbia University.

16. Herbert A. Gibbons, *John Wanamaker*, 2 vols. (New York: Harper and Bros., 1926), vol. 2, p. 393.

17. New light on this dramatic instance of political protocol is provided by Frederick M. Davenport, "Did Hughes Snub Johnson—An Insider Story," *American Political Science Review* (April 1949), pp. 332ff.

18. *New York Times*, January 26, 1915.

19. *Ibid.*, July 2, 1960.

20. Garland C. Routt, "Will Hays: A Study in Political Leadership and Management" (Master's thesis, Department of Political Science, University of Chicago, 1937). See also, Will Hays, *Memoirs* (Garden City, NY: Doubleday, 1955).

21. *New York Times*, December 21, 24, 1960.

22. Merlo J. Pusey, *Charles Evans Hughes* (New York: Macmillan, 1951), vol. 1, pp. 367–68.

23. *Ibid.*, p. 403.

24. *New York Times*, June 28 and December 6, 1916, January 16–19, February 1, 12, 1917.

25. *Ibid.*, January 16, 1916.

26. *Ibid.*, December 21, 1916, January 19, 23, February 11–14, 16, 1918; Hilles Memorandum on the Election of Hays, Butler Manuscripts, Columbia University.

27. Routt, "Will Hays," pp. 66–67.

28. *Ibid.*, pp. 81–83; *New York Times*, February 23, 26, 27, March 2, 3, 13, 14, April 5, 14, 1918.

29. *New York Times*, April 13, May 4, 1918.

30. *Ibid.*, June 30, 1918.

31. Routt, "Will Hays," pp. 85–86.

32. *New York Times*, January 11, 1919.

33. *Ibid.*, December 12, 1919, April 27–28, 1920.

34. *Ibid.*, January 29, February 5, May 19, 1920.

35. For further detail on the Republican fund-raising operation, see that committee's report. Senate Committee on Privileges and Elections, Hearings before Subcommittee, Pursuant to Senate Resolution 357, 1920–1921, 66th Congress, 2nd and 3rd Sessions.

36. Routt, "Will Hays," p. 100; *New York Times*, February 26, 1920.

37. Letter to E.E. Whiting, Taft Manuscripts, quoted by Greenlee, "The Republican Party," p. 293.

38. *New York Times*, November 1, 1919.

39. For a careful analysis of the factors in Harding's availability, see Richard C. Bain, *Convention Decisions and Voting Records* (Washington, DC: Brookings Institution, 1960), p. 206.

40. *New York Times*, June 8, 1920.

41. *Ibid.*, June 4, 1920.

42. Routt, "Will Hays," p. 101.

43. Greenlee interview with Hays, January 23, 1950, reported in Greenlee, "The Republican Party," p. 409.

44. *New York Times*, June 23, 1920.

45. For the problem of the South, see the *New York Times*, January 31, June 9, June 19, and October 27, 1921. Less than a year after he entered the cabinet, Hays resigned to become head of the motion picture industry's new association of producers and distributors, at a reported "annual stipend" of between $100,000 and $150,000.

46. *New York Times*, April 30, May 19, 1920.

Chapter 17

1. E.E. Robinson, *The Presidential Vote, 1896–1932* (Stanford, CA: Stanford University Press, 1934), p. 21.

2. James M. Cox, *Journey Through My Years* (New York: Simon and Schuster, 1946), p. 324.

3. *New York Times*, January 9, 1921.

4. *Ibid.*, January 21, 1921.

5. *Ibid.*, February 8, 9, 1921.

6. *Ibid.*, February 11, 12, 13, 14, 17, 18, 1921.

7. *Ibid.*, February, 19, 21, June 11, 1921.

8. *Ibid.*, October 9, 11, 25, November 2, 3, 1921.

9. Cordell Hull, *Memoirs* 2 vols. (New York: Macmillan, 1948), vol. 1, p. 115.

10. *Ibid.*, vol. 1, p. 113.

11. *New York Times*, May 4, 1922.

12. Hull, *Memoirs*, vol. 1, pp. 120–21.

13. *Ibid.*, vol. 1, pp. 117, 118.

14. *Ibid.*, p. 114.

15. Harold B. Hinton, *Cordell Hull* (Garden City, NY: Doubleday, Doran, 1942), p. 173.

16. *Washington Post*, November 13, 1923; *Literary Digest*, December 1, 1923.

17. Carter Field, *Bernard Baruch: Park Bench Statesman* (New York: Whittlesey House, 1944), pp. 72, 204–5.

18. *New York Times*, March 26, 1923.

19. Lee N. Allen, "The Underwood Presidential Movement of 1924" (Ph.D. dissertation in history, University of Pennsylvania, 1955), pp. 276–77; Cox, *Journey*, p. 328.

20. *Evening World*, July 7, 1924.

21. *Herald Tribune*, July 1, 1924.

22. *New York Times*, July 19, July 20, 1924.

23. *Ibid.*, July 27, 1924.

24. *Ibid.*, August 12, 1924.

25. Cox, *Journey*, p. 331.

26. Elliott Roosevelt, ed., *F.D.R., His Personal Letters* 4 vols. (New York: Duell, Sloan and Pearce, 1947–50), vol. 2, p. 566.

27. *New York Times*, November 19, 1924. Cf. Allen Sinclair Will's proposal below.

28. *Ibid.*, February 20, 1925.

29. *Ibid.*, November 7, 17, 1924.

30. Much of the following account is based on James M. Burns, *Roosevelt: The Lion and the Fox* (New York: Harcourt, Brace, 1956), pp. 95–97.

31. The Roosevelt-Walsh correspondence is reported in the *New York Times*, March 9, 1925.

32. *Ibid.*, March 9, 1925.

33. *Ibid.*, March 22, 1925. A detailed proposal for a midterm conference was offered by Allen Sinclair Will in *North American Review* (March 1925), in which he suggested that the number of delegates should be equal to the number of senators and representatives in Congress from each state, plus a limited group of special members including the candidates on the last two national tickets, the national chairmen in the last two campaigns, and a group of Democratic leaders from both houses of Congress. He also suggested that the call for the conference come from the members of both houses of Congress assembled in caucus.

34. Compare the resistance of congressional Democrats to the Raskob conference in 1931 and again to the establishment of a Democratic Advisory Council under the auspices of the national committee in 1957.

35. Letter of July 14, 1928, in Elliott Roosevelt, *F.D.R.*, vol. 2, p. 640.

36. *New York Times*, January 9, 1927, July 12, 1928; *The Outlook* (August 22, 1928), pp. 645–49; *World's Work* (September 1928), pp. 486–92; Edmund A. Moore, *A Catholic Runs for President* (New York: Ronald, 1956), pp. 121–26.

37. *New York Times*, April 27, June 29, 30, July 3, 6, 11, 1928.

38. *Ibid.*, July 12, 1928.

39. Letter to the author, September 19, 1949.

40. *Ibid.*

41. Burns, *Roosevelt*, p. 99.

42. "The Reconstruction of the Democratic Party," *Yale Review* (September 1928), pp. 18–27.

43. Paul T. David, Ralph M. Goldman, and Richard C. Bain, *The Politics of National Party Conventions* (Washington, DC: Brookings Institution, 1960), p. 460.

44. *New York Times*, November 8, 1928.

45. Telegram of November 12, 1928, and Elliott Roosevelt, *F.D.R.*, vol. 1, p. 7. See also *New York Times*, November 12, 1928, and January 14, 1929.

46. *New York Times*, November 11, 1928.

47. *Ibid.*, November 8, 9, 11, 1928.

48. *Ibid.*, December 4, 5, 7, 12, 13, 18, 1928.

49. *Ibid.*, December 10, 1928, January 14, 1929.

50. *Ibid.*, December 6, 1928, January 17, 1929.

51. *Ibid.*, January 16, April 17, 1929.

52. *Ibid.*, May 1, 1929. At forty-nine, Shouse had a long political career behind him. He had been a Kansas state senator, representative in Congress, and assistant secretary of the treasury under Carter Glass in the Wilson administration. In 1920 and 1924, he was one of the most active of the McAdoo leaders. He shifted his support to Smith in 1928,

was active in the New York campaign headquarters, and assisted Raskob after the election with the problem of clearing up the deficit.

53. *Ibid.*, May 5, June 11, 1929.

54. Charles Michelson, *The Ghost Talks* (New York: G.P. Putnam's Sons, 1944), p. 15.

55. *Ibid.*

56. *Ibid.*, p. 21.

57. *New York Times*, June 9, 1929, January 17, 1931.

58. *Ibid.*, June 15, 16, 19, 30, July 12, September 18, 1929.

59. *Ibid.*, April 8, 9, May 29, 1930.

60. *Ibid.*, October 28, 1930.

61. Elliott Roosevelt, *F.D.R.*, vol. 2, pp. 143–44.

62. Samuel I. Rosenman, *Working With Roosevelt* (New York: Harper, 1952), pp. 48–49. Rosenman was a state legislator who had been recommended to Roosevelt in 1928 by Governor Smith as particularly qualified in the preparation of policy statements and speeches on legislative issues.

63. Hull, *Memoirs*, vol. 1, p. 141.

64. *New York Times*, November 6, 1930.

65. *New York Times*, February 11, 1931.

66. Hull, *Memoirs*, vol. 1, p. 142.

67. Elliott Roosevelt, *F.D.R.*, vol. 2, p. 179.

68. Hull, *Memoirs*, vol. 1, pp. 142–45; *New York Times*, March 6, 7, 1931.

69. *New York Times*, December 15, 1931.

Chapter 18

1. Lela Stiles, *The Man Behind Roosevelt: The Story of Louis McHenry Howe* (Cleveland: World, 1954), esp. chap. 9; Frank Freidel, *Franklin D. Roosevelt: The Triumph*, 4 vols. (Boston, MA: Little, Brown, 1956), vol. 3, chap. 12; James A. Farley, *Behind the Ballots* (New York: Harcourt, Brace, 1938), chap. 2; Edward J. Flynn, *You're the Boss* (New York: Viking Press, 1947), pp. 83ff. Apparently Roosevelt asked Flynn to take on the job of rounding up national convention delegates. Flynn, who considered himself a poor "mixer," preferred to remain in the background, and saw his big-city and anti-Prohibition images as possible liabilities in the search for southern and western delegates. Flynn heartily agreed with Louis Howe that the most logical manager was Farley.

2. *New York Times*, July 3, 1932.

3. *Ibid.*, July 21, August 4, 5, 6, 11, 1932; Freidel, *Franklin D. Roosevelt*, chap. 21.

4. Farley, *Behind the Ballets*, p. 323; Freidel, *Franklin D. Roosevelt*, p. 360. Scientific sampling of public opinion did not become popular until 1936 and then became known generically as the Gallup Poll. That was the election in which the *Literary Digest* poll proved so inaccurate a forecast that the magazine went out of business. It is not clear what techniques Hurja used in 1932 that gave him such a reputation for accuracy in forecasting. In 1936, however, he was apparently as wrong as the *Literary Digest* poll.

5. Laurin L. Henry, *Presidential Transitions* (Washington, DC: Brookings Institution, 1960), pp. 423, 432.

6. Farley, *Behind the Ballots*, pp. 233–38; James A. Farley, "Passing Out the Patronage," *American Magazine* (August 1933), pp. 20ff.; Henry, *Presidential Transitions*, p. 433.

7. James A. Farley, *Jim Farley's Story: The Roosevelt Years* (New York: Whittlesey House, 1948), p. 70. This second of Farley's memoirs gives particular attention to what Farley regards as Roosevelt's "ingratitude" and "discourtesy."

8. Ernest K. Lindley, *The Roosevelt Revolution: First Phase* (New York: Da Capo, 1974), p. 57.

9. *Ibid.*, p. 293.

10. Robert E. Sherwood, *Roosevelt and Hopkins* (New York: Harper, 1948), p. 47.

11. *Ibid.*, p. 51; Jonathan Daniels, *The Man of Independence* (Port Washington, NY: Kennikat, 1971), p. 166.

12. Sherwood, *Roosevelt and Hopkins*, p. 68.

13. Farley, *Behind the Ballots*, p. 307; Richard C. Bain, *Convention Decisions and Voting Records* (Washington, DC: Brookings Institution, 1960), p. 249.

14. Farley, *Jim Farley's Story*, p. 62.

15. Samuel I. Rosenman, *Working with Roosevelt* (New York: Harper, 1952), chap. 8; Elliott Roosevelt, ed., *F.D.R., His Personal Letters*, 4 vols. (New York: Duell, Sloan and Pearce, 1947–50), vol. 3, p. 595.

16. Roosevelt, *F.D.R.*, pp. 598–601.

17. Farley, *Jim Farley's Story*, p. 64.

18. *Ibid.*, p. 68.

19. *Ibid.*, p. 65.

20. Rosenman, *Working with Roosevelt*, p. 147.

21. Farley, *Jim Farley's Story*, p. 73.

22. *Ibid.*, p. 92.

23. For a relatively detached and thorough evaluation of the Farley candidacy and its implications for Farley's relations with Roosevelt, see Charles Michelson, *The Ghost Talks* (New York: G.P. Putnam's Sons, 1944), chap. 11. Michelson observes that Farley loyally and energetically used the headquarters staff to help with the fight for passage of the Supreme Court bill, but was openly reluctant to be associated with the attempted purges of conservative Democrats in the 1938 primaries.

24. Farley, *Jim Farley's Story*, pp. 49–50.

25. Quoted by Rosenman, *Working with Roosevelt*, p. 178.

26. Farley, *Jim Farley's Story*, pp. 153–54; Elliott Roosevelt, *F.D.R., His Personal Letters*, vol. 4, pp. 835–36.

27. The details of the conversation are preserved in Hopkins' extensive notes, which are reported by Sherwood, *Roosevelt and Hopkins*, pp. 93–100. The quotations that follow are from Sherwood's account.

28. Farley, *Jim Farley's Story*, pp. 175–76, 255. There are innumerable accounts of Roosevelt's third-term decision and his choice of a running mate. See relevant pages in Sherwood, *Roosevelt and Hopkins*, Rosenman, *Working with Roosevelt*, and Michelson, *The Ghost Talks*.

29. Farley, *Jim Farley's Story*, chap. 24.

30. Rosenman, *Working with Roosevelt*, p. 205.

31. Cordell Hull, *Memoirs*, 2 vols. (New York: Macmillan, 1948), vol. 1, p. 860.

32. James F. Byrnes, *All in One Lifetime* (New York: Harper, 1958), p. 119.

33. Rosenman, *Working with Roosevelt*, pp. 213–21.

34. Byrnes, *All in One Lifetime*, p. 125.

35. Flynn, *You're the Boss*, pp. 159–61.

36. Roosevelt, *F.D.R., His Personal Letters*, vol. 4, pp. 1012–13.

37. Michelson, *The Ghost Talks*, p. 160.

38. Flynn, *You're the Boss*, p. 161.

39. Rosenman, *Working with Roosevelt*, p. 229.

40. Flynn, *You're the Boss*, p. 167.

41. *Ibid.*, p. 170.

42. Telegram dated January 18, 1943.

43. Michelson, *The Ghost Talks*, pp. 148–49.

44. Flynn, *You're the Boss*, p. 178. Cf. Henry A. Wallace, "How the Vice-President Is Picked," *U.S. News and World Report* (April 6, 1956), p. 88, and Daniels, *The Man of Independence*, p. 210.

45. Quoted in Hannegan biography, *Current Biography, 1944* (New York: H.W. Wilson, 1944).

46. In an interview with Robert Hannegan in later years, columnist Leonard Lyons learned that Roosevelt sent a longhand draft of this letter to Hannegan, who edited it somewhat before dictating it to Roosevelt's secretary, Grace Tully, for typing; *New York Post*, October 10, 1949, p. 22. The general Roosevelt strategy is reported in Daniels, *The Man of Independence*, p. 244.

47. Sherwood, *Roosevelt and Hopkins*, pp. 881–82. Other accounts of this nomination from different perspectives may be found in Byrnes, *All in One Lifetime*, chap. 13, Daniels, *The Man of Independence*, chap. 15, Rosenman, *Working with Roosevelt*, chap. 22, Flynn, *You're the Boss*, pp. 180–84, and Wallace, "How the Vice-President Is Picked."

48. Rosenman, *Working with Roosevelt*, chap. 24.

49. *Ibid.*

Chapter 19

1. Quoted by Claude M. Fuess, *Calvin Coolidge, The Man From Vermont* (Hamden, CT: Archon Books, 1965), p. 335.

2. *New York Times*, May 2, 1924. The reference is to an investigation of Wheeler's financial activities by George Lockwood's *National Republican*, which continued to be identified as the organ of the national committee, although technically this was not so.

3. *Ibid.*, May 1, 1924.

4. *Ibid.*, November 19, 1924, April 15, 1925.

5. *The Autobiography of Calvin Coolidge* (New York: Cosmopolitan, 1929), pp. 230–32. The autobiography was probably written between winter 1927 and fall 1929.

6. *New York Times*, September 15, 1925. Also, December 10, 16, 1925.

7. *Ibid.*, September 26, 27, 1925; July 7, October 25, 31, November 3, 1926.

8. *Ibid.*, April 26, May 14, July 12, October 4, 1926.

9. *Ibid.*, November 3, 6, 17, 1926.

10. *Ibid.*, April 22, 1927.

11. Details about the preparation and announcement of Coolidge's cryptic statement of withdrawal are carefully set forth by Fuess, *Calvin Coolidge*, pp. 390–400. This account includes the authoritative version of Presidential Secretary Everett Sanders, who was directly involved.

12. *The Autobiography of Calvin Coolidge*, pp. 239–45.

13. *Ibid.*, p. 247.

14. *Ibid.*, p. 246.

15. *New York Times*, October 6, December 6, 7, 8, 1927; Fuess, *Calvin Coolidge*, p. 424 n.

16. *New York Times*, June 12, 1928.

17. *The Cabinet and the Presidency, 1920–1933: The Memoirs of Herbert Hoover*, 3 vols. (New York: Macmillan, 1952), vol. 2, pp. 190–94.

18. Harry S. New to Nicholas Murray Butler, April 26, 1936, Butler Papers, Columbia University.

19. *New York Times*, June 5, 1929.

20. Quoted in Edward C. Latham, *Meet Calvin Coolidge* (Brattleboro, VT: Stephen Greene, 1960), p. 220.

21. Harris Gaylord Warren, *Herbert Hoover and the Great Depression* (Westport, CT: Greenwood, 1980), p. 153.

22. *New York Times*, March 7, 1929.

23. *Ibid.*

24. *Ibid.*, January 19, March 27, April 1, 1929.

25. *Ibid.*, June 5, July 7, 1929.

26. *Ibid.*, June 11, 26, 27, August 2, 1929.

27. *Ibid.*, August 6, September 4, 6, 9, 1929, December 21, 1920.

28. *Ibid.*, August 8, 1930.

29. *Ibid.*

30. *Ibid.*, July 29, 1930.

31. *Ibid.*, August 7, 14, 24, 1940.

32. *Ibid.*, November 6, 1930.

33. *Ibid.*, November 13, 17, December 6, 1930.

34. *Ibid.*, December 21, 1930.

35. *Ibid.*, December 4, 30, 1930, March 28, May 5, June 30, October 30, 1931.

36. *Ibid.*, October 30, November 20, 1931, April 12, June 12, June 13, 1932.

37. Letter dated June 17, 1932, quoted by Latham, *Meet Calvin Coolidge*, p. 198.

38. *New York Times*, June 28, July 22, 1932.

Chapter 20

1. *New York Times*, May 6, June 5, 1934.

2. *Ibid.*, June 8, 1934.

3. August 23, 1934, Knox Papers, L.C.

4. *New York Times*, January 3, 6, 14, 15, 20, 1936.

5. Most of the information regarding Hamilton's incumbency as national chairman was drawn from the following sources: Henry O. Evjen, "The Republican Strategy in the Presidential Campaigns of 1936 and 1940" (Ph.D. dissertation in History, Western Reserve University, 1950); Karl A. Lamb, "John Hamilton and the Revitalization of the Republican Party, 1936–40," *Papers of the Michigan Academy of Science, Arts, and Letters* (1960), pp. 233–50; an unpublished paper by Dr. Lamb on the "The Opposition Party as Secret Agent: Republicans and the Court Fight, 1937"; an unpublished manuscript by Professor Joseph Boskin entitled "Politics of an Opposition Party; The Republican Minority in the New Deal."

6. Boskin interview with John Hamilton, *ibid.*, chap. 3.

7. Walter Johnson, *William Allen White's America* (New York: Garland, 1979), p. 460; Ralph D. Casey, "Republican Propaganda in the 1936 Campaign," *Public Opinion Quarterly* (April 1937), p. 30.

8. *Saturday Evening Post* (February 27, 1937), p. 92.

9. Interview with Landon, cited in Karl A. Lamb, "John Hamilton," pp. 236–37.

10. For details of the organizational developments under Hamilton, see Lamb's "John Hamilton."

11. *Ibid.*, p. 237, n. 11.

12. *Ibid.*, p. 250.

13. The Republican national committee did not establish a pension plan for regular employees until 1956, *Washington Post*, July 20, 1956.

14. Karl A. Lamb interview with John Hamilton, reported in "The Opposition Party."

15. *Ibid.*

16. Quoted by Lamb, letter from Hamilton to Landon, May 6, 1937, personal files of John Hamilton.

17. Lamb, "John Hamilton," pp. 244–45; *New York Times*, August 21, 1937.

18. *Atlantic Monthly* (September 1937).

19. *New York Times*, January 7, 1938.

20. Donald B. Johnson, *The Republican Party and Wendell Willkie* (Urbana: University of Illinois Press, 1960), p. 79.

21. *Ibid.*, p. 108.

22. Raymond Moley, *27 Masters of Politics* (Westport, CT: Greenwood, 1949, 1972), pp. 49–50.

23. *Ibid.*; Henry O. Evjen, "The Willkie Campaign; An Unfortunate Chapter in Republican Leadership," *Journal of Politics* (May 1952), pp. 241–56.

24. Evjen, "The Willkie Campaign," p. 245.

25. American Institute of Public Opinion poll released in August, 1940; Sam Lubell, "Post Mortem: Who Elected Roosevelt?" *Saturday Evening Post* (January 25, 1941).

Chapter 21

1. Democratic National Committee Press Release, February 12, 1947.

2. Jack Redding, *Inside the Democratic Party* (Indianapolis: Bobbs-Merrill, 1958), pp. 88–93.

3. *Ibid.*, pp. 37–40, 89.

4. Harry S. Truman, *Memoirs*, 2 vols. (New York: Signet Edition, Doubleday, 1956), vol. 2, p. 186.

5. *Ibid.*, vol. 2, p. 178.

6. *The Future of American Politics* (New York: Harper and Bros., 1951), pp. 9–10, 12.

7. For an evaluation of the implications, see Arthur Krock in *New York Times*, October 9, 1949.

8. *New York Times*, August 14, 1949.

9. Several professional political scientists in the administration presented Truman with a copy of the report. Because of the relevance of the party council proposal for the development of an advisory council during Paul M. Butler's subsequent incumbency as national chairman, it may be useful to quote at length the proposal upon which the president commented. Given Truman's disapproval, it is important to note that the Democrats were the "out" party during Butler's incumbency and disbanded the advisory council when the party was "in" after 1961.

> We [the Committee on Political Parties] propose a Party Council of 50 members. Such a Party Council should consider and settle the larger problems of party management, within limits prescribed by the National Convention; propose a preliminary draft of the party platform to the National Convention; interpret the platform in relation to current problems; choose for the National Convention the group of party leaders outside the party organizations; consider and make recommendations to appropriate party organs in respect to congressional candidates; and make recommendations to the National Convention, the National Committee and other appropriate party organs with respect to conspicuous departures from general party decisions by state or local party organizations. In presidential years, the council would naturally become a place for the discussion of presidential candidacies, and might well perform the useful function of screening these candidates in a preliminary way. Within this Party Council there might well be a smaller group of party advisors to serve as a party cabinet.

Committee on Political Parties, American Political Science Association, *Toward a More Responsible Two-Party System* (New York: Rinehart, 1950), p. 5.

10. *New York Times*, November 1, 1951.
11. *Ibid.*
12. Truman, *Memoirs*, vol. 2, pp. 491–92. The rest of this story is documented in several places: Kenneth S. Davis, *A Prophet in His Own Country* (Garden City, NY: Doubleday, 1957), pp. 388ff.; Paul T. David, Malcolm Moos, and Ralph M. Goldman, *Presidential Nominating Politics in 1952*, 5 vols. (Baltimore: Johns Hopkins University Press, 1954), vol. 1, "The National Story." The historical accuracy of President Truman's observation about presidential control of the national conventions was, of course, debatable. See Paul T. David, Ralph M. Goldman, and Richard C. Bain, *The Politics of National Party Conventions* (Washington, DC: Brookings Institution, 1960), chap. 6.
13. David, Moos, and Goldman, *Presidential Nominating Politics in 1952*, vol. 1, p. 106.
14. *Ibid.*, vol. 1, p. 131.
15. *Ibid.*, vol. 1, p. 125.
16. Truman, *Memoirs*, vol. 2, p. 500.

Chapter 22

1. *New York Times*, November 9, 1952.
2. Kenneth S. Davis, *A Prophet in His Own Country* (Garden City, NY: Doubleday, 1957), p. 434.
3. Adlai E. Stevenson, *What I Think* (New York: Harper, 1956), pp. ix-x.
4. Letter to author, August 30, 1955.
5. *New York Times*, April 5, 26, 1954.
6. *Ibid.*
7. *Ibid.*, May 6, 1954.
8. *Ibid.*
9. *Ibid.*
10. Sidney Hyman, "The Collective Leadership of Paul M. Butler," *The Reporter* (December 24, 1959), p. 8.
11. *New York Times*, December 7, 1954.
12. *Ibid.*, December 5, 1954.
13. Davis, *A Prophet*, p. 440.
14. Butler interview with author and others, February 9, 1955.
15. Harold Leventhal, "The Democratic Party's Approach to its Convention Rules," *American Political Science Review* (June 1956), pp. 553ff.
16. For additional details on final action taken at the national convention, see Charles A.H. Thomson and Francis M. Shattuck, *The 1956 Presidential Campaign* (Washington, DC: Brookings Institution, 1960), pp. 117–24.
17. Butler interview with author and others, February 9, 1955.
18. Stevenson, *What I Think*, pp. ix-x.
19. *New York Times*, December 4, 1954, April 3, 1955, and James Reston column of April 13, 1955.
20. James Reston in *New York Times*, June 19, 1955.
21. Hyman, "Collective Leadership," p. 10.
22. For details of the campaign and the convention, see Thomson and Shattuck, *The 1956 Presidential Campaign*, and Richard C. Bain, *Convention Decisions and Voting Records* (Washington, DC: Brookings Institution, 1960). For loyalty pledge details, see

Abraham Holtzman, "Party Responsibility and Loyalty," *Journal of Politics* (August 1960), pp. 485–501.

23. Hyman, "Collective Leadership," p. 10.

24. *New York Times Magazine*, November 18, 1956.

25. *Ibid.*

26. *New York Times*, November 7, 8, 10, 11, 18, 1956.

27. Douglas Cater, "Who Will Speak for the Democrats?" *The Reporter* (November 29, 1956), p. 22.

28. *New York Times*, November 27, 1956.

29. Hyman, "Collective Leadership," p. 11.

30. For example, Cabell Phillips' analysis in the *New York Times*, December 2, 1956, and various press association reports during this period.

31. *New York Times*, November 28, 1956.

32. *Ibid.*

33. *Ibid.*, December 19, 1956.

34. *Ibid.*, December 4, 9, 13, 14, 16, 19, 1956, and January 4, 1957.

35. *Ibid.*, January 19, 1957.

36. The research agency was Press Intelligence, Inc., whose surveys covered 650 newspapers and press associations. A press release of the Democratic Advisory Council, October 20, 1957, described the Press Intelligence findings.

37. *New York Times*, April 14, 1959.

38. *Charlotte (North Carolina) News*, December 8, 1959.

39. John B. Oakes in *New York Times Magazine*, December 22, 1957, p. 8.

40. *New York Times*, May 7, 1957, report of May 5 broadcast.

41. *Ibid.*, August 11, 1957.

42. *Ibid.*, July 7, 1959.

43. *Ibid.*

44. *Ibid.*

45. *Ibid.*

46. *New York Times*, July 20, 1959.

47. Paul T. David et al., *The Presidential Election and Transition 1960–1961* (Washington, DC: Brookings Institution, 1961), chap. 1.

48. *Ibid.*, p. 9.

49. *New York Times*, March 16, 17, 1960.

50. *Ibid.*, July 11, 12, 1960.

51. Columnist Doris Gleeson, *Chicago Daily News*, December 13, 1961.

52. Thomas B. Morgan, "The People-Machine," *Harper's Magazine* (January 1961), pp. 53–57. On the campaign, see Stanley Kelley, Jr., in David, *The Presidential Election and Transition*. On the net effect of the television debates, see Charles H. Thomson, *ibid.*, pp. 106, 109–10.

53. *New York Times*, January 22, 1961.

Chapter 23

1. *New York Times*, January 13, 1941.

2. *Ibid.*, November 12, 1940. The account of Republican developments between 1941 and 1944 is based on Donald B. Johnson, *The Republican Party and Wendell Willkie* (Urbana, IL: University of Illinois Press, 1960), particularly chapters 5 and 6.

3. *New York Times*, November 12, 1940.

4. Johnson, *The Republican Party*, p. 168. See also, *Time* (December 9, 1940), p. 18.

5. *New York Times*, January 13, 1941.

6. Johnson, *The Republican Party*, p. 170.

7. *New York Times*, February 13, 1941.

8. *Ibid.*, March 24, 1941.

9. Charles D. Hilles to Col. R.B. Creager, the national committeeman from Texas, February 21, 1941, copy in Nicholas Murray Butler Papers, Columbia University.

10. *Ibid.*

11. *Ibid.*

12. *Ibid.*

13. Quoted in *New Republic*, January 26, 1942, p. 115.

14. *New York Times*, April 21, 1942.

15. *Ibid.*

16. Reported by Johnson, *The Republican Party*, p. 217.

17. *Chicago Tribune*, December 7, 1942, quoted by Johnson, *ibid.*, p. 225. Other quotations in previous paragraphs are also based on Johnson's account. The meeting was reported in the *New York Times*, December 7, 8, 9, 1942.

18. Johnson interview with Pryor, quoted in Johnson, *The Republican Party*, p. 224n.

19. See Tables 16.3 and 16.4 in Paul T. David, Ralph M. Goldman, and Richard C. Bain, *The Politics of National Party Conventions* (Washington, DC: Brookings Institution, 1960).

20. *New York Times*, February 8, 1944.

21. Johnson, *The Republican Party*, p. 291.

22. Letter from Charles D. Hilles to Nicholas Murray Butler, July 5, 1944, Butler Papers, Columbia University.

23. *New York Times*, July 1, 1944.

24. *Current Biography, 1944* (New York: H.W. Wilson, 1944), p. 77.

25. Based on notes of an interview between Professor Emeritus Charles M. Hardin of the University of California at Davis, then of the Rockefeller Foundation, and John Danaher, in August 1945.

26. The Senate policy committees, as employed by the major parties, were given early assessments in Hugh A. Bone, *Party Committees and National Politics* (Seattle: University of Washington Press, 1958), chap. 6, and Malcolm F. Jewell, "The Senate Republican Policy Committee and Foreign Policy," *Western Political Quarterly* (December 1959), pp. 966–80.

27. *New York Times*, March 16, 1947.

28. *Ibid.*, March 4, 16, November 26, 1947.

29. For a full account, see Seymour Z. Mann, "Congressional Behavior and National Labor Policy: Structural Determinants of the Taft-Hartley Act" (Ph.D. dissertation in Political Science, University of Chicago, 1951).

30. Jules Abels, *Out of the Jaws of Victory* (New York: Holt, 1959), p. 142. An excellent source of information about the campaign is a senior thesis in the Department of Politics at Princeton by Edwin W. Stockly, "The Republican National Committee and the 1948 Campaign" (April 1949).

31. The research is reported in Bernard Berelson, Paul Lazarsfeld, and William McPhee, *Voting* (Chicago: University of Chicago Press, 1954).

32. *New York Times*, January 26, 1949.

33. *Ibid.*, December 25, 1949.

34. *Ibid.*, July 9, 1949.

35. *New York Herald Tribune*, October 16, 1950.

36. See chap. 21 for details of the Boyle case.

37. *New York Times*, July 4, 1952.

38. *New York Times*, January 20, 1952.

Chapter 24

1. Walter Johnson, *1600 Pennsylvania Avenue: Presidents and the People, 1929–1959* (Boston: Little, Brown, 1960), pp. 317–18.

2. *Look* (April 21, 1953).

3. *New York Times*, March 28, 1953.

4. *Ibid.*

5. *Ibid.*, March 30, 1953.

6. *Ibid.*, April 3, 1953.

7. *Ibid.*

8. *Ibid.*, April 4, 1953.

9. *Ibid.*, April 8, 1953.

10. *Ibid.*, April 10, 1953.

11. *Ibid.*, April 11, 1953.

12. For details on the Republican return to power, see Laurin L. Henry, *Presidential Transitions* (Washington, D.C.: Brookings Institution, 1960), part V. On Hall's conversion of the national headquarters into, in Stewart Alsop's words, something like the "home office of a large and successful business concern," see Hugh A. Bone, *Party Committees and National Politics* (Seattle: University of Washington Press, 1958), passim, and "Barnum of the G.O.P.," *Saturday Evening Post* (May 26, 1956), pp. 26–27. Much of the discussion of Senator Taft's relationship to the Eisenhower administration is based upon Henry.

13. Henry, *Presidential Transitions*, p. 578.

14. James Reston analysis of June 25, 1956, and press report of August 28, 1956, both in the *New York Times*.

15. *Ibid.*, June 24, 1956.

16. *Ibid.*, November 6, 1956.

17. *Ibid.*, June 9, 1957.

18. Philip S. Wilder, Jr., *Meade Alcorn and the 1958 Election* (Eagleton Foundation Case Study in Practical Politics; New York: Henry Holt, 1959), part 2. Much of the account of Alcorn's incumbency is based upon Wilder's account.

19. *New York Times*, March 8, 1957.

20. *Ibid.*

21. *Ibid.*, March 17, 1957.

22. Wilder, *Meade Alcorn*, p. 15.

23. *Ibid.*, pp. 15–16.

24. *New York Times*, April 4, 1959.

25. This account of the 1960 Republican preconvention developments is based on Theodore H. White, *The Making of the President, 1960* (New York: Atheneum, 1961), chap. 3.

26. Paul T. David (ed), *The Presidential Election and Transition, 1960–1961* (Washington, DC: Brookings Institution, 1961), p. 3.

27. White, *Making of the President*, p. 76.

28. *Ibid.*, p. 376.

29. Quoted in a discussion of "Leadership Problems in the Opposition Party," by Senator Thruston B. Morton, in David, *The Presidential Election*, chap. 11.

30. *New York Times*, November 30, 1960.

31. *Ibid.*, December 2, 1960.

32. *Washington Post*, December 1, 1960.

33. *New York Times*, December 2, 1960.

34. *Ibid.*, January 7, 1961.

35. Morton, in David et al., *The Presidential Election*, p. 298.

Chapter 25

1. E.E. Schattschneider, *The Semi-Sovereign People* (New York: Holt, Rinehart & Winston, 1960).
2. Chester A. Barnard, *The Functions of the Executive* (Cambridge, MA: Harvard University Press, 1938).
3. For a pertinent theoretical exposition, see John Galtung, "A Structural Theory of Integration," *Journal of Peace Research*, no. 4 (1968), p. 377.
4. Ralph M. Goldman, "A Theory of Conflict Processes and Organizational Offices," *Journal of Conflict Resolution*, 10:3 (September 1966), pp. 328–43.

Chapter 26

1. William F. McCombs, *Making Woodrow Wilson President* (New York: Fairview, 1921), p. 220.
2. *New York Times*, January 29, 1920.
3. *Ibid.*, April 25, 1920.
4. *Ibid.*, January 29, February 5, April 25, May 22, 28, 1920.
5. *Ibid.*, September 22, 24, October 15, November 2, 5, 6, 7, December 15, 17, 1937, August 6, 1938, February 17, 25, 1940.
6. *Ibid.*, September 2, 1943.
7. *Ibid.*, December 26, 1949, January 4, 6, 8, 12, February 2, 7, 13, 23, 1950.
8. The dilemmas in U.S. out-party leadership are fully stated in Paul T. David, Ralph M. Goldman, and Richard C. Bain, *The Politics of National Party Conventions* (Washington, DC: Brookings Institution, 1960), pp. 501–6, and Paul T. David, "A New Role for the Opposition Party Leader," *New York Times Magazine* (September 18, 1955), pp. 15ff. See also, David Fromkin, "Leader of the Opposition: An American Lacuna," *Interplay* (February 1969), pp. 12–14. Opposition leadership in the British parliamentary system also has its dilemmas, as described by Max Beloff, "The Leader of the Opposition," *Parliamentary Affairs*, vol. 11 (Spring 1958), 2, pp. 155–62.
9. Fromkin, "Leader of the Opposition," passim.
10. David et al., *Politics of National Party Conventions*.

Indexes

Index.

Name Index

Subject Index

About the Author

Ralph M. Goldman is professor emeritus of political science at San Francisco State University. While at the Brookings Institution in Washington, he coedited, with Paul T. David and Malcolm Moos, the five-volume *Presidential Nominating Politics in 1952* and coauthored, with Paul T. David and Richard C. Bain, the definitive *Politics of National Party Conventions.* He has written three histories of the Democratic party, the most recent entitled *Dilemma and Destiny.* Over thirty of his articles on American party politics and elections appear in scholarly collections, journals, popular magazines, and encyclopedias. In a unique volume on *Transnational Parties: Organizing the World's Precincts,* he anticipates the emergence of a world party system. He extends this view in *From Warfare to Party Politics: The Critical Transition to Civilian Control,* in which several case studies describe how party systems have developed into the institutional alternative to warfare. Dr. Goldman has been a political commentator for RKO-General Broadcasting and Voice of America and has served as senior consultant to the National Democratic Institute for International Affairs.